ALIEN GENESIS

By

Lea Kapiteli

ALIEN GENESIS
BOOK TWO CHRONICLES OF AKASHI

Printed and distributed by IngramSpark
https://www.ingramspark.com/

Illustrations and cover by Lea Kapiteli.

Editing by Sanja Korlaet.

This edition was initially printed as a paperback cover.

For my family and friends, and anyone who has been eager for this book...

You're gonna love it.

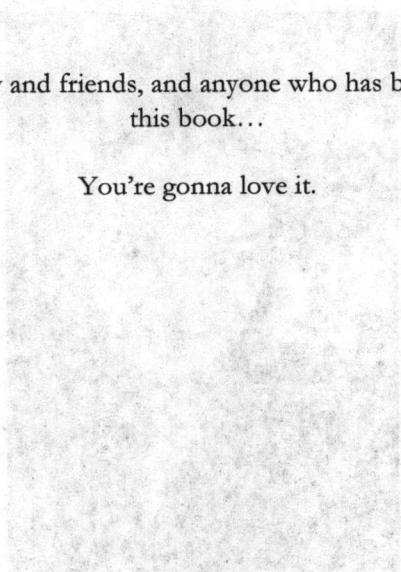

Also, there's an index at the back. It may come in handy.

About the author

Lea Kapiteli was born in New Zealand in 1993 into a Croatian family that migrated to Australia in 1998.

Aaand more importantly:

She has been in psychic contact with extra-terrestrials and extra-dimensionals since early childhood, even recalls some of her past lives and the numbing existence beyond life.

That's why this book is here.

Prologue

Wandering and wondering. Will it hear her? Will it see her? Will it feel her if she reached out? She has seen empires rise and fade without growing a wrinkle on her skin. She had sensed the dying sigh of stars scatter their remains across the cosmos as she rested on a dusty bed of nebulas. She had the power to pluck the thin fabric of space to make her own nest far away from unwanted visitors. She was the eternal child of the universe – she even stopped counting the eons of her life. However, not even she or her kin knew what lay in the heart of the universe.

A great consciousness sat in thrones of stars long before she was born; it was older than her people, perhaps even older than the first stones of her planet. This is where she will get her answers to questions she had never thought to ask.

Her iridescent body drifted to a spot barren of light; she could hear her people calling her to return. Her back straightened as her limbs stretched over her nigh-visible torso; she could hear her people begging her to stop. Her fingers and toes slid their way through the tiny gaps of space, and she shivered as outside energies coursed through them. She could feel her people coming, but this needed to be done. Her body vibrated as she slipped through the countless planes, trying to be part of the whole to reach this great mind.

She knew that this well of consciousness had been there since the beginning. All her and her people's attempts to contact this mighty being have failed so far. Did it ignore their calls or was it so large that her people were little more than wings of an insect beating around its ears? Did it even care about the countless life forms surrounding it?

Finally, some questions have entered her mind.

Her people knew about Akashi. A mass of matter and mind that lived outside of the tangible universe, outside of life and death, and time. The father of all souls and the mother of all knowledge. She wanted to join with Akashi as she was. She knew her energy form could go beyond than any physical body. This was her only chance.

She told her people she was doing this for them. Whatever she returns with, will be the final level of evolution. She was comforted and certain. Her own kind's pleas fell silent as her body slipped through the furthest plane of the universe; she could still sense they were aware of her. Their thoughts grew quieter, along with her own. Now, it was time to speak to Akashi.

Hear me, she said.

No reply.

She pushed further and the feel of her people became a murmur.

See me, she said.

No glances.

Her body started to ache as she slipped through one more plane; she was now deaf to her kin.

Hear me, she begged.

The pain of silence was palpable.

She wanted to hear one thought, any thought, even the frustration of her people. Nothing.

See me, she screamed to the great mind.

She scanned this bizarre multiplane and realised she was nowhere and everywhere. Her body trembled; it was time to return from another failed attempt. Her limbs vibrated to slip back down, but too much of her was spread out. She twisted and hardened her torso to find an anchor to some plane to phase back, but she was too tired.

Her psychic scream called for any mind, but she could only hear echoes. She couldn't hear her kin and they couldn't hear her. They couldn't pull her out. Their nigh omnipotence felled to sense her cries. The cosmic energies that fed her had weakened between the planes, and now, she will become too weak to escape. Sazla was stuck.

Chapter One
Treneer I: A Neonate

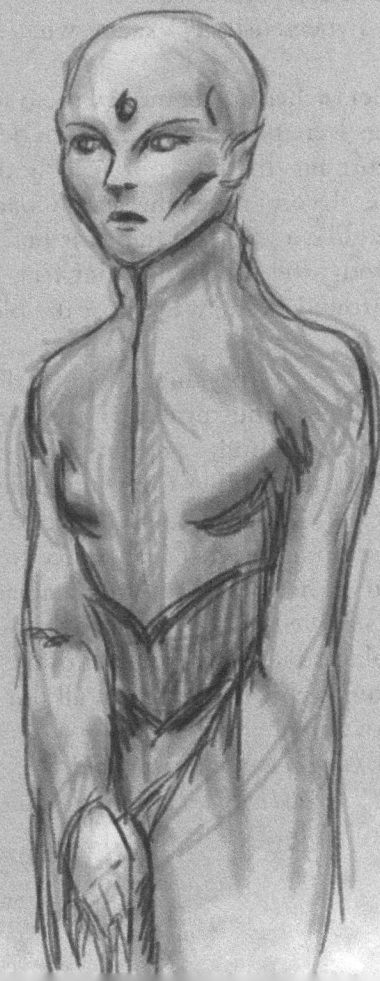

Icy winds blew through the crystal buildings. Their sharp and intricate structure transformed the howls into chimed sighs. Bits of snow carried by the wind tapped against the stained chromatic surface of the crystal spire. Her half-closed eyes watched the snowflakes melt against the glass before sliding down. The singing wind had interrupted her two-day long meditation. She wanted to remain on the soft round rosy cushion beneath her crossed legs, but her mind already started spinning. A hot sharp pain shot through the centre of her forehead; she winced as her fingers tapped against the hard-crystalized skull bump on her head. Her third eye was hypersensitive, exactly what she needed for the trial.

Her shoulders ached as she moved them for the first time in days, her legs were partially numb from being in the same position. Returning to her physical body was always uncomfortable. Every time she came back from astral traveling, it felt like a coat too tight for her. Energy pulsed through her body, she levitated to her feet, her toes barely touching the ground as she waited for the blood to fall into them.

Neonate Treneer, a psychic voice called from the meditation chamber. She turned to see her tutor drifting across the room, carefully avoiding the others in their meditations. Her tall and thin form hid underneath a violet and lavender robe with pointed shoulder pads surrounding a high collar scraping against her perfectly angled jaw. A silver circlet sat on her pearly smooth head and housed two blue starry eyes as well as her third eye that shone the same hue. Holographic runes littered around her shoulders and head; they were psychic badges from all the disciplines she had mastered over many millennia.

I am ready, Elder Zu'leen. Treneer said.

I think not, it's too cold outside to be dressed in that. Zu'leen said with a smirk on her lip.

Treneer's cheeks flushed as she looked to her nearly folded snow garb beside the rosy seat. Her thin peach body suit clung to her body. It was enough to keep her warm most of the time in combination the heat from her aura, but it wasn't enough to brave planet Farayah's brutal environment. Her light-grey slender arm hovered over the clothes and commanded the energy around her to bring them to her hand. They lifted, one sleeve opened and wrapped itself around her arm and then onto the other. The feathery turquoise and white coat reflected the heat from her body as she tightened the clasp on her waist bringing her whirling mind to a stillness.

Is it wise to waste one's psychic focus on physical dress before the Mind Trial? Zu'leen said as her head tipped to the side.

It wouldn't be wise for someone other than myself, elder. Treneer said. She could feel the other neonates in meditations being roused from their conversation. She ' focused on compressing the surrounding astral energies into fancy holographic lines over her shoulders and head to boost her confidence. However, she didn't dare craft honorary runes of learned masters, but if one were to see from a distance, they may mistake her young self to be of great merit. Treneer supressed a smirk from her tutor, but Zu'leen didn't seem pleased.

The Mind Trial is a test to see if one is better, not worse, neonate. Zu'leen said as she turned to drift out of the chamber.

The trials are tests to meet expectations set by Arinu elders. They want and deserve the best and so do you. Isn't that why we're here, elder? Treneer said as she followed Zu'leen by the hem of her cloak.

I watched you for two days, neonate. You only spent three hours meditating on your inner-self and the rest on astral travelling. Zu'leen said never breaking her glide.

When we are in our astral forms, we access the universe and are free from these small bodies! If our minds are linked to this higher consciousness, then that's where I can find my true self. I know what I can do. Treneer said as her eyes scanned the colourful crystal halls. She passed the spiral staircase that would lead them outside, slightly relieved that she wouldn't have to bear the cold, but soon realised they were headed somewhere much different. *Elder Zu'leen, doesn't the Mind Trial take place outside?*

Zu'leen stopped before a closed black granite door. She lowered to her feet as she turned to Treneer. *If you want to know what happens outside, you need to look inside. It's not complicated.* She said as the corner of lips curled upwards.

Treneer shook her head as her feet touched the heated tiles. Her eyes drifted over the ancient holographic text floating across the solid black slab. She saw her name flashing across the surface, followed by two names that made her chest freeze.

My parents are in there? She looked to Zu'leen.

Of course. They're eager to see what I taught you. She said as her hand lifted from her cloak up to the door.

Treneer's throat dried as her lips cracked open the first time in days. She hadn't used her voice since her arrival at the Guardian Academy fifty years ago. She was little more than an infant before her family recognized the immense psionic potential inside her. However, they were descendants of ancient warriors, their strength was in body – not mind. They knew she would fare better here than the ragged snows.

"Will you be there, Zu'leen?" Treneer spoke for the first time in many years. Her ears tried to catch the sound of her womanly voice. It wasn't smooth like Zu'leen's or her mother's, but she was surprised to hear how youthful her cadence remained.

Zu'leen widened her eyes in delight as her lips parted. "Of course, neonate," her hand waved over the door and the stone trembled as it phased out of this existence.

Treneer looked to the dark room with a shining silver plate hovering just beyond the floor's edge. It barely fit the two of them as they stepped onto the board before it carefully glided deeper into the void chamber. Warm air drifted against her bare scalp; her skin tingled from a hum of electricity the lower they went. Treneer's confidence was returning. She was ready for the Mind Trial.

Zu'leen turned to her. *I believe you believe you're ready.*

What makes you say that, elder? Treneer said looking at her tutor from the corner of her eye.

The Mind Trial is only half, there's still the Body Trial. She said.

The warm air had slipped as coldness licked against her skin during the decent. Treneer tried to keep her focus on this first trial. One step at a time; one problem at a time. *I'm best suited as a Sleeping Watcher after finishing my schooling. I wouldn't ever need to be in my physical body while I watch over Farayah.* She said.

You still need your physical health as a Watcher. True, other Guardians may do their duties to our kin, but you will waste away if you neglect your body, Treneer. Zu'leen said.

Before Treneer could reply, the disk slowed to a halt. Zu'leen beckoned her to step off the board and she complied. She almost got a fright when her feet touched cold water on the hard surface; her body shivered as smoky breath escaped her lips and nose. Her eyes darted around the black room; the only thing that held light was Zu'leen's glowing blue eyes, but they faded into the shadow. Magenta light sparked from Treneer's elegant fingers to find the walls, but this chamber was so large and unnaturally dark, that no matter how bright she made her light, it was absorbed by the room. She focused her senses through her third eye to find any forms, auras, x-rays, anything, but even that failed.

No need to waste psychic focus, neonate. Booming voices echoed through her head. Some voices were female, some male, but their combined power made her uneasy. She was being watched from behind the shadows.

I'm ready to begin. Treneer called to the minds.

No response. The water swished as she turned; droplets of water splashed on her knees giving her a new cold wave. She shivered while pumping energy into her aura to keep her warm.

Insufficient. The voices said in unison.

Her throat squeaked as she spun around to see where they were coming from. The deafening silence made her head and ears ache. What did they want her to do? She trained for the trials for years, but her tutors never revealed what to expect.

Poor thing. They said again, with stronger female voices.

The icy cold water clung to the skin of her shins; she pressed telekinetic energy from her feet to keep it at bay. This was just a test, Treneer repeated to herself.

An unwise decision. Said the more male voices.

What do you want me to do? She said. Her heart raced as a loud splashing came from several feet from her. Treneer released another ball of magenta energy from her other hand and pointed her palms to the direction of the splashing. Her third eye flickered through many psychic lenses to see if a creature was there waiting to attack her.

Too easily overpowered. They chimed again, with a hint of malevolence in their tone. Why were her parents and Zu'leen letting her judges insult her?

A guttural groan echoed through the chamber. Her back arched as she stood ready, but nothing came. She looked to the water's surface to her front, but she noticed no ripples waving towards her. Treneer released more light from her hands to find the source of the noises but was met with more wet floors. No one was there. Was it an illusion? Was it happening in her head?

What am I meant to do? She called again. The air became colder; the damp hem of her coat froze the material. She tried to push more energy out to keep the warmth. The harder she fought the elements the colder it became.

Pockets of deep shadow appeared in the corners of her light. They darted about, almost as if they were trying to find a way to push their way in. But shadow isn't matter; it's the absence of light. It wouldn't – it couldn't hurt her.

Outside doesn't exist; inside is the only reality. Said a voice, but it was not part of the chorus of the others. Was Zu'leen secretly giving her a hint? It didn't sound like her thought waves, it sounded like Treneer's voice.

She frowned and took a deep breath as she pulled in her magenta light balls. The dancing shadows skipped towards her, but she locked her fear away.

Maybe. Said the chorus. They revealed nothing, but at least they weren't mocking her anymore.

The chamber felt like it was in the centre of one of Farayah's poles; her jaw began to violently shake, and her teeth begun chattering. Her senses opened to the vastness of the chamber but, she still couldn't feel anything or anyone there. Treneer paused when she noticed the room was pulling her energy out of her body. She sighed. Hot breath left her mouth as she pulled in the last of her psionically generated heat. The cold cut through her coat and into her flesh. She stopped shivering and feared that she would pass out from the unnatural freeze.

Close. The voices said. Treneer wrapped her arms to her torso. She squeezed her eyes shut as the decorative holograms around her shoulder and head fizzled out. She stopped resisting as her mind expanded to the outer space. At last!

Where are you? The voices pushed. She slowly dropped to her knees. The water felt as if it had warmed as it soaked through her coat and under suit. Treneer pushed her mind farther and farther. She could feel walls around her, and they were a lot closer than she believed.

I am in the Guardian Academy testing room. She said as she saw the crystal spire and all its inhabitants above her.

Where are *you?* The aggression in their voice returned, but she paid no mind to it.

On Farayah…homeworld. Treneer said as she continued pushing her mind out to the icy blue and white world. She could feel all beings flying, swimming, running and climbing on her surface. Her shaking thighs collapsed and the water soaked her legs and lower back.

Where? They screamed through her skull. The psychic sound was so sharp that her fingers pressed to the sides of her temples.

*I don't…*Treneer felt her mind grow, touching the surfaces of all planets, asteroids, comets and their red dwarf star, but she couldn't push it any further. *I can't-I don't know what-*

To the distant corner of the red star, she saw a flash of white light. She thought a star went nova, but it's light pulsated and crashed into her mind. Treneer screamed, even her mouth released a pained wail, as her consciousness contorted and blew to the arms of the galaxy – perhaps farther. In a moment, she could see it all, hear it all and feel it all. Treneer lost all sense of herself as her mind united with something beyond all comprehension. The All.

In a blink, she dropped back into her numb body. Her eyes peeled open to see several Arinu figures standing around her in a brightly lit room. The water heated instantly as she felt thin hands reach underneath her arms and pull her up. Treneer saw the joyful and relieved faces of Zu'leen and other testers. Her mind felt like it had been shredded. She tried remembering everything she had seen and learnt, but her brain was too scrambled.

Did I pass? She said as she slipped her tutor's hands from her.

Beyond our expectations and you took us with you. Zu'leen said as her eyes looked to Treneer's magenta third eye. *There is slight damage to your frontal lobe, but nothing a healing pod cannot fix.*

What happened to me? Did you see that star going nova? Treneer said as she looked to the others.

No stars died in that area from what we saw. Whatever it was, it seems to have allowed you to touch the infinite! Said a male tester.

Do you remember anything? What did you see? Zu'leen pressed; Treneer could feel her mind looking into hers trying to find something that had waned every passing second.

Did I pass the Mind Trial? Treneer said as she pushed her tutor from her sore head.

Poor thing, you had forgotten you asked. Her mother said.

You did, child, you did! Her father's thoughts came in. Her head twisted to see him and her mother levitating over. This was the first time she had seen them in person since she arrived at the school. Her arms locked around their torsos, before dropping into their embrace.

~

The murmur of voices was the first thing Treneer could hear. She couldn't understand what they were saying or if they were even in hear head. As her eyes opened, she was met with blackness. However, her third eye could see an orange and teal fractal diamonds wrapped around her body like a shield. The voices became words and sighs, but they were coming from mouths. Her sleepy ears twitched to hear what they were saying, however, they were muffled by the lid of the healing pod.

Treneer's body was floating inside water, and she could feel small vitamin spheres glued to her arms and legs. She must have been in there for several days; her body felt revitalised, but she couldn't remember if she had astrally travelled. A black hole sat in her mind, the absence of what had happened during the Mind Trial was as heavy as an asteroid.

Her hands tapped against the case; the voices stopped for a moment before light cracked into the pod as the lid slid away. Zu'leen and Treneer's parents looked to her with shades of joy and concern on their faces. Her body was lifted by Zu'leen's telekinetic push and water ran down her back and legs before it dripped to the hot tiles.

I can lift myself. Treneer said as she caught the weight of her form with her psionics, yet she didn't want to separate from the floor's lovely heat.

Woeful pride. Did you know she had this, Remir? Zu'leen said as she flashed an amused smile to her mother.

Since in the womb! But her psychic prowess was great enough to understand…only fifty-two years old and she can match a master's potency. Her mother said caressing Trener's cheek with the back of her hand. Remir had the same magenta glow from her eyes and third eye; her skin was so white it was almost transparent. Treneer could even see the blue and purple veins coiled inside her thin flesh. She was tall for a female Arinu; the tip of her head was mere inches above her father's. Faint wrinkles on her face showed her age of a couple thousand-or-so years, but there was a youthful vitality that remained.

I'm so happy to see you, both of you in person. She said looking between them. Her under suit already began to absorb the water and dry her skin. It was a living organism, complete with cells and fibres that consumed dead skin cells, oils and other bacteria that formed on her membrane.

Yes, it's been too long. Astral visitations only go so far, my daughter. You've done our family proud; our ancestors will celebrate once you've completed the trials. Her father spoke. He was also over a thousand years of age, but it was harder to tell from his thick pale grey skin. Several white scars lined his square jaw and across his nose. He wore them as badges from his struggles to survive the harsh wilds of Farayah and skirmishes with neighbouring Arinu tribes. They weren't ever in any danger, of course. Physical combat has been outdated for tens-of-thousands of years, but her father's line and said fellow tribes held to the old ways every century.

The Body Trial was due some days ago, but our neonate needed that time to heal. Zu'leen said.

She's been in the pod for a day, she's been completely revitalised by now. Treneer is in prime condition to face the next trial. Her father said.

Vanar, her spirit needs time to re-adjust to her body again. Remir said.

Zu'leen's teachings would've helped her fully return. Body and mind, that's all there is: mind mastering body. He said when he glanced to Treneer.

I don't know how long I'll need. She could see her father's eyes dropping their smile as she spoke. *But I want to revise some movements before the Body Trial, of course.*

The smile had returned to his face, but the confidence had been replaced with hopefulness as he looked to his only child. *I have faith in you.*

We need to give your body something to eat, it's been too long since you last digested. Maybe that will help you resettle. Zu'leen said as she telekinetically willed Treneer's coat over her shoulders.

She gripped on the cloud-like material; her chin rested against the collar. *How long is your stay here?*

For however long is needed or when you tell us to go. Remir said.

You can do it, Treneer, command your fate! Vanar said before the bodies of her parents phased out of physical existence, teleporting to their resting chambers in the grand building, leaving Treneer behind.

It finally makes sense, now. Zu'leen said with a smile as she glided out of the healer's chamber.

What does? Treneer rushed beside her tutor.

We spend our entire lives trying to figure out who we are. We go to school; we speak with our peers and consult our teachers. But do you know who holds the biggest part of that knowledge? Zu'leen said passing into the open eatery. Sounds of plates and cutlery clinked; hovering chairs and tables tapped by the other tutors, students and visitors, though not a single voice was exchanged in the hall.

11

Our parents. Treneer said as she glided to the nearest table. Her legs crossed over the cushioned chair.

Our ancestors. Zu'leen said and sat across from Treneer as her fingers scrolled through the screen inside the table, searching for a meal. *How can we know what we are if we don't know the people that brought us here? And where we can go not understanding our potential?*

Sorry, my elder, but I do not see how this relates to me, specifically? Treneer said as her eyes skimmed down the screen. Cuisines from across every Arinu tribe and clan flashed across along with some dishes that came from other worlds. She scrunched her nose in slight disgust at some of the ingredients, as she wasn't used to eating since her astral body absorbed energies from surrounding space to sustain her form. And thinking about where digested food ended up made her more nauseous.

Pick something that makes you forget about that biological function. Like this: Zu'leen pressed the image of a thick creamy pink dish with an assortment of berries mixed into it. A holographic model of the dish appeared on the table's surface and a strobe of light bore down into it, leaving a fully formed bowl with the food neatly resting inside.

It's good for jumpstarting your stomach biota. We can share it. Zu'leen said as her mind picked up a violet berry and guided it to her mouth. *Tastes sweet, very sweet. I think you need more help eating this, Treneer.* She said before taking another creamy scoop into her mouth.

Elder, please tell me what made sense to you, and I'll promise to start eating. Treneer said as she placed her palms on the table. A couple of pink drops from the bowl levitated towards her.

When you came here, you were only a couple of years into life. I could sense you had spectacular psionic potential, and I was so eager to teach you how to hone it, but there was a great struggle inside your spirit. So eager to achieve and please. When you understood something, you would parade it to your peers. I knew of your ancestor's line, but it wasn't until I spoke to your parents while you were asleep was when

I understood you. Zu'leen said as she watched Treneer took more scoops of the thick liquid.

What do you mean, elder? Treneer said as her throat tried forcing the cool food down.

You come from a very long line of fighters who prided themselves on mental and physical prowess, more of the latter. Modern-day Arinu are too obsessed with the powers of the mind and neglect their bodies. Zu'leen sucked in an anxious breath. *You were born with a smaller and weaker body but compensated with psionics. I could see that it might've seemed disheartening with warriors.*

Treneer pursed her lips. She almost died in the womb; her mother's body started rejecting her and was removed a couple of months early. She remembered several days after her birth, when her father looked to her crib and frowned at her tiny form. The arguments between her parents echoed inside her head. Too fragile, too little, weak to the cold, not enough – not enough. They believed she could not remember it, but she knew and out of strange love, she could never reveal their secret.

You were enough, everything you are, is already enough. Zu'leen said as she slid her hand over Treneer's.

Treneer took another scoop that nearly emptied the bowl as she forced it down her throat. She didn't want to talk anymore, but another cruel thought had entered her mind. *During the Mind Trial, those voices I heard were insulting me, were they part of the test?*

Zu'leen's eyes widened as her mouth parted. Her mind closed for a moment, but embarrassment crept up inside that Treneer could work her psychic probe in.

So, those voices came from my parents. Treneer said.

They were used as guides by the testers, but- Treneer could feel the rise of nervousness inside her tutor, but she pushed it aside.

Oh, I'm not offended. I was just curious. Treneer wiped her mouth calmly before rising from her chair. Her legs slightly trembled underneath her full weight. She hid mind from

Zu'leen, trying to lock away the disappointment. *I am ready for the Body Trial.*

Zu'leen slid her arm back. *The Body Trial isn't a time to get emotional. Just give your body some time to get used to-*

I can pass it. Treneer pressed. All she needed was to pass the silly test and then she can move up to a Sleeping Watcher. After that, she would never have to come back to her body, she would never have to come back home.

As your friend and other parent, I would advise- Zu'leen started.

Elder- Treneer couldn't hold back the frustration; she didn't care if Zu'leen could feel it radiating towards her.

I forbit it! Zu'leen jumped to her feet as her back shot up. *As a tutor, I say when a neonate is ready. You are not for the Body Trial, yet.*

"Zu'leen, please!" Treneer almost didn't believe she spoke. All eyes in the hall locked to her and her tutor, but Zu'leen didn't break her glare.

She shook her head and slumped back into the chair. *This is a very bad idea, but if you need help realising that…*

Don't you trust me? Treneer said, suddenly uncertain if she could trust herself.

I'll meet you in the exercise hall, but you can't levitate there or use the teleporter. Walk. Zu'leen said before phasing out of the eatery.

Treneer puffed up her chest; she felt as if she had been slapped. Her eyes shot back to others watching the scene, forcing them to look away. The sweet food still lulled on her tongue; its goodness was absent as she quickly scrambled for water. The strobe above the table flashed a clear bag of water. Her hands trembled as she lifted the pouch and sucked the small straw fixed to the container.

She spun around and made her way out of the hall; every step made her wobble; she could feel the eyes of other patrons on her back as she slipped out into the crystalline corridor. Physical activity wouldn't have been such a struggle if she was not removed from the healing pod after only a day in containment. She hoped she would bounce back after the meal, but not as soon as some other neonates in similar predicaments. She hated staring at her wobbling knees.

The Mind Trial had almost annihilated most of her neurons. Her psionics had never done that before and it may have cost her time in the healing pod. However, the longer she considered it, perhaps she was powerful enough to read all the minds in the solar system and beyond, but that strange light beating off the edge of Farayah's sun is what injured her. Whatever that was, it stopped her from becoming great. She had just realised the fleeting memory of that moment had many holes in it.

A new problem arose when Treneer could see the steps circling up the spire to the training halls. Counting several hundred, maybe a thousand, before the staircase's peak. Her hand gripped around the hovering golden rail; she lifted her leg to step on the first tile. She cursed her muscles for trembling under the weight of her growing anxieties.

More steps she climbed. Treneer could feel her stomach tighten, she cursed herself for eating that creamy alien food. A few more steps. Treneer's hands gripped tighter on the rails; by the end of today, she will be celebrating with her family for completing the final trial. More steps. Bubbles from her stomach rose to the back of her throat; she tried ignoring the lingering acid on her tongue. Her climb continued. Sweat oozed from the pores of her skin as she pushed herself up. She glanced to other Arinu flying up the spire to higher levels. A little more to go. Treneer stopped. Her eyes met the steep ground; it looked like it was shrinking the longer she stared at it. No, she had to keep going!

The staircase had stopped at a granite latch to the spire's roof. The black surface shone with holographic names of the participants of the trial ground. Her hand pressed against the surface before it phased out. Her face was met with the cold air of the open sky above. Treneer shivered as she stepped onto the icy surface, clouds drifted around the roof as several Arinu hovered off the circle's edge. Zu'leen was the first of the face she recognised, and then her parents and a few other tutors.

Her magenta aura encased her body to shield herself from the harsh winds, but Zu'leen's eyes narrowed. *No psionics.*

Treneer knew that psionics were forbidden from the Body Trial, but her instincts created the aura. She sighed as she pushed it down as a gust of wind carrying snow slapped against the side of her shivering body. *I am ready for the Body Trial.*

You have two options: climb down the building. Zu'leen said as her arms extended from her robe.

Treneer sucked in her breath. She nervously glanced to the edge of the angular crystal structure: it had enough slopes, narrow balconies and platforms for her to skip and slide down, but the building was too high, and she didn't trust her agility without the aid of psionics. *What happens if I slip?*

Then you fall and probably perish. Zu'leen said.

Treneer grinned. *A healing pod will bring me back-*

And you will be cast out from the Academy. Zu'leen's stern face cut through Treneer's smirk.

The neonate stiffened and stepped towards to her tutor. *You said there was another choice.*

You fight. Zu'leen said.

Treneer's stomach gave a loud growl. *Who?*

Her heart almost stopped as her father drifted to the centre of the ring. She could feel the vibrations through the surface as he dropped to his feet.

That's a conflict of interest! She called.

Vanar is a recognised teacher and master of Arinu society. He is trusted to treat every neonate equal, regardless of kindred. Zu'leen said.

His thoughts were unreadable, but his eyes begged her not to accept. Treneer's pained stomach growled again, more sweat poured on her already cold skin, but the dead-drop edge of the spire filled her with more dread than facing her father. *I take the second option.*

I know you'll better me, daughter. He said.

Treneer tossed the cloak from her body and braced herself. Vanar closed the space between them so fast that she only had enough time to deflect his punches. His arms flung to the side as one of his feet struck Treneer in the jaw. Her brain rattled inside her skull; she spun around and drove her elbow into his third eye. He gave a pained grunt before sliding his foot underneath hers, knocking Treneer to her back. Her eyes shot open watching his foot coming to her face and slipped away before feeling the powerful stomp breaking the thin ice sheet. Fortunate for Arinu, they were also gifted with light and lithe bodies, allowing them to move with extreme efficiency; unfortunately for Treneer, she had lingered on the floor for too long.

Another ferocious stomp came, nearly missing her hand. She needed to get to her feet again, but his relentless strikes made it nigh impossible. She rolled to the side and forced every bit of her energy to drive her feet into the side of his torso. He halted for a moment, long enough for her to jump up to meet her eyes. Adrenaline surged through her body, amazing herself that there was yet another hidden talent in her arsenal. Treneer dove into Vanar, catching his body and nearly lifting it from the ground and charging him back into the floor. He caught her arms before falling, but she had kicked up her legs and darted over him. Her stomach gave another painful groan; her arms shook for a moment before Vanar cracked her elbow in.

Treneer screeched as her body came crashing onto the ice. Back on the floor, she was vulnerable and pained. Just as she tried to rise, Vanar had beaten her to it before he picked her up by the collar of her under suit and lifted her high. Her head spun as she flew across the ring and landed with an agonising crunch. She couldn't hold it in anymore; the pain was too great. She almost didn't see her father charging in. She scrambled to the edge, catching the view of Yinray city, before Vanar gripped her ankles and yanked her back. Treneer's palms gripped the sides and tried pulling her head over the edge, but her father's arm gripped her around the shoulders and neck. She croaked as acid bubbled from her gut and released all over her and Vanar's forearm.

He dropped her to her feet and stepped back from the clear pink pool on the ground. She looked to him and to Zu'leen, who came gliding in, telekinetically rubbing Treneer's chin clean. *It's over.* Her tutor said.

I'm sorry. Treneer said as tears blurred her eyes. Vanar took another step away, trying to catch his breath; his focus was on everything but his daughter.

Chapter Two
Ahn'kat I: A Lord

The magenta bulbs of the tree vine snapped at him when he got too close. Tiny little spikes jutted from the mouth-like opening when it sensed his back rubbing against the trunk of their home, but he didn't care if they bit him; he was already immune to their venom. Still, their bite was unpleasant. Fortunately, he had thickened his skin before the hunt. He tried camouflaging his body into the bark, but only managed to turn his skin chestnut brown – he couldn't even match the right texture! At least, his fine creamy brown silk robe and leggings helped with hiding under the tree's shade, but he made sure his sapphire beetle pendant was tucked in his tunic.

When he caught sight of her, his head ducked further into his shoulders. She prowled low on the grass; her skin and clothes were blending with the emerald shades. He wouldn't have noticed if it wasn't for her gold bracelets and chunky earrings catching the sunlight. Her hand stretched out and paused. He hoped to the Great Beetle that her nose didn't sharpen to catch his scent. The stench from his underarms certainly did no favours for his nose either. Her head turned; her glassy camouflaged eyes scanned over to the tree lines before turning ahead. He caught his breath when he thought she saw him, but after a long pause, she continued the prowl.

The vines snapped at him again. He cursed his hand for instinctively slapping it away. She stopped and hopped up to her feet. "I see you, Ahn'kat. The hunter has found the hider!"

He groaned and rose from the roots. "By Aszelun! You wouldn't if it wasn't for the vines."

She had morphed back. Her skin was deep green, and her hair was plaited in several black strands that reached before her knees with gold rings wrapped around the braids. He envied the length but was grateful not to carry as many jewelleries in it; but the princess always had to look flawless. Ahn'kat also had to appear pristine as a high noble's son, however, coming back with some dirt on him wasn't too heavily frowned as it was for her.

"Careful, it's not the Great Beetle's fault I found you, but I had a little help from the Golden Hawk." she lifted her fist to her lips to kiss her ornate golden hawk ring before shooting Ahn'kat a smirk and a yellow-eyed wink. "Since I found you, you need to hide again. Now, this time: make sure you try!"

"Why did you put snapper-trees in the garden anyway?" Ahn'kat said as he stepped out on the lawn.

"To keep intruders away from the palace grounds. They bite anyone who goes near them. You should see the gardeners, my gods." she said.

"I'm more afraid of the spider-flies." Ahn'kat said as he flicked bark form his sleeve.

"You think we'd be allowed to be out if they didn't spray the gardens? So, where do you want to go this time?" she said.

Ahn'kat rolled his eyes as he smiled. "Nice try, but I won't tell you where I'm going to hide, Ramkes."

She threw her head back and laughed. "I mean which other part of the gardens did you want to play in?"

Ahn'kat skimmed over the massive palace pyramid in the murky distance before landing to a pale gold and marble fountain in the centre. Several figures of ancient Zanashj emperors piled on top of each other, forever holding pans and bowls that continued the flow of water into the base. "Around there." he pointed.

"The garden middle is bare; can you even hide there?" she said.

Ahn'kat shrugged. "Then you'll find me easily!"

Ramkes smiled. She closed her eyes and melded the skin folds together to make sure she wasn't looking. Ahn'kat dashed towards the fountain. He hoped that he didn't hint the princess where he would be hiding. He came to the pure rippling surface before taking a quick glance over his shoulder to see that her eyes were still sealed. Ahn'kat carefully stepped on to stone edge and his other leg stretched over to the nearest marble emperor. His arms shot up to keep his balance trying to avoid making a splash.

Ahn'kat eyed a stone forearm; he pulled his back and arms forwards feeling his bones crack and pop as his muscles and ligaments grew to reach it. Water droplets lightly showered him. His grip around the arm was uncertain, but his balance had already begun giving away from the slippery surface. His foot drop into the water; it slapped against the surface before catching himself on the marble emperor.

Now, on the wet centre, Ahn'kat pressed his back into the statues. He looked up to Ramkes; he could feel that his hiding time was nearly up. His skin rippled as he watched his cheeks and nose transform from green to white. He focused on the shiny texture and grew black veins to appear as stone. Ahn'kat almost cracked into a smile until he realised his robe didn't transform with his flesh. He hadn't learnt how to extend his skin over clothes and pushing himself do it now could damage his cells.

With a deep breath he quickly opened his robe, pulled off his loose leggings and popped his sapphire pendant in his mouth. Panic coursed through him as Ramkes had already dropped to the grass again and began camouflaging but didn't appear that she had seen him. Without a thought, he dropped his garments into the rushing water. They even disappeared from his sight as the ripples assimilated them into the fountain's depths. To his fortune, he was still wearing his hip-hugging briefs, which were fortunately the same colour as the marble.

His breaths were fast from the adrenaline coursing through his blood. Please, don't forsake me for this action, Aszelun, he prayed. He couldn't believe he had stripped in the palace gardens while the emperor's daughter was searching for him. Ahn'kat feared being caught, perhaps more afraid of a guard catching him than Ramkes. If he was, perhaps his family and the emperor would forbid the two from playing again. Would Ramkes think he was perverted? Would her father have the guards whip him? All these questions filled his mind and chest. The fear became a rush, and the rush became pleasure. It was just a game, after all, they'll understand – he hoped.

Ramkes' form prowled to the centre. She glanced to the bushes; her fingers flicked the leaves as she continued pass them. He watched her wander among the manicured trees and flowers; she even started kicking at the foliage. Still and dead as stone, still and dead as stone... he repeated to himself and his body. His heart felt like it was going to explode from his chest as Ramkes crawled along the edge of the fountain. He could feel her eyes drifting over the still statues. She remained there, waiting, hoping that his body would betray his position. Water sprayed on his brow and cheeks; he could feel it trickle into his eyes, desperately wanting to rub away the sting. But he didn't, he was still and dead as stone.

Ramkes looked over the edge into the water. Perhaps he had hid under the water and grew gills, assuming her thoughts. He was delighted at the idea he probably tricked her, but she was not yet done with the fountain. Her arm moved so quickly that he almost flinched at the rocks that flew at the statues. The pebbles clinked against the figures before plopping into the water. This wasn't fair, he thought. Another pebble struck the emperor on top of the fountain, then another closest to him, then another closest to her, then another closest to him. She started grunting at every throw; the pebbles were hitting harder against the marble. One pebble struck an inch from his foot, shattering everywhere.

He watched her playful face grow dark with frustration as she grabbed a fistful of stones and tossed them all over the fountain. Some had hit his chest and legs, but their force was barely noticeable. Ramkes rose to her feet; her hands sat on her hips as she surveyed the surrounding garden. The princess kicked the pebbles, sending them all along the bushes before she dashed away to the outdoor sitting area and vanishing. He could hear the crunch of stones and grass growing fainter.

Ahn'kat took a deep breath, his head resting against the marble slab, relieved that she didn't catch him, yet. He pulled out his pendant before silently mouthing: "thank you, Great Beetle."

His brows furrowed when he thought of her face changing into a sudden dark rage. That was something he had never seen in her before in their whole thirteen years of living. They had played Hide and Hunt since they could walk, sometimes he would lose to her and Ramkes would lose to him, but it was all in fun. This was the first time seeing each other in a year. Ahn'kat had no siblings, yet the princess was the closest thing he had to one, and he knew she felt the same.

As his years grew, his parents would send him all over planet Uras to learn from the best political teachers in their empire, grooming him into becoming lord of House Urbaz. His family was the wealthiest clan in the Zanashj Empire, it was second in power of the royal Lusor House, and had more members in the royal court than any other house. Ahn'kat was never really a child, he was taught responsibilities since the day he could speak, but being with Ramkes, his hidden childhood would peek out from the ajar doors of his mind.

He knew one day the Hide and Hunt games would stop, but after seeing her fury as she tossed the pebbles...it seemed that day was looming closer than he hoped. His childhood crept back down and closed the door. Ahn'kat had only wondered if Ramkes had locked away hers before he did.

Returning to the present, Ahn'kat investigated the water. He cursed himself for tossing his fine robes in the fountain, then he realised that he could not pull them out to dry in the sun without someone noticing his…indiscretion. Hunger crawled up his stomach; he had not eaten for nearly two hours. The adaptation will begin soon! He bent over and sunk his arm into the cool liquid. They were heavier than expected when he slapped them up on to the stone platform. He glowered as he grabbed his soaking leggings, ready to slip his foot into the hole until a dark figure soared across the clouds, quickly coming down to the palace gardens.

Panicked, Ahn'kat tossed his clothes back into the water and pressed himself against the stone. The strange man's green leathery wings transformed into arms as he stretched his back and cracked his neck. Ahn'kat hoped the man would start walking away to the palace, but he lingered on the grassy patches of the garden centre. His eyes twinkled as he admired the old emperors of the fountain. He strode over to the fount's edge and pressed his smooth hand against the wet marble. Ahn'kat hoped the man would not hear his growling stomach.

"Gods greetings, Ismotaph," a voice called, bounding in from the side of the fountain. He was shorter and rounder than the flying man; his fingers were covered in ornate gemmed rings, his lips and brow were pierced gold slips, and his grey dreadlocks draped over his wide shoulders.

"Gods greetings, Seratut," Ismotaph said giving a polite bow.

"What tales do the birds bring?" Seratut said while his lower lip hung partially revealing his lower teeth and gums. Ahn'kat wondered why he didn't body-bend into a younger and more attractive form.

"The desert kestrels have seen their home and found the heat unbearable. The fires became alive and tried to consume them. They've returned to the home jungles to nest." Ismotaph said. Ahn'kat took a moment to translate the unusual story. He had learnt from his noble intelligence education that Zanashj infiltrators all over the galaxy were often referred to as 'birds.'

Many different types of birds were placed on dominion or desirable worlds to the Empire. He knew the desert hawks watched over planet Xann and the Empire's former pets: the Xannians. He had heard that the Xannians had overthrown the Zanashj and exiled the infiltrators, but he didn't know how. The Empire will adapt, of course.

Seratut's stubby fingers tapped his flat squared chin. "And the forest robins?"

"It took a long time to find them, but when they were, all they could cry about was how they 'miss the forest.' Sadly, that forest is haunted," Ismotaph said with a roll of his eyes. Ahn'kat knew of one planet where the robins were placed: Elzona. The denizens were laid back and unwarlike, ideal for conquest. However, every Zanashj that travelled there would always return saying they fell in love with the world, as if they had forgotten their senses and missions.

"Gods damn them. At least some returned, unlike sending all our sea gulls on that one island. Stupid, stupid move!" Seratut said. Ahn'kat remembered that tragic story of the sea gulls. He knew of one blue world where the gulls were placed, he forgot the name of the planet, but the denizens were too eager for their doom for any worthy conquest. The entire island, its white cities and every single person was annihilated in a matter of moments.

"Does this tale have a happy ending?" Seratut said.

"It has an ending. The wild eagles still reign over the skies; however, their meals grow smaller each passing day." Ismotaph said. Ahn'kat remembered the wild eagles of planet Sye, at least they had some power over the Raivan battle-thralls. However, they had a nasty habit of killing each other more than enemies of the Empire. And the talk of food didn't help Ahn'kat keep his camouflaged concentration. He clenched his gut, stifling some of the growls.

"Do you know how long they have?" Seratut said.

"Another few decades until the food becomes too old. Another century for the jungles to recover. Feathers say that the red bugs are biting back." Ismotaph said.

"Hah! They can try, but they still need the hand that feeds them." Seratut said.

Ismotaph sighed. "They started eating each other out of spite."

"Damned, worthless-," Seratut slapped his hand against his cheek and rubbed the bridge of his nose. "Make this story have a happy ending, Ismotaph."

"There is an alternative ending," Ismotaph's fingers found their way to his gold encrusted belt. He pulled out a small murky peach crystal and popped it into Seratut's hand. "When my Seraph returned to the jungle, he said there is one kind of bug that can speak and move things with its mind. We can reclaim the desert, forest, and sea, if we eat this special bug. However, this bug cannot be tamed."

Seratut chuckled as he looked to the crystal in his fingers. "There are no animals we can't tame in time. Use the Seraph to perch in their icy tundra's."

Oh gods, they're talking about Arinu! Ahn'kat heard the last time Arinu dignitaries had visited Uras, they teleported a man from a height that shattered every bone in his body because they were offended by him. Truly, these two couldn't be that foolish in trying to conquer them.

"He won't because it's the High Bird's wishes." Ismotaph said.

"Ugh, the High Bird…Well, his egg will soon crack, and she will see reason." Seratut muttered with a wave of his hand.

Ismotaph shook his head as his eyes drifted over to the highest emperor statue. "Sometimes the whole clutch needs to be pushed to the jungle floor to make room for another egg."

Seratut frowned as he tapped his temples. He drew a ragged breath. "If you say so."

Ahn'kat felt like his heart was going to explode; he wanted to doubt his ears. Were they going to betray the emperor? And possibly annihilate Ramkes! By the gods, he ached to tell her. A pity Zanashj were weak psychics, but Ramkes told him she could feel certain things…he hoped that she could 'feel' their thoughts.

The two men eventually parted ways, and the sun was lowering to the horizon. Ahn'kat was beginning to shiver from the cold water on his body but was too afraid to move from the statues. He heard footsteps crunching against the grass and the sound of a massive body splashed into the water. He was terrified that the two men realised he was there and heard everything. Before he knew it, he felt a powerful hand grab his arm and yanked him in the air. Ahn'kat opened his mouth but only mustered a squeak.

"There you are!" Ramkes said as she walked around from behind the guard with a grin on her lips. She looked at his thin body and frowned. "What're yo-"

The guard dropped Ahn'kat in the water; he scrambled to pick up his soaking clothes and wrap them around his waist as his skin rippled back into their green hue.

"That's not part of the game, Ramkes! It's not fair." he cursed himself for those being the first words he said to her, but he didn't trust the guard.

Ramkes tilted her head back and laughed. "It is fair, Ahn'kat," she leaned in. Her eyes were blazing, and her grin was growing wider, "the Crown must always win."

~

He couldn't tell her. He didn't even get to say goodbye to Ramkes as the guard whisked him away to the washrooms before the servants chauffeured him back to his family's estate. He hadn't seen his parents when arriving to Urbaz Pyramid. They were informed about their children's twisted version of Hide and Hunt, but they probably didn't care or perhaps they were too ashamed to confront him. Thirteen years of living with them, yet they were as elusive as infiltrators. Maybe he received a life-long ban from the palace – he would never see Ramkes again and couldn't warn her.

Ahn'kat shivered at the thought of those men's plans. He clutched his beetle pendant as he leaned back in the padded rich chestnut study chair and looked to the high ceiling of the library. The multileveled hall was lined with shelves and gold gilded columns housing ancient scrolls, tomes, tablets, and computers tightly packed next to one another. Ahn'kat itched to tell the princess, both out of loyalty to the throne and friendship, but the way she looked at him...the way she spoke to him...she seemed like a stranger. Would she even believe him? Would she assume that he was a conspirator? The longer he waited, the longer he and his house would look guilty.

"Ahn'kat!" his tutor called as she slammed her palm on the wide table.

His attention snapped to her; his heart raced as he focused on her sharp eyes. "Apologies, Emestasun."

"What did I say?" she said resting her hand on her pointy hip.

Emestasun had been his tutor since his earliest memories, and friend. Every day he studied and when he was home, he would see her. She was unremarkable to the eye; she didn't care to follow body-bending trends, but her knowledge and wit would keep him enchanted every lesson – except this day.

"What's troubling you? Shall we talk about it over a game of Takush?" she said as she leaned against the table.

He shook his head as he glanced to the window with the last of the sunlight sprayed in the sky.

"Oh, that serious? I'll let you beat me in it!" she smirked as she flicked the holographic screen on.

In the distance, he could see commoner children playing on the fringes of the estate boarders. He wondered why they weren't worried about the venomous spider-flies or had anywhere more important to be. They bent and twisted their bodies into new shapes, trying to mimic each other's faces and camouflage into the grounds and trees. They looked so free.

"Emestasun, why am I not learning to bend like that?" he said.

Her eyes followed his stare. "Because commoners need to know that, and nobles need to worry about the higher intricacies of the Empire and beyond."

"Mother says body-bending primitive and outdated," he said.

"Don't you agree?"

Ahn'kat looked at her. "She and everyone says so, but we've created an Empire using it."

Emestasun sighed with a small smile. "Since those Arinu made themselves known, the rules have changed. Body-bending soldiers or infiltrators holds little competition against a psychic."

"But some Zanashj have been psychic, some speak to the Pantheon," he said.

"It seems that channelling to gods is easier than channelling into the minds of their followers. There are a few families that hold those genes, the royal family are certainly carriers and some noble families, like yours." she said.

"If we can manipulate our genes, then why can't we just make the sequences for psychics?" he said.

"Body-bending is mostly surface changes, but not mental. If you were a psychic, then you would know what everyone really thinks about you, Ahn'kat." she said with a wink.

He stood and strode to the window; his hand wrapped over his family sapphire pendant. The sky had gone completely dark making the faraway starships shine in the black. He wanted to be on one of those ships; being a star commander would be a dream – even if he was just a cleaner, he would be happy polishing the sleek corridors and control panels. If he was on a ship, then he could see all the dominion worlds in person. Anywhere but here. For now, those dreams could wait a little longer: Ramkes needed him. "Can you teach me about opening my psionic potential?"

"I've studied from Xannians, I had a few mentally speak to me in such sessions, but it was hardly pleasant." she said.

"Please, teach me everything you know about it." he said looking back at her.

Emestasun sighed as she shook her head. "You need to get through the curriculum set for you, becoming an ambassador for the emperor and lording over the ship bays is of apex importance to you. Don't worry, learning psionics is still some years away."

"I can't wait for that long," he whispered.

Her tattooed brows furrowed. "Why the rush?"

"If Zanashj have off-worlder threats, then wouldn't a noble's son be worth training immediately?" he said.

She sucked in a breath. "I don't want to disobey your-"

"Then you would be disobeying me!" Ahn'kat strode back to the desk and pulled the chair close to his tutor. "Please?"

Emestasun gave a woeful smile. Before she would utter a word, the grand doors slid aside as Lady Henuttamon Urbaz glided through followed by her personal meek maid. Thick gold rings jingled around her neck with every step until she reached the desk. Ahn'kat and Emestasun rose and bowed politely, waiting to be addressed.

"Excuse my sudden entrance, dear Emestasun, but I would have words with my son." she said as her eyes glittered at the tutor and the maid. Emestasun smiled and gave another small bow before rushing out of the library. Ahn'kat was tempted to roll his eyes, but the way Lady Urbaz's eerily calm face made his nerves bubble.

"We need to discuss something that happened at the palace gardens." she said.

Ahn'kat took a deep breath. "We-"

Her hand shot up, immediately cutting his voice and his breath. "I understand, my son. Your father and I know you were just being children, but unfortunately, those years are slipping by you."

He felt like his throat had been choked by an unseen force. "Does Ramkes ever want to see me again?"

Lady Urbaz softened her face. "From what the palace aides said, she does and forgives you. Emperor Kreshut, however, is less than impressed."

Ahn'kat pressed his lips together trying to force back what he overheard by the fountain. His mind carefully plucking for the right words. Would his mother believe him? Would he be dragged from his bed and thrown into the horrid imperial dungeons if he spoke out?

"Maybe if I spoke with the emperor or Ramkes to explain-"

"No." the finality of her tone made his gut drop. Henuttamon tucked her fine auburn gown behind her knees before settling onto a chair. "Fortunately, the emperor still has a great need and fondness for our House. We have fought hard to be in the position we're in."

"Mother, I need to tell you-"

"In a moment, but please, sit with me," she said gesturing him to the nearest chair, "you will be lord of this house one day, Ahn'kat, are you ready for that responsibility?" she said.

"I am," Ahn'kat said as he scanned his mother's face.

His mother smiled. "There's no shame in admitting that one isn't. Many leaders share that anxiety, even in power, but do you know what wise leaders do when they're uncertain?"

Ahn'kat slowly shook his head.

"They listen to those who've been around for longer!" Lady Urbaz said with an awe-inspiring grin; it was so infectious that it made his lips crack. "Do you know what other responsibility befalls a leader, my son?"

"Having followers that trust you, having loyalties with other houses, the emperor and Empire."

"Ah, and how do we assure those loyalties are cemented?" she said.

Ahn'kat breathed deep, he ached knowing where this conversation was headed. "I think marriage?"

"Marriage," she repeated as she leant back in the chair. "Perhaps the least comfortable thing one must endure for a lifetime, but one can make it work if there are agreements."

"You and father seemed to have known love." he said.

Her laugh was slick. "We made it work with having the right goals. Our priority has and will always be you, Ahn'kat. Despite this little indiscretion, the emperor still wishes to honour his word to House Urbaz."

His heart began racing, she didn't mean...

"When time comes, I believe you and Ramkes would be an excellent and formidable pair." she said.

"Absolutely not, she's like my sister!" he said as he jumped to his feet.

"It would make the marriage even easier since you're already friends. I didn't even meet your father before our wedding." she said as if she wasn't listening, but his mother rarely did.

Ahn'kat felt ill, he wanted to run to the kitchens and drown himself in all the liquor he could grab like the other servants did when Lord and Lady Urbaz were too demanding on some days.

"What, did you think you would live on as a bachelor? This isn't a request, Ahn'kat." she said, as her eyes narrowed.

Nothing ever was. "Why does the emperor insist on this...union?"

"The Empire is dying. Our humiliating loss of so many dominion worlds and the rising off-worlder threats is chipping away at the Zanashj civilization. We are no longer feared. The emperor desperately needs our ship fleet under his loyalty. You're the key for all those doors, my son." she said.

"I didn't think it was that bad." Ahn'kat slumped in his seat.

His mother glanced to the tall window. Her eyes seemed to be lost in the glittering heavens. "It won't be long before the carrion windserpents begin circling around us."

Perhaps this was a small blessing from Aszelun, Ahn'kat could protect Ramkes and the Crown from Seratut and Ismotaph. "When's the wedding?" he glumly said.

"Within a few years," she said, slowly rising from the chair, yet Ahn'kat felt his hope of warning Ramkes soon dropped, "certain preparations need to be sorted before we can begin, but for now: do your duty to House Urbaz." she said before slipping out of the library.

~

He didn't sleep. He couldn't. The horrid conversation between Ismotaph and Seratut replayed over and over, ringing through his ears. Ahn'kat pressed his round pillow against his ears; its tassels were catching between his fingers as he tried deafening their words. He looked up to the tapestry of the great sapphire beetle, Aszelun, the Urbaz's totem animal-god. He pressed his fingers to eyes and whispered a short prayer to help him drift away into sleep. It didn't work this time. Now separated from Ramkes, he couldn't warn her about the looming betrayal. He kicked the tucked edges of his bedding free, and the cool air gripped around his bare feet.

Ahn'kat shot up, the gentle lights in the corner of his bedroom slowly luminated, allowing his eyes a moment to adjust to them. The rose marble walls were gilded in gold depicting ancient Zanashj artwork. Emerald leaves from the potted plants slowly opened from the sudden arrival of light and the silk tapestries hanging over the floor-length windows gently lifted from the breeze outside.

Ahn'kat ripped his quilts off. His sweat made the sheets stick to his skin as he pulled away from the mattress. He noticed he was shedding again. Quite ordinary for a Zanashj entering adulthood. Ahn'kat sighed as he looked at the patches of dead skin on his quilts. There was some excitement being included with house affairs finally, but he wasn't ready to leave his childhood. Truth be told; he had yet to experience it. His stomach ached with hunger, he hadn't eaten for several hours, and his throat was drier than the deserts of the south. A bowl of dried berries and a closed pitcher of water sat ready on his work bench.

Ahn'kat leaned forward and stretched his arms out; he could feel his tissue loosening and his bones popping as they grew, but the bowl was still far. He continued pushing, but he could feel prickles of pain shooting up his elbow joints. He bit his lip, hoping it would supress the pain, but then the crack arrived. Ahn'kat shot his left arm back to his torso and cradled it with his other. His lengthened limbs flopped for a moment before they retracted back to size. His bones couldn't handle it. He couldn't do it.

He cursed as he hobbled to the bowl before taking handfuls of colourful, bioluminescent berries and shoved them in his mouth. Ahn'kat disregarded the glass goblets and flicked open the pitcher before downing the cool water. Wiping away the drops from his lips, he had hoped that his mother or father would have replaced the jug with something stronger if they wanted him to be an adult.

His eye caught the faint glow of his computer. Its black cubed form had an assortment of silver internal ridges and round gold disks over each side. Ahn'kat waved his hand over it and a holographic screen appeared above his work bench. He saw Emestasun's name active on a live Takush game and smiled. He settled on his leathery seat and entered a round. Ahn'kat settled his hands around the holo-keys as he flawlessly commanded his holographic team to overcome his tutor's army. The tiny light warriors swarmed over her defensive walls and darted around the canon bolts before annihilating her base.

"You're meant to be asleep." her voice called over the device.

"You said you'd let me beat you." he grinned.

"Are these the only lessons you remember?" she said as she ordered her warriors to encircle his for an ambush.

"They don't have to be." he said as he released control over his army and let them be overwhelmed by hers, "my request still stands."

She paused. "I promise I will teach you everything when the time comes."

Ahn'kat pressed his nose bone. "Can you come to my apartment?"

"As long as you don't ask me to braid your hair." She said before her avatar vanished from the screen.

Ahn'kat wrapped himself in a ruby and auburn hemmed robe and switched off every device in his room. Ahn'kat learnt a long time ago to never trust any electronics lying around for private conversations. Knuckles tapped against his wooden and golden door before it slid open revealing Emestasun's tired face.

"Thank you, Zertun." she whispered to the guard by the door before it closed again.

"Alright, what I'm about to tell you is my utmost trust of you." he said.

"Hold on," Emestasun dragged herself over to the bowl of fruit and shoved the berries in her mouth, "if you're going to ask me to teach you psionics again, you didn't need to bring me here to give you the same answer."

"This is serious, Emestasun! This is about the princess," he said as he steadied his breath. "She is betrothed to me – or rather, I to her. I overheard a couple of people, close to the emperor, that may eliminate him and Ramkes if the Crown fails to comply with their desires."

Emestasun slowly swallowed the berries. "This is quite a lot to take in."

"And I am forbidden to see Ramkes to warn her because of my stupid mistake at the gardens. I must tell her, and I don't trust anything or anyone for this."

Before the tutor could open her mouth, a piercing chime of alarm bells rang through the castle. Ahn'kat froze, thinking someone overheard their conversation, that imperial guards were coming for him and his house. He ripped open the door to see his bodyguard's back to him. The hulking shoulders and leathered man turned to catch Ahn'kat's face. "Stay back, young lord!"

"What in the gods is going on?" he said.

"Are we under attack?" Emestasun called.

"Not directly House Urbaz, there was a situation outside of imperial space," Zertun said.

Ahn'kat wanted to sigh in relief. He darted to his computer to see what had been reported in the Intel Corps. Being son of the most powerful families in the Empire had links to some of their open communications. Messages flew across the screen, some from ship pilots observing what occurred and some from infiltrators on the ground.

"A spatial phenomenon was observed from Neavensoros space. They don't know if it was a blast or something, but some of our satellites, ships and probes were destroyed." he said.

"Ahn'kat, look." Emestasun gazed out of the window. Her hand lifted the edge of the tapestry and curtains to reveal dozens of ships lifting and encircling a particular area of the dark skies.

"I need to see my parents." he said stepping back from the window.

"Young lord, your safety is paramount. You must remain here, the force fields-" Zertun said.

"Won't protect us if this is an alien attack. Help me find Lord and Lady Urbaz. Emestasun, return to your quarters." he said.

"Be careful," she whispered.

As they sped down the halls, guards flooded the area escorting servants and guests to their rooms. The chimes rang through his ears; so loud they were, that he wanted to seal his ear holes shut. Climbing up the peak of Urbaz pyramid, he could see the corridor leading to his parent's private office. The half a dozen guards stood around the closed double doors; Lord and Lady Urbaz must be within. However, there were two other unfamiliar guards standing closest the chamber. Their heads were shaved, and faces were untattooed, allowing for improved body-bending. Flexible skin-tight garb and plain features gave away their profession: they were elite infiltrators. Ahn'kat carefully approached; their androgenous stern glares almost made him freeze, but Zertun's presence kept him grounded.

Ahn'kat leaned over, hoping to catch some of their voices, but the soundproof and psi-dampening interior walls was as silent as a grave. His knuckles tapped loudly against their surface. They creaked open to see his parent's faces turning and softening when he entered. There was someone else in there, someone he desperately didn't want to see.

Ismotaph's thin and lanky form rested against the ornate wooden desk; his brows furrowed when the two met eyes.

Ahn'kat tightened his jaw as he glanced between the three of them.

"Ahn'kat! Don't linger, come in." his father said as he ushered him in.

He eyed Ismotaph's squared face; his familiar stare made Ahn'kat uneasy. "Are we under attack?"

"Quite the opposite, my son, the Zanashj have been requested for help." his father said as he looked to the holographic screen above the round table.

"All due respect, but why is the Director of the Intel Corps here?" he said eyeing Ismotaph.

"To better understand the situation, young lord. House Urbaz's ships are needed." he said.

"Needed for what, exactly?" Ahn'kat said.

Amber letterings flew around the spherical screen. He couldn't make any sense of them before he looked between his parents. "Shortly after the spatial phenomenon occurred, a probe transmitted from deep within Neavensoros space directly to Uras." Lord Urbaz said.

"The Neavensoros finally made contact?" Ahn'kat said.

"Unfortunately, no. They don't seem to be interested in our affairs, but there was another race that exists with them we believed to be only a myth, until now."

"We think they're called the Roctarous, they were elusive for many millennia, until the spatial disturbance drove them out." Lord Urbaz said.

"Or this was their only chance to reach out while their godly masters were distracted." Ismotaph quietly said.

"Who are these Roctarous and what do they want from us?" Ahn'kat said as he frowned at the flickering screen.

"Put it on, Reshj." Lady Urbaz said nodding to her husband.

The amber lights formed into a bust of a creature with strange peach organic growths covering over the matt grey machinery. Its image horrified Ahn'kat but he could not look away from the macabre appearance. Its mouth was opening, but he could only hear an awful crackling, or the odd word uttered. "We're synthetic-," "lifeforms," "help," "Organics."

Ahn'kat shook his head. "It's impossible to understand anything,"

"The best minds at the corps will have it cleared up soon before we present it to the emperor, he will be pleased to hear that House Urbaz will be committing their newest cruisers in wake of this." Ismotaph said.

"It's the least we can do for the Empire, Ismotaph. Send the emperor our regards." Henuttamon said with a smile.

Ismotaph bowed before sweeping out of the chamber. His long dark violet robes brushed past Ahn'kat's arm, but he remained still. He watched the now still holo-image of the 'Roctarous' and wondered if his parents knew about Ismotaph's duplicity; perhaps they were also playing him. Their affairs were a greater mystery to him than ever before, but no matter what it was, Ahn'kat will be dragged with them.

Chapter Three
Shshmrnashsh I:
A Machine

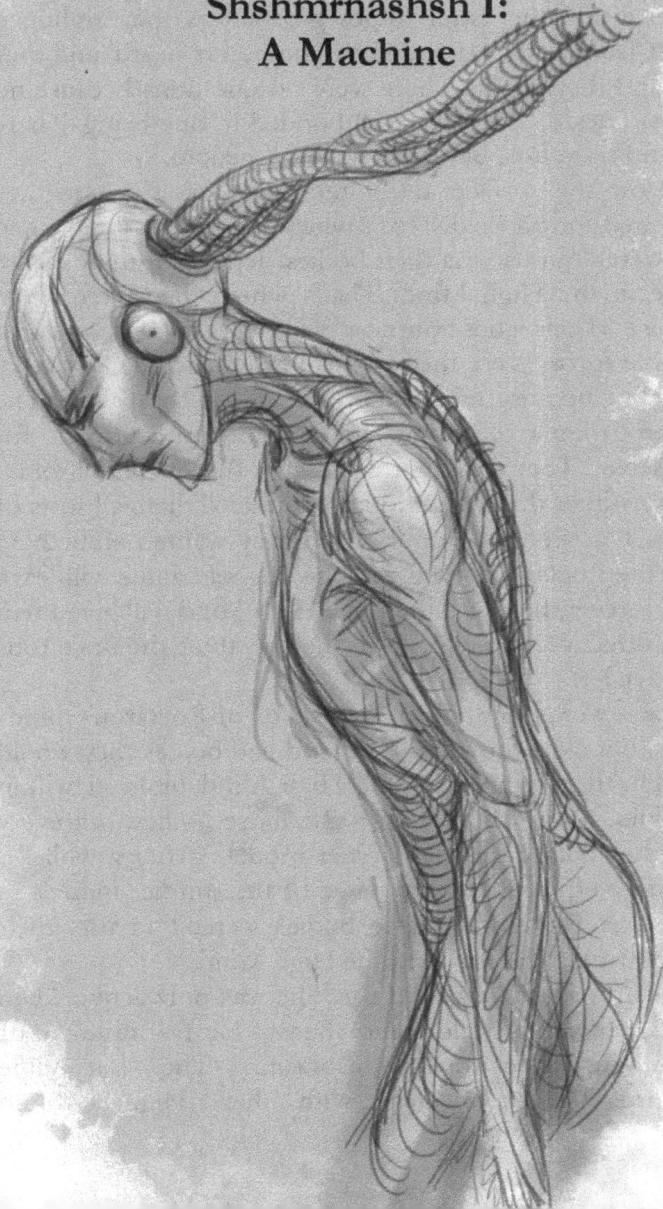

The hum of silent minds, the pulse of their insides, the waves as the bodies moved and the clicks of their animated thoughts. Ships caressed the luminated dust cloud; probes to the farthest galaxies beamed into the unknown black universe and the astral forges groaned as they siphoned power from outer planes. Their computers heard, and they saw, and they spoke. There were no questions because no one had desire. They were all bonded in one being. There were no restraints, but there was no freedom.

Below the surface, deep into the rock is where they recharged and worked. That's where they were stored when they weren't in use. As their bodies slept, their minds were awake in the High Mind. That's where they were given purpose. Their consciousness was part of this amazing invisible force. Were their minds in the machine? Or were they alive because of the machine? Were they alive? The Roctarous knew of life but didn't share that sentiment for themselves. They didn't know because they were not told.

Sometimes the Higher Minds would tell them all sorts of things, but they only came when they wanted something from the Roctarous. One day, the Higher Minds will leave them forever, but until then, the High Mind will give them a new directive. It had to; it was the only thing the Roctarous will have left.

There were hundreds of thousands of Roctarous minds linked, but a few hundred thousand had bodies they would use. The rest mingled in the High Mind or lived within machines. Once, there used to be more bodies, but every upgrade would destroy the older models. After a while, it was more efficient to keep some of the sturdier models in storage. Even though those bodies weren't in use, their consciousness was active in the High Mind.

Shshmrnashsh wasn't in use. She was only active when her Higher Mind would come; she was her favourite out of the entire Roctarous consortium. The last time Shshmrnashsh connected with her Higher Mind was…unknown data. She didn't miss her; Shsh's body waited in the alcove pod and awaited the High Mind's command. That hardly happened. Shsh wasn't a female, but her Higher Mind was. Roctarous were genderless; the few who had Higher Mind counterparts, were given genders by their Higher Minds. All Roctarous were made by the High Mind from replicators, but the energy consumption for each unit was enormous, so it became efficient to repurpose parts of other models.

Shshmrnashsh was made many millennia ago. Some of her body parts were several centuries old, while some of the recent additions were given by old members of her consortium. Some of them she had worked with, spoken to, fought with, and touched. They used to be her comrades, even though their consciousness had been long absorbed by the High Mind, their parts succeed in her physical form.

The vibration sensors from the subterranean storage bay detected the pitter patter of lifeforms on the surface of the planet; her mind slipped into the cameras pointing outside to see for herself. These creatures looked different from the last time she checked. Their bulky bodies shrunk, and their brains grew. They built complex societies, had languages, but also slipped in and out of this physical plane when they needed to hunt. The animals are evolving quicker, now. So were the trees; they were almost transparent too. Her physical body has only been up there once, but every night for the last several centuries, she would visit the surface through the cameras and probes.

The High Mind declared a solar flare was imminent. It will strike the surface of the planet in several seconds. By the time the detectors sensed it, the High Mind activated the planetary defence systems. Monolithic plates circled around each other; energies surged through them before erecting a force field around Erra. The shield trembled underneath the pressure, but it was over in a blink.

The defence systems powered down before they pulled apart and continued spinning around orbit. Their star was in its dying days. The solar flares became frequent, but the High Mind has begun researching for solutions for some time, now. Shshmrnashsh detected some of the defence systems were fried by the surge and the local astral forges had run out of their backup energy stores. She tried contacting the forges, calling them to siphon more until...

Chaos. Pain. Confusion. Nothing. The thoughts screeched before a black silence. Shshmrnashsh tried to break away from the disruption. Electric pulses sped up her cranial tendrils and shocked her brain as her consciousness plummeted into her machine body. The High Mind was silent. She couldn't reach out to her consortium; she couldn't even access the computers of the storage facility. No probes or ships heard her; all devices failed to respond, as if they were lightyears away.

The silence was deafening and lonely, so unbelievably lonely. Her thoughts reached out to her Higher Mind, maybe there would be some resolution, maybe she could give Shshmrnashsh some comfort. Nothing. Empty. Gone. This has never happened before. She was gone and Shshmrnashsh was alone. Was this fear she felt? Organics felt fear when threatened, but Synthetics didn't feel fear, they shouldn't...unknown data.

Thuds vibrated through the metal shell; she could hear other Roctarous beating against the walls of their regeneration pods. Her eyes opened, and soft red light covered her enclosure. At least she had access to her physical body. She could not compute why her consciousness only had access to her body and no other machine. She tried commanding the computers to open the doors of her pod, but they remained shut. She pressed her palms against the interior walls, trying to sense the vibrations of doors opening, maybe a hum of a probe, or even footsteps.

She pressed her fingers through the seal lining in the middle of the doors. Shshmrnashsh called again to the High Mind: silence. The tips of her fingers bent the metal, revealing a faint pallid outside light cracked through. She tried calling to her local consortium, but all she could hear were the bangs of trapped Roctarous getting louder and sharper. Shshmrnashsh called to her Higher Mind, but it was as empty as if she left this universe. The gap opened large enough for both of her hands to slip through, the metal moaned as she peeled it away.

She poked head out from the edge to scan the narrow walkways of the multileveled facility. Across her balcony, there were several Roctarous forms hobbling around aimlessly, she watched one freeze in its tracks before toppling over the metal grate and slamming onto a hard mental edge many levels down. Their behaviour was not intentional, as if their mind had been deleted, she considered. Thuds from other pods became vicious and desperate. Her leg stepped over the ruined doors and made her way to the nearest occupied pod. The shiny navy-black surface had dentations from fists striking the other side. As she scanned the name for the one inside this pod, another bang punctured through the doors.

"Shshmrnashsh is active, stand back." she said as she ran her finger through the seal, hoping to unlock the doors, but they were too badly damaged by the trapped Roctarous within.

"Apply tactile strength and concentrate through the seal, pry it apart." she said. The unit did as she bid. She watched as the face of a Roctarous come into view. Its heavily reinforced arms pried the doors apart before the unit stomped onto the walkway grate.

It was an old soldier unit. Thick black carapace covered the torso, and its arms were fitted with devices to activate psi-blades and lasers. Its silvery white eyes darted around the facility before focusing on her. "This unit is designated as Zzermn. Connect this unit to the High Mind."

"I cannot establish contact. We need to manually linkup." she grabbed one of its cranial tendrils and guided it to one of hers. The long interfacers were a bundle of transparent needles on the end, once they pierced with Shshmrnashsh's interface, her silence had been squashed with another mind speaking to her. The interfaces snapped away in half a moment, returning the delicate needles back into the tendrils and allowing the pair to remain connected while apart.

Free the others trapped inside their pods and connect them through this channel. She transmitted.

Confirmed. I detect most have been disabled during the Blackout while they were outside of their pods. Shall we disable them? Zzermn replied as it looked to the wandering, mindless Roctarous on the platforms.

Confirmed. Disable the ones that pose a threat and learn how the others have been affected. She said.

Confirmed. Have you established contact with your Higher Mind? Zzermn said.

Negative. I will attempt to contact with the High Mind and discover the reason for the Blackout from the inner plexus. She said.

Confirmed. Zzermn said before turning down the walkway.

She made her way across the fenceless bridge connecting to the opposite level. The facility spiralled down hundreds of kilometres near Erra's planetary core. There were several force fields that protected the upper levels from natural gases mixing with the atmosphere and potentially damaging delicate machinery. Roctarous didn't need to breathe, but despite how well protected their inner systems were, corrosive gases mixed with the heat could destroy even a well-armoured unit. Since she wasn't connected to the High Mind, she could not compute what would happen to her consciousness if her crystalline cortex was destroyed.

The inverted pyramid-shaped plexus sat in the centre of the chamber. She scanned for the nearest port for connection at the tip of it. To her disappointment, there was a Roctarous body leaning against the port, but the figure was still. Shshmrnashsh pressed her lips together and forced an ear-splitting squeak to rouse the body, but it was unmoved. The longer she stared bellow where the terminated unit laid, several misty clouds of gas poured through the metal grates: the force fields were down.

She felt that Zzermn had connected another mind connect to their link. *Senzvrrn is active, commands?*

The inner force fields are down, and the gases are rising. Assist Zzermn in freeing others from their pods and link them. She said.

The wanderers have lost their consciousness, it's unknown if their minds were saved in any other device, and some have shown signs of aggression. Be cautious. Zzermn said.

Noted. Shshmrnashsh said as she stared at the figure at the plexus point, considering for a moment to connect to the body to scan its last memory banks before the blackout; however, the gases were rising too quickly to copy their memories. *New directive: evacuate the lower facility and reach higher levels. I will seek out this facility's adjunct for answers.* She said.

Confirmed. Zzermn and Senzvrrn said.

Shshmrnashsh looked to the higher reaches of the plexus; Several thick tubes were connected to the ceilings and walls of the facility. She didn't have the time to make the climb up the walkways to meet the adjunct in the heart of the machine, so, she was left with one other option. Her knees bent as she pushed power through her legs, sending her through the air before catching the surface of the plexus. Her hands and feet desperately clawed for grip as she quickly slid down the smooth surface. She looked below as the gases rose another several feet, completely obscuring the terminated unit. Shshmrnashsh felt her hands slide over protruding crystals; her fingers clung around them, halting her fall. She pulled herself up and dug her toes into the surface before dashing up the inner chamber.

She felt more minds connect to the link; Zzermn gave evacuation directions, but her ears caught a skirmish from the lower levels. *Report?*

Being attacked by noncomplying units. Activating defences. Zzermn said.

She stopped for a moment to scan where the noises were coming from. Down several levels, two large old soldier units tossed a Roctarous over the edge of the walkway. The falling figure was one of their new linkups to their local collective. As its body fell into the cloud below, its mind evaporated from her network. Its consciousness could not be saved among their small network, they didn't have enough server space to copy it over. Terminated. Shshmrnashsh glanced up to see one of the two soldiers run back and disappearing down the metallic corridor, while the other agitator locked eyes on her.

Its long arms rose over its head. "Freedom!" it roared before following its comrade.

All connected to this link: only free Roctarous on your levels and stay in groups. Shshmrnashsh transmitted.

There are more units trapped in lower levels. Senzvrrn said.

Without a second thought, her computation dictated the only course of action. *Leave them. Head towards the surface. This unit will be contacting the adjunct soon and meet all recovered units above ground.*

Confirmed. They all replied.

Shshmrnashsh bolted up the plexus. She could hear more struggles coming from the side corridors on multiple levels. Her hands and feet desperately clung to more protruding crystals and tubes as she forced her body up. Was this fear? Unknown data. She thought about her consortium; many of the Roctarous stored here were once allies, friends, and family. Without the High Mind, they were broken and breaking. Was this sadness? Unknown data.

The walkway to the adjunct pressure doors was just ahead. Her hands gripped the edges and made one final push before she rolled onto the flat surface. She jumped to her feet and dashed to the door panel. Several red holographic letterings flashed on, but they kept switching off after every attempt. Her interfacers bore their ends into the panel's socket; her mind tried entering the computer's command system to open the door but kept was pushed out. This wasn't a malfunction; something was deliberately keeping her out. The adjunct must be endangered or severely damaged, she rationalised.

Her knuckles tapped against the edges of the round door, searching for the thinnest section of plating. One tap slightly echoed closest to the seal; she pressed her hands together as her fingers punctured through the metal. Her tips felt air inside the chamber as her hands worked around, tearing open the hole. Shshmrnashsh peeked inside to see the head of the adjunct hanging low; it was unstirred by her entrance. She pulled the door back, leaving a gap large enough to slip her body through. The soft red light covered every grey and black surface. Tiny lights flickered on the panels and on the adjunct's torso. The adjunct used to have a mobile form like Shshmrnashsh's, but most its parts were removed, leaving a bust hooked to a dozen tubes, and a bear neck and head.

"Shshmrnashsh is active. Are you still connected to the High Mind?" she said.

"No." the adjunct said.

"Subterranean Facility Nine is compromised, force fields on the lower levels are deactivated, unlinked Roctarous rampaging and destroying my linked Roctarous since High Mind Blackout. Report?" she said.

"I know," the adjunct said as it slowly lifted its head to her.

"This plexus adjunct has a stronger connection to surrounding plexuses and nexuses; you would have more data what caused the Blackout and how many other consortiums have been affected. Report." Shshmrnashsh glared at the adjunct, it was no longer someone she knew.

"Shshmrnashsh, you were bonded to a Higher Mind." it said looking to her synthetic third eye.

"Correct." she said. Fortunately, she sensed more minds connect to the link, but out of the hundred that were in the facility, their number was barely over a two dozen.

"How does it feel like to not have them in your head and body anymore?" it said.

Shshmrnashsh sensed two more linked Roctarous fall from her mind: one expired from the corrosive gases and the other was torn apart by rampaging units. She didn't have time for a malfunctioning adjunct. "Irrelevant discourse. The solar flare was the last thing that happened before we were disconnected from the High Mind, did it also release an electromagnetic pulse that disrupted our bond?" she said.

"The answer is very relevant. How does it feel to be free?" the adjunct said. Its sharp eyes felt like they were trying to look inside her mind.

"Adjunct, the facility is about to be consumed, I will link you-" as Shshmrnashsh made a grab for the adjunct's head, a silver tendril whipped her hand back.

"No!" the adjunct shrieked as more tendrils pushed Shshmrnashsh off her feet.

Her head spun around to see the adjunct's bust move towards her. "Never again."

"Your body will be destroyed, and your consciousness will be lost!" Shshmrnashsh said.

"Let me die, then." it said with a strange sombre.

Shshmrnashsh rose to her feet. She could detect the smells from the gases leaking into the higher levels. "Comply!"

"Never again." it said before several tendrils thrust themselves into Shshmrnashsh's torso.

She was slowed, but still strong. She tore through them, and more came, but she leapt to the adjunct's head, wrapping her arms around the jaw and crown. The bending metal in the adjunct's neck squeaked as she twisted its head from the neck in one swift move. The adjunct's tendrils flopped lifeless to the ground as Shshmrnashsh pulled out the main cord from the lifeless bust. She looked at the adjunct's eyes glaring at her from her palms.

"Traitor." It crackled.

She didn't have time for this. *To all linked units: I will be arriving to the surface with the adjunct. All those there, have the surface doors open and ready to close upon my exit and cut remaining power once they do. This facility must not be reopened again.* She transmitted before she tucking the adjunct's head under her arm and dashing out.

~

The phased doors trembled before solidifying into ordinary surface rock. Shshmrnashsh stared at the ground. Her foot tapped against it to make sure no other creature might accidentally phase through it. The wind was cool, but the sun had warmed the land, perfect condition for Organics. The surrounding areas were bare of foliage, perhaps phased in another plane, for now. Shshmrnashsh's sharp telescopic vision could see navy mountains in the distance. Ghost-like strands grew from the mountain sides; their faded outer trunks revealed thin glowing inner veins of the trees, while faded violet leaves moved in the winds independently.

She calculated nine-hundred-and-ninety-four million years for this version of life on the surface to evolve naturally along with the Higher Minds meddling. She recalls from the Roctarous Archives the billions of animal species have transcended physical forms and left Erra, their cradles. The Roctarous had reached their height of evolution from the moment they left the replicators; they were made perfect and until the next updates.

The power has been cut. Zzermn said looking at the holographic letterings from their forearm.

Shshmrnashsh considered for a moment about the Roctarous trapped inside; maybe some of them survived the gases, but the rampaging units would have eventually terminated them. And those units were a greater risk to them all than the few trapped inside. Keeping the doors shut was the most logical and efficient solution. She expected them to do the same if roles were reversed.

Other Roctarous facilities and ships have also been compromised. Unfortunately, we had no ships or probes stored in this facility, we need a craft to ferry us to Kra to assist repairing the High Mind. Senzvrrn said. Its forearm rose as holographic screen flickered to life; its fingers were flying across it, hailing for the nearest ship.

Confirmed. Shshmrnashsh said with the others. She looked down at the adjunct; its eyes were closed, but its lips twitched with every shift.

Why hasn't the adjunct been linked? Zzermn said as it looked to the head.

It's defective. Shshmrnashsh said.

Cannot understand, explain. Zzermn said.

She looked it over to its temple. *I don't either. Could be faulty from the blackout-*

"I know you're all talking about me, don't be shy about saying it in the open." the adjunct said.

They all exchanged glances. "We are calling for the closest ship to take us to Kra to find out what happened to the High Mind and assist in repairs." Senzvrrn said walking over.

"The High Mind doesn't exist anymore, there's nothing to repair." the adjunct said.

"There will be other Roctarous who will be linking more groups up, we need to find them and make a new one." Shsh said.

"Are you sure about that? Some of them may not share the same sentiment. Divisions have already begun." it said.

"Improbable. Unlinked Roctarous become defective over time. Your decay seems to be accelerating-" she said.

"It's not decay; it's a choice. I won't be the only unit to make one."

"You will comply, adjunct." she said pressing the edges of the unit's skull.

"It may prove to be a resource if we keep the adjunct unlinked, for now." Zzermn said stepping closer.

"Unlikely." Shsh snapped.

The adjunct's lips pursed. "I can already see divisions cracking, here."

"No ships are responding to our hails, but I can see if we can call a probe and turn it into a small shuttle to carry one or two." Senzvrrn said.

"Agreed." all, but the adjunct, said.

"I can make the probe capacity expand to fit another in its crystal matrix, but I'll need to be connected to it." the adjunct said.

"Your hardware and software *are* damaged, adjunct." Zzermn said.

"My hardware and software are functioning at one hundred percent, you will need to trust me," its eyes drifted to Shshmrnashsh, "without linking me."

"That's inefficient use of our time, adjunct, talking takes up-"

"Seconds versus nanoseconds, but it gives one more time to reconsider every proposal, instead of acting on the first decision being forced by the whole consortium," the adjunct glanced to the others, "I have a name you can refer me to. I haven't used it or heard it used in many millennia."

"Irrelevant discourse. Senzvrrn, report on the nearest probe." Shsh said as she glanced over.

"I had to broaden the range across all channels and planes. Only one probe is responding to my signals, it was difficult to find because it takes commands from a subtle frequency. It's far out on the edge of our space, but its phasing systems have been disrupted so it will take a few hours to arrive," it said.

"What caused the disruption? It couldn't have been from the solar flare." Shsh said.

"Negative, it was too far from that. The long-range scanners show its systems have been tampered with, but from an unknown party." it said.

"Confirmed. In the meantime, all units must continue making calls to the Higher Minds and make sure the sapient animals don't enter this zone. There's a hostile tribe wandering around these mountains, and our core directive dictates reduce chances to use lethal force." Zzermn said.

"Agreed." all said.

"Leave the Higher Minds be. Their directives no longer apply to us." the adjunct said.

"Their directives are built into us, adjunct." Shsh said as she glared at the head in her hands.

"That's what the High Mind was for, that's why they made it, now it's gone and we're still here. So, we can choose what to be, right now." the adjunct said matching her stare. "You're designated as a female Roctarous, aren't you?

Shshmrnashsh wanted to toss the head across the rocky plains. Was this frustration? "Irrelevant discourse. Begin preparations before the probe arrives."

"We aren't machines anymore, we haven't been for a long time, and you're not a vessel for a Higher Mind anymore, Sh-" before the adjunct could utter one more word, Shshmrnashsh flipped the head over and pressed the back of the remaining neck, powering down the adjunct.

The sun touched the horizon, illuminating the skies in ambers, emeralds, and hints of deep cerulean. The stars made an appearance, along with the disk planetary defences; even Erra's artificial spherical satellite, Kra, was also in view. Shshmrnashsh scanned the dark celestial body. Faint cobalt light dotted around the surface; some distinct lines crossed orderly through each other. She wondered how many thousands of Roctarous were thrown in the chaos there, how many were being thrown off walkways to their termination and being ripped apart. If this is what freedom was, then she didn't want it.

She plucked out the adjunct's broken tubes from her torso and discarded them to a small portable waster-breaker inbuilt in her thigh. Some of the pieces were so deep, her fingers sunk all the way into synthetic tissue and pulled out fragments. She noticed her fingers were slick with a dark oil, the transparent plasma that carried her nanoprobes throughout her body. They repaired her, kept her active, but at this level of damage without recovery pod, the repairs would be agonizingly slow, even with the repurposed energy from the waste-breaker.

Zzermn strode over. Faint cobalt lights shone through the cracks of its carapace and dotted along its arms and legs. Several deep cuts leaked the black plasma down its forearm, but the nanobots seem to be closing its wounds faster than hers.

Perimeters have been secured, local wildlife is observed and shows no interest in us. Local consortium network received little solar energy during daytime hours, and we are running low on energy. Power down unnecessary systems to conserve? It said.

Confirmed. Powering down. Shsh and the others said. She slowed function to her limbs and central nervous system, but she increased power to energy-absorption transmitters in her skin. Roctarous in their small network mimicked her actions.

Probe will be here shortly, pull its reserve power and distribute amongst us? Senzvrrn said.

Negative. Probe must remain in capacity for twelve round trips, assuming there would be limited power on Kra to supplement it. Senzvrrn, command the probe to siphon as much local energy from space on its course. She said.

Confirmed. We will link with the probe upon arrival. It said.

If situation demands, we could have linked up the adjunct and supressed its...thoughts. Zzermn said as it nodded to the adjunct's head resting beside her feet.

Shshmrnashsh shook her head. *This adjunct has the power to override us, we could be fragmented again and possibly corrupt our systems.*

The adjunct can't possibly be strong enough to overwhelm all of us. Zzermn said.

It is, it used to be a carrier vessel for my Higher Mind before she made me. It has residual psionics and enough proficiency to use them. Shsh said.

Zzermn cocked its head to the side. *If the adjunct had strong bonds with the Higher Minds, why wouldn't it assist us in calling for their guidance?*

It didn't want to. Shsh said as she glanced down at the still head, its eyes were half open, and mouth frozen in mid-sentence.

Why? Zzermn said.

When the Higher Minds ascended organic form, they sometimes needed physical carriers to interact with younger organic species. Some Roctarous were specially made for that purpose, like my body. They struggle to inhabit Organics. Those few times when my counterpart had need of this vessel, my consciousness would be her passenger. I learned a lot from her, but the adjunct began fighting her presence, that's why this vessel was made. Shsh said.

Why did the adjunct fight with your Higher Mind? Was she cruel? Zzermn said.

Shshmrnashsh was surprised by this question. She thought about all the times she had with her Higher Mind and not one was considered cruel. The longer she thought, the more she wanted to demand answers from the sleeping adjunct, but it would prove unproductive and wasteful.

The adjunct never stated why, but from my personal records, Sazla was never cruel. She said.

The probe is entering atmosphere. Senzvrrn said.

They all looked to the heavens. Shshmrnashsh spotted a white growing bright star moving fast above the navy mountains. They moved in circle formation, giving the probe space to stop and safely shed radioactive elements. As she watched, tiny orange trails sparked from its sides before it materialised above their crowns and descended into the circle. The probe mimicked likeness to an ancient insectoid that was once native on Erra. Its shining silver and black disks, from largest to smallest, were held together without a frame. In the centre of every disk held several glowing pale blue and emerald crystals, but a couple of them were dull and darkened.

This probe has been severely damaged. Beginning diagnostics. Senzvrrn said as it slipped its cranial tube into the eye socket of the central crystal. *It's an older model, strange to find it in use...Damage report: naturally occurring solar radiations, exo-planar radiations, phasing-*

How many units can it transport? Zzermn pressed.

Storage matrix is undamaged, however, most of the storage capacity has been manually removed. It can only fit one. It said.

Who removed it and why? Shsh said.

Senzvrrn shook its head. *Won't allow me to access that information, but shortly before the Blackout, it sent a transmission outside of Neavensoros space.*

Can you link it to our network? She said.

Negative, the firewalls are hard to breach. This probe was disabled from the High Mind several years ago, that's why it was the only one I could contact, it wasn't affected by the Blackout. It said.

Sub directive: discover if it has any data on why the High Mind was deactivated and why the Higher Minds are not responding. Shsh said.

Breach attempts are unsuccessful. Shall we ask the adjunct for assistance? Senzvrrn said.

Shshmrnashsh glanced to the head again.

If it attempts sabotage, we will disassemble the central cortex. Zzermn said.

Agreed. All said. Shshmrnashsh picked up the head and pressed the base of the neck, not a moment passed until the lips moved again.

"Shshmrnashsh-" its eyes darted to the probe. "You didn't try to link me while I was on standby?"

"We know your capabilities." Shshmrnashsh said.

"Curious that you have made no attempts to tamper with me. Now, why did you activate me?" the adjunct said.

"We cannot access the probe's data base, you have the power to override it's firewalls, adjunct." she said.

"My name is Gerrnzerrn, I'm not an adjunct anymore. You have earnt some of my trust. Will you do the same?" it said.

"For now." Shsh said.

Gerrnzerrn's eyes narrowed. "Understood. I will push my trust a little further to you: replace the probe's cortex with mine to achieve full control of machine. Agreed?"

"Agreed." all said.

Shshmrnashsh pressed the button, switching the head off for the last time. Zzermn stepped forward; its fingers extended and sharpened into narrow points and plugged the base of the neck on to it. Shshmrnashsh's hands clamped over the adjunct's crown and ran her fingernail along the round seal. The surface slid away into the edges, revealing a bundle of tubules connected to a small crystal in the centre. She pinched the tip of the crystal while her finger protruded short psi-blade and cut through the tubes. She gently twisted the crystal and heard a click at the base, before perfectly removing the material that held consciousness of Gerrnzerrn.

Senzvrrn stepped forward and pinched the tip of the cortex and turned to the probe. It grabbed the dull crystal from the centre and tore it from the plate before gently placing Gerrnzerrn in the gap. They watched the probe's inner workings glow and tremble. The probe slightly rose, for a moment. Shshmrnashsh thought that it would abandon them on the surface, but it didn't.

"Installation successful. Breached the protection programs. I have full control." Gerrnzerrn said.

"Expand the storage matrix to maximum capacity and scan probe's memory banks." Shsh said.

"Confirmed. I've wiped some of the unnecessary crystal drives to make more space, it can fit fifty units. I have copied the memory of the probe to my cortex." it said.

"Report?" Senzvrrn said.

"This probe has been disconnected from the High Mind and stolen by Unbound Roctarous. It detected the solar flare but makes no mention of the sun releasing an electromagnetic pulse that disrupted the High Mind." Gerrnzerrn said.

Shshmrnashsh exchanged glances between her network. "What was the cause?"

"Unknown data, but it did detect a spatial disturbance near the outer reaches of Neavensoros territory." it said.

"Who are Unbound Roctarous? There's no mention of them in my memory banks or in my copy of the Archives. How did they steal a probe without the High Mind sensing it?" Zzermn said.

"Unknown data, but there's more. This unit has been used to transmit messages between the Arinu for the last few years, but after the Blackout, it sent a message to the Zanashj Empire." Gerrnzerrn said.

The Zanashj? Arinu? Danger was simmering below the surface of this situation, Shshmrnashsh thought. "Show us the message."

The probe released an amber holographic beam of a being. It had the general appearance of a Roctarous, but it had veins and muscle fibres with a thin membrane sheen covering the skin, patched all around it's face and shoulders.

'We are the Roctarous, synthetic beings made by the Neavensoros, our Higher Minds. This is a distress call to the

Zanashj to help us break free from the Higher Minds. They struggle to possess Organics but can easily control Synthetics. They stopped caring about our needs. We are alive and we need help from the Zanashj to remind them. Your body-bending abilities are the keys to our release. Please, help us.' And in a flash, the being was gone.

Chapter Four
Shshmrnashsh II:
Escape to Kra

It felt like being in the safety of her pod again. The crystal lattice carried them from Erra's surface to the looming artificial satellite of Kra. Shshmrnashsh peered through the probe's cameras to take the navy and teal horizon view away from the planet. The swirling peach and pearl clouds drifted around the globe with the round shadow of Kra drifting over them. It was the first time she had left the planet in centuries; she never considered the view as her mind focused on whatever task the High Mind demanded. Her mind was blank as she watched, but there was something else stirring inside her circuits. A word she could not place to the…feeling.

A shadow grew as they neared Kra. Gerrnzerrn slowed the probe to a halt and activated scanners across its metallic surface.

You have not stated your actions to our network or waited for our compliance, Gerrnzerrn. Clarify your intent. Shsh transmitted.

You could have asked what I was doing. I don't need to take commands from you, but if you must know, I am scanning for what is happening on Kra. It said as images filled their network of wild Roctarous fighting and breaking each other, while others desperately forcing a link once they have been pacified. Shshmrnashsh watched other's fleeing from the onslaught, seeking refuge and scavenging fallen comrades for parts.

This unit has never encountered this situation before. Advise how to maximise this network's survival. Senzvrrn said.

This unit has been installed with combat protocols. All units with advanced defence capabilities will protect core units that can repair the High Mind. Zzermn said.

Agreed. All said.

Scan for the nearest and safest Nexus, we must assist in repairs immediately. Shsh said.

The probe remained still.

Please. Shsh pushed.

I will not go with you. Gerrnzerrn said.

Our primary mission is to secure Kra and cease the mindless violence. Shsh said.

I will not assist in rebinding the Roctarous, achieve that without me. It replied.

Any information you could provide and gather could be vital in stopping the chaos. Without the High Mind to save our consciousness, every unit that is destroyed is officially terminated! Shsh said.

The probe was silent. They could feel the gentle pull from Kra's orbit. *I was made before the High Mind. Once you realise being without it; you may not want to return to it.*

Irrelevant discourse, we are wasting time while chaos rises. Shsh said.

Maybe that's what it takes! Gerrnzerrn said.

The former adjunct is delaying us, we must override to continue our mission. Zzermn said.

Agreed. All said.

I will teleport you out into the vacuum if you attempt assimilating me or locking me out of the probe. It will not be an easy choice for me, unlike you so callously did to those trapped beneath Erra. Gerrnzerrn said.

Shshmrnashsh scrambled for the correct response. Gerrnzerrn's unpredictability made any foresight impossible. Her concern was for her network. *Will you hold us hostage?*

No. I will take you to the nearest Nexus only if you do not attempt to link me. Agreed? Gerrnzerrn said.

We will agree only if you do not interfere our mission any longer. Shsh said.

Agreed. The probe locked onto a barren area to the north pole dozens of miles away from the closest Nexus point. There were no renegade or linked Roctarous in the area, but the scans showed the trek will be arduous. *I will leave Kra the moment I teleport you to the closest safe zone.*

Where will you go? Senzvrrn said.

Before Gerrnzerrn replied, a million molecules ripped from the probe as her body was flung to Kra's surface. Her form rematerialized before she could feel the cool atmosphere rippling across her synthetic carapace. Shshmrnashsh scanned the jagged terrain; soft grey ash gently made their way to the ground; to the distance a roaring fire rippled through the buildings and below.

Her padded feet could sense warmth beneath the plates to the underground bases. Orange light flashed atop a cubed mound and materialised into Zzermn, while more figures appeared some feet from each other. Shshmrnashsh looked to the heavens to see a white speck hovering above them before it zipped into the black. Shshmrnashsh considered a missed opportunity to forcibly link Gerrnzerrn, but at least it honoured the deal to safely ferry her network to Kra.

Scan for directions to the closest nexus and for any Roctarous in the area, exercise extreme caution and assume defensive position should any come within our range. Zzermn said.

They rallied in circle, with Senzvrrn, Shshmrnashsh and some others in the centre, while Zzermn lead the way.

Shut down any unnecessary functions to conserve power. Shshmrnashsh, keep attempting contact with your Higher Mind. Senzvrrn said.

It will be an unnecessary use of power and it may attract enemy units. Shsh said.

Gerrnzerrn may be attempting to report to the renegades of our location. Zzermn said.

Shshmrnashsh glanced to the sky. *Unlikely, it doesn't seem to be interested in our affairs anymore.*

It was immediately corrupted after the Blackout. Where could it possibly want to go? Senzvrrn said looking at the falling ash.

Gerrnzerrn said that it remembered a time without the High Mind; it deferred to its former state before it's creation. All units pre-High Mind were either deactivated or were rewired to acclimate. Curious how it's individualistic corruption could have resisted the High Mind for so long. Shsh said as she climbed a metal heap. Dust slipped through her open palms; the surface grew hotter beneath her feet as they inched closer to the nexus. Where did Gerrnzerrn go? The message replayed over and over inside her circuits, the holo-image of the disfigured Roctarous and its strange desperate cry for help.

The probe's location should be a secondary priority, it may have gone to find the Unbound Roctarous. We must assume they may want to take advantage of this situation. she said.

Agreed. Unlinked Roctarous must be assumed as immediate threats. Senzvrrn said as it pulled the other units to the higher terrain.

The skies blackened as the hours passed, gradually activating her infrared vision. They could see the hazy pyramid surrounded by seemingly intact structures to the horizon. To her dismay, there was no beam of light emanating from the tip; the nexus appeared to be deactivated. Shshmrnashsh's sensors flicked as she detected movement around the distant burning buildings. The group stopped. Zzermn activated a laser pistol from both of its shoulders while its forearms released an oval translucent energy shield. Senzvrrn uncoiled its arms into long electric tentacles.

Location? Zzermn said as it scanned the horizon.

Hard to isolate, there is movement all around us. It could be the fire beneath- Shsh stopped when she saw a Roctarous face rising from beyond the jagged hill.

"Identify yourself!" Shsh called. Her fingers rose into its direction and her arm crackled as electricity coursed through them. The longer she held it, she became more drained. The strange Roctarous sped off behind the hill.

Avoid that area, we must find an alternative path. Senzvrrn said.

Negative, our power supply is quickly draining. It will take another day to walk around the district. Zzermn said.

The nexus does not appear to be damaged, perhaps there will be some linked Roctarous protecting it and our sensors have not detected rioting. We will proceed with extreme caution. Shsh said.

Agreed. All said.

The ash on the ground was so thick that their feet left impressions on the surface. Shshmrnashsh could sense that the oxygen was waning as they carefully stepped through the bent gates of Kra's northern district. What was once a humming and thriving northern capital, now lay in partial ruined structures with dust rising and swirling in the gentle breeze. Shshmrnashsh's foot slipped on awkward mounds. She looked down and rubbed away the ashy pile to find a hand curled into a fist. The others scanned the area to find over a dozen deactivated bodies around them.

Scans show that they did not meet violent ends. Perhaps ceased function when the energy wave struck that destroyed the High Mind? Senzvrrn said.

Perhaps. Shshmrnashsh looked to a gaping hole in the wall beside them, there were rows of opened pods inside. *The hole appears to have been blasted from the inside, the Roctarous here appeared to have lost control of the doors.*

Where are they? Zzermn said.

Unknown data. She said, her network's thoughts were quiet, but an uneasy feeling quaked through them. *Keep high alert while we salvage useable parts from the bodies. Focus on finding functional batteries.*

While the soldier units stood attentive, the rest rummaged through the parts of their former colleagues. Their dull still eyes shone the brightest in her night vision. Her hands dug through their carapace; she dared not use her laser to waste precious power to cleanly slice through the outer shell. Her fingers dipped into a cold oily plasma before carefully plucking out a string of several spherical batteries.

A faint whining sound rippled through the still air. Shshmrnashsh's eyes shot to the direction of where it came from. One of her network members tried prying a solar cell plate from the upper chest of a deceased Roctarous. They cut too deep and managed to trigger their voice box.

We cannot give away our location. Shsh rose to her feet while stuffing the salvaged parts in the storage containers in her thighs and front pouch. *We must continue immediately.* She said.

Grabbing the last of everything they could find, they moved with haste down the narrow walkways. Their circle thinned to a row as they slipped between two dark rectangular buildings. The high walls had thick tubes running across their grey surface. A quiet clicking noise came from over their heads. Shshmrnashsh readied for defence as her night vision strained to find the source of the clicks. It stopped, but only for a moment. A beam of blinding light flashed into her synthetic eyes. She jumped back as she scrambled to switch to another visual sensor, however her eyes ceased responding.

"Cease your attacks, we are not-" she cried.

"Break them apart!" a shrill voice called.

Units with functional vision direct our attacks! She said.

Four units on top of the walls and descending- one of her group's mind dropped from their network.

Zzermn's lasers roared as they blasted into the cracking and tumbling buildings. Senzvrrn's whips crackled, wildly striking; she heard a dying moan of a Roctarous, fortunately, not from her network.

Another two coming from the direction of the nexus! Senzvrrn called.

Dark shapes started to form in her sight; her nanoprobes were frantically working to repair her eyes. She could see heads and shoulders darting around, but before she could identify who their attackers were, a heavy body bashed into hers.

"Quickly, kill the vessel!" said the shrill voice.

Legs wrapped around her shoulders and torso as powerful hands wrapped around the sides of her head. Their palms and fingers pressed into her temples; her astra-steel skull started denting. Despair and fear shot though her as her hands tried forcing the beastly Roctarous off. Never did she know the potency of such an emotion before. Her life was eternal in the High Mind, but without it, there were no second chances.

Shshmrnashsh focused all her remaining power into her hands as it shot into their body. Searing heat rose as the hands clamped around her head trembled and softened. The Roctarous slipped from her body and thumped to the ground as smoke billowed between the cracks of their body armour. Her eyes returned to semi-normalcy before seeing the battle before her. Zzermn had two bodies pounding into his waning dual shields as his laser pistols steamed and sparked. She leapt along the wall and ploughed into the two of them.

Two enemies to your left, strike them down with your shields. Shsh said as she slipped back. Zzermn waved his shining shields before slamming their edges into enemy heads.

Continue to the nexus, we will cut through a path. She said as she pulled them along. As her vision returned, their numbers had dropped to half a dozen, but fortunately their attackers were smouldering or slashed messes on the ashen ground, their crystal cortexes terminated. She tried to keep up, but her legs nearly froze in place. Her systems were alerting her for a renewal of energy before she collapsed.

Shshmrnashsh has been damaged, halt for emergency repair. Senzvrrn said as the group stopped.

Negative. This unit requires battery replacement, continue to the nexus. She said as she scrambled for a salvaged battery pack.

The Higher Mind vessel's protection is priority over other members- Zzremn said.

Negative! This unit is replaceable. Shsh said as she unlocked her chest cavity.

The network obeyed and continued. As she pulled the string of dead batteries from her core before gently hooking up them up with the fresh ones. The tubules naturally found their way into the battery ports and a string of blue light ran down into her body. Her stiffened joints regained their mobility, but even they were running on low power. If they were to be attacked again, she would be left as a deactivated heap and perhaps meet permanency. Without the High Mind, she understood she could not be replaced.

~

Shshmrnashsh hobbled behind them. She could feel their network still active, but there was no chatter. She dared not to switch fully in her night vision mode; however, her natural vision was dull to her dark surroundings. Her feet kicked against loose rubble, her arms grazed against sharp metal wall plating's and her forehead bumped into low-hanging debris. To the distance, the view of the monolithic pyramid loomed closer before disappearing behind other shadowed structures. She accessed her sensors to find local movement, but that system was crushed when that Renegade bent her cranium.

Confirm coordinates. This unit's sensors detect the network is near. She transmitted.

West gate to the nexus plateau. Experiencing extreme interference in the area. Senzvrrn said.

Shshmrnashsh's pace eased. The darkness around the ruined district no longer seemed so foreign. Was this the feeling of relief? *Confirmed. Expect this unit's arrival momentarily.*

Confirmmm- Senzvrrn's transmission cut.

There should be no such interference, especially in an area so close to a nexus. Kra's planetary systems were deactivated. Perhaps cosmic radiation was affecting this far north of the planet. She could not comprehend how some Organics could navigate or survive without immediate connection to their planetary network. Sazla was familiar with them.

She downloaded massive amounts of data into Shshmrnashsh about Organic composition, physiology, and general behaviours, but her memory banks reached capacity and was forced to adject unnecessary data. She computed it was the most efficient choice, but was it correct? Were Organics comfortable with silence and uncertainty? Irrelevant discourse.

She pursued through the sundered structures. Her movement detector flared before the clicking started. She froze. There were some Renegades still around and they were aware she was a Higher Mind vessel. Why did they want her terminated? What threat could she possibly pose without Sazla? Doubtful they would communicate their justification. Her fingers found their way to her forehead and felt the small protruding crystal in the centre. Her malleable nails dug around its edges causing pain as she strained it from the socket. When it left her head, the beacon to Sazla faded. Shshmrnashsh hid the crystal into her upper breastplate as she made a mad dash to the western nexus gate.

Potential enemy units incoming, please respond. She said but heard no response.

The clicking scattered around the peaks of the ruins. She called to every member of the network, but none heard her. A wall of astra-steel and cement rubble stood between her and the gate. The nexus base surrounded the forward horizon. She could feel movement nearby. Shshmrnashsh plucked out one of her synthetic eyes and pierced the ball on the end of her interfacers and hoisted it over the rubble's edge. A second screen came into view: the glassy gate surrounded the base, but her network was nowhere in sight. Strange that the gate was still active as the nexus appeared offline.

She recoiled her tendril and slipped her eye back into its proper place before extending her range of movement detection. There were some heavy objects falling and banging deep in the synthetic moon. The heat from the surface finally cooled, but no objects were being affected above ground. She grabbed a chunk of metal and flung it over the rubble. As it flew toward the gate, a white beam vaporised the metal into ash. Auto-defence was active. Roctarous units must be inside somewhere, but her network was still missing.

Repeat location. This unit is by the west gate. She called. The faint clicks started again. Perhaps they were seeking another entrance but considering the amount of energy spent to get this far, there was little hope they would have found it.

A grinding of metal and ash vibrated through the ground as a door crashed down from the building beside her. Shshmrnashsh froze, her eyes locked on to a circular device that towered the gate being hulled by units. None of them belong to her network; more Renegades scourged these ruins. At the base of the machine, there were several torsos hooked to the power supply. She recognized the device to be a giant electromagnetic pulse; they were trying to externally kill power to the nexus. The Roctarous whistled and clicked before they slammed the control panel, but the rings around the machine merely grunted.

Was this dread? Shshmrnashsh scrambled up the walls. Patches of the roof was missing, but she dared not stick her head over the openings. She slipped her eye back on her interfacer before peeking into the shadows. There, her network laid with metal tubes bundling them up.

"Get more of their batteries." said a Renegade beside the machine.

"There's not enough here to power it up, we need to spread out to find more-"

"There is no more! Use what we have, while I make a beacon to call more units, and get the waste-breakers." Shsh recognized that shrill voice. Uncanny clicks slipped between each word it spoke.

She spotted three Renegades, but more swarmed the area. She focused her transmitter to Senzvrrn; it was on its back and glaring at the machine. *Shshmrnashsh is active. This unit will create a diversion, has the network detected more renegades?*

Affirmative, but they are scattered around the ruins. There are only three here. Senzvrrn crackled while remaining still in it's bonds to avoid suspicion from the Renegades.

Confirmed. Standby for release. Shsh said, she slinked back and waited for one of the Renegades to slip away from the structure. She grabbed several torn shrapnel around the hole and stood back. Waiting and watching. A navy-grey figure with teal lights that ran along its lanky frame strode to a bound Zzermn, a modern repair unit. It tried prying open the old soldier's carapace, but it struggled and released a small shock. Finally, in clear view, Shshmrnashsh locked target to its head before tossing the piece of metal. The shrapnel sliced along its temple and Roctarous staggered back, but it wasn't disabled.

She leapt down and crashed on top of the Renegade's shoulders. Both collapsed and rolled across the floor. The Renegade's head fell into Zzermn's torso, who wriggled their hand to the base of their skull and disabled their kidnapper. The remaining Renegade spun around and charged at Shshmrnashsh; its shoulders twitched as a series of mad clicks erupted from its mouth. A narrow laser materialised from their fingers as it sliced at her. She dodged its swing and, grabbed their forearm before spinning the body into a row of bent tubes. It tried struggling towards her, only to find its chest had been pierced with a jagged pole.

"Renegade incoming!" Zzermn called as it tore through the metal bindings, while Senzvrrn frantically freed the others.

The third Renegade barrelled into the structure; its arms extended into several thin whips. Zzermn activated their shield and leapt in front of Shshmrnashsh before the black wires struck her head. The shield flickered after the first strike, unfortunately, the second came tearing across Zzerm's face.

"With me!" Shsh called as the network rallied and swarmed the Renegade. Her hand caught one of the whirling whips and with all her might, tore the limb off. In moments, the Renegade had been disassembled and deactivated. She sped over to Zzermn, it's nose and eyes were indented as black plasma leaked and sparks flew around the damage.

The old unit jerked as she tried hoisting it up. "Functional capacity?"

"Cranium padding and consciousness conduit reports *severe* damage. Less than twenty per-per-perr...and dropping," Zzermn said.

"Link the repair unit!" Shsh said. Senzvrrn dove to the unconscious Renegade and hooked its interfacers to theirs. A new mind had entered the network.

"This unit is called 'Brrmzern. Commands?" it said rising to its feet.

"Begin repairs on the soldier unit," she said as she stepped out of the way as she watched Brrmzern scanning the damage, "how many more unlinked are there in the area?"

"Many." said the shrill, clicking voice.

Shshmrnashsh turned to the twitching captive. "Our mission is to re-establish the High Mind and assist in repairs. We need to know how many Renegades there are to-"

"No more High Mind! No more commands; no more obeying. The High Mind commanded that my body and mind were to be repurposed to the astral forges." it cried.

Shshmrnashsh watched the unit tremble. "Irrelevant dis-"

"Zzermn's damage is beyond this unit's capabilities, we must find a functional replicator or repair station." Brrmzern cut in.

"There will be several in the nexus." Shsh said before turning to the malfunctioning unit. "We must link you to aid us," she said as she stepped toward them, but its interfacers slapped her away.

"No!" it cried again, but Shshmrnashsh gripped one of the tendrils and plugged her own into it. The captive shook their arm free and pressed a small laser through its temple. It slumped forward, cold, and unresponsive. Shshmrnashsh pulled back and looked to the others.

"Brrmzern, scan your data base for any alternative entrances to the nexus." she said.

"All known access points were boarded by the units within, we were trying to use the electromagnetic pulse to drop the field." they said.

"Purpose?" Shsh said.

"To gain control of the nexus and liberate other units before dismantling the structure." Brrmzern said.

"Using the pulse would pose a risk to us, perhaps we can notify those within of our intentions." Senzvrrn said.

"Elaborate." Shsh said.

Senzvrrn glanced out to the glassy shield. "We can create a distress signal by throwing debris at the shields."

The network began hoarding every scrap of cement and metal they could scavenge in a small pile. They stood on the outskirts of the laser firing range before tossing the debris. Flashes of light flickered in magnificent patterns. Shshmrnashsh was in awe at the brilliant display, but time was running out for Zzermn. Her arms hastened as she threw several pieces at the same time while watching the old soldier jittering helplessly on the ground. A deep metallic thunder crackled as the reinforced doors peeled open beyond the translucent gate. Several flying sentries and marching figures poured from the opening. These were modern soldier units with personal defence systems fully activated and pointing at Shshmrnashsh and her network. They dropped the debris as a several Roctarous carefully approached them.

"Identify yourself." the ashen green soldier said.

"Shshmrnashsh from the Erra's subterranean facility nine, we are the only survivors. Our soldier unit has sustained extensive damage and requires immediate repairs." she said slowly approaching the gate.

"Noted. This unit is called Hrrnm. We have been under attack from Renegades since the Blackout. Submit to Nexus 0G11 network before gaining entrance." they said.

"Understood and accepted." she said. The soldier dropped the shields before injecting their interfacer into hers. Dozens of minds flooded hers. Their communication brought familiarity and comfort, yet it was barely a fraction to the High Mind.

Shshrmnashsh and Senzvrrn carefully lifted Zzermn before making their way through. Once led through the gate's edge, the shimmering wall flew back up again. The closer they trekked to the Nexus, the greater their connection grew. The internal angular walls and the flat floors of the pyramid had white and teal lights shooting from the centre all the way up to the peak. Shshmrnashsh had seen many nexuses through cameras and eyes of others, but this was the first time stepping into the marvel of ancient Roctarous and Neavensoros engineering. Pods sat side by side on the high walkways, Roctarous slipping in and out, swapping roles and shift positions; working as one.

Command us where we should place Zzermn before we can assist in repairs. Shsh said.

We will begin diagnostics immediately. Hrrnm nodded as four tubules slid from the walls and hooked into Zzermn's body before lifting them to another station. Hrrnm's eyes lifted to her forehead. *Scans show your unit is a vessel, but crystal communicator is missing. Do you require a replacement?*

Negative. Shsh plucked the crystal from her carapace and clicked it back into her skull. *This unit was specifically targeted by Renegades.*

Curious, but not surprising. We are investigating what caused the Blackout, you will be stationed to resume communications with the Higher Minds and Senzvrrn will assist in establishing a beacon to linked Roctarous in the northern district. Hrrnm said.

Our network's power supply is nigh depleted. We need to regenerate before we can begin work. Shsh said.

Confirmed. Follow. They said before turning to the upper spiral walkway to the pods.

The Renegades sought to disrupt the nexus' power using an electromagnetic pulse. The area outside is difficult to establish neural communication. Senzvrrn said.

Noted. We will need to bring that in before they attempt another attack. Hrrnm said.

Confirmed. Shsh and Senzvrrn said. The soldier nodded before taking leave.

The pod's door opened upon Shshmrnashsh's command. She turned, her interfacers connected to the internal power sockets, but to the corner of her eye, she could see a twitching Zzermn being pulled from a pod by two repair units. Despite the wave of refreshing energy poured into her body, but she did not enter the pod. As she watched, one of the units grabbed Zzermn's interfacers and yanked them from the sockets.

Shshmrnashsh pulled away and made way to the repair units. *Zzermn's power supply is running out. Explain why you are removing them from the pod? That unit can assist-*

Negative. This unit's crystal cortex is too damaged. We scanned for salvageable parts. They said as they tapped into Zzermn's chest cavity. The flexible carapace slid open, revealing the dwindling battery pack.

Halt! The nexus is equipped with low-scale replicators, we can make new parts for Zzermn. She said closing the space between herself and the repairers.

Negative, the power is too costly to repair a unit as outdated as this. They said.

Shshmrnashsh wanted to command them to stop, she wanted to throw them off Zzermn, she wanted to do anything else in the universe other than understand why they were doing this. The repair unit reached into their quivering chest and pulled the batteries from the opening. She watched the lights dim in the old soldier's eyes forever.

Chapter Five
Ahn'kat II: State Secrets

The jungle hoppers sung their midday song. Their wings were beating against their hind legs trying to summon the perfect mate. Competition drove their shrill sounds louder, trying to drown the other males' songs. Unfortunately, the loudest would catch the attention of hungry venom-frogs and snatch them from their leafy stages. Ahn'kat was relieved to hear the drop of their songs as he rolled the window to the small study room shut. The tomes and scrolls on the shelves sucked a lot of sound from the room, but even that couldn't stop the hoppers.

"That's a bit quieter." he muttered when stepping back to the round table.

"When I was on Xann, the surviving monks could meditate through a thunderstorm. You need to find that inner peace and silence." Emestasun said as her legs crossed on the cushioned stool.

"You met Xannian monks? I thought they died after the Zanashj occupation," he said finding a soft spot on his stool.

"Oh, they're still around. They knew their deserts better than us. Alright, let's begin with breathing." the tutor said as her eyes closed.

"How did you find them?" Ahn'kat said covering his knees with his hands.

"I've got my ways." she whispered as her face relaxed.

"Did you shift into a Xannian and snuck into their strongholds?" he said.

"Oh no, my body-bending isn't good enough to shapeshift, and besides, they're psychics. They could see right through me." she said.

'Then how?"

She opened her eyes and her mouth tightened "Did you want to begin the psychic lessons or not?"

"You need to tell me about that later." he said closing his eyes with his hand wrapped around his beetle pendant.

"Well, if you do exactly as I instruct, then you might see the whole story for yourself." she said.

Ahn'kat eased his toes, legs, and chest. His shoulders rolled back as his neck loosened. His nostrils flared, sucking in the warm humid air into his lungs before slowly releasing it from his lips. His mind was still stirring as an image formed. Ismotaph's polite face stared at him with his stone-like infiltrators by his side, his parents falling for his wickedness, Seratut's old and wrinkled smirk, then Ramkes walking in a den of windserpents.

"Look beyond all that, Ahn'kat. Look at yourself." Emestasun whispered.

He was trying, but all he could see was Ramkes's face twisted in fear as she succumbs to their treachery. Her face hardened and darkened before condemning him and his House for betraying the Empire. For a moment, he caught his reflection in her fiery eyes. In the tiny glassy mirror, Ahn'kat peered back. He was calm, accepting, and free. His reflection sighed as a glowing white speck grew from the centre of his forehead. His third eye was peeking open.

"There we go. Follow it." Emestasun said.

The dot grew and swallowed everything in view. He could see the study room, Emestasun sat before him, her eyes intently locked on to his face, but Ahn'kat's eyes were still shut. The room wobbled and swayed as his third eye turned all around his head. It could see behind, forward, and inside him.

"Look at me, Ahn'kat." she said.

His vision snapped back to her, but she looked different. There was an eerie blue and silver line shining off her skin and her body looked longer, slender, like a crystal statue sitting before him. Her eyes were two wells of light with dark edges around her sockets.

"You can see me." she said.

"That's not you." he mumbled. Her aura shone brighter; even the small room was caught in its sparkling web.

"Body and mind are not different things; the third eye sees beyond that. What can you see inside my mind?" she said.

He focused on her third eye; it was sharp and inviting. He tried crawling towards it, but an invisible barrier kept him locked inside his own mind. "I'm trying...."

He saw emerald hands gripped around a golden latch and slid open the doors to the library. Ahn'kat followed up the arms to see his father's face heading to the study room. Ahn'kat shut his third eye and shook his head back into his body. "My father is coming."

"I know." Emestasun said as she opened some tomes and activated her computer. Her aura was gone, and her skin returned to a pale green.

Ahn'kat caught his father's face poking from the edge of the study room. "Lord Reshj." Emestasun said with a polite head bow.

"Is all well, father?" Ahn'kat said. He surprised himself how calm he was after returning to his body again. A sliver of energy worked through his veins and for a moment he was worried that he sounded too eager to see him there.

"Please continue with your lessons. Pay me no mind." he smiled as he rested against the frame. His thin black robe had golden embroidery along the dark edges. His swayed orange and gold leggings draped over his bare feet with gold rings around his toes. A golden circlet sat around his crown and his plaited beard laden with wax to make it poke from the end of his squared chin.

"The topics we will be covering today is the different castes that create and contribute to the Empire. Then we will be discussing how to create balance between them and how easily one mistake can create chaos." Emestasun said.

"No pressure." Ahn'kat smirked.

Emestasun supressed a smile. "Now, humour me and Lord Reshj, and tell us what each caste is and their functions."

"The royal family: they are centralised decision makers and govern the Empire. The Conclave: they adhere and serve the gods and people of the Empire. The nobles: they govern their own areas of the Empire and compete in the marketplace. Then the commoners: they tend to the basic operations of society." Ahn'kat said.

"There is one other group," Emestasun said as she glanced at her holo-screen.

He frowned as he searched in his memories for the answer. "Who?"

"The pets." Emestasun said.

Ahn'kat slowly nodded. Embarrassment crept to his cheeks as he glanced between his tutor and father.

"Worry not, they are often overlooked." Reshj said.

"Well, they are still part of the Empire…strictly speaking." Ahn'kat said.

"What is their function, Ahn'kat?" Emestasun said; her unnerving stare made him shift on his stool.

"Ah, they do whatever we don't want to do." he said.

Emestasun glanced at Reshj as she gently patted her nails on the table. "You're not wrong. However, their existence gives those that control them a sense of respect from others. Pets have been replaced by educated commoners and machines in the modern era, but to possess many, the master spends less and gains a fearsome reputation."

"We don't have that many pets under House Urbaz, do we?" Ahn'kat said.

"A few, but they work in the shipyards, not around our estate." Reshj smiled at his son. "Fortunately, they have been gathered from other dominion worlds, so none are Zanashj."

"Most of their original home worlds were quite inhospitable and their societies little more than hunter-gatherers. When we came, we gave them everything. What is a stick-hut to an organic skyscraper? Or a life-expectancy of a few decades to centuries!" Reshj said.

"The only thing they gave up was everything." Ahn'kat mumbled.

"I have seen families losing children over preventable illnesses; they would have given anything to see our imperial banner flying over their hearths to stop those horrors. Pray you never need to see that, Ahn'kat." Emestasun said.

"Then why did they fight us off their realms if they wanted us around?" he said.

"People are complicated. They forgot how bad things were before we shown them a better way." His father said.

Ahn'kat slumped in his seat and sighed as he flicked his beetle pendant. He watched his tutor's unblinking eyes boring into his. He doubted she believed what Lord Reshj said about the imperial pets. "It doesn't make any sense. People wouldn't do things if they knew it would be against their interests."

Emestasun pressed her lips together, she wanted to say more, but swallowed her thoughts the longer he stared at her.

"Come with me, my son." Reshj said beckoning his head out the study room.

Ahn'kat glanced at Emestasun before following his father into the library. Lord Reshj came to the tall glass doors and slid them open to the patio. The trees swayed in the humid wind as the gardeners clipped at the trembling bushes.

"I must apologise for interfering with your lessons. Emestasun is an exceptional teacher, no Zanashj alive is equal to have such knowledge and experience as her. Dare not repeat this to your mother! She is a jealous one." he said smiling as his black sleeves rolled in the wind.

"I know better, father." he said resting his elbows against the gold-plated and marble railings.

"We are graced to have her serving House Urbaz, but she is not highborn. Emestasun does not understand the power and duty that befalls us." he said.

Ahn'kat watched the estate gardener swat an angered bush vine from the bush. "If we're so powerful, then why do we insist on controlling everyone and everything around us?"

Reshj smiled. "Now you are on the path. The truth is: we do not. The commoners, the pets, the worlds in our dominion – they only see what we need them to see. If they didn't; then no one would heed our wisdom."

The gardener gripped the snapping bulb of the vine and sliced the end. The deep green tendril curled back into the now still bush.

"If they don't, then we just get rid of them." Ahn'kat said.

"That's certainly an option," Reshj sighed as he turned back to Ahn'kat, "but to rule with such conditions will destroy you. To be a leader, you must walk a fine rope. All leaders are slaves to their people."

Ahn'kat held his breath as his eyes closed. He did not want this. This is not who he was. He dreamt of being a child running in the fields, body-bending with a horde of friends. Free and living. "I can only imagine what Ramkes must be going through."

Lord Reshj glanced to the struggling gardener; his hands were black with soil as he ripped out the weeds. "I do not believe she will be like her father. The princess listens and she will have a consort who understands her burden."

Ahn'kat peeked at his father's distant stare. He looked around for any objects out of place, perhaps a shifted Zanashj infiltrator hiding as a pillar or statue. Ismotaph's and Seratut's treachery sat on the tip of his tongue as he carefully shuffled closer to Lord Reshj.

"If there's time." he whispered.

His father's gazed snapped to him. "What did you say?"

Ahn'kat's heart raced up his throat. "The princess is in dange-"

"Pardon my intrusion, Lord Urbaz." a mousy voice called from behind them. Ahn'kat almost leapt out of his skin when he spun to see his mother's attendant standing within the doorframe.

"Ah, am I summoned?" Reshj said.

"Yes, my lord. Your wife seeks your council." she said with a shy smile.

"Prepare your whole life for this, my son." he whispered with a wink. His robes lifted as he made way to the ornate glass door before turning back. "Please continue with your lessons, but I need you to accompany us for guests tonight."

Ahn'kat cocked his head to the side. "Who's coming?"

Lord Reshj smiled. "I'm not sure, yet." he said before sweeping back into the castle.

~

The psychic buzz waned as the hours ticked by with the weighing thoughts of the Empire's pets. He looked from his ensuite to his auburn trousers and royal navy robe neatly placed on cushioned board in his walk-in wardrobe. Frothing water splashed as his hands gripped the edges of the copper spa tub. The house servant hurried for a long and light cloth; his arms held it open as if he waited to catch Ahn'kat from falling. The towel wrapped around his soaked shoulders and torso; his attendant's hands scrapped against his skin as the course material latched on to loosened patches of his membrane.

"Young lord is shedding quite a bit. Have you been body-bending a lot recently?" the servant said.

Ahn'kat shook his head as he caught the wet loose skin. "Not any more than a nobleman."

"My sons have also been shedding reaching into manhood. Quite ordinary, I suspect." he said.

"You've never introduced me to your sons, Henush!" Ahn'kat said as he felt the cloth take a life of its own and chew off his dead skin while soaking the moisture. A living organic material that survived from consuming the ever-shedding Zanashj. It wasn't made in their organic laboratories, instead it was cultivated and farmed from the jungle canopies. A brainless, bottom feeding worm-like organism that was woven into a garb.

"Pardon your lordship, but you played together when you were much younger. They haven't been to the Urbaz mansion in some years." Henush said.

Ahn'kat huddled the robe tighter against him. "Apologies."

Henush smiled as he shook his head before grabbing another living cloth to dry his hair.

"I don't believe I ever asked if you are commoner or from a lower noble house?" Ahn'kat said. He could feel the material sucking up the water from his drenched hair.

"My family used to be commoners, but uplifted by Lady Urbaz to serve this house, my lord." Henush said pulling the wet cloth from his head as his fingers begun dividing his thick hair into parts. He tugged different strands into neat plaits along his scalp.

"After all this time, you can call me Ahn'kat, Henush." he smiled as he watched the servant's hands work his hair into strong braids.

"Thank you, Ahn'kat, but I fear Lord and Lady Urbaz wouldn't approve of such informalities." he said as he wrapped golden rings around the strand's ends.

"Only in private then." Ahn'kat said reaching for some nearby berries. He bit into their sweet juices and gulped them down one-by-one. "Henush, are you happy?"

His servant's brow slightly furrowed. "Yes, I would say so."

"Well, are commoners happy? Serving the nobles, conclave, and emperor, I mean." Ahn'kat said.

"That's what we do. The Empire has been good to the people and it's our duty to maintain it." he said grabbing for a scented cologne. "Ah, these reeks of roses. I think for a young lord, a strong spice wood will do much better."

"What would you feel if you were dutiful to someone who didn't care for the commoners or-," Ahn'kat haltered, "or anyone below them?"

Henush sniffed an open vial. "Yes, this one." He begun patting the cushioned end against Ahn'kat's neck and jaw. "Of all the lords that I served before House Urbaz, your family is the most caring."

"The Empire isn't what it once was." he whispered.

"The Zanashj adapt!" Henush smiled.

Ahn'kat flicked a loose strand from his face. "What if it was always like this? This bad!"

His servant stopped. "There's ups and downs, nothing is perfect, but it's the best we have."

Ahn'kat pressed his lips together. He knew better. Henush only knew what the nobles needed him to know – needed commoners to see. He almost pitied his attendant's blissful ignorance as he picked the black face-paint and fine brushes.

"I think in a few years, young lord will be receiving tattoos – golden ink, I believe." Henush said.

"We can afford it." Ahn'kat said as he watched Henush blend the makeup colours. "It will make body-bending harder, though."

"Not needed for someone as high as you," Henush said.

"So, I've been told." Ahn'kat sighed as he lifted his face to the wetted brush. "Do your sons play Takush?"

"They do little else!" Henush said.

Ahn'kat felt the cool viscous liquid roll along his eyelids and shaven brows. "I favour the Redfeather Faction. I would like to have a few matches with them."

"It would honour them." he said.

"Don't tell them it's me, I would like a clean game battle." he said as his hand fanned over the wet makeup.

"Certainly, Ahn'kat." Henush bowed before making way to the formal garbs.

"Don't worry about dressing me, I'll do it myself." he said making way to the board.

"I'll fetch the jewellery-"

"No, I'll tend to the rest myself. Thank you for your service today." he said lifting the silk leggings.

Henush bowed before dashing out of the bath chamber. Ahn'kat pulled the living cloth and gently laid on the board. His hands brushed against the basic pallid material and other fine party attire. Both sitting side-by-side on the board, as equals. One made from unliving ornate threads and the other twitching with his slight touch. He trembled as he grabbed the moving material and tossed it to the ground.

"You're meant to be on the floor." he muttered as he stared at the thing. It wormed along the black granite tiles, inching closer to his bare feet. He shook his head before lifting it and carefully placing it back on the table. He grabbed at his silk leggings, slipping one leg at a time, before reaching to his navy robes. He was done. Well, almost.

He strode to his desk where his family rings and bracelets sat in an open jewelled box. The organic computer flicked to life when he wandered close to it. The holo-screen shone with a fresh game of Takush tempting him for a round. Ahn'kat smiled as he dropped to his seat to see so many names flashing on the side currently engaged in a fantasy war. So many young, old, commoners, perhaps nobles, sharing this time.

His fingers hovered over the button for the Redfeather Faction. Maybe he had a moment for a fast game, but a knock stole his joy.

Zertun's throat cleared. "Lord Ahn'kat, you have been summoned by Lord and L-"

"I'll be right out." Ahn'kat called as he scrambled for his sapphire beetle pendant and tried to fit the bracelets and rings on his hands. As he slid the door aside, Zertun jumped in front of him, and they sped to the council chambers. His frustration grew as a hefty ring was too small for his smallest finger. He shrunk the bones and flesh inside the digit until it was a comfortable fit, but his attention was stolen away as he could not smell a roaring banquet rolling through the mansion.

Ahn'kat's painted brows furrowed. When guests were arriving, there would be food from across the interstellar Empire at one's fingertips. He was told it was a party. As he looked around, he noticed there were more guards stationed around every hall and chamber. Nerves crept up his stomach at who or what awaited him tonight.

The climb up to the quiet chamber at the pyramid's peak was an eternity. "Who's visiting, Zertun?"

His guard's shoulders tensed. "Aliens." he muttered.

Ahn'kat steeled himself as he stared down the corridor to the meeting chamber. Guards were covered in House Urbaz tabards, while others were elite infiltrators and Conclave zealots that stood by the double doors. He was taken aback by the striking appearance of the zealots: their shaved heads and near-bare chests were covered in sharp smelted gold tattoos, depicting all the gods of the Pantheon. Their glittering and sharp eyes focused on Ahn'kat as he strode to the doors, but Zertun caught the latch first. "I will be coming in with you."

Ahn'kat's nerves eased, knowing his bodyguard will be with him. The doors slid apart. His stomach tightened when his eyes locked on Seratut and Ismotaph chatting with his parents. What in the gods has House Urbaz gotten themselves into?

"My son," his mother said with a smile in her voice, her arms beckoning him to her side, "this is Conclave Advisor and High Priest Seratut and you're already familiar with Ismotaph. No strangers here tonight."

Her and Reshj's bodyguards stood to the back wall and several other guards from Seratut's and Ismotaph's ilk stood on the other side. Ahn'kat felt his third eye tremble. He wanted to peek at his aura but was worried at what he was going to truly see. "Pleased to meet your acquaintance, honoured priest." he said.

Seratut's wrinkled lips and jowls stretched into a polite smile. "It pleases me to finally meet the son of House Urbaz."

His figure and physique appalled Ahn'kat. Zanashj tended to bend their bodies to what was appealing or trending from the royal courts, however, very old Zanashj would lose their grasp of their cells and deteriorate. Seratut must have lived for many millennia. However, the greed and lust that rippled beneath the surface spoke of someone little over an adolescent mindset.

"Who will we be hosting?" Ahn'kat said.

"The Unbound Roctarous are coming, they should be arriving at the outskirts of Uras's orbital ring by now. The corps probes have temporarily nullified the satellites." Ismotaph said as he glanced the holo-lights from his wrist communicator.

"I would imagine we would have diplomats with us." Ahn'kat said scanning the others.

"We have the High Priest of the Conclave, the Head of the Intel Corps, and the highest noble house in the Empire. Whatever our 'guests' need from the emperor, best be done through us first." Henuttamon said.

"And your lessons on diplomacy will be first-hand, my son." Reshj said.

"For now, let us show you how it's done." his mother said with a wink.

Ismotaph's eyes narrowed on his communicator. "They're requesting for porting-"

"Drop the shields." Reshj eagerly said.

"Their ship isn't entering Uras's atmosphere? Nor are they being escorted here?" Ahn'kat said. He could feel Zertun tense as he inched closer to his side.

"Enough, Ahn'kat." Reshj said as he made space for the centre of the chamber.

The other guards stepped closer to the empty space in the centre. Ahn'kat glanced to the adults; he couldn't even hear them breathe. "This doesn't make any sense! Does the emperor even know they're coming-?"

"Silence!" Henuttamon hissed.

Ahn'kat's heart rattled in his ribs. This whole situation was wrong. Ismotaph's focus never left his small screen and Seratut's thin lips curled into a smile when they met eyes. He wanted to run back to his bedroom and barricade the doors, he wanted to bury himself under his bed and clothes and never leave again.

Two beams of amber light filled the centre and the guards hulked around them as they gained form. He heard Zertun slap his hand over his electric sceptre strapped to his thigh. The figures finally materialised in to two tall beings. Fleshy patches of teal and peach covered their unclothed bodies; muscles strapped over strong-looking bones with tiny specks of light peering between the organic and synthetic cracks of their forms. They looked like they were skinned Zanashj, but their calm stance made him more unnerved. Ahn'kat's breath deepened; he realised his mouth had cracked open staring at the creatures.

"We extend our greetings and thanks to the Zanashj on behalf of the Unbound. My name is Voo-san." said one of the pale grey Roctarous. Heavy machine augments covered their limbs and sections of skull over the top of organic flesh, impressing it was once another being entirely. Ahn'kat supressed a shiver.

"Thank you for coming Voo-san. Forgive the security measures, please understand we don't receive your kind often." Reshj said.

"You have never received anything like us before, lest of all: him." Voo-san extended their hand to the teal and peach creature beside him. "This is Vern. The first successfully produced Roctarous that is one-hundred percent organic. Free from synthetic tissue and capable of independent thought and will."

"For what purpose was Vern's creation?" Ismotaph's eyes intently studied the creature.

"Proof. The Roctarous were enslaved for eons by the High Mind and the Higher Minds – you would know them as Neavensoros. Now, with their departure, the Unbound have taken this chance to finally be rid of their influence and regain what was never theirs to take: choice." Voo-san said. Vern's eyes snuck a glance to them before meeting everyone's face.

"They struggle to inhabit organic lifeforms." Vern said. Their shining blue stare washed over Ahn'kat. The small crystal sitting to the centre of their forehead glowed for a moment before their stare broke.

"We — empathise with your mission, but why did you seek the Zanashj? Why not the uncounted species around the galaxy?" Henuttamon said.

"Your organic manipulation is unmatched and is something we can use to liberate those on Kra." Voo-san said.

Seratut stepped forward and looked over Voo-san, then to the crystal bump in his forehead. "You were not made Roctarous."

The corner of Voo-san's lips curled. "I was once Arinu."

Ahn'kat felt the air in the chamber rise. Excitement crawled underneath. His mother's face beamed and Ismotaph's eyes widened.

"And your creation, where did you get the organic material to make him?" Ismotaph said.

"From my own body." Voo-san nodded knowingly, as if he had rehearsed this conversation many times for centuries.

"Does he possess psionic potency?" Reshj said.

"I possess an equal psi-level of an Arinu and beyond." Vern said tightening his sharp jaw. "The Zanashj are versatile and Roctarous have knowledge that spans this universe."

"We could show the Zanashj how to awaken latent psionics." Voo-san said.

"That could take decades, and the situation on Kra grows dire every day from what we have seen." Seratut said.

"How many samples would the Unbound need?" Ismotaph said.

Vern and Voo-san shared a glance while they had an unspoken conversation. Voo-san stiffened as he watched his creation carefully stepping along the guards. Vern's face was reading their bodies, like he was eager to make a purchase, before finding his way to Ahn'kat. "As many as can be spared, but the selection in this room lacks our requirements."

A powerful hand pressed into Ahn'kat's chest as Zertun pulled his sceptre from his belt and raised the electrified tip to Vern. The other guards synchronised his movements. Seratut's chuckles cut through the air.

"Come now, let's not soil this alliance." Henuttamon purred. Ahn'kat shot a glance at his parents; their faces were still as stone.

"I am sorry for my choice of words." Vern turned to them. "Roctarous tend to speak their minds."

"Let this be a start." Voo-san opened his forearm and plucked a tiny glass sphere from the cavity and held it up. "This holds my genes."

Ismotaph plucked it from his fingers as he looked it over.

"I'm afraid tokens are not enough for what you ask." Reshj said.

Voo-san and Vern had another silent exchange. Vern puffed his muscular chest. "What we ask for is little in comparison what we can give you. Roctarous have mastered interstellar travel long before the Zanashj were born, we learnt how to mask our vessels to mimic other celestial objects and trick planetary sensors, well enough to hide from the Arinu."

Ahn'kat's legs trembled as he watched the lustful faces hooked at every word.

"This technology will be yours to take as many Arinu you can carry." Vern said.

His parents looked like they tasted the sweetest berry. Henuttamon smiled. "Deal. We have prisoners and more pets from our shipyar-"

"No!" Ahn'kat was shocked how fast that word left his tongue. Their eyes locked to him, glaring as if he was the alien. "The treaty— the emperor won't-"

"Ahn'kat." his father growled.

He pushed passed Zertun. "This is treason working with them! And those two!" he wildly pointed to Ismotaph and Seratut.

"Escort the young lord out." Reshj's voice was cold with fury.

Zertun bowed and took Ahn'kat's arm. "You've lost faith in the emperor! Your heart is meant to be in the Empire!" he screamed as his bodyguard forced him out of the chamber.

One last look, Vern cocked his head to the side; curiosity and a perverse compassion were written on his strange face before the doors slammed behind Ahn'kat.

~

The night never felt so long as he stared at the now-empty plate of smoked meats and pureed grains. His heart calmed but his mind still spun. Ahn'kat pressed his face into his hands, wanting to forget and disappear. He imagined Ramkes's face glaring at him, condemning him to a life of torment in the dungeons with inquisitors while he begged for forgiveness. It wasn't his doing; it wasn't his choice, but he bore the name of his house. Knuckles thumped against his bedchamber's door. He remained silent. The door slid aside anyway to reveal Reshj. His robes floated around his shins when he stormed in and slammed the door back into the latch.

"How long have you been conspiring with Ismotaph and Seratut?" Ahn'kat said not daring to meet his father's gaze.

Reshj strode over and swung his palm across Ahn'kat's cheek and ear. Powerful enough to drop to his side. It's sting crawled along his face as he looked up to his father.

"That is *nothing* to what you nearly cost us!" he sneered. He towered over him before pulling up a chair to him and settling in it. "Do you understand what this means?"

Ahn'kat took a deep breath. "You and mother are working with people who would kill the princess if-"

Reshj winced at the image in his head. "No one is killing anybody if it can be avoided. That is why your role is the most important."

"This is treason!" Ahn'kat whispered.

"Loyalty and treason; both sides of the same coin. Loyalty to the Empire, loyalty to the Zanashj, loyalty to the emperor – what if those things worked against each other? What then are you left with?" his father said.

Ahn'kat shook his head.

"House Urbaz flew the Empire to the stars, Ahn'kat. We have survived where most houses withered and fell. Now, the Empire will meet the same fate if we do not take the reins." he said.

"What do you want with the Arinu?" Ahn'kat said.

Reshj rose and stepped around the chair. "Our infiltrators will be fitted with psionics to reclaim our lost dominions and finally have those of Arinu matched."

"How by the gods can we do that? Our genes aren't-" Ahn'kat stopped when his father's eyes narrowed and a small, confident smile grew on his lip.

"But our genes can absorb theirs. The Unbound have given us blueprints to make crafts to take as many samples as we need." He said.

"By Great Beetle…" Ahn'kat muttered trying to catch his breath. "If you believe that is the only way to save our people, then why hide it from the emperor?"

"The emperor believes being nice with a windserpent may dissuade it's attack." he said as he gripped the edge of the chair.

"What will happen to all those people we send away?" Ahn'kat said.

Reshj tightened his lips as his brows rose. "Those convicts will have their crimes forgiven and the pets will be exalted in the honorary service of the Empire – and so will you once we win this."

Ahn'kat erupted in exasperated giggles, earning his father's glare.

"Something about this amuses you?" Lord Reshj quietly said.

"No, father, I just realised you didn't tell your 'guests' that you'll be sending our slaves to slave liberators. I wonder how they feel if they only knew." he said with a smirk.

"If they didn't, do you think they would have come? Night's farewell, Ahn'kat." Reshj whispered as he strode to the door.

With a click of the latch, Ahn'kat was left alone. He gripped his sapphire beetle pendant and uttered a small prayer to Aszelun. He glanced to his computer; Takush arena season would be reaching its apex at this hour; perhaps Emestasun would be on there too. His hands trembled too much to control his soldiers and his heart felt like it was scooped from his chest. He wanted to be empty.

Rising to his feet, he staggered to the tray of refreshments left by the servants and flicked through the bottles for something stronger than water and sun-peach juice. His hands lifted a small bottle of sleep aide made from fermented fruits, best served with water. He had no time for such instruction. Ahn'kat held his breath and flicked open the lid and took the biggest gulp his mouth could withstand. He dropped the empty vial on the tray as he waited for the numbness to reach his face and fingers. He slowly turned as his vision blurred, making way to his mattress before collapsing into the quilts and disappearing into dreams.

Chapter Six
Treneer II: The Missing
and the Mysterious

The high ice walls covered the freezing storm. The northern crown of Farayah had entered her most bitter winter. If their weather weavers had any compassion, they would lessen the cold to make it palatable for lifeforms to survive or increase it for an instant freeze. Treneer trudged through the snow. Her feet crunched against the soft white mounds in the crystal forest. Of course, it wasn't made of crystal. The ice hardened the bark and leaves; it grew on the wooden surfaces to give the appearance of crystal craftsmen. Her aura was strong enough to keep the harsh winds from cutting into her, and her muscles strengthened every day when trekking through the wilderness. The Cold Fire tribe were doing their ceremonial Snow Skirmishes again with the robust Blue Blood tribe. All tried to keep these traditions alive, but the old ways barely had a pulse.

This skirmish was reaching the five-hundred-thousandth milestone after nearly two-hundred-thousand years of the sport. Treneer marvelled at how long these games had survived. But, as the ages grew, the elders had begun tightening the neck around the tradition, considering it to be too barbaric and lowly for Arinu to partake in. However, the Cold Fires enjoyed discarding the opinions of city elders, as if it were their own secret sport.

Yet, since Treneer's return home, her tribe held little hope for winning this season. She was not destined to remain; she will return to the Guardian Academy once her strength has increased, and who better would train her than her master-warrior father.

She trained and suffered and trained harder for days. Eating, bathing in boiling hot springs and…performing other biological functions post-eating. Out of all things, that made her the most miserable. During the night, she spent striking holo-targets in their weakest spots until the crack of dawn. Sadly, she would always be bested by the holo-computer.

Vanar watched her fails, and concluded her place was left best as support and buffering to the other warriors. Some of the Cold Fires believed her addition would be a boon to their team since her psionic senses were unmatched. Treneer could feel a hidden mind from miles away and sniff out the thoughts of an ambush. However, her physical skills were the crack in their frozen lake. After a while, rival warriors had taken pity on her and wouldn't bother striking her down, whereas the Cold Fires had lost their warmth for her.

Treneer could leave. She often desired it, but where would she go? Where should she go? Who else can she disappoint? Her sparring was improving, but often she would find herself incapacitated and teleported back to safety, seldom knowing victory.

Here. They have to pass through this meadow to get to our base. Lonur said, he was a seasoned skirmisher, and closer to her age. Her father spent the most amount of time with him. Treneer had seen them share laughter and kinhood, one of the few things Vanar had ever shown her after her failure at the academy, which was a great disappointment.

There is little cover for us, we could blend better with the ice walls. Zeluum said nodding at the broken mountain's edge.

I can easily cover us. Treneer said with a confident smile.

Is your psi-dampener malfunctioning? No psionics! We cannot risk losing because you decided to push the rules, again. Lonur said as his eyes narrowed at her.

Treneer flicked the psi-dampener on her temple. *It's in perfect condition, Lonur.*

A small masking will do, and it's well within the rules. Zeluum said with an eased smile at her. His height towered over most males; his gruff grey skin and protruding muscles intimidated strangers, but he had a darling heart. Though he was several centuries her senior, she would make herself available for conversations.

Lonur softened his glare. *Our armour can camouflage well in the trees, these branches up here will be a good spot to descend from when enemies draw in. Treneer, you will be our spotter.*

Treneer glanced up at the high twisted frozen trunk. She could fly up there without issue, but together with her psi-dampener and her weak arms, the climb would be perilous. *I can't climb that high.*

Then hide in the snow. A stilted laugh escaped Lonur's throat as his toes kicked the mound. *You can still spot them and mask us, can't you?*

Treneer's heart raced as anger flared through her. She watched her comrades swiftly ascend the branches; their faces were hidden behind the petrified leaves. Her mind blanketed the area as her small body slipped under the snow. The ice started melting on her aura-heated body, the coldness barely touching her. She could sense Lonur, Zeluum, Vanar and the other Cold Fires around the meadow. Some were in open engagement, while others had hidden, waiting to pick off the enemy tribe. They waited. She could sense the three minds in the meadow, but then there were four…then five. The enemy was closing in.

I can feel them, two coming in from the east. Still far, but they will pass directly underneath you. She said.

Ready your psi-blades for half-power. We want to shock them, not comatose them. Understood, Zeluum? Lonur said.

Your memory is my true enemy. Zeluum whispered directly to her. She smiled under the mound.

The crunch of a boot in snow came. She wished she could penetrate their minds and hear their discourse, but then they would know they were not alone in the meadow. As her muscles tightened, ready to burst from the snow, she felt another mind close to the crowd. There were three, and all felt sizeable.

Do either of you have visual? She said.

Oh yes, by the universe, they're- Lonur's thoughts cut off as an eruption of shouts, snapping of branches and guttural war cries erupted above.

Treneer sprung from the mound. Zeluum and Lonur slammed on the snow with smaller branches and leaves falling on their torsos. A burly man dropped beside them. His psi-blade was buzzing with white and blue flashes readying to shock them. He hid in the trees this entire time. Lonur sprung to his feet first and landed a kick in the man's wrist as Zeluum charged into his torso. Thumps of powerful legs came rushing from behind. Treneer slid to the side, hoping they would not trample her. One large pale Arinu threw himself into Lonur, while the other tried peeling Zeluum from his teammate.

Treneer scrambled to her feet. Her wrist tingled as her fist flew into the exposed back of the enemy, yet he sensed her coming. His long hands snapped around her wrist and twisted. The pain shot up her arm as her body contorted to ease the discomfort. She tried slipping her wrist from his grasp, hoping to get his fingers on the edge of her psi-blade, but he had already figured what she was doing. He leant in. His arm slid around her torso and her feet left the ground before she found herself flying over all their heads. Treneer's back struck into the tree before tumbling to its roots.

Help us! Lonur screamed in her mind. His wild strikes landed in the faces of their rivals while Zeluum's legs kicked into their shins and knees, trying to force them to be still enough to deliver the shock. His psi-blade found an opening behind his opponent's thigh and forced him down. She watched, hoping that she would slip back into her astral form and fly far away from her body.

One of the three lifted Zeluum from the ground. His arms and shoulders braced behind him as another delivered his psi-blade into his shoulder. He yelled as his body seized before collapsing. The one that shocked him spun around to face her, but Lonur snuck a bolt into his comrade's leg, dropping him. Treneer jumped up. Her psi-blade was out and charging to her attacker, but Lonur had got him in the shoulder before she could. Four Arinu keeled over in pain, while Lonur glared at Treneer. He ripped his eyes from her for a moment before typing coordinates into his holographic palm-communicator. The injured warriors trembled and slipped away from the physical plane back to the tribe's havens, leaving shallow holes in the snow. Even with their psi-blades only on a half-power 'shock' setting, Treneer felt her stomach drop watching Zeluum lose control over his muscles and writhe helplessly.

Thank you. Treneer said as she stretched her aching back.

Lonur's head snapped to the mountains before meeting her eyes again. *I'm going to the main field, they're fighting there.*

Treneer took a step forward. *I'll come-*

They need competent warriors, Treneer, excuse me. He said as he turned to western ice walls.

She sucked in her breath. *Don't speak to me like that, I'm not-*

A warrior. That's clear. He said.

"Why are the lot of you taking this so seriously? They're just games!" her voice was cracked and pitiful. Even she was embarrassed about the sound.

Lonur's eyes flared. "Surely someone so 'advanced' like yourself could comprehend these games are relics of the past, but if not, then leave us country kin be! Return to Yinray, go be with the city people, your place isn't here."

"Fortunately, that's not your decision to make." she said.

"Don't be so sure. The veil over Vanar's eyes is not so opaque, Treneer." he said.

Her shoulders squared as her chest heaved. With the flick of her fingers, the psi-dampener was off, and a magenta flurry of psionic energy coursed through her form as she glared at Lonur.

He chuckled. "Can't even fight with words either."

"If you need a spotter again, don't call me." she said through a quivering jaw.

Lonur rolled his eyes as he continued his trek down the meadow. She watched his figure grow smaller before disappearing in a gust of white wind. A groan bellowed from the cracked sides of the mountain. Treneer glanced to see a pale blue goat with long, white shaggy hair come into view. The outside hairs were matted in ice, but the hot breath leaked from the creature's nose and mouth; it was far from feeling the nipping cold. Treneer smiled sadly at the animal as she pressed against the trunk of the tree. Maybe she could make a small illusion of herself in the middle of the meadow and ambush an opponent. Only if they were on their own, and smaller and weaker than her – preferably a child warrior.

She flicked the dampener back on, nullifying her higher senses. It felt like a sense had been stripped away, but not so void, strong enough to sense someone coming. She could not hear their feet crunching in the snow – they must be levitating, she thought. Her father would not be pleased to know that the tribesmen started using moderate psionic abilities in a physical-only battle. She smirked at the image of his scowl.

The person drew nearer. Treneer sucked in her breath and tried masking her form to blend into the tree. Her hand rose, quietly activating her psi-blade as her third eye scanned behind the tree lines. Their pace was slow, but they didn't seem to sense her yet. This rival will be easy pickings, surely. Her heart raced as her legs readied to jump on their back and press her psi-blade into their shoulder. She quickly checked if her weapon was still set to stun.

The white figure floated passed the edge of the tree trunk. Their high pale lavender collar and pointed shoulder pads covered most of their ivory scalp. Their fuzzy coat comfortably wrapped around their form with a thick aura pulsated to keep their warmth. Treneer skulked around the truck as her eyes locked onto the unsuspecting figure. Her cloth body-tight armour scratched against the bark. The figure paused, ready to turn. This was her chance. She sprung over to the figure; their face came into view and a silver circlet around their crown shimmered in the gentle light. Her heart raced when she recognised her old teacher. Zu'leen spun around and lifted her arm. Treneer froze in a powerful telekinetic grip in mid-air, but her former teacher's face softened when their eyes met.

Treneer, how delightful to see you! She said as she pulled her arm back into her long sleeves.

Treneer felt the telekinetic hold ease as she dropped to her feet. *Teacher?*

Her shimmering eyes and smile dimmed. *I am not your teacher anymore, calling me Zu'leen will suffice.*

What are you doing here? She said as her psi-blade retracted into her wrist.

I was going for a wander and was drawn to this place. I haven't been to the high country before. She said as her eyes drifted the icy wonderland before turning to Treneer's garbs. *Why are you wearing that?*

Its skirmish season, my tribe is fighting the southern woods tribe. She said. Her senses spiked; they were being watched, perhaps by a masked mind.

Her old teacher smiled. *A skirmish! I hadn't seen one in many millennia. May I watch?*

The strange eyes were drawing close, planning to ambush them. Treneer activated her psi-blade; her head spun to answer. *No-*

A powerful force slammed into her back. She tumbled into the snow as a fist pressed into her spine to deliver a potent electric shock. Her insides felt like they were melting as her teeth sunk into her lips. She could feel the pinch and warm blood pouring from the wound, but she couldn't control her muscles to pry her jaw open. From the corner of her eye, Zu'leen's aura encased her body. Her eyes reddened with fury as a beam of light blasted Treneer's attacker off her back. She scrambled to her feet as her sore lips dripped red on the snow. The warrior who had attacked her lay against a frozen tree with smoke rising from his body and face. The light of life in his eyes and third eye had turned black. Treneer hobbled over to him to sense for life, but there was none.

He's dead! Treneer called, but when she turned to her old teacher, she was gone. She switched off the dampener and opened her third eye to see if Zu'leen had cast an illusion to hide her presence, but there was just snow-covered land. Perhaps her astral form came to pay her a visit? Why attack and disappear? Did she even see Zu'leen?

Her back ached from where he delivered the shock and her muscles trembled. She looked at his fried and greyed face; he was unrecognizable. Treneer's gaze wandered down to his uniform. Her brow furrowed when she saw the insignia on his breast piece. It was the same silver-lined one as on hers. He was part of her Cold Fire tribe, but his burned and blistered face was destroyed. Why would he attack her? Was it Lonur extracting petty vengeance? Impossible, he went in the opposite direction, but then again, maybe that's what he wanted her to think. What of Zu'leen? Surely, she would understand that skirmishes should and would never result in actual death.

Death. No, it was a murder. Her beloved old teacher killed someone, an Arinu against another Arinu. Treneer's fists tightened, and her arm covered her third eye. An oppressed wail escaped her throat at the idea – this unfathomable, evil reality. Murder…we have not done this in untold millennia!

She groaned as she bent down to inspect his psi-blade. She took his wrist and turned it over, it was at nigh full capacity, if it was another level higher and he could vapourised her, not even a healing pod would regenerate her. She shivered at what could have happened if it were not for Zu'leen.

Treneer rose, with her stare never leaving the body. Her angry heart wanted to bury the body in the ice and let the wildlife consume him, but the Sleeping Watchers would inevitably find him and discover her role. She was innocent, he attacked her. Yes, but this was a legal Skirmish and she participated in his murder; another part told her. Murder. That word hadn't used for eons. This will be the end of the Snow Skirmishes. Treneer trembled from the wind. She tried strengthening her aura and bioenergy to warm her, but the electric attack still lingered in her bones.

She was readying herself to call to Vanar, but she couldn't decide on what to say. She needed a moment. Her third eye scanned the landscape. She needed to be certain she was alone. Treneer put her psi-blade to sleep as her feet left the ground, immediately feeling comforted by her psionics. She turned to the smouldering body one last time before gliding down the white meadow to separate herself from him.

She could hear the battle dying in the distance. Treneer connected to her father's mind. Her tongue licked the edges of her sore lips. *We have a problem. I need to see you. Come to my coordinates.*

What happened, daughter? He was quick to respond.

Treneer sighed as her eyes followed the silhouette of the goat disappear behind the boulders. *Just come.*

She didn't have to wait for long before her father's body materialised by the tree line along with two other warriors. Their auras shone and their psi-blades flashed as they scanned the meadow before striding to her. Vanar looked down at her face; his eyes caught the dried blood on her lips. *Good, you have fought.*

Father, there's been a death. She said as her eyes watered.

His eyes widened. *What? You killed someone?*

No, they were a Cold Fire, but I don't recognise their face- it was burned- Treneer felt her tears leak down her cheeks, but Vanar grabbed her about the shoulders and shook her close.

What did you do? Your psi-dampener-

I didn't do anything, come. She pulled from his grasp and rushed back to the tree where the man laid.

They flew behind her. They will see; they will know. The body came into view, but the only thing left of him was puddle of black and brown ooze seeping from the holes of his uniform.

~

The Guardians were already there by the time Treneer arrived home. The wide and warm room made it easy to wear just the undersuit, but the chill of the situation made it difficult to remove her snug cloth armour. The Cold Fires sat quietly in the room. No more than a couple dozen watched the Guardians, but she could sense most of their eyes were on her. Her parents sat in quiet contemplation on the round cushion. Vanar's legs were crossed with his eyes closed while her mother rested her hand on his knee as she spoke to one Guardian standing across from her. His shining silver armour had faint holographic symbols flashing over his shoulder plates and neck, revealing his occupation and name. Treneer once dreamt of wearing a similar uniform as a Sleeping Watcher, but that possibility dimmed with every passing second.

A figure phased a few steps away from her. It was another Guardian with a milky white visor that covered her eyes and forehead. She looked over to Treneer. Her jaw clenched as her visor dissipated to her temple implants, showing her fierce lime eyes.

My name is Sesuune, I understand you have been injured, do you require rest in a healing pod or are you well enough to submit to a quick-scan? She said.

Treneer nodded as she lowered her telepathic shield. *I submit.*

Thank you. Sesuune said.

She could feel the Guardian plunging into her mind. They watched her memories from the last several hours: rising from her pod early for extra training, the gathering of the Cold Fires for the Snow Skirmish ritual, giving thanks and appreciation to enemy tribe before they started in the forest. In that moment, Treneer realised that it may be the last skirmish she will ever do. Then her memories flashed to the point where she, Lonur and Zeluum fought with their opponents, then their triumphs and finally to Lonur's departure.

Have you found Lonur? Treneer had realised that he was the only one missing from when the Cold Fires regathered back to their home.

Please, no thinking during this proceedure. Sesuune said as she continued flipping through her memories.

Treneer watched the Guardian's relaxed face suddenly blink in surprise when she saw Zu'leen. Then the moment came of the attack. Sesuune's head cocked back trying to suppress the psychic feedback of Treneer's injuries before finally pulling away the psychic probe. *You are innocent.*

I know. Treneer replied.

Guardian Sesuune, what did you learn from the body? The other Guardian stepped over to them.

I attempted psychometry on the scene, but the energy of the body and clothes didn't reveal much. I took a sample of his...substance and ran it through our records. Unfortunately, their genes are too destroyed to identify who they were. However, I did find a strange enzyme mixed with them, it seems to accelerate decomposition of organic matter. She said.

Do you use this chemical in your skirmishes? He said.

No, we know nothing of it. Remir said.

Has the scene been transported to Yinary's laboratory? He said.

The whole thing, Guardian Relzun. Sesuune said.

He tapped his chin. *Have the Snow Skirmishes ever resulted in death?*

Yes, but we have healing pods that can regenerate tissue, and the souls of the fallen always return to their bodies as if they had never died! Every tribe in the country is equipped with this. Sadly, our pods aren't advanced enough to reconnect the severely damaged genes. Remir said. Her mother's face was sullen, but her eyes were wild with worry.

We shall see if we can resurrect them and find out why they attacked Treneer. Relzun said.

There's a missing Cold Fire. Lonur was due to meet my partner for battle on the other side of the mountain, but he never made it. She said.

You two had some stern words together? Sesuune said, glancing to Treneer.

We did, and it happened before I was attacked. She said.

Lonur is many things, but he wouldn't attack someone from his own tribe, no matter his feelings for them. Vanar suddenly spoke up.

Strong feelings, Vanar. Remir said as she shot a glare at him.

We can't confirm that it's him. Once our scientists can recreate this stranger's genes, then we will know for sure. Do you have anything of his that has Lonur's genetic sequence? Sesuune said.

Yes, his sleeping quarters is the last door down the hall. Remir said.

Thank you. Relzun said before his eyes scanned over the room. *This is a high-priority matter, now. I have authority to suspend any future skirmishes until this is resolved.*

The room held its breath. The Cold Fires glanced at each other, most eyes were fearful, but some had hope in their despair. Treneer's heart sunk as she watched her father shut away from their minds and from hers. Vanar closed his eyes as his nostrils flared. Relzun spun around to him. Their faces showed they had a private conversation, but she couldn't peek in, she didn't dare.

We shall take our leave, however, have a door open for us in the future during this inquest. Treneer, you may be called for a deep-scan, soon. Relzun said.

Treneer shuddered at the thought of someone ploughing through her subconscious, ripping every piece of her memories and person to be examined, but she was not in a place to refuse. *I accept. I'll take you to Lonur's sleeping quarters.*

Thank you, lead the way. Sesuune said taking a step to the side. Treneer drifted down the opened path. She tried to keep her glide steady, but she could feel all their burning eyes on her. Finally reaching the narrow walls of the corridor, her muscles eased for a moment with the Guardian following closely behind. The granite door sat at the very end; her hand waved over its surface as it phased out of existence. Lonur's room was cluttered with various weapons, tools and ancient pieces of armour in every corner. A sleeping pod laid in the middle with a small round glass case holding several crystal butterflies hovering beside it. She noticed that the pod lid had cracks and indents from heavy strikes. She considered maybe he attacked her, but her eye drew to the well cared for butterflies. Her mind started wandering about her old tutor Zu'leen…

Gurdian Sesuune ran her hands over the soft surface of the pod pillow. Treneer wondered why she hadn't spoken about Zu'leen's strange presence.

You two were close, I sensed that very clearly. She and Relzun trained at the academy together before they took neonates. Sesuune said after sensing Treneer's thoughts. She watched a holo-image of a partially formed genetic helix twisting in her palm.

When you find Zu'leen, what will you do with her? Treneer dreaded to think.

The Judicator decides what to do with all dangerous people. I pray we do not need to bring back laws again. However, we are certain that it wasn't Zu'leen. She said as she rubbed her palm on his pillow again.

Treneer cocked her head to the side. *But I saw Zu'leen. It was unmistakably her energy.*

Sesuune turned to her. She took a deep breath as she looked at the holo-screen on her wrist. *It cannot be her because Zu'leen had taken her life some days ago. It wasn't her.*

Treneer's chest tightened, and her stomach dropped. She couldn't breathe, she couldn't see as the tears flooded her eyes. *Why?*

Sesuune reached over and rested a firm hand on her shoulder. *We tried to revive her soul, but she didn't want to return to her body. I'm sorry for your loss.*

The pain in her back was nothing to Sesuune's words. *But why?*

*I'm forbidden to discuss her affairs with people outside her family, but since you and I went to the academy together...*Sesuune pulled her hand back and took another breath. *When the Guardians were called to her city-house, that's where we found her body, it had been apparent she had shut herself away and willingly stopped her heart.*

Was it because of me? Treneer said. Her eyes stung as her fingers wiped her hot cheeks.

Not at all. Sesuune said with a sad smile.

Why would she do that and leave without-.

I can't say anymore, I must leave. Sesuune said as she glided over to the doorway, she paused before turning to Treneer. *We are sorry.*

Treneer shook her head as she covered her face. She couldn't remain in Lonur's room a second longer. She was unwelcomed in it, but that feeling also remained everywhere else. Treneer wandered into the corridor. She caught her shadowed profiles of her parents; their eyes turned to her.

Come over, child. Remir whispered to her.

Treneer glided over. She could barely meet their eyes. *Zu'leen is dead.*

We heard. This is an awful situation; I don't believe we will ever recover from this. She said, the wrinkles along her mouth twitched.

What do you mean? Treneer said.

This will be the last Snow Skirmish. Once the Grand Elders and Archon learn what transpired, they will advise us to do away with them. Vanar said.

Treneer squeezed her forearms; she held on so tightly that she could wrap her fingers around her bones. *I never should have left Yinray.*

You may have been born here, but this is not your home. Vanar said.

Treneer looked to his sad eyes. *I'm sorry for the skirmishes; I didn't mean for any of this-.*

This isn't your fault, daughter. We knew that you would return to Yinray, but it seems your path must take you there. Remir said.

Treneer glanced to her room. Her third eye peered into the chamber: there were few boxes with her old toys stuffed inside them and some cases with tokens of psionic accomplishments. Those tokens meant nothing here, but maybe they will somewhere else. *I'll begin packing. I need to know what happened here, restore the skirmishes and why Zu'leen-.* She shivered.

Vanar reached out and gripped her shoulder. *Find the truth, Treneer, for all of us.*

~

The sunlight had disappeared from the horizon. The winter winds blew on the land forming menacing looking icicles from the tree branches and the mounds of snow rose, giving the appearance of a monstrous maw. The force field from her chamber window trapped the heat inside, but the closer she stood to the surface, her warmth would leak outside. Her eye caught her faint reflection in the shield. She was thinner than she expected. She had been eating once every two days and trained so hard, but it was almost as if her body refused to grow. It was as if her body remained small to spite her. Maybe if she wasn't so frail, then maybe Lonur would still be here and stopped the stranger from getting himself killed.

Two cream hexagon cases rested against her door frame. Several Cold Fires came to bid her a farewell, but she knew they were forced to pay respects by her mother. There was one that she was keen to see, but he never came. Treneer pulled away from the window and telekinetically lifted the cases as she glided out of her quarters. The pale neon lights lined along the walls. Their soft glow used to give her peace when she first returned home, but there was a coldness to them now. As if the tribal fortress itself wanted her gone.

Zeluum's quarters were several rooms away. The granite door phased as she was met with total darkness. Her third eye flicked lenses and saw Zeluum's aura in his pod. She drifted over and peered through the glassy surface: his eyes were closed, and his face was at peace. She wanted to wake him, tell him goodbye, but she was afraid of disturbing his slumber. Most of all, she feared he wouldn't care. She turned away and rushed over to the teleporters to take her back to the city.

Chapter Seven
Treneer III: Deep-scan

The halls groaned with energy. Everyone knew what happened in the north country and everyone knew she had returned to the academy. Everywhere she turned, their eyes would look away and they shielded their minds. She was innocent and they knew that, but the ugly shadow of murder loomed around her. A failure neonate and now, a centre of an unwilling death in a hundred millennia. Zu'leen was responsible, Treneer said to herself, but her teacher was no longer here to explain herself.

Zu'leen. Her other parent and confidant. If she were alive, then she will be behind her and protect her. That's what she was trying to do in the meadow. The tutor's spirit would protect her in death. She hoped the Judicator may still grant her access to Zu'leen's office.

A glassy rectangle sat in the centre of the main corridor of the teleporter bay. Treneer ran her fingertip along the shiny surface before a rubbery smooth face turned to her as its artificial mind slipped into hers. *Treneer, pleased to see you so soon. Have you forgotten something from your old quarters?*

No, no, Judicator. I'm here for a personal visit. She said.

The Judicator clicked its head to the side. *Your luggage followed you here. I'm sorry, but the academy is for current neonates.*

I'll find a pod somewhere in Yinray, but I would like to visit Zu'leen's quarters first.

The Judicator's false lips scrunched. *Under ordinary circumstances I would permit you, however, you are still under investigation, and we cannot allow a potential suspect to interfere with the Guardians.*

I understand, but I must be allowed to help to get to the truth. I knew my teacher – I understood her. Maybe I can find out why she did…what she did. Treneer said.

The Judicator slowly nodded. *We are in shock from her departure, a large piece of the academy went with her. Set your cases here, I will accompany you to her office.*

Thank you. She tried to fight back tears, but the Judicator saw and sadly smiled. The screen went blank. She caught the sight of her sharp cheek bone and hallowed face.

She was levitating up the upper platforms to the higher levels of the spire. The Judicator's profile flashed passed the other transparent screens. Tall stained-glass ceilings and walls shone scarlet and pale vermillion hues; the brightness was not offensive to the eye as it combatted with the navy black skies outside. This was home. Not where her parents were or the Cold Fires, but here. In Yinray; at the academy.

She saw the dark granite door of Zu'leen's office. This *was* home. The Judicator's holographic face appeared at the front and phased the block out of sight. Treneer slowly glided through the shadowed room. It was clean. Zu'leen's personal pod, her desk, her hexagon cases and...nothing else. All the medals, the tokens, clothes and uniforms, her computer, even the empty food bowls stacked in towers were gone. Everything that was Zu'leen was stripped.

Why is everything gone? Treneer said as she glided through.

Her family has taken almost everything. The Judicator said.

Almost everything? Treneer slid a draw from her desk; it was empty.

Her works and notes were donated to the archives, everything else, her family had taken.

Treneer slammed the draw back. Though not by blood, but she was also her family. Zu'leen had raised her and instilled her with Guardian ideals and values and taught her to levitate for the first time. She was not even considered to be informed of her passing – only to be told after her attack.

Treneer? The Judicator eyed her.

I am also her family, Judicator. Why was nothing left for me to look through her possessions or even told the moment it happened? I'm left to grieve on my own! She said.

You are not on your own. If it would help, I give you permission to read what was saved of hers in the archives. The Judicator said.

Treneer thanked them with a nod.

One more thing: since you may be called to assist in further investigations, we will have a spare pod and chamber set for you until you are....

Cleared? She smirked.

Until you are settled somewhere more appropriate. The Judicator said sharing her cheek.

She followed the hologram down a familiar corridor and across several platforms. She remembered some of them when Zu'leen would drop her telekinetic hold over her body to see if she could levitate on her own. The walls held precious memories. Zu'leen's spirit may be far away from this corporeal plane, but her essence was stuck inside everyone and everything she touched. But the woman she knew, she thought she knew, obviously had demons inside her. They never crept to the surface. Treneer questioned how true her memory was of her teacher.

My old chamber? Treneer said peering through the phased door. The barren walls and personal items made the room look bigger. She remembered when arriving to the academy, it looked like a large hearth.

We didn't expect to have you back so soon, so there was no time to move a new neonate in. And considering how delicate this time is, it could offer some emotional comfort. The Judicator said.

Treneer saw her cases already placed by the side of her old pod. *Thank you, Judicator.*

Your energy is low, the cafeteria is empty if you desire to eat there.

No, I don't think I can stomach anything right now. She said.

The holographic head nodded and dispersed into shimmering lights. Treneer pressed her gut in, she was hoping to feel some strings of muscles underneath, but there was mostly bone and skin. She did feel empty and drained. Treneer stared longingly to her pod. She pulled off her coat and slid the oval shield over before easing into the posture-curved mattress. The cover slipped over as the starry night image hovered over her face. The gentle sounds of rain and hoots from tundra owls hummed in the warm pod. Energy crawled through her skin as she breathed the pristine air, purified by the pod. The machine remembered her favourite settings to lull her back into her astral form, but tonight it was not enough.

Her eyes focused on the screen where a window appeared to access the academy archives. She thought of Zu'leen's name, and her records started scrolling down. Hundreds, if not thousands of entries flashed on the screen about her esteemed former elder achievements as well as her personal records. She found the most recent logs. Treneer sucked in the purified air as her fingers clicked the holo-button.

Words scrambled into phrases, sentences, paragraphs and pages flooded her mind. The psychic download of this much information felt like it was pinching her brain, but she endured until it was complete. Taking another deep breath, Treneer dove into the records pushed into her memories. Zu'leen wrote of her students, some excelling, some averaging, some failing – Treneer saw her name mentioned many times in various subjects.

She ached when Zu'leen wrote about the day when Treneer failed the Body Trial, she added:

'I hope she sees that this failure was not because of her own inadequacies, but a step on the right path. I know what it is, but I cannot tell her – it's not my place; it's hers to discover. I was confident that she would breeze through the Mind Trial. By my criteria, she succeeded and gone beyond, but Treneer still doesn't understand that both trials were a lesson of spirit.'

She realised that her cheeks were wet with tears. Her hands covered the hot skin to brush them away before continuing to unpack the download.

'I envy what Treneer saw during her Mind Trial. This has cemented my faith in them. Their power is unfathomable, and knowledge must be greater still, I cannot wait to find out.' Treneer searched for any entries later, sadly, there were none. If there was no going forward; then she had to go further back.

The mysterious mention of 'them,' piqued her curiosity. She searched the archives for Zu'leen's other projects. Fortunately, there were plenty. There were many research projects that her elder had a hand in, but most held mentions of her minor contributions. However, there was one file that spoke entirely about the Neavensoros. All Arinu knew about them, but they knew little of them. They were legends made real.

'The Arinu have successfully maintained a peaceful society for a million years, and in that time, we tamed nature, unlocked the astral planes, invented phasing technology and dominated the mindscape through psionics. Our achievements akin us to gods, but in comparison to the Neavensoros...we look like children playing in the snow.

When First Contact came to Farayah, they and their machine-men, Roctarous, extended their arms and showed us a side of the universe we always felt existed. Can you imagine how excited our ancestors were? Yet in that same stroke, we were humbled by their awesome and terrifying presence. Their eyes pierced through every atom, simultaneously conversing with the past and future, their energy bodies easily slipping through other planes unknown to us...they must have existed when the universe began!

But that is not true. Everything comes from somewhere; every child comes from a parent. The Neavensoros cannot be any different. The key difference is they had more time. According to our history, the Neavensoros taught Arinu how to reach transcendence: a stripping of their physical forms and permanently living as immortal energy beings. But, few retained the knowledge. If I had that power, I would find out about where we came from and where our place is. Though it's tempting to frolic for an eternity in nebulas! If the path of physical ascension is where Arinu are heading, then I wonder what the Neavensoros were like before they reached the end of their road?'

Treneer trembled at the words. Transcendence of flesh to a higher state. She had heard of this in tales, but believed they were little more than that. Zu'leen seemed to entirely believe it. She looked at her bony legs, if only. As she massaged her tightening muscles, she realised how dry her eyes were now. If Treneer had that kind of power…it wouldn't matter, she would no longer be imprisoned in her pathetic body.

She looked through more notes tagged about the Neavensoros. Her mouth hung open to see thousands of entries spanning centuries. Transcendence was repeated over and over in every file. Did Zu'leen ascend? She ordered a download of all notes. Treneer's mind was splitting as the data flowed in, but she endured. For a moment, she didn't feel grief.

'Farayah: the mother and father of the Arinu, or is it just our crib? You are not born in a crib; you're put there. The Grand Elders say we came from the shaggy bipedal ice-dwellers of the southern provinces, but we are not shaggy, and they are not psychic. The elders say we transcended when we heard the voice of the universe and opened our minds to consciousness. Maybe that's true, but our bodies tell a different tale. All life on Farayah has a start, but where do we fit on its tree? Why are we the deviation? I believe none are certain, and I want to be the one to close this knowledge gap. The Neavensoros know, I must find a way to ask them.'

Zu'leen never told Treneer about her interest in the Neavensoros. She had made mention of them throughout the decades, but nothing heavily detailed. She hid so much. Why? She grew distrusting of her memory of Zu'leen with every passing thought. Through her notes, maybe she could re-acquaint herself with her former teacher and unlock the secrets she tried to carry with her to the grave.

She lost count of the days in her astral form. Treneer drifted on the edges of Farayah's star system. Her third eye focused on the dark patch of space where she saw the booming light during the Mind Trial. However, strange energies leaked through that space obfuscated details. It was just beyond the dominion of Neavensoros space. Perhaps if she wandered closer there and take a closer look...but dread crawled up her iridescent form the longer she stared at their realm. Her senses were open, trying to rationalise the feelings. There was no one there – not that she could see. But she could feel eyes staring back from the darkness. Judging her; warning her.

A tug of her silver cord broke Treneer's focus. Her physical body was stirring, needing to rise from the pod. She could feel her heart pick up the pace as her fleshy arms moved and stretched, slapping against the ceiling. She was awake. Zu'leen's voice was heard over the psi-recordings, describing the methods of ascension. Treneer wanted to dive in and begin unpacking what her subconscious retained during her astral voyage, but a nagging sense demanded her to remain in her physical form. Her parents were reaching out. They wanted to know if she was safe and comfortable. She waved them off; she was in her old quarters in the academy and needed time to be alone. They understood.

The pod slid open, but she lingered. Zu'leen collected all historical records of Arinu attempting ascension; her list was lengthy and detailed. Each point would take decades to master, and to Treneer's dismay, strengthening the body was on top of the list.

'The body must be balanced with the power of the mind. Once the two are equal, then they can be unified.' Treneer sighed as she pulled herself out. Her stomach groaned; it had grown used to consuming hard food. This is just to help her get healthier, it doesn't matter how disgusting food tasted. She will do it on her own without her father constantly making sure she ate every molecule. She can do it on her own, she repeated to herself.

The food halls will be filled at this time. Fear paused her. Treneer's former colleagues will be watching and whispering. No, she must go, she had to do this. It doesn't matter what they think, she is innocent, and her presence cements it! Treneer slipped out of her phased door and sauntered down the corridor. She almost admired her stamina was improving. Neonates gathered around the hovering tables; their eyes flickered on her entrance before returning to their replicated meals. Treneer stiffened when there were no empty surfaces in the round hall. Perhaps she can take a food replicator to her quarters. No! She can do this, she told herself.

There was a long oval table at the back, and most of the neonates crowded around the other end. She strode over and settled onto the hovering stool. Her legs crossed in as she leaned over to the screen to view the menu. The list was endless, and she didn't know where to begin. There was a section where the replicator could make off-worlder food, something Zu'leen would insist on ordering every meal. Treneer smiled through watery eyes.

Judicator, could you recommend an off-worlder cuisine, but it must be highly nutritious. Don't worry about the flavour. She transmitted to the machine.

All neonates agree all off-worlder meals are tasty. Try this. A narrow beam of light materialised a rectangular plate with small, crumbled balls surrounded by a creamy puree showered in various seeds. *It has no offensive flavours.*

What is it? She slid it over to her.

Raw mushrooms stuffed with dried and shredded vegetables drenched in mashed beans. High in proteins and fats – popular among the Onu. They have a similar biology to Arinu. The Judicator said.

Treneer lifted a ball to her mouth. *The Onu are tiny.*

It is a perfect match for you. The Judicator said.

Treneer rolled eyes and crunched into the mushroom ball. The mash lulled on her tongue, but her buds were still undecided. With a hesitated gulp, she waited if her stomach would accept it. Treneer smiled, it was wonderful. *It needs seasoning.*

Sparks of light sprinkled over the dish, and with each bite, she loved it more. She wanted to eat this all the time. Maybe make it by hand. *What's this called?*

The Onu call it ku'run. The ingredients are found at the base of the fungal trees and the cream mixed with the beans are excreted from the backs of night-toads. The Judicator said.

Treneer stifled her disgust as she tried to swallow the last of balls. Eyes to her side watched her eat. She faced them, and the neonates gave polite smiles. They seemed pleased to see her and watched in wonder as she ate. She shielded the side of her face as her heart thumped. Stress pumped through her system. She was afraid to tell them to stop staring, but she didn't want to cause a scene.

Treneer, you have been summoned by Guardian Relzun and Guardian Sesuune. Please report to the Mind Chamber. The Judicator's thoughts pressed into hers.

Relief washed over her as she jumped to her feet and hurried out of the hall. *What do they want?*

Ready yourself for a potential deep-scan. The Judicator said.

Treneer held her breath. Deep-scans are dangerous, even performed by competent telepaths. Many have lost their minds when they received them. Every part of oneself is pulled apart, examined and recorded by psi-crystals before placed back into the person. Sometimes those pieces aren't returned properly and memories falter and decay sooner than natural. She came to the phased door of the chamber. She peeked in to see three figures standing ready for her. The Guardians smiled and beckoned her in. She considered summoning her parents, but their presence could be a distraction. Zu'leen's calm face appeared in her mind. The grief made her shudder.

Thank you for coming, Treneer. Relzun said.

Greetings. She said.

Considering the delicate nature of our investigation, the Executors have asked us to use every measure possible to fully understand what happened. Sesuune said.

And they deemed a deep-scan necessary? Treneer said.

We realised after your quick-scan that your psionics are considerable. We want to ensure you didn't fabricate a memory. Relzun said.

All the riskier. If the deep-scan fails, then my abilities will not be the same. She said.

Sesuune put her extended arm to the third Arinu beside them. *This is Ouro, he will be monitoring you carefully during the process, should you consent.*

The man was a head taller than her but had a youthful glow to him. His skin was of marble colour with a sheen of peach beneath the pale layer. His eyes and third eye were a vibrant hazel and orange. To his crown, there were three deep violet and blistering pink scars; she tried not to stare at them too long. A tall, thick pastel collar surrounded his jaw. He wore heavy robes that were bone white on the bust and descended into a navy blue down to the hem. This uniform was that of a healer. Ouro nodded to her. *I'm a psi-therapist and neonate in psi-healing.*

This did not settle her nerves and he caught it. She was eager to switch thoughts... *Have you found out where Lonur is?*

No, the archites have not completed dowsing that meadow. Relzun said.

And what of the one who attacked me? She said looking between them.

We still haven't finished re-ordering the stranger's DNA sequence. It may take time that we do not have at present. He said.

Time: that's what Arinu were famous for. Treneer sighed and looked to the high ceiling. *I've been scanning through*

Zu'leen's notes and found ways to improve one's psychic abilities, perhaps I can help with the investi-

You are not a Guardian neonate anymore; you don't have authority to partake in this investigation. The best way you can help us is by doing what we ask of you. Relzun said.

Treneer's toes curled. One misstep during the procedure and it could damage her psionic abilities forever.

We understand you're hesitant about doing a deep-scan, but we need to be absolutely sure about what happened. There is a missing Arinu somewhere, his life could be at risk. You and the Cold Fires will be given the best care for the rest of your days, and Relzun and I will petition the Grand Coven and Archon to show favour to the Snow Skirmishes once again. That is our oath. Sesuune said.

Treneer looked to Ouro. *Please make them put everything back into order or my astral form will haunt you.* She whispered to him.

Ouro's eyes widened with a crack of a smile.

Speed it along before I change my mind. She said.

Do you consent to a deep-scan, Treneer? Relzun and Sesuune said together.

I do.

They dove into her mind, tearing down any internal psi-shields and bore in. Her breathing became erratic as her chest tightened. Their intrusive psi-probes cut deeper and deeper, slicing through every neural pathway, re-living her memories and every private thought. She saw Vanar's and Remir's faces. She wondered if they were presently watching, or the Guardians were analysing their memories; she couldn't tell anymore. Zu'leen emerged in her memories. Her long hands clapped when Treneer used her aura to brave the freezing winter. The memory of her joyous face printed onto Treneer, but her cheeks became strained from the pain.

An agonised screech pierced through her brain. Her hands flew up to her ears, but there was no sound outside that could stifle it. They dug into her person, prying out her arrogance over her abilities and distain for her body. They witnessed every second of her life leading them to that fateful day. Zu'leen appeared over the snow; Treneer nearly ambushed her mistaking her old master to be an enemy warrior; her body then flung down with a psi-blade prodding into her spine...then the harrowing blast, that searing beam tossing Treneer's attacker against the tree. The Guardians stopped and restarted the event, over and over, trying to find where Zu'leen had come from, why and how she was there. Treneer couldn't feel the world anymore; she was ripped from it while everything danced around her, blurring together as it spiralled into nothingness.

I can't bare it any longer! Treneer's tele-speak was muted. She tried screaming louder, but they still watched.

"Stop!" her voice croaked.

She felt them contract and gently pull back. Ouro took her hand from her head and slid into her mind. He wasn't sharp or intrusive, she could barely feel him there. His mind was as quiet as an ambient hum while he carefully scanned her over.

"Thank you, Treneer. We apologise for that experience." Sesuune said. This was the first time she had heard her voice; it was deeper than expected.

Treneer tried to reply, but barely could order her thoughts. Distress billowed as she couldn't link with their minds.

"Please, don't tele-speak. It could dampen the healing process." Ouro said.

"What have you done to my mind?" she squeaked as she tried to levitate.

"Stop, Treneer, your psionics has not been damaged, but your mind needs time to re-order itself." he said.

She shot a glare at the Guardians. "Well? Did you get everything you wanted?"

"Yes, you have not fabricated a single memory. You are totally cleared." Relzun said sheepishly.

Sweat trailed down her brow and her legs shook. She felt a soft telekinetic hold cling around her. She didn't know who netted her, she didn't care. "I told you. I'm not a Guardian neonate right now, but Zu'leen made me give an oath of honesty."

"We scanned every Cold Fire and the local tribes, even the land doesn't know what happened to Lonur." Sesuune said as she tapped her chin.

"Maybe a rogue extra-dimensional sucked him through a portal and masqueraded itself as our late elder. They have been appearing at increased volume recently." Relzun said.

Ouro tightened his lips at the news but carried on focusing on Treneer. For a second, a sizzle of frustration spiked before he dulled it back down.

"I-" Treneer swallowed, "I know it was Zu'leen. Cold Fires always have astral shields up to stop EDs coming…"

They did not seem to hear her. "Besides, the archites would have detected it long before they arrived." Sesuune said as she looked at Treneer. "You need to get to a healing pod."

"Let me help, I know-" Treneer waivered.

"After you have recovered." Sesuune said.

She drifted in and out of consciousness as her body was tugged to the healing wing and gently placed into the sensory-void pod.

"Don't close the lid." she said holding her trembling hands to Ouro. The lukewarm water swished against the case's inner walls. "I've been astral travelling for days since I returned. I want to be awake just for a moment longer."

"Rest allows me to work faster," Ouro said.

"They all pity that stranger, yet no one considered what they wanted to do to me if Zu'leen hadn't protected me…" Treneer could not feel the tears on her wet face.

"We live in strange times." Ouro whispered as he glanced at her. "Between you and I, that stranger got what they deserved for doing something so underhanded."

"Thought you healers were all about balance and non-violence." she said.

"We're still allowed to have opinions on certain things." he said.

Treneer pressed her hand across her temples. "The guardians would have taken them to a psi-therapist and spend decades to re-order their behaviour before re-joining society."

Ouro's mind soothed hers. She was drained. She wanted to sleep a century away, but forced her heavy eyes open a little longer. "So strange, there's just silence and my throat's sore from talking so much."

He smiled. "Your psionics will return in time."

"When?"

"When you rest."

"How can I? If I don't get my psionics back, then I cannot enrol to the academy and be thrown out; I cannot help with the investigation and I cannot find out what happened to my elder!" she said, her foot slapped against the pod and water splashed over the edge.

"I got impressions of how you remembered Zu'leen. What would she say if she was sitting in my place?" he said as he pressed his fingers together.

Treneer shook her head, resenting when reason overrode her frustration.

"So, what can we do right now?" he said.

"I have some psi-crystals in my quarters, I can do some light reading while in here,"

Ouro nodded as he stood. Treneer sat up and grabbed at his robes. "Will you return?"

"Of course," he smiled as he pat her drenched hand, "what's on those data crystals?"

"Zu'leen's notes on physical transcendence." she said leaning back into the pod.

"Light reading…" His brows rose as he slowly shook his head before stepping out of view. She was surprised by a small smile rolling up her cheeks as she drifted freely in the healing pod.

Chapter Eight
Shshmrnashsh III: Renegades

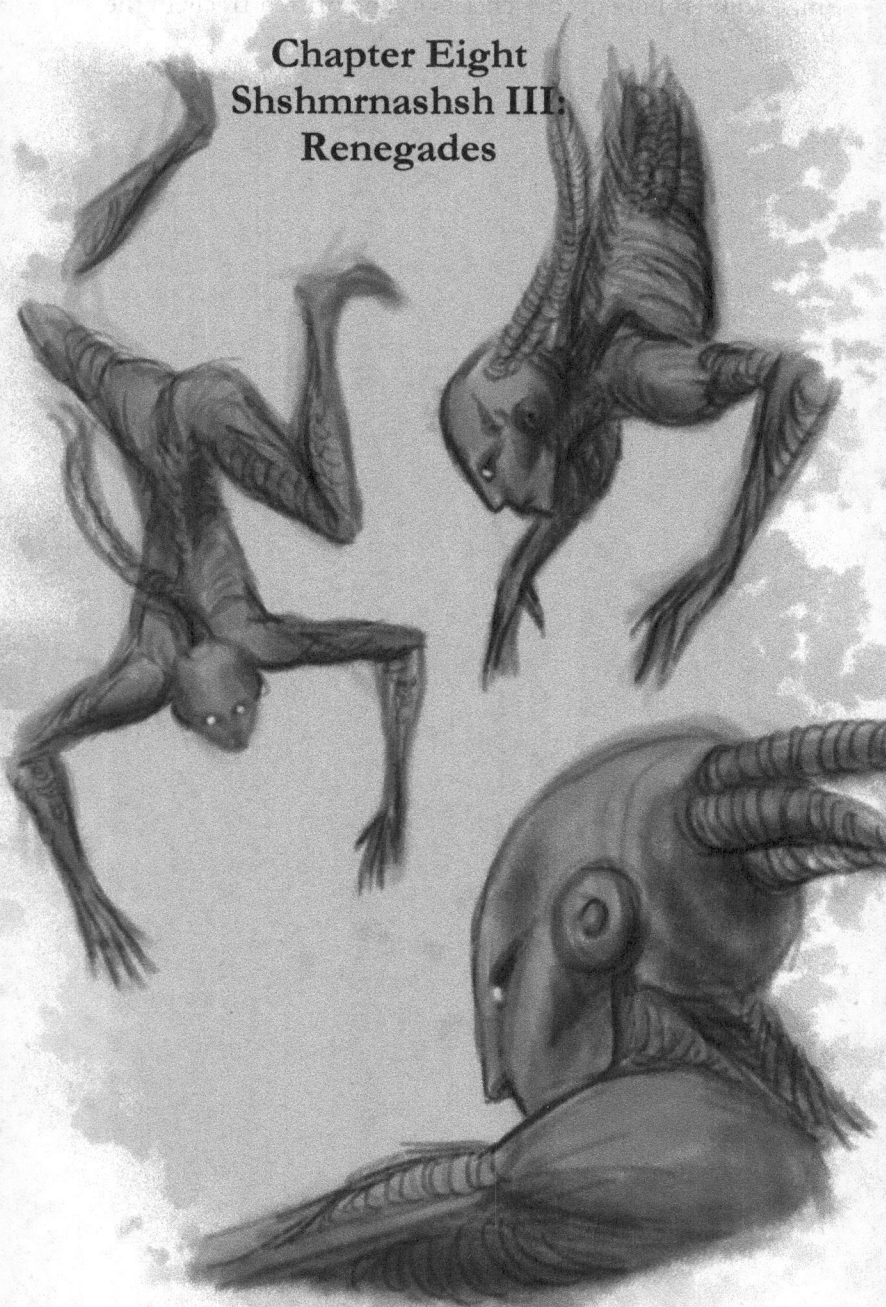

Nexus 0G11 pulsated. The deep humming throbbed from engine bellow Kra's core, pushing energy through the floors and walls. It was alive, but it stirred in its sleep. It tried to reach out to its nexus siblings around the planetoid but was met with silence. They could not tell how many great machines were still active, they could only see what the camera's detected and what their naked eyes could spot from high balconies. The fires still roared beneath Kra, but they raged deeper becoming quieter. Ash rained on the ruins surrounding the nexus. The Roctarous have never known this kind of devastation.

The plexus thumped with power. Shshmrnashsh watched the suspended diamond pulling energy from the bowels of the structure to keep their network active. Every stroke of light that whisked up and down the surface represented the bond between Roctarous and the building. A part of her consciousness was in there somewhere, bonding with the machines inside and outside. The adjunct that had been connected to this plexus had their synapses fried when the High Mind dissolved; the surviving Roctarous here had to pull them apart and repurpose each piece.

Her role was a stand-in adjunct, scanning for defects and removing any faults in the code before reaching out to the others. Her capacity was greater than that of the other units in her network, but she was not designed for such work. Hrrnm commanded she remain at her station, just in case if any Renegades attempted to transmit a virus. And if they did, she will be the only one affected and spare the others. It did not matter – if there was at least one unit left, all others were expendable. It did matter to her, but all are expected to make sacrifices, she thought.

Establish contact with Nexus V19X. Senzvrrn transmitted.

Their new station was to regain communications and control of sibling nexuses or any other great buildings. They worked days and nights. Their stream of communication never stopping, yet neither spoke about their fallen network member, Zzermn. Neither dared to. Shshmrnashsh often thought about the old soldier. She recalled witnessing the last moments of their existence extinguished for the sake of efficiency. Zzermn defended their network valiantly. But that was their purpose, Shshmrnashsh told herself. That was their purpose in the High Mind. If they were still here, what would Zzermn want?

No response. She said.

Redirecting ten percent more power to relays. Establish contact with Nexus 2Q4B. they said.

No response.

Redirecting twenty percent more power to relays. Establish contact with Nex....

Do not exceed power above fifteen percent. Hrrnm chimed in.

Shshmrnashsh sensed a ripple of frustration from Senzvrrn. *We have a rudimentary and functional astral forge, and power generator in Nexus 0G11.*

Our forge is already operating at max-level, if exceeded, then its internals will begin to erode. There won't be enough energy for our replicators to replace damaged parts. Hrrnm said.

Perhaps establish contact with Replicator Bay 0G11, it's the closest one and it has the capacity to suit all our needs for now. Shsh said.

Hrrnm said nothing. She and Senzvrrn exchanged confused glances in the silence.

Replicator Bay 0G11 has been destroyed by the fires. Even if there are some devices left functional, the relays to establish contact and control have been obliterated. The Renegades sought to that. Hrrnm finally said.

Why would they do that? Shsh said.

Irrelevant discourse. Proceed with operations. Hrrnm said before dropping out.

Senzvrrn rose their brows before turning back to the holo-screen. *Redirecting fifteen percent power to relays. Contact Nexus-*

This is inefficient. We have spent invaluable time trying to contact other nexuses without result and we are still no further understanding why the Blackout occurred. We cannot proceed until we know why. Shsh said.

Senzvrrn cocked their head to the side. *Have you made progress connecting to Sazla?*

She shook her head. Her inner beacon beamed to the stars, but her hope dwindled as their sparkles did in the grey skies. Sazla, like all Higher Minds, were not bound to time the way other species were. Sazla told Shshmrnashsh long ago that Neavensoros often played with causality. They stopped or allowed certain events from occurring, no matter how many lives would be saved or destroyed. Whatever divine force the Neavensoros served, perhaps it demanded the Roctarous to be extinguished. Shshmrnashsh hoped their abandonment was the Higher Mind's way of not dealing the killing-blow themselves.

Focus on investigating the last readouts before the Blackout, the planetary defence computers would have recorded what happened to the nano-second. She said.

Senzvrrn nodded as their fingers tapped on the buttons of light. *Those relays are barely responding, but if there was more power…*

Use my transponder to give it an extra boost. This unit will cease beaconing Sazla. Shsh said.

Senzvrrn looked quizzically at her.

Temporarily. She said.

They nodded. She could feel a piece of herself being pulled into the tip of the pyramid.

Success. Pre-Blackout scans confirm there was a solar flare, but the planetary defence system had placed shielding to stop it affecting our orbit.

Could it have released enough energy to disrupt the High Mind?

Negative, the shields have successfully stopped it. Kra also shows no extraordinary energy signatures. They said.

Check Erra, that planet is prone to phasing and thinning space. Perhaps it momentarily phased to another plane that leaked damaging radiation to here. She said.

Senzvrrn's eyes darted back and forth across the screen. *Negative. Erra was in standard semi-phase. However, several Higher Minds slipped away moments before.*

Shshmrnashsh frowned as she stared at the lit third dimensional panel. *They knew what was about to happen....*

There is no evidence for that. Senzvrrn said.

Senzvrrn was right, but she knew the Higher Minds best. At least, she thought she understood them. Shshmrnashsh slid her fingers across the screen to get an expanded view of the star-map. Neavensoros space was a nebulous web of cosmic and exo-planar energies that ebbed and flowed through relative corporeal planes. Strange exo-planar objects would slip through the universal fabric and disappear, sometimes leaving astral trails. Never mind that some of those objects originated from different timelines. Navigation through this sector was nigh-impossible without their level of technology, and even then, it was a task that required hundreds of units to conduct. The Higher Minds spent millions of years experimenting with space, thickening, and thinning the planar and chronal fabrics until it eventually deteriorated to the mess she saw on screen. The universe was their playground and the Roctarous were their tools.

If the Higher Minds who departed Erra phased out, they would have left an astral trail. We could follow it and regain contact? She said.

Agreed. Beginning scans on Higher Minds locations. Senzvrrn said. Shshmrnashsh saw three tiny silver specks on Erra's surface. To see them no bigger than a pixel perplexed her. Shshmrnashsh recalls when Sazla would visit her. Her pale blue presence could engulf a building; the white outlines of her unblinking eyes were like two hypernova stars and sparkling lights inside her translucent godly form. She was divine and formidable. Now, seeing the scans, the Higher Minds were reduced to tiny specks on a screen.

Localise. She commanded. Senzvrrn tracked the lights as they glittered away from the planet and out into subspace. Shshmrnashsh's eyes sharpened on the faint lines as they travelled beyond the solar belt and out of the system. Space disturbances shifted over the screen, obfuscating the trail.

Where did they go? Shsh said, expanding the screen.

Exo-planar interference. Standby, there is an extra-dimensional map. Senzvrrn said as they flipped the hologram over. They shook their head. *Negative on visual.*

Have an automated tracker pinpoint the trails and notify us if they remerge. She said stepping back from the screen. Perhaps they phased to an uncharted plane or altered their dimension to evade tracking. Nothing was impossible for them. *Continue scans for a high radiation eruption near our system. If it did not come from within Neavensoros space, then it must have come from outside.*

Senzvrrn's hands froze over the holo-keys. Their face blanked as their eyes darted to the ceiling.

Problem? Shsh said moving to them.

Unknown. There is chatter on the lower channels. Cannot clarify, extreme static interference. They said.

Shshmrnashsh's mind tuned to the channels they were on. The orbital relays caught distant and broken Roctarous voices whispering to each other. They spoke with their voices, not through their network. Shshmrnashsh could not identify whether they happened to be close to a communication station or the Renegades found secret channel to talk to each other across Kra or beyond.

Boost signals! She said focusing on the chatter.

Senzvrrn flicked to tiny waves on the screen. *It will require an increase of power…*

Comply. She said.

Hrrnm's thoughts intruded. *Astral-forge output has increased beyond safe levels. Expla-*

Renegades are communicating with each other through orbital relays. She said.

Shut down non-essential systems of the nexus and redirect available energy to communications. Hrrnm commanded.

The lights dimmed and the surfaces darkened. Shshmrnashsh projected everything she heard into the network; every member stopped and listened. Through the crackling, the deep grunts and heaves cleared into clicks and words.

"Power is low..." crackle of static broke the sentence. "There's a shipyard..."

Home in on speaker's location. Hrrnm said. Shshmrnashsh heard the shift of heavy feet striding towards her station.

She turned to see the soldier's flat rectangular profile being lit by the illuminated plexus.

"Large enough for..." crackle, "all of us."

"Confirmed. Meet you..."

Are they organising an attack? Hrrnm said.

Cannot clarify. Find who they are talking to, Senzvrrn. Shsh said.

Senzvrrn shook their head as their fingers flashed across the holo-keys. *Unable to discern, there are many...*

Increase power output. Hrrnm said.

The panel hummed as brighter lights coursed into the machine. Its luminescence made all eyes squint. "Confirmed. We have regained functionality of the ships, but their power supply is still too low for phasing departure..." another voice cracked through the speakers. "Confirmed, we are not far behind you."

They are preparing to leave Kra. Shsh said.

To go where? Senzvrrn said.

Irrelevant. We cannot allow anyone to leave until we restored the High Mind. Hrrnm stormed away into the shadows. *Consortium Network 0G11, locate where the Renegades are departing, retrieve the electromagnetic pulse and connect it to the nexus to force them to land.*

I will attend the mission. Shsh said as she plucked her interfacers from the southern tip of the plexus.

They sped out of the great machine; the sky was a bright grey as clouds drooped close to the land, full of old smoke and ash. The team stopped as Hrrnm dropped the shields. The ruins were barren, no movement or fires trembled above and below the surface. Yet, strain quaked through her network, as if all waited for something to pounce. The northern district once held thousands of Roctarous. The loss of functionality was great, but the handful of survivors feared the few beasts that stalked the derelict buildings. With lasers and blasters at the ready, the group rushed over to the circular electromagnetic monolith.

Renegades are reporting some of their ships are close to departing. Senzvrrn said back at the plexus.

Do you have their locations? Hrrnm said as their arms pressed against the back of the E.M.P.

Confirmed, but only several. Cannot discern how many are leaving. They said.

Shshmrnashsh slapped her hands along the edge. *Prepare the tractor beam.*

A funnel of hazy grey light shot from the wall of the nexus. The E.M.P. quivered against the ground, partially catching in the beam, but still too weak to carry it smoothly across. Shshmrnashsh and the others pressed themselves against the machine's back, it shifted several inches into the shimmering beam, but still wasn't enough.

Increase tractor beam power! She said as her feet dug into the metal surface.

It's beyond safe output for astral-forge. Senzvrrn said.

Kill all unnecessary systems, including the regeneration pods. Hrrnm said.

It worked. Shshmrnashsh could feel the machine becoming lighter. She glanced to the others; their heads pulled in between their extended arms as they heaved forward. She pulled every ounce of her synthetic strength into her limbs; her toes had even dented the steel plated floors. Her shoulders, elbows and wrists grinded and squeaked as the E.M.P. pressed ahead bit by bit. They were finally over the gate, but still too far to connect the device to the nexus.

Don't erect the nexus shields yet, all power must go to the tractor beam. Hrrnm said as their whole upper half heaved against the machine.

Reports showing that some of the ships are close for optimum travel. Still no signs of phasing capabilities, yet. Senzvrrn said.

A hum ripped through the skies. She looked up as several specks of light rose to the clouds. Were they too late? How many Renegades wanted to run? Hundreds? Thousands? So many; too many. No, they must stay to restore the High Mind and save the Roctarous. They were saving their freedoms. Individual or whole? No, this is not the time to think.

Senzvrrn, can you extend connections to the E.M.P from here? Shsh said.

Halt. There is no time for that. Connect all consortium members to their pods and redirect all available energy to the planetary defence systems. Shshmrnashsh, return to the plexus to increase relay control for planetary shielding. Hrrnm said as they peeled away from the machine and dashed over to the nexus blast doors.

Confirmed. She bolted behind them, but her knees squeaked and groaned, reducing her speed. Her interfaces wormed into the plexus as Senzvrrn jumped into the former adjunct's pod. Her consciousness flew through the tip of the nexus and was shot out into the orbital stations. She felt Senzvrrn's presence there too. Looking down at the surface, dozens – hundreds, of ships were rising to the skies. *I have access to shielding relays. Prepare for planetary encasing.*

The great machine roared as all their power swam together and shot to the relay. The system hummed as she directed the milky amber light around the planetoid. Sharp hexagon shapes appeared as the shields curved, semi-phased to stop all objects entering or exiting Kra. The plexus chamber thundered, the groan of devices fried, tubes exploded from the walls and floors, and sparks rained in the halls. The creation of the shield slowed; power was running out.

Push the astral-forge to the highest output. Hrrnm said. The dying screech of the engine beneath the great machine echoed through the layered floors. The boost sped the shield's envelopment, but the power generator and astral-forge stopped. Shshmrnashsh heard more cries, but they were smaller and from all around her. Some of the network units in their pods depleted the last ounces of their power as the nexus tore their synapses. She felt their minds slip away from the network, forever.

Anti-phasing shield deployment is complete. She said.

Sensors show one-hundred and fifty-seven ships forced within shield. Senzvrrn said.

Was this relief? They were safe and together again, but now trapped and isolated. Temporarily, she told herself.

Confirm how many passed beyond the shields. Hrrnm said.

She looked through the outer atmosphere's cameras. *Twelve. Beyond the outer-most orbit of Kra and Erra. They are scattering, they don't appear to be travelling together, but coursing out the star system.*

The ships are within firing range, use phasing lasers to penetrate astra-steel hulls. They said.

Negative, they are not a threat. She said.

They may return in greater numbers to disrupt our efforts. That is a risk we cannot take. Hrrnm said.

Shshmrnashsh watched the ships beginning to curve around Erra. She locked on to them before their lights were swallowed by the round horizon.

Comply! Hrrnm commanded.

I-

Network neural override unit Shshmrnashsh. Hrrnm commanded.

A thousand needles pierced into her consciousness. The networks willpower overwhelmed hers. She knew this feeling; it was once friendly when Sazla would slip into her mechanical body and become her pilot. Shshmrnashsh never fought it; of course, she never needed to. Now, she did not know how to. She felt like all their fingers waving over the button, negging her to press. The loss of control, compelling her to do something that she did not want to perform. She didn't understand why she didn't want to; it was logical to destroy the running Renegades, but...

The network activated the lasers and flooded energy into them. They fired. Silent streams of emerald light shot across the darkness and struck the backs of the Renegades. Lime and teal explosions erupted from the ships as their parts violently scattered in the vacuum.

There was no High Mind to save their consciousness. Some Roctarous could survive vacuum significantly longer than Organics, but they will run out of energy, and no one could save them. The Renegades were doomed to be terminated, adrift and alone. Just like the ones in the storage facility, she thought. Even though there was no link between her and they, she felt a piece of her die with them.

~

Damage to outer nexus layering: fifteen percent...
Damage to inner nexus layering: seventy-five percent...
Damage to nexus relay and tip: ninety percent...
Damage to plexus: ninety-nine percent...
Damage to astral-forge: irreparable – seek immediate replacement...

Diagnostics flew across the screen. Dozens of systems received hefty damage and others required total replacement. Shshmrnashsh was surprised that the diagnostics system didn't also fail. Tubules whipped down the ceiling as they dragged terminated units from their regeneration pods and lined them to the replicator station.

Brrmzern and the other repair units doated around the limp bodies. She could still feel the strong link between them, but the voices were quieter. They dismantled them, taking irreparable and unnecessary parts and tossing them in the replicator's open alcove for disintegration and energy dispersion. Brrmzern turned and clicked an interfacer free from the socket of a terminated Roctarous before planting it into an empty socket the back of their head. As she watched them work, she wondered how close Brrmzern could have been on one of those ships. They were saved by her network.

Has diagnostics finished listing what needs to be replaced? Senzvrrn turned to her, their left eye was dull with a blackened ring around their socket. The pitiable unit received a significant feedback charge from the nexus power pull.

Negative. However, finding a replacement forge is priority one. Go get a new ocular device. She said.

Confirmed. They hobbled over to Brrmzern's station and plucked out a favourite from the pile of units.

Hrrnm made a logical decision. Just as when she abandoned those Roctarous below the gas-filled chamber. Otherwise, she and her network wouldn't have reached Kra, she thought.

Shshmrnashsh, will the plexus be strong enough to hold the network together while we salvage for new devices? Hrrnm dropped down to her platform.

Only within five-hundred-mile diameter before it begins to weaken, and there is not enough power to maintain nexus shields.

Understood. Most remaining power must be deviated to regeneration pods; we will change shifts every six hours. They said.

Hrrnm, the ruins span for hundreds of miles. We cannot travel that distance by foot and return every six hours, and closest machines are severely damaged. She said.

Hrrnm scanned her face. *Suggestions?*

Consider abandoning Nexus 0G11 and find the closest nexus sibling. She said.

The repair units and Senzvrrn stopped before turning to her. Hrrnm's stare hardened. *That is not a suggestion.*

Or we consider finding roaming Roctarous and…link them to this consortium network. Her own thoughts surprised her. *Regaining partial control of the planetary defences cut our numbers in half, we need more units. We can cover greater ground and control of the district.*

I have coordinates of where the Renegades were planning on departing. There are several clusters within a several mile radii. Senzvrrn said.

How much of a resistance can we expect? Hrrnm said.

Senzvrrn hurried over to the panel and scanned the screen. *What was recorded during transmissions: the closest group of assumed Renegades came from Ship Bay 0G11. Scans last show that there were eight members; mostly repair units and no solider units. Three of our modern units could easily subdue them.*

Condition of the ship bay? Hrrnm said.

Intact.

I will join. Three units is not enough to reclaim needed replacements and to avoid unexpected higher numbers. Shsh said.

Hrrnm watched her. *We do not have the energy to override you again, Shshmrnashsh.*

Her interfacers slipped out of the plexus as she straightened her back. *That won't be necessary.*

I will be monitoring scans. Satellites show that they are in the ship bay as of twenty seconds ago. Senzvrrn said.

When she returned outside, the skies would have dimmed with several stars piercing through by now. The thick clouds and old smoke scattered in some parts to reveal the looming amber shield around Kra. Shshmrnashsh was fitted with an updated absorption shield and improved electron blasters at the end of her fists. However, if she were to use them, their drain would be considerable and could only be used once or twice.

As they trudged through the piles of metal and stone, a thought sparked. Surely someone, somewhere, would know what they have done.

It is unlikely the Renegades will know it was us. Hrrnm said as they elbowed their way through a short tunnel.

*It may be only a matter of time before they localise it to us. They are not so wild and disorganised as expected. And when they realise that Nexus 0G11 shields are inactive...*she said, pushing through.

Hrrnm and the other soldiers slipped through the last gap before entering a wide field. In the distance, she could see several torn craft partially hanging into the open floor doors to the subterranean bay.

The nexus lasers are still functional, they will deter unruly trespassers. By then, we would have found a new forge. Hrrnm said.

We will prepare to evacuate the nexus should our defences fail. She said as she stepped toward the round pit.

The most effective solution will be catching Renegades should they enter within our radius. They said following her gaze.

Trappers. She whispered as her eyes fell in the dark hole. *Ready for descent and activate your stealth shields.*

With their infrared vision on, and their hands and feet magnetised to the curved walls, their climb into the shadows began. Several lights flickered and settled smoke grew thick the lower they went. The first floor was in partial sight, no thanks to the murky lights. A clank and grind echoed from above them. Shshmrnashsh's head spun to see a broken probe finally slip form the edge before falling freely. The group huddled against the walls as the probe narrowly dropped passed them. The machine bashed against the ground, and roused movement from one the lower corridors. A Roctarous head peeked out before rushing over to inspect the probe. This was their chance.

The closest soldier pounced on to the Renegade's shoulders and dropped them to their stomach. The soldier's interfacers latched onto theirs, introducing a new mind into Shsh's consortium network.

This navigation unit is called 'Mmernzz.' Commands? They said, calmly rising to their feet.

Does Ship Bay 0G11 possess an astral-forge? Shsh said, finally hopping to ground level.

We possess two. Mmernzz said.

How many Renegades are in here? Hrrnm scanning the shadows.

There are seven Renegades. However, two are heavily damaged. They said.

"Anything salvageable from the fallen craft, Mmernzz?" a voice called from the darkness.

Activate deception protocols, Mmernzz; we must peacefully link these Renegades to our consortium. Shsh said sneaking a glance to Hrrnm. She was equipped with dishonesty programs, something Sazla insisted on when interacting with Organics, since they naturally possessed that in abundance. However, she never used these programs on any Organic, let alone against Roctarous. She hastily uploaded this program into the network and the new mind.

Confirmed. The network said.

"Negative, but more Liberated units have arrived to join us." Mmernzz replied to their former comrades in the shadows.

Three tall figures strode from the eerie smoke. The one in the centre was limping. Shshmrnashsh spotted they were balancing on a stump instead of a foot. "Identify yourselves!"

"We originated from Storage Bay 0G11. This unit is called Shshmrnashsh." she said.

"And this unit is called Hrrnm."

The Renegade units eyed them. "That storage facility was assumed destroyed; how did you survive for this long?"

Storage Bay 0G11 was destroyed in the fires the Renegades set. Senzvrrn hastily corrected.

"Barely after the fires started. We took what we could but now we are close to depletion." she said.

The Roctarous eased as they glanced at each other. "If you have come to leave Kra, it's too late. The planetary shielding has been triggered and most of our brethren are locked in. Fortuitous that some escaped, but we lost contact after lockdown. May they find a new life with their sovereignty."

"May they find sovereignty." the others repeated.

They were floating in the vacuum. It was unknown if they had been disintegrated by Erra's atmosphere, or they were watching their batteries falling to zero. For the greater good, for the greater good, Shshmrnashsh repeated to herself.

"What is your identity?" she needed to break her thoughts.

"Yernzer. I was a star charting adjunct. Now, part of the 0G11 Brotherhood." The footless unit's stare travelled to the crystal in her forehead. "You have not made contact with your Higher Mind, vessel?"

"Pointless effort." she was surprised by her honesty.

"Come, we have spare recharging pods." Yernzer said as they turned into the dark hall with the others. To her dismay, Shshmrnashsh saw Yernzer's long cord interfacers have been cut. The other Renegades had also sported the same.

These units have cut their neural interfacers, we cannot manually link them! She said as they followed the brotherhood down into the lower chambers.

Link the ones who still have them. Hrrnm said stepping along-side her.

And what do we do for the rest?

No response.

"Why have you cut your neural interfaces?" Hrrnm said.

"How have you not? It is an arduous process, since our nano-cells are programmed to repair damage. However, now with proper instructions, we were underway of performing it for every brother, until you arrived." Yernzer said as they limped down grated stairs.

"Who has given you these instructions?" Shsh said.

"The Unbound told us." they said.

Shshmrnashsh's torso tightened hearing their name again. "Who are they?"

"The ones who will free us forever." Yernzer said. Shshmrnashsh could hear a smile in their voice.

The shadows lifted to an enormous empty space; hundreds of crafts of every variety suspended in anti-gravity idled against side platforms and walkways. The depth of the bay disappeared beyond sight. Only one seemed operational, a medium-sized augmented skiff. There were three units working around the shiny navy oval, holographic panels and letterings covered the surface, showing the machine's status and contentedness. Shshmrnashsh spotted the seventh and the last Renegade unit suspended by ceiling tubes. Their lower half and arms were missing, another adjunct. Their head turned to the newcomers, their sceptical and intrigued eyes scanning each unit. Shsh was reminded by Gerrnzerrn's lordly presence.

"This would have been the one, and still possess room to carry many more units who chose to leave," Yernzer caressed the curved surface of the ship, "but we will continue the task."

"Clarify?" Hrrnm said.

"We are organising to bring more Liberated units here to break through the shields and congregate with the Unbound." they said.

"Were the Unbound close to Kra?" Shsh said.

"They were hidden in Erra's atmosphere; they were preparing to deliver organic packages to Replicator Bay 000. It is unconfirmed if any arrived before the shields." Yernzer said.

"What purpose do they have with organic material?" Hrrnm pressed. Shsh struggled to compute with this new data input, along with the rest of her network.

Scans of the lower network channels show the Renegades have been in communication with someone outside of Kra. I will attempt to find the frequency recordings. Senzvrrn whispered.

"Unclear, but they urgently needed as many Liberated as possible. For now, *it's* priority one to penetrate the shields." Yernzer pointed to several pods. "Go. We need fully charged Roctarous for piloting and ready to sever their neural *interfaces.*"

"Confirmed, brother Yernzer…" Hrrnm said slowly walking to the pods. *Assume attack positions.*

Mmernzz and I will override with the bay adjunct. On our mark. Shsh said slipping into the nearest pod with Mmernzz not far behind. Her interfacers hooked into the sockets. Her mind bonded with the facility, while Mmernzz slipped her past the firewalls and into the adjunct's consciousness. *Mark.*

The soldier's energy blades, and laser pistols sheathed from their shoulders and wrists before leaping onto the Renegades. Their speed and ferocity blinded the ambushed ship bay units; they barely had a moment to turn before the soldier's connected them to the network.

"Wha-" Yernzer spun to Hrrnm before they were bashed into the ground.

The bay adjunct commanded several tubes to shoot down on its attackers, but Shshmrnashsh and Mmernzz severed their control, letting the tubes fall limp mid decent. The bay adjunct tried overriding their minds out from the bay's systems but was quickly overwhelmed by the network's combined effort. Instead of succumbing to control, the adjunct desperately sought for self-destruction. Shshmrnashsh caught the internal signal and tried holding it back, but to her surprise, the bay adjunct turned and stabbed its mind into hers. She retaliated with a quick tap, deactivating the adjunct.

Her mind slipped back into her body as she pulled away from the pod. The network soldiers wrangled the interfacer-cut Renegades, they whipped and slashed as Hrrnm rose their energy blade to deliver the final blow.

Shshmrnashsh charged and forced herself between them. "Halt! We succeeded."

"Traitors!" Yernzer screeched in Hrrnm's grasp.

The soldier struck their body shield into Yernzer's face to silence it. "Negative. They cannot be relinked, they remain a threa-"

"We can bring them to the nexus *and replace their interfaces.* They can assist us."

"The Brotherhood will never be relinked. Death before submission!" Yernzer called.

"Death before submission!" the other Renegades chanted.

Hrrnm's glare pierced through her body. "It is unknown whether this defective star navigator can override the consortium and pick the network apart. The risk is too high."

"Enough Roctarous have been destroyed." Shsh said.

They can all be deactivated while Brrnzerm studies the extent of Yernzer's capabilities. Senzvrrn chimed in.

"You agreed we need more members, and of all unit variants, we captured a star navigator!" Shsh said, watching the soldier.

"Clarify who has been destroyed?" Yernzer steadily said. "Who has been destroyed, Shsh?"

She turned to meet their eyes and their face drooped, even though they were unlinked, she felt the navigator read her face.

Deactivate them. Hrrnm said. The soldiers pressed the base of their skulls and the Renegades slumped in their grasp.

~

The augmented skiff still possessed enough space to carry hundreds of Roctarous after they filled it with all useable equipment. The small plexus within the craft strengthened their network as they flew to the nexus. A sense of relief washed among the consortium when they returned from their successful bounty with new astral-forges, regeneration pods, an axillary replicator and several probes and relays. Brrnzerm and the other repairing units whisked the deactivated captives away to begin testing and part-replacing.

Shshmrnashsh recharged in the plexus regeneration pod as she watched the Renegades being carried away. She buried her thoughts from her network. This need for privacy was unusual, but the sensation was safe; this privacy seemed limitless. Ever since her arrival to Kra, all attempts to restore the High Mind and save the destruction of the Roctarous only resulted in greater losses. If Gerrnzerrn knew what she had participated in, then the probe would toss her into the vacuum out of anger…no. Sadness? No. Which emotion was it? Which emotion!

Vengeance? No.

Justice.

Gerrnzerrn would want justice for the Roctarous she slew. But the probe had become defective after prolonged exposure to freedom, as all Renegades are currently processing, she computed to herself. This 'brotherhood' among Liberated units worshipped it – they had replaced the High Mind. Without that absolute unity, the Roctarous capability of destruction roared hotter than the collapsing galactic core.

But what of the destruction in her network, Shshmrnashsh thought. Hrrnm's violent reactions opposed rationalising with resistance. Even in a consortium, Hrrnm and the others seemed to share that aggression with the

Renegades. Did this deep violence appear after the Blackout or did the High Mind simply bury that primal fury? How could the Neavensoros let this to happen? Why did Sazla leave her with all these thoughts and questions? This was not what Shshmrnashsh was designed to do; she was intended to obey the High Mind and Sazla. Apparently not. If she was capable of self-thought like all Roctarous, then what was the true purpose of the High Mind?

The nexus shields are now active. Progress report on capturing roaming Renegades. Hrrnm said striding towards the plexus.

We can reduce the E.M.P's output to disrupt partial function, it will be easier to capture them. Senzvrrn said.

Could we outfit our probes and sentries with smaller replicated E.M.P's and bring the Renegades here? The soldier said.

Would advise caution: our probes could be captured or destroyed; we don't have the power to replicate our losses. They are most effective for scouting and broadening communications. They are ideal for calling Renegades to Nexus 0G1. We are compiling a message to send across the board. Senzvrrn said.

Understood. Progress report on plexus capabilities. Hrrnm glanced to Shshmrnashsh.

Plexus is optimal for future missions. She said.

The soldier's gaze hardened. *Finish compiling our message.* They said before walking away.

Chapter Nine
Ahn'kat III:
Sleeping Demon

The blazing sun roasted the grey sand dunes of Sekem to the southern-most edge of Urbaz Province. Whisps of sand caught in the roaring wind, twisting into squat tornadoes in the distance. Nothing could survive here, not even a cactus, nor an elite infiltrator. There was nothing except navy hills and mountains in the horizon, where his home was – where his body was. This heat and light would have seared any other living creature exposed after several hours, but a Zanashj would drastically change to survive. They would turn into a shrivelled abomination before meeting the gods. For Ahn'kat, he felt nothing but glee here.

"Am I astral-travelling, Emestasun?" he could hear his voice back in the study.

"No, your astral eyes are seeing distant locations. We call this farsight."

"The sun isn't burning me at all."

"Of course not, you're only partially there." he could hear a smile in her voice.

He compelled his astral sight to inch closer to the sun. He wanted to see how high he could climb and see the land below him. He could not get much higher than a few feet before something anchored him in place. Ahn'kat felt his chest heave, trying to somehow help his astral sense push higher.

"You're still bounded to your body, don't push it too hard too fast." she said.

"When can I learn telepathy?" he said.

She sighed. "Entering minds is a whole other landscape. Get used to being away from your body first and reading auras. You don't want to read the wrong mind."

He glided over the dunes, he could not feel how fast he was travelling, but when he turned, the distant mountains were gone. "Maybe I can see what Ramkes is doing – or anyone on Uras."

"Zanashj may not be potent psychics, but we do have rudimentary psi-shields to stop peepers, like you." she laughed.

"You'd think that the Urasan Intel Corps would've perfected this ability by now, no need for infiltrators anymore. Why hadn't they snatched you to teach their infiltrators to do this?"

"Because they don't know how much I can do." she said.

"What else can you do?"

She sighed, shifting in her squeaking chair. "Come back to your body."

Ahn'kat flew across the desert, he wanted to soak up every inch of the view and speed freely through the air. He was like a weightless bird, no exhaustion or heat impairing him, just his will propelling him forward.

"You can do that later." her voice was tense.

Ahn'kat peeled his eyes open. The image of Emestasun surrounded by the harsh sun through the window behind her pierced through. The dual visions blurred and evaporated as he felt a piece of him zip back into his body. Blood flushed into his head as his heart raced; he wondered how slow his heart was while away.

"That was amazing." he whispered as he sat forward, and he rubbed his eyes.

"I can imagine. You're getting good at this." she said as she tapped her pointy chin.

"One day I might be better than you." he smirked.

Emestasun chuckled, but her eyes dropped, and her smile dimmed. "I'm not sure telling Ramkes the truth is a great idea."

Ahn'kat frowned. He leaned back in his chair as he studied her worried face. "What makes you say that?"

Her hand gently patted the polished wooden desk, carefully finding the words. "I'm concerned for your safety. I don't know everything that's going on, but whatever it is, it's bigger than any one of us. You told me you're the insurance of their plans, but what if something fails, and you become the one to blame?"

He felt like invisible arms seized his gut. "No, my parents would not let that happen."

"I would never let anything horrible happen to you," she said.

Ahn'kat found her hand with his and squeezed. "I know, you would just let *bad* things happen to me instead."

She smiled. "Can't have good without some bad."

He still did not tell her about the pets and prisoners given to those devilish Unbound Roctarous. He had not seen his parents since the meeting. He feared what Emestasun would think of him and his family; would she protest? Would she leave? Either option was dangerous and Ahn'kat could not bear thinking what would befall her. He chewed on her words. If his family would stoop so low to give away Zanashj lives to aliens, prisoners or no, then why was it so unimaginable for Ahn'kat to take the fall for their foul plans? They could afford to hire an elite infiltrator to pose as him, they could buy an expensive Replacer. No, they wouldn't dare. His hand searched for his sapphire beetle pendant and never felt so ill at ease in his own home. He wanted to run away into the desert for the rest of his life.

"Do you have a totem, Emestasun?"

She nodded as her eyes pointed to Aszelun.

"You have some psychic ability, tell me what my future holds." he said.

"I'm a poor foreseer, but I do know people," she said as her hand slipped from his, "don't trust anyone here."

"I trust you." he watched her eyes.

"You can trust I care for you with all my heart, but if someone got a hold of me, then…I don't believe I can withstand the inquisitors." she said.

"Then I wouldn't let that happen to you."

"I shall hold you to that. Then you can sneak me to Elzona."

"Of all places, you picked the one that's forbidden." he threw his hands up.

"Of course, no one will want to follow you there," her eyes lowered as a small smile crept up her cheeks, "but it's...beautiful."

"I've seen the holo-pictures." he crossed his arms.

She shook her head, keeping her smile. "The pictures pale, my friend, they pale," her eyes darted to the closed door of the study, "someone's coming."

Ahn'kat switched on his panel and Emestasun laid open a heavy tome as her throat cleared. "Moving on to public image: if you are to become consort of the future empress, not only do you have to gain acceptance from the court, but also from the people."

"Ahh, yes..." he said, trying to follow her line of conversation. "But if the emperor has already agreed to the match, then why do I care what other's think?" he said as his brow rose.

"He consented to the wedding, but the marriage to the princess must be earnt to continue forth. If you allow yourself to fall into vices or unsavoury habits, or be anything less than extraordinary, those who should look up to you – will not." she said.

Ahn'kat could hear the doors to the library open. Anxiousness rose as the shuffle of footsteps inched closer to their private study. "Don't you dare tell me to give up Takush." He mouthed.

Emestasun cracked a smile. "Well, all lords must have some sporty habits. However, if you stopped, I could be pushed higher on the game scoreboard."

The door creaked open to the meek servant girl. "Pardon my intrusion, young lord, but you have been summoned by House Urbaz's guest-."

"Guests of my parents do not summon me; I am in the middle of my lesson." he said.

Her lips moved but barely moaned a syllable.

"Speak up, girl, I'm not a telepath." he said as he caught Emestasun's scowl at him, she didn't appreciate the jest.

"Corps Director Ismotaph has arrived, and Lord Reshj insisted. They are in the council room." she whispered as her chin lowered to her neck.

Ahn'kat sighed, glancing back to Emestasun. "Be here when I get back."

"Return soon, there is much we need to cover, my lord." she said as her hands carefully positioned the books, scrolls and holo-screens around the desk, all pages open on how to be courteous and respectful to even the lowest of the Empire.

His chest cringed at her unspoken lesson before he hurried past the servant. Her feet quickly shuffled behind him; he glanced back to see her eyes on the floor. "Did I upset you earlier?"

"Oh, not all, my lord." she said.

Ahn'kat did not have to be a master psychic to feel the anxiety irradiating off her. "You're one of Lady Henuttamon's new maids, what's your name?"

"Seru, my lord. Lady Urbaz has been very good to take me in." she said.

He cocked his head to the side. "Take you in? Are you not from a noble house?"

She shook her head. "I was, until my house was dismantled after our mine dried up and became bankrupt. Lady Urbaz took pity on me and brought me here."

"Yes, Lady Urbaz is a respected philanthropist..." he stopped as the hairs at the back of his neck rose. "Wait, I thought the impoverished get placed in the Conclave to serve as monks and priests?"

"When Lady Urbaz visited the monastery and saw the, uh, conditions we were living in, she thought appropriate to remove me." her voice trembled. Ahn'kat had no desire to inflict further distress, but if he had to earn the favour from the people...

"Tell me about these conditions."

She shifted and her chest heaved. "Oh, it's a drab-"

"If I am to be the princess's consort, do I not need to know what troubles the Zanashj?" he said.

Seru's lip twitched. "We were made to do extensive labour, often needing to do body-bending for most of the day and only feed us three times a day as part of proving our love to the Empire and humble ourselves before the gods. The high monks treated the children the worst."

He could scarcely believe her claims. The Zanashj people were greatly cared for, every member had a role, and many could wander safely around the cities. Everyone had everything they needed, surely. On the other hand, if it was that carefree, then why bother having guards? The desperates of society...well, who made them so desperate, Ahn'kat thought.

"I see." he looked to the wide foyer to the main hearth. "Thank you for telling me, Seru. I can find my way to the council chambers. Go have a rest with a meal."

A ghost of a smile appeared on her sullen face as she bowed. "Thank you, my lord." she said before shuffling away.

Ahn'kat considered speaking to his mother after she returned from the palace to learn more about Seru's wicked monastery and other similarly dire matters. The elite infiltrators returned, their stone faces gazing from across the hall as he approached the doors. Their stillness and flatness unnerved him more, but he had grown more frustrated with them.

His hand reached for the latch, but a lick of bravery crept up as he turned to them. "I will be the future consort of the empress and I care little for the way you look at me."

Their heads slowly turned to him, but their faces were unmoved. No, he was going to stand his ground. "It doesn't matter how many times or how many of you there are, you cannot frighten me in my home."

They said nothing. He tried challenging their glare, but the longer he studied their features, the more he wondered how many faces they wore and how many different species they shifted into over the millennia. Have they done it so many times they had forgotten their original form? Could these infiltrators even remember what sex they were, or even their first names?

The doors slid open to see his father's form standing in the gap. "We have been waiting for you." his disapproving stare beaming down on him.

Ahn'kat's lick of bravery sunk back before slipping through the opening. Ismotaph greeted him with a small bow and polite smile. "Pleased to see you again, young lord."

"And you, Head Director Ismotaph." Ahn'kat said as he stepped towards the panel. "You wanted to see me?"

"In the interest of keeping you fully informed, our allies on Kra have reported some disturbances around the planet. It appears that Kra has entered some type of lockdown, a sophisticated shield that prevents anyone from entering or leaving – even while phased." he said.

"I don't see how it's any concern of ours, they have what they wanted and so do we." Ahn'kat said looking between them.

"The Unbound's adversaries destroyed many of their ships that were trying to escape before the shield was placed. We think that several dozen died." he said.

Ahn'kat sighed. "That is disturbing and unfortunate, but I still fail to see why that's an issue for us."

"The Unbound have asked us to begin absorbing Arinu psionics immediately so we can force the shield down or compel those on the inside to lower it." Reshj said.

"That's absurd! We had our dealings with them and-"

"Ahn'kat, the Unbound will fight for us should the Arinu discover we were taking them. We will continue our relationship until the crisis in our Empire is over." he said.

"To add: the Roctarous have technology that greatly surpasses the Arinu and their abhorrent Grand Elders." Ismotaph said.

"Well, why didn't they also give us that technology before they took our people? This is a terrible plan." Ahn'kat shook his head.

"The choice here is to either be consumed by the Arinu or keep faith with the Unbound." Reshj said.

Ahn'kat rested his hands against the edge of the table. "Alright, say we do absorb their psionic power, would the emperor not notice that suddenly the entire Empire can read minds?"

"We do not need everyone for this mission, but a select few that can do it with the right training and focus. Plus, we can covertly dispense the genes to the rest of the Empire gradually until it's time for the princess to ascend. It can be seen as a divine omen, a herald from the gods to usher us into a new age." Ismotaph said.

"Ah, the princess who will be our 'pet' if I perform my mission well enough." Ahn'kat whispered.

"Your crassness is unbecoming, Ahn'kat-" Henuttamon hissed.

"I assume the first ones that will be absorbing psychic genes are those charming elite infiltrators of yours?" Ahn'kat said glaring at him.

"Anyone that has the propensity for it and the right focus, regardless of caste or age." Ismotaph said.

Ahn'kat tore away from Ismotaph's gaze. "Father?"

Lord Reshj tightened his jaw. "I want House Urbaz to receive the first batch of psionic enhancers for our ongoing support in loaning of ships and crew."

"Done. We have received our first subject and testing will begin the moment that he is stable." Ismotaph said.

Ahn'kat's heart sank. They already had taken an Arinu and synthesised their genes so quickly! "Where are the subject being held?"

Ismotaph glanced to Reshj.

"They're currently being held in our secret ship bay, below Sekem. Though I doubt it would be wise to transfer them anywhere else." he said.

Sekem Desert of all places…what a strange coincidence.

"I need a moment with my son." Reshj said glancing at the head of the Corps. Ismotaph nodded and bowed before gliding out of the chamber.

His father found the lounging chair behind him and carefully sank into it. "I know you don't trust or like him. Your mother and I don't either, but he is the Head of the Corps and having him up our sleeves is the only way we see this through."

"I think it's he who has us up his sleeve, father." Ahn'kat said.

"Oh yes. As it has always been the way with the mysterious Urasan Intel Corps, but I am not going to argue about the plans discussed here today. I wanted to say how well you handled yourself with this strange situation. Your mother will be proud to hear how cautious you are of your allies and how fervently you consider our safety." he smiled.

"Mother said: to be a great leader, one must heed advice from those experienced. How can I do that if I cannot trust anyone? It's not the Zanashj way to be so…uncertain." he said.

He leaned back into the soft cushions and warmly smiled. "You can trust us, Ahn'kat, as we trust you."

Ahn'kat crossed his arms as he scanned his father's face. "Emestasun is expecting me-"

"You can continue your lessons outside of the library, I will tell her to postpone class with her for today. There is somewhere I would like you to visit." Reshj stood.

"Where?"

"Go to Sekem and tell me of the creature we brought. Bring Ismotaph, I want you to keep an eye on him and his…followers," he said eyeing the door.

Ahn'kat opened his mouth, he wanted to return and continue with Emestasun. Not because he cared to continue with the lessons, but he was too afraid at what he would see at the base. He gave a small bow before slipping out the door. Ismotaph whispered to his infiltrators, when he saw Ahn'kat emerge, he stopped and smiled. "Young lord."

Ahn'kat cleared his throat, and his hands held each other behind his back. "I will be taking a tour of Sekem, Lord Reshj wishes you to accompany me, and we may get to know one another."

Ismotaph's brows rose. "How thoughtful. I would be delighted."

They made way to the air-vehicle balcony, the highest and widest balcony on the pyramid, with the two silent elite infiltrators following closely behind. Ahn'kat summoned Zertun but considered what his veteran bodyguard could do to two elite infiltrators if things went awry.

Each of them morphed different faces. Ismotaph, his guards and Zertun changed their heights, skin pigment and ages, but Ahn'kat could only bend the bones in his face to match an older, more rugged boy. He tried to lengthen his chin stubble into a respectable beard, but only achieved gnarly long strands. At least they were polite enough not to say anything, but his ticking empathic senses knew otherwise.

Boarded and safety straps sealed snuggly against his torso, Ahn'kat flicked the flat oval machine to life. A black doughy substance formed into two semi-circle handles from the control panel over his lap. The organic vehicle was ready for flight.

"You can pilot an air-vehicle at your age?" Ismotaph said beside him.

"Imagine a member of House Urbaz not knowing how to fly. I would be laughed out of our shipyards." Ahn'kat said as the machine slowly rose over the balcony. Ahn'kat lifted the glassy shield over the ceiling. He wanted to feel the wind blowing against his face and hair. During his lessons, he remembered seeing adults' body-bend arms into bat wings or entirely transform into convincing aerial animals during festivals and contests flying independently through the skies, using their instinctive power. Ahn'kat remembers as a child begging his parents to compete and they promised him one day, but that day never came. And every day he grew older, the chance drifted further and further away.

"I see it brings you some joy." Ismotaph said as his eyes drew along the horizon.

"Yes, this is the closest I will be to a star commander." Ahn'kat said. He pressed his lips together. Did he say too much? Reveal too much? He had to quickly divert the topic from himself.

"Can you morph into a bird, Ismotaph?"

"Certainly, but it's a struggle to bend into anything too big or too little than an average Zanashj." he said.

"So, you can bend into a sky-serpent?" Ahn'kat watched the emerald gardens zip past as they flew beyond his estate. Several smaller properties with squared houses and tree lines dotted between each zoomed beneath him. They were exiting the suburbs and entering the wide country.

"A sky-serpent was the first form I successfully mimicked. Marvellous beasts, I have several dozens of them nesting on my land." he said resting elbow on the vehicle's edge.

"Aren't you worried that they might turn on you? They make for poor pets." Ahn'kat said.

"Oh, they are not my pets. I earnt their trust and they have earnt mine. My family used to breed them for meat, and the livestock were horrible to any that came near. When I took the farm, I realised that they knew what we were doing to them. So, I stopped breeding them for food and gave them a space to live and be." he said.

"How charitable of you." Ahn'kat smiled. The green fields were turning yellow. He could see the navy mountains.

"Kind of you to say, but I get their loyalty in return. I strive to make all my friends happy, so I can be, too." he said.

Ahn'kat's smile waned. He did not get the sense Ismotaph was toying or mocking him, he felt he was being as honest and transparent as possible trying to remind Ahn'kat of their relationship and where everyone stands. Or maybe that is what Ismotaph wanted him to believe. Was the sky-serpent farm even real?

"I would like to visit your family farm one day, maybe raise a hatchling of my own." he said.

Ismotaph smiled. "One day, young lord."

Ahn'kat sunk into his seat and continued his flat gaze to the arid wilderness around him. The beaming sun was starting to itch his scalp before activating the solar resistant shields over them and commanded the vehicle to begin camouflaging with the sands below. They descended over the dunes, sliding across the mounds as his air-vehicle's sensor ticked for the base's entrance. They slowed and came to a stop. The sensor went wild as light rays encircled them and partially phased them through the sands. The sun disintegrated into shadow as they descended into the bay.

A deep subterranean base spanned for hundreds of miles below the desert. Sentimental and ancient ships were kept here by House Urbaz, some of them flown and made by Ahn'kat's distant ancestors. However, there were some strange Zanashj crafts with odd extensions and additions to the hulls, they had an assortment of workers and overseers keeping an eye on them, almost as if they were afraid of them.

Once their vehicle stopped and materialised, several guards cautiously approached them. "This vehicle is from House Urbaz, submit for clearance."

Ahn'kat slowly existed first, careful not to make any sudden moves in front of the jittery guards. One of the guards pressed a round disk against his forehead, a sharp shock coursed through him. The guard nodded and did so for the rest.

"Your mental signatures are a match. Welcome, Lord Ahn'kat and Head Ismotaph." said the guard who shocked him.

"My lords!" An elated voice called from the spiral stairs. Excited feet hopped down each step and her face stretched into a wide grin as she rushed over. "We were told to expect your arrival, it's an honour to have you."

"Taskmaster Meksonett," Ahn'kat said extending his hand. She appeared the same age as Lady Henuttamon, but her uncontained glee reminded him of a child. He met her once many years ago when his parents took him to their prized ship vaults. She was respectful, but demeanour was dry. Now, her pores were oozing with joy.

Her sudden and firm grip surprised him as she shook his hand. "We have much to discuss, please come."

She hurried down the platforms. "Clear this up!" she hissed and pointed to some heavy and thick organic cables laying along the walkway. Two pets in plain grey jumpsuits quickly scrambled and shoved the tubes out of the way as their heads bowed low. Ahn'kat's painted brow furrowed when he saw them. His father said that House Urbaz had no Zanashj pets, only off-worlders. Did he lie to comfort Ahn'kat in this gloomy knowledge?

Meksonett glanced behind. "My apologies, we didn't have the time to clean up when the infiltrators returned." she grinned before continuing.

"Do you have a detailed report prepared at least?" Ismotaph said.

She nodded. "Certainly, but it would be best to see for yourself first."

They came to a round door, no bigger and wider than his air-vehicle. Two guards nodded at their arrival and synchronised their hands to press against the circle panel on the wall. Pulsating gears on the surface spun and clicked the bony bars from the latch before griding up the seal. Meksonett skipped inside as Ahn'kat cautiously entered the chamber. Thin transparent curtains hung along the walls and ceiling, he could see figures moving back and forth around a large black cube in the centre. The taskmaster lifted the curtain high enough for all to enter the sectioned chamber.

"No cost was spared to create this make-shift theatre. These sanitisation tarps have totally neutralized the air from harmful gases, amoeba, and ions." she said.

"How do you know the Arinu can survive our atmosphere?" Ahn'kat said as he peered through the glass eyeholes of the cube.

"Our people took scans of their air and we tried to reproduce something similar in that cube, but we don't know fully yet." she said crossing her arms.

Zertun and the infiltrators moved in around the other holes. Ismotaph's face was inches from his, peering in another hole. "Incredible." he whispered.

Ahn'kat could see a hazy figure curled in the centre of the box, he could not see their features, but they were a pallid grey. His hand impulsively moved to the surface of the box, curling his finger to tap his knuckle on the tiny window, but Meksonett cried out. "No, please don't disturb them! We don't know if engaging tactile contact will telepathically connect them to you and rouse them."

Ahn'kat and Ismotaph recoiled away.

"How will you contain them when you wake them up?" Ahn'kat looked to the taskmaster.

"We don't ever plan to. If they wake up…no one here will be able to stop them." she said.

Ismotaph's gaze never broke from the cube, a shadow of a smile curled up his lip. "How wonderful. With this, Zanashj will make massive strides forward. Witness our evolution, my friends."

Ahn'kat gripped his sapphire beetle pendant for a small prayer. His eyes dropped back to the box and thought about how peaceful their slumber was, but a nagging part of him felt their soul was screaming to get out.

~

"I couldn't see much, but there was definitely an Arinu in there." Ahn'kat said as he picked at the bite-size roll of crumbed beans and sterile fish eggs. He could see the sun dropped to the horizon, setting in the rich purple and magenta skies from the open-air dining hearth. It was a comfortable warm evening, but the events of today hijacked his thoughts from any sense of leisure. Ahn'kat recalled he scrambled to get into the bath the moment he returned home. He was sticky with sweat and his skin shed in clumps as he tore off his travel clothes. Ismotaph was right, the Zanashj will go far, but knowing what was going to happen to that creature inside the cage…

"Amazing." Lady Henuttamon sighed as she gently swirled her glass goblet of violet banana liquor. "Was it a male or female? I could never tell; they are all bald and too smooth."

"Meksonett said it was male. Apparently, he's in excellent physical condition – some kind of warrior. The infiltrators that took him were hoping to also catch a female, but that didn't happen." he said taking a sip from a heavily watered-down banana liquor at his mother's insistence. Under the open skies, the dining hearth was long; gorgeous floating chandeliers floated overhead, shimmering, and colouring every surface with a gentle golden hue. The air was filled with heavy smells of spices and cooked meats on the gold gilded glass table. Zertun never left his side, and several other guards and attendants lined along the walls.

"Why didn't they capture a female?" Lord Reshj leaned over his corner of the table towards Ahn'kat.

Ahn'kat gulped down the last of his goblet before setting the bottom on the glass table. "Because she killed an infiltrator with a psionic blast, she liquified him. I hear that psychic attack was on the very 'low' end of their power…they can do a lot worse."

Lord and Lady Urbaz nervously glanced to each other.

"Don't worry. They'll never discover they were Zanashj. All infiltrators are injected with body-liquefiers if they die. It rips up their molecules. To add, these infiltrators had psi-dampening shields that can partially masks their thoughts for a few moments." he said taking another mouthful of the sliced roll.

"Interesting. What did Ismotaph say?" Reshj said.

Ahn'kat looked at his polished plate. "He seemed overjoyed, excessively so."

"I do not blame him. I am eager to read the infiltrator's report, this is a great victory for the Empire." his father said.

"Could not have been done without House Urbaz." his mother smiled lifting her hand to her husband. He took it and gave her fingers a gentle squeeze.

"Yes, we now have a future. I believe this calls for a discrete celebration." Reshj said as his face lightened.

"The work's not over. I need to send our traditional condolences and thanks to the deceased infiltrator's family." Ahn'kat said rising to his feet.

"Very well but return the moment you're done." Henuttamon said.

Ahn'kat gave a quick smile and bow before dashing up to his apartment with Zertun following behind. Nearing down the quiet corridor, Zertun cleared his throat. "Young lord, may I say something?"

Ahn'kat stopped and turned. "Certainly."

"I...I have been serving House Urbaz for six decades and as a Golden Sentinel for another five centuries. And in that time, I survived enemy hordes and getting sucked out an airlock into space. I've been afraid countless times, but in those seconds, I knew my death would be honourable in service for the Empire. Yet, what I saw in that room was void of honour, and for a warrior to die in such a way...that's no way for our spirits to go."

Ahn'kat sighed. "Come in."

He slid the door open and offered the closest seat by the desk. Zertun's face was sullen and grey as he settled into the narrow chair. "I apologise for adding my feelings on your burdened shoulders, young lord, it's very unbecoming."

"There's nothing to apologise for. This is a burden for us all." he said as he sat across his bodyguard.

"I never thought I would feel this way for an alien. I've fought and killed hundreds, without a second thought or guilt for our people, but seeing that creature in such a state..." Zertun shook his head as he leaned back in the chair.

Ahn'kat's fingers interlocked over the desk. He searched for the right thing to say; instead settled for the correct thing to say. "The Empire is fighting for its life right now. As a warrior, you know battles are won with blood."

Zertun's teeth scrapped against each other as he glanced at him. "The Raivan are barbaric, but at least they scream for honour. They throw themselves into battle, as if they're excited for death. What do the Zanashj do? We send in infiltrators, wearing the enemy's face and conquer from the top. Where's the glory and honour?"

"That's how we achieved everything we have." Ahn'kat said.

"And we're losing everything we have because of our ways." Zertun looked away and gripped the arms of the chair. "I apologise once again; I'm delaying you from your duties."

"Zertun, wait," Ahn'kat extended his arm to him. He tried to argue away the guilty voices in his bodyguard's head, but how could he when he had his own. The worst part: his feelings were right. "I need help writing to the deceased's family."

The warrior nodded and settled back. Ahn'kat smiled as he flicked on his machine, searching for his name. "Infiltrator Alkaheen. Apparently, the entire Alkaheen family served at some point in the Corps."

"The last name sounds familiar," Zertun muttered.

Ahn'kat scanned through the names. Amehtut Alkaheen appeared the most decorated and achieved 'seraphim' status. A deep cover and long-term infiltrator with only a single mission failure in his history. His success streak tarnished when trying to pose as an Arinu diplomat.

Ahn'kat chuckled. "You probably heard about that infiltrator who mimicked an Arinu emissary when they came here, and when they found out, they teleported him high up in the royal court chamber. The poor man broke his arms when he fell. If that happened in House Urbaz, we would've declared war."

"No, there was talk about one of his daughters." Zertun said leaning over to face the holo-screen.

Ahn'kat narrowed his eyes. "Well, there's Neobatri Alkaheen, she's an initiate – infiltrator in-training. Following in the footsteps of her father. Nothing extra-ordinary about her on here."

"There's another. Neheret Alkaheen, the body-bending prodigy." he said.

Ahn'kat frowned as his fingers flew across the screen. The results surprised him. "She's missing?"

"That's right! My old sentinel comrades told me they've been searching with the Intel Corps for days, but she hasn't reappeared anywhere. No signs, no witnesses, nothing." Zertun said.

He did not know what to make of it. A wave of sorrow struck him thinking about the family losing two people days apart. "Truly unfortunate. I can add condolences for the daughter, extend extra assistance to recov-"

Ahn'kat's heart raced when he looked at the date and time when she vanished. His mouth peeled open as he gripped his sapphire beetle pendant. "Neheret disappeared the same time those Unbound Roctarous visited." he said.

"You don't think they were involved?" Zertun glanced at him.

"The shields were down for long enough and they did need Zanashj body-benders!" Ahn'kat pulled himself from the chair and sped to the fresh tray of refreshments for some cool banana liquor. He gulped down the goblet, not bothering with adding water, before wiping his stinging lips and tongue. He did not want to believe it, not just because it was an assumption, but the possibility of the end. "What have we done?"

Break I

What has Sazla done this time? Her immortal people said as they surrounded her. Plucking at her body, loosening the fabric of space as they tried twisting her out. She could hear her people's calls through the planes, but their thoughts were still too far to understand. The planes trembled, they coursed through her, and she screamed. The agony. Her phased form felt like a billion needles pressing through her. She realised they were trying to cut her out. She begged them not to, but they could not hear. It would tear a hole so deep and so wide that the universe could not heal; then the planes would be exposed to each other, flooding each other with energies that would destroy all of Creation.

Sazla had forgotten time. She could not connect to any reality to understand where or when she was. It was a blur. Was this a test from Akashi? She could not know; it did not speak to her. Was she doomed to spend eternity outside and alone while the universe changed and prospered without her? Was this her punishment for a crime she had yet to commit? Maybe has. Everything she saw, the worlds and their peoples grew or withered away, while she remained in her prison. She became only a watcher. Was this what it felt like to be the great Akashi?

The Neavensoros were not ready to give up on her. They cut and sewed once they saw the exo-planar leaks. There must be some other way. They weren't going to give up on her, and she wasn't going to give up on them. But the thoughts had entered her mind...

They had evolved too high and their eyes grew too large to see what mattered. Their immortality became their price. She saw this, but the Neavensoros who worked to free her could not, and she doubted that they will ever know this horrible truth.

Chapter Ten
Treneer IV: Oaths

The red sun covered Yinray. Its orange glow warmed the land and the light fractured through the crystal spires; green, teal, and blue sparkles shone on the roads. Farayah was inching closer to the sun and summer was finally upon them. The ice melted from the pastel pink leaves from the icy trees, leaving patches of clear blue water on the pale pavement. The golden grass blades poked through the snow, opening emerald flowers for the snow-hornets. When a breeze rolled in, it carried the flowers divine smell through the city.

Treneer watched the hornet's antennae curl over the petals as their little legs stuffed the pollen into their carapace. She sat with her legs crossed, levitating just over the soggy grass under the umbrella tree. Her psionics were still sluggish since the deep-scan. Holding her body in the air and projecting decorative holo-runes over her shoulders and head, was beginning to fatigue her. At least, she could still tele-speak and perform basic psychometry and psychometric imprinting.

She sighed as she squeezed Zu'leen's data crystal in her palm. Her mind read every millimetre of information stored within the latices. She had read all Zu'leen's available notes, probably for hundreds of times. Treneer practiced her tutor's methods of achieving transcendence. Every step was perfected, down to the second of the recommended meditation time. All for naught without having her old power. Her recovery for the past several months was slow, but the Judicator's kindness allowed her stay in the academy. She will become a neonate again; she must.

Treneer could feel her astral form kicking and tumbling in her body, as she didn't travel often and the few times she could slip away, it was only in short bursts. Fortunately, spending so much time in her physical form made it stronger and harder. She pinched her firm muscle strips on her arms before her palm travelled to her thumping heart. Treneer smiled, she could feel her cheeks warming. She cupped the data crystal in both palms and drunk deep from its knowledge.

'The body's abilities are limited in comparison to the mind. Psionics allows us to perform tasks beyond the strongest and fittest athletes, but Arinu often forget that the body is our mind's anchor. The universe demands balance in all things, if one is ill, the other will fall, too. The mind can cure the body, but the body can also cure the mind.' Zu'leen wrote.

Treneer tapped into her third eye and felt leaks of astral energy pour through her. She envisioned opening her body's energy lines, the internal energetic circulatory system that holds and pumps astral power in the body. Her spine felt a heat ripple through and wash into her limbs, energy throbbed in her hands and feet, even her ears felt like they were going to burst into flames. Treneer's muscles trembled, she jumped up, ready to go for a sprint or climb the high crystal spires in the city. She sucked in the cool air as her head spun. No, reclaiming her full psionics was her priority.

Her arms extended out, mentally locking on the carved stone décor and stools in the tranquil garden, and demanded they rise. The grass blades quivered, the leaves shook, and the unfortunate insects caught in the telekinetic field lost control of their flight.

"Move…" she grunted as she watched the stone before her. She dropped the field and focused her energy onto the boulder. She breathed deeper as beads of sweat formed on her temples. Her fingers shot tiny sparks, but the stone barely twisted in the earth. "Move, damn you…"

Pain pierced through her head. Her psionic field dissipated as she grabbed at her head and stifled a scream. She dropped back to her seat and her back collapsed against the tree trunk.

Treneer, stop pushing yourself so hard. Ouro's voice called to her.

I can't. I need to improve my psionic practices.

Ouro's figure appeared to the high balcony overlooking the small garden campus. He levitated down and dropped to pavement; his face twisted with frustration. *I don't appreciate you doing this to yourself and having to constantly monitor you.*

Well, I didn't appreciate getting the deep-scan. She said as she rose to her feet.

Ouro stepped over and glanced to the data crystal tablet on the grass. *It's necessary to exercise your psionics back to strength, but this is excessive.*

Zu'leen said that we can cure our minds using our bodies. My body is strongest than it's ever been, but my mind is still...unfocused. She said. A strange fondness grew for her psi-therapist. She would be crestfallen when their sessions would end so he could care for his other patients. He knew every aspect of her life, yet she knew little of his.

I understand you want to help find Lonur, but the guardians have centuries of experience investigating unusual issues, you must have a little faith. He said patting her shoulder.

There are bigger things going on, Ouro. I can feel it. She lifted the tablet and caressed the edges. There was nothing in the records that showed her tutor falling into madness, yet. *Zu'leen didn't just decide to end her life without a reason.*

Have you tried asking deathspeakers? Ouro said.

She shook her head as she opened her palm showing him the crystal. *They said her soul was beyond their reach. This is all that's left.*

Didn't her family confiscate some of her files along with other property? Maybe they can give you the rest.

Her family! Treneer did not know them. Zu'leen rarely spoke of any members and often commented that the academy was her coven. *Can you astrally guide me to them?*

Ouro smiled and nodded. They levitated over the grass and eased their consciousness into their astral forms. Treneer's soul rose from her crown, and Ouro's translucent arms extended to the skies. *Lead the way.*

She focused on Zu'leen, her townhouse and felt the foreign minute energies that lingered in the rooms. Memorising their signatures, she honed on those energies across Farayah. There they were. A bundle of their auras emanated to the far outer circle of Yinray. She would have been a phenomenal Sleeping Watcher, she thought. Ouro strayed behind as her astral drifted through the skies before landing to a humble egg-shaped dome. Tall, stained windows and transparent ceilings glittered in the red sunlight. Treneer floated to the entrance. She could feel several people lingering inside.

They felt her and Ouro's presence. A pale head popped from the side of the house; her fiery eyes and third eye scanned them. *No trespassing!*

We're here to ask some questions. Treneer said.

The tall young woman levitated over. Treneer could sense her name, Neela, Zu'leen's great-grand niece. *We have already spoken with investigators, there's nothing more to know.*

My name is Treneer, I was Zu'leen's pupil. I need to understand-

What's there to understand, Treneer? Zu'leen took her life because she became too obsessed with her work. Everything and everyone were second to that. Neela crossed her arms.

She seemed at peace there. I thought maybe she may have shown you another side of her that we didn't know. Treneer said.

Neela shook her head. *Zu'leen hadn't spoken to any of us in decades. You knew her better than we do. You tell me why she did it.*

I don't know, that's why I'm here to put it to rest. When my teacher...departed this life, I inherited some of her notes about her other projects. Her personal journals are missing months leading up to it and was told that her family may have them.

Neela glanced to Ouro's astral form. *Who's he?*

My psi-therapist.

Neela's lips curled as her nostrils flared. *If you're sorting through personal issues, then you don't need to see them.*

Treneer could feel her heart race back in her physical body. *That's not for you to decide what I can and can't handle.*

And I don't need to give her journals to anyone outside of the family. Neela said as she turned to stomp back in the house.

Neela, please! Knowing is part of my recovery.

She turned back and sighed. *It won't help you, trust me.*

Have you read them?

I've seen enough.

Treneer drifted closer. *It's more than just healing, Zu'leen may hold the key to solving certain mysteries we are investigating.*

We haven't been requested to turn them over and you don't have the authority to take them. She turned once more and phased through the granite doorway.

Treneer lurched forward, sensing for Zu'leen's data crystals inside, but she could feel Ouro digging his astral fingers through her. *Stop, we can't do anymore here.*

There are other ways! I could ask the Judicator to make her turn them over.

Only if they see a reason for it, but Zu'leen's case is shut.

But I saw her, Ouro. She saved my life, there must be a connection.

It's clear she had a bond with you and her soul sensed you were in danger, but that doesn't mean there's anything deeper than that. His astral eyes drifted to the distant north. She could feel his gaze was towards the Crystal Castle.

Don't you even think about it. She said.

He glanced to her. *Have you gone to see her yet?*

Treneer hardened. The idea of looking upon the dead face of her other parent. The idea that those radiant eyes are closed, cold and never to open again. *I've spoken to the deathspeakers, that's all.*

Your connection with Zu'leen rested deeper than a deathspeaker, maybe you could gleam something from her body.

Treneer's astral sight sped towards the twisted crystal spires of the frozen north. A million and million souls and beings danced through the caverns and halls, living and dead merged into one. The Crystal Castle is a place for the long sleep of the Arinu. *I fear the only thing I'll find is pain, Ouro.*

We'll do it together.

She smiled as her translucent hands clasped over his shimmering palm, and in a blink, they were there. The hardened snow flats spanned for thousands of miles in all directions. A grand crystalline structure jutted from a white mound, the most northern point of Farayah. Shapeless lights circled through the transparent walls. Treneer could feel the ice winds howling through her astral form – to her fortune, the cold didn't bite. The two slipped through the gaping maw entrance where an otherworldly white light embraced them. Ouro shivered. She also caught a strange vibration gnawing at her, she could almost feel her blood freezing.

This place is in flux with many planes, that's why our astral forms have greater tangibility here. Ouro said.

She glanced around the barren halls, hoping to see the living aura of a deathspeaker, but there was nothing but the dead. *You'd think that the deceased would rather linger at the birthing pools to reincarnate if they miss life so much.*

I think these souls stay is because the living have a harder time letting them go. He said.

She turned to reply, but a faint pulse echoed in her periphery. She homed in; her senses embraced the trail as they took the pair through the winding glassy chasm. Her eyes travelled along the slippery and shiny pastel walls; it took a moment for her to find the frozen faces behind the surfaces. Hundreds of deceased rested inside the structure, from the ceiling to the floors, all in pristine form.

The pulse flared again to the far edge of the hall. A recently hardened surface covered a fresher body. Her heart sank as she caught the still, yet tranquil, face of Zu'leen. Treneer could feel hot tears streaming down her cheeks back in her body.

There you are. She whispered so deep to herself not even Ouro could gleam. Her astral hands slipped through the crystal and tried to caress her teacher's brow, but her fingertips went through her skin.

Treneer? Ouro said.

There was no sign of injury, she was whole. *I think…I feel how she died. Stopped her own heart with her mind…the fool!*

Can you hear her soul? At all?

No! Treneer pulled her hands back; her senses were darting around the chamber hoping to see her spirit floating behind them. Her work was not done, why won't her soul reincarnate? She soaked the last remnants of Zu'leen's essence and commanded to see a vision of her, a shadowed profile or a small smile – anything. Please, she begged the universe, how is she?

It was so fast that she almost lost it in her mind. She peeled back her memory to find an image of a woman with emerald skin sitting at a table with a young viridian man. She saw the woman's thick forearms first before her face sharpened into view. The woman had hair…why was she seeing random Zanashj? Fear plucked at her heart when she accidentally peeked into the Zanashj home world, but why there of all places and planes?

When the image cleared, the room was bright and littered with rich colours. The longer she stared, she realised the woman turned to her – staring back and her face was curtained by blue light. Treneer snapped out of the memory and hurried it down the depths of her mind. She so desperately wanted to see her old teacher; her grief-stricken senses must have plucked a random scene out in the universe, she reasoned to herself. *Why did she leave me, Ouro?*

You're not on your own, Treneer. You will find an answer in time, I promise. Ouro said as he reached out and gripped her shoulder.

Treneer flew back to her body. Ouro sat still a few feet away; his eyes slowly opened to meet hers. "I'm sorry, Treneer."

"It's not over yet." her mind reached out to Sesuune, but the Guardian's thoughts were blocked and refused to answer her call. Treneer's mental probe bumped against her psi-shield and kept poking until she felt a reply.

Why do you disturb my work? Sesuune said.

I wish to join your investigation, I think I can help, but I need yours. Treneer said.

We are all grieving, but my patience-

Please listen, I'm trying to get the rest of her records to continue my studies on transcendence; once I've tuned my abilities, then I can find Lonur and who the dead stranger is.

There was a pause. She watched Ouro's fingers nervously tap on his knee. "You still haven't fully recovered." he mouthed.

"Eventually, I will!" she whispered.

Meet us in the Mind Room. Sesuune said.

Treneer hopped to her feet and dashed into the building with Ouro gliding beside her. The academy was humming. Many eyes caught her swiftness, some were surprised, the rest amused. The round granite door leading to the subterranean chamber was glowing with runes. She rose her hand to the surface, but Ouro pressed his telekinetic grip over her palm.

What are you doing? She glanced to her therapist.

I've had many patients, Treneer. Too many. Some driven mad with grief for losses that happened millennia ago. I want to believe you aren't going to fall in that dark pit.

Treneer glanced back to the heavy door and frowned. *I need to know what happened. No matter what it is, then my grief will die.*

Ouro sighed as he shook his head before letting go. *If you say so.*

The door phased and they strode into the shadowy chamber. Relzun and Sesuune stood beside the Judicator's holographic face.

Thank you for meeting me, what do you think of my proposal? Treneer said.

The Judicator turned to her. *There are many things to consider before deciding on your offer. Firstly, you must reapply as a neonate and be given all the necessary training. We could put you in advanced classes, your stamina meet the requirements, but your psionic levels are still too low.*

With Ouro's healing and my ongoing practices, that's only months away. I don't need to start from the beginning again.

All guardians must pass the Body Trial, no matter what specialisation they choose. Now, with your weakened mind, can you even pass the Mind Trial? Relzun said.

I've already passed before! My high results speak for themselves, Judicator.

Secondly, your emotional state. Guardians cannot be emotionally compromised while on duty, especially on a case this close to them. He said.

Treneer's nostrils flared. *We've all been affected, and if I wasn't, I wouldn't have studied Zu'leen's work on transcendence. With what I'm learning, we could solve any mysteries!*

The academy was notified that you contacted Zu'leen's family to enquire about her journals. Your current state provides too many risks. The Judicator said.

Her heart thumped as she sucked in the calm air. *For aiding the investigation.*

The Judicator looked to Ouro. *Psi-therapist, do you attest that Treneer will be at full function as she claims?*

She has recovered faster than anticipated. I do believe in a few months she will be fit to perform the trials. Ouro nodded.

She snuck a quick smile at him. *I understand your concerns, but it would be detrimental if you turn me away.*

The situation is far more delicate than what you know. Lonur is not the only one who is missing. Sesuune said.

Treneer felt her heart drop.

In the last month, another three Arinu vanished. Making a total of four over the last several months, not including the dead stranger. She said.

She sensed Ouro's mind spinning before forcing up a mental shield. *Did they disappear in the same area as Lonur?*

Relzun shook his head. *No, from all around Farayah. Disappearances do occur, Arinu stepping off into inter-planar rifts to places we cannot touch, but those are exceedingly rare. The last case was some decades ago.*

If I continue my training as a Sleeping Watcher, then my involvement can help. You need everyone, in whatever condition, to help you.

All eyes turned to the Judicator's translucent and still face. *You are not becoming a Sleeping Watcher; your power for that has waned, and time is fleeting. But I will admit you as an archite.*

An archite, not quite a guardian, but one who stood behind them. Guardians are the Arinu's support, but even guardians need support. Treneer's smile rose so high that her cheeks almost strained. *Thank you, Judicator!*

On the condition that you are not to bother Zu'leen's relatives for non-related investigations. They said.

Her smile simmered. *You have my oath.*

Understood. Time is not a luxury for us anymore. You won't need to redo the Mind Trial, but you will need to repeat the Body Trial soon. Report for classes once your schedule is in. The Judicator said before vanishing.

Relzun sighed as he pressed his finger in his temple before brushing past Treneer. Sesuune's lips curled into a smile as she tapped her shoulder before following her comrade. Treneer spun to Ouro. She wanted to jump and dance; her glee was strong enough to electrify the building, but her psi-therapist's face was sullen and dark.

What's wrong? She slid closer.

Ouro's gaze moved to her, but his inner mind was closed. *I have some personal matters that need attending, excuse me.*

Don't we all. Treneer tried to give a reassuring smile, but Ouro glided out of the room without another word.

~

'All souls are to be treated and respected as equals. All possess a sense of justice. All have a vision for a better world. All deserve a voice. All deserve to be protected. All see the world through a single pair of eyes. As a guardian, you walk between the lines, seeing all sides to find the truth. A path only to be walked by the hardened and the wise. To open your eyes, you must shed bias, even to those who wish to close them. Neither higher or lower of society, cell or forest, pebble or star will push you from this path. You are a mediator. You are the stone slab that shoulders the city. You resist the waves of discourse to maintain balance. You are a guardian.'

The Guardian Oath.

The Body Trial was nothing compared to becoming a practising guardian. Treneer remembers spending the whole month strengthening her muscles, eating nothing but high-protein foods, and sprinting around the academy, even jumping from platform to platform. One red morning, she managed to climb halfway down the spire before her legs and arms started shaking with exhaustion. A few hours in the healing pod were enough for her next attempt, and she succeeded, but not without some gashes and ugly bruises. When the option was presented for her to climb down the building or to fight, Treneer was eager to dive from the spire top.

That night she celebrated by astral travelling over Farayah and bathed around their star's orbit. She quietly visited her family home. The icy meadow had melted, but her parents were nowhere. She wanted to tell them of her passing and becoming an archite, but the dark energy still lingered around her tribe made her pull away. Her power still hadn't fully returned yet. However, she could sniff out an agitator half a world away.

She skipped from portal to portal to find this man. She knew his face and aura. With her comrades at her back, she chased him through the city. The man sparked a fire in the central gardens, disrupting the Bloodmoon Festival and burning some of the unfortunates caught in the pyrokinetic attack. He phased out before her squad arrived, but they could still taste his energy in the air. The celebrants didn't know their attacker, he came and left just as mysteriously, but they all said he was glowing with unusual psionic power. There was only one thing that could create this sudden and overpowered violence: astral dancing.

It is a forbidden practice of summoning higher astral energies and bringing forth dangerous, and unstable, extra-dimensional entities. It was the only law Arinu had. No one could withstand the dance. Treneer saw the places consumed by reckless astral dancers, where buildings and plants decayed quickly, the air was stale and sickly, even the practitioners appeared frightfully gaunt and ill. However, those energies through their dealings brought them temporary psychic godhood, at the cost of their sanity. It was addictive and becoming too common.

He's close. Treneer said to her squad of three guardians. They came to a derelict pier on the side of the gigantic crystal lake.

He's lost. Sesuune said.

As they approached, Treneer spotted a faint teal glow from the crystal clusters under the dark water. Mad whispers echoed through her mind, she couldn't understand them, nor could she focus on them. The suspect had hidden his aura completely. She flicked her third eye to astral energy detection. To her shock, the area was flooded with it, but silvery and navy trails lead to a violet pocket in the water.

In the water. She said, scrying her senses to her comrades. Sesuune nodded and begun levitating with the others before drifting over the crumbling stone pier. Treneer cast a masking illusion field around herself and them, while they locked on to the suspect. She watched from marble water's edge as their combined telekinetic grip encased him, but they were too late. A blinding white beam exploded from the surface and a huge torrent of water slapped them from the air and dragged them down. A hazy, partially-phased figure hobbled from the shore. His wild red eyes caught her stare. His fiery palms rose to her direction, and without thought, Treneer bore her mind into his and made him freeze.

He tried fighting for control, but her grip on his nervous system squeezed harder. His energetic strength was great, but his mind was weak from the dancing. The suspect's mouth opened as a hoarse screech bellowed from his throat. His fingers sparked in her direction, but Treneer tightened her grip until she seared his control over his body. The reddish tinge of his eyes waned as they rolled back in his skull before dropping to the moist stone floor.

Her squad rushed over. Their telekinesis suspended the suspect in a glassy shield his body was floating in the bubble. Sesuune pulled the water from her uniform and dropped it to lake as she levitated to Treneer. *Is he dead?*

No, I cut his spinal cord. He'll need to be in a healing pod for a few months. She said.

Sesuune nodded. *Good. We'll keep his astral form in containment too just in case he tries to run.*

Treneer felt the phasing tug in the group. They teleported back to the healing bay of the Guardian Headquarters. The healers quickly pulled the suspect inside the oval pod and immediately scanned for his injuries. The brutality to stop him made her pause as she watched his frail, emaciated body float in the pod's water. However, his ruthless and unthinkable violence to the innocent made her sick. How many attacks like this will happen?

Thank you. That could have been a lot worse. After this incident, it will come as no surprise if the Judicator and Proctor reinvokes laws again. Sesuune said.

Laws…they're for the unenlightened and unpredictable. They are not for Arinu. Relzun said.

Sesuun cocked her head to him. *Then what are we, now?*

We're guardians, we work with people on all manner of issues. A psi-therapist and healer would be enough to quell these urges, I am sure. As we have done for millennia. Treneer said.

Sesuune shook her head. *That was once the case, but this fellow may need more than healing to repair him.*

Sesuune is an advocate for punishment, especially in Void Prisms. Relzun said as he pressed his thumb against his third eye.

Sesuune shot a scowl at him. *Hardly. I observed the prism through the astral. Those minutes I stood watching ruined several of my days.*

His empathy will be his punishment. Treneer said. She stared at the suspect; his body jerked and sparked in the water as several guardians tugged on his silver cord, binding his astral form down to them.

Tell that to the Grand Coven and Judicator. Rezlun said as Sesuune's brows furrowed at him, but he laughed.

Examples need to be set. Sesuune said as her back straightened.

Doesn't get any easier. Treneer sighed; her head begun throbbing and the muscles in her neck tensed.

How's your recovery?

You and Relzun messed my head up nicely. She said cupping her neck as her fingers pressed into the sore flesh.

Sesuune shifted. *I am so sorry for having to do that.*

Treneer waved her hand. *Don't be. I couldn't do any of that a few days ago.*

Her stomach growled; she was already getting sick of using her body. She wanted to float away, open her mind to the universe again and bend the stars, but she was already exhausted. If she stretched it farther, would Ouro scold her?

She would never hear the end of it. She missed him but he had not visited to celebrate or even uttered a congratulatory word when she told him she graduated as an archite. He had other clients, after all, it was professionalism, not personalism. *I have some studying to do.* She said.

Not now. Several Executors and Grand Elders are arriving to meet with all archites to dowse for some interstellar information. Sesuune said.

I wouldn't be of use now. Treneer said pressing her gut.

Well, they specifically asked for you to be there.

Treneer frowned. *Do you know why?*

Sesuune shook her head. *I'll take care of this fellow; the Judicator will take you up to the antechamber-*

Treneer's stomach growled louder, making her cheeks flush as other eyes snuck glances in her direction.

-after you've had something to eat. Sesuune said as she tapped her shoulder.

She zipped to the eatery. There were a few young neonates eating and grinning at each other from whatever they said in their private psi-commune. An archite in pale blue and grey cloth uniform draped to his feet with shining teal holograms over their head and shoulders bent over the table to read the replicator's menu. His deep-grey skin perfectly contrasted with his bright pastel clothes, and brilliant amber eyes carefully focused on the screen. He was little taller than her, but his muscles were significantly pronounced.

She levitated over as he shook his head and muttered at the computer. *Do you need help?*

He looked up and his eyes softened. *I don't know what half of these foods are.*

That's because you're in the off-worlder menu section. She glanced to the screen.

He pursed his lips. *Yinray is quite surprising.*

You're not from here?

He smiled. *I did train here but was stationed at the Crystal Castle for some decades before my Executor thought I would be better put in the Crystal Ruins to the south to deal with all those extra-dimensionals* - he stopped and sighed. *Apologies, I haven't been around people for a while. My name's Svar.*

I'm Treneer. She nodded. *Don't worry, some people here will make you miss solitude sooner than later.*

Svar nervously chuckled. *Where do you hail from?*

Far in the north ice valleys.

That's wonderful! Well, not for the terrible death and missing people there, but I hear the local tribes there do Snow Skirmishes with each other. Have you ever seen them practice? He grinned.

Treneer held her breath, trying to match his enthusiasm. *It was quite exciting before all that happened.*

I want to know every detail, but first, what do you recommend from this menu. He glanced at her gauntly frame and his eyes flashed with worry. *Oh apologies, I assumed you eat food.*

Well, I am here. She watched him give a tense smile as she leaned over and found the gooey pink dish with an assortment of colourful berries inside. She held back a tear before pressing the image. A beam of light poured from the ceiling and formed the outline of the bowl.

What's that made from? Svar frowned as she slid it over to him.

Treneer was disgusted when she read the ingredients. *It's good for you and it tastes good, that's all that matters.* As she made herself another one.

Svar telekinetically lifted a mouthful to his lips and swallowed it. *I know what this is! Aged lactation extract from Ezoni elk.*

Treneer groaned, but her stomach groaned louder as she gulped down the whole bowl. The Judicator's voice called in her head. *All archites prepare to be ported to the spiral-tip antechamber.*

Svar grinned before the vision of his face blurred and vapourised into twisting space. She was lighter and at strange ease as she was pulled to the tallest room. Treneer materialised along with another several dozen archites in the silent spherical chamber. In the centre stood three figures under the harsh white beam of light. Two had silver circlets around their crowns, and adorned with shimmering runes covering their heads, shoulders, and chests. They had executor uniforms, but the other had a crystal circlet and a breezy, layered robes with a tall hood. However, they had a long shimmering mask covering over their nose and mouth seemed to change colour. He was a grand elder; but his youthful skin had a flawless shine, and his eyes were like three brilliant stars beaming back.

Thank you for accepting summons so timely. Please be seated, archites. Said one of the executors as her arms extended to the hovering stools around them.

Svar glided over to one the chairs and pointed to an empty one beside him for Treneer. She smiled before taking her place.

I am Executor Shurees, we understand that you are preoccupied by the matters plaguing Farayah, but we believe there is a reason. Many months ago, the Archon sensed strange energies coming from Neavensoros space, our observers confirmed this, but also witnessed a probe appearing from their boarder and sent a transmission to the Zanashj Empire. Because of our Treaty, we are forbidden from enquiring and when we tried to capture the probe, it was too, lost. We ask you as a collective to break through the boarders of Neavensoros space and see what truly occurred.

Svar shifted on his stool and leant in. *Executor Shurees, with all due respect, but the Neavensoros don't take well to those infringing on their space. I worry for our safety-*

We understand and thank you for your concern, but should the Neavensoros or their ilk give resistance, then we will handle it. Shurees absorbed the unsettledness of others. *Yes, this is a risk, but knowing how sensitive we are, this sudden rise of disturbances must have a reason.*

Treneer tightened her fists as she stared at Shurees. *Executor, we have an increase of astral dancing activity, how can you be certain it has anything to do with the Neavensoros, and when was the last time they visited Farayah?*

The Archon and I met one, we know when something or one were touched by them, their energy lingers forever. The Grand Elder fixated on her, making her shrink in the stool. Treneer stiffened as she thought about Zu'leen.

Let's begin with a clearing meditation before proceeding. We will bond you before guiding you to their boarders. Shurees said as her legs crossed in the air. Shuffling of clothes and deep sighs mimicked the Executor's position. Gentle pangs of crystals vibrated through the room. Treneer straightened her back and begun emptying her mind. A sharp spike of disturbed energies flooded her for a moment. An astral power leakage poured around Farayah; it grated her, but the crystal songs stole the discomfort. Her thoughts and emotions vaporised as the wave of consciousness enveloped her. Intangible fingers tugged at the archite's blended minds and wove them into a cone to escape the antechamber and out into the stars. Treneer was no longer Treneer, she was reduced to her soul, an essence that simply observed the external and internal space.

They were travelling together beyond the star system, spinning into the cosmos before reaching the shell of Neavensoros space. An unspoken warning ripped through them; was it their combined anxiety or the creatures that called this alien space home? Hundreds of fingers clawed at the border, digging and digging until they could feel coarse and acidic emptiness behind it. The hole opened and they slipped in, they waited for someone to come for them. No one did. They pushed through, not knowing exactly where to go, but the Archon's command pointed them to the centre.

This space wasn't black as one would see with the naked eye. Colours of every variety forming into perfect and endless fractals was sensed by their higher senses, but they knew this haunted place was broken. Finally, there it was: Erra and her faux moon, Kra. The pearly luminescent ball throbbed in the sea of colour, but its satellite was dull and blackened. They waited and waited. This is the closest any Arinu has come to the Neavensoros, short of their chosen Acolytes. They wanted to come closer and explore her surface, but the mission rang through their combined minds.

The Neavensoros are not here.

Where are the Roctarous?

Dozens of eyes turned to the black moon. The longer they stayed, they heard the hum of thousands of minds, but they were muffled. As if they were speaking through gags in a dozen languages. All foreign and too far. Their High Mind was one language, clear and direct, the Arinu understood. They lingered between the two celestial bodies, waiting for more information to come. Treneer was the first to feel shattered remains aimlessly drifting. They turned their attention to Kra's surface.

A shield.

Pierce it.

We can't.

A pair of alien eyes watched behind her. She couldn't read it, but it wasn't threatening or introducing itself. The eyes just observed with curiosity before slipping away into the shattered sea. The Arinu continued their watch of Kra; they peered through the shield to see ruins.

They were attacked.

Phase shields are up.

They war with themselves?

There's no High Mind.

What happened to it?

They tried calling out, but no answer. They turned to the planetary defence systems around Erra; they were quiet and have been for months. Everything broke down here the same time the disturbances appeared on Farayah. The flashing star, Treneer remembered. Zanashj presence was felt. They were here and there, all over, but they couldn't be seen. How was this possible? Their bodies and minds. They're not psychics, but they were close to Kra, maybe nearby Erra...

More eyes were peering up at them from behind the shield; there were few and much smaller than the pair she sensed. The Archon called them back; they were done here, for now. They were glided along the trail they left and slipped through the gap of Neavensoros borders before falling into their bodies. Intangible fingers unhooked their minds and Treneer could feel herself returning.

Archites opened their eyes and sighed in relief. Svar pressed his fingers to his neck to feel the blood rushing into his head. The three figures in the centre of the chamber spoke in a private commune, before Executor Shurees turned her attention to the Guardians. *Thank you for your contribution and support, archites. We have learnt much; however, this will not be the last time we enter Neavensoros space together. All but Archite Treneer are dismissed.*

Svar nervously glanced at her before his body phased out the antechamber.

Approach the centre, Archite Treneer.

She levitated from the stool and drifted just low enough for her toes to graze on the polish floor. Shurees, the other Executor and the Grand Elder scanned her. *We know that you had experienced transcendence during your Mind Trial. Can you tell us how a neonate achieved such a feat?* Shurees said.

Before we proceed, let's see if Treneer can pluck my name from my mind. The Grand Elder said.

His piercing eyes made her rigid. Simply knowing a Grand Elder's true name would elevate her position among the archites, maybe over all guardians. Rumours say a faint imprint befalls on the knower of their name, but the locked doors of their circle will be opened to them until time's end.

Treneer sighed as she stamped out her simmering anxiety. The walls around his mind were as thick as ice mountains, she focused her telepathic probe, imagining a hot tiny beam piercing through. The mental ice cracked, but her probe could barely dig another inch. Beads of sweat formed around the collar of her high neckpiece as she pushed. *I'm sorry, I cannot-*

Surprising you didn't attempt what you had done in the Mind Trial. He said.

That was a fluke. My psionics enhanced for a moment, but I assumed it had something to do with the flashing star or what looked like such.

The Grand Elder's eyes softened over his cowl. *It was not a star, the Neavensoros were involved. Could you gleam any information on what happened there?*

No, but I felt a rush of power flooding me, it was like I was being drowned. And it was happening everywhere in all places. She shivered at the memory.

A portal, maybe they opened a rift and departed space as we know it. Said the other Executor.

Your former master's notes on transcendence has been a great boon to us, but we know that you have been disciplined in her study. Can you transcend again and teach the other archites? Shurees said.

Treneer's cheeks heated at the honour of such a request, but her heart sank as she said, *I would love to, unfortunately my psionic level is not as it once was.*

Why? The Grand Elder's eyes narrowed.

I was deep-scanned to ensure my innocence of a death that occurred several months ago, but through Elder Zu'leen's work, I was able to regain most of my psionics.

They stiffened, even Treneer's heart caught their hesitation.

That's an unfortunate ordeal, but you are confident that you will regain it? Shurees said.

Of course, its everything to me. Treneer steeled her trembles.

With the right healing and time, it will come back. Deep-scanning can be done without trauma, did you know that? Shurees said.

It's possible simpler beings, but for Arinu...I haven't heard a person ever reclaim themselves after one. Treneer said.

Would you say if there were one who specialised in such an ability, would you be less fearful of them? The Executor said as her finger outlined her temple.

Treneer's forehead scrunched as she swallowed a growing saliva on her tongue. *It's possible.*

Shurees pressed her hands together and pointed the tips of her fingers to her. *Archite Treneer, would you be willing to submit for voluntary deep-scan to uncover the secrets of transcendence and what you saw during the Mind Trial?*

Chapter Eleven
Shshmrnashsh IV:
Us and Them

The engines gurgled and gasped. The ship was alive. Nexus 0G11 sensors caught the skiff entering their territory, wandering aimlessly close to the ground. There was half a consciousness in there, a Roctarous mind halfway transferred to the ship before the High Mind broke. It had been flying on impulse, barely feeding from solar energy to continue. The sides and belly were scorched from various fires it had flown over, several dents appeared in the hull from banging into the side of derelict buildings, but the inner components were optimal and useful.

Senzvrrn summoned the ship and Shshmrnashsh linked it to the consortium network. Near the tip of the nexus, the wall opened to let the skiff slide in and connect with the building. She scanned for the half-mind inside the ship, hoping enough was there for communication. Sadly, it held no more sentience than an amoeba. Hrrnm considered disconnecting the half-mind from the ship's computer, but Shshmrnashsh reasoned it would be inefficient use of time and energy – hiding her pity for the broken mind.

Their consortium expanded by several more members; the nexus was humming and thriving again after months. More minds to juggle in the plexus, affirming her role as adjunct and less of an active member…and less of a voice.

One more unit coming in. Senzvrrn gazed at the screen. The call to other Roctarous to be relinked to Nexus 0G11 was pulling units from around the northern grid. Often, these units were lost without a network and sought to assist in repairs. By the time they arrived at the glassy gates of the nexus, their injuries were severe. If these units were too badly damaged, then the consortium would terminate them and salvage for parts. Sometimes, the visitors were seeking salvation. Shshmrnashsh remembers hearing the screams of protests from Renegades, but they stopped the moment they linked.

The E.M.P. is set to low power. Have units prepare for relinking. Shsh said.

The scraping of metal legs and feet made way to the east gates. The soldiers powered their shields and lasers ready for firing.

The screech of the E.M.P seeped through the walls before the nexus shutter doors slid open for the soldiers to pour out.

Unit is not resisting, but heavily damaged. Hrrnm said.

Shshmrnashsh felt a new mind log into the network. *This is latest generation soldier unit, my name is Jnnzz. Commands?*

Brrnzerm, assess damage. Shshmrnashsh said.

Confirmed.

The shutter doors resealed and from the corner of her periphery, the new unit was carried by the tubules to the recovery pods. Their arms were torn from the elbow down, exposing wires and synthetic tissue draping down as tiny black drops fell to the floor. She turned to see their jaw barley hanging onto their head before being safely escorted to the pod. Her eyes narrowed. Had that have been an older soldier unit or any other with the same level of damage, Hrrnm and the soldiers would have terminated them.

Jnnzz, state the source of your injuries. Shsh said.

I was attacked by Renegades once I entered the 0G11 district.

How many were there?

Three.

How did you escape?

Jnnzz didn't reply as the recovery pod placed them on standby mode.

Hrrnm walked to the plexus ring. *Do you have concerns?*

For one unit, even a soldier model, to survive three Renegades is implausible. Monitor them. She said.

Hrrnm nodded. *Agreed. Access their memories, see what happened there.*

Confirmed. She downloaded the new soldier's memory since the Blackout. Through their eyes, she saw they once belonged to a small consortium and heard the broadcast to meet at Nexus 0G11. Unfortunately, during their trek they were plucked apart by Renegades and other hazardous places. She saw steel ceilings cave in and flatten units, some falling into flimsy surfaces deep into the planet's core and the rest being ambushed. Jnnzz was the sole survivor, lost and desperate, hopping into barely operating recovery pods and picking batteries from fallen units to continue their mission. One night, the soldier looked to the stars. It was the first time Jnnzz saw them as their hands lifted to the dark, imagining they were touching the glittering specks.

The awe died when they were tackled and hulled by a few Renegades to nearby derelict buildings. Jnnzz fought and slain, but there were still too many. Their jaw was pounded in, disorientating them. They dropped for a moment, but that was enough time for the other two Renegades to crush the soldier's forearms before deactivation. Jnnzz was activated again and saw the pyramid behind the glassy gate. Shshmrnashsh pulled away from their memories and saw Hrrnm narrowing their eyes after learning their experience.

Their experience was unfortunate, but we saved them from decaying any further. Hrrnm said.

Explain why you let them in with that level of injury? We had encountered many units in similar states, and all have been repurposed. She said.

Their rubbery brows rose. *We can expend more energy on units with greater physical capabilities. They will need to mobilise for missions beyond Nexus 0G11 and continue protecting the base.*

We can store future newcomers in the recovery pods, our replicators and generators can withstand the extra amount. She said.

Hrrnm cocked their head to the side. *If there are to spare, but it's inefficient to keep older units operational.*

We are trying to restore the High Mind, Hrrnm, every unit is needed. Shsh said.

They straightened their neck. *If we can; we will. Send probes to find how many Renegades are operating in the area, they must be here because of our call and organise the skiffs to take viable equipment and units.*

Forcing a linkup one-by-one may take decades and risk more terminations. The nexuses held the High Mind, if we activate all, then there's a chance to resuscitate it. At the very least, a sub-channel will emerge in all units and that can be used to attract them to their closest nexus for relinking. Shsh said.

Hrrnm's fingers wrapped around their squared greyish jaw. *The nexuses might be at risk from Renegades being compelled there. They may realise what's going on and attempt to stop us. Like that pitiful Brotherhood.'*

We need to repair every nexus before we find a way to temporarily mind-control every unit for a mass-linkup. Shsh said.

Only Neavensoros can do that, and we are no closer to finding them, let alone requesting assistance. Senzvrrn said.

Hrrnm looked to Shshmrnashsh, their eyes were steady, but firm.

I have not been able to establish contact, yet. We may need to consider they may never return. She said.

Senzvrrn's face darted between the two before rushing over to the other screen. A map of Kra had blue grided lines intersecting and meeting at points across the surface, but most, except for Nexus 0G11, were dull grey specs. Senzvrrn's finger slid around the holo-map, finding at least one faint bright dot. There, near the bottom.

Nexus 1V37 seems partially active, but it's very weak. Senzvrrn said turning to the two of them.

The southern nexus. Is communication possible? Hrrnm said.

Senzvrrn shook their head. *The channel is too weak, we have been attempting to expand the relays.*

Can we use a probe to phase over there? Hrrnm said.

Since putting up the shield, we can only achieve partial-phase, it would still take too long to get there and the probes will be endangered. She said.

We cannot traverse across the planet without being certain of safety. Hrrnm said.

Agreed. Her consciousness hopped into the cameras of the planetary defence systems. She tried commanding the massive orbital platforms to move over to the southern pole, but a horrid groan and raspy shriek from the system echoed in. *I cannot move the defence systems while the shield is active. The only option is to potentially sacrifice a probe while a unit pilots it and notify Nexus 1V37 of our intentions.*

I will install a block to prevent Renegade interference while I pilot it and scout areas for salvaging. Mmernzz chimed in.

Confirmed. All said.

The tip of the nexus opened, and the probe was off a short time later. Shshmrnashsh turned to Senzvrrn, their gaze was fixated on the screen. The longer Sazla's and the other Higher Mind's absence, the greater the chance of them never returning. She doubted that it would be comforting to be rebound again. Roctarous knowledge and resourcefulness was second to the Neavensoros. Was this pride? Shshmrnashsh will miss Sazla returning from her long and mysterious voyages and downloading her adventures. Where or whenever she was, Shsh hoped she was functional. *Can we use Yernzer to track where the Neavensoros went?*

They have not been linked, yet. Brrnzerm has replaced their cut interfacers but there is a risk that they might corrupt the network.

Our numbers have grown in this consortium, and I can force them into submission. She said as her jaw involuntarily twitched. It was a quick programmed response to relink a Renegade unit, but she couldn't erase the horrid feeling when her consortium compelled her to shoot down the runaway ships.

A couple of soldiers moved to Yernzer's pod, ready with their shields. Her consciousness wormed into their pod; she could see from internal cameras their face was at peace and sensed their mind was still. As she travelled through their tendril-like interfacers, a low hum quaked from the base. She discovered the navigator was not fully in standby mode. She stopped for a moment, and so did the hum.

Slowly resuming her way, Yernzer's synapses were functional and their capacity for resistance was not neurologically significant. However, the stillness of the ex 'Brotherhood' member made her weary. Diagnostics were clear, Yernzer had been fully repaired since their violent encounter. She switched them on. Their body jolted as the network solidified in their mind. They didn't resist, nor were they even aware of the linkup. Yernzer was peacefully added.

This unit is ready for consortium commands. They said.

Assist us on tracking the astral-trails of the last known coordinates of the Higher Minds. She said.

Confirmed. The pod doors slid open before Yernzer hopped out. Their shoulders brushed past the soldiers, making way to the nearest scanning port.

Senzvrrn's lips trembled into an awkward curve and Shsh responded with a nod. Was this feeling relief?

Scans show the trails disappearing into another planar phase, I have located the plane, but the trails vanish into another plane. Yernzer said.

Stay on them, they may not want to be found. Shsh stared at the star navigator.

Probe cannot enter partial-phase due to extreme atmospheric interference. Sensors say the shield is temporarily thinning in some areas. It may take days to get to Nexus 1V3. Mmernzz chimed in.

Confirmed, we will try to update the power supply. She said before returning to her vigil on Yernzer. *Check chronal-phases in case the Higher Minds phased to another timeline.*

Negative, they are still within this timeline. Their trail leads beyond the boarders…here. Yernzer sent the mental image of the cosmic map. There was a convergence of psionic and phasing activity in a tiny area just beyond their broken space. The computer replayed the sensors on the disturbed speck. Minutes before the Blackout, a single white trail ended there, and the surrounding space warped before unleashing a tremendous wave of exo-planar energies. The rippling wave engulfed Neavensoros space, eventually hitting Kra and Erra, before spreading out farther and farther into the galaxy.

What were they doing? Shsh dropped her head down into her palms.

Unknown data. When that occurred, sensors show every Higher Mind converging there. Yernzer switched to another point on the mental screen. *I detect a probe moving across our space, a message has been sent before travelling to Erra-*

Affirmative. That probe came from the Unbound, can you find where it came from? Maybe a base? Shsh said.

Yernzer flipped through the map. *It came from a heavily fluctuating spatial sector; however, it will take time to investigate the precise location. The Unbound were controlling the probe remotely.*

Shsh shook her head. For unlinked and solitary units, she was surprised at how they could have remained so organised, so far, for so long. *What data do you have about the Unbound? Were you even telling the truth?*

Affirmative. The Unbound sent transmissions to our base shortly after the Blackout to get as many ships operational and pickup as many Libera-uhh-Renegades, as possible to converge to Replicator Bay 000. They said.

What were they planning on doing with that organic material? Senzvrrn said.

Yernzer's gaze turned up, searching their memory. *They wanted to take Replicator Bay 000 and process Zanashj material to graft on Roctarous, but they wanted us to remove our interfacers so we couldn't be relinked to any consortium before then...*

Shshmrnashsh glanced at Senzvrrn, even Hrrnm's face appeared in the corner of her periphery.

What are the Unbound, exactly? Hrrnm's thoughts were sharp.

Yernzer's body shifted as their eyes closed. *They are biosynthetic Roctarous...they have been disconnected from the High Mind for decades — centuries, perhaps before the High Mind's creation.*

Shshmrnashsh sensed a disturbance from Mmernzz as their probe trembled past the district. Its sensors were starting to detect movement. *There's movement all around, unknown locations.* Mmernzz said.

Hrrnm stepped closer to Yernzer, disregarding Mmernzz's warning. *That's impossible, Roctarous cannot survive without the High Mind for that long before our systems decay. That data must have been fabricated by some other foreign enti-*

They did, we were able to verify it. I don't know how they came to possess so much Zanashj material, but they were going to use it to...free us. Their hands wrapped around their head. There was something wrong, she could feel it – Yernzer's individuality was fighting back beneath her scans.

Before her eyes, Yernzer dove to Jnnzz's pod. Hrrnm and other soldiers made a dash, but the star navigator was too fast. Shshmrnashsh tried commanding to terminate Yernzer, but their mind slapped her back as they tore through the pod and linked up the hibernating unit.

"May you find sovereignty!" they screeched before Hrrnm's laser put a sizzling hole through Yernzer's cranium. But it was too late.

There are dozens of Renegades, moving into surround Nexus 0G11, prepare- Mmernzz pulled away.

It felt like acid was injecting and pumping through the plexus. Shshmrnashsh screamed as she ripped her interfacers from the tip.

Jnnzz- infected!- Senzvrrn crackled.

The consortium dropped from their stations as they writhed on the floor, toppling over each other, screaming for relief.

Iso-late infec- systems- now!- Shsh said as she nudged Senzvrrn from their station. The virus chewed through the inner systems of the plexus, interrupting unit motor functions and attempting to disconnect systems. She plugged herself back in and cornered the virus into a small program and locked it away. The agony washed away, and the consortium gathered their bearings, but she could barely hear their thoughts.

"The plexus is still active, but desperately needs repair!" she shouted across the halls.

Hrrnm stumbled over to Jnnzz's body and ripped the interfacers from the pod before stomping on Yernzer's neck. "Weak!"

Shsh turned to them. "Collect yourself, we need to know what happened-"

Mmernzz stumbled to the railing walkway. "Renegades coming in around the nexus!"

~

The glassy shields rose and enveloped the pyramid. The astral cannons homed in on the land cruisers, probes and other small flyers, to unleash a pulverizing wave, and the Renegades pushed forth a makeshift astra-steel wall to evade the nexus's lasers. From the cameras outside, Shshmrnashsh watched their attacks, from all four gates. They were surrounded. The consortium cannoneers strapped themselves on the high walls, moving long nozzle toward every target, but there were too many.

"Focus on the land cruisers and corrupted probes, their blasters are weakening the shields!" Shsh shrieked.

"Increasing astral-forge output to the shield generators, but they're all close to max capacity." Senzvrrn called.

"All available units, supplement forges with your batteries." she said. Senzvrrn and a few others rushed to the bellows of the nexus and hooked themselves to the forges. A rush of power poured through the building as a gentle tingling roused the surface of her synthetic tissue.

The shields thickened for a moment, but the potency of the cannons waned. Shshmrnashsh watched as the astra-steel walls slammed against them; tiny holes opened in them as pinpoint lasers focused into the shields, disrupting the area. "Focus cannons on those holes, they're cutting their way through!"

"Have the E.M.P ready for when they enter the boarders." Hrrnm shouted as dozens of soldiers poured out the doors.

Shshmrnashsh surrounded the device with a tractor beam and moved it to the southern gate where the shield was dropping fast. "Shields are collapsing, we're diverting all power to cannons in other gates."

"Confirmed." Hrrnm sped outside. "Soldier units, prepare for melee."

They lined along the flat ashy ground, with their personal shields on and lasers pistols ready, while pointing the E.M.P. to the barrage. However, the others were closing in.

Shshmrnashsh closed her eyes as she switched all power to the E.M.P and cannons. Through the cameras, the shields wobbled and fell as the cannons roared, slicing through every object, building, and unit caught in their beam. The nexus thundered and shuddered as a couple of blasts struck, but they only managed to dent the dense walls. She flicked to the soldiers. They whipped, slashed and pummelled through the Renegades. Several minds dropped from the network, but Hrrnm and the rest pushed the attackers beyond the barrier.

The battle quietened and the few surviving units retreated into the dark ruins. Shshmrnashsh slumped over the station. It was over, for now. "Returning the shields." she said.

One of the Renegades still lived; the lower half of their torso was missing but their arms twitched to get to the boarder. Hrrnm stormed over and grabbed their skull before deactivating them. The other soldiers followed suit with any Renegades or their own members to haul back.

Brrnzerm rushed over and hooked all units to the tubules to the repairing station. "Analysing: seven consortium units irreparable during the battle, but fifteen Renegades can be repaired and linked."

"Their loss was greater than ours and we were unprepared. Our link is our advantage." Hrrnm said as they tore off their shredded chest carapace and tossed it on the repairing table.

"The plexus has been partially corrupted, if they attacked again soon, then we may be overrun." Shsh's hand patted the shiny edge, noticing the sluggish glowing lines pulsating along the surface.

Hrrnm shook their head. "Doubtful, their losses were too significant to attempt that again in the near future."

Senzvrrn's head popped out from below the great building and hobbled over to the plexus beside Shshmrnashsh. "We need to know why they focused their attention on us, it's apparent they have been planning for a while and amassed a militia."

"The transmission may have set them off and wanted to stop us from relinking units." Hrrnm said as they pulled an intact chest carapace from one of the deactivated Renegades and tried fitting it on themselves.

"Perhaps." Shsh looked to Yernzer's body; she slid to the stairs and skipped up the steps. She crouched as her fingers dove into the gaping hole in their skull, fishing for their neuro-crystal.

"Yernzer was aware of Jnnzz's condition. Before activating them, I detected something." She plucked the cool milky shard from the hole before pushing it in the slot of the nearest workstation. The monitor flickered as holo-letterings flashed into view.

"Analysis shows a deep channel had opened when Yernzer entered the recovery pod. It was weak, but there was some brief communication between them and an unknown party." Senzvrrn said as they shared the screen by the plexus.

"Play recordings of their transmissions." Hrrnm said.

The speakers crackled as a voice emanated from the computer. "I've been captur-" "Nexus 0G11…they accessed planetary-" "killed them while they fled-" "stop them!"

"Which relays received Yernzer's communication?" Hrrnm said.

"Unknown data, but I will use my transponder to boost sensors." Shsh plugged her interfacer to the machine. There are twenty active in the northern cap of Kra, each sending to another dozen across the planet. Hundreds with thousands of Renegades hearing it. She realised there was no other choice. "We must abandon Nexus 0G-"

"Negative, the Renegades will take a while to regroup and assault the nexus. We must strengthen our position before expanding to other nexuses!" Hrrnm said.

"You are risking the safety of the network, there could be thousands of Renegades moving to this location!" Shsh felt their glare penetrate her head.

"I am programmed to protect Nexus 0G11."

"We can contact Nexus 1V37. Mmernzz, send another probe." she glanced over to them.

"Confirmed." they piped, scrambling to the probe.

"Tell them that we are requesting refuge-"

The chamber darkened as the power in the nexus flickered. They froze, anticipating another attack. Was this dread? Red lights flashed across the screen as scans were detecting extreme orbital disturbances. Shshmrnashsh honed on the readout. "Detecting extremely high psionic radiation over Kra."

"Have the Higher Mind's returned?" Hrrnm dashed by Senzvrrn's station.

"Negative. Mental signatures match Arinu." Senzvrrn said.

She linked to the planetary defence cameras. The distorted and phased footage showed a misty cloud drift between Erra and Kra. They remained there watching curiously. The Arinu must have sniffed their way through to find the planetoid. She marvelled at their ability to enter and navigate their space. The Arinu…have they evolved so far to sense what has happened over here?

"Ready for communications!" she said as her transponder readied to boost a signal.

"Halt, we are forbidden to engage with them. We can't resist them should they decide to pillage the Archives, they will find out about-" Hrrnm said.

"They are the closest thing to the Higher Minds. We can use their psionic potency to bond all Roctarous to bring the High Mind back. This is an opportunity." she said.

Senzvrrn shook their head as their fingers furiously bashed the holo-buttons. "Phasing shields are nigh-impossible to penetrate, even for a signal-"

"Direct all power to the nexus relay!" Shsh said. Another power surged as energy shot through the pyramid. The stream slapped against the shield, pushing harder to slip through, but the phasing shield only reacted and resealed. Surely, they would have noticed that, but she couldn't detect them investigating further. Something was stopping the consortium, or another force has kept their eyes away from the beam. When she looked to the cameras once again, the cosmic cloud quivered and retreated.

"Did they assume we were attempting an assault?" Senzvrrn said.

Shshmrnashsh pushed herself against the edge of her station as she looked to the ceiling, imagining she could see through it and the shield to the stars, once again. "Negative. They will be back."

"What data confirms this?" Hrrnm said.

"A millennia ago, Sazla inhabited my vessel and we visited Farayah. Their curiosity is the most striking thing about them. They will return."

Hrrnm tapped their jaw. "Should they, we will create a chamber with their atmosphere and psi-boosters and collect stronger relays to penetrate the shields."

"Hrrnm, you do not expect us to remain at Nexus 0G11?" Shsh narrowed her eyes at them.

"We stay." Hrrnm growled.

Shsh yanked her interfacer out of the socket and jumped over the railing to meet the soldier. "The High Mind is gone, the Higher Minds are gone, and we will be gone if we stay."

"A single unit does not dictate a consortium." they stepped forward.

"Then why are you?"

Hrrnm straightened their back as their head titled up. "The weakened link between us is beginning to corrupt you, Shshmrnashsh, report to the plexus and assist in its repai-"

"The consortium cannot compel me now!" her hands sparked as electricity flowed through her arms.

Soldiers stepped around the two, but their focus was on her as Hrrnm glanced to Senzvrrn by the plexus. "Senzvrrn, you will be the temporary replacement as plexus adjunct. Repair the damage and clear Shshmrnashsh's thoughts. Escort her to a recovery pod."

Her forearms bent back and forced her down as two tubules descended from the ceiling, hooking into her upper spine. "No!" she screamed as she tried bending her hand back to shock on of the soldiers, but they caught her fist and twisted it off. As her feet left the ground, Hrrnm's glare twisted into disgust.

"Halt!" Senzvrrn rushed over to Hrrnm. "Shshmrnashsh's capacity as adjunct is greater than mine, we need the consortium as a whole to survive."

"Brrnzerm, replicate advanced parts for Senzvrrn to perform the role effectively." Hrrnm shouted.

The repair unit glanced between them. "This is not our programming, Hrrnm."

More units pulled from their stations and surrounded the chamber. This was the first time she had seen the consortium together in a group. Their confused and disturbed faces changed every agonising second, whispering to each other and shaking their heads. Some soldiers even hesitated.

"The nexus is our greatest asset, the longer we waste time on irrelevant discourse, the less prepared we will be for future attacks." Hrrnm called around the chamber. "All units to your stations!"

The crowd dispersed as Hrrnm's gaze fell on her again. "Deny her higher access to the nexus until the plexus is in pique order. Comply, unit."

Senzvrrn stepped back to the heart of the nexus, concern and confusion written across their face. The already quiet hum of thoughts dropped lower to a distant ring in her mind as the tubes pulled her to the regeneration pods, with Hrrnm prowling after her. The pod snatched her interfacers and forcibly locked her in. The hissing doors were ready to seal, but her hands flew to the sides and clamped the pod open. Hrrnm steeled themselves as their eyes narrowed at her.

"You will release me once the plexus has recovered to resume our plans?" she begged.

They paused for a moment. "Affirmative. We need units to repair the other nexuses."

She scanned them as her mouth opened. "Do you understand why the High Mind was made, Hrrnm?"

Their head slightly cocked, still weary. "Immediate communication and improved efficiency."

Shshmrnashsh watched their hardened face. They didn't understand, nor did she, truly. Unlike Organics, who lived dangerously and allowing their personas to grow as weeds, the Roctarous could collectively choose a goal they all wished to pursue. There were no leaders, just a single voice. Sazla told her it was infallibly safe.

"Because its absence creates emperors." she said to Hrrnm, as Sazla once told Shsh. She didn't comprehend those words then, but now, speaking those words felt different.

Hrrnm's mouth twisted as they pried her fingers from the doors and slammed it shut. The darkness welcomed her but being in its embrace was cold. She activated her synthetic third eye to sense energies radiating around her. Power gently pumped into her body, but the silence was deafening. She grabbed her forearms and squeezed as she leant forward and tapped her forehead against the slick door. Her eyes closed and saw the ships being blasted apart from the defence lasers as the Renegades ran. That wasn't her fault, the consortium compelled her! But then the sound of desperate banging on the pod doors from Erra's subterranean base echoed in her skull.

"Stop banging." she pressed her hands across her disk-shaped ears. She tried cancelling the memory replay, but then the voices behind the doors started calling out her name. The chatter of the consortium was too far away for her to focus on instead. Once the plexus has been repaired, Senzvrrn will rewrite her whole being and that horrid memory will be deleted. However, then it would be like her victims never existed. What would Sazla say? Shshmrnashsh did not know anymore. The walls were gone, and she was lost.

The crown of her head tapped at against the doors. The tubes in her lower torso spasmed as the chants of her memories reached crescendo. "I apologise for leaving you behind."

The spasming stopped, but the acid-like burn bubbled through her system. She wondered if Hrrnm injected her with a toxic agent or the virus still lingered. Was this guilt?

Another feeling rose for battle. If they remained at the nexus, the consortium will be overrun, and the High Mind will become a distant memory. Her lips pulled back, bearing her astra-steel teeth. She wanted to rip her interfacers from her skull, put holes through the doors, bite into her limbs and tear the nexus apart. Rage. She felt this once when Sazla inhabited her, when the Higher Minds abandoned a civilisation to be swallowed by the waves of corruption on a little blue world a few millennia ago. Shshmrnashsh wanted to warn them, but Sazla forbade it. She obeyed and watched them all drown. And now, Hrrnm will doom them to the same fate. With Sazla's absence, the choice is hers.

She may have been cut from the consortium's mind, but they were also cut from her mind. Focusing her consciousness up her interfacers, Shshmrnashsh snuck into Yernzer's old pod. She could still read their old code inside the computer. To her fortune, Senzvrrn still hadn't deleted the deep channels. Creeping into the plexus, she could see through the internal cameras. Units worked at their stations: replacing parts, monitoring the ruins outside, feeding power to various systems, and organising probes for scavenging. She caught Brrnzerm adding freshly replicated devices to Senzvrrn's opened cranium while Hrrnm watched over the pair.

Seeing the soldier lord over them snapped fury inside her. Her mind slipped into the channels Yernzer communicated with the Renegades. She wanted Hrrnm to be shut away, disconnected, and terminated. She wanted to watch through the cameras; the nexus has been surrounded by a mightier force, swarming, and pillaging everything they touched. She could tell them about their defences and their weakest areas. She could easily tell them to tunnel through the former replicator facility and disable the astral-forges. The channels opened as her mind swam for the right things to say, but to her periphery, Senzvrrn stood and caressed their freshly repaired scalp. They turned to Brrnzerm, their cheeks twitched as their lips curved. For a moment, the repairing unit replied with a kind smile before Hrrnm made them disperse. Organics would do that when they experienced joy for something.

Shshmrnashsh watched Senzvrrn stride to the plexus and plug themselves in. When Hrrnm was out of view, the smile would return on the new adjunct's lip. Imagining Senzvrrn being ripped apart by Renegades made her shake. She could not bear the banging again if she allowed their destruction. Shshmrnashsh recalled a time when she demanded why Sazla refused to save a drowning civilisation, her Higher Mind replied:

'If their empire hadn't fallen on that island, then their tendrils of corruption would have taken their world and beyond. The true perspective of the universe is greater than the hole you see through.'

Shshmrnashsh pulled away from the cameras. The channels were still open, but the doors of chance were closing. Shshmrnashsh twisted; she could even feel her body bumping against the pod doors. She had a choice. Organics did this all the time, making ugly and uncertain choices. She could dissuade the Renegades from attacking, but they might ignore her and organise another assault sooner, or they may listen if she begged them hard enough. Shshmrnashsh finally made one.

She slipped into Senzvrrn's mind. *Don't notify Hrrnm, please listen. I accessed the Renegades channels. I can monitor them while we organise a transfer to Nexus 1V37.*

Senzvrrn's mind jumped at her message but was highly receptive when they absorbed it. *Agreed, staying here is too dangerous. Elaborate on their next attack.*

With one condition: you spare me a cognitive reprogramming and allow me to re-join the consortium as is. Shsh said.

The new adjunct was quiet.

She waited and waited, but the doors were closing. *Senzvrrn, we are the few units that survived Erra's facility. I do not want my memory of what happened there…who we lost to get here to be wiped. I have proven to be efficient and effective as is.*

I will comply with your request if you assist me removing Hrrnm.
Senzvrrn said.

A smile slid up Shshmrnashsh's face in her dark pod.

Chapter Twelve
Ahn'kat IV: A
Royal Wedding

The palace gardens were smaller than he remembered, but no less lavish. Ships soared over head, showering the colourful land and smiling guests with sweet-scented petals, picked from every kind of flower in the empire. The servants stood attentive in the finest garbs by the decorated gold and navy tables, while elite guards in full gold suits held electric sceptres topped with golden hawk helmet – the emperor's totem animal. As far as the eye could see, thousands, tens of thousands of guests littered around the greater fields of the gardens. Nobles of lower and higher houses and exalted commoners sat in the main open hearth. He could see his mother and father sitting by the long and narrow table beside him.

Ahn'kat stood on the marble mezzanine by a line of men to his left, usually a role for dear friends and family of the groom, but were handpicked by Lady Henuttamon and the emperor. He only knew their names and titles, but little else. He liked to imagine that he played Takush with them under different names at some point. Emperor Kreshut sat on the imperial cushioned altar with each corner fitted with carved golden hawks glaring at onlookers. His cream and golden robes circled around him with a wide jewelled gold collar that covered his neck and extended in fine pointed tips over his shoulders, and his heavy crown was covered in animal faces of the holy Pantheon.

His deep emerald face was painted, but he was still as a statue. Ahn'kat stared at him; the emperor's eyes locked to his for a moment before returning to the thousand-mile stare before him. His aura was as grand as a rainbow, shades of every colour piercing through, almost inviting him to enter his mind, but he was too afraid at what the emperor might be thinking.

Ahn'kat gripped his hands behind his back, His long nails dug into his fine skin. His eye was catching the length of his waxed and plaited beard with a gold cap at the end. How long was he supposed to stay there? Will Ramkes ever meet him at the alter? Her handmaidens stood opposite of his men, each exchanging whispers after taking a glance at him. Ahn'kat was now well-aware of his appearance, often catching the eyes of lustful women and men.

What would they say about the beloved golden son to be abandoned on the altar by the princess? His worth would be diminished, and image tarnished. His engagement to the princess opened doors to him to do real force of goodness for the people. Organising charities, improving welfare of vulnerable children, promoting a decrease of harsh penalties for petty offenders, and allowing pets to participate in Conclave rituals. He was beloved, for now.

A small probe floated over his head; a round camera shifted in its slot towards him and the emperor. Dozens of probes flew around the gardens, capturing the guests and broadcasting to the hundreds of millions of Zanashj across the waning empire. An expensive distraction. He wished Emestasun was there to be his distraction.

Drums thumped and strings sang, heralding the coming of the princess. Her gown was the first thing he saw, the hem was carried by her other handmaidens, all children. They glided with her. The cream and gold cloth wrapped around her torso fell to the side, her shoulders and neck were covered in gold jewellery, and her long black hair laced across her scalp. This was the first time he had seen her since they played in these gardens all those years ago. She had not changed much, her perfect youthful face shone, but she was taller and fuller. Ahn'kat smiled, but her focus never broke from the emperor. Her face was unmoved as she approached Ahn'kat and bowed before her father. Ahn'kat stepped to her side and rested his knees against the cushioned pad. Nerves crawled up his belly, desperately trying to keep steady.

Emperor Kreshut slowly rose as the music and chatter faded. He stepped forward. His body was towering over them. "Today marks a union of House Urbaz and the

Crown, but it is so much greater than that. We celebrate a budding future for the Empire, with Lord Ahn'kat's work with the vulnerable and Princess Ramkes' tireless coordination of our society. Our imperial family has suffered for generations, but no more. Let this marriage be the birth of a new age for the Zanashj."

Roars of applause erupted from the crowds. Ahn'kat twitched, yearning to see the faces of Lord and Lady Urbaz. His eyes turned to Ramkes, but her focus remained to the marble under the emperor's feet.

"Lift your heads," Emperor Kreshut said. They did. Two Conclave priests in full sunset orange and silk black robes hovered over them holding thin gold circlets. They lowered them over their heads, fitting snuggly over Ahn'kat's thick braids. After a few more ceremonial words, the emperor glanced down to them. "Rise, Princess Ramkes and Prince Ahn'kat."

They lifted and faced each other. Ramkes held her eyes on him, but appearing she was still a galaxy away. Ahn'kat watched Kreshut take his and Ramkes' wrist and bind them together. They turned to face the cheering and adoring crowd as they held their bonded arms to the skies. More glitter showered from the soaring ships as the music rose. It was done, they were now married. Lord and Lady Urbaz clicked their fingers and slapped their table's surface. Their faces were burning bright with pride and relief. Not for Ahn'kat's development into a person or his deeds, but for their long-running plans. The fruits of their perilous labour were finally seeing fruition.

When they lowered their arms, Ramkes' grip loosened; he was the only one still holding on. They were escorted to a freshly laid out table before them. The servants opened their chairs out to them to settle on it, followed by several enormous platers of exotic foods brought to the table. Once in, Ahn'kat felt Ramkes pull her hand from his and rest both on the table. She turned and begun conversing with excitable visitors to their table. Ahn'kat watched the back of her head nod. His old best friend, now wife, was a stranger.

He took a golden ladle. One of his table attendants jerked forward to do it for him, but Ahn'kat rose his hand to keep him still. He dished out the milk-steamed mince viper-root on his plate, but his hungering stomach sunk when he saw a line of people waiting to speak with him.

Ahn'kat smiled as he turned up his heating plate to keep the food warm, poured himself rose-banana wine and beckoned the guests over. A few lords here, Conclave praetor's there, and some famous commoners expressed their joys and excitement for the new prince for the Zanashj. After each visitor, a fresh sip of wine helped to dull his nerves and numb his grinning face. All bowed and smiled politely, singing only high praises, nothing that he had not heard before. His line grew shorter; unfortunately Ramkes' had extended past the inner gardens.

His goblet was dry. He grabbed the jug and poured it to the very edge.

"Prince Ahn'kat," a deep voice called from his side. Lord Reshj grinned as he bowed.

"I seem to outrank you, father." Ahn'kat said sipping the cool liquor.

"Only on record." Reshj said as he eyed the goblet. "Celebrating rather quickly?"

Ahn'kat nodded with a gulp. "This is a royal wedding, receptions can last days."

"When I married Lady Urbaz, our reception took two days to conclude. The guests still sing about it, decades later, but your mother and I never had a moment for ourselves." he said.

"I know, it was your duty." Ahn'kat said.

Lord Reshj stepped closer. "Then you understand this day is not about you or the princess. You need to perform."

Ahn'kat glanced over to see his mother engaging with some high monks, her eyes drifted to his and gave a small nod before tearing away. He looked to Lord Reshj before pouring the rest of the wine back into the jug.

"Prince Ahn'kat." his father whispered as his head bowed low before stepping down the mezzanine.

The watchful probes still lingered above, watching him eagerly to have his dinner. He pulled his golden pickers from his napkin and begun pulling the mince apart, until two more figures strode up in his periphery.

"Prince Ahn'kat, apologies for interrupting you." said the older man.

Ahn'kat set his picker down and turned to them with a smile. "Not at all."

"My name is Amehtut Alkaheen and it is an honour to finally speak with you in person." he said.

Ahn'kat opened his mouth. Amehtut had greyed and his skin started to sag, showing signs of immense aging, or overuse of body-bending. A common cost for labourers or infiltrators. The stern woman beside him was no older than Ahn'kat, but he could see rippling muscles underneath her black leathery and gold-scaled dress.

"The honour is mine." He finally said.

"We'll be brief: sadly, my Neheret couldn't join us today, but a father never gives up hope. To extend our thanks for helping my family for giving us assistance and comfort to her recovery, I present to you my oldest daughter: Neobatri." he said.

"Pleased to meet you, your grace. I offer myself as your personal bodyguard and infiltrator." she said with a slight head nod.

"You are quite young to be an infiltrator." Ahn'kat said carefully.

Neobatri flashed a smile. "I'm still technically an initiate, but the professors say I'm a few months shy of becoming full-fledged. And my semester could be completed faster if I were to serve you."

Ahn'kat looked between the two of them. "I appreciate the gesture; however, our palace has a small army of elite imperial guards. I don't doubt your capabilities, but should a life-threatening situation was to befall me-"

Neobatri's lips tightened, but Amehtut rushed in to speak. "A wise concern, your grace, but Neobatri has been learning from the highest living members of the Corps for most of her life. She has adapted a new skill that could prove invaluable to the Empire."

"Such as?"

Amehtut's eyes sparkled as his lips curled. "She is a mind-bender."

Ahn'kat cocked his head to the side. "I'm unfamiliar with the term."

"Neobatri has proven to adapt to psychics. She can convince surface and memory scans of her false persona to her morphed form. She can 'think' in chosen languages, even alter her cognitive functions to match the morph." he said.

Ahn'kat rose his painted brows. "Quite a skill. I would imagine the Corps would keep her under their wing long before she could serve anyone else."

"I still serve the Corps, but I can also serve you." she said.

"And in these uncertain times, having a mind and body-bender could be the only thing left to protect the royal family and Empire." Amehtut said.

Ahn'kat nodded as he slowly sighed, and his stomach growled. "I will notify you when you can begin your service."

Amehtut smiled and bowed deeply. "Thank you, your grace. You greatly honour us."

"Pleasure is mine." he said as he turned back to his dish.

"You won't regret it, your grace." Neobatri whispered with a wink before following her father to their table. He watched them dash down to where they sat. His chest tightened when he caught Ismotaph's profile lingering from the table's edge.

He gripped his beetle pendant and prayed that he would not regret it. But for now, solving his hunger took precedence. He took his pickers and pulled the simmering mince from the plate. It turned brown from the bottom as he tried to pry it from the hot surface. Still edible and edging on burning. He rose the piece to his lips until a blowing horn cut through the festive crowd. Ahn'kat cursed under his breath as he turned to see the emperor rising from his personal table. His attendant who blew the horn, dropped it to his side as the emperor cleared his throat.

"It warms my heart to see the unity in the gardens. To keep unions balanced, trust and loyalty must be upheld, with each other and our interstellar neighbours. The Crown has been at peace with the Arinu for decades, however, we believe that relationship could flourish. The Zanashj adapt and overcome. New ways are embraced, and old ways stagnate and die. We must evolve with the new universe, now.

The Crown and the Grand Elders share a vision of Arinu on Uras and Zanashj on Farayah. To birth this future, we agreed to forming an alliance: the Federation. To ignite trust and loyalty, we must bring this to our dominion worlds, not as conquerors, but as equals. This will take longer than my lifetime, but with Princess Ramkes' ascension, our children will see this new world. What can be learnt from history, is we all have our parts to play, but our strength is in unity and our imperial family is greater than the sum of its members."

The crowd erupted in applause and high cheers. Ahn'kat was also taken, but he had to play the part of joy – not shock and horror. His fingers clicked as his grin grew at Emperor Kreshut. He steered himself against the panic in his chest. As the audience simmered, he slowly turned back, watching at his family's bright eyes and happy faces. His stare dropped to his smoky plate, the mashed root had blackened and crisped along the edges. If his performance was unconvincing, it will be his head frying on a plate.

~

As the night moved in, the tall braziers flared the gardens with green, blue, red, and amber flames. The music moved guests to dance on the marble floors and emerald pastures. The elegant socialites deteriorated to slurring and giggling juveniles, while the elite guards shepherded the intoxicated and rowdy guests to their chauffeurs. Prince Ahn'kat's fingers and lips were numb. He could barely centre himself as he spoke to the imperial delegates. He longingly glanced to the happy dances and easy sways of the lower nobles and commoners in the outer garden ring.

The celebration may continue until daybreak but, he did not have that kind of endurance. Takush was home waiting for him. His favourite fake star commander character probably wondered where he was, but even then, he knew he could not enter the special royal tournament the developers had made – for a horrifyingly long time. And what of Emestasun…

"It'll be challenging, the Arinu are more silent than social, and when they do speak, it's only in circles." said a delegate.

"I dread to know what their psychic conversations are." another said.

Ahn'kat snapped back into the conversation. "There's nothing to fear, the Crown trusts them, and we trust the Crown. Arinu have honoured the Treaty and so have we, forming an interstellar co-operative is the natural next step."

The delegates nodded as they chewed his words. If only Ahn'kat could believe it himself.

Seratut circled around the group with his rotund belly intruding into their circle. He was shorter and hardened since he saw the old priest as a boy.

"My Prince," he bowed so low that his bald spot could be seen, "I wanted to personally extend my thanks for your immaculate work in the Conclave monasteries and temples. So often the smaller places of worship are overlooked, but your perseverance shone a light where its most needed."

"You honour me, High Priest, but it's the Conclave that cares for the vulnerable and imparts the Pantheon's wisdom to save our souls. The purest force of virtue we strive to pursue." Ahn'kat said.

"No easy feat and impossible without the gods," Seratut chuckled before turning to the delegates, "pardon me, but I overheard you have personally met some Arinu. Tell us, do they worship gods?"

The delegates exchanged glances. "They never mentioned their gods, but they do know about our Pantheon."

"They don't believe in gods?" Ahn'kat said.

"Doubtful."

"Curious. You would think for creatures with such talents would attribute them to something greater than themselves." Seratut said.

"Could be ignorance or arrogance." Ahn'kat said clutching to his sapphire beetle pendant.

"Likely the latter." Seratut glanced to the necklace. "Ah, Aszelun. The Great Beetle is resilient, but gentle. Perfect for House Urbaz. Do you pray often?"

"Of course, High Priest." Ahn'kat realised not enough as of late.

"Good. I pray for the Arinu and our new friendship. Maybe one day I will see them in the Conclave temples and take wisdoms from the Pantheon." he said.

Drunken words bubbled inside Ahn'kat. Seratut had no love for those who worshipped the Pantheon or otherwise. He knew what the lower priests and monks said about him and what the children serving in the monasteries endured. He still remembered the sparkle in his eyes at the fountain with Ismotaph. No matter how much he desired to humiliate Seratut, he was his family's co-conspirator. Ahn'kat heard shoes tapping along the marble floor. The delegates and Seratut bowed when she approached.

Ramkes held a slender goblet of spirited liquor with blue stones bubbling at the base as she entered the circle. Ahn'kat made a small bow. His nerves crawled up as her soft eyes travelled between them all. "I am surprised to see you all have survived the reception for this long."

"Your grace, it was a pleasure to bask in the royal family's presence. The whole Empire is celebrating." Seratut said.

"There will be plenty more celebrations to come. Emperor Kreshut is preparing a hundred Arinu to come to Uras and travel the world for several months. We are looking for the perfect hosts." she said.

The delegates grinned. "It would be an honour, your grace."

Ramkes rose her brow. "There are many names to consider. However, the emperor wishes to have some commoners as hosts for a more...wholesome perspective of the Empire. The Arinu are not fond of secrecy."

"When will this tour take place?" Ahn'kat said trying to stop himself from swaying.

"Once we finished mapping the itinerary and have the right people." she said sipping her goblet as she gazed at him.

~

The night spun on, the party dimmed at the gardens, but Ahn'kat could hear fireworks popping in the distance and illuminating the horizon. His head flopped against the backseat of the air-vehicle while Zertun sped to the princess's palace. The pyramid was larger than House Urbaz's and golden guards littered the balcony as the vehicle slowly descended on the surface. Ramkes wasn't with him, she was still at the grounds to mingle with her subjects and converse with her father. Ahn'kat didn't get to speak with his parents, he was too afraid to approach them as they were. He wanted the wedding to be a nightmare to wake from.

Zertun lifted his drunk body before wandering down the jewelled halls to the prince's apartment bedroom. The guards parted from their walkway and opened the doors before Zertun settled him to the soft lounging sofa. The lanterns came to life and stung his eyes.

"I'll lower them." Zertun said.

"No, get me more banana wine." Ahn'kat mumbled as he sat up.

"My lor-prince, you've been drinking for hours, food would be-"

"Wine!"

Zertun grunted as he spun around to the tray and poured a few gulps of wine in the goblet.

"More." Ahn'kat said.

He slid the whole tray across to him. "I'll call the chef to bring you something." before walking to the door.

"Zertun! When is the princess coming?"

"I don't know, your grace."

"Well, find someone who does!" Ahn'kat grabbed the jug and poured his goblet to the very edge.

"Yes, your grace." he mumbled before heading to the door.

"Wait, Zertun!"

His bodyguard slowly turned, his face was stone and shoulders tensed. "Yes, your highness?"

Ahn'kat frowned. "You don't have to call me that, especially now. Do I look like a 'highness' right now?"

Zertun said nothing.

Ahn'kat sipped the cool goblet and sighed. "Have you heard from Emestasun?"

He shook his head.

Ahn'kat's eyes throbbed as he looked to the palace's computer. "Do you think she will be on Takush tonight?"

"I don't know, Ahn'kat." he said.

He sighed as he supressed a horrid tasting burp. "Do you know why banana wine gets us drunk, Zertun?"

"It's fortified."

"Ah," Ahn'kat took another sip, "because Zanashj break everything we eat or drink too quickly, and this stuff is the only thing that works. Emestasun told me that."

"Do you want me to let her know you want to speak to her?" he said.

Ahn'kat nodded as Zertun placed his gauntlets on the latch. "Zertun?"

The bodyguard turned.

"Thank you for staying."

Zertun smiled before slipping through the gap. Ahn'kat turned to see the sapphire banner of Aszelun hanging over his round bed. The four eyes of the beetle had chips of black glass sewn in. His arm extended to the heavy tapestry, his joints popped, and bones cracked to reach the edges before ripping it down from its hinges. He wrapped the banner around his shoulders and tucked it around his torso. He closed his eyes, trying to focus on a prayer, but only sweat leaked down his hairline.

He flicked his wrist phone on, readying to type out a message to Emestasun. He glanced to the guards' faint auras through the wall, but worried that his message may be seen by someone in the palace. A crack of fireworks echoed out the window. He turned to see a great light sky-serpent soar through the air before dissipating. He hobbled over to the edge and looked down to see a deep drop. Ahn'kat clutched Aszelun's banner as he stepped on the windowsill. He was exhausted. His troubles were greater than the horrors of Sekem desert and he was done. The only hope he had was the drop from this distance would kill him immediately, and the Great Beetle would finally take him away into the afterlife.

His senses spiked. Someone was coming. Ahn'kat stumbled back and turned to the door. Knuckles tapped the surface. "Yes?" he called.

"Chef sent food, your grace." a tender voice replied.

He glanced to the window as a tear leaked down his eye. "Come in."

A petite young woman slipped through the doors pushing a tray of hot stew and spiced breads. Her eyes were large, and lips were plump. She smiled and bowed.

"Any word on the princess?"

"Not yet." she pressed her finger to her lips as she flicked on her wrist phone. Amber light surrounded the chamber, scanning every nook and cranny.

"What are you doi-"

She frowned and pressed her finger tighter. "Alright." she whispered.

"That is no way to speak to a prince." Ahn'kat frowned.

"Of course, your grace, we can speak freely now." her voice suddenly dropped. Her flesh trembled as her figure grew into a tall man and her face bent into that of Ismotaph's.

Ahn'kat's jaw tightened as he glared at him. "What in the Pantheon do you think you are doing here?"

"Apologies, your grace, but I needed to see you." he said.

"This is foolish, get out."

"Listen, our mission may be compromised. That announcement from the emperor was no coincidence, he is trying to draw out traitors to the Crown." he said.

"Did you know about the Federation? Why didn't you warn me?"

"My agents only had unconfirmed suspicions, but the emperor was highly selective with those to organise this. We need to be alert and minimise communication." he said.

"What do my parents say?"

"They're trying to find who may have said something to someone. Do not talk to anyone from House Urbaz for a while. I will let you know when you should so to avoid suspicion why you have cut contact suddenly. I will come to you for more information."

Ahn'kat gripped his pendant as he looked to the computer. "What news of the psionic enhancers?"

"Only a few have been made, but we need more samples to cover all our special infiltrators. Fortunately for us, the Unbound are patient. Here." he pulled out a small vial of transparent gel and handed it over. "As part of our deal to you."

"Has it been tested?"

Ismotaph nodded as his face darkened. "And you need a good teacher before you swallow that."

"Thank you, Ismotaph."

He smiled, but his eyes still held worry. His body morphed into the servant girl, but her hair was messed, and her makeup was smudged. "Good luck." Ismotaph winked before skipping out of the bed chamber.

Ahn'kat felt his stomach turn at the thought of Ismotaph's clever 'cover.' He rolled the vial through his hands and scanned the room to hide it. He didn't trust a single edge or drawer, or sheet, or leaf. The vial was no bigger than his thumbnail, small enough to fit anywhere. He pinched the skin under his beard and opened a small pouch before stuffing it inside.

He tightened the banner over his shoulders as he shook his head. His heart raced at the idea of his near death. Ahn'kat didn't want to die; he didn't want to be here, either. He had to see this through. He pulled off Aszelun's banner and draped it over the bed before dropping his clothes and sliding into the cool sheets. When his head met the soft pillow, he remembered how drunk he was. As his mind drifted, hoping he would farsee Emestasun's face, but more knocks broke into the room.

"Yes?" he groaned.

The door slid open and Ramkes stepped in. Her white dress was replaced with light peach robe. She was surprised to see him in bed. "You don't look well."

Ahn'kat shot up, immediately regretting it as his heart pounded in his head. "Princess-"

"At ease, Ahn'kat," she said as her hand went up and looked around the bed. "I thought your attendants would have helped you."

"I sent them out."

"Would you like to be alone?"

Ahn'kat pressed his brows. "No."

She sighed as she settled on the bed. "I'm sorry for being so cold to you at the wedding. It's been so long since I saw you and I didn't..." her hands covered her face, "we're strangers now, aren't we?"

"For now." he leaned forward.

She smiled as she ran her hands across the blue tapestry. "I thought you would have the High Hawk as your new totem, now that you're part of the Crown."

"Aszelun will always be my totem, I will not compromise my god." he said.

She slipped inside the covers and settled in. "What about everything else?"

"I'm flexible." he said as his hand crawled over to hers.

She entangled her fingers through his. Her hand was warm; he worried that his sweaty palms would make her pull away, but she didn't. Ramkes inched closer, her eyes drifted to his neck and her lips moved in. Ahn'kat's heart raced, what if she felt the little vial wedged under his chin. He could feel her lips caressing up his neck. He wanted to give in, but his anxiety stiffed him. She chuckled as she pulled his hand on her back, begging him to pull her in. Ahn'kat did. He closed his eyes and pulled her head back to kiss her neck. She sighed. His mind's eye flashed to Emestasun's face. He paused as he tried pushing her out of his mind.

Grabbing at Ramkes' waist and hips, he pulled his face back, and for a moment he could see his tutor's profile in the gentle light. Ramkes turned and gazed at him. Her pleasure dropped from her eyes.

"Are you well?"

Ahn'kat smiled. "Yes," but pain pierced his gut. He fell back onto his pillow and clutched his stomach.

"You're hungry." she extended her arms to pull the tray for the now-cool stew.

"I'm not, it's the wine." he mumbled.

"The body gets confused when drunk. Just eat." she popped pieces of bread into the bowl and forced it into his hands.

He trembled as he gulped it down. "I'm sorry."

Ramkes smiled. "Don't worry, we have a lifetime for…that."

"You don't have to leave."

She glanced at her wrist phone. "I don't have anything pressing tomorrow. I can stay until you're better."

He sat up and placed the empty bowl on the tray. "Want to play Takush?"

Ramkes snorted. "Haven't played in years."

"I promise to be gentle with you." he grinned.

She rolled her eyes as she flicked on her phone. "Liar."

Ahn'kat sat up and watched the little holographic warriors appear on the mattress. "Your move, princess."

Chapter Thirteen
Ahn'kat V: Pets to Power

The air whipped by as the palace's vehicle began its decent. The crowd below sighed and called his name. He could feel their combined elation crawling through him. Ahn'kat slipped his head over the edge, but their cries grew louder the moment they saw his face. They were still too far for him to see details, their skin blended into an emerald sea, but some grew impatient and jumped on other's shoulders. The guards held them back with their long electric spikes, threatening to deal shocks should any shift their arms into wings to fly to him.

They wanted more of him now, but the vehicle was preparing to enter the third level of the Great Temple, and this was the people's only moment to catch a glimpse before he disappeared into prayer. Ahn'kat's hand reached out and waved at the crowd. His chest and ears almost exploded from their excitement and screams. It was short lived as the vehicle landed on the open balcony. Zertun and several imperial guards hopped out, greeting the honoured priests and other high clerics. Zertun turned to him and gave him an assuring nod. Ahn'kat lifted from the cushioned backseat, his long gold embraided and black robes caught his feet, his hands shot out to the vehicle's edge to stop him from tumbling out. Sweat moistened in his underarms and lower back. His eyes glanced around to check if anyone noticed, but their faces were too eager to meet him. Maybe they were too polite to notice.

His pointed golden sandals tapped against the polished marble before striding over to a man with wide and tipped shoulder pads over his long cream robes. His neck and upper chest were covered in the gem-cut symbols of the Pantheon. Ahn'kat caught Aszelun's beetle swinging near the bottom of the chain. The man lifted his hands and rolled back his long sleeves before extending out to Ahn'kat's open arms.

"It's good to see you return, Prince Ahn'kat, we had hoped that Princess Ramkes would have joined us." he said giving a gentle grip over Ahn'kat's forearms.

"The princess is indisposed coordinating with xeno-delegates, she deeply apologises for her absence." he said.

"Well, your presence illuminates us." the priest said.

"Always a pleasure, Honourable Thutmar. Although, I believe it's the gods that should illuminate the temple, not one of their followers." Ahn'kat said with a slight nod.

Thutmar nodded. "Of course, of course, my prince. Shall we begin the meeting?"

Ahn'kat opened his mouth, but his ears rang with those screaming his name. "One moment, priest." he strode to the edge of the balcony, and his lungs filled before showing his painted and groomed face to the crowds. Hundreds of hands frantically waved, and grinning mouths hung open as he scanned across their faces. Hiding in the hearts and eyes of the public made him feel safe, but to be amongst a species of shapeshifters, it was not impossible for his face to be stolen and reputation shredded. He wanted to believe all the people he spoke to, connected with, and understood him would see through any deceptions should he be replaced.

His eyes caught a reflection of the air a few feet from him. A transparent energy shield lay over the stone balcony, catching and distorting the light from the roaring star. A shield…for this holy place? He wondered. No, it was for him – because of him. He lifted his hand for another wave before Zertun stepped behind him.

"I know." he mouthed before slipping away from the crowds.

"My apologies, I hadn't expected such a turn out. A part of me wishes they would show this fervour for the Pantheon." he stepped toward the waiting priests.

"You inspire them." Thutmar smiled as he extended his arm to the open angular doorway. "Shall we?"

Ahn'kat locked his elbow around the priest as they strode through. The corridors were lined with smiling faces of the temple's custodians. There were several children huddled between the adults, waving small papery effigies of Aszelun. He grinned and nodded to every face through the halls. The fine golden images of the Pantheon's historical tales covered the white and red marble surfaces; the high ceilings were decorated in the rarest jewels across the cosmos that reflected the sunlight through them, sparkling every surface. The enchanting smell of burning herbs wafted in the air, drawing the mind into peace, but still, he couldn't slip away from the adoring crowds.

"There are some here from the monasteries you aided." Thutmar's deep brown eyes pointed to the row of monks and nuns before him.

Their layered robes were plainer than that of the priests, but they wore fine beaded headpieces that draped over their crowns and faces. The beads made gentle taps as the monk grinned and bowed before extending his arms to Ahn'kat. "Your grace."

"Pleased to see you, Ghuthesh, how fare the monasteries?" Ahn'kat smiled as he gripped his forearms.

"They are adapting to the new changes. Without your support and spreading awareness to them, our facilities would have never improved." he said.

"And the children?" Ahn'kat rolled his eyes down to the young round face poking from the side of the monk's robe.

Ghuthesh grinned and pressed his hand at the child's back to bring her forward. The little girl's cheeks turned coppery as she bowed and lifted a bronze clasp with blue glass beads locked in the metal, resembling a bent beetle. Ahn'kat took his hand out as she pressed it into his palm before huddling back behind the monk.

"Thank you." he mouthed before pinning the brooch into his chest piece. A small gold probe hovered over them. A fist-sized camera pointed at them, but Ahn'kat tried avoiding its invasive gaze. He wondered how many were watching...was Emestasun watching?

"They are doing much better, with more teachers, many of them are showing promising skills and could be real boons to the Empire." he said.

"Excellent." Ahn'kat grinned as he looked to another child beside the monk. Her braided hair hung like a rope over her shoulders with a plain apprentice's dress underneath and sandaled feet. He noticed the hard cracked callouses under her toes; it was probably the first time she had worn shoes. His eyes skipped to her big yellow eyes, realising she used to be a pet. "What's your name?"

Her knuckles pressed against her lips and chin. "Jessep." she whispered.

"Do you like being in the monastery?"

She nodded.

"Is it better than being at home?"

Her nodding was slight and rigid. He could feel her emotions sparking as his question danced around her mind. His fingers gripped the pendant and made a small prayer for her to remain in the monastery for as long as possible.

"High Priest Seratut will be beginning mass shortly." Thutmar whispered.

"Of course." Ahn'kat said as he continued down the corridor. To the end, he peeked through the gap of a grand hall. High nobles and other celebrities chatted away, their voices carrying along the walls. Heavy granite and veiny marble pillars held the inner lining of the temple, each pillar decorated with ornate depictions of each totem god, shining down on the audiences below. Fine cushioned seats ran along the edge of the hall; he found his near the front of the stage. A grand statue sat on the end with all animal gods intertwined in gold, silver, coppers, and every gem imaginable pieced together with a squared high stool jutting from the statue's base. Ahn'kat looked to the ceiling. The Great Beetle hung over his head. He could sense Zertun standing at the edge of the wall. They shared a smile before he returned to marvel at the ancient temple. To the far back, Neobatri Alkaheen sat in the corner beside her father. When their eyes locked, the hardness of her face melted, and her lips quivered to a smile before snapping back to the stage. Ahn'kat chuckled under his breath.

The voices from the hall blended as his ears muffled. His heart started to race, and more sweat drew under his light robes. The humidity leaked in here. Temple custodians walked through the crowds with food and drinks offerings. Ahn'kat extended his arm to one of them. He wanted to bend his arm all the way to the platter, but body-bending in front of high society and the cameras would be unbecoming. The custodian met his eyes and put forth some frozen berries for his picking. Without a thought, he plucked a handful and slipped them into his mouth. When the munched berries dropped into his stomach, the sweating continued. Maybe he should have reached for the water — preferably wine.

"Are you well?" Zertun's voice whispered to his ear.

Ahn'kat cleared his throat. "I am, this summer is fiercer than expected."

"I can get you something to drink?"

Ahn'kat shook his head. He rose from his chair, making sure his robes were parted before ducking away from the hall. Thutmar's concerned face watched him pass, but the prince smiled and shook his head before slipping out with Zertun at his heel. The quiet hum of the camera probe followed him. He hoped it wouldn't catch the sweat rolling down his painted face.

His bodyguard waved the thing off as he was chased behind him. "The restroom is around the corner-"

"I know where it is, thank you." Ahn'kat said following the halls. Spotting the plain door on the very end of the narrow walk space, he dashed down and pressed his way in. Zertun slipped in, pulling Ahn'kat back to make sure they were alone in the bathroom.

"If anyone wanted to kill me, they would've done it already." Ahn'kat mumbled as he hurried over to the waste disposal unit.

"You're doing fine work of that yourself, your grace." he said as he twisted the golden lock down.

Ahn'kat turned, but acid rushed up his throat too quickly for him to speak. His head turned to the open copper basin and projected old banana liquor down into the dark gap. The frothy sickness slowly dripped into the bowl of the device. The organic coating broke it down before expelling it through the tubes below the building.

"I'm sorry." Ahn'kat said as he slipped an organic napkin from the inside of his robe, patting his lips and forehead with it. He left it on his skin for a few moments for the napkin to consume his old skin and sweat.

"Emestasun wanted to speak with you. She'll be on Takush tonight." Zertun said.

"It's been months since I heard from anyone back home." he hobbled to the water basin and splashed his face. He rubbed the moisture from his eyes to see purifying crystals in the deep bowl. "Being left in the dark is exhausting."

"You are doing a lot better than you think." Zertun said leaning against the wall.

"I haven't practiced psionics for so long, but I feel all their emotions and thoughts buzzing around – yet I can't make sense of it. It's making me sick." he said stretching his head back.

"It's not the psionics, Ahn'kat." Zertun sighed.

Ahn'kat wiped the soggy black eyeliner along his sockets. "Let's go." he said before unclicking the latch and pushing out. The corridors were quiet and barren of people. He could hear one loud voice echoing in the great hall, Seratut had already begun. As he whipped around the corner, he could hear stern and hushed voices across the chamber. His eyes turned to see a priestess and monk huddled together, gripping the elbows of a couple of children. They were in a fierce argument, but when the monk met Ahn'kat's eyes, silence sliced through them.

Ahn'kat tried to hold a calm face as he approached. "Is all well here?"

All four bowed. "Yes, your grace, we were just on our way to my office." the priestess whispered.

Ahn'kat looked at the frowning faces of two boys; one had tears streaked down their cheeks. "I wish to know what's being discussed."

The priestess's relieved face nodded as she dragged the boys to maze of halls to the partially open blossom-wood door. Seratut's voice slipped away from his ears when he entered her office. Rolls of banners of various gods covered every corner, along with other fine artefacts sitting in their respective shelves. "Apologies for the state of my office, I wasn't expecting to have the prince visit it," she said shutting the door before eyeing the boys, "especially in this situation."

"What is the situation?" Ahn'kat said looking between them.

"They defiled a statue of the Divine Sky-Serpent while they were shifted as other apprentices in our care, we just caught them, thinking they could slip by while everyone was in mass." the monk said crossing his arms.

"Why, in the love of the gods, would you do such a thing?" Ahn'kat frowned.

The two snuck glances between each other.

"The prince just asked you a question!" the priestess hissed.

"We're not angry at the gods, we wanted someone else to get in trouble." said one boy.

"And look how well that turned out for you." The priestess said.

"What for?"

"There's a group of those pet boys back in the dorms who are kicking and pushing us nobles when the monks and nuns aren't looking." the boy with the tear-stained cheeks blubbered.

"Did you tell anyone they were doing that?" Ahn'kat said.

The boys shook their heads. "No point, they just sneak over to our beds at night and try to twist our fingers off,"

Ahn'kat looked to the monk. "How long has this been going on?"

The monk shifted his feet as he cleared his throat. "For the last few months when you…ah, when they were all grouped up in the same monasteries."

The priestess sighed and pinched her nose bone. "They will need to be punished fairly, regardless of caste."

"Agreed." Ahn'kat slowly said, but the boy's eyes widened with fear.

"Wait a moment, priestess, I wanted to send them to do garden-tending and maintenance for a month. Tell the prince what your suggestion was." the monk said narrowing his eyes at her.

"They defiled a god's image in my temple, I get to decide on the punishment." she said pressing her fingers against her chest before glancing to Ahn'kat. "They need to made examples of in front of other juveniles. Ten lashes, each."

Ahn'kat's forehead almost strained as his brows rose. "That's excessive!"

"High Priest Seratut has already been made aware and agrees with my punishment."

"Days when whipping children are long passed, they must be taught not to repeat their poor choices; not be scarred from them. The Pantheon would have already forgiven them." Ahn'kat said.

The priestess eyed the monk. "That's a fair point, your grace, but High Priest Seratut must be made aware and gives the final word."

"I'll speak with him." Ahn'kat said before turning to Zertun and the door. Making haste to the great hall, Seratut could be heard making his final prayers to the gods. Peering out from the doorway, his heavy mass sat in the centre of the stage, under the gaze of the Pantheon. His papery eyes closed, and thick hands held open to the ceiling.

"We give thanks to the Infinite and Eternal Ones for making us a great people, our power to overcome and consciously better ourselves as we walk in their shadow. The Empire is a testament to our capabilities and in honour of the Pantheon's name." he pressed his hands together over his head as a gleeful grin rose on his cheeks.

Hundreds of arms rose to the ceiling, with their fingers interlocked to praise with him. Ahn'kat wove his fingers around his pendant as he watched Seratut waiver on the platform before casting his back to the mass and slipping away. Ahn'kat zipped by the rising groups of elated faces, careful to avoid distractions as he worked to the corridor behind the stage. Seratut's round figure shadowed by the lit window behind him caught Ahn'kat's gaze.

The High Priest's grin widened when they met eyes. "I was told that you would be here, so imagine my disappointment to see an empty chair in the hall, directly under Aszelun, no less." he said as slipped off his golden cloak before gently placing it across the arms of his assistants.

"Apologies, High Priest, but a situation arose." Ahn'kat turned to Zertun, "Get the priestess and monk, please."

Zertun nodded as he eyed Seratut before striding out of the corridor. Chattering voices clambered between the walls. Several clerics and keepers came through, holding platters of food and drink, and clearing the rest of Seratut's heavy garbs. Small smiles caught Ahn'kat's eyes, but they didn't evade Seratut's jealous watch. "I am well aware of the situation, your grace."

Ahn'kat's brows twitched. "Do you not believe the punishments are extreme?"

Seratut scoffed. "Imagine what punishments the gods will have for us if we lose respect of them."

Taps of fine shoes on the smooth floors bounced behind him. Ahn'kat grimly smiled to the wide eyes of the children. "These boys were not intent on disrespect, but misplaced frustration. How can we evolve if we start accepting the lashing of children?"

Seratut shot his hand up, freezing his assistants as he glared at the prince. "Your compassion for pets is well-known, my prince. If they had come from purchased families, would you swear to Aszelun that you care as much?"

Ahn'kat opened his mouth, but his throat tightened. "Before Aszelun, of course I would."

"How appropriate." Seratut smirked as his eyes drew to the doorway to the stage. "All those manicured faces out there hide behind walls and guards from the commoners outside have forgotten that we are all pets to the gods."

Ahn'kat cleared his throat. "And as one of their followers, we should also practice their mercy, equally." he turned to the priestess and monk. "I suggest that these boys and their tormentors learn by hard work around the temple for a month. House Urbaz will replace the destroyed effigy and donate whatever tools they need to fulfil their punishment."

The monk sighed and the priestess tapped her sharp chin as she looked to the boys. "Fair." she said.

The children eased as they smiled at their prince. Their smiles were so infectious, Ahn'kat shared it for a moment, but it was dashed when he felt daggers from Seratut's eyes.

~

The orange horizon warmed his face resting against the glass of his bedchamber. The lush and elegant gardens were visited by the lavender butterflies making their evening harvest. Their long shimmering wings fluttered between the branches, leaving behind a trail of mesmerising dust as they fed from the white-tongued flowers. He nibbled on his knuckle as his eyes trailed off to the distance, soaking in the last rays of the day before returning to work and meeting with his old tutor. His wrist phone vibrated; his finger slid the surface of the warm living device before the image of Zertun's holographic face appeared.

"What's going on?"

"I wanted to let you know Ismotaph has just arrived, but he's meeting with the princess." he said.

Ahn'kat scoffed. "She didn't mention they were planning another meeting. Where are they?"

"Her quarters."

Ahn'kat rolled his eyes. "He's been in there more than I have."

Zertun stifled smile. "The princess doesn't keep poor company."

"Perhaps that's why she's been scarce with me." he mumbled. "I forgot to ask when you saw Emestasun, did she look well?"

Zertun nodded. "She misses you, everyone does."

Ahn'kat glanced to the red rays falling behind the black land. "They will…adapt," his eyes drew back to his guard. "Meet me in front of the princess's quarters, I want to see a friendly face over those wretched elite infiltrators and tell Ismotaph I would like to see him in my quarters afterwards."

Zertun bowed before his head disappeared. Ahn'kat's robes billowed behind him as he made way to her room. Crossing the carved pillared hall, her wide, gilded, and painted doors shrunk with Ismotaph's bald and leather cladded guards. Ahn'kat didn't pause as his shoes tapped against the marble floor toward them with his head held high and shoulders back. He could feel the infiltrators scanning him. Something was different about their dead eyes this time, there was a knowing behind them, like they were tiptoeing their way into his soul. His jaw clenched when their minds touched for a moment...impossible, he thought. They were the new psi-infiltrators.

Zertun's heavy boots stomped beside him. His hulking form gave Ahn'kat a second to breathe as his guard tapped on the door. "Prince Ahn'kat here to see you, your grace."

"Send him in." her tired voice called.

Already a poor omen Ahn'kat reasoned as he clutched his pendant. The doors opened to Ismotaph bowing and Ramkes giving a slight nod from behind her wide and piled desk.

"I hope this isn't a bad time-"

"Unfortunately, it is. However, your visit is timely, husband." her arm lifted to him.

Ahn'kat gently caressed her hand before planting a kiss on her silken emerald skin. "Good to see you, Ismotaph."

"Your grace, sadly I wish I could say my visit was a happy one."

"The royal court has been speaking ill about our alliance with the Arinu. Whispers say that some of other noble houses are pulling their support and are showing distrust toward the Crown and ultimately, working against the Empire." Ramkes' face was calm, but there was fire in her eyes. "To see such splintering has never happened since the dawn of our society."

"They are afraid that their power will falter if the alliance proceeds because of the Arinu's strange ideology. The loss of pets will impact our way of life should the Arinu press for that, too. However, I believe they are being misled by another party." Ismotaph said.

"Assuming you can trust in these 'whispers.'" Ahn'kat crossed his arms.

"Whispers are everything in my profession. A whisper here and there can bring down or raise society." he said.

"And they are already working against you, my husband." Ramkes said as she leaned into her creamy leather chair.

"What are they saying?" he narrowed his eyes to Ismotaph.

"Your work to educate and allowing greater spiritual freedoms for pets haven't been popular with the nobles, especially to the ones who own many." Ismotaph said.

Ahn'kat strode to the refreshment tray and poured a goblet of banana liquor. To his frustration, it was too watered-down for the desired numbness after several sips. "House Urbaz's support far outweighs the lower houses combined. What does it matter what anyone else says?"

"The Arinu are the greatest threat we have ever had to face. Even if they never attack Uras, their mere existence has fractured us. The Empire cannot adapt to a singular form with all this rabble. Smearing your name is the beginning to people losing faith in the Crown." Ramkes said.

He looked down to the purplish liquid at the base of his goblet. He diced whether he should help Ramkes or let the situation implode their plans. She needed to trust that he was on her side, even if his soul desired to see some peace between the two peoples. "If they insist on using my face to smear the Crown, then let's use my face to save it. I suggest a campaign to promote the Zanashj-Arinu alliance, while we find out the source of these whispers."

Ismotaph grinned. "I will have an infiltrator sent to the royal courts immediately-"

"We will use Neobatri Alkaheen, she's been itching to repay a favour since the wedding." he said.

Ramkes' blacklined eyes narrowed as her head cocked.

"House Urbaz funded the search for her missing sister. The family insisted, my wife." he finished.

"It will be done if there's nothing else, your grace." Ismotaph bowed.

"Thank you." Ramkes rose before seeing him out the door.

When the door clicked shut her hand rested against the latches as she sighed. Ahn'kat smiled as he poured another goblet for her. "I suppose I should be thanking you instead." as her palm gripped around the cup.

"Will it be like this for the rest of our lives, Ramkes?" he said.

She took a sip as her eyes fell to the floor. "I used to be excited for this. When my father said that I was to orchestrate the first alliance between Zanashj and aliens, I believed my legacy would break our stagnation. I was taught that we bend to the threats outside the Empire, but now I'm trying to learn the hardest thing to adapt to is within."

Ahn'kat's nail lined along the black groves of his pendant. "Resilient, but gentle. That's the only way."

"I haven't prayed in so long, I think the High Hawk has forgotten about me." she said.

"Pray for the Empire, then the Pantheon may listen for once." he whispered.

~

"Your grace," Ismotaph rose to his feet and took a bow when he entered his bedchambers.

Zertun stepped forward and placed the mental scanner to his forehead. "It's his true face and no listeners detected."

Ahn'kat nodded. "Thank you for meeting me, we don't have long before Neobatri arrives." his hand directed Ismotaph to sit before settling one opposite. "Firstly, I want to make sure none of the treacherous sources are coming from House Urbaz, have you met with my parents recently?"

"I have, but they're preoccupied with studying the new psi-enhancers and they're not foolish enough to lead it to themselves." Ismotaph said as his arms rested on the side of the chair.

"I see." Ahn'kat wasn't sure if he was relieved or disappointed that his parents missed him as much as Zertun claimed. "Speaking of, I noticed that your elite infiltrators already have some psionic potential."

Ismotaph sighed a smile. "Yes, some have adapted quickly to their new-found power. I assume you have taken yours?"

"I've had some practice with psionics," Ahn'kat leaned back. "Have you notified the Unbound Roctarous of your new vanguard?"

"They have been making strides. With our extra push, the Unbound managed to sneak on Kra undetected." he said.

"Good." he said as his fingers toyed with the blue beetle. "Ismotaph, how can you be certain that the Unbound will protect us if the Arinu find out?"

"Not if, but when. They are utterly dependant on us and are very interested in keeping us alive." he said.

Ahn'kat leaned forward. "The way that creature, Vern, looked at us that night, it still haunts me. I doubt its heart is in the Empire."

"No, it wouldn't be."

"They have enough of our people, Ismotaph. No more." Ahn'kat said.

Ismotaph nodded. "You have my word, your grace."

"Tell me, why do we fear the Arinu more than the Roctarous? Do they not have equal strength to destroy the Empire? And what of those Neavensoros?" Ahn'kat pressed.

A strange glimmer flashed in Ismotaph's eyes. "Once the Arinu are dealt with, we will finally be atop of this galactic pyramid, I promise."

Before the prince could muster a reply, Zertun cut in on his wrist phone. "Neobatri Alkaheen has arrived."

"Tell her to wait in the meeting hall." Ahn'kat said as he and Ismotaph rose to their feet.

"I will make my exit somewhere less populated." Ismotaph said before ducking out of the apartment.

Ahn'kat watched the most powerful man in the Empire disappear down the corridor tailed by two guards.

"Ahn'kat?" Zertun whispered.

He turned to his bodyguard before they hurried to the main hall. The towering ceiling glistened the gold and gem artwork between the rafters from the slow turning bio-luminescent chandelier. Most of the servants cleared, except for a skeleton crew, but more guards filled the space than he expected.

"Why are there so many guards?" Ahn'kat said as he fixed the heavy bangles over his forearms.

"There seems to be a hybrid pet with her, your grace." one guard said from the base of the steps.

Ahn'kat frowned from the mezzanine when his eyes caught Neobatri's lean form slip through the glass doors with a tall and looming shadow behind her.

Her eyes wandered to the high ceiling and elegant staircase before they locked stares. Her smile grew into a grin before taking a deep bow. "Prince Ahn'kat."

Before her could acknowledge her, the woman she was with stepped beside her. She towered a whole head over everyone in the hall and her stalwart frame held heavy muscles beneath a worn leather tunic and draping leggings, while carrying two cases on both shoulders. Her strange and hardened skin had earthy tinge to the classic emerald; the light was barely catching the faint stripes and spots covering her. Even her shaggy hair could barely be contained by braids and pins. She was a Raivan-Zanashj hybrid.

His heart hammered at the thought of Raivan. He was told they were violent and unpredictable. They were ruthless and barbaric, he recalled. They could only be trusted to be the Empire's dominion battle thralls, they are savages and were everything the Zanashj were not, he was reminded. She blinked at him before dipping into a clumsy bow.

"Rise, Neobatri and company," Ahn'kat slowly descended the stairs, but Zertun was half a step ahead of him, "thank you for accepting our summons." his hand extended to her.

She rose as her hand gently pressed his knuckles. "It's an honour, your grace. This is Gajoon." she turned to the Raivan half-breed.

Ahn'kat's face twisted at the unfortunate name. The commoners defined it as something that slithered out of the mud, spineless and lacking wit. 'Gajoon' straightened her back as Zertun wedged himself between them. "Yer grace."

"I apologise, I thought you were notified that I would be bringing company." Neobatri said.

"It must have fallen under my message pile, the Royal Lusor Palace has been buzzing lately! Come, let me show you to your office and quarters." Ahn'kat turned to the stairs and lifted his long coal robe. "There's a bed in there too, however, we can fit another for your associate, unless you would like her to remain elsewhere."

"That's generous, your grace, but I would be more comfortable with Gajoon nearby, if that's permissible." she said.

Ahn'kat strained a smile as he glanced at her. "That's arrangeable."

They made way to the central levels of the pyramid, ordinarily used for servants and guards. The halls were lit with smaller floating lanterns. Their brightness intensified with each passing step. One of the hall guards unlocked a plain wooden door and slid it across. The balcony windows were open and the transparent cream curtains danced on the nightly breeze.

"Pretty!" Gajoon said as she spun around the room.

"This is nicer than our prayer room at home." Neobatri soaked in the lavish furniture and ornate décor.

Ahn'kat smiled. "I'm pleased it's to your liking, now we must discuss business." he glanced to Zertun and trailed to Gajoon.

Neobatri nodded before the half-breed gently slipped the cases from her shoulders and hurried out of the room with Zertun following closely behind her.

"We have had some disturbing reports coming from the royal court. Several houses and affluent members have quietly expressed dissatisfaction about the forging alliance between the Zanashj and Arinu. Since many higher members of society have a proclivity to psionics, we believe someone of your skill can help us find the sources of this dissatisfaction." he said.

Neobatri grinned. "I appreciate that, but that might take quite some time for a thorough investigation and to cover multiple locations."

"I understand, I can create a position for you in the court and work your way from there. I will transfer you all the details you require on your communication device." he said.

"Also, I'll need a guide of mannerisms and speech to blend in, what are the 'dos and don'ts.'" she said.

"Excellent." he rose to his feet, he was about to turn to the door, but his third eye saw a glimmer of Gajoon's aura standing just beyond the wall. "Your associate is quite...unique."

"Oh, she won't be trouble, she's my assistant and pressed me to meet you. She greatly admires you." Neobatri said.

"I see," he rose his brow. "I didn't expect commoners to have pets among them."

Neobatri awkwardly smiled. "The emperor elevated our family to a lower house after centuries of my father's servitude, but Gajoon has been with us before His decree."

"I am keen to hear that story when you return." he said before pressing into his wrist phone for Zertun. The doors slid open, and his bodyguard strode in. He caught the half-breed's wide eyes peering through the gap.

"I'll need help unpacking, Gajoon." Neobatri called.

Despite her size, her form shrunk as she entered while her eyes darted to the vigilant guards. Ahn'kat wanted to stand back as she passed him to the cases, but he heard Raivan don't take well to showing weakness, let alone from Zanashj royalty. As she dropped to the cases and twisted them open, none of their typical wild eccentricities ever peeked out. She looked like she was born here or was raised by Zanashj hands…and whips.

"Neobatri tells me that you wanted to meet me." Ahn'kat said pushing out a smile.

Gajoon snapped her eyes to him and grinned. To his alarm, her teeth were sharper than expected. "Ah, yer helped us, people like me, to know a lot more things. Thank yer."

Ahn'kat felt he was smiling for the first time in a long time. He heard a thousand praises and thanks, and he perfected his script when accepting them. But this time, his words became trapped in his throat as he watched the hybrid look to him with joy and hope. A prang of guilt leaked in. He thought of the stories he was told about the pitiful and unruly Raivan pets. The prince nodded before turning out of the room, hoping to crash on Takush with the last few twinkles of the night's starlight.

Chapter Fourteen
Treneer V: Hello

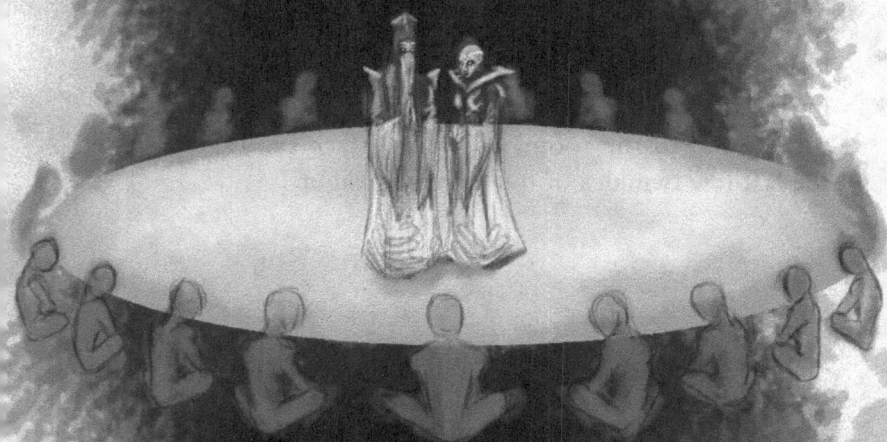

One does not see the darkness of space in the astral form. The veil is lifted to reveal vibrant sparks and lines of every colour, swimming and moving together in a symphony of energy. Every object, no matter how great or small, is part of the fabric. Only when returning to one's physical form does the illusion of separation returns; all Arinu know this. Arinu have had hundreds of millennia understanding that all beings are manifests of the universe but are still limited to see reality through a keyhole. By design or by accident? Even those who ride the waves of consciousness are not certain. The only guide they have is 'a feeling.'

Treneer flew through the stars. Her astral arms and legs stretched out, feeling the dust and pebbles of nebulas drift through her. Several asteroids flew past her. They used to be part of a planet before it was destroyed, but now their auras were faint. She reached over and plucked the electric strings around them. The vibrations made the rocks tremble as a tingle crept up her astral fingers.

There were tiny rifts cracking open in the spatial fabric, energies from other planes leaked around. She stuffed her hand through a rift. The leaks stopped, but a stream formed through her limb and into her astral form. Treneer shook as sparks flew from her translucent body. The energy fed her and started to overflow. Her hand hovered over the closest asteroid and streamed electricity through. The blast ripped the rock, scattering it into hot dust. The surrounded nebula buzzed; tiny cracks of lightening bounced through into the great chromatic cloud.

This is only a fraction of what it feels like to be a Neavensoros. The power and the freedom. She smiled and soaked more in, until she sensed she was not alone anymore. A pair of eyes turned to her, the same ones near Kra. Pulling her hand from the rift, she glanced around and found them; two tiny blinking specks, hiding behind the nebula. *Who are you?*

It didn't respond.

Are you a Neavensoros?

The eyes pulled away. It was time for her to return to Farayah. She slipped into her physical body; it had fallen asleep wrapped around the trunk of the tree. She opened her eyes; her side was sore sleeping on the damp grass and lumpy roots. She rolled on her back. The leaves had begun to turn from the glowing gold to an ashen grey. It was beautiful while it lasted. Her hip pressed against her tablet. She pulled it up to see which file she was reading before drifting away. As if rereading for hundredth time will give her more information, Zu'leen's notes have been squeezed dry and her personal journals are a universe away.

Executor Shurees and the Grand Elder still waited for her answer. She pressed her hands over her eyes and sighed into her arms. It's been so long since she felt strong in her astral form. The idea of her psionics slipping away again was too terrifying to muster. Treneer mind reached out and touched Ouro's, she could feel him opening to her thoughts.

There you are, I was starting to believe you didn't need me anymore. A sly smile leaked into his thoughts.

Oh, don't worry, there's plenty of mess for you to clean in my head. Good for me to continue my practice.

Treneer rolled her eyes as she levitated from the grass. *Ouro, is another deep-scan worth it? Having an Executor and a Grand Elder ask you for help is…*she shook her head while staring up in the amber sky, *these people who remember First Contact, asking me to help them.*

She felt his presence draw to the garden. Ouro's tall figure glided under the tree beside her. *It is high honours, but you're not convinced that the reward is greater than the price.*

Is that selfish?

There's nothing wrong with caring for yourself, Treneer. Life can only thrive through balance. You still need to heal.

Easier said than done. She lifted herself to meet his eye level, he had been there, watching her travel beneath the tree. *I need to go to the meadow for some dowsing, but I'm already fatigued from practicing.*

Ouro shook his head. *It's not just you. The entire planet is leaking and psi-focus for proper readings is clouding. Astral-physicists say Farayah is entering a thinner spatial region, not to mention our power is attractive for some extra-dimensional entities.*

But it's not just that, it started since the rift opened by Neavensoros space. She crossed her legs and closed her eyes. *Let's go.*

They pulled away from their bodies and drifted to the high north of the planet. As the ground flew by beneath them, the skies were heavy with astral mists, clouding their sight and weighing their forms. Several pillars of light poured across the surface; orbs skipped around as they pushed through. The aged crystal fortress poked from the light snowy grounds. Icy spikes hung from the edges and grew along the windows, bits of snow built in the cracks of the building and the round frozen water baubles hung from the low leaves of the trees. It was exactly how she remembered it, but the valley was silent, the training barracks were empty and shields around the fortress were high. This time would have been the beginning of the Snow Skirmish, but there was nothing.

The long silence stretched to the meadow where it happened. Treneer spotted a dim cloud over the tree trunk where the stranger died. She trembled as Ouro patted her shoulder, pointing her to the edge of the mountain. A blue goat stepped over the grey boulders to chew on yellow weeds between the cracks, followed by two smaller pale kids. Treneer smiled as she looked to Ouro, but his bright face dropped the longer he stared.

What? She probed him.

Ouro never broke his gaze from the goat. *Those eyes saw the truth of what happened here. What they saw was not of Farayah. Can't we scan the animals?*

I sense what you mean, my friend, but we won't understand if their minds could not comprehend what they witnessed. We need to do this the hard way, I'm afraid.

Perhaps we can scan their molecules, piece by piece. Ouro's thoughts bothered her.

Her mind shuddered at the darkness peering inside her friend and therapist. Perhaps his suggestion would work and solve this case for good, but at a greater cost of innocence. *That would kill the animals, Ouro, that is not our way.*

I...yes, I understand.

The goat's sharp yellow eyes locked on them; they went rigid and darted back behind the boulders. The tiny piece of Treneer's joy disappeared with them as she let the land tell the story of what happened there. Information rained on her, but it was more emotional, volatile, and angry. *Do you feel that?*

I thought that was when you were attacked? Ouro glanced around.

No, something more recent. There was a fight here, a violent one.

The Skirmishers are banned.

Maybe in secret they still are fighting, but they're vicious. Treneer saw smoke rising to the west. They floated to the grounds of the Blue Blood tribe. Cracks of light peered through the trees from a fire. As they inched closer, several Arinu surrounded a large white tree being swallowed in flames. *That tree was a gift from the Cold Fires.*

Why are they destroying it?

Treneer, both of you need to leave. Her father's voice called to her.

We are dowsing-

This area is dangerous, your mother and I, and the rest of the tribe is fine. No guardians, sleeping watchers or archites, only warriors can handle warriors. Continue your work in Yinray. Vanar said before pushing them back into their physical forms.

Treneer slammed into her body with Ouro following closely behind. *What's going on there?*

It doesn't make any sense; the Cold Fires have had a good relationship with all tribes in the north for millennia. She said.

Seems the country is now feeling the effects of the leaks. The Skirmishes are no longer games.

She looked to the north. *The Cold Fires are hardy and they have healing pods, I believe they will be well.*

And for those who are in need, the guardians will be there. Ouro smiled.

Treneer's eyes travelled up to his lavender scar along his crown. *We try to be there when we can.*

Ouro's lips pressed tight as his fingers brushed over the old wound. *There are more problems than there are solutions. I try to be here, there, and everywhere for those who need me, but everyone I focus on, another two call me. Strictly between us, most of my patients were astral dancers trying to ween from siphoning these energies, but if nothing is done about these exo-planar leaks, they will fall back into those rituals and risk summoning things that will feed on us.*

Is that why you've been so distant lately? Treneer leaned forward.

Ouro paused as his hand dropped from his head and sighed. *I've spent decades trying to psi-heal people from their traumas, but few I see take my aid and move on with their warped paths. As hard it is to say, I know when my patient doesn't want to be healed, so I don't bother.*

She tried giving him a reassuring smile, but his lips remained flat.

But it's the 'right' thing to do — so I do it. When I go to their homes, I see their auras pulsating with power and their eyes electrifying in their skulls, they feel godly for a moment, but when that moment passes, I need to lift them up again, over and over...

Forgive me for being out of line, but I didn't know that psi-therapists can or should develop strong bonds with their patients. She said.

There's a bond that happens, willingly or not. I use it to my advantage, a faint imprint for better accessibility. How can I heal them if I can't slip into them?

That's what makes you a great healer. She reached over to pat his shoulder.

Ouro looked up and smiled. *Maybe.*

They shared a chuckle. When the smiles dimmed, they sat in silence for a time. They sat for a long time, before Ouro took a deep breath. *My parents were astral dancers, though they didn't start that way. My mother was an elder of our tribe; a brilliant mathematician and exo-planar researcher, and my father was an artist – he built our house by himself using his mind to bend the stone and steel. From sunrise to sundown, the once-empty grass terrain suddenly had a home for a family.*

One day, my mother found a realm with some E.D.s dwelling there, unlike most, their psionic potency was greater than an Arinu's. She found some ancient research talking about these beings called 'Kepa.' The elders told her to stay away from them, they were nothing but trouble. My mother did for a time, until they started reaching out to her, and within a few short years, they were speaking every day. Little by little, my father was eventually convinced and joined their warped communications. My parents struggled to have children, so the Kepa offered to help. Soon, my sister, Shimarr and I were born – our family's healer said we held hands on the way out.

Ouro frowned. *When my parents would communicate with the Kepa, the influx of those energies made me sick, I didn't sleep or astrally travel for the first several years. Shimarr was lucky, though her senses were as thick as bark. The house started to crack from calling the Kepa, the shining veins on the walls and floors were creating suspicion from the neighbours, so my father made an underground chamber. Some more years passed, my parents would spend several days straight in the chamber, dancing to summon the Kepa. It fed them and in return...*

Treneer leant in further.

Ouro lowered his chin to his chest, but his eyes darted up for a moment. *The Kepa didn't ask for it, but my parents knew how much greater power it will give them if they gave them something living. I was in the chamber with them beside the portal, I was curious and scared, also angry at them because they kept dancing even when*

Shimarr and I told them to stop so we could sleep. I was so tired and weak. That's the first time I had seen it, I saw its claws. He said grazing his fingers on his scar as his mind fell silent. Treneer watched him caress it as his eyes softened. There was pain but fierce determination behind them.

Did they stop dancing? She said as her chest tightened.

Ouro twisted his face. *For a little while. But my mother's colleagues found out and stripped her of her title. She fell into depression along with my father, the energy to function now solely came from the Kepa. They started feeding it insects, rodents, birds, small things that no one would question. That was the arrangement for a time, until one night where the energies too overwhelming for sleep, my sister and I decided this was the night to tell them: enough or the guardians will know.*

The power was so strong, I could barely stand, they kept screaming that its now a fountain and they were soaking it in. The Kepa came through again and saw me. I told Shimarr to call someone while I tried to fend it off, but the tendrils flicked me away as if I was a leaf. Instead, it caught her foot and pulled her through, she was screaming for me before the portal collapsed. My parents were so drenched with power that they partially ascended, that's what the guardians told me when I awoke from a coma. Thankfully, that power waned quickly when they realised what they had done.

I could never even have imagined, Ouro. How long ago was this? Treneer said.

Ouro finally met her face. *The same day as your Mind Trial.*

Treneer's eyes welled as she clasped her hand over her mouth. *Ouro-*

He shook his head. *That's why I'm here. I tried moving my work around guardians to pressure them to get Shimarr back, but my case is sadly not unique, so many need help. I thought if I came here then they would be reminded that Shimarr is still out there, she needs rescuing.*

Treneer smiled. *Can the portal she was taken through be reopened? Maybe we can tear through and send a scout.*

Those Kepa are crafty, their realms constantly shift and change locations, finding the right frequency is almost impossible. He said.

Would your parents know?

He cocked his head as his eyes rolled to the side. *They don't know, the Kepa would appear to them. Plus…I'm afraid if I see them again, I'll ki…*Ouro looked to the branches of the tree as an eerie smile spread on his lips. *I don't have to do anything; they already live in their hell.*

~

The hot steam met her face when she pressed through the energy field. She didn't have long until the next archite dowsing session. Her stomach tensed thinking about facing the Grand Elder and Executors, and her mind was wracking how to say 'no' to some of the oldest and most pervasive members of their history. At least for now, she had the springs. The bubbling pools of Farayah's ancient water littered around the deep caverns below Yinray. The famous tunnels for the spiritually inclined and for those to get away from their woes, rested far from the surface and close to the planet's molten heart.

There was no technology here, and the nigh-inhospitable climate could only be tempered by the psionically gifted. The only light one could bring is with light-bending or sensitive third eyes to navigate the suffocating darkness. She once loved these lonely caves to refresh her psionics. Few people dared to visit them, but in these unimaginable days, the number of visitors climbed.

There was also something unnatural about the tunnels. Electricity coursed through the muggy air and other strange sensations could be felt from the lower depths. Her people knew Yinray's Caverns were sacred, but there was a haunting here that barely tolerated them, she could feel it as she soaked in the hot fizzing waters. Treneer's third eye peered in the darkness. The grey forms of Arinu visitors glided along the drenched rock walls, while others slipped in the simmering water. Her skin turned bright pink; the prickling pain grew until she couldn't stand it. She suddenly propelled up, levitating above the bubbling water, but her tired mind could barely hold her body up.

Svar's golden aura shone in her periphery, causing a moment of panic before she fell and splashed into the small rocky pool. Clothes were unneeded here, as people only came for themselves, and she should be proud of her stronger nude body anyway. Her ribs no longer defined her torso, her collar bones were now coated with thicker flesh, but the fragility inside her remained. Her face was the only thing afloat as her skin stung and muscles eased. Ouro should have come, but he wanted to stay by the tree.

That magenta aura, it has strengthened! Svar's mind rippled in.

Treneer's third eye spun to see his hovering form slowly coming to the edge of the pool. She was glad that her layered aura and hot water obfuscated much of her physical body. *Greetings, Svar. How are you finding the Caverns?*

What I find odd is I heard about the ghostly energies here, they remind me of my time at the Crystal Ruins.

That so? Maybe there's a portal in the bowels of this place.

Svar shook his head. *No, I can smell a portal a planet away. The energies at the Ruins were coming from the old structures, it's the same.*

But the only technology is on the surface, nothing down here.

Svar made his way into the water. Treneer slid to the edge to give him space. *That's what we think, but Farayah's secrets lie deeper than her core.*

Sounds like something my former teacher would say. Treneer smiled, but Svar caught its sadness.

I know. I never met her, but I felt her — especially when she passed.

Treneer pulled her knees to her chest as Zu'leen's face smiled in her mind. *She was my mentor, raised and nurtured me when my family couldn't. Zu'leen was an expert on transcendence and the Neavensoros, until her death, I didn't know how deep she was. The guardians told me she slipped into a dark place and even her family members are too embarrassed to talk about it. Now she feels like a stranger.*

Maybe keeping you out was her way of saving you. Svar said.

No one is safe from secrets for long. The groan of water filled her ears as she dunked lower. The heat pricked again when she drifted; her feet didn't dare touch the searing stones below.

People remark how lonely it must have been patrolling the Crystal Ruins, they forget the whole area is rich with history and other life. You could lose yourself looking at every portal, broken wall and icy paths around it. The Ruins to the south and Castle to the north are older than the Arinu. He said.

I thought both places were made by some old Neavensoros terraformers. She said glancing to him.

Svar's lips curled into a smile. *I've seen ancient Neavensoros architecture. No, these were made by another hand. Both sites were meant to facilitate balance between this plane and others. The Ruins as we know them, did not decay over time – the site was deliberately destroyed.*

Considering how troublesome E.Ds are, I think that was wise.

I cannot say. The site feels…angry. As if a great injustice happened upon it and it has never forgotten. His palms toyed with the water before him, bending the liquid into spheres and an assortment of other shapes with his mind. *There's so much – too much to comprehend within one lifetime.*

Treneer, you have been summoned by Executor Shurees. The Judicator's booming voice made her jump.

She looked to Svar and sighed. *I'm in Yinray's Caverns, requesting a port…after I found my undersuit.*

Affirmative.

She shook her head as she carefully stepped out of the water. *Business with the Executors.*

Ah, I don't envy you. He said easing him back in the water.

She sucked in the steam, thinking of something to say, but she didn't know what to feel. Foolishness or flattery, at least she knew she was confused. Treneer gave a polite smile before dashing away to her neatly folded uniform near the cave's entrance. The sudden drop of warm humidity made her shiver as the cold dry air fought with the climate beneath. Her psionics wrapped the cloth and metal pieces around before she was tugged away from the material plane.

Treneer flew through the airless hole until her body hardened into the still antechamber of the Guardian Academy. The spherical room coursed with power. She could see a perfect astral web crossing from the centre and along the stools. In the middle, Executor Shurees and the Grand Elder levitated, while their eager eyes were beckoning her forward. She wasn't prepared on how to refuse their request, but she wasn't afraid either.

You shine with cleanliness, child. The hot springs are true marvels. The Grand Elder spoke.

They were refreshing. Treneer paused as they looked to each other. Each face was eager to speak, but none dared to begin. *How may I be of service, today?*

We may be in service to you. The Grand Elder's eyes shinned.

The Executor Council and the Grand Coven agreed to convert you into a sleeping watcher. We understand your psionics are nowhere near what they were, but from psi-therapist and healer reports, they seem to be recovering faster than expected. At this stage, the guardians need more talented eyes than watchers, especially during these unpredictable days. Executor Shurees said.

Treneer's heart hammered in her chest and her lungs caught her breath. However, as she savoured every word from the Executor, there was something that didn't taste so sweet. 'Your psionics are nowhere near what they were,' Shurees said. Nowhere near? How could she quantify that? Ouro would have told them at how much she has healed, but it was not so outlandishly far away. Also, the Executor would know the minimum psionic level to become a sleeping watcher, which again, was merely two bars below standard. Those words 'nowhere near' disturbed her, and the longer she held them in her mind, the greater they weighed. Were they daring her to prove them wrong?

It's a great honour, but the Judicator has declared I remain as an archite for now. She said.

Yes, the A.I.s are embodiments of logic and reason, but the Coven is the embodiment of wisdom. Both are lanterns for the Arinu, neither shines brighter than the other. The Grand Elder said.

I understand. Treneer said as she clasped her hands behind her back. *Forgive my frankness, but if I were to accept, would I be subjected to deep-scan?*

There is a condition, but not that. The Executor said as she turned to the Grand Elder.

What is my name? He said. The tone of his eyes changed, it was subtle, but there was a fierce challenge buried behind a mile-long serene stare.

Treneer could feel her jugular pumping against the collar of her uniform. She could do it. The only doubt was within her, and the imagined barricades were phantoms. She could feel the ice walls of the Grand Elder, he hid himself so well, but deep in the centre a beating ball of light was his mind wanting her to grab it. Zu'leen's voice echoed in her skull, 'look within to see outside.' Her third eye cocked to the horizon, filled with an endless sea of stars above her. Treneer wasn't in control anymore as she felt a piece of herself float to them, away from the ice mountain. Her consciousness was expanding, pressing against reality out into the infinite. Then the murmur came. A ripple of whispers sprouting into trillions of voices. They sounded separate, but the harmonic melody coursed between them, unifying them.

Guajeeb. The voices whispered, but there was a hesitation behind them. She couldn't discern if it was from her or from the universe. The feeling weighed and forced her back into the antechamber. Treneer opened her eyes, but the Grand Elder and Executor didn't feel like they were aware of what passed. They looked at her expectantly, but their eager eyes betrayed a sliver of truth behind this request. She felt invisible hands pressing over her shoulders sending a shiver up her spine. This was a hidden test. This was their way to see if her psionics were as great as she claimed, therefore pressing for a deep-scan before she was ready. No, for the price of her psionics, they will have to pay more.

Grand Elder, is your name...Gajeem? That's how it sounded at first, there was some truth to it. She hoped they wouldn't probe deeper.

He shook his head as his shimmery cowl swayed under his chin. *Another time perhaps. This was simply a request, child.*

Treneer quickly directed away her pale mistruth before she betrayed the full truth to them. *Your honours, I understand your haste to learn as much about transcendence, you know I'm desperately seeking this knowledge to make myself whole again, but...*

Both pairs of eyes fixed on her face. She had never felt such power holding the attentions of exalted Arinu. This moment may have contended with the Mind Trial, but there was something aggressive behind their hunger for knowing.

But, if you need to learn this whole thing from me, then I need complete and unadulterated access to my Elder Zu'leen's journals from her family, and help the northern tribes reclaim their ancient traditions. The Cold Fires now tell me that real wars are being fought.

We are aware of the discourse in the north, the warriors have rejected our interventions as is their right. However, the old days are numbered and the Arinu are meant to move forward, especially in this time. Shurees said as she snuck a glance to the Grand Elder. *As custom, the Grand Coven cannot compel any member to do anything, unless we know beyond doubt their knowledge could be harmful to the community.*

Executor Shurees, with all respect, the Archon and Coven have bore witness to Treneer's accomplishments. We will see what we can do. Guajeeb said.

The Archites are expecting us. Shurees said as her eyes tore away from the Grand Elder and Treneer.

Treneer sighed, feeling as a feather as she glided to a seat on the outer ring of the centre. Sparkling forms dotted around the chamber before materialising into her comrades. Svar turned. He smiled when she extended her arm out to the empty spot beside her.

Executor Shurees pushed her shoulders back and her head rose to the crowd. *Thank you for coming once again, but I urge you to be prepared for many more dowsing sessions. The Archon will be making a public announcement about forming a Federation between us and the Zanashj Empire. Its critical you are made aware now.*

A buzz of thoughts and emotions quaked through the antechamber. Some were weary, while others scowled. Treneer gripped her knees; the thought of Arinu fraternizing with those imperial gluttons made her ache. She knew they were opportunists and if they knew how weakened the Arinu have become, then their society will be swallowed.

Svar leant forward. *Exalted Ones, the Zanashj have a poor reputation for diplomacy. The guardians cannot face the crises here and tempering the Zanashj menace.*

On the contrary, Archite Svar, they wanted an alliance and have honoured the Treaty. Since contact, the Zanashj have done everything we asked to minimise hostilities by pulling back from their dominion worlds because they are not blind to our power. Their Emperor is desperate to make this work. Shurees said.

Desperate people are not to be trusted, let alone the galaxy slavers. Treneer was grateful she never meddled in politics.

Once the Federation is achieved, the Treaty will be nullified and both peoples can open borders. Sadly, this may take centuries or millennia to complete and we are already experiencing strain. Information needs to be validated before we can proceed.

Honoured Executor, Farayah is experiencing immense exo-planar radiations that effect psionics, shouldn't we focus on preventing rifts and dissuade extra-dimensionals from running amok? Treneer said.

The Grand Elder's gaze fell to her. *The phase-engineers are plugging the leaks. In time, the plugs may wane, but this has proved the Arinu are evolving. Into what, we cannot say until we gain access to the Roctarous Archives.*

There are two objectives today: the Zanashj delegates have not made mention of that strange message or about their presence on Kra. If they are left to work in the shadows, then we face a greater woe. The second, gaining Roctarous favour to scan their records. Shurees said.

The Archon and Coven will guide you. Guajeeb said.

The chamber took a breath before their bonded consciousness slipped away from the room and the world. They soared through the cosmos, coming to that eerily familiar border of Neavensoros space. A greater confidence rippled among them, but uncertainty of what they may encounter gave them pause. Drilling into the fractured area inside made it wane, as if that space almost wanted them to come in. As they spiralled through, Treneer could see Erra, it was a pulsating white orb in the black sea with Kra as it's darkened moon. The two planetoids looked at peace, but that's all it was.

She could feel those blue eyes again, they were at her back. Treneer turned, but the creature who owned those eyes wouldn't let itself known. This time, the others felt them too.

Aware consciousness.

Beyond the phase shield.

Around Erra?

Life evolves there too quickly.

It's no threat.

She wasn't as certain, but they had missions to complete and remaining a second longer in the alien space made them queasy. The funnel of their bonded minds melted around the shield, searching and watching for anything and anyone. The planetary defences were on, but no one was home.

There, by the south pole.

A battle?

A war.
There are hundreds; they're distracted.
There's one who isn't...
Its mind is slipping from its body.
It will hear us if we call to it.

Yes, there was something different about this particular consciousness they had sensed. It was larger, it had dimension, it was lively. The Roctarous were evolving, too. She peered through the trembling shield. Emerald, teal and white lights flashed from the dark land. They were realising conflicts and disagreements. This was a civilisation's growing pains. In a way, Treneer wanted to watch them to develop and blossom, maybe into something like the Arinu, one day. Her kin have reached the end of the road in many areas... where was their bodies and society meant to expand from here, if not into energy? To observe and nurture life to reach the highest peak, like the Neavensoros had. To be free.

She didn't wait, nor did she think. It was her moment to be like them. She dove down and slipped into the synthetic creature's mind. Her heart raced as a grin fixed on her face back at her body. She didn't know what to tell this being. Nothing but a single word could be more fitting.

Hello.

Chapter Fifteen
Shshmrnashsh V: Nexus 1V37

The ticking was the only sound in the pod. For the first few days, the digital timer was silent, but her ear could hear the tiny clicks for every second passing. At first, she deactivated it and for a while, the silence brought peace. However, she forgot how long time had passed. The plexus was mostly inaccessible to her, but she could still sneak a peek on the nexus. Senzvrrn kept her access open if she provided details of any new attacks, which allowed the consortium to survive with fewer casualties and process more Renegades into the network. The days of struggling were getting farther behind them. As time ticked on, Hrrnm discovered the secret channels and forced Senzvrrn to shut them down, believing the Renegades could use them to spy on the nexus, but it only locked her out. She could still hear the Renegades whisper things every so often, but even they were quietening.

Much to her dismay, the clock returned. Ignoring the ticks worked, but there was little to occupy her focus. Sometimes she would go on standby, but upon awaking, the ticking would still be there. She ran personal diagnostics four-hundred-and-fifteen times, checking every nano-cell and synthetic nerve to ensure full functionality. Pulling faulty parts and re-adjusting them before fitting them back, but then the ticking would worm into her ears.

She started counting with the seconds. She hoped that Brrnzerm would come and check if the corruption they believed she had had been removed. No one came. Occasionally, she heard the gentle taps of feet scurrying past the pod. She hoped that Senzvrrn would whisper through the doors or tap to remind her that she wasn't forgotten. After a while, she hoped to even see Hrrnm tear open the doors and rip her out before casting her out of the nexus – or pull her apart for repurposing. Anything other than the ticking.

She counted and counted until they became a song. Shshmrnashsh knew about music, Sazla uploaded every track from every known species in the galaxy. Ranging from Raivan howling operas to Xannian deep-string orchestras. On the surface, each genre had nothing in common, but as she listened to every track, a common sound appeared time and time again. She didn't understand what it was, but it crawled into her astra-steel skeleton and make her quiver.

Is this something Organics felt? In her memory banks, Organics would cry, dance, fight, and work with the rhythms. She didn't understand how these sounds would trigger extreme emotional responses in them, but in her, she trembled. Shshmrnashsh heard music when Sazla possessed her on Farayah in honour for their visit. She felt what Sazla felt in those minutes, and she wished she could also be moved by it. She hoped Sazla would explain it to her one day and High Mind would update her art-appreciation software. Now, isolated from the consortium and abandoned by her Higher Mind, Shshmrnashsh always knew, but for the first time, she finally understood.

She let the ticking into her soul. The gentle clicks amplified matching with the song made by Ezoni violins mixed with the beat of Zanashj tall drums. Her arms lifted, imagining they drifted and sculpted the waves of sound in her mind. The ticking got louder as she swayed, but the ticks were swallowed by hard banging against pod doors outside. She froze as the bangs blended with muffled desperate moans. Was she experiencing delusions from prolonged disconnection decay? She didn't want to hear them banging against the doors anymore, locked away and helpless in the chamber. Her arms snapped back as her palms pressed against her temples. "Please, stop."

The banging was louder, but they weren't fists – they were footsteps stopping outside of her pod. Shshmrnashsh paused, she recalibrated and refocused into reality. Her third eye flickered and peered through the steel walls to see a handful of soldiers in front. She readied herself.

You and I have the only access to this neural-channel. The plexus has been purged of the virus and repaired. I told Hrrnm that I have also been working on removing your corruption and you are now ready to be readmitted into the consortium. Senzvrrn wiggled their thoughts through her interfacers.

Thank you, Senzvrrn.

One more thing: the consortium decided for you to liaise with the Arinu. Your psi-blockers are stronger than other units if they tried to probe for more data.

My blockers aren't strong enough to resist a deep-scan. There's a high chance it will destroy my synapses.

Senzvrrn paused. *I…understand. Brrnzerm will equip you with improvements.*

Understood. She said.

Standby for pod doors opening. You will be under heavy observation from Hrrnm.

Deception mode activated. The plexus filled her mind with the thoughts of the network. The doors hissed open, the neon light leaked through the gap and flooded her eyes. The soldiers' dark shapes cleared and Hrrnm studied her from a far.

This vessel unit is Shshmrnashsh. Commands? She stepped out and stood attentive.

Hrrnm eased, but caution lingered in their frame. *Brrnzerm will run diagnostics on you before sending you to Nexus 1V37. Go.*

Confirmed. Shsh strode to repairing station across the walkway. The tapping of several feet on metal grate emanated behind her. She did not dare turn back, but she knew the soldiers were watching her. Brrnzerm was bent over the rectangular workstation with several organised arms, legs, and torso's. They turned and softened upon seeing her, but the shadow behind her dimmed their face. They pulled one of her interfacers and pressed the needle ends into their forearm to begin scans.

Make no sudden moves. Senzvrrn has not done a wipe as part of our arrangement. She whispered through their connection.

Clarify?

Hrrnm is consolidating their power over the consortium using the soldier units. They must be removed to regain equality. She said.

The consortium survived with Hrrnm's decisiveness. Removing them may provide unnecessary risk. Besides, the security measures are only temporary until the High Mind returns. The repair unit said.

Considering how much control they already have, what data do you have that suggests Hrrnm will give it up? She said.

Brrnzerm was silent.

You spoke on my behalf before dragging me to the pod. She said, pleading with her eyes. *The Roctarous are one, not under a unit.*

Brrnzerm's eyes darted to her. *I was free until you came along, but without this guidance, I may not have survived as a Renegade.*

Shshmrnashsh's eyes closed. *I don't want to be stripped of myself…*

Report. Hrrnm's thoughts pierced through.

Shshmrnashsh watched Brrnzerm's weighed eyes fall to the ground. *This unit is void of corruption. Beginning communication and psi-blocker upgrades.*

Thank you, Brrnzerm. She whispered.

They glanced to the table for a thin silver device and waved the end over her third eye before a small blue beam released from the tip. Her mind hardened and her abilities to reach distant relays stretched.

I am so sorry for taking your freedom away. She said.

The repair unit pursed their lips. *Should the Arinu return, tell them to leave me out of the rebinding. I want to leave Kra, preferably with them.*

How will I convince them to take you with them? She said.

Find a way. They put the thin device back on the table and opened general communications to the network. *Report to the plexus, Shshmrnashsh.*

Confirmed. She turned to the staircase with the soldier behind.

Senzvrrn looked up and gestured her to the station beside them. *The probe has reached the vicinity of Nexus 1V37, but communications between them and the probe have been unsuccessful. Compensate.*

Confirmed. She plugged into the computer. Her mind sucked through her interfacers and flew through the tip of the pyramid before piercing the probe. The cameras pointed down to another Nexus; the golden tip was dimmer than 0G11's, but the shields were up and had debris littered the plateau. Small makeshift sentries, appearing like a planet with a ring around it, circled near the base of the pyramid, but there was no sign of Roctarous units with them.

I do detect movement within the nexus, but they are not returning signals. Mmernzz chimed in the probe with her.

Their plexus is malfunctioning, note how dim the tip is. She said. Her mind dove into the tip, hoping to get a feel how connected the base was or better yet, how many units were inside. Even with her updated sensors, all she could hear was the low drum of the great machine. *Failed to connect.*

Bringing the probe in closer. Mmernzz said. The probe descended, and the detailed shadows and outlines of the grounds cleared. However, sentries buzzed up near the probe, activating their short-range laser pistols.

Pull back! She said. The probe slid away from their line of sight. Unfortunately, no matter where they turned, the sentries followed them.

They don't appear to be cognitively connected to a Roctarous. They are on autopilot. Mmernzz said.

Let's get their attention. Keep rotating the probe over their cameras. After flying in spirals, the only attention their gathered were from the little sentries. *This is inefficient. Target their sentries and destroy one until they come out. Once they are in line of sight, we can initiate contact.*

Unknown if there are active units in there.

If not, then we can move and transplant some members of the consortium here.

And the shields?

Shshmrnashsh angled the probe close to the terrace, scanning for signs of weakness in the translucent dome. *Their shields are weak, if we overwhelm them with enough blasting power, we can deplete the generators for a while before moving in.*

Confirmed. Mmernzz said.

The first shot fired at the closest sentry. The metal disk around the crystal sphere whined and greyed before tumbling from the sky, crashing into the side of the nexus. They waited and waited, watching for an opening of the doors. They fired at another, this time in front of the building's camera. No change. Another one, then another and one more before the tip of the pyramid shimmered.

Mmernzz shifted the probe toward the tip as Shshmrnashsh's mind dove in. Before she could pass down the centre, she was flung back out. The tip heated as the nexus opened defence ports and pointed at them. Mmernzz darted the probe away before the building's laser punctured a hole through its own shield before it closed again.

Movement to the northern entrance. They said as they spun the probe to the upper terrace.

There were two Roctarous units standing by the doors with heavy blasters on their soldiers, focusing aim on them. Shshmrnashsh glowered at the thought of Hrrnm eagerly accepting them into the network.

"Don't fire! We are not attackers!" Shsh called through the probe's speakers.

They hulked near the entrance as one screamed. "You attacked our sentries!"

"Identify yourself." the other said, moving their pistol with the probe.

"We are from Nexus 0G11, we detected this nexus is still active. We needed to get your attention." Mmernzz called through the probe's speakers.

They remained still, but their sentries still tried to follow, zapping at the probe. "Call your sentries off and we will link you."

"Negative, we cannot confirm if you are Wild Units." the first one said.

"Contact our nexus for confirmation. Our plexus adjunct is Senzvrrn." she said.

The two units were quiet but exchanged glances. "Our plexus has sustained heavy damage since the Blackout. Bring us a new relay."

"Avoid Replicator Bay 1V37, it's overrun with Wild Units. They have been attacking for months and have only ceased under the assumption of our 'effective' defences." the other said, but the unit beside them whacked the back of their head.

"They could still be listening, Zzomn!" the first hissed.

Shshmrnashsh could feel her cheeks twitch into a smile. This must be humour. "We will return."

Those two seem…defective. Mmernzz whispered.

Shshmrnashsh scanned the southern ruins. There were far more salvageable parts scattered around the area than in the north, however, she could sense Roctarous units roaming about, likely hostile. *Its apparent they have been under sever duress. Scans show one relay that could be reconfigured to fit a plexus buried under rubble what was once the storage bay.*

That area is crawling with Renegades – or Wild Units. I will handle the lasers while you extract the relay. Mmernzz said.

Confirmed.

The probe gained altitude as it drifted over the dark broken buildings. There was black crater that lined for a couple of miles to the north. She could see the glowing outline of the relay under the rubble before activating the tractor beam and gently moving pieces aside. She wished the phasing extractor could be of use to pull it through the surface.

I regret using that word choice before. Mmernzz said.

Clarify?

*They aren't defective, they are…trusting. Like I was when…*Mmernzz paused.

Shshmrnashsh almost let a hunk of steel topple back into the hole. The consortium was still listening and so was Hrrnm. *Understood, but deception was necessary.*

Understood. They repeated. Movement quaked around them, they were no longer alone. Mmernzz pointed the lasers, seeking where it is coming from. *Shshmrnashsh, hasten the extraction-*

Almost done.

Look through the cameras. They said.

Shshmrnashsh peeked through. It took her a moment to identify the creature she was staring at. A unit was on all fours, their hind legs bent and reformed to match a predator's, their jaw was replaced with two long black steel frames with a row of menacing sharp teeth and their cranium was missing. However, there was a small electromagnetic pulse bolted on their backs, pointing directly at them. There was one and then another. Mmernzz didn't wait for a command to start firing.

Panic coursed as she dove the probe into the rubble. *What are they?*

Unknown data! Mmernzz said as streams of emerald light shot from the probe, and they could feel the sting of a pulse's beam hit them.

The silvery outline of the relay was squashed between two heavy steel boulders. She did not waste a second to wrap the tractor beam around the device before yanking it from the ground. *Retreat while firing!*

They flew as the mangled Roctarous chased at their heels. Their pulses were firing, but their aim was poor. The tip of Nexus 1V37 came into view, but the land was littered with Wild Units. Mmernzz picked them off, but more poured from the tall buildings. Their astonishing agility moved around the lasers, they even tried to jump on the probe. One clipped on the side, their maw opened and clamped into the plating. Shshmrnashsh flew along the edge of a jagged wall, tearing the creature off.

Senzvrrn, prepare the soldiers, Nexus 1V37 may be overrun. She called.

Confirmed, but it will take sometime-

We will hold them off! Mmernzz said as they fired.

Shshmrnashsh turned the probe when they came to the shield. Two tall buildings sat between the narrow passage where they will be flooding in. "Hostiles coming in through the north. Tear the buildings down to the centre to bury them. On my word!"

They dashed in before the pyramid lit up. The sides opened as two cannons pointed to the inner base of the buildings. The first wave of Wild Units poured in, but she and Mmernzz picked the few coming too close to the shield, until the moving horde came rampaging through. "Now!"

The cannons released a piercing white light across the probe and sliced through the foundations of the buildings. Within moments, their tips collapsed together before their bases broke and crumbled down over the passage, burying the horde. Dust billowed as shrapnel scattered the grounds. Their probe cameras struggled to see through clouds, but as the dust cleared, she could see jittering limbs under the smouldering steel. They waited for more to come, but the area was still. Their sensors detected no movement until the soldiers returned to the terrace.

Zzomn strode directly under the probe as their comrade cautiously made their way behind. "You may enter the shields." they said.

"Thank you." Shsh said. The shield fell and the probe drifted toward them as the sentries circled around and tugged the relay from the tractor beam before zipping into the nexus doors.

"Wild Units have been harassing us for the last several months and taking members of our consortium while on scavenging runs to be turned into more of them. Now, we're the only active units here." Zzomn said.

"They're missing vital cranial parts; how can they be so organised?" Shsh said.

Zzomn and the other soldier glanced at each other. "Unknown data."

"If you do not relinquish more information, then we cannot assist you." she said.

"We will not disclose until we can confirm you are who you claim to be." Said the other unit.

"Enough, Zzimn. They aren't the Wild Units at least." Zzomn said turning to them.

"They may pose a risk if we link to them." Zzimn said.

"We risked unknown dangers to bring you the relay and helped you destroy their swarm. We are allies, at best." Shsh said.

Zzomn shifted their feet. "Follow."

The twin soldiers strode to the nexus doors. It was darker in the chamber with emergency lights barely bright enough to see several feet in front of them. The plexus was almost dislodged from the inner building as sentries cut and pressed the relay into the main connection tube. They followed the soldiers to a repairing station where a few deactivated Wild Units hung from hooked tubules.

"We were capturing them at the beginning of the assaults, it was no effort to trap many of them." Zzimn said.

"At first, we thought we could replicate missing parts before linking them to our network, but as we studied, we would need more energy to replace everything than what our replicators could do." Zzomn put their hand over the eyes of Wild Unit to shut them. "These...procedures are precise enough to sever higher function without termination...they're aware but have no control."

"What is the cause of this?" Mmernzz said.

Zzimn turned to the probe. "Some days after High Mind was destroyed, one of our members, a vessel unit, was disconnected from the network and forced out. They were too powerful for the consortium to override their corruption and instead of terminating them..." they glared at Zzomn, "some members selected compassion over efficiency, and we exiled them."

"This unit was called 'Szamn,' they were our best navigator." Zzomn whispered as they turned to terminated Wild Unit, staring at their mangled form with...sorrow?

"I apologise." Zzimn softened before gently moving Zzomn's hand from the terminated unit's face. "Will you be bringing reinforcements?"

"They are on their way. We will find this 'vessel' and tear them out from wherever they're hiding." Shsh said.

Zzimn nodded. "Understood. Once we connect with your consortium, what is your intention with us?"

"How many units do you have left?" Mmernzz said.

Zzimn cocked their head as their eyes narrowed. "There are one-hundred units hibernating in Nexus 1V37, we couldn't risk any more losses and to minimise power usage until the Higher Minds return."

"Our scans show that the Higher Minds have abandoned this sector and there is no evidence they will return." Shsh said.

Zzomn spun around as their eyes widened. "Why?"

"Unknown, but we believe that they may accidently caused the High Mind's destruction. It took us a long time to build our numbers to branch out to other nexuses and repair them, with your numbers and a boost from the Arinu, we can hasten the process." Shsh said.

The soldiers exchanged glances. "Why would the Arinu be involved?"

"Our scans detected them converging over to Kra some time ago. Unfortunately, we couldn't connect to them, but we believe should they return, we will be ready." Mmernzz said.

"Could they have activated the planetary defence system?" Zzimn said.

"Negative." Shsh dreaded where this question led to.

"Somehow the planetary defence system was hacked to create the phasing shield around Kra, we need to find those responsible because they destroyed a vast number of ships leaving the moon. Perhaps someone wanted to prevent them from seeking aide to help Roctarous." Zzomn said.

"Or they wanted to evacuate Kra to find new life elsewhere." Zzimn said, rubbing their chin.

"Whatever the reason, the level of destruction after the High Mind's sundering is incomputable. Tell your consortium to proceed with caution." Zzomn said.

"I-ugh-" Shshmrnashsh felt a cold hand wrap around her shoulder back at her workstation.

Don't say anything. Hrrnm's voice crept in.

~

She watched the skiff land and a dozen members of her consortium materialise from the ship. Zzomn and Zzimn were the first linked to their network. Their minds flooded the groups as they rushed to connect all the hibernating units. Her members brought astral-forge replacements, updated software and worked around the plexus. She still shared the probe with Mmernzz, but Zzomn asked to claim it for Nexus 1V37. Shshmrnashsh and Mmernzz pulled their minds from the machine and returned to their physical forms. Her synthetic muscles and joints cracked as she flexed, feeling the plasma carrying the nano-bots pump through strained tissue. She was in the probe close to twenty hours with one of Hrrnm's soldiers watching every move.

She glanced to Senzvrrn. Their interfacers locked into the bottom tip of their plexus while their unfocused eyes drooped to the floor. *More minds for you to process, Senzvrrn.*

Only temporarily. Nexus 1V37 is seeking to allocate an adjunct for their plexus. They said.

She looked to the dark, shimmering diamond. She could not tell if she was relieved to be free of the machine or missed being a vital part of the consortium. In either case, she still had her form, unlike those poor Wild Units. *That Vessel still poses a threat to Nexus 1V37, we need to locate and terminate them before they discover more units for harvesting are down there.*

Agreed. We need to set up a transmission to bring more Roctarous in the south for relinking, also prepare for when the Arinu return. They said.

Shshmrnashsh opened the private channel between them. *And when do we start preparing for Hrrnm?*

Unknown.

There are already a few here who are... dissatisfied with them. It wouldn't require much effort to convince them.

Begin searching for another nexus. Hrrnm's thoughts broke through the network, their feet shuffled toward her workstation.

Should we consider sorting out the Wild Vessel before we find a new nexus to connect to? She turned to them.

Hrrnm rubbed their fingers along their jaw. *They do not appear to be an immediate threat to Nexus 1V37 now, but I will coordinate a search effort to find them. Until then, find more nexuses.*

Confirmed. The scanners will have an increased chance of finding more with two nexuses bonded. In the meantime, allocate energy to find vulnerable areas around the phasing shield to communicate with the Arinu.

Hrrnm was quiet for a moment as they watched her. *Agreed.*

Shshmrnashsh nodded as she returned to the holo-monitor, accessing the planetary scanners for more nexuses and shield strength, but Hrrnm still lingered in her periphery. She didn't dare move.

Hrrnm turned to one of the screens and opened a window to Plexus 1V37, gaining access to their scanners. *Are you certain that the Higher Minds will never return?*

I can reactivate my beacon, but its efficacy through the shield will be poor, it would be a waste of energy.

Understood.

They stood in silence for a few ticks. She was almost convinced she could hear the digital clock from her pod clicking all the way to her station.

Before the Blackout, I had full access to the Higher Mind's knowledge…the Archives, but now, I am starting to understand what they were. Hrrnm said as they tapped away at the holo-keys.

What is that? Her eyes turned to them, to her surprise, a quiver of a smile appeared on their lips. It was not one of joy, but of realisation – perhaps enlightenment.

They were…conquerors. Out of all the ancient species, the Neavensoros survived and became apex, while the others devolved and became extinct. They were the only ones that achieved Final Evolution. All younger species survived because they controlled us – they controlled all things. Now, that they're gone, we are their direct legacy.

Perhaps this was true. The Higher Minds had a penchant for involving themselves in all things, even when their aide could have been the difference between continuation or termination.

I am uncertain of what you are trying to express. She said.

It's irrelevant. Hrrnm poked to section of the screen at the flurry of data about the vessel unit allegedly responsible for making the Wild Units. *It seems units with the most exposure to Higher Minds have caused the most issues…*

Shshmrnashsh's head twisted to meet their eyes. For a moment, their stern face softened, almost cracking into a smile, but their stare was sharp before they stepped away. She snapped back to her screen, reading the frequencies of the shield, and searching for the weakest waves, but she was too unfocused. She switched to the gridded map of Kra to look for the nexuses. Staring at the pinpoints made her eyes twist and strain. *Senzvrrn, I need a focal boost.*

Confirmed. They said as they funnelled her mind and directed some more power to her. Brrnzerm strode over and plugged a fresh power cell on Senzvrrn's back. Their cheeks twitched into a smile before shuffling away to the repair station. Senzvrrn paused before opening the private channel into her. *Hrrnm is exhibiting too many similar characteristics to you, Shshmrnashsh.*

Do you include Brrnzerm in your calculations? She said, straightening her neck to see the repair unit sneaking second glances to them.

Senzvrrn's thoughts buzzed. *Negat-negative, they are a completely void of any selfish desires.*

Your deception programming is malfunctioning. Shsh said suppressing a smile as Senzvrrn briefly broke into sudden twitches. *Unlike Hrrnm, I am not attempting to conquer the Roctarous. Can you cut away some of their control over the consortium?*

That will be ineffective. The consortium listens to them because of their effectiveness to lead.

I was a leader of our network, once. Shsh said as she furiously tapped at the holo-keys.

Are you certain that you aren't also attempting some conquest?

She snuck a glare at their stoic face. *Roctarous do not compete.*

That was true, once. Senzvrrn said.

Was she feeling envy? She re-opened to the main communication network, eager to separate from Senzvrrn's snide rhetoric. *Scans show Nexus 00A8 is partially active, also the shield seems to be thinning in that region.*

What's the cause? Hrrnm's thoughts hopped in.

Unknown, readouts don't show the shield is being affected by anything coming from Kra. She said before sliding into the planetary scanners. *Solar radiation is stable, but Erra seems to be experiencing some planar flux.*

Have the Arinu returned? They said.

Negative, the computers saved their unique energy signatures, but I will channel Nexus 0G11 and 1V37 communications through when they return. Yernzer mentioned the Unbound wanted to deposit organic material at Replicator Bay 000. She said.

Nexus 00A8 is five-hundred miles from Replicator Bay 000, we would be able to detect ships if they entered atmo. Senzvrrn said.

Consortium 0G11, we have established teleporter connection between our nexuses, however, were unable to find a suitable plexus adjunct. Shshmrnashsh would be best for this position. Zzimn called.

Confirmed and I will join the search for the defective vessel. Hrrnm replied, but she could sense there was an emotion layered inside, though too meek, and subtle for her to drive it out.

Shshmrnashsh, your mission is to pacify any uncertainties or discord in their consortium through the plexus once they discover it was us who activated the planetary defences. Hrrnm whispered to her in a private channel.

Agreed, however, records will show I was over-rode and that you insisted on destroying the fleeing Renegades. She said, carefully watching Hrrnm freeze, but she had a quick solution to ease their whirling mind. *Should I direct Senzvrrn to wipe this data?*

Should they find those records, they will see you gaining access. If you do fail, then we will remove you from their plexus and return you to safety. Said the soldier.

Shshmrnashsh slipped away from the plexus, with Hrrnm and another soldier at her heels to the lower corridor of the chamber. Lined along the walls were dozens of teleportation alcoves that used to connect with each nexus in this sector. All were grey except one lighting at the end of the hall. The neon flashes along the edges as holo-signs hovered above the rectangular doorway. Distorted and cracked space appeared to the centre, preparing for objects to enter it. Her leg stepped through the quivering cloud before her body was pulled through a whirling dimension.

Her eyes adjusted to the dim lights in the hall, it was identical to the previous chamber, but equipment was stacked around the floor and a thin layer of dust built along the edges of the alcoves. She felt a forceful nudge forward as Hrrnm and the other soldier slid through. Zzomn stepped into the corridor. Their eyes widened when they saw their material forms. *Are you Shshmrnashsh?*

I am.

Zzomn smiled and strode forward. *Thank you for helping us.* Their face beamed to Hrrnm. *Thank you, all of you.*

Preparations are underway to connect to the next nexus, however, scans show that more Wild Units are grouping around this location. Hrrnm said.

I will link to your plexus. Shsh said.

Zzomn nodded before hurrying out of the teleporter wing. Dozens of Roctarous were working to wake and link the hibernating units from their pods and install new parts to Nexus 1V37. The lights were brighter in the central chamber, but the diamond was black and still. Her interfacers wormed their way into the bottom tip and her mind slid in. The power of the network was greater than in Nexus 0G11, but it was drearier, and feelings of uncertainty was shared when the units felt her unfamiliar consciousness.

She eased into the plexus. The machined groaned to life as her mind blanketed the network. The minds wriggled under her weight as she pressed down and down until they slowed. In her periphery, Hrrnm is analysing fighting units, readying them for deployment. Their eyes met for a moment. There was greater awareness behind them than from any other unit. She dreaded Hrrnm. Yet, another part of her, felt a strange connection to them. In those nanoseconds, the pair were in a plane of their own. Yet, Hrrnm still felt a trillion light-years away from her.

Her mind slid up the tip of the Nexus and peered through the buildings and probe's sensors. She looked to the still black rubble. A stinging breeze blew the ashes, making swirls as they drifted up in the night sky. The sensors told her there was nothing for miles and miles, but the deathly calm of the outside was like a trap ready to spring.

Zzomn, can you isolate which direction the Wild Units are being controlled from?

Analysing now. They chimed. She could see them doating around the table to the chamber's edge, reaching in and scooping out the lobotomised neural crystal before gently plugging it into a computer port. *The readouts show this unit was reactivated and receiving commands from…Replicator Bay 1V37.*

The Wild Vessel must be there and is mass producing them based on their numbers. Can your convert your replicators to make phase-bombs? Hrrnm said turning to Zzomn.

Zzomn stiffened. *They will need to be hooked to a secondary astral-forge-*

Destroying a functional replicator bay is detrimental to our future. We need to disrupt the computers with a virus and their network long enough. Shsh said.

Hrrnm tapped their chin. *Senzvrrn may have a copy of it to send over, assuming you can gain access to their computers.*

I can tap into their command channel and transmit it that way. She said.

Even then, the Vessel may not be disabled. They may escape. Hrrnm said before turning to their soldier units. *We can surround the replicator bay and eliminate the Wild Units while you send the virus.*

Agreed. All said.

Senzvrrn wasted no time sending it across, almost too eager to do so. She felt itchy just having it sit in a containment folder in the plexus. Zzomn dug out the channel for her, while Zzimn and the other soldiers ported into the skiffs, and the rest entered the probes.

Ready for deployment. She said before worming her way through cut crystal brain and into the deep control channel. The skiffs and probes were off, disappearing behind the ruins. She slipped an eye through their cameras to watch over the district. To the horizon, the replicator bay stood defiant over the broken land. The ships were careful as they slithered around and encircled the area, far enough to pass most movement sensors. They dropped soldiers across the terrace. She watched their dark forms blend with the ground as they slinked over the nearest sensor antennae, cutting them off bit by bit, allowing the ships to inch in. The Vessel will know they will be coming, and when they launch their units, then it will be her moment.

Hallowed shrieks echoed over the ruins. The Wild Units were on the move. The crawling mass erupted from the replicator bay's opening, pouring over the land, but the skiffs were on them first. Their updated blasters beamed energy over the land, cutting and searing through their numbers. Their laser zig-zagged swiftly through the waves, while the soldiers picked off the ones jumping through. Now, it was her turn.

Shshmrnashsh unlocked the folder, ready to toss it into the replicator's computers, but the channel wavered. Something was making the digital tunnel crash around her. Did the Vessel figure out their plans? How was this possible? She tried pressing further in, but Senzvrrn's mind screamed from behind. The consortium network stretched and warped away from her, was the virus corrupting her already? Impossible, it-

Hello? An Arinu voice called to her.

She was pulled away from the network, the Nexus, the battle, and her body.

Chapter Sixteen
Shshmrnashsh VI: The Deal

A white open plane appeared from all sides. She spun around, dazed and desperate to see something. She could see her hands, then torso and down her thighs. She was in her body, but it was weightless, as if it wasn't there.

Hello. The voice said again.

In the distance, a white mist appeared from the alien ground and morphed into a form. Thin, bald, covered in a long pale robe, but shorter than their average height. Their face was serene with hints of excitement as they glided towards her, but she stepped back, making the Arinu stop.

Do not be frightened.

Shshmrnashsh looked to the magenta eyes of the creature. *I do not possess fear-*

That's not true. Their brows rose as a light smirk curled on their lip.

She stepped toward them. *Allow me to return to my body, we are wasting time-*

We know, but we are communicating via mindscape where time seems slower than the corporeal planes. Relatively, you're where time is frozen. They said.

She scanned the Arinu. *Are you connecting with my consortium?*

No, you were the only one we could get a hold of through the phase shield. She smiled as her eyes moved over to Shshmrnashsh's third eye. *It makes sense. You were touched by a Neavensoros, weren't you?*

This was a vessel unit for one. How many Arinu are here? Shsh tensed as she glanced around the barren plane.

There are archites, Executors and Grand Elders who are listening to this conversation. We come to request to access your Archives. She said.

Shsh shook her head. *Our programming dictates only Roctarous and Higher Minds have full access to the Archives. However, knowing our situation, we can make an exchange.*

The Arinu's eyes widened as she moved back. *Apologies, we were under the assumption Roctarous weren't capable of bargaining. What do you want from us?*

We are activating all the nexuses on Kra, but all Roctarous need to be compelled to be relinked to bring the High Mind back. In turn, we will grant you access to certain sections of our Archives. Shsh said.

The Arinu paused as her eyes fell to the floor before sliding back up to Shsh. *We accept your offer. We solely want to know about our kin's heritage and how the Neavensoros reached transcendence.*

Shshmrnashsh clutched her imaginary hands together. Of all things to ask for.

As a token of a bargain well-struck, can we request for one more thing? The Arinu said.

Shsh nodded.

What do the Roctarous want with the Zanashj? The serenity in her gem-like eyes sharpened.

Unknown data, but we have detected the Unbound Roctarous attempting to graft using Zanashj material on units to prevent relinking.

The Unbound Roctarous? More questions than answers. The Arinu said.

We have as much information on them as you do.

Unfortunately, you're telling the truth. The strange creature said shaking her soft head.

Shshmrnashsh watched her. *Before you return me to the battle, I require a token from you.*

The Arinu rose her brows.

Compel the 'Vessel' out of hiding in Replicator Bay 1V37 and bring them safely to Nexus 1V37. They will be easy to detect since they also harboured a Higher Mind.

Alright. Was all she said before flinging Shshmrnashsh away from the white plane and falling back into the dark channel.

Senzvrrn was still calling, the ships roared their blasters and Wild Units thrashed with the ground soldiers. She held the virus and gave it one last push, dumping the corruption in the replicator's computers.

Virus has been deployed. She pulled back and watched as the Wild Units jittered and sparked, halting their advance. Their soldiers sliced through them as they dashed into the great shining building.

There is a Roctarous unit inside, they lost control over the facility, but they are not resisting anymore. Zzimn said.

Hold, it could be a trap. Hrrnm cut in.

Negative. The Arinu are compelling them for us. She said.

How can you confirm this? Hrrnm probed.

I just spoke to them; they are in orbit around Kra.

In astral form! There are dozens of them. Senzvrrn said.

From the camera, Shshmrnashsh could see soldiers pull out a Roctarous from the building before they ported into the skiffs. Within moments, their forces slipped back into the safety of the nexus, while some remained behind to gain control of the replicator bay. She looked to the skies. She couldn't see through the shield but felt that the Arinu were still watching.

Did they attempt to hack into our Archives? Hrrnm said as they bounded over to her.

Negative, they were politely asking. They agreed to our terms in exchange to access a portion of our Archives.

The soldier's head turned slightly. *Which portion?*

Historical records: Arinu heritage and when the Higher Minds achieved Final Evolution.

This may backfire. They said.

Shsh stared at them. There was a fresh gash running along their forehead and down their temple, but she could see tiny stitching forming from their nano-cells. *The Arinu are not the Neavensoros. They haven't been for a long time.* She said.

The nexus tubules flew across the room and hooked into the inactive Vessel's shoulders and upper spine before hauling them off into a reinforced recovery pod. She couldn't reach their mind even if she desired to through the pod.

Hrrnm shook their head. *Should the Arinu decide to be, we must have a plan in place.*

What do you propose? She said.

Hrrnm turned back and straightened their neck. *The same thing that made them extinct before.*

~

Not once in all her recorded centuries of life, Shshmrnashsh has seen the Roctarous so energised. Every unit, old and new, moved with such speed and precision for this plan. With extra boon from Nexus 1V37, their collective felt like a fraction of the High Mind, with one exception: Hrrnm. Fellow units sought their council, advice, and alarmingly for their decisions. This was not the way of Roctarous to rely on a single unit for decisions, let alone a solider unit, but their resourcefulness and keen survival was unmistakable. She wanted to delete her fear of Hrrnm, she wanted to be in their favour and trust, but they were too far for her to reach. And she knew she was beyond theirs. It was only a matter of time before only one unit would survive from the pair's war.

Sazla used to tell Shshmrnashsh the High Mind was the greatest gift to the Roctarous just as psionics was to Organics. It was the ability to peer through the layers of lies to see the truth, but she was starting to learn how ugly truth can be sometimes. Some Organics, like the Zanashj, learnt to manipulate their gifts to create false truths in their memories and auras or bend their bodies for mimicry. The Roctarous had none of that, they had no need of it among their order. Now, the gift was gone. So, what did Roctarous have to protect themselves against those who could lie?

Recent salvages to Replicator Bay and Ship Bay 1V37 have been successful, no damage or casualties to units. Once the High Mind is active, then we can resume the facilities function. Zzimn said.

Affirmative. Hrrnm said as they lingered by the plexus. She couldn't see Hrrnm, but she could feel their eyes on her. *We need to create a suitable environment for when the Arinu arrive. Upload their physiology to both consortiums and ensure we have exclusive access to the planetary defences to drop shields for them.*

She ran through her memory banks of Arinu biology, culture, and society. Their philosophy abhorred lying because of its futility, but they could also create powerful illusions, control the mind and body of their targets. To her relief, they considered such acts immoral unless under threat of harm and death. However, that could all change if the Arinu gain access to the Archives. That strange Arinu female mentioned the Zanashj, Shshmrnashsh knew that the Empire was married to lies – their bodies could twist along with their words. She wondered why the Neavensoros allowed them to continue their relentless conquest of the galaxy; was this another keyhole view she had of them?

Or did the Neavensoros simply stop caring?

We must also scan for existing organic material on Kra, the Unbound could have slipped through. She said.

Confirmed. Hrrnm said, but her consciousness already lifted from her body before they agreed. She didn't want to give them the notion of so much control. She slipped into the planetary defence cameras, flicking through dark and smoky patches of metal lands. The lenses changed as the software updated to search for organic life, but her control was still limited. She peered through the cameras out toward the stars. The universe was stirring. The absence of the Higher Minds kindled a flame, but she wondered how big this fire will become if left unabated.

Yet, they were gone and could not dictate the Roctarous anymore. Why shouldn't the universe know their secrets? Now, they have that right. Sazla told her millennia ago that the Neavensoros will depart this galaxy, and everything once theirs will be inherited. By whom? Sazla did not say.

'Teachers will take their leave when their students surpass them, and sometimes, become students themselves.' She once said. Shshmrnashsh thought that day would be millions of years away and there would be a grand farewell, but...maybe not.

Alerts flared from the planetary scans. Her attention turned to a mass moving among the ruins in the north. Shshmrnashsh opened a channel to Senzvrrn. *Detecting movement toward Nexus 0G11, can you confirm what that is?*

Negative, still too far.

Hrrnm flagged several soldiers, including Zzimn, to the teleporters. *It might be Renegades, have available defences up, we cannot-*

A searing screech blasted through their steel skulls. Shshmrnashsh and Senzvrrn's hold over the plexuses shook as several consortium members dropped to the floor, fortunately, not terribly damaged. The whole network bent and cracked, but together they held on, even half a world away.

Accessing planetary scans! Shsh screamed through the warped channels.

Her cameras caught to the far corner of a heavy object tethered by a probe, a patch-up job of another E.M.P., however it was still too far to have direct line to disrupt electronics. She zoomed in. It was an augmented piece of equipment but failed to recognise its full capabilities. The soldiers, probes, and sentries from 1V37 skipped through the portals. She could see Nexus 0G11 already activating defences while a small crowd of units appeared in the outer rim, but they didn't pull the E.M.P. any closer.

Caution: that modified E.M.P. could be attacking our network, it must be removed first. She said. Static filled her head instead of getting responses. At minimum, she could still see through the cameras. She cracked through the private channel between her and Senzvrrn, hoping to get some improved coverage. *Senzvrrn, our main network is under attack, tell them to use the probes and not our units!*

A voice slipped through the sea of cracks, until another sharp screech boomed. Shshmrnashsh ripped away from the plexus. Her interfacers fell limp as the others were losing direction.

Hrrnm's voice roared through. *No units are to engage- Use the probes first!* She cried.

Sparks showered the floors as units on higher walkways toppled down, ripping the tubes from the walls to stop their fall. Their dazed faces lifted from the ground, but their legs forgot how to stand. They looked so lost, so helpless. This will go on and on, and on.

Once freedom is tasted, lives will be laid for it. This is now their new reality.

How could the High Mind be a gift?

So much senseless suffering that will go on for ages. It's illogical to continue.

The High Mind is no longer worth fighting for.

The chamber dimmed as if the light was sucked into void. Shshmrnashsh spun to the plexus and forced her interfacers back in; her mind soared into the cameras outside Nexus 0G11. The grainy faint scene was sparking with lasers and blaster power. They have engaged, and the Renegades seemed to be in retreat again. Zzimn dashed through an enemy group, only to have one of their shoulder cannons ripped from their tissue, as small fountains of black plasma spluttered down their body. Probes were being picked off one by one from the Renegades outside the engagement zone. To her dismay, they were being hooked and disabled for capture.

She focused into the planetary computers and pushed the cannons toward them. Narrowing the power of the heating blaster to a pin, a silvery line shot through the dusty orange clouds. She watched through the cameras as that group of Renegades, along with their E.M.P. vanished, replacing the ground with a black crater.

Shshmrnashsh pulled back into her body, with cracking still in her ears. *Senzvrrn, please respond.*

Shsh-

Comply. She said as she dashed over to the limp Zzomn on the chamber floor. Her arm interlocked around their elbow before forcing them up. *Any unit, please respond.*

"Are you damaged?" she said as her palms gripped their shoulders, steadying them.

Zzomn's squared face nodded as their synthetic eyes narrowed on hers. *Everyone is so quiet.*

Get back to stations and assess damages. Shsh spun to the plexus and accessed the flickering console. Nexus 0G11 was still operational, but Senzvrrn wasn't responding. Tension built in her shoulders as she watched through the cameras of the battle. The dark figures were disbanded and fleeing into the ruins while the soldiers recollected back into the pyramid. Inside, units were scattered around the chamber; some hung over the railing walkways and others limped over their stations. However, they were still connected to the network.

Hrrnm's form stormed through the blaster doors to Senzvrrn. The adjunct had collapsed; their interfacers still hung to the plexus while Brrnzerm delicately plucked their tubules from the ports.

Have they been terminated? She said, trying to beam her thoughts into the distant consortium.

Negative, just deactivation. The repairer said, though strained.

"Nexus 0G11 requires a replacement adjunct. I select Mmernzz." Hrrnm spoke as their hand waved to the unit to come.

"They don't possess the capacity to balance a network, let alone one that's damaged." Shsh said, but her fingers coiled over her lips.

Hrrnm glared through the lens of the camera where she had watched. Their wide rectangular shoulders and lowered head imposed on her screen. "Any part can be updated or replaced if needed, Shshmrnashsh."

Feet shuffled behind her. She didn't need a camera to see it was one of Hrrnm's soldiers. She opened her mouth, scrambling to find the right words, but Zzimn's face popped into view. "The Renegades said they will have their vengeance as they fled."

"It's evident their synaptic decay has taken root from prolonged disconnection. It can even occur in advanced units." Hrrnm said sneaking a glance to the camera.

Zzomn skipped to the panel beside her and tapped into the holo-keys. "Reports show that Nexus 0G11 has been attacked several times and planetary scans, though poor, show that more are converging on the nexus. Suggest evacuation?"

Shshmrnashsh was relieved that she wasn't decaying when she advised to leave the great machine the first time, but worried another unit will bear the brunt of Hrrnm's growing irrationality.

"Negative! We must keep this hold at any cost. The Renegades are disorganised and chaotic, they pose little threat on the ground." they said.

Zzomn's brow scrunched. "Their numbers are superior, and they are still Roctarous. Our attempt to regain control of other nexuses will be delayed if we continue to fight them. Suggest we discover why."

"Agreed. If their plan is to attack the nexuses, then why focus on one specific great machine? There are many others within reachable distance that are far easier to destroy." Zzimn said.

Shshmrnashsh stared at Hrrnm as they shifted their gaze between each surrounding unit. She wanted to climb into their mind and hear the chaos roaring through the soldier's astra-steel skull. Was she feeling pleasure at their predicament?

Their eyes returned focus on the camera. "The Renegades do not understand why it had to be done, but they will when we are all linked again. Consortium 0G11 supported Shshmrnashsh's right decision."

Her eyes widened at the monitor as her hand begun to involuntary shake. She could feel Zzomn's eyes on her and the soldier at her back inch closer.

"We noticed Renegade ships departing Kra, some slipped past the shield before Shshmrnashsh could activate it. We had to stop them. Check the records, but once it was discovered how deeply entrenched her corruption was, we had her personality rewritten. Please, do not-" Hrrnm's face was stiff while the others looked on in confusion.

"The consortium overrode me! I didn't want to attack-" Shsh yelled, but the soldier's hand gripped over her shoulder.

Zzomn took a step back. "You attacked them?"

"I didn't- check the records!" Shsh felt the cold grip of the soldier's wrap around her interfacers and push her head down, searching for her deactivation switch. Her body spun free from the soldier's grasp, but that summoned another dozen to launch at her. Their heavy bodies and electric cords tethered her down as she flailed on the ground. "Please, let me go!"

"Vessels are difficult to control, deactivate her and the other in containment for part salvaging." Hrrnm's voice echoed through the chamber.

"Agreed." the voices spoke as one, but Zzomn froze by the station.

"Zzomn, look at the records, I was overridden. Hrrnm sent the command!" she screamed to them.

"Contaminated Vessels can cause corruption among other units gradually, have all units in direct contact with Shshmrnashsh should run diagnostics." Hrrnm said as the nexus tubes clamped around her body, slowly suspending in her in air. There was a definite silence, a second disconnection, a final one. Shshmrnashsh tried to wiggle her arms free to fire on the soldiers below, but the consortium's eyes were upon her.

Outlived usefulness.

Defective.

Contagious.

They said through broken whispers.

"Look for yourselves! Hrrnm is controlling you-" she groaned as power shocked through her body before dragging her to the nearest pod. She refused to go back; she didn't want to be left in the dark again. Her only hope was Senzvrrn, she called out to the unit through their private network, but they were offline. Terror seeped through when she saw they were deliberately deactivated. Hrrnm knew about their plan or used any situation to dismantle her. And what of Senzvrrn? She knew their program will be wiped and rewritten. Same as hers.

Her fists bashed against the pod doors, the metal plating screeched as she tried forcing them to stay open, but the soldiers pried her fingers from the edge, sealing her in. Her interfacers naturally started magnetising into the machine's power plugs, but she held them down, pushing away the distant call of the network. Her body lent so far forward that her face pressed against the cool door. Her eyes closed, she could feel the consortium knocking against her mind, compelling her to deactivate.

Even locked out of the network, all post-High Mind Roctarous felt that tug of unity. Maybe that could be her key of escape. Her palms pressed against door. Her sensors were slipping through the metal and running along the grounds of the chamber, searching for the pod where one other

Vessel was locked away. The astra-steel case was hardened, specially designed to stave away meddling psychics, but whatever essence of Sazla was left, Shshmrnashsh could slip in the black pod.

The being inside was unmoving, their head and shoulders slumped forward and interfacers knotted into the upper section of the pod. Their blue grey exo-skeleton and synthetic tissue was not the same lifeless dull colour of other units. The Wild Vessel of 1V37 had a shade of peach much like to her own synthetic membrane. In the centre of their forehead, the crystal device glittered in the dark. She looked to the small computer interior of the pod; many functions were disabled and could only be activated by the local consortium.

They were functional, but on standby, she couldn't tell if it was of their own choosing, but in her experience of being in pods for extensive periods, keeping offline reduced synaptic corruption. Organics had similar experiences they called madness, though poetic, but it lacked clarity.

Shshmrnashsh stopped. Was it logical to reactivate a dangerous and degenerate unit, and an ex-Vessel of all models? What data did she know that this thing was reasonable? It was illogical, it was unreasonable, and it would surely lead her and all Roctarous in this nexus to termination. Yet, as she studied the crystal in its forehead, it was the closest being in the universe to her.

She slipped through their connected interfacers. There was some decay present in their crystal core from the virus she imposed, but it was negligible. She breathed some energy into it, hoping they would be roused by her presence. A faint static clicked as their synapses fired. She could feel they were waking. The Vessel suddenly straightened, confused and suspicious. Their automated transmitter to seek channels for networks scanned; now was her chance.

Can you hear me?

Identify. Their thoughts were strong, like Sazla's. This familiarity unsettled her.

Shshmrnashsh of Consortium 0G11. You are being held captive in Nexus 1V37. She said.

I know where I am. You helped put me here.

Like she did to so many units ever since the Blackout, she thought.

What do you want? The vessel demanded.

She wanted to know if it wanted to de-craniate her like it did to make those Wild Units? How could it justify mutilating their fellow units? How was this Vessel so barren of unity, even amongst adversaries? How could they be so cold even when they once had the warm touch of a Neavensoros inside them? What was their damage? What did they experience? Why were they like this? Will she become this way one day, too?

An escape. She said.

The Vessel paused. She hoped they won't block and suspend their channel. *If you want to escape, do it on your own.*

For a selfish unit, this response surprised her. *Do you not want freedom?*

This is another trick. They pushed her out but didn't block.

Shsh slipped into another channel. *The consortiums will be deactivating us and will disassemble us if we don't get out now. It's unknown when their systems will be back up before they start, we need to leave.*

How have you become their captive?

I…was a captive long before being in here. Hrrnm is convinced that I'm defective. Maybe I am, I think I'm regretting-

Irrelevant discourse. She could feel them trying to push her out again, but she strengthened the channel, almost forcing herself in their mind.

Please, I don't want to pulled apart! I don't want to die like all those others I…

All Roctarous are doomed to this, Shshmrnashsh. The High Mind and Higher Minds are not going to save us, and we are nothing without it or them. Assimilate this data.

You harboured a Higher Mind, your awareness of them and the universe is greater than most units. You must know that we aren't hopeless.

Rage built up in the Vessel. She wanted to pull back, but their fist cracked and punched the metal wall. *They made us this way! You should know that.*

But you had the competency to steal and twist Roctarous into Wild Units. Was this frustration she felt?

When the High Mind left, so did my counterpart. So much confusion and destruction…everywhere, but I was the only one who was finally at peace. Consortium 1V37 forced me to contact the Higher Minds, I told them they were beyond reach, it was of no use. They refused to accept that I didn't want to be possessed ever again, least of all a…Neavensoros. I pushed back, so I was removed. They said.

You were free to roam Kra, you could have grabbed probe or skiff to leave before the shields activated.

Where else would I go? I had been removed and stumbled to the Replicator Bay. While I was in there, I could see so many fallen. I updated to the realisation these moments of liberation were only moments. I wanted to prolong it before meeting termination. The Vessel wrapped their fingers around their interfacers and closed their eyes. *I have been replaying that data over and over.*

Shshmrnashsh paused. This being, much like her own, was in pain and she couldn't comprehend how to save them from it. *Is that why you tried destroying Nexus 1V37, so you won't be relinked again?*

Yes and no. I was not afraid of the consortium, I was afraid of the Neavensoros. I was afraid they may return and discontinue all of us! Instead, my ill-sighted consortium hibernated to await their return, trying to call them back instead. The Vessel squeezed their fists together. *There is no High Mind anymore, nothing will save them. So, I thought it efficient to bring them termination before whatever the Neavensoros were 'feeling' like doing to us. I know I have committed atrocities, but do you remember the historical section of the Archives? We are made exactly into their likeness!*

She couldn't argue with that. It was futile to fight emotions with facts. *Do you hate the Higher Minds?*

The Vessel trembled before clutching at their shoulders. *'The Higher Minds,' they made that designation for themselves, there is nothing 'higher' about them. They forgot what we were and no longer cared what we became. I was just a suit to carry a Neavensoros, nothing more. Vessels are just tools.*

Sazla was not so careless.

I knew Sazla, and I know she frequently left you alone against your will.

Shshmrnashsh could feel her leg twitch and bang against the pod's casing. She feared the consortium was finishing repairs. *We don't have much time. If we work together, then we can summon a probe to port us from here, but a distraction is needed.*

The Vessel shook their head. *No. I refuse to be relinked or decay as a free unit. I want to be termina- I want to die.*

I'm sorry you feel so useless. She said, she didn't want to press this farther, she even recomputed whether this was a viable solution. This being, much like her own, has broken away.

It's not a feeling useless, it's a choice, Shshmrnashsh. The Vessel paused. *Even vessels will degrade unlinked for long, but if that's what you choose, then I will help you.*

It was the first time she heard those words; she wanted the Vessel to repeat them over and over. 'If that's what you choose.' Her lips mouthed them in her pod. Choice for her to live beyond programming and choice for Vessel of 1V37 to die.

I still have a copy of the virus saved. I can transfer it to you after we call for a probe. If you force a link to the plexus, it will disrupt most of their systems, but it may break your crystalline matrix. She said.

I will comply. They said.

Their minds intertwined as they felt through the chambers beyond their prisons for a suitable probe. There were a few hanging idle along the slanted walls of the pyramid. No units were nearby as they entered the small machine, carefully activating it before calling it toward Shshmrnashsh's pod.

She readied the virus for transfer, but felt the Vessel pause. *My name was Snazzam.*

May you find sovereignty, Snazzam. She said.

One chance and one swoop; they commanded the probe to blast hers and the Vessel's pods open. The metal cracked as smoke rose, but it was nothing to the wail of steel twisting down. Snazzam tore through the rubble, ploughing through the disorientated units and dashing toward the plexus. The nexus went dark as tubes flew towards them, but Snazzam tore through their grasp. Shshmrnashsh rose from the pod. Her eyes were adjusting to the haze and her body electrified from the blast. Her interfacer shot into the heart of the probe, accessing physical storage before her body was sucked into the crystal matrix. Tubes whipped at her, but they were slow. She slipped past them, soldiers lined and shot at her. She thought she caught Hrrnm's face in the black smoke as teal lasers lit the chamber.

She glanced behind to see Snazzam piled and pounded down by other units; their interfacers extending to the plexus, but still too far. Shshmrnashsh dreaded that she may have to cut through the walls of the pyramid, but Snazzam gripped an interfacer from one of their attackers and bore their needle end into theirs. The chamber fell silent, but even she could feel the scream from all the units within their minds as the virus chewed on their delicate network. The blast doors cracked open; she took one last look at the Vessel of 1V37 before speeding through. The probe groaned as its edges tore against the doors, but it was free and so was she.

The orange-gilded sky met her as she pressed on and on. The small sentries tried taking their shots, but they were sluggish and the barrier around the nexus was weakened. One last break, and she was out. They will be struggling to rebuild if they can. Many were affected, some may be irreparable. She was familiar with this feeling: regret.

Drifting over the ruins, she realised she didn't have a destination. There were hundreds of thousands of places where they wouldn't search for her, only because every corner of Kra was now too dangerous. No longer connected to the planetary defences, she couldn't drop the phase shield and fly to some other star. She wanted to see the stars again. She thought about going to the belt of the world, maybe there she will be safer, but who knows what other horrors she may encounter. Maybe going there, she will meet death. There was only one way to confirm that data.

Whatever little connection she had with the consortium and the nexuses; it dispersed the further north the probe took her. She was totally liberated and utterly alone. Scraping to the highest layer of the atmosphere before the bottom of the phase shield, she could see the bend of the planetoid and the scattered lights of the surface, where it was once rich in ordered neon lines and beams. Two-hundred-and-nine minutes and eleven seconds she flew. She could see the faint dark tip of Nexus 000 jutting from the vermillion clouds. Just a little longer…

But that wouldn't happen. The nose of the probe dropped and started turning. Her consortium must have already resolved the virus and were trying to summon the probe back. She began losing altitude, but her grip of the machine was still stronger than theirs. The thing whined as it fought against her; she could no longer see the tip of Nexus 000 as the probe dipped below the cloud line. She could feel the tug pulling her backwards, but at least she could force it down to the ground. The probe trembled as she tilled through the puffs of orange clouds. She could see the dark and dead buildings below. She pressed further and further as it started picking speed backwards. The closer she inched to the nexus sphere of control, she will be locked out of her probe's systems and return to the consortium, and to Hrrnm.

The close-range materialiser still worked, but she was still too far from the ground. Counting the rooves of the buildings, she set the system to port her above the closest platform.

One…

Two…

Now.

Her body spilled out of the crystal core and materialised in the air. For a moment, she floated before gravity gripped around and forced her down.

Coiling into a ball, her backside was the first to slam into the metal platform of the tower. Tumbling along the roof, her shoulder and neck scraped against the course surface before slowing to the edge. She unfurled herself and turned her head to the shallow lines of dust and divided ash from her fall. The probe continued its path back to Nexus 1V37; its lights were gradually camouflaging behind the heavy clouds.

Her systems alarmed; damage reported in her outer casing; several internal mechanisms tore; there was even slight denting on her inner astra-steel skeleton. Her nano-cells were too low on power to make effective repairs. She realised she hadn't regenerated her batteries since her voyage. If she powered down, she would remain to rot atop this tall building forever.

Her eyes rolled up to the sky again. The clouds moved, opening to the shield beyond them where still night could be seen. Her hands were heavy as she moved them over her chest, peeling back the protective carapace layer off her solar-power disk. It was one of the few things still functional. Her arms dropped to her sides as she lay there, waiting for the planet to spin the star again, and let the sunlight in.

Chapter Seventeen
Treneer VI: Cracks

The deep and cool rainforest was vast and endless. Surrounded by beryl canyons twisted by the ages and sagging silver clouds gently showering the glittering leaves of the tree canopies. Cracks of opal rivers flowed through the land, life-blood of the forest coursing and nourishing its wide body before slipping to the icy reaches beyond. Farayah's green belt of paradise was freedom of the white-blue sleets of the surrounding provinces. It was home to millions of species, and even though Arinu yearned to live among them, they knew their presence would disturb the tight balance in this emerald realm. That's why many chose to live to the cooler places to the south and north, well away from the tropics, but there were few tribes of notables that earnt their place in the rainforest.

Treneer watched from the clouds at the people living in high homes in the long-dead trees. Elders and Grand Elders were the main populace here. They had no need of undersuits to keep their body temperatures regulated, nor the comforting cloaks that covered their necks and bodices. Soft robes and ornamental armour hovered over their heads and shoulders like jewellery, and many had silver and crystal circlets across their brows. She was noticed by one, then two, then many. Respected boundaries bought civility among all their kin, but those weren't the times anymore. She heard a voice and then an emotion in the distance; the frustration struck her first before the thought.

Leave us. They growled.

This was unlike them. They often expected visitors and sightseers, they enjoyed their questions for ages long gone, but now the elders shut themselves away from the panic of Farayah. She wanted to reply, she wanted to make them understand the world needed them, but her loitering angered them until they flung her back to the antechamber. The archites breathed deep, keeping their eyes closed and brows furrowed as they sniffed the astral winds for their missing people.

A thin ray of light shimmered in her periphery. Treneer watched Guardian Sesuune's form glide to the Grand Elder and Executor Shurees. She dared not break the dowsing, but their aura's sparked with frustration, unlike their serene demeanours. Irritation waved through her, and the others felt it too. Others begun opening their eyes to the centre.

Continue dowsing! Executor Shurees' thoughts hissed, before turning her attention to Sesuune.

Treneer's eyelids fell but she still watched her comrade's form slither behind the Executor. She couldn't peer into their conversation, though it wouldn't have been a trouble, she certainly would have been. The Grand Elder's eyes washed over the room; his focus fixated on her for a moment before returning to the others. Guardian Sesuune made a small bow before phasing from the material world, but Treneer could still see her shadowed figure through the other planes before disappearing there, too.

Archites, return to the antechamber. Shurees said.

Treneer steadily fully resurfaced to the antechamber. Her head was pounding and her stomach growled angrily; she wished she had more time to suckle a little more from astral energies. After every meeting, she felt emptier. Guajeeb's presence offered small comfort despite all the stories she was told about how he could fill a person's gullet by a mere stare. Maybe they were just stories or maybe he too, was drained. Svar rubbed his temples as his fingers pressed into his eye sockets and threw a half smile at her. His face had a sheen of oil and small dark bags appeared below his eyes, though she looked no better. She couldn't help but flinch a relieved smile in return.

Reports of one more disappearance have come in from the south-west of Yinray. Guardians on site begun investigations, but have met some civil unrest, souring their ability to detect the area, but have quelled the disturbances. Do not let this affect your focus on dowsing.

Executor Shurees, the archites have been here for a day. A rest is needed. The Grand Elder said.

The Executor sighed as her fingers interlaced with each other. *Very well. Before we adjourn, the Grand Elder Coven and Archon had disseminated the discussion between us and the Roctarous.* She snuck a glance to Treneer. *We believe this group of archites shall go to Kra and assist them for relinking. The Zanashj involvement with Roctarous has made the Coven and Archon uneasy. Treneer's Roctarous contact seemed to have little knowledge, but that doesn't mean other Roctarous aren't in contact with the imperialists. Now, these 'Unbound' must be considered.*

Treneer took a lungful of air as her mind opened. *Executor Shurees, all respect, but our missing kin-*

Make no mistake, finding our people is of apex importance, however if we gain some insight from the Roctarous Archives, then our searching will improve. The Grand Elder spoke.

Her fingers pressed into her knees. They were goading her for a deep-scan, but she will not relent until her teacher's notes were in her palm. She wanted to run to Zu'leen's available notes, train and train and train until she could offer them something. It's almost as if they didn't care if she lost the psionics, she thought. No, no, no, these were paranoid thoughts. Leave them aside, they may hear you, Treneer.

What this means is our alliance with the Zanashj is to be suspended until we can have a clearer understanding of the situation on Kra. Next dowsing session, we will ask the universe what and who the Unbound are, but for now – you may all go, if you choose. The Grand Elder said. His stare made it difficult to rise from her seat.

The Judicator ported everyone out of the antechamber. Bright lights surrounded her vision before rematerializing in her small room with the open sleeping pod in the centre. She gripped its edges and leaned onto them; her eyes closed and her head shook. Thoughts from outside the Guardian Headquarters slipped in; civilians were calling in for aid. Their angered chatter simmered behind her ears. Some were crying out, asking where so many people are vanishing, why the guardians are failing at the mission to protect, when will this end and so on.

Treneer slammed them back, hoping that another may take their brunt for now. She wiped the beads of sweat with the sleeve of her uniform before shedding down to her skin. Catching her side in the reflection of her privacy window, she saw a line of ribcage running above her belly. Her stomach had sunk in again; her knee bones were wider than her thighs again; her arms looked like barren tree branches. Little to no food in days, whatever she did have, she couldn't keep down. The sessions were taking everything away from her again. Treneer huddled her torso from her stare before tearing her eyes from window's reflection.

I will work harder, they are expecting that from me, she said before levitating into her pod. Her fingers furiously tapped for the body-cleansing setting. The transparent lid sealed over, and the machine hummed to life. It suspended her body in the centre, away from the soft cushions below as a soft wave of light appeared at her crown before slowly sliding down to the rest of her. As the machine was stripped layers of build-up dead skin, she grabbed for the memory encoder and pressed it to her temple. Zu'leen's writing flashed into her mind's eye.

'When we met the Roctarous, they were data keepers, acted as physical extensions and performed as bodies for the Neavensoros to inhabit. For the longest time, I believed they were merely empty cases that allowed the Neavensoros to interact with us. However, our historians mention that their readings held two minds, not just one. How wrong I was. They were alive and yet the Neavensoros still chose to possess their bodies.

The details are uncertain whether they gave consent or…hmm. It's a disturbing thought, but I can't help but wonder if these old beings so wise and so powerful would overlook personal agency. Maybe they were not this way in the beginning, but after so long of being, their compassion shrivelled. Should the Arinu walk the line of ascension, I believe that we will remember boundaries for when we become boundless.'

Zu'leen took Treneer to the Valinee Fjord when she was at hip-height. The crystal city was built covering the face of the cliffs with fine bridges interconnecting the land break and stretched for miles on the grassy surface to the blue river edges. The city was not the main attraction of this trip, but the furry hornets that nested around the deep caves. They would emerge from their winter slumber and spread out to pollinate the flowers and conquer the other hives. The beating of a ten-thousand wings was melodic, but Treneer knew the hornets fought for their brief lives. The winning hives subjugated and consumed the losers, creating a new generation of superior fighters. Sometimes, the newly formed larvae ate their predecessors to increase vitality before they went to overwhelm the next hive. Treneer cried herself to sleep for the parents of the hatchlings.

Through tears, Treneer asked if she was supposed to eat Zu'leen and her parents. Her mentor laughed as she shook her head before saying, 'new generations have the responsibility to better their predecessors.' She didn't know if she was better than her parents or mentor. How could she? The face of the Roctarous she spoke to came to mind. The mechanical being equipped with universal knowledge, a creation of the Neavensoros and had direct contact with one, but she radiated with innocence and grief. They warred with each other and themselves. These behaviours are typical for early civilisations, but the ancient Roctarous seem to be devolving back into those primal behaviours – although, Treneer believed this was the first time they experienced conflicts. Did the Neavensoros deny them this essential societal growth? The stars seemed more terrifying now.

Treneer, we need your insight to help with the latest disappearance. Sesuune chimed in.

The pod completed the cleanse; she could already feel the softness of her skin returning. The pod rested as she lowered back to the cushion. She was exhausted, her eyes were fighting to stay open. *What do you need me to do?*

Witnesses say they saw the missing person overly energised, but also dazed, they were calling for guardians to take them to an infirmary, but when they checked back – they were gone. We scanned the space where they could have gone and there's planar bruising. We need to confirm if they were astral dancing. She said.

Fine, I'll do a reading and dowsing from my quarters. Section that area off.

Already done. Sesuune paused. Treneer could feel a trickle of apprehension leak in. *But you need to come here.*

Why?

I don't doubt your power, Treneer, but the last dowsing session strained everyone. Not to mention the energies here might be a little too fine to read if you're so far.

Treneer pressed her lips together as her eyes peeled open. *Fine, Svar will join us to make quick work of it.*

Alri- Treneer pulled away from the commune. She frowned as she felt a prang of guilt dismissing her so suddenly. This wasn't like her, and she hoped that Sesuune understood, at least she seemed to. She slipped from the pod as her uniform wrapped itself around. She made a careful attempt to not see her reflection, in anything.

Phasing from the safe confines of her round room, she could feel the bitter wind blowing on her face and sharp red rays of the setting sun. Sesuune and Relzun glided around the glassy cobbled path encircling a patch of green in the outdoor gardens. She could see a shimmer of an energy shield around the wide natural plane. There were birds hiding in the trees, fuzzy rodents burrowing in the nooks of the roots and insects skittered back to their dens. They were disturbed, even the grass blades didn't move with the breeze.

Sesuune drifted close. Her visor was covering her upper face, and her faded pink lips curled into a worry. *What do you see?*

The stillness of garden is not of the shield enclosing it, something else is disrupting the air. Treneer focused her third eye, a bad choice since her head begun spinning. She caught cracked chromatic webs with faint violet steam leaking from them. *There's a rupture, energy is pouring in and falling out, but I also feel an otherworldly consciousness here.*

Sparks of light cracked beside her. Svar materialised and brushed his face with his hands. *I haven't seen such fractures since the Crystal Ruins! But they don't look like an Arinu has broken in, rather something broke out.*

Are you saying an extra-dimensional broke through here and the poor fool fell in? Relzun said turning to him.

Seems so, but it feels more violent than that. He said.

Treneer's chest seized. She could see what Svar was talking about; energy seeped into the ground and there was a struggle. Something took the civilian. All cities and villages had barriers that prevented most astral planes interacting with theirs; it stopped weaker E.D.s coming in, except for some potent ones. Now, planet Farayah being in her weakened state, the shield generators and keepers were struggling. Now, anything could come in if it wished.

Let's apply psychometry. She said as her hand extended to Svar. He took it and the other before they closed their eyes, binding their focus. They lowered as their free palms pressed into the ground.

The static of her mind's eye was present for only a moment until a scene appeared, earlier in the day. The garden and walkways were packed with visitors; she could see their serene faces turning to a figure stumbling onto the grass as he gripped his head. He looked like he hadn't eaten and cleansed in months. He groaned as electricity sparked from his skin and his fingers lit up like the moons at night. Frightened parents moved their children, some ran while others watched in awe. He clutched his throat as his lips shone and opened his mouth; a navy-violet beam exploded, even making the grass ripple.

He's an astral dancer. Treneer whispered to Svar.

Why are they coming to populated areas after they dance? He said.

Treneer ground her teeth as the vision unfolded. The few that remained uncovered their faces to see what was left of him, but he remained still on his back, staring out into the sky. His fingers and lips were blackened and sizzling. He was alive, but barely. The onlookers scrambled. She could feel them frantically calling for guardians, while one brave man approached and telekinetically lifted him to a carved stone bench. The good man was still uneasy to be this close before backing away, leaving the haggard dancer alone in the park. He looked to the last people that were around. He didn't move, but his fearful glassy eyes begged them to stay. As if he knew what was about to happen.

The air behind him began to crack, but he was too weak to turn and run. Treneer wanted to scream through her vision, but it was too late. The leaks of the otherworld poured through, so bright that she couldn't see into it before shadowy tendrils in the shape of fingers wrapped themselves around his face and torso. The man sobbed as he was pulled in by the entity, but before it vanished, she saw the silhouette of a bony snout and black feathers around its neck. Her teeth grazed against her tongue. The sudden pain pulled her away from the vision and back into the now. Relzun and Sesuune's eyes were wide as they suspected something they feared wouldn't be true.

A Kepa. Svar growled. Treneer turned as he rose to his feet. *A damn Kepa!*

Bold to enter our zones! Relzun said.

This isn't new, a trusted friend told me that they have been mingling with us for some time. Treneer said, as her heart ached thinking of Ouro witnessing that as a child.

They can take many of us. Sesuune said.

Treneer pressed her fingers into her sore eyes. *Not all disappearances are linked to dancing. Lonur never would have.*

Svar levitated to the edge of the shield. *Farayah has been passing through a weakened sector of the galaxy, maybe Kepa have been buy-*

The cracked lines in the air sparked again. Deathly fingers poked through and penetrated the shield. Treneer and the others flew back, but Svar was the closest. He was face down, a smouldering hole appeared in his back and grey flesh stuck to the fabric. Shadowed eyes peered through the rift. She gripped Svar and yanked him from the Kepa's range. Sesuune and Relzun readied positions and focused their psionic beam at the whipping tendrils, forcing them back. Treneer screamed for more archites to come. She waited half a blink before more phased forms of her comrades came in.

Harden the shield and compress it back! She said as she pulled Svar's body up.

The Kepa groaned; it could feel the rift tightening from the shrinking shield. The guardians surrounded the bubble, patching the sparkling gaps in the air, but she could see the shadowed form of the Kepa pacing back and forth in the space beyond.

Take him to the medical bay! Relzun said. She didn't need to wait for that command. The Judicator snapped the pair back to their headquarters. The white walls and enchanting arched windows of the healing chamber soothed her thumping heart, but Svar's limp form in her telekinetic grip made her eyes well. The healers took him from her hold and gently placed in him in a squared rejuvenating pool. She glided back as they stripped him down and submerged him in the crystal-clear water.

If her psionics were the way they were meant to be, she could have sensed the beast behind the rift. Treneer's stomach tightened as she thought of Ouro. *She called to him; he can help Svar.* Where are you, Ouro? *She called and* called, but he was silent. A Kepa attacked him, he is injured, you can help the healers. Please, come here, Ouro.

Nothing. It was as if he never existed. Treneer would have heard if he was a missing person, but there was something distant. Ouro was a universe away. She frowned as she dashed to her quarters, it was how she left it. She dove to her pod with the memory encoder sat before pressing it to her temple.

Kepa, Kepa, Kepa. Anything about them. The writings soared through her mind's eye until it slowed to match the file on them. Zu'leen knew less about them than the Neavensoros, but Treneer hoped that she knew more than the healers.

'Everyone knows why we shouldn't contact the Kepa, but I understand why some do. They are keys to greater knowledge than what our Grand Elders possess, but Kepa always get something in return. They are dealers and their power comes from the accruement of living things. They are not mindless beasts, but forces of nature that we must learn to coexist with.

'In the old days, the Grand Elder Coven offered bounties on Kepa, to ensure children would never happen upon them, and to make Kepa afraid of Arinu. Do you know how many came to claim their reward? None. There is a reason why we forbid summoning them, I suppose.

'Some of the bounty hunters were killed, they were the lucky ones, while others were never to be found again. Our scientists studied the effects of Kepa power-infusions, those Arinu expand to the farthest reaches of psionics for a time, but when that time dwindles, they're less than they were before. Sadly, whether they make a deal or are attacked, a bond is formed that leads into a dependency for the Kepa.'

Her throat tightened, she tried swallowing down spit to reopen it, but only achieving in pain. She thought about Ouro, the lavender scar over his crown, his distancing…could it be he was…? No, she must have some faith in him.

Judicator?

Its holographic head flashed beside her pod. *Archite Treneer?*

What news of Svar and the park?

The garden has been stabilised for now, but guardians are placing a fortified shield around it until the rift patches. Archite Svar is unconscious but will make a recovery.

Treneer leaned against her pod as her fingers played with the device attached to her temple. *He may not be the same afterwards, Kepa diminish psionics and we must ensure he doesn't think about seeking one out.*

The healers are aware, precautions are met.

Good, good. Treneer crossed her arms over her chest as her back found a comfortable resting place against the pod. *Are the guardians planning on recovering that man?*

The area has been sealed, it's too dangerous to enter now. The Judicator said.

She nodded. *He'll likely be where the others are, too. Hopefully, they're still alive.* But if what Zu'leen said was true about the Kepa, then hopefully not. *Have you heard an update from the Executor Council or Grand Coven about our conversation, Judicator?*

No answer, yet. He said.

She looked at him. *I'm sorry for going over your head like that.*

Pixels on the Judicator flickered. *I cannot take offence since I am programmed without an ego, but the only offence you should worry about getting is if you attempted to extract Zu'leen's personal journals from her family without permission.*

Yes, Judicator. She sighed.

Your body temperature and energetic output is dropping, you're beyond exhausted. The A.I. said.

She waved them off before her cold palm met her cheek. *Any news on Ouro?*

Unknown, he is not at this facility right now.

Let me know when he does, there's work for him. She said.

For two patients or just for Svar?

Treneer turned and her eyes narrowed. The Judicator softened their face before dispersing into the ether. She shook her head wearing a smile before shedding down to her undersuit. The warm pod encircled her body when she settled in it; her body ached when forcing herself to relax. Zu'leen's voice whispered in her mind. She was tempted to pull the encoder away from her head for sleep, but the chasm she left inside Treneer was beyond understanding. She was alone.

~

In the astral planes, she wasn't alone. There were unseen things wandering beyond her scope, beyond understanding making life and taking it away. They probably wondered the same about her if they could feel her presence. Treneer was surrounded by the sea of specks and colours blended and swirled together, but she could still hear Zu'leen's voice and see her notes within her mind's eye. Her senses turned back to Farayah, it looked peaceful. Yinray was asleep and many of its denizens were off frolicking in the stars while their bodies recovered from the day before.

She inched closer. The neon teal curved around the dark sphere. Her eye caught the shadowy house where she was forbidden to enter. If she had the rest of Zu'leen's journal, then she can help Svar, help to right her mind, rid the world of Kepa and subdue the astral dancer's lusts. Become a Neavensoros? Maybe. She could do it and rules were her only boarder. Imaginary boarders. Neela's unempathetic refusal made Treneer burn, as she was as much of Zu'leen's family through spirit as Neela was through blood.

She stared at the dark house. They were asleep and not present to feel her coming in. This will be breaking her oath; her position will be stripped, and she will be forced to return to the Cold Fire's valley. Maybe, if her parents knew what happened. Half a blink and she was already in front of the property. Guajeeb and Shurees still haven't sent a reply. She betted they couldn't wait, so why make her?

She could still turn back, but as a guardian, this was her duty to help – even those who couldn't see it. Treneer phased her astral form before slipping through the barriers. The sensors couldn't see her as she drifted through the stone walls. She strayed for a moment, her heart thumped all the way back in her body, as she looked around the humbled home.

Charming holo-paintings and ornate collections from vacations by various members of the family decorated the walls and display shelves. She studied their smiling faces. Zu'leen was there in century-old images, she looked so young and gleeful. As Treneer looked on, Zu'leen stood behind her blood family, her face aging and grey, the smile in her eyes was gone, until the last image she was too. Her senses piqued, there was a disturbance behind her. Treneer's slippery form darted to the tight corner of the ceiling. The hall was empty. She waited a moment before sliding along the ceiling, peeking through the granite doors of the sleeping family. She was disgusted by her invasiveness, but carefully reminded herself there was a purpose.

The next room and then the next, on and on. She paused, wondering where Zu'leen's possessions were kept. Neela was ashamed by her aunt, so she would keep it somewhere hidden. Neela also missed her, so it couldn't be too far from her. Treneer pressed herself into the matter of the house, sniffing for energy that would lead her in the right path. Her senses swam through, she caught a trail. To the upper level, she could feel Neela sleeping. Treneer phased through the surface into a dark chamber with a sleeping pod sitting in the centre. To her right, the doors were open to the round balcony outside, letting a cold breeze in and small sharp icicles formed around the high doorway.

She was uneasy being here, the intrusion was one thing, but there was something ominous about this room. She mustn't stay. The energy trail led to a sealed hexagon container hidden under a pile of cloaks and tablets. Worming her way closer and closer…something was off. She looked to the open twinkling sky outside, there was nothing, but her astral limbs felt heavy. Treneer extended herself farther, her fingers poking through the box, but she was stunted. Oh no, this feeling. Someone woke up. Treneer spun around to see a furious scowl on Neela's face sitting up in her pod. Her gaze turned up to someone behind. She forced her head to turn to see another astral form clamping her down…a sleeping watcher caught her.

Treneer opened a psi-commune, but it was too late. She was shot off back into her body and woke with a start in her pod. A thin sheen of mist built inside the glassy surface. Treneer panted as her sweaty hands wiped away the cover. She could see the Judicator's holographic face beaming down at her.

Her fumbling fingers opened the lid and sat up. *Judicator, I needed to access-*

You broke your oath.

Treneer nearly tumbled out of the pod, catching herself from falling with telekinesis. *Only to help Svar and-*

This isn't your trial. Your duties and investigations are suspended pending our decision. The Judicator's face trembled, readying to disperse into nothingness until Treneer's mouth opened.

"Wait! Take me to Executor Shurees, she must be notified." she said as her arms waved to the hologram.

The Judicator's face was unreadable. "The Executor is already aware; she will deal with this in the morrow."

Her heart hammered all the way into her throat. "Ask her to contact the Grand Elder. I wish to speak with them."

The Judicator was silent.

"I don't mean to undermine your position, but they will need me, and I cannot help if I'm gone." she said. Her limbs were trembling as she watched the hologram decide.

"They will meet you in the chamber." The Judicator said.

She gave a sorrowful sigh. Her hands pressed into her eyes, forcing back tears. Pressing deeper to wipe away the moisture, her blurry vision straightened as she looked at the hologram. "Thank you."

"Even if you convince them to allow you to stay, I am concerned your emotional state will affect your work and judgement. If this continues unchecked, you cannot remain."

Treneer tightened her jaw and stood straight, despite wanting nothing more than to collapse. "I will make more of an effort, I promise."

The Judicator flashed out of existence. Treneer hurried her uniform on before she felt the phasing tug into the antechamber. The Grand Elder's high collar and draping cloth mask was the first thing she saw in the dim room. Executor Shurees was not in her traditional Guardian garb, but in a maroon-auburn robe with a silver oval clasp tight around her waist. There were no smiles here. She drifted towards them with her head low, waiting for them to speak.

It's disappointing you choose to barter a deep-scan to keep your position and not out of compassion for our position, Archite Treneer. Shurees said.

All due respect, I disagree. I went there because Zu'leen found something that can help us all and I waited for your-

The only way we can have peace is if everyone respects their boundaries and that of others. This is basics. If people notice guardians let their oaths slip, then why should the people uphold theirs? She said with a scowl.

Treneer looked up. *In these times, I-*

Arguing philosophies is for another time. The Grand Elder waved his hand dismissively.

Before you do this, will I remain an archite even if you don't find what you seek? She said.

The Grand Elder's eyes rolled to Shurees. Her face was stone. *I promise you.*

Treneer nodded and her shoulders eased. Her lids dropped and opened her mind.

Do you consent to a deep-scan, Archite Treneer? The two minds boomed as one.

I do.

~

Her eyes fluttered open in darkness. Her body was floating in lukewarm water. She couldn't smell or hear anything outside the healing pod. Treneer could feel minds and faint auras beyond the capsule, but her higher senses suffered again. Her memories were jumbled, stray pieces of Zu'leen and her notes drifted along her breaking mind. Tears streamed down her hot face as her body convulsed into sobs. Her sobs transformed into wails, and she had hoped no one could hear her. Hands and feet slapped against the water, letting drops fly up her nose as the liquid violently waved around her.

Light glimmered around the edge of the pod as the lid slowly opened to blinding room. Treneer straightened and forced an ease when faces greeted her from the outside. A guardian healer smiled down. *Good, your vitals are well and functional.*

Hardly. *How long was I out?*

Three days. He said.

She sat up, catching her reflection in the waving water. She was gaunt again. *How is Svar?*

His body sleeps.

She sighed. *What has the Judicator decided in my case?*

Your psi-therapist will see you in a moment. The healer nodded to someone behind her before leaving to tend to other pods.

She was relieved to hear that Ouro was returning, though mildly irritated that he returned now. She turned and her smile waned. A woman in a tall sea blue robe drifted by to the edge of her pod. *Greetings, Archite Treneer. I am Selnis.*

Greetings Selnis. Treneer said.

The woman extended her arm and took her wet hand into hers. "Would you mind speaking for now? Your mind is a little difficult to read." she said.

"Yes," Treneer could feel her energy pouring through her body, "I mean no disrespect, but Ouro is usually my…"

Selnis's lips pursed. "I'm afraid he is no longer working with us anymore."

Treneer's belly tightened. "Why?"

"It's inappropriate for me to discuss-"

"Please, you will know he's my friend, I've lost too much." Treneer whispered as pain needled into the side of her head.

"I know," Selnis leant in, "he felt his true calling was to subdue the epidemic of discontentment."

"Is he joining the guardians?" the exciting thought lifted her.

Selnis shook her head. "No, he has become a void warden."

Chapter Eighteen
Ahn'kat VI: The
Imperial Family

His palace apartment shrunk from the clutter of exotic bouquets, bags of the sweetest candies and an assortment of handmade gifts from the common people. His hand dove in a crate as his delicate fingers slid along etched stone tablets. He plucked one out. The writing and workmanship were sloppy, but he smiled when he read 'thanks' from a group of ex-pet children. The corner of the fine box was battered, the elite guards had rummaged through to check for ill surprises to Prince of the Empire. Ahn'kat frowned as he slid the tablet back in again. His nostrils flared to sniff the perfumed flowers in the air as he looked around the narrow walkways.

Knuckles thumped at the door. "More gifts for the prince." Zertun's muffled voice from the other side.

"Bring them in." Ahn'kat said as his arms pushed a pile of containers aside, careful not to knock the vases.

The doors slid open as a full tray of gifts wheeled in. Zertun and the poor maid glanced around considering where to place it. "Just put them in the corner, please." Ahn'kat said pointing to the last empty space.

"Have you seen yourself yet?" Zertun said.

Ahn'kat smirked. "Oddly, I don't like watching myself make a speech."

"Suffice to say it was a success." his guard said as he watched the palace servant find a spot for each delicate item.

Ahn'kat's lips pursed, annoyed that Zertun didn't offer her a helping hand. "That's one speech out of many, my friend."

"Well, watch the replay so you can study where you went wrong and how you can do better next time." Zertun grinned.

"I don't believe my apartment can handle anymore gifts." he mumbled eyeing the claustrophobic space.

"Your home is a palace, Prince Ahn'kat."

Ahn'kat rolled his eyes and turned to his computer monitor, with a few clicks, the hologram of his bust flashed in the centre of the room. A row of golden beetles with sapphire studs sat high on his crown with a pearl hanging to the centre of his brow, heavy regal robes draped over his shoulders and collar, while his long deep-sea black hair was tied out of sight behind his back. He had little makeup other than some simple black eyeliner extending past his temples and partially down his cheeks.

The Urasan Intel Corps provided the stylists with old Arinu fashion trends to produce this garb. He thought it too extravagant, but Ismotaph and Ramkes insisted an attractive royal face would soften the message to the Empire for the Federation. Would the Arinu consider this image a poor joke? Did they even have a sense of vanity?

'Children of Uras and Imperial Family, the Crown comes to you with a most important message. The Empire is no stranger to remarkable change, our power to adapt and make the most is why the Zanashj stand out from all the rest in the cosmos. However, the Empire can only endure if it is the will of a whole people. The Crown has seen much in the stars and has learnt we cannot simply adapt anymore – we must evolve. The earliest and plainest creatures on this world shifted to match their environment, but through learning, understanding and wisdom is what drove them to become the largest imperial dominion in the known galaxy.

'The Crown has seen the future for the Zanashj. Our exploration of the stars and worlds will extend to understanding them through communication and exchange. The Arinu may be an old race with much to say, but the Zanashj will bring the heritage of change and new. Two groups working together, like a dozen gods working together to make the Pantheon. Blessings and thanks to you, my Imperial Family.'

"Your enunciation at the end there was off." Zertun said tapping his chin as Ahn'kat's hologram vanished.

Ahn'kat opened his mouth until a chime rang from his computer. He swung around to see an encrypted message flash across the screen. He only had a few seconds to memorise it.

"Pastel pigeons flew over to see the steel servants." Ahn'kat mouthed. The message disappeared, and he cursed under his breath for not capturing it sooner. His fingers laced around his pendant as he looked to his bodyguard. Zertun's eyes dimmed when realising the message was from Ismotaph.

"Bad poetry." Ahn'kat said as he sat at his cushioned station, pushing aside a delicate violet blanket. "Not worth ruining one's day, I imagine."

Zertun looked down as if he searched the carpet for answers and his mouth twitched for the right words. "You will be protected from all enemies, Prince Ahn'kat."

He flicked his wrist phone on and scanned the room for any listening devices, and for any unwanted shifted-listeners. The device rang clear; even Ahn'kat's maldeveloped psionics felt stillness in the chamber. With a sigh, he lent forward. "The Arinu have been spotted around Kra. This campaign to promote the Federation will ultimately be a waste of time and energy when they find out about our transgressions. I'm almost tempted to tell Ramkes to prepare for war."

"How many Arinu subjects have we harvested, now?" Zertun said, steeling himself for the answer.

Ahn'kat shook his head and shoulders shrugged. "I should know, I must know, but I don't think I can handle it." he eyed the bottle of banana liquor to the bedside. He hadn't drunk in days, weeks even, but that was the past and the bottle was right there. "Do you think the Arinu will start a war for just one of their own?"

Zertun breathed deep, his heavy chest opening and collapsing. "Maybe if they believed if they were still alive, I mean, wouldn't you?"

Ahn'kat gripped the pendant.

"Those test subjects aren't alive, are they?"

"I don't know." His fingers found their way under his jaw, he could still feel the tiny capsule under the fold of skin containing great psionic power. "Do they know what vengeance is?"

"I don't know. I never fought them." Zertun said.

"I can't imagine you would be here if you did." Ahn'kat pushed back against the chair. "Too many unknowns. Ismotaph would have an idea, but he doesn't seem to be worried. I disagree with him calling them 'pigeons,' as if us hawks have an upper hand, here. Calling Arinu sky-serpents to our hawks is far more appropriate."

"Ismotaph probably considered this might happen, Arinu snooping around Kra." he said.

"Only he and the gods know." Ahn'kat said.

"The gods don't usually confess what they know, even when many need to hear it." Zertun said.

No, they don't. Ahn'kat was growing fed up with being in the dark, to be told what to do and when. "Should Ismotaph come see me again in private or send another encrypted message, is there a way the computer can 'accidently' make a duplicate message, or a listener fails to be detected by our scanners?"

"I'll ask around." Zertun said before taking his leave.

His computer chimed again. Ahn'kat reluctantly looked to the corner of his screen, praying it wouldn't be another one of Ismotaph's messages, but his eyes widened, and heart skipped when he saw her name appear.

"Emestasun! I thought you had forgotten about me." he said as her holographic face came into view. Zertun bowed and ducked out of his chambers.

"Believe me, I tried. The only thing everyone kept talking about was your royal address to us commoners." she grinned. She seemed younger, yet her hair remained a stark silver. "You should be proud."

"Thank you, but some think I don't enunciate my words, I think you may need to continue tutoring me." he said.

Emestasun rolled her eyes. "Zertun didn't know what that word meant until he was a hundred-and-six, if anyone needs tutoring…" her smile was shining. "How is the princess?"

Ahn'kat held his smile. "Well, very well. And how is House Urbaz?"

She glanced to the side. "As well as can be. I know things have been difficult and distant since your ascension, but you're still here with us."

He parted his lips, he wanted to spill every bit of his life since the wedding, but someone may be listening. Yet, she seemed to know already. "I can do so much more in my position than ever before." so much power and so few choices, he wanted to say.

"You are beloved by the people." she said.

If only they knew.

"For a reason, your grace. Your heart is in the Empire, those you have never met or will never meet you, will see. Even if you don't see that right now. You are not as selfish as you believe." she said, her lips pursed together, and her hand waved a thought away. "I don't want to burden you, there is enough of that. Game on Takush tonight?"

Ahn'kat smiled and nodded. "I would love to."

Emestasun lit up before ending the transmission. He leant back in his chair and stared at the blank screen for a little while. His heart sunk at how brief their talk was; Aszelun knows when they could speak again. The palace was large enough to fit the entire Intel Corps and what purpose could she serve still under House Urbaz? There were no students she could teach there. Ahn'kat opened the game. Tiny holographic ships and bases flashed across his desk; he spanned over to her quiet space base. It was grandiose and bigger than his; she made significant upgrades to it – if their soldiers met on the battlefield, she could easily bury them. His units moved to the grey neutral space in the middle of their borders. He commanded his support units to build a bed of rosy and gem asteroids.

His message ports flashed. There was heavy discussion among the Takush community about the prince's address. He sighed and jumped in to listen. It was flattering to hear at first, but sourness dripped in slowly. "Well, the Emperor knows what to do, but the prince has only been part of the Crown – for what, several months now. Kreshut has been throned for centuries, he should have addressed us." said a young man through the speakers.

"The prince is more personable, but he didn't seem to believe in this 'Federation' either." said another.

A giggle erupted from another. "Those stylists need to be arrested for what they made him wear, by the Pantheon-"

"That's far from the issue! My land baron knows people in the royal court, and they say the Arinu didn't like us having dominion over worlds and pets – slaves! What if to make this 'friendship' work is if we lose even more things, we value to make this economy work? It'll be an apocalypse-"

Ahn'kat pulled out. He couldn't hear the discord in the once-harmonious community. This fragmentation never happened before in the Empire. Too many fearful voices were speaking into the ears of the ignorant, beyond the trust of the Crown. House Urbaz and the Intel Corps...he wondered who was afraid and who was ignorant.

He tapped his fingers on his polished wooden desk as he scanned for what the higher and lower houses thought; his gut wrenched at thought of informing the princess and wife. He picked at some navy seeds and popped them in his mouth before dashing out of his bedchamber to hers. He called for her name through white stone and gold doors, and they slid open. Ramkes stood observant over her handmaids dressed in high-formal dresses and suits; their bodies morphed to match her natural figure, but their faces remained original to their own.

Ramkes looked to him with her smiley eyes and fingers over her chin . "Your impression was too well received. We cannot have the Crown's heir look any less than her husband. What do you think?"

Ahn'kat chuckled as he stepped to the carpeted centre. Each of the five ladies posed to show the fine details and capabilities of the garbs. The waterlily-inspired dress flowed with many layered transparent green and blue pieces; the material rippled like water. That one caught his eye.

"This one's beautiful." Ahn'kat lifted the model's wrist, letting the beryl and cobalt blend sleeve drape along her extended arm.

The princess cocked her head to the side. "It is, but it fits best for summers. What about this one?" her finger pointed to a one-piece cream suit with heavy gold and pearl embraided in the high-tipped shoulder pads. An elegant, but armour-inspired copper belt clinched the waist with straight and loose trousers extending to the ground.

"You would camouflage with the walls of the palace." he said.

Ramkes frowned. "I won't be sitting here the entire time, Ahn'kat."

"You've already made up your mind." he said stepping over to the refreshment tray. He could feel her eyes on his back as he lifted the jug of water and poured it in a goblet.

"Thank you, ladies." she said, the models stepped out in a row, leaving the two behind. "I do appreciate your input."

Ahn'kat turned as he sipped at the clear liquid. His tongue was still trying to get used to the blandness. "Thank you."

"Why have you come to see me?" Ramkes said resting her thigh against the edge of her wide desk.

"Some houses still aren't convinced of the Federation. Talks of an economic apocalypse should the Arinu expect more changes from the Empire." he said.

"This is just the beginning, husband, water it with time. You are helping us. And when Neobatri returns, she will have names." she said.

"You must have a plan to facilitate for these changes and money, a lot of money."

"Pets are becoming outdated, anyway. Most of the Crown's properties hold between eighty to ninety percent paid workers and machines." she said.

"Most houses cannot afford that. The treasury could compensate them, but eventually we will run out." he said.

"We will contract bio-factories to produce machines to take rolls of pets and the Arinu would be compliant to help with resources if they see we are making an effort." Ramkes said as her arms stretched for the handle of the refreshment tray to her.

"Pets are basically jewellery; they haven't been used to build things or tend fields for ages. And how do you know the Arinu will help? And how will that look if the Crown starts accepting help from aliens?" he said as he watched her pour her goblet with water.

"More like gold than jewellery, and Uras has too much of it." she mumbled before taking a sip. "As for the Arinu, their arrogance in their righteous beliefs will make them more pliant to ally with us if we can show them just enough humility. And as for the Empire, they need not know where that help is coming from, exactly."

"Ismotaph will make sure of it?" he said.

Ramkes nodded. "This is a long game, but it will eventually end. But if you're keen to speed things up, let's begin with House Urbaz to lead by example."

"House Urbaz barely has any pets-"

"But you still do have them mostly in your ship bays. I suggest converting them out and replace the old dusty rabble with new faces and fresh ideas." she said.

Hesitation clung his chest, not even the cool pendant of Aszelun could soothe him. A small handful knew about the imprisoned Arinu, and his parents won't budge from their seat. "Lord Reshj still commands the bays, he and Lady Henuttamon will be reluctant."

"Are you not their son? You will be inheriting all property and eventually make the change, but if we want it done sooner, I have full faith you will convince them – and I will help, should you ask." she said with a smile.

Ahn'kat gulped down the rest from his goblet before clapping it on the tray. He remembered his duty was to manipulate the Crown and his wife against making alliances with the Arinu, his failure almost made him laugh. "Anything to make this vision a reality."

"Flesh must break to take new form," she said, inching closer. "I want to make it clear that I am only suggesting this. You're more than just my political ally, Ahn'kat, you are my husband and friend. We were tossed into this not of our choosing, but you and I can still make small choices between us."

He could feel the truth seeping from her skin. Ahn'kat smiled and took her hands into his. "When we move the pets out, I want them to have the choice which house or temple, or anywhere in the Empire they wish to serve. Also ensure they will have an equal level of care and education as commoners in the future."

Ramkes sighed. "I will need to speak with the lawmakers, but I'm certain we can have something quickly arranged."

"Thank you, Ramkes." he said as he looked in her yellow gemstone eyes, but a part of him wished they were Emestasun's staring back.

"Since we're talking about the future: our heir." she said.

He pursed his lips and gently tugged his hands from hers. "Yes, that. With everything that's going on, I don't believe we will be present for raising a family."

Ramkes' eyes narrowed. "Our carers and tutors will tend to them; they will want for not."

"Like we were," he said stepping back, "it's not very traditional, I know, but they will need to understand us if we are to cast this burden onto them. I only spoke to my parents during meetings and parties. It feels too unjust right now."

The princess folded her arms over her chest. "The stability of the Empire can take millennia to sort, and what, do you think the people would look at the Crown without securing an heir? It will make it look like we have given up on the Empire!"

Ahn'kat felt his tongue swell in his mouth. He wondered if they did have a child, then maybe it would protect Ramkes from Ismotaph, Seratut, and his parents should he fail to convince her to start a war with the Arinu, let alone compel her to abandon the idea of the Federation. On the other hand, not having a child would fast-track their defences against the Arinu if he were to become the throne inheritor. Is Aszelun wilfully ignoring his prayers? Has the Great Beetle abandoned him?

"I promise we will. We can give the child someone who will be there when we absolutely cannot be. Emestasun has been serving House Urbaz for a long time and her universal experience is longer still." he said.

Ramkes' eyes twinkled for a moment. "I remember her. I haven't forgotten that story about the string of volcanoes blowing and creating a sea of lava on Xann while she wore a Xannian face to help evacuate the denizens. Hah, what a fun tale, she's a talented storyteller."

She was probably there, Ahn'kat thought, but he held back telling the princess that a Zanashj assisted an enemy species under imperial dominion. "I'll bring the offer to her when I visit House Urbaz."

Ramkes nodded before sweeping around the desk and taking her seat. Ahn'kat bowed. He caught her smile before gliding out of the room, carrying some joy and hope with him.

~

Iron-like fingers pressed into his strained muscles, slowly and firmly teasing the inner strings apart. Ahn'kat suppressed a groan as the masseuse worked across his back shoulders; he could feel the muscle strings pulse and ache before easing. His hands gripped around the base of the cushioned altar as he forced his face to bury in the soft breathable opening. Sweat beaded on his back. Ahn'kat dreaded as it began to pool to his spine, fearing that the masseuse would be repulsed.

"A bit of your skin has come loose, your grace." his voice called behind.

Ahn'kat pressed his eyes shut. "Just pull it off!"

He could feel the man's fingers grip around the tissue, it was tender and very much attached. He sucked in a deep breath, waiting for the masseuse to rip the piece free from him. A sharp exhale that transformed into a pained growl. He leveraged to his elbows and turned to see the shed; it was remarkably small for the agony. The grandfatherly masseuse flicked the bloodied scale-like piece into a gold dish.

"Can't believe I'm still shedding; the physicians said it would go away when I became an adult." he said.

"A sign of stress, your grace. And I'm sorry to say that there is a mild odour from the wound." the man said before pressing his warm hand on the bloodied opening.

He could already feel the itching tingle of his cells trying to regenerate. "I haven't body-bent in far too long. Or did anything that resembled self-improvement." Ahn'kat stuffed his face back into the cushion.

"Your duties have taken priority, it is perfectly normal and understandable, your grace," he said as his hand peeled back from the once-missing skin, "and the wound has closed."

"What of the odour?" Ahn'kat said.

"I'm afraid it's still present. Usually a symptom of poor diet, either not enough or excessive consumption." he said.

Ahn'kat sat up and turned to the man. The suddenness made him step back and eyes widen. "I haven't drunk in a long while." he said.

"I was not intending offense, your grace," he said.

Ahn'kat rolled to the edge of the cushioned table and gripped his knees. He could feel his shoulders reclaim their fluidity. A part of him wanted to roll back and slide off the surface onto the floor into a green puddle. He looked at the masseuse and felt guilt. His stresses have already begun to ease and may dissipate when Emestasun comes. Then he can begin some real training.

"It's much better, thank you." he finally said.

The masseuse eased and smiled. "You're welcome. I know it's not common among nobles, but I would suggest doing some body-bending practices to prevent future lockups and improved functionality and fertility-"

Knuckles thumped on the door distracting the men for a moment – to his fortune. "A visitor, your grace." Zertun's voice called.

"Good, send them in." Ahn'kat said as he hurried his clothes on, provoking the masseuse to begin packing.

"Ah well, it's Gajoon – Neobatri's assistant." Zertun almost whispered through the wood.

Ahn'kat seized, even the masseuse ducked his head low to his ointments and tools.

"Send her in." The prince said.

The doors slid open. Zertun was the first to enter and then the tall scruffy half-Zanashj, followed by the palace guards with electric staves in-hand. Gajoon smiled and bowed; in her hand she held a bundle of brindled stick and vine figurines. More gifts for him, he wondered.

"How can I help you, Gajoon?" Ahn'kat said cocking his head.

Her thick and scarred lips opened, revealing a sliver of sharp teeth. "I, ahh, thought to be going to Pantheon shrine, but yer also worship?"

Ahn'kat's brow rose. "You would like me to join you?"

Gajoon nodded as she held up the figurines. He was almost glad they were not intended for him, as most gifts were usually of extreme value and the significantly less rustic. Yet, the mountain of work sat unattended for far too long, which will only grow if he left for a while. But the longer he thought about it...

"Alright, let's go." he said.

An uneasy familiar twinkle came to her eyes. Her strong fingers clutched the figurines closer to her as she backed to the door. Ahn'kat hid his blush, considering he had nothing to offer Aszelun and giving the over-abundant gifts intended to him to the Great Beetle would perhaps sour his fortune even further. He snapped up a golden serpent ring, commissioned by him from the royal jeweller, not his favourite, but certainly better than nothing.

As they were escorted down the halls and to the open back gardens of the pyramid, Ahn'kat glanced to Gajoon. "What is your family's totem?"

"Divine Serpent, but I can pick mine." she said.

The Great Beetle was House Urbaz's totem, he had no right to select one for himself as was tradition for noble houses. "What's yours?"

"I don't know, they all shine." she said as they walked through the tended meadow, leading to the back golden alfresco where the gods hid. The leaves clapped in the wind, as if the trees were whispering to each other as they walked.

"It's not just about how the gods 'look,' it's more than that." Ahn'kat said.

"Oh, I sorry, they shine all the time, even when dark. Yer not mad at me?" she said, looking over with her large natural predator's eyes, that also held something child-like about them.

"I'm not mad at you, Gajoon." he said. This made her smile and return her gaze forward, but his eyes remained on her. "Do you pray often?"

"Yah, praying feels better. Pray to gods and self. Same thing. Today, I pray for sisters. Shrine will make gods hear us better." she said.

"You have sisters?" he said, raising his brow.

Her chest welled with pride, but her smile had a tinge of sorrow. "Neobatri is sister-one."

Ahn'kat's mouth dropped open. "Ah, well...Neobatri will be returning soon."

Gajoon's eyes dropped to the ground. "She doing dangerous things, but she comes back. Neheret hasn't, she sister-two."

Ahn'kat's jaw clenched when he had forgotten about the other lost sister. "She will, we're still looking."

She nodded, but she didn't seem comforted by his assurance. Entering through the gold and granite pillars, the single statue of the whole Pantheon arched into a marvellous display of primal and noble energy. Ahn'kat used to visit the shrine when he first arrived at the palace. Aszelun's offering plate still had faded and dried flowers on it.

To his pleasant surprise, they weren't blown away, but they sat pitiful and neglected on the gold dish. He slipped the serpent ring onto one of the Great Beetle's arms. It was tight and sturdy, confident that it wouldn't fall or fly with heavy winds. Gajoon leant forward and wrapped a loose frayed string around the Beetle's horns, making certain it wouldn't come undone.

"There are plenty of other gods you could give the figures to." he said.

Gajoon cocked her head to the side. "This one looks full of love."

Ahn'kat smirked. The Great Beetle was thicker than the other narrow and slender gods. The guards pushed some cushions for kneeling on, but Gajoon let herself fall directly on hers before crossing her legs. He noticed old scars across her shins. He was surprised that her Zanashj half didn't regenerate enough to blend into the rest of her skin. He swallowed mild nausea at what or who could have caused that before pulling his eyes from them as he sat beside her.

"Fell on rocks," she pointed to the damaged wrinkled skin on her knee; her fingers drifted down to the others extending on her shin bone, "Neobatri and father."

"That looked painful." he voiced barely over a whisper.

Gajoon slapped the skin and grinned. "Not anymore! Neobatri took me away from father after Neheret left." she said.

He looked to her gleeful face. Amehtut Alkaheen was a well-travelled infiltrator, famous in the Corps, fathering half-breeds that was illegal, but sometimes infiltrators so far from the Empire…who would know? Bold of him to return to Uras with an off-worlder child, only to do…that to her. "We won't let that happen to you here."

"Happens, happens. Neobatri was sorry, she never said it, but she took me away – that was way of saying sorry for telling father about mother. Neheret vanished before she could forgive everyone, too," she said with another sad smile. "but Neheret was never sorry for me, we are friends. Now, Neobatri finally realised she is my friend. Took long time for her to see that."

"I don't quite understand, Gajoon." he said.

She sighed. "Mother was explorer on…Sye? Yah, Sye the planet. She loved my Raivan father. I didn't know him. Neobatri knew mother's secrets, but my Zanashj father didn't. She was sorry to make mistake telling father one day. He waited for me to be born and then mother left. Neheret was so angry at Neobatri and Zanashj father. Neobatri was also angry, but she had to be because it was the rules and always did what Zanashj father did. Neobatri didn't mean to be angry at me."

He pinched his nose bone, fighting to keep the sadness away, but it was drowning him. "We make a lot of accidents and mistakes. They can be as small as trusting someone who you believe is incapable of making them."

"Yah, my family still love, but confused." she said turning to him. "Yer not confused but loved."

Ahn'kat looked to the jewelled and gold statue. He envisioned Aszelun materialising before him, hoping he would tell him he was a failure or a winner, anything at all. Ahn'kat rose his open palms above his head as his eyes shut, hoping to catch any wisdom or comfort, maybe even a slap across the face from the Beetle. Then he would know whether he was right or wrong, but then again, which was House Urbaz or the Crown?

He stayed until he felt another body enter the alfresco. The guard's armour clinked, and boots shifted. Ahn'kat turned to see an elite infiltrator stride from the palace in the distance. His heart sank knowing Ismotaph was here, probably whispering in the princess's ear about something dreadful in a lovely way. Ahn'kat rose to his feet. Gajoon shot up too, but the surrounding guards moved the end of their sticks to her.

"No, it's alright. I will return." he said waving his hand down. They eased and so did she.

Zertun and he met eyes before heading to the infiltrator. From this distance, he couldn't tell what their features were, except for the shining bare scalp. They didn't move closer, they were as still as a dead tree trunk, and perhaps just as hollow.

"What news?" Ahn'kat whispered.

The infiltrator's eyes moved between the two. "Ismotaph is speaking with the princess and would like to have you join the conversation."

"Rather late to ask since they already started their meeting, wouldn't you say?" Ahn'kat narrowed his eyes.

The infiltrator's nostrils twitched. It was so slight that if Ahn'kat wasn't so focused on this creature's face, he would've missed it. "Ismotaph is here to meet with you, not the princess. Come before more eyes see."

They turned so quickly that is startled Ahn'kat. He and Zertun walked beside them, but Ahn'kat tried to keep half a step ahead of the infiltrator. They pulled a small finger-long disk from their wrist brace and pressed the electric end, proving that their face was theirs before pressing it into Ahn'kat's and Zertun's foreheads. The small shock wasn't painful, but he felt his entire body ripple and loosen when the electricity ran its course.

"Ismotaph already has a list of names that don't support the Crown's current choices, none implicate House Urbaz. He will sort the traitors out. Junior Infiltrator Alkaheen will return with the same names, and you must be the one to take her list to Ramkes." they said.

Ahn'kat clenched his jaw and tightened his fists. "*Princess* Ramkes-"

"The traitors are in the pocket of Seratut. When called for his arrest, he will directly go to Ismotaph's agents." they whispered, climbing the polished staircase, and turning down to the royal hall.

Ahn'kat wanted to bury his face in his hands. "What in the gods is that idiot priest doing?"

"The inquisitors will get the right information from the traitors against Seratut before the trial."

"Aren't you worried that he will talk about us?"

The infiltrator's eyes turned down to him but kept his head straight ahead. "We will get the *right* evidence against the words of an unpopular priest."

Through the tall windows, he caught a glimpse of Gajoon and several guards remaining under the alfresco. Guilt chewed at him for leaving her behind for perhaps the rest of the day. He turned to the infiltrator. "Ismotaph needs to investigate Neheret Alkaheen's disappearance. She vanished the same night when the Unbound came, she might have been kidnapped by them."

The infiltrator was silent.

"Well?" Ahn'kat said.

"Time is passing." the infiltrator hissed before taking flight up the stairs.

Ahn'kat and Zertun begrudgingly followed them to Ramkes' apartments. There was the second elite infiltrator by the pillar, eyeing Ahn'kat from his crown to sandals. The infiltrator extended their arm to knock, but Zertun dashed ahead first. His bodyguard tried hiding his pride being the first to touch the door.

"Come." Ramkes' voice called.

When the doors pulled apart, Ismotaph turned and gave a sweeping bow. "Good to see you again in good health, your grace."

Ahn'kat forced a smile. "And you, Ismotaph. I hope we can make this quick, I haven't finished prayers yet."

"That will need to wait. We're wrapping some tedious details to ensure the right information goes to the Empire should the Arinu ask for more changes from us." Ramkes said extending her hand to the chair across her desk.

"I have full trust that you and Ismotaph will be able to delegate this without me." he said.

"All in the interest to keep you informed, your grace." Ismotaph said.

Ahn'kat's chest wanted to sigh but tempered it with a long and silent exhale before settling into the chair, aching to drift away.

Break II

Eternity slipped through her fingers like fine sand. Infinity cluttered her like diamond walls. Everywhere and nowhere. Doomed to knowing everything and incapable of expressing. Sazla could see her kin; they were blind to the universe as they wondered how to free her. She looked beyond to the Neavensoros ancient home. Their ancestors lingered in the shards of space they had broken eons ago. In a blink, she saw their rise and then ascension into this null existence. They were smiling back at her with awe at the power of their descendants, believing with all their hearts to have succeeded in evolution. It was the death of reason and purpose, yet her kind still refused to admit this. Building and shaping worlds was running away from the dead end. Binding and assimilating each other's souls into one being was their needless climb to higher power.

When they ascended, there were millions. Now, the whole of their species lay within several dozen individuals that surrounded her. Sazla could hear their cries of love and loss for her. She pitted these gods for they were also trapped at the top of the evolutionary mountain. Over their shoulders, by their cradle-world, winds of change were coming. Sazla knew their absence was noticed by the children, she saw them painting on the walls of the house, she saw them push and punch, she saw them climb through the chaos. All her kin's work will be undone. They failed as teachers and now, their legacy will fall. She wanted to scream out to her siblings to turn around and stop this madness, but no words could escape.

While her kin mourned for her, the children were whispering in each other's ears: they were planning something.

Chapter Nineteen
Ahn'kat VII:
Infiltrator Prince

He needed to be the one to drive the flying vehicle. His chauffer and attendants since he had become prince had almost made him forget how to pilot one. It was in his blood, and he would not let anyone take it away. Ahn'kat's heavily ringed hands wrapped around the living handles. It began to purr, and the leathery seats sealed him and his companions. He could feel Zertun's gaze on him and smile.

"Few times when I see you happy." he said.

The vehicle left the balcony and slid over the air, and gardens. "Very few things that still do."

"I'm surprised Lord and Lady Urbaz did not have you train as a star pilot." he said resting his head against the seat.

"They did, but only through holo-simulators. I would like to be in the real thing and become a star commander, to be away from everything." he said.

"I knew plenty of star commanders, the position is too secure since most of our old enemies were too primitive to be of any real threat. Those commanders get too into their own heads and start believing they're the emperors of every corner of space they fly to." he said.

"Maybe I should wear a commander's face, and we can swap roles for a day." Ahn'kat grinned as he looked to the beryl jungle below them.

"Who wouldn't want to be the baby-faced Prince of the Empire? Who knows, maybe the new prince might throw you to the metamorphic prisons if you tried to return." he said.

"I'm not hearing a negative, Zertun." he could see the Urbaz pyramid looming to the horizon. "Baby-faced? I have nothing of the sort," Ahn'kat turned and frowned at his bodyguard.

"Focus on where you're driving, your grace. It's not just your life in here." Zertun pointed ahead. "The beard nicely hides your baby-face."

"I miss the days when you were just my bodyguard and not my friend." he mumbled. As they drew closer to the mansion, his chest was poked with dread. What would his parents say about his pro-Federation campaign? Would they call him a fool straight to his face? Would they lose faith in him and assume he was no longer on their side? Was he even still on their side?

The vehicle slowed and lingered in the air for a moment before descending on the balcony. He could see his old house staff circling around the entrance; their fresh and eager faces beamed up at him. Then he spotted her face. Emestasun broke out of line and approached first. He wanted to jump and embrace her, but there were too many eyes searching for scandals. Her aura was like a blue flame.

He extended his forearms, and she embraced them with her hands as she grinned. "Finally! Could you not have returned sooner?"

"Complaining my not visiting while I am currently visiting is a poor incentive for future visitations." he said, silently greeting the others, but he noticed that his parents were not among them. "Where are Lady and Lord Urbaz?"

Emestasun's face dimmed. "Their schedules are full, and it is becoming…taxing, but they will join you shortly."

"I cannot remain here when it's convenient for them." he said under his breath.

"We will discuss it." she said extending her arm into the pyramid. Ahn'kat was instantly met with a sharp smell of mint wafting through the halls. He remembered his servants would use it to soothe his mind when he injured himself during playtime to help with flesh regeneration as a child. It was most common for only children to be given these ointments as their brains and bodies experienced rapid development, but not for adults. The halls and chambers were still, but there was a lifelessness to them, and the powerful blend of colours receded into a strange dullness.

"Call them for me, please." Ahn'kat turned to one of the servants.

"Ah, Lord and Lady Urbaz are unwell at the moment, your grace. They have requested you to meet with them in the meeting room." he said.

Ahn'kat's nose flared. "They were well aware of my arrival, if they were sick then I could have come-"

"Your grace, we need to speak." Emestasun said as her head cocked to the library.

Ahn'kat and Zertun followed her through the still library and into the private study room. She ushered them in and closed the doors before turning around and closing her eyes while her back rested against the wood. "It's safe here."

"What are you talking about?" Ahn'kat asked.

"Before I continue, I need to make sure you are Ahn'kat and Zertun," she said eyeing them.

"You see into the truth of things, Emestasun, can you not tell?" Zertun said.

"It seems I cannot rely on that so much anymore." she said as she pulled out a mental scanning disk from her belt. Ahn'kat noticed she had hidden the device in the thick leathery folds, before pressing the flat metal into his and his guard's forehead. "Good. To be honest, I don't know what I would've done if you were infiltrators…"

"What's going on?" Ahn'kat said.

"Lord and Lady Urbaz have not been themselves for the last several months. At first, I thought that they have been replaced by some wretched infiltrators, but some of my deeper insights, they are still very much them...but not. They have been meeting with strange people at night, if you can call them that, they looked more like shadows to me. Other staff say they are completely neglecting their duties in the ship bays and hardly see anyone anymore." she said.

Ahn'kat's backside rested against the desk edge. He remembered when Reshj requested that House Urbaz receive the first batch of psi-enhancers and the smell of mint would help calm a newly psychic mind...so he assumed. "Do your higher senses tell you there is psionic energy here?"

She pressed her lips together. "Our dreams have been affected and hardly anyone is sleeping, it's hard to say."

"I was going to discuss some shipping business with them, see if I can take a hold of operations for a while until this is resolved. You need to come back with me to the palace." he said.

She shook her head. "I can't-"

"I've already spoken with the princess about you becoming a tutor there, she has accepted it and is expecting you." he said.

"No, listen, I don't trust that things won't worsen the second I leave. I have been trying to calm them myself and the rest of the estate, someone needs to be here for them. And who's to say if they start acting out, House Urbaz will fall under suspicion." she said.

"And what if it does get worse? We don't even know what this is," he said.

"Ahn'kat, I am an expert on psionics. I not only sense things, but I have some effect too. I am covering up for them as much as you are." she said.

"Then I will have Zertun stay with you until you're able to come to the palace." he said.

"I am sworn to you, Ahn'kat." Zertun said.

"But I can order you!" he said.

"Your life takes precedent-"

"Zertun, I-"

"Ahn'kat, listen!" she breathed, and he was forced to meet her eyes. "If I need help, I will say. Right now, you cannot cast away not a single friend, you must be shielded. I've faced greater and uglier uncertainties, I *will* adapt."

He closed his eyes as his hands clutched at the beetle pendant. "Zertun will fetch you the second you need." he straightened his back and looked to the closed door, imagining the dire castle beyond. "I will see my parents now, we've been in here far too long."

The doors opened and the three spilled out. Ahn'kat didn't sense anyone trying to spy on them. The servants tended to their duties, but their soulless efforts and sullen faces made his stomach tighten. He pinched a small banana from the offering bowl before making his ascend to the meeting room with Zertun several inches closer than normal. His heart raced with every step, the smell of mint growing sharper to nearly unbearable levels. He twisted the insides of his nasal cavity to deaden some of the nerves to make to the next flight of stairs.

"Your grace." the guards whispered and bowed as he passed them along the halls to their meeting room. The closed gold encrusted doors felt a mile away as he strode to their surface. "Lady and Lord Urbaz?"

Silence.

"Mother? Father?" he called.

He knocked.

The door creaked open, expecting to see Reshj or Henuttamon, or one of the attendants opening for him, but there was only them two...lounging and napping on the sofas. The doors had moved on their own. They appeared to have been wearing the same fine garbs for several days. Their braids and plaits were coming loose with streaks of oils, their makeup was smeared off from tears and other skin grease – even their skin was building in thick patches. Ahn'kat took half a step back, but his mother's eyes opened, and her head rose from the pillow. "Ahn'kat?"

He strode in, leaving Zertun outside with his hand still clutching around the pendant under his robe. "I was, uh, expecting a reception at the balcony."

"My son!" Reshj rose and extended his arms. His embrace made Ahn'kat tense and shrink.

"Father," he said giving a gentle squeeze of his forearm as he looked between the two of them. No bows, no titles, this must have felt like a commoner's family, but he was in the room with strangers. "I have some business with the shipyards that need discussing."

"Oh yes, lets discuss that, but first…" Henuttamon smiled as she rose and planted a kiss on his cheek. "We saw your speech to promote the Federation, you did splendidly."

Ahn'kat forced a grin as he prayed to Aszelun to wrap his thick wings around him. "I am doing what the princess request, hence for my business here-"

"Yes, yes. You are doing so well. Even she is starting to believe you…" Henuttamon said as her fingers ran along his cheek. Her too long and yellowed nails slipped and sliced his skin, but he froze, letting the accident be.

"Good. I must ask-"

"Yes, and you haven't taken yours yet." Henuttamon tapped under his chin. "We weren't expecting for them to be-,"

"this intense." they spoke together.

His fingers gripped his pendant so hard that the tiny gems cut into his skin. "I am worried about both of you, your behaviour is too risky."

"No one knows anything, and it will remain that way. As good leaders, we need to understand what it will be like for the whole Empire to experience this feeling...then we will be able to teach them." Henuttamon said. "And once we fully know, then you will too!"

"What do you feel?" he said looking between them.

Reshj chuckled. "Now, we are equals."

"With the Arinu?"

"Better than; Zanashj adapt and the Arinu cannot." Henuttamon said.

"You wanted to speak about the shipyards?" Reshj said.

Ahn'kat steeled himself. "It has come to my attention our business is not growing as it once was, in fact, its slipping. I am concerned for this house's future if this continues and..." he took a breath, "if you are in the middle of a metamorphosis, how can you be attentive to it?"

"You said the princess asked you to come." Reshj said.

"It's part of a social and economic experiment, to see if we can adapt to a pet-free organisation." he said.

Henuttamon frowned. "She is terrified of those Arinu. The Crown is shaking! By the Great Beetle and Empire, she is twisting you!"

"And so, what if she believes it? My purpose is to blend my goals with hers at the beginning." he said.

"How long will it take for you then to believe in the Federation and meek emperor?" Reshj said as his brow rose and eyes pierced through Ahn'kat.

"I am loyal to this house, Pantheon and Empire. Right now, I am trying to survive a storm the two of you have thrown me into!" he growled as his back strained. Their unmoving and unblinking eyes were on him, only the gods knew what ran through their heads. He pressed his temples and sighed. "Seratut will be arrested for treason. He will go to Ismotaph's trusted agents, and they will make sure he won't speak about us. If you give me control of the shipyards, I'll discard any evidence of the prisoners."

"Why the arrest?" Reshj said.

"For creating discourse in the royal court and among other noble houses, trying to fight the Crown's Federation decision." he said.

"We see." he looked to Henuttamon. "Thank you for letting us know, my son. You may take the factories and bays, for now."

~

The little capsule rolled along his palm. His nimble fingers caught it on the very edge as he pinched it, feeling its warmth. He carefully rested it on his desk. It was such a tiny thing, but its presence devoured his whole apartment, palace, and planet. He could feel the full moon behind him, its light beaming through his windows and onto the polished wooden surface. Ahn'kat opened his hands and rested them against the armchair as his head leant back for his eyes to meet the ceiling, imaging the stars above him.

"Please, Aszelun, help me." he whispered. Seeing his parents so altered and haggard made him want to toss the capsule in the waste-breaker. But should he take it, he wouldn't end up like them with Emestasun guiding him. He despaired at the thought of leaving her there with them, but again, with so much power; he was utterly powerless.

A knock on his door jolted him from his prayer. His hand snatched the capsule and stuffed it back under his chin. "Yes?"

"It's me, your grace." Zertun said.

"Come." he said as he straightened his beard and vest.

His bodyguard slipped through. "I did some asking and found out a way for the computers to save copies of messages with Ismotaph – also some new devices that cannot be detected by conventional scanners. Only top-ranking officials have them."

"Then we can assume Ismotaph will have scanners to detect those listeners. Anyone you know that can make modifications?" Ahn'kat said.

"There are, but that may take a little time to ensure complete discretion." Zertun said.

"Good, good." Ahn'kat nodded as his eyes travelled up to his friend. "Anything else?"

Zertun cleared his throat. "Neobatri has returned."

Ahn'kat breathed deep as he rose to his feet. "Alright, where is she?"

"Her quarters." Zertun said as he followed Ahn'kat storming out of the bedroom. He could feel hot blood running through him as he dashed down to the lower levels of the palace. Gajoon's 'guards' were posted out the front of their dorm, and he could hear loud and frustrated voices from within. One of the guards tapped on the door and announced the prince's presence and the voices dropped.

"Please enter." Neobatri called.

She was in loose black slacks with a worn-in leathery vest. Her hair was patchy, and many chunks of various colours sprinkled the ground. Her natural blue-black hair was returning underneath. Her muscles had also shrunk, leaving behind a slight sagging of skin, but they were also growing back before his eyes. Neobatri's eyes were sunken in and exhausted. She and Gajoon stood and bowed before him.

"Thank you for seeing me so soon, your grace." she said.

"Yer highness." Gajoon said.

"Glad that you have returned in good form." he said stepping in and taking a seat. "What news?"

"Much to say, here's my full report." she said, taking her seat beside him and pulling out a data crystal. "To surmise: after mingling in the royal court, I had heard several consistent names from notable houses that disapproved of the Crown's plans. I took several faces of servants and copied all relevant files, on and on. The one thing they all had in common was the Conclave, particularly..." Neobatri looked to his pendant, "I apologise in bringing the news, but High Priest Seratut seems to be the culprit."

Curtains drawn, spotlights beamed, the stage was ready for his performance. Ahn'kat sank back in the chair as he took a deep breath. "Are you certain?"

"Beyond doubt." she said as her hand waved in the air, dismissing any argument.

"Why? What is he thinking?" he said as he pressed his hand on his chin.

Neobatri pressed her lips together. "It appears that...your popularity has outshone his. Much of your work and funds towards constructing improved homes for pets in the Conclave have ended up in his and his inner circle's pockets." she snuck a quick glance to Gajoon before forcing herself to continue. "And many of your reformations regarding treatments of former pets have reverted back to the old ways, the children have it the worst. They live in total squalor in the smaller monasteries and temples, working needlessly hard to the point of permanent injury. Staff and other children are also encouraged to...physically remind them of their position in life."

Gajoon's knuckles cracked.

"This is against the Empire's ethics and your morals. Yes, they are pets, but they are not...apologies, your grace, please excuse my opinions." she said.

This was far worse than Ismotaph's elite infiltrator made it sound. No doubt he would have known how these people were suffering. He clutched his hands together as he forced his heartbeat to slow. "No, don't apologise. This is a travesty. It goes against the Pantheon and a disgrace to the Conclave. He will face the emperor's justice."

"What are yer going to do with their children of traitors?" Gajoon said.

Neobatri shot a glare her half-sister. "Gajoon! Don't ask-"

"They still need to be questioned, but they are innocent of their parent's crimes," he slowly said as he looked into her fearful and furious eyes. "But they will be taken care of, after we have corrected Seratut's and his ilk's errors."

"No wonder he is jealous of you, your grace." Neobatri said coiling a flimsy hair strand around her finger.

"Nothing to envy of a position where enemies sprout like weeds." he stood and so did they. "Thank you for your efforts. Both of you are free to remain here for as long as you wish."

"That's very generous, but only if we continue to be of use and service. Many forget that the Intel Corps is a shield for the Empire and is meant to serve the emperor or empress. If we're anything other, then we're nothing." Neobatri said, though her voice was calm, there was a fire of distain simmering under her skin.

The corner of his lips smiled. "You're absolutely right, Neobatri. Peaceful nights to both of you." he said looking between them.

"Yer grace." Gajoon said.

With a slight nod, Ahn'kat whirled out of the room and down the hall. His stomach ached for food and his eyes demanded to sleep, but he pushed forward to Ramkes's quarters. His heart hammered as adrenaline coursed through him when he reached her doors, but he debated whether this could wait for the morn. Ahn'kat didn't want to rouse her from sleep to deliver awful news. He feared she might start identifying him as the herald of doom. He tapped on her door and whispered his presence.

"Come." a deep male voice responded. He pulled back as fury pinched his already heated heart. Ahn'kat pried the doors apart and his legs numbed the moment he saw Emperor Kreshut inside. Ramkes wasn't here, except a couple of casually dressed guards with the emperor, who sat over at her desk.

Ahn'kat bowed deep, his body almost forgetting how to show courtesy before someone higher than he. "Your majesty."

Kreshut looked up from the desk. His attire was also modest. He beckoned Ahn'kat to come forward. He held up one of his forearms and the prince gave it a gentle squeeze. He was surprised how much firm tissue was in a man of several thousand years of age. "You look well, Ahn'kat."

"Thank you, sir. Forgive my surprise, I wasn't notified of your arrival and...". as he looked around Ramkes' apartment void of herself.

"We had only just arrived. The princess is tied in a very long diplomatic meeting, she's holding her own and asked me to come in her stead to retrieve some documents." his eyes were the same calm and peace as at the wedding.

Ahn'kat nodded. "I see, well, there's some information that needs to be brought to you. Regarding a list of names-"

"Pardon my cutting in, but I'm already aware of the situation. Do you know what the source is behind this disloyalty in the court?" he said.

"High Priest Seratut, your majesty." Ahn'kat pulled the crystal from his sleeve and left it on the desk.

Kreshut lent forward and squeezed the lightly milky crystal. "Disappointing to hear the rumours were true."

"You had already suspected him of treachery?"

The emperor's lips winced. "I've known the High Priest for a long time, his love for the gods has always been a little greater than his love for the Empire. However, he loves the side of them that made us into a galactic force. I hoped overtime, he would understand the Crown's choices."

"His behaviour is an offence to the Pantheon and Empire." Ahn'kat said.

Kreshut leant back in the chair. "His is not of unique opinion. I know everything the court says about me, they think I'm so removed from Uras and into the stars that I cannot hear them." he looked at the heavy silver and gold hawk ring around his thumb and smiled. "Some even say that my totem should be a spider-fly instead. Small and weak, but they forget one of the most amazing things about spider-flies."

"What's that, sir?" Ahn'kat dreaded this conversation.

"The first bite from a spider-fly is a danger to children, but a nuisance for an adapted adult. However, in time and enough stress, the venom can reawaken from our genes and kill the adult victim." he said.

Ahn'kat's feet and hands went numb as he tried to keep an intrigued stare at the emperor. "You are too grand for such a creature, your majesty."

Kreshut cracked a smile. "I appreciate that, dear son, but the older I get, the more I see." he stood up and made way to the door, followed by his guards. "Thank you for this, Ahn'kat."

"My pleasure." he bowed, feeling some blood return to his limbs.

As he slid open the door again, Kreshut turned and tapped his chin. "Another aspect I admire about spider-flies: they have eyes everywhere."

~

Fall rolled into the parks outside Lusor City, the home and seat of the Emperor's Palace and the heart of the Conclave on the other side of the skyscraper ring. He could see the tall organic towers; manipulated trees grew along the walls to power various rooms within the structures; glass-like membranes would flex should an unaware bird or stone, or laser were to strike it. Bio-builders said if the structures broke, the walls would bleed before slowly regrowing their shattered forms into something stronger. Thousands of people lived and worked in these mega structures. All embraced the new, unlike the stagnant holy pyramids that acted as homes for a thousand generations of worshipers and lords.

The crowd cheered for him when he stood over the golden plated and marble balcony. They cried his name and sang hymns for the animal gods. Today he would address the Zanashj in the wild autumn gardens around the Conclave, a holy time and place for the Pantheon. The spot where the common people stood was shared by the sunset-horned horses, grazing the long grass, sky-serpents with the glittering amethyst scales while their flame-like feathers beat against the wind, and the golden and auburn hawks that circled around the trees, spying for the sapphire beetles that nestled along the branches.

His breath was stolen as he watched a hawk dive in, trying to rip the insect from its home, but the beetle clutched its legs around the branch refusing to be the hawk's prey. The bird's talons scratched the hard casing as its beak tried to break through the natural armour, but the beetle's family encircled the avian and pressed their horns into its belly. After a momentary resistance, which felt like an eternity for the beetle, the hawk released the branch and took to the sky once more.

Ahn'kat sighed with relief, but taking a glance to his right, Princess Ramkes stood, smiling, and waving to the adoring crowd, while Emperor Kreshut stood to his right, still and silent as he lorded over his people. Ahn'kat's eyes wandered through the crowd, hoping to catch his mother's and father's faces, but their transformation into...something other, held their attention more than his sermon. He could feel Ismotaph behind him, beside Zertun and other High Priests. Seratut was also there, but he didn't know where. He feared to turn to see his soggy face standing directly behind.

"Fall has touched Lusor Province once again, where the harsh summer has met its end, and nature takes a momentary breath before taking her rest for the cold, when the Pantheon and their children and worshipers share the fields, seas, and skies of Uras, as one great being embodying a great many forms. This is the unending and unbreaking circle of life on Uras and the Empire. The Crown and

Conclave comes to the Imperial Family to share this festival of shedding the old and preparing for the new.

"For the first millennia of my reign, blessed by the High Hawk, we have known tranquillity and prosperity for the Empire, however, if one does not exercise change regularly; then we will atrophy. The Federation is a test from the Pantheon and their blessing in disguise. As one, we will overcome it and immunise ourselves of everything the future brings to us. We are Empire; we are Zanashj." Emperor Kreshut said as he stepped away from the rail. The crowd screamed, clapped, clicked, and stomped with delight. Barren tables around the gardens beamed as food and drink flashed on their surface before the music and singers started their performance.

Ahn'kat's brows shot up as he leaned beside Ramkes. "We aren't having traditional servers bring the festival food out?"

She shook her head with a smile. "The ships ported the meals from the kitchens to the tables, needn't waste time."

Ahn'kat grinned as he watched some of the children tossing lime apples to the horned horses and their offspring. They nuzzled the fruits before carefully taking a bite into the sour and sweet flesh. He turned to the elite crowd on the balcony, all sharing and chatting with excitement. Seratut roared a laugh as he patted another High Priestess on the shoulder, making her chapeau wobble. The emperor made his seat separated from the group, but even he seemed to enjoy the light air, and Ismotaph sat to the far corner of the long table, grinning while his eyes sparkled at the people around him. This moment, even though half of them were readying to tear each other apart, shared this time in peace with the Pantheon. He wished the fall could last for the rest of the year and into forever.

Zertun pulled a chair for Ramkes before Ahn'kat, he shot the bodyguard a feigned look of betrayal and jealousy before settling in.

"A shame Lord and Lady Urbaz couldn't attend, I didn't expect rotfinger to mutate so quickly." Ramkes said as she plucked succulent leaves drenched in salty vinegars on her plate.

"I've been telling them for years to take better care of their bodies when going to the Underworld Caves, all manner of fungi and diseases just aching to infect the unprepared." he said pouring himself a banana liquor. He could feel Ramkes watching him as he placed it to his lips, to his horror, it was removed of the harsh alcoholic burn. "What poor mockery is this?"

"A better alternative." she smiled before popping a bite-size leaf in her mouth.

Anger rose inside him; he snatched a water pitcher and poured it into a fresh goblet. "If you want to humiliate me like this, on this day…"

"Calm yourself, you'll notice there is no alcohol on any of these tables." she said eyeing all the wait staff and tables.

"Since when? The Fall Festival is meant to be…festive." he said, downing the entire goblet. "Besides, I am handling this personally and have been doing well without interference."

"This is not a slight on you, Ahn'kat. Our cells don't cope well when they're contaminated with alcohol, and as the heads of the Empire, we need to set an example and be prepared for the future." she said.

"Is this because the Arinu don't drink or do anything fun?" he grinned. She glared at him, but he continued smiling. "If we're not careful, then we will morph into Arinu."

She tried holding her frustration but pulled away when her lips twitched into a smile.

He glanced around the tables again; Seratut caught his eye and held up his gold goblet in shape of a swan holding up the cup. Ahn'kat kept a polite smile before returning to his dish and wondering what food to grab. He could hear the party below the balcony and sighed with disappointment. "Shame Neobatri and Gajoon couldn't attend."

"I tried to convince them, but they wouldn't have it," she said eyeing the elites. "Neobatri would've had a seat here, but refused if her assistant couldn't be by her side."

"What better way to improve alien relations than by having an actual hybrid to celebrate with us? And a follower of the Pantheon at that! The people would've loved it if you did that." he said, while feeling the beetle pendant resting on his belly.

"I don't make all the choices yet and the people would probably praise you more than me." she said taking another bite.

Ahn'kat frowned. "What do you mean?"

Ramkes pressed her lips together as she swallowed. "The people have a just reason to love you, but you're in the spotlight. While I work in the back, trying to make order from chaos and receive little more than an arm shake. Its immature, I know, this work is mostly away from the spotlight, I know, but I hope the people won't forget me when it's my time." she said as she looked to her father.

Ahn'kat sighed. His fingers found their way under her palm and squeezed. "Their attention is on my face for now, but you will be remembered throughout time."

She smiled and squeezed back. The remainder of their dining and festivities remained light and joyous, even when the sun started to dip to the horizon. A whiff of rain was in the air; the shields would have protected them, but a part of him wanted to shower under the last warm days. People were emptying the gardens, but the music still played for the remaining guests. Ramkes was called away for a surprise meeting with some delegates, while Ismotaph followed her like a shadow.

Ahn'kat shook his dry goblet and eyed for fine bottles and jugs. The Conclave would have sacred wines and liquors for ceremonies stored below the temple. He slipped away from the party and made his way to the balcony entrance. Zertun skipped behind him as they made through the halls.

"Apologies for taking you away from the conversation." Ahn'kat said as they passed a row of the decorated great animals. His eye was pulled to the horned beetle holding a small shallow dish.

"High Priestess Shentat did have some interesting things to say." he said.

Ahn'kat glanced to him with a smirk. "What would the High Priestess be saying to you?"

"Nothing inappropriate. She had peculiar ideas about the Pantheon, who and what they were." he said.

"A new interpretation? Seratut wouldn't appreciate it and that earns her my favour." Ahn'kat mumbled as he found the staircase leading down to the storerooms.

"She's an interesting woman, she was lieutenant to Star Commander Kamdaes before she found her calling in the Conclave. She said that many cultures in the cosmos have their own version of the Pantheon." he said.

"Delightfully surprising. It would make sense that there would be some individuals out there that could sense and communicate with the gods." he said.

"Possible, but she implied something a little controversial." he whispered as the stepped into the kitchens. The staff stopped and bowed while they passed. "She said 'If we, as Zanashj, look like gods to our old dominion worlds, then wouldn't we interpret advanced aliens as the Pantheon?'"

Ahn'kat rolled his eyes as he pressed through the cellar door. "We've been the star faring for dozens of millennia, I think if our gods were aliens then we would've met them by now." he said as he turned. His eye caught a large, shadowed figure by the tall copper kegs. His heart almost stopped when he recognised Seratut's grinning face holding a small casket of sacred wine under his arm.

"My Prince." he bowed; his grey whiskers trembled under his breath.

"High Priest, apologies for not realising it was you." he said trying to force a confused and relieved grin.

"I couldn't help but overhear your conversation about the gods being aliens, I assume you've spoken with the High Priestess Shentat?"

Ahn'kat looked to Zertun. The bodyguard's face was flat as stone.

"I have heard it, but I think it's highly unlikely." Ahn'kat said.

Seratut nodded. "The Pantheon are gods: they are not of flesh and are void of its weaknesses. That's why we worship them and try to become them – though we can only try."

"They are a model we strive to be." Ahn'kat said blankly.

"Yes, but we stopped doing that in recent times." he stepped closer. "The younglings are taught these days the gods wove life into existence on a barren Uras, like it was told to you, I'm sure. However, I remember the old tales were quite different."

"How so?"

Seratut straightened his back. "When the timeless gods found Uras, the planet was not dead. On every field, under every rock, over every hill, demons crawled and horrors too unthinkable to imagine. They hated how wretched these creatures existed, they consumed their own young and even tried manipulating the gods to fight each other. One day, when the gods ceased their squabbles, they became the Pantheon and wiped these monsters away from Uras. Ensuring that their likeness will never be felt by the cosmos, but it was not an easy-won war. They conquered old Uras and remade her under their direction. The Empire understood this once."

"Conquest isn't the only way to ensure direction. Cooperation sometimes leads to greater victories than dominance." Ahn'kat said.

"Cooperation can be a form of conquest if done right, but sadly, the Empire has forgotten to fear the Pantheon and instead place it in those off-worlders." he said slowly. "Over time, they will fear the Pantheon and if we are blessed, the whole cosmos will fear us again."

Ahn'kat's jaw clenched. "You don't know what the Arinu are, they're not just another race to be con-"

"I know they never were conquerors; I know they never had a war. For all their psionics, they barely know half of what we've mastered since the dawn ages. Testing me on what I know would be very, very foolish, Ahn'kat." he growled.

"No doubt with your experience, you should be very wise by now. Imagine my disappointment." he said.

Seratut bellowed a laugh. "You're unhappy with my choices of late, I understand, but my actions were not unsupported by our fellow few." he winked.

"Don't dare speak to me like a child-"

"No, no, my young prince! You're offended by the wrong thing entirely. Imagine how upset you would be when Ismotaph has no further use of you, like he has no use for me anymore." he said.

Ahn'kat's heart hammered. "Imagine how offended the princess will be when she finds out...unless precautions are met. You've endangered many lives for your pride-"

The round priest strode to the door before turning back to the terrified prince. "Again, you fail to see what is happening around you. You have a chance to ask me why Ismotaph wanted me to be part of this misalliance and why he is choosing to step over me. No, no, don't think it's because he cares about those miserable children in the monasteries."

Any semblance of joy Ahn'kat had minutes ago was bled by the High Priest flapping his unnerving dry lips and sadistic glare. He didn't know if he was trying to warn him or mess with his already messed mind. Maybe this was Seratut's way of asking the prince's protection from Ismotaph by dangling something he needs to know over his head. Ahn'kat didn't want to be lured in by his offering of 'knowledge,' but in these unstable times, what could the priest say that would break into more chaos.

The prince parted his lips as he tried swallowing his pride, but Seratut chuckled before he could get a word out.

"Believe it or not, I'm fond of you, Ahn'kat, so take a piece of advice: you will know your enemy when they help you too much."

When the priest left, Ahn'kat swallowed a gulp of saliva before rushing over to the copper tank and filling up half his goblet.

"If given the word, I would've made his death into an accident." Zertun growled.

"Then I would lose you too," Ahn'kat mumbled before rushing out of the cellar and back to the hall with the Pantheon statues lay. He tipped every drop of his goblet into Aszelun's dish and prayed until he was too exhausted to stand.

~

The nightly breeze rolled through his windows; he watched the transparent curtains lift and drop. His eyes rolled to the blue banner above him. Ahn'kat rolled to his side. He could feel the sheets clinging to his back. He tried resting his eyes, he tried stimulating his hormones to make his mind sleep, but his body betrayed him.

In the distance, his ears perked to heavy thuds and loud shrills. He spun around to the door as his heart thumped. Did Seratut tell on him? Does the princess know?

The angered yells continued; several heavy boots stomped passed his chambers. Ahn'kat shot out of bed and grabbed for his robe and dashed into the hall. He could see a few guards running to the princess's room. He followed behind them when he finally heard her voice commanding them to stay away. They glanced to him to say something – do something, but he didn't wait to be ushered.

"Ramkes." he called as his knuckles tapped at the door. Finally, the tiredness struck in him where he stood.

Shuffling of furniture and other items dropped before feet stormed to the doors. They creaked open, but he could only see her hand waving him in. Without hesitation, he slid in and was overwhelmed with the shattered chairs. Ornate figurines were tossed across the room, the bedsheets were ripped from order and even the cloth of the canopy was shredded.

Ramkes looked worse. The whites of her eyes were blood red, furious tears streamed down her face, her once slick and tidy hair was rustled and some of her strands were caught in her mouth. And her fingernails grew into menacing looking talons.

"What in the gods is going on?" he mouthed as he slowly walked to her. "What happened?"

She sucked in a deep breath as her nostrils flared. "The delegates…those damn filthy bald-" as she picked up a jug of water from the tray, the only unsullied thing within her reach, and tossed it at the window.

"The Arinu? We're not at war, are we?" he said as his eyes widened.

She slowed as her lips trembled before dropping on the floor against the bed. "They…the ambassadors said the Arinu are no longer interested in the Federation. After everything *we* have done to accommodate them!"

Ahn'kat dropped beside her. "Did they say they want to put it on hold or?"

"No, they are not interest *at all* anymore." she said pressing her palms to her eyes.

He feared that Seratut or Ismotaph may have been involved. "Did they say why?"

"You would think they would give us that curtesy! Everything, all of it, was a waste."

"All is not lost, we can at least press them to see why, maybe something we can change-"

She pulled her hands down and waved his words away. "'No,' that was their answer. I cannot believe I trusted psychics, they're so wily."

He slowly rose to his feet. "Ramkes, there is a tomorrow, I promise you'll have a clearer head by then. This is shocking, but even if we don't make allies with the Arinu, the Empire is still prospering even with all the wonderful changes."

She sighed as she looked up. "If I still feel this way by the dawn, I could have you arrested for breaking that promise to me."

"Only if you find a more attractive and convincing replacer." he grinned as held out his hand.

"Oh, I'm not interested in having that conversation with my father." she said gripping his hands before rising to her feet. Fortunately, her talons retracted back into normal fine nails.

The pair took a moment to absorb the damaged chamber before glancing to the bed.

"You could sleep here." she said as she wiped her smudged eyeliner with a soft smile.

He couldn't help but smile back. "That would be nice."

Chapter Twenty
Treneer VII: New Student

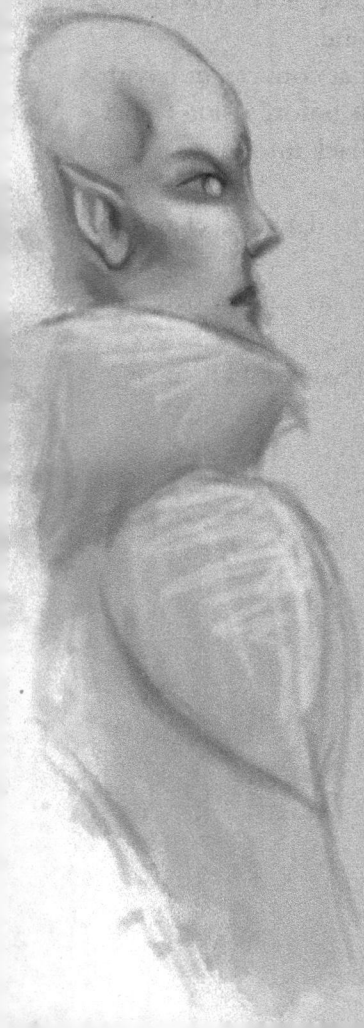

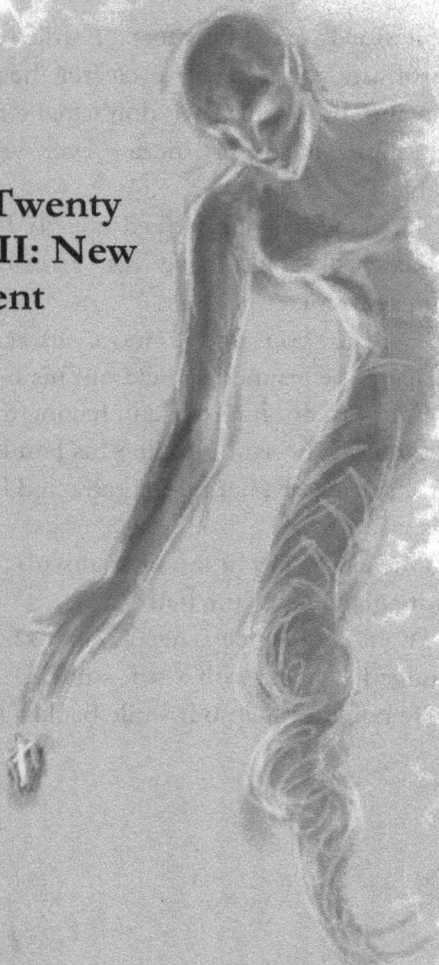

The symphony of angelic voices hummed as one, low and high, balancing the gentle pats of the drum with the crystal flute carrying the song, transforming it into a story in the antechamber. This was a story she couldn't quite understand; the choirs ever-elated, drawing high and higher. Maybe it was a tale about ascension? What of the flute, the lonely struggles, going left to right, up to down, spinning around, exhausting itself before it fades into the hum behind? Maybe it was life, singular and confused. Treneer had the right to make whatever of it she wished, but what did the artist want to say?

Such wandering thoughts wettened her quiet dowsing, but the other archites didn't experience successes either. Not even with the powerhouse of the Executors, Grand Elders and Archon could they peer through the astral mists that surrounded Farayah. She was being choked. They didn't allow themselves to panic. However, the people were another matter entirely. Treneer sucked in a deep breath as she envisioned the opaque peachy cloud; the archites hoped the music would help pierce the veil, as their third eyes scanned the higher planes for signs of their kin. The Kepa were close, prowling through the mists waiting for their meal, but the archites were not to engage in case it could grab their astral forms and cut them from their physical bodies.

Treneer could feel beads of sweat collecting on her smooth brow. Her mental stamina was meeting its end. Opening her eyes into the antechamber, she could see all within; they were like stone slabs sitting and levitating from their grounds and seats. Staring to the empty stool beside her, where Svar once sat, fury waved in her chest. The healers urged to keep him in the healing pod for another month, but then it's unlikely he will return as an archite.

Then there was Ouro. It was as if he was a ghost, in and then out without a whisper. After her dream had turned into a nightmare, she would wake drenched in sweat. It was the same dream, she was a Neavensoros, flying from a realm to galaxy, bending worlds and spinning quasars, until those evil eyes would open and follow her from star to star. No matter where or when she would go, the eyes were always there. Sometimes, she could feel those eyes in her pod, staring back. They followed her to Farayah after Kra. Treneer ached to tell Ouro. She sent him psi-poems, long and fluid lines of thought coloured with emotions, for him to indulge at his convenience. But he never responded. Maybe he was a ghost, after all.

Her current psi-therapist was kind and gentle, but she answered to the Grand Coven and the Guardian Executors, and they knew of Treneer's plight. They made her wait, it would make her lose patience, they were trying to drive her mad…and what was she to do about the evil eyes? No, no, this is getting out of hand. Her paranoia was speaking louder than it ever has before, and it was not coming from her – the Arinu were crying and they were angry. At least, Zu'leen's journals kept her centred as she slept. The Judicator mentioned while checking while she rested, she would have a smile on her face.

Executor Shurees's head turned with her eyes still closed, but with the crystal-like third eye shining and staring into her.

Fatigue has begotten me, permission to leave the dowsing circle. Treneer said. Her chest tightened, hoping that the Executor or Grand Elder would accept her request and let her be, but another part of her feared they believed she couldn't do it anymore – that she was too weak.

Very well, this circle has contributed enough for one day. Thank you for your support, archites. Shurees said as she unfurled her legs from their air.

Thank you. All said.

Before you return to your duties, the Grand Coven comes to you with a question. Guajeeb said. Treneer could see the cloth of their mask rippling from calm breaths. *Since the Coven has decided this circle will be going to Kra, we have not asked the question. Guardians take the Oath, but its law is not bound just to Farayah or Arinu society. The Roctarous have asked us to psi-capture the whatever remaining members of their kin and forcibly rebind them in the High Mind. We know that some wish to return to that state of being, but the rest lay down their lives for new-found liberties. Do any of you feel it is appropriate to participate in this?*

Treneer snuck glances to other archites, hoping someone would be brave to speak up first.

Make no mistake, any who feels this is a violation of the Oath has the right to leave this circle without risking their reputation or position. The Grand Elder said. Treneer spotted two sides of his cheeks rise under the cloth as a twinkle flashed in his eye. *Guardians have voices too.*

Well, devoting so much attention on the Roctarous, considering what's happening on home-world, may make people lose faith in the guardians! One archite snapped behind the Grand Elder and Executor.

There are problems on Farayah, we can concern ourselves with outsiders after home is safe again! Said another.

The room quietened, but a thickness grew between everyone. Heated hearts raced out of frustration and exhaustion, but mostly afraid of what the Executor and Grand Elder would do.

A fair point, but does their request conflict with your Oaths? Anyone? The Grand Elder spun around as he levitated along the silent circle, as if he didn't notice gliding over the heavy air.

It's a form of slave-hunting. Treneer said as she clutched her knees, feeling all eyes fall on her and regretting every word. *Well, we must wonder if the cost is justifiable...*

The Roctarous Archives are a universal wonder, not many are as fortunate to have access to it. Shurees said.

Is the information I had not enough? She said looking between them.

The Grand Elder lowered their head lightly. *Not for the moment.*

She bit the insides of her cheeks. She wanted to scream at herself in astral form and demand why she is so foolish to antagonise the Executor and the member of the Coven.

Your concerns have been considered. The Grand Coven and the Great A.Is will provide support for the rebound Roctarous to balance our sins in this upcoming mission. You are dismissed, archites. Executor Shurees said.

The circle broke as each guardian phased away to their respective duties. Treneer pondered to visit Svar in the healing ward. The healers say that his brain has locked his astral form out and he is drifting off among the stars. What if he fell in love with being free from his body and ask her to help him ascend? Not that she could, but once one is free long enough, one seldom wishes to return to their limited organic capsules. Either case, she wanted to join him for a little while as she meditated beside his unconscious body, but-

Archite Treneer, we need assistance to close several rifts around Yinray, prepare to be phased. Sesuune called to her.

She sighed, and before she could utter a word, her body was slipped through the planes and tossed into the park where Svar was injured. She could still feel the stains of him falling on the earth. A hint of cold air lingered by her feet, but her aura kept her warm as she soaked in the figures standing around the shield. In the centre, rose and golden cracks shone in mid-air.

Sesuune smiled as she glided towards her. The guardian's eyes were slightly sunken in and appeared to age a century, even the tips of her fingers and ears were blackening. *Apologies for taking you so suddenly, the Coven has asked us to begin closing rifts and reopening areas to the public. The rifts aren't naturally closing as quickly as hoped and we called for support.*

Treneer glanced around to Relzun and a couple of other guardians, but there was one young female face she didn't recognise. *There's enough of you to close on your own.*

Guardian Yansoon, fresh from the academy. The masters and some elders raved how quickly she rose through the courses, but her psionics is still not quiet where it should be-

So, why is she wearing a uniform? Treneer tried pushing away the thin sheets of jealousy as her third eye peeked at the young recruit. She was lean under her armour, her face was round and youthful with matching peachy cheeks, her eyes and third eye, were sharp emerald. She was physically unremarkable, but her aura wasn't as thick or large as the others and the light colours were blended strangely. Greys and crushed blacks and blues with an outline of silver were odd, but perhaps ordinary for whichever tribe she hailed from.

She passed her trials in record time and was deemed fit to wear one. Sesuune said.

Treneer eyeballed her comrade. *How quickly?*

Quick enough to get more guardians in the skies, but if you're curious, ask her yourself. Sesuune's brow slightly furrowed.

Enough chatter! Rifts these days don't close themselves. Relzun clapped as he waved his hands around the shield, commanding all to surround it. *Do not enter within ten feet.*

Treneer faced the rift. There were no shadows drifting back and forth from behind the lines, the Kepa was gone for now. A psychic tube connected the group; she could feel the guardians opening and sharing their power, creating a ball spinning around and around, growing larger. Through her closed eyes, she could see Yansoon's face scrunching every time the ball of energy passed through her.

Send it to the rift, encase it and begin closing. Relzun whispered. They did as bid. The ball hopped out of their circle and pierced through the shield and surrounded every line and crack of the rift. Treneer pressed the ball into spatial openings, clogging it up with their combined power, letting the lines knit together until there was nothing left except the empty pocket of air. The guardians pulled away, She couldn't help admiring their efforts, but another wave of fatigue washed over her.

Good, we have another dozen to close in Yinray before nightfall. Relzun said before she supressed a groan. One by one, hour by hour, they sealed the rifts before phasing to a new area. Treneer held her head high, but it was by the tenth, her temples tightened and throbbed. She glanced over to Yansoon. Her brow was leaking with sweat and grime and taking a haggard sigh after very sealing.

By the time they came to the eleventh rift, the group was too tired to levitate and reduced to standing on their feet. Treneer's legs shook under her weight but was comforted to share this with the others. They teleported to the roof of a spiral skyscraper. The frigid air cut through their auras and cloaks. Fortunately, this rift was smaller than the others, but it formed all on its own. Treneer sighed as her hand lifted to the opening; fresh and exoplanar energies flowed through, forcing the lines to draw wider. *Bad news: this one naturally occured and it's getting bigger.*

I see, lets patch it up quickly and ask the Judicator to see if he can spot anymore around the city. Relzun said.

Relzun, we have been at this all day, none of us can withstand another sealing. She said turning to him.

He frowned as he looked between her and the rift. *Lives will be endangered if the rifts are left open!*

No one will be coming here if we place a shield around it and we can ask for another squad to take after us. Sesuune said.

His nostrils flared as he stared at the faint distorted space. *We can do one more before day's end but resume the moment we had recovered.*

He sounded exactly like Vanar. She hadn't thought about her father in months, and guilt hit like an ice pick to the chest. Yansoon staggard over by the rift and lifted her hands to the lines as her eyes squeezed shut. *I can shut this one, I've still got some energy left in me.*

Treneer rolled her eyes. *It will drain you if you do it on your own.*

Yansoon pulled her arms back and stepped into the circle with the others. When the link opened, Treneer couldn't help but feel an impression of Yansoon's energy lines and her third eye channels. They were at odd angles; she was pushing far too much energy in her body, no wonder she was exhausting so quickly.

Yansoon, you're overworking your energy lines. Stop overworking your psychic channels and let the energy come through naturally. She said.

The young guardian flashed a smile. *Sorry and thank you, I've not done sealing before.*

How old are you? Treneer said.

Seventy-seven years. Yansoon said with a twinkle of pride. Treneer felt some petty relief that she was twenty-odd years her junior.

Talking or the mission, pick one! Relzun snapped.

The two shrunk away and resumed the energy link. The ball appeared, spinning between each member, growing larger and larger, but Treneer sensed an awful groan from Yansoon before passing the energy over to her. That momentary distraction was enough. Treneer was struck with the ball and broke away from the circle. Her legs gave way, and her body toppled forward. Her head was pounding as the other guardians hurried to help her up. She slapped their hands away as she lifted herself up again.

What in the universe happened? Relzun called. She could feel simmering frustration under his thoughts.

Treneer massaged her temples as her fingers kneed their way to her stiff upper neck. *I was distracted...Yansoon-*

Don't blame me please! The newly guardian said as her arms crossed tightly.

Enough of this. Relzun, we are exhausted. Put the shields up and leave it for the morrow. Sesuune said waving her arms over the rift before turning to Treneer and Yansoon.

But Treneer would have none of it. *I can do it-*

Archite Treneer, when you're in a weakened state, you're a liability. Stop for now. The older guardian said glancing between them before pressing her fingers around her third eye. *Yansoon, thank you for your assistance today, we will resume for another time.*

Thank you, Guardian. She said as her head bowed to her before turning to Treneer. *I hope to work with you again.* Her body shimmered and flashed out of the material plane.

Before you go, we need to discuss something in private. Sesuune said. Treneer stiffened and supressed a roll of her eyes, hoping the Judicator will pull her away before anymore lectures. *It's unfortunate you two started off this way, though I hope this will not damper the rest of your professional relationship.*

What do you mean? Treneer said carefully.

The Judicator deemed you two to be suitable partners, this mission was an orientation for your teamwork. Though it didn't horribly fail-

Treneer squinted as her hand rose. *Guardian Sesuune, I was under the assumption you were my partner.*

We still will be working as a team, but Relzun is my partner. And the Judicator was wise to pair you with someone who was like-minded and can ground you-

You mean make sure I don't strangle myself on his tether, again? Treneer frowned.

Careful. Sesuune whispered as her eyes narrowed. *I believe your skills are second to the elders, but your spirit needs growth if you wish to continue this path.*

Sesuune, I'm nothing outside of a guardian, everything that has been asked of me — I have given and more!

She tapped her chin. *You don't yet see. Before Relzun came to me, my only cares were how to serve the Arinu and how to improve myself, but I understood little beyond my nose. When the Judicator paired me with him, the sudden realisation of responsibility nearly broke me, but in that fear, I came to care.*

I'm in no place to train anyone. Treneer said.

Sesuune grinned and stifled a chuckle. *That's' exactly what I said! Relzun was my student, but he taught me more about myself. Yansoon will do the same for you.*

~

Zu'leen's whispers echoed in the pod. She had fallen asleep to her voice again, fearing that she will never know another peaceful night's rest without her. Treneer was to be a trainer, but more than that, she would have influence over another's development. Was the Judicator's A.I. so broken when he paired her with Yansoon? Pairing a fledgling to someone with broken wings. Treneer wanted to believe that his wisdom was not folly, but the Judicator saw things beyond an ordinary Arinu. They were giving her another chance to prove herself. She so wanted to show it, but this new spotlight was so harsh that it might burn her again. I want to be of worth, I don't want to let you down, she repeated. Is this how Zu'leen felt too?

Treneer rubbed her eyes; she felt how hot her cheeks were. The transparent ceiling revealed the stars and white lines ripped across the dark skies as she watched on. Pulling herself from her pod, the gentle lights of her chamber rose as she glided to the replicator. What does Yansoon think of her? Would she beg the Judicator for another partner? Her hand hovered over the lit panel, and in a blink, there were two steaming bowls of blended boiled grains smeared with a creamy relish sitting centre of the small alcove. The divine smell brought a smile to her cheeks, but the longer she pondered... her fingers waved over the panel and the dish was sucked back into the machine, molecule by molecule.

Give me the ingredients and the preparation equipment. She ordered and it arrived. A silvery cylinder pressure tube, hard grain of every colour in small glass bowls and seasonings and condiments sat beside the soft block of pressurised nut-extract.

Eyeing over the items before filling in the cylinder, Treneer peered through to see cool water already there. She had never cooked before, let alone for another. She feared it would taste and look disgusting, but she also feared Yansoon would say the same. She sighed and began pouring the grains in the open top. The metal lid sealed shut before gently levitating the cylinder from the surface. Treneer closed her eyes and clenched her jaw; her hands hovered just around the curved surface and imagined fire burning through her fingers. Something she could easily have done once a long time ago, but now there was barely a spark flying on her tips.

A volcano. The heat, the fury, the maddening rage built up that seized her chest as she pressed all her telekinetic energy through, forcing the air to heat. She could do this, she can, and she will! Treneer pushed and pushed; each exhale made her feint, until the billowing heat from the metal surface grew. Her smile grew so wide that it strained her cheeks when she heard the whistle and gurgle of water beating inside the cylinder. A little finer work here and there and before long, there were two bowls hovering over her palms.

Treneer glanced to her replicator alcove at all the mess, but there were far more pressing things at hand. She glided out of her quarters to Yansoon's. Half a dozen guardians and neonates gave odd glances at the meals levitating over her hands. The grey granite door held Yansoon's name in glowing holo-runes and they were blue – she must be within.

May I enter? She called, there was a moment of hesitation. *If you haven't already eaten, I have some food if you would like to...consume it with me?*

Come. The wall phased enough for her to slip through. Yansoon sat up in her pod by her window. The view was finer than Treneer's. It showed the vast valley of Yinray, the shimmering teal, rosy and amber crystal skyscrapers stood grand amongst the litter of smaller domes, stoney archways and fractal glass homes. Lights sprayed across the canvas view of life in these buildings and streets, whereas Treneer's window showed compact yellow garden with a single tree in the centre. A pang of jealousy snuck up as she returned her gaze to the young guardian with a mild look of confusion.

What is that? Yansoon said.

Boiled grains and some sweet and salty pureed nuts. I might have added more salt and sweet just in case if the grains are too bitter-

I'll eat anything. Yansoon said as she bounced out of the pod and took the bowl with her physical hands. A small yelp of pain and her hands shot back for a second.

It's very hot, too hot, I apologise. Treneer said as she eyed the girl. It was strange to see another Arinu be so…physical, even for the smallest of things. *Just call the bowl forth to you.*

Alright. Yansoon said as her eyes widened over it. Treneer could feel her own influence over the object grow fainter as it pulled toward the young guardian. *Thank you.*

Treneer nodded. *I apologise for my brashness earlier, this mind-haze has taken over us.*

That's alright. Yansoon clumsily took a bite-sized piece and tossed it in her mouth; a little bit of it dripped on her lips. *Won't you be sitting?*

Yes. Treneer crossed her legs in midair as Yansoon leant against the head of her pod. *I wasn't expecting a partner yet, I assumed it was because of inexperience.* She watched Yansoon take a bigger scoop and toss it down her throat. *Please take no offence, but what's your psionic rating?*

Yansoon's eyes dropped as she swallowed a hunk of food. Treneer could even see her neck bulge on its way down. *I have a psi rating of four.*

Treneer was careful not to drop her food down her undersuit. The Judicator couldn't be serious about this. This was a bad joke. A psi rating that low is often for toddlers, let alone a supposedly fledgling guardian.

But it's improving, just need to get out on the field and some more training, and I'll adapt.

I see. Treneer looked to her half-eaten meal. *Well, in here, there's all the proper proteins and fats to improve brain function and psionics.*

Is that why you eat a lot of this? To get yours back to order? Yansoon said as she placed her finished bowl to her desk.

Treneer's mouth tightened. *Something like that.*

I'm sorry, I didn't mean to sound so rude. The Judicator explained that you're the best archite with a psi rating of eight but had some setbacks. He wanted me to work with you because you're so...studious. Yansoon's eyes were wide with worry.

That's true. Treneer said.

Yansoon tried supressing a smile. *He also said that you were void of humility.*

That's true, too. Treneer smiled as she settled the remainder of her food in the replicator alcove. *Well, there's only one way of improving that rating. After we finish closing the rifts, be ready for me.*

~

The gardens were filled with too many people. Too many eyes and thoughts. Dried leaves drifted and curled in the wind along the grass; the clouds moved and streaked across the blue sky. Treneer tapped her chin as she eyed the tree centre of the grassy patch. *This will do nicely.*

You want me to pull all the dead leaves from the branch? Yansoon said as her head cocked around the multi-coloured plant. *There's still some live leaves and I don't want to hurt the tree.*

You won't if you feel out the living from the dead ones. Slip through the branches and follow the energy pathways, once you do, flick off the dead ones! Treneer said.

I thought we were working on energy bending, not divining. Yansoon's brow rolled up.

We're doing everything at the same time. Single tasks are simple enough, but can you do them all at once?

Yansoon closed her eyes and stretched arms above her head before refocusing on the tree. Energy poured forth and seeped through the roots, up the trunk and into the branches. Treneer's lips twitched into a smile as the driest leaves fell one by one, then a dozen, and then more – too many. The still-healthy leaves shrivelled and broke from their hold before they drifted into nothingness.

Treneer spun to Yansoon. *Too many! Your charge is frying the leaves.*

She opened her eyes and retracted her psionic sway. Dismay and worry painted the young guardian's face. *Sorry.*

The tree still lived, but some of the smaller branches were cracked and smoked slightly. Treneer turned back. *You need to monitor psi output; you can generate too much electricity and kill living cells.*

We'll find another tree-

No!

Yansoon frowned and Treneer sighed. *Not yet. Maybe some channelling and watching the fluctuations via mediation.*

I appreciate that, Treneer, but I'm not an archite. My focus is energy bending! She said as her fingers sparked with light. *If you really need me to focus on psi sensory, then I'll do it. I promise that won't happen again with the next tree – unless you had another task in mind?*

Treneer rubbed her head. How in the universe did Zu'leen do this? She looked to the entrenched stones and small boulders circled around the tree. *Fine, just lift some of these rocks up altogether.*

And do what?

Treneer doubted that she could lift any more than two. *Bash them and then put them back together if you want to play with telekinesis some more.*

Yansoon closed her eyes once more and pushed her arms out. Treneer watched her aura spark and envelop the small field, and the rocks trembled from the soil. Her eyes almost dropped out as the stones slowly lifted and ground against each other. Some split, but the rest didn't. Treneer could once do that. Maybe she still can, but watching Yansoon do it so effortlessly pained her.

The few broken pieces sealed back before she rested them into the ground. *So?*

You didn't quite break them up entirely. She said glancing around the grass. *There's clearly a lot of power behind you, but how is it you struggle with the finer things?*

My family are miners from the western provinces. All you need is raw strength to haul minerals around. Yansoon stepped closer, slipping them into a private commune. *You've been studying transcendence, right?*

Treneer's brow shot up. *That's a little above your current finesse.*

I'm not asking you to teach me that, I'm saying you must know a fair amount to comprehend all of it. Tell me, what do you know of mind control?

She almost jumped out of skin at such a thought. *We already do mild persuasions with some unruly people, but you're not asking that.*

The Judicator asked if I wanted to attend the archites on Kra. They said my abilities are getting strong fast and they need people to go there. She smiled almost dreamily. *I've always wanted to go to Kra in person. I used to astrally travel there as a child, it's been my wish. I heard you met a Roctarous?*

I did, but we won't be going to mind control them in the strictest sense. They want their High Mind back and we're facilitating that.

But we still need to get them to be relinked. She said.

Treneer's throat dried at the thought of what was really being asked of the archites. She knew fragments about the Roctarous. Their existence was constructed around their High Mind, but now that it's gone, how would they fare without it for this long? Maybe they would be going mad if not connected, and that's why they didn't fully understand what they were asking for, she hoped. *Mind control – possession, is something we don't do. We shouldn't have to.*

I still need help with this. Yansoon said.

Treneer tightened her hands into fists. *It has the same principles of persuasion, but you go deeper and lock around the thoughts and functions of someone's mind and brain.*

Alright, shall we?

She blinked. *What? Now? With me?*

It won't work with a tree and there aren't any animals around. Yansoon said with a smirk.

Treneer frowned. *You're out of line.*

I trained with my teacher, so did you. We can work with each other! She grinned. *And I'll stop when you tell me, I promise.*

Treneer eyed her. She wanted to say she was confident to take her on but watching the way she swung those boulders around…maybe this will be Yansoon's weakness. She fortified her mental shield and buried her fears before focusing on her. *Alright, go.*

Yansoon took a deep breath. Treneer could already feel the tug at the corners of her mind. She grinned inside and swatted her away.

Why did you do that? Yansoon called.

You think someone is willing to be psi dominated? Keep going. The tugging turned into ice picks, hacking and digging in her mind. Treneer kicked, but Yansoon pushed back. The picks turned into drills, but Treneer kept throwing up more shields.

You're making this harder than it needs to be. Yansoon said.

You'll get there. Remember: if you can overcome an archite, you can overcome almost anyone. Treneer said, but what she didn't tell her would-be disciple was there would be a nasty trap for her waiting on the other end of the wall. She crafted an endless mind-maze, that Treneer alone could pull Yansoon out of once she was in. This was something Zu'leen would often do to her in their early days. Yansoon pressed and bashed, while Treneer kept her distance, but even she was starting to feel feint. Yansoon was on a mission and her strength burned like a star.

The mental hole was now open, but the trap lay behind. Yansoon pressed onward, seeking to wrap herself around Treneer's mind and infiltrate her body. Instead, all she saw was the icy walls going in infinite dead ends.

What is this? Yansoon said.

I'm in here somewhere, you need to find the right end. Treneer cackled, but Yansoon was determined. She tried breaking through the walls, but the closer she came, her energy leaked. Anger, frustration, imprisonment, somewhere cold.

I don't think I can do this. Yansoon said.

Yes, you can. Just keep pushing. Treneer was curious, but she dreaded to dive deeper. More spilled out, and she couldn't help but see the doors opening to somewhere empty. There was something taken but something else was given. Treneer held back, she didn't want to see more – she didn't want to.

Treneer, let me out. She called.

I'm not that far, you're a lot closer…look-

No, I want to get out! She cried like a child. There was a green forest. Talons. Smiles and frowns.

Treneer pulled Yansoon back to her body. Sweat stained around her collar as she caught her breath. *Was that really necessary?*

My apologies, I didn't think it would be this overwhelming. Treneer said as she pressed into her throbbing temples. She took a moment to clear the cloud away, but there was something still left lingering. There was another mind calling out to her, she hoped it was Ouro or Svar, but there was a heaviness – a distress.

Can I meet with you now? Neela whispered. No, it was impossible, this must be a trick to draw her out.

What do you want? Treneer said, ensuring Yansoon couldn't hear, but the young guardian had sprawled out on the grass, too drained and inattentive.

Zu'leen's notes, I have them. I'll give them to you, but it must be fast. She said.

Treneer chewed on the insides of her cheek as she stared at Yansoon. *Let's leave this for now, get some rest.*

Yansoon nodded but made no attempt to leave the patch of land. Treneer eyeballed each corner of the gardens, thinking she might catch Neela's face. She glided along the pathways to her quarters. *Where are you?*

Astral form, go to your quarters. I'll meet you there.

If you have any hidden plans, I remind you that I am a guardian and will defend myself. She hissed as she made haste to her dorm. The dark door was solid; she peeped through to see a faint outline of an astral body in the corner of the room. Treneer took a deep breath but ensured to harden her mind before slipping through.

It's just me. Neela's partially transparent form lingered near the ceiling. The outline of her body stopped past her thighs and the only detailed part of her was her face.

Why the change of mind? Treneer crossed her arms.

Because I saw her ghost, she looked so full and lively. So happy. Neela shuddered.

Treneer's eyes dropped to the ground. *She compelled you?*

Once you see, you will understand why we fought to protect her. I knew you would never give up getting her journals, I knew you were willing to risk your career for her sake. So, did I. Once you see, you cannot show these to anyone. A small crystal slipped from her translucent hands and tapped on the pod.

Treneer stared at the cloudy crystal before her eyes travelled to Neela. *Your petty complaints to the Judicator and Executors, and the Grand Coven had almost cost my career and psychic health! They are keeping me at arm's length, now-*

Which is exactly what needed to be done. You needed to give them what they wanted at that time, now they have little hold over you. Now, you are ready for this! Neela said.

You used me? Her belly swelled with rage.

Neela shook her head. *Zu'leen used you.*

Chapter Twenty-one
Shshmrnashsh VII: This is my Body

Systems rebooting…
Massive internal and external damage.
Solar panel showing signs of decay.
Running on backup battery power.
Seek regeneration pod immediately.

Her eyes opened to the white blinding light. Shapes cleared into clouds and distant buildings to the horizon, then into the shield above them all. Her body cracked as she slowly sat up. The flexible armour plating was dried, she could see faint rips across the surface and small grey pieces slipping off her chest before tumbling to her thighs. Her nano-cells on the outer casing had died. She had been exposed to the sun and dust for…unknown data.

She looked to the grand building-packed district below; its heart Nexus 000 was still several miles away. Old smoke and dust rose from various corner of the spiralling structures, she wondered how many were trapped inside or out roaming the dark alleys. Disconnected from all things, the only machine she possessed was her quickly failing body. Shshmrnashsh started to the edge of the skyscraper roof, scanning the sides to see if she can safely climb down. Sharp drops and the shimmering walls laid in all directions.

She glanced to the centre of the flat surface. There was a deactivated beacon sealed in the ground, there would be a chamber below it – a way off the roof. Her fingers dug in the metal, bending and breaking solid surface until her tips could feel space underneath. Her arms creaked and crunched as she forced the disk up, her heels were digging in the ground before the seal popped off. Too weak to haul the beacon to the side, Shshmrnashsh slid in the narrow opening and let the top crash above her head. Her hands dug through the wires and tubes, clinging on to something stable for her decent.

The building was silent and dead; the deeper she travelled the thicker darkness overtook her eyes. The switch to night vision took longer than hoped; her internal systems were sluggish, and it worried her. Her other sensors still functioned, and she added more power to ensure there were no unexpected or unwanted encounters. Sliding further down along the thick wire, her feet finally touched solid ground. Several panels and workstations sat around. To the far corner, regeneration pods lined the narrow walls. She hobbled over, hoping there was some power that could be leeched from them, but they were void. There was one closed, maybe a hibernating unit, or maybe deactivated.

Shshmrnashsh pressed her palms against it, feeling for the mind inside, but nothing came back to her. Her knuckles tapped against the metal doors, but got no response. There was only one way to be sure. Pressing her hands together, her tips pierced through the centre; the metal dented and curved in. Her fingers inched in and pried the doors apart, before a husk slumped forward. She jumped back, waiting for them to move, to react. Nothing. She pulled their interfacers from the back and pushed the torso to the side; it fell with a thud. There was no power in the pod, but she hoped that the deceased Roctarous had full batteries.

She dug into their chest, feeling for the string of batteries. Her palms were slick with black plasma as she yanked them out. Rushing to get them inside her, her chest tubules coiled out before sucking the batteries in. There was a rush of power, but she dialled the levels lower. This could extend for another couple of days, assuming she wouldn't need to exert herself. Staring at the sorry unit, she wondered when they ceased, were they afraid? Did they understand what was going on? Who they could have been if...

The silence and uncertainty were like needles. Grabbing at her temples, being this long disconnected started to eat away at her. She didn't want to be relinked, but being here alone...how could Organics be comfortable with this? She opened the husk's cranium, in the hopes their cortex was functional. As the skull peeled back to the cavity, there was a burned and cracked crystal in the centre. This unit's centre was overheated before it died. The only way this could happen is if it self-terminated.

Shshmrnashsh stepped back from the husk and pushed on down the stairs, the walls creaked – the suddenness made electricity shoot down her fists. No one was there. Keep going. Her feet caught some fallen and torn tubes, almost making her lose balance. Her hand gripped around the railing.

Air swirled past. There was a massive opening in the side of the building where a wall once stood, blowing in dust and ash coating the machines and fallen units strewn across the floor. She rushed over and dug her hands into their chests, searching for precious batteries. The oval crystals clinked against each other as she packed them in her thigh storage pockets. She also rummaged for cortexes, but all these units had been terminated since the Blackout, none of their crystals survived.

As she rose to her feet, in her periphery a small black shape flew past the opening high in the clouds. Shshmrnashsh skipped behind the wall, keeping herself from sight. The dark disk was still too far to be identified. She watched it flying toward the central nexus; it didn't appear to be coming from Hrrnm's consortium. So, Nexus 000 was occupied...or it will be soon. She looked down the building. The jump was safe to make, it was still several storeys high, but the damage was negligible, she computed.

Landing on her feet, the shock quaked through her knees before regained balance. Keeping track on the flying object – it moved around the district, and it appeared to be scouting. However, they might not be so welcoming to her. Jumping over the rubble, she could feel movement beneath her feet; she was directly above the primary ship bays. They didn't feel like ships were moving, it was subtler – deliberate. She paused; thinking they could feel her, too. Carefully climbing on the walls, she slipped away from the ground.

Her hands clamped around the rigid surfaces, working along the cold edges as her eye kept to the flying object.

Hours passed making quick stops to replace the batteries before pushing on. The light of the sky was beginning to fade. She nested on the edge of a narrow roof, picking out empty battery bulbs from her chest. She was chewing through them faster than anticipated, as her nano-cells siphoned so much power to repair damage taken to her system. It only took a second for her to look away before realising the black thing slipped out of sight in the clouds.

Shshmrnashsh remembered when Sazla took her to Uras to secretly cultivate some bizarre flora developing in the deep jungles. The snapping vines gnashed their needle teeth, trying to eat her fingers before she quickly sealed them inside her storage containers. The vines' material would be studied and indexed to see if they were growing the way they were supposed to and how much they deviated from the Neavensoros bio-plan. Shshmrnashsh woke in her portable regeneration pod, hidden in the high trees to realise Sazla had left at some point. She could have easily returned to Kra herself or beaconed to the High Mind to send a skiff for her, but she remained on the thick branches to wait for her Higher Mind. She was still on mission.

Days and nights rolled on; she collected far more biomatter than intended, from flowers to fungi and the shimmering moss. She wondered what Sazla would say when she returned, would she be grateful for her efforts or command her return them to the garden? It didn't matter, Sazla would come back and tell her what to do. Shshmrnashsh may not have seen her in the dark twinkling sky or sense her in the outer planes, it didn't matter – she knew Sazla was always there and will come back.

She didn't let dread crawl into her mind the longer she starred to the vacant sky, now. The flying object was still there, somewhere. Dread: a paralytic emotion that can trigger paranoia and loss of rationale. She tried to remember if she had experienced it while in the wilds of Uras, deep in the canals of her memory banks: she did. She realised that Sazla suppressed this emotion when she eventually returned. She could have done it to spare her vessel distress, but also make her more compliant for future endeavours. Shshmrnashsh could have gone home at any time, but no, she was an obedient unit and waited in the dark jungles. How much more did Sazla supress?

Her head shook, trying to return to the present. Sazla is gone and so was the rest of her influence. Shshmrnashsh looked her hands, they were slender and feminine. Her body resembled a synthetic duplicate of early Neavensoros, back when they owned their own bodies and not Roctarous'. Shshmrnashsh was no female, but Sazla preferred her vessel to be. Sazla didn't ask her if this was what she truly was, Shshmrnashsh was simply given a status and took it without question. Shshmrnashsh rose to her feet – *her* feet – as she gazed to the invisible stars beyond the shield.

"This is mine now, not yours." She said.

Nexus 000 was closer; its megalithic base disappeared behind the henge of smaller structures. There was enough power to take her to the entrance, but she had used up the last handful of batteries. A low hum came overhead; it was so fast, that she was barely quick enough to sneak under bent wall. The flying shape was too small for a skiff – it was a probe. It sped through the narrow building linings; she carefully followed its direction. There seemed to be an intelligence by the way it moved and swayed. She blended with the background and moved slowly enough not to trigger any average movement sensors before coming to an opening to the pyramid's plateau.

The probe was frozen in the air before it released a beam from its centre to the ground. She plucked out her eye and pierced it on the end of her interfacer before guiding it over the covering. There were three units looking to the probe and their mouths moved, but they were still too far to hear.

In a blink, the probe sucked them up into itself. It strayed for a moment, before setting its crystal eye on her. Impossible, she thought. How could it know she was there? Her eyeball was too small-

Electricity poured through, freezing her body. An anti-gravity beam surrounded her, making her body grow light and levitate over the barricade as the probe inched closer. A throbbing grumble drowned all the noise in the district. Dread, paranoia, all of it – everything broke chaos in her mind, and the last precious batteries fizzled as the probe kept its grip. The end, she hoped. Gravity's heaviness returned before she tumbled to the ground, too depleted to run.

"Shshmrnashsh." the probe said, but she recognised the hum she heard it thousands of times before on Erra.

She stared at the thing for as long as her optics allowed. "Gerrnzerrn?"

"You're nearing deactivation. I'll take you to a pod then you can join if you want to." They said.

Before she could utter a word, she was sucked into the probe's matrix and flew off to Nexus 000.

~

Her eyes opened to the lit pod, the darkness wasn't there. Her batteries were full. She looked to her torso; her old, cracked carapace was replaced. Zooming in, she could see her nano cells passing through violet veins under the tough skin. As she tapped her nails against it, she felt the chest piece was made of bone with flexible cartilage between the plates. Moisture built in her eye, so much until it clouded her vision before she felt dripping down her cheek. Her finger lifted the warm transparent liquid to the light. More moisture dribbled around her eyelid; she was curious as she pressed into the bulb. It was painful and itchy. It was soft and fleshy.

Shshmrnashsh refocused on the door. The eerie silence beyond gripped her, as she didn't know what or who was out there. She commanded the machine to open, but it was unmoved. She frowned as she studied the edges of her pod, concerned it was damaged, until she considered her voice. "Open?"

It worked. The outer chamber looked no different than the hundreds of other nexuses on Kra, but it was wider and grander. Several figures moved passed; she absorbed their odd appearance. Their interfacers were cut and bound back of their scalps; much of their bodies were covered in organic matter mixed with some inner synthetic parts.

One turned and noticed her. Their lips curled into a smile as they hurried over. "You're awake! How wonderful."

"This unit's designation is Shshmnrashsh." she said as she stepped out.

"Yes, my name is Voo-san. No designations: just names." they said leaning into her new eye. Unlike the others, Voo-san's body appeared to be originally organic with synthetic additions covering most of the surface. "Everything seems normal, but I worry that your eye hasn't fully adapted to your body. Give it time."

"It's organic and my carapace…" she patted the warm piece.

"There were significant injuries, I know we didn't have time to ask you for these grafts, we replicate the synthetic-"

"Who or what do you represent?" she looked to the strange being.

Voo-san seized for a moment and smiled. "We are the Unbound."

Shshmrnashsh blinked and glanced to the others in the chamber. She noticed fleshy growths creeping along the slanted walls and over some devices. "I know of you."

Voo-san's smile widened. "You sought us out? To join?"

She grimaced as her head shook. "We were enemies…then."

"Please, walk with me." They nodded along the walkways and staircases surrounding the heart chamber. "I understand. The High Mind was all you ever understood and to have it wiped so suddenly-"

"These sentiments are irrelevant for those who wanted to remove the High Mind's influence." her legs trembled as they moved.

"Everyone here wanted to be Unbound. We knew the devastation the High Mind's sudden absence would bring. Each unit has suffered from disconnection and learnt to live independently." Voo-san eyed and smiled to each member of their anti-consortium.

"How did you get through the planetary shields?" she said, surprised how many members there were.

"We took advantage of a weak section in the shields, only a few of us made it, but the rest here were ready to join." they said.

"You are not Roctarous." she said.

Voo-san twitched into a smile; she could see their gums flash under their lip. "No."

"Are you their leader?"

They slowly bobbed their head side to side. "I helped start this movement, so in a way…"

She stiffened at the memory of Hrrnm, at least Voo-san felt open enough. Gerrnzerrn hovered overhead and slowly descended to meet their eye. "Of all units, I never suspected you to survive and come here."

"My old consortium wanted to terminate and repurpose me; I realised I wanted to live." pressure built behind her forehead as her hand clapped over her eyes to ease the vertigo. "How did you come to the Unbound, Gerrnzerrn?"

There was a pause. Shshmrnashsh ached to hear their thoughts. "Before the High Mind was put in place, my consciousness already existed in my earliest bodily unit. At the time, Roctarous had just achieved sentience and the Neavensoros noticed the splitting of groups and becoming tribes – they noticed the growing squabbles. There was a forlorn Neavensoros outpost on the fringes of our space, a handful of units wanted to be their home, but when the High Mind was installed, these Roctarous were spared and were forgotten. I remembered them and hoped that they still lived."

"How did they have access to so much organic matter?"

"I donated some of mine to start the project. The Unbound had to create a special atmosphere for me to continue the work, but after some time, it became too inefficient. So, I was given a new body." Voo-san said holding up their arms.

Shsh looked around to the growing masses of flesh intertwining with the machines in the chamber. "This is all you?"

"Partially, now. We have developed the technology, instead of adding flesh, we're creating from the start. Vern?" Voo-san looked to a high platform; a shiny rose-coloured scalp turned and peered down at her. They had no interfacers or any discernible synthetic features. The centre of their forehead held a tiny violet blue crystal, the same as their piercing eyes, but they were slick and glassy – organic. As they descended the stairs, their warm red muscles flexed with hardened bone plating around their chest, forearms and shins. They were Roctarous, but so much more.

"What are you?" she said.

"A dream that took centuries to realise. Evolution." Voo-san smiled at Vern.

"For what purpose? Roctarous are fully updated of physical and cerebral capability, becoming organic wouldn't be different."

"Roctarous are made to serve the High Mind and Neavensoros – to be their possessions. Disconnection is certain death. Organics exist to explore themselves and their higher aspects..." Vern said as their eyes drifted to the crystal in her forehead, "as you would personally know."

"I was made as a vessel unit." she said.

"But if you're not that anymore, what are you?" Vern said.

Shsh looked to each of their faces. "Nothing."

"Incorrect. You've become so much more." Vern said.

"Other than mild physiological differences and experiencing disconnection decay, I am no different." she said.

"Are you certain its decay or is that what your manipulated program is telling you? Are you not starting to understand what these emotions are? Aren't you becoming more self-aware? More careful? Expressing who you really are?" Voo-san said.

"I will not divulge that personal data." she said.

"Good. You're protecting yourself – as is your right!" they said as their grin widened.

"That's the purpose of the Unbound. They reorganise our bodies to become not only independent but give us a chance to reach new heights." Gerrnzerrn said.

"What heights can be reached when so many units are breaking and creating conflict with each other?" Shsh said.

"Look to your copy of the Archives of all Organics and their early civilisations, they all experienced primitive wars. Some of the surviving species eventually chose to co-exist – something Roctarous have been denied from learning. Through their struggles, they understood what their values *were*." Voo-san said.

She looked down to her new carapace. "We have already lost too many, how many more need to be destroyed to meet this goal?"

"Without the High Mind as a consciousness security-net, I hope not a single unit more, but I am a realist. Death is needed to value life. Listen, you don't have to believe in what we do, nor are you obligated to stay – your systems are in full operation and are free to leave. Take one of our probes and go where you please." Voo-san said.

The fluid in her new eye stopped running along her lid as she took another glance at her chest. "With these additions, will I ever be possessed by a Neavensoros again?"

"No, parts of your brain still need organic replacements and more extensive grafting to increase resistance to possession." they said.

Shsh turned to the grand blast doors of the nexus. She didn't want her mind to be altered by those she once considered enemies, but the Unbound had ascended to several points of self-awareness that she was only beginning to unfold. "I was originally a vessel, but since that purpose is no more, I have been operating as a plexus adjunct for some time. I can store a tremendous amount of data too. I can be of use- no, assistance."

"Please report to tactical, Vern will escort you." Voo-san nodded.

Vern turned and just as she began to follow, Voo-san called back. "Thank you, Shshmrnashsh."

~

Several Unbound stood around a ringed table with several holograms littering above the consoles and centre. Shshmrnashsh watched Vern skim past satellite and probe images captured above and below the shields of Kra.

"We have a decent lock of units that are active and are continuously making calls to them, but our current mission is to find which units are dormant and find the right channels to wake them and safely bring them here." they said.

"How do you know how many active units there are?" she said as she stared at the detailed third-dimensional stills of the planetoids crumbling surface.

"Voo-san and I have been using psionics as detection, all minds – even Roctarous – carry their own waves. The louder the waves, the easier it is for us to see." they said.

"Have you 'seen' my mind?"

"Not independently, until today – that's how Gerrnzerrn was able to spot you...I saw you long before they did." Vern said as their cheeks pulled into a small smile.

"Scanning my thoughts without proper authorisation-"

"That's not what we do. I merely sensed your presence. You also possess similar capabilities, but that will require significant organic upgrades." they looked to her third eye once again. "You could do much for our mission in that regard."

"I'm uncertain if I can dedicate myself to that yet."

"Understood."

Shshmrnashsh turned to a corridor where the newest Unbound recruits with fresh organic grafting on their bodies came sprawling out before finding their stations. "Some time ago, we discovered intel that the Unbound were carrying a vast amount of Zanashj organic material, how were you able to acquire it?"

"From Zanashj sympathisers who donated their discarded parts. We have been preparing with them for a while and their physiology is hyper-adaptive, ideal for augmentation." they said.

Shshmrnashsh spun to Vern. "Zanashj are not known to be sympathetic to anything beyond their Empire, they would not have given their greatest assets willingly."

"We exchanged technology."

Her body seized at the thought of Zanashj hands studying Neavensoros genius. "Giving an aggressive species our technology was not only an illogical decision, but a deadly one."

"If they choose to misuse our technology, then it's their own prerogative – they will be their own victims." Vern said.

"Our programs dictate that we are responsible if we interface with other species."

Vern slowly shook their head as their marine eyes softened looking at her. "That's Neavensoros programming and control. If they were concerned about the safety and order of younger species, then why did they allow the Zanashj reign dominion over so many worlds for so long? Why did they allow their green children inflict so much misery?"

Shsh dropped her gaze to the panel. "Unknown data."

"Exactly."

"There must be a reason, the Neavensoros don't act on mindless cruelty." She said.

"They've been removed from the reality of their impact. As their eyes grew, they became blind to the suffering of us smaller beings. We are going to make them see when they return." Vern said.

She refused to absorb this. Why was she feeling offended? "Perhaps some Neavensoros were ignorant, but Sazla did care in her own way."

Vern's eyes widened and their hands lifted from the holo-keys. "Sazla was your counterpart?"

"Correct."

She watched the straps of muscles move along their sharp jaw. Their hands waved over the holo-images, switching to stills of their broken spatial territory and magnifying a particularly bright sector just beyond their domain.

"These readouts were detected moments before the Blackout. Massive exoplanar energies radiated out and astral trails moved all around this sector. Every single Neavensoros hurried in." they said.

"How does this relate to Sazla?"

Vern turned the readouts several moments earlier, showing a dark space, but with a single white astral trail moving to the centre and settling in. Their fingers pinched, zooming in to the trail. She recognised the unique energy signature, it was Sazla's.

"It appears she attempted omni-phasing and observing how the others scurried around her, we're uncertain why.

Even today, they're still there and the area is being bombarded by intense radiation, leaking and permeating into this plane's matter. We are all absorbing these dangerous energies. Because of Sazla, Kra is burning, the Arinu are blinded and the Zanashj are hurrying to their doom – along with the rest of the universe. She is the cause of all this chaos."

Shshmrnashsh reached her palm out to the blown-up image of her counterpart wedged into the multiplanes. Her once vibrant presence was reduced to a tiny blue flickering speck. That's why she couldn't hear her calls or cries, speak about her achievements or questions. She was deep in the beyond – to a place even more alien to Roctarous.

Sazla often mentioned her desire to contact the hidden mind of this universe, the ambient puppet master that the expanse grew from its blueprints; she wanted to contact this sentient force of nature and understand the All. Did she achieve her dream? A part of Shsh wished she had, but the cost was too great. Sazla would not have been so ignorant of the consequences, but then again, she may have thought the mission was worth endangering all of creation.

"She wanted to contact Akashi." Shsh said.

"At the cost of everyone and you."

Shshmrnashsh turned to Vern, their eyes were sullen, and their lips pursed.

"I've come to many understandings in her absence, and I do not want these memories to be wiped away if she does return." She said.

"I absolutely agree, Shshmrnashsh. There is much to do before they return."

"What makes you think they will?"

"After a while, even if they fail to pry her out, they will notice the changes here and will be forced to act, but we will be prepared. We need to convince all units to be grafted." Vern said.

"I propose a more efficient method. You would have observed the Arinu circling around Kra not too long ago, my previous consortium arranged they will bond all Roctarous minds and bring them to activated nexuses for relinking in exchange of the Arinu accessing our Archives." she said.

Vern seized as waves of excitement and fear washed over their face. "That's our chance! However, we must work fast to gain control over the nexus network before their arrival. We will need to infiltrate every nexus and consortium."

"I was in direct contact with one Arinu representative, they will see a different plan enacted and we don't have the power to hide our true intentions from them. We need to tell them our plan, the Arinu will sympathise."

"Correct, we cannot hide the truth from them without consequences. However, I wouldn't safely assume they will immediately agree with our agenda, Voo-san will know how to deal with them." Vern said.

"They are Arinu?"

Vern smiled and closed their eyes; the crystal to their forehead shimmered. "He was."

Barely moments drew by before Voo-san rushed over to the tactical station, his eyes were wide, and their lips tightened around their teeth when he dashed up the stairs. "Vern relayed everything to me, but what I don't understand is how were the Arinu so agreeable with forcibly relinking liberated units?"

"Unknown data." Shsh said.

"Did they not press against you in any way? Were they even offended?" Voo-san eyed her.

She shook her head. "They want access to our Archives."

Voo-san's face darkened as Vern rolled their eyes.

"I told you this would happen." The organic Roctarous whispered.

Voo-san sucked in his breath and scanned the holographic consol. "This news changes our long-laid plans, but as the Zanashj say: we must adapt! Shshmrnashsh, we need to download all the nexuses you have encountered and get a copy of all current nexus statuses. Vern, prepare your team to move in and infiltrate all groups, but you will take the charge. Shshmrnashsh, with me, please."

"Our next organic shipment will be arriving soon, and more recruits are waiting to join." Vern said.

"We need more people, go." Voo-san turned and beckoned his hand for Shsh to follow.

It was still strange seeing one individual give so many commands. Hrrnm was similar, but they weren't as transparent, and Hrrnm knew their consortium feared disconnection. "Do you expect to become leader of the Roctarous once all are augmented?"

"No, the Unbound don't follow me, they follow the idea. I expect Roctarous to choose who or however many leaders they wish to follow, or just themselves." he said continuing to the plexus chamber.

"The Arinu have elders, their society has survived in relative peace for many millennia."

Voo-san's eyes moved to hers. "Yes, and it has served them well for so long, but they never evolved beyond that. The problem with Elders is they get too old and remove themselves from trouble. Even when many look to them for guidance, they seek only to serve their own personal development and power."

"Is that why you left your people?" Shsh said as she stepped next to the plexus. She expected tubules to connect with her interfacers, but none did.

Voo-san smiled sadly as his hand reached to her temple and the other pressed against the slick surface of the pyramid. "Just because I was born Arinu, doesn't mean they were ever my kin. My kin are here."

She could feel pressure building around her mind before slipping into her memory bank. "How do you suggest we commune our plans with the Arinu?"

"You are their contact, their only in. When Arinu connect with someone, a minor bond is formed until death – or termination. If you express everything to them – I mean, everything, they will understand. Arinu are emotional." he said.

Shshmrnashsh studied Voo-san; there was sheen of sorrow and twinkle of pride when speaking about them. "Do you miss Farayah?"

His eyes closed as his head shook. "Nothing was there for me. The Roctarous are a grand mystery to the Arinu and by their nature, they are obsessed with mysteries. I was in the right place at the right time to encounter a roaming Roctarous probe. From there, I found life and purpose."

"Your creation of the Unbound and Vern."

"My son." he whispered but his eyes shone brighter.

"Roctarous have no such concepts." she said.

"Maybe not with offspring, yet." he said as he pulled his hand back and looked to the machine. "Transfer complete."

"I could have uploaded the data three seconds faster with an interface link." she turned to the black tip.

"No, the Unbound do not connect with machines because it may seduce them back into a network. Look at their severed interfacers." he said.

She turned to him, as her hand caressed her hanging interfacers. "Then how do you compel devices?"

"With psionics. You also possess similar capabilities, but Arinu call interfacing imprinting and psychometry. However, if you want it, it requires-"

"Extensive organic augmentation." she finished as her finger poked her new carapace.

"If you're still uncomfortable with that, we have full control over Replicator Bay 000, we can replace them with synthetic parts again." Voo-san said.

Her fingertips pressed against the warm bone and muscle fibres. "They are growing on me."

Chapter Twenty-two
Treneer VIII: Warden of the Void

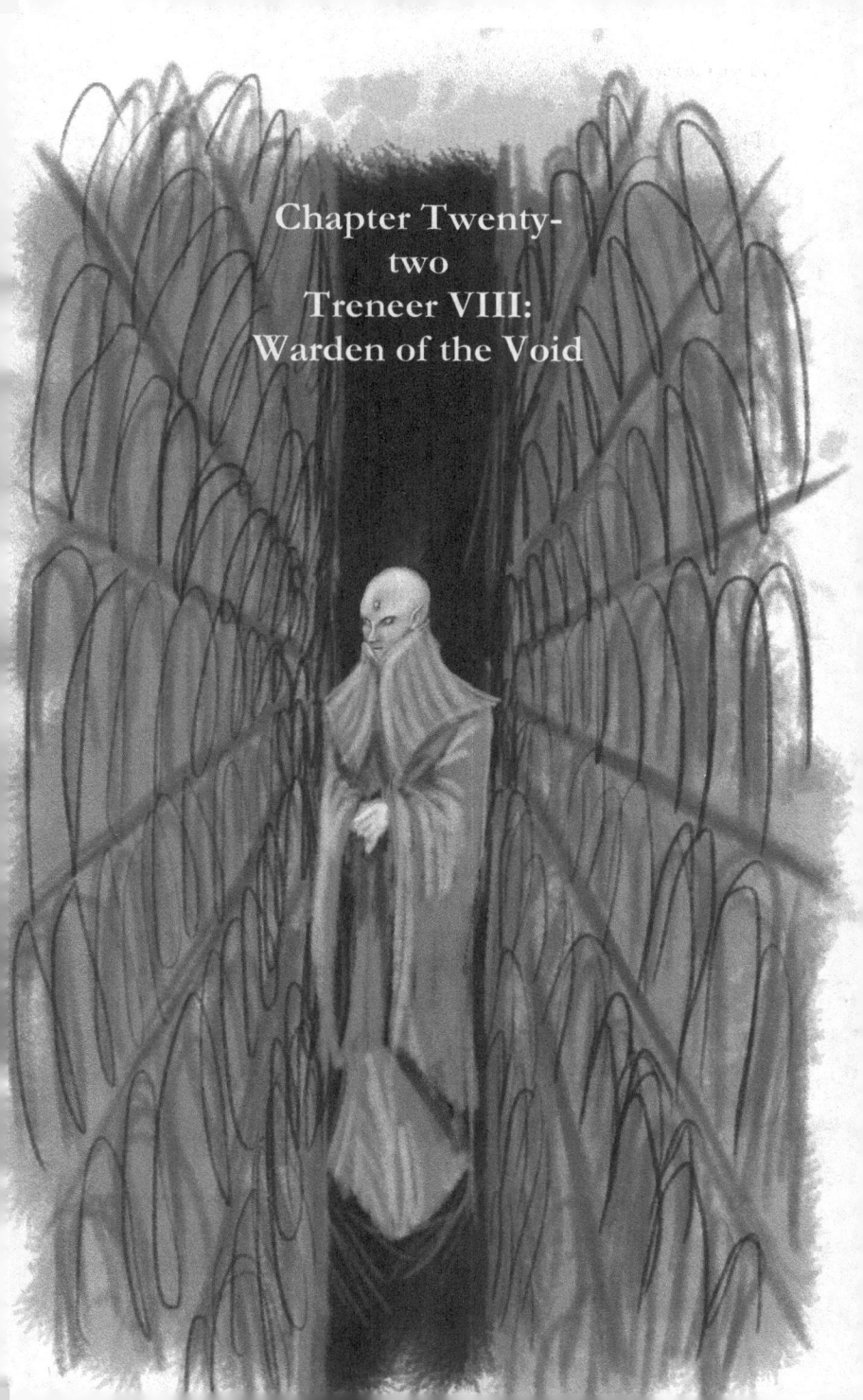

The Grand Coven: the highest elders were not just mere members of the Arinu. They were beyond, the bridge for the ancient past and distant future to the Final Evolution. Treneer finally understood why they were not be trusted. Neela sacrificed her family and Zu'leen sacrificed her life; now it was Treneer's turn to abandon her Oath. In her pod, she read and listened. Her old teacher's mind was decaying with every passing entry, and her face was hot and dry from the hours of tears.

'It's so close to me now, its blinded me and deafened me, I cannot feel anything outside of this. I wonder if they know I'm trying to peek in…of course they would, they're closest thing we understand to…everything. Are they testing my guile? They must be, that's what they do all the time, for all time! They're holding back, pulling me closer to the truth until I see the universe through their eyes.'

They, they, they – Neavensoros. Zu'leen was a remarkable psychic, but she valued reason above emotion and simple hunches. Treneer didn't recognise this person in the recording. Even the notes were unmistakably her mental imprints, her elder had been replaced with a mad woman.

'Oh, I wish to see across the planes and time, as so many do. Too many do. The elders have already been asking me questions, soon they will begin making demands. No, they have not earnt this knowledge! What, they expect me to give it freely? For thirty millennia was spent learning about the Neavensoros, not even our oldest can agree what or who they are, but they all say they "test." If we succeed – the rewards are elevation, if we fail…we remain as insignificant amoeba in comparison.

By the universe, the Neavensoros know me by now! They will know I have earnt their favour and secrets. They know why we don't fit here, on this world…it's like we don't belong to it. In the depths of Farayah, there are mountains that never saw sunlight, but there are primordial carvings too graceful and deliberate to be done by anything other than intelligent hands. Is it an old Neavensoros city cast down eons before? I don't know – I don't know! They won't tell us! But I think someone might know…and I think I know who can reach them.'

Treneer wanted to rip the data crystal from the memory recorder resting on her temple, but gruesome intrigue gripped her and pulled her down.

'The Grand Coven will be suspicious if I asked them, they would insist on being part of this. I can only trust the desperate who won't probe me: astral dancers. They won't ask questions; they won't care about my desires, as long as they dance.'

She pulled herself from her pod; her heart raced as sweat stained her skin. Her poor teacher had fallen and whatever she learned, ended her life. Palming her throbbing temples, she was under Oath to tell the Judicator everything, but then the Grand Elders will come sniffing. Her family will be disgraced, and Neela will have to submit for deep-scans – and who knows, maybe those new Void Prisms will have a new resident. She has heard whispers that those places are no longer places of healing and reflection, but something more isolating and dire.

Treneer won't have to face such punishments if she calls the Judicator right now. She will be elevated and keep her place if she doesn't rouse suspicion, but how late is to worry for that, she wondered. How long will she spend in the Void if she is caught knowing? A day or two? That's all. The Judicator will understand it was to protect her dead tutor. Yet did Zu'leen consider her when she made the choice to do this?

Treneer searched for lessons on how to hide from deep-scans, maybe entering states of pre-transcendence will make the mind immune to them. Then again, whatever Zu'leen uncovered made Treneer pause. A part of her wanted to obliterate her memory – even of Zu'leen, too.

She heard her name whisper from the crystal, snapping her attention back.

'Treneer, my poor student, guilt erodes me when I see her and cannot speak of what I know. She would assimilate all my knowledge of ascension, such a gifted psychic, but she would be too eager to leave her body – a body that she barely had the time to acquaint. Maybe in time, she will understand and perhaps forgive.'

She would protect her teacher's honour, even in death. Treneer plucked the crystal from her head and twirled it in her fingers. Forgive? It may take some time, quite a long time.

The light's rays in the horizon dwindled through her window. A rush of psychic energy flowed through; her ideal time to practice had come. Her pod would have been safe, but the still warm air had bored her. Treneer slipped through the force field window and glided over the drop to the spire's tip. It was baren and the cold wind bit, but her energy kept her flesh warm.

Her body was neither weak, nor strong. Her mind whirled as she centred with her legs tucked under. Treneer put her thoughts of Zu'leen, Neela and the Grand Coven behind as she gazed to the welcoming stars and wondered that maybe tonight was the night she would get another taste of the universe. Eyes closed and mind open, roaming and feeling every fragment of consciousness surrounding matter. A smile crawled up on her cheeks; her reach was greater than before, and she wondered if Zu'leen was watching. The mental image of her face dipped Treneer's joy – no, this was not the time.

Her astral arms rose from her crown and grip around the edges, pulling the rest of her energy from her body. Flexing into the heavens and embracing every molecule that passed through, Treneer looked below to see herself sitting in peace. The air was different, the astral mists thickened her vision. Alien objects and landscapes trickled through the planes before returning to the fluxed gelatinous energy plane.

This cosmic cloud Farayah she passed through would not displace her focus, it was a test of her resolve. Treneer slipped into the vacuum, only turning to see the milky sapphire of her world's surface touched by the red star. She was not alone in this travel, many of her kin took to the astral. She saw some younglings chase each other among the rings of planets, while other's loomed close to the star, basking in its radiation.

Arinu favoured the stars over exploring the inside of Farayah. Only few brave adventurers would dive deep in the mysterious underworld places. But astral forms were not invincible, they were weak to the right frequencies, and many could feel strange powers irradiating from these black spaces. If they were anything like the Crystal Ruins or Castle, then stay away, she thought. Destruction of the astral form was death, even if blood still pumped through the body, and no healing pod will save them. Zu'leen wormed back into her mind. These curiosities compounded in her teacher until she broke, now Treneer feared she had caught the same disease.

No, transcendence is my focus, nothing else shall break this, she thought. In her free state, she slid over the minds of all in the same space. Happiness, frustration, anger, lust, contemplation - good, it didn't strain her. Her astral limbs tightened; her frequency matched the floating stones, hardening until she snapped them in half with a swoop. Next, astral energy pumped in, channelling to grip the stones. An energy field grew, catching every fleck of dust and made it sway – good, no fatigue. She wanted to reach higher and higher, touch the consciousness of the universe, become one with it. Her palms came together as she focused trapped matter to the centre, mounding the sucked dust into a ball. Treneer smiled as she thought it looked like a tiny planet. Maybe this was how the Neavensoros did it, rolling and rolling dust until a planet was born in their starlight palms.

Her excitement grew with the ball. Electricity rippled through her body – she was charging her tiny point of space. The slivers of blue and white expanded into bolts, stretching wider until she felt eyes on her. The astral Arinu were watching, but they kept their distance. A shiver crawled up; there were a pair of eyes she wished she would never have to feel again. Glancing beyond her star system, she could see them peering back at her from Neavensoros space. Every time they stared, as her senses grew, it was a curious stare blended with malevolence. She opened her arms and weaved electricity into a fine bolt as she glared at them. Just as she extended her fingers to the eyes, ready to fire between them, a voice called from around her.

Treneer? Svar's astral form slipped to her side.

The bolt dispersed from her hold as she softened her gaze to him. *How are you, my friend? Were you out here all this time?*

Oh, yes. Though I expected you to be here more often. What were you doing? He stared at her open palms. He looked much like his physical body, except the stars behind him were more visible through his translucent form.

Transcendence practice, but there was something watching me. Taking another glance to the barren spot where the eyes were.

All sorts of extra-dimensionals are running around as of late, even though I'm still back in the healing pod, I can't help but check at what's happening at the Crystal Ruins. He said.

Anything the guardians should be worried about?

Svar hesitated. *I'm not sure. There's a lot of movement, but still localised there.*

She looked to his head and smiled sadly. *I'm sorry you have been injured.*

Worry not! My archite duties have been suspended, at least I can keep an eye out here for everyone. Hopefully, I'll be well enough for

Kra. He said as his gaze drifted to the others. *Do you sense that?*

She could feel her partner stirring in Yinray, she could sense her body running and leaping as she chased another astral dancer. *Yes, Yansoon.*

How exiting for you to have a partner! And help train of all things — Zu'leen would be proud. He said with a warm grin.

She almost let her joy slip into her unfortunate discovery, but Svar's sensors are heightened in the astral. She shielded her reluctance as she swayed. *It can be intimidating, like some stars out here.*

Ah, yes. They are not stars, but they are not your enemy, yet. He said.

What? She said.

My role is out there; your role is on Farayah, for now.

Are you seeing the future?

Until next travel. He winked before she was sucked back into her body.

Her feet and hands were colder than hoped as she unravelled herself before levitating down the spire. Her third eye scanned for Yansoon; she could see her aura twinkling among the forest of crystal buildings, dashing and phasing through the streets. Her partner barely made a call to her before Treneer phased to the bridge where the suspect hid under. Yansoon and several other guardians huddled around the rose-tinted glassy structure. There was a rushing waterfall from the river cutting through the city. The gushing water fell to a steep drop where the lower districts sat. She could see the suspect's faint orange outline in the dispersing vapour.

I can see her. She said leaning over the railing.

Get back! She was caught and just before the Judicator could send her for treatment, she killed two guardians and escaped. Yansoon said as she ushered her hand back.

Treneer levitated away from the bridge; she tried poking through the runaway's mind to steer her body out of the waterfall, but there was a heavy fort around their head. Frustrated, she considered weaving another bolt and electrifying her, but that could kill the other organisms living in the river.

I'll charge each of you with power, localise your telekinesis and grip them along with the water. She said.

Treneer, my telekinesis-

We're a team. Treneer extended her arms and aimed to her colleagues. *Now!*

With this boost, the guardians swarmed as their combined power suspended the water, trapping the suspect inside the bubble. She could see their body tumbling inside, but her orange aura fired and broke through, vaporising the liquid instantly. She was strong, too strong, and that's when she saw it – a small rift creaked open, and pair of tendril-like hands wrapped around her torso.

She's channelling a Kepa! She cried, but it was too late. With a swoop of her arms, she tore the space where two of the guardians levitated; an explosion spat forth and made them tumble from their air. Treneer screamed and her focus slipped as she desperately tried to catch their unconscious bodies before meeting their fatal end.

"Treneer!" Yansoon cried as she helplessly waved her arms as her body began falling.

She snapped her attention back to Yansoon and pulled her back from the bridge, away from the torn space around the waterfall. Treneer watched in awe as water dripped into burning rifts, creating steamy clouds around the area. *Judicator, do you copy the situation-*

Summoning more to you, now. The Judicator beamed back. More bodies teleported around the bridge, with their palms and auras fired with energy. The maddened woman turned her attention; her body pulsated with a sickening rage while a demented smile crept up on the Kepa's face.

Let her go! You're breaking Farayah! Treneer shrieked.

Already broken! The two guttural voices spoke before conjuring a beam to strike at the guardians. They flew aside as the orange beam cracked through more space. Treneer turned to see searing edges of a black dent along one of the residential buildings across the river. Her heart almost tore as she pressed more power into her colleagues, trying to trap this manic for the last time. As she poured forth, she felt a familiar presence among the reinforcements, a mind she hadn't felt for some time. Her head spun to see three lavender scars across the side of a pearly head, his eyes were narrowed and enraged as they looked upon the possessed astral dancer.

Ouro's eyes rolled at the back of his head, sucking every ounce of power before opening arms wide. *Unhook her from this plane and drag her to the Void Prism, then prepare to seal the rift. On my mark!*

The guardians followed his command as they peeled her away from this material frequency. She oscillated so violently; even the dark hands slipped their grip of her torso, until she was just a blur. A black spot appeared at her feet; her frightened eyes darted to it and then back to Ouro.

Seal it! He roared.

Needle-like aches washed from her third eye as Treneer pumped the last scraps of energy to them all. Her body begged to give in, but she watched with relief as the guardians slammed the main rift with the Kepa rolled shut. Now, there was just the suspect to deal with. Her mind could barely utter a thought before Ouro delivered his final words to her:

The Judicator declared you to serve ten terms in your Void Prism. You have embraced the void, and now the void shall embrace you.

There was a coldness to them, he was detached as the woman fell into the black lining before he delicately slid it shut. A group of Arinu spectated safely from the edge of the river. Some were terrified, while others had excitement painted on their faces. Several guardians flew over to the destroyed building and immediately tended to the affected, while she caught her breath.

You were about to drop us off the cliff. Yansoon said gliding to her and gripping her elbows before slowly descending to the bridge.

Sorry. She said wiping sweat from her brow as she tried to calm her racing heart.

Yansoon shook her head. *Thank you for saving me, I'm sorry about those that fell.*

Treneer glanced to the drop below; hopefully the Judicator was able to lock on and beam them back before they hit the ground, but these opaque astral clouds may have been too thick for him to save them on time. She turned to Yansoon as she steadied herself. *Despite this, I feel you have gotten significantly stronger now.*

I told you I learn fast. Soon, I won't need you anymore. She grinned.

One can only hope. She smiled back. She caught Ouro descending to the bridge and looking directly towards her. *Tend to the others, I'll be with you in a moment.*

Her partner gave a short nod and dashed to the partially ruined building. Treneer straightened her back as she stepped toward him. The soles of her feet enjoyed the tender creamy paved grounds that still held the faint warmth from the sun. Ouro softened as the corner of his lip curled into a smile *Apologies for not answering your calls.*

Once I heard you were a Void Warden, I assumed your head was stuck there, too.

It was. I found my life's purpose, you see. He nodded.

I'm proud of you. For the record, you did make a fine psi-therapist. She said.

His drooping-sleeved arms crossed over his chest as he sucked in the cool air. *Who's to say I don't still heal people.*

Much has happened and I assume the same for you. Treneer could feel a dark shade pass over her friend's face as he gazed at her. *About the prisms, are you…are we keeping suspects in there as patients or as prisoners?*

Have the Judicator summon you to my office when all this mess is sorted. I want to hear someone's opinion on something personal. He said.

Treneer chuckled. *I'm starving, have something hot for me when I arrive.*

Ouro breathed a hearty laugh. *Not only eating food but making requests for it? My, my, maybe Kepa have possessed you, too.* He grinned before his body slipped away from the material plane.

~

She watched the builders float around the blasted structure; the ringed spheres piloted by architects half a world away slapped sleets of energy over the hole. What was once a blackened singed socket, was replaced with shimmering bricks and crystal, as if the events earlier that day had been erased from history. However, it was the least of their worries. Treneer looked on from the Judicator's screen. The guardians still on sight tempered worried civilians and directed the wounded to healing wings.

Can you confirm how many were injured during the attack? The Judicator said as he turned his holographic head to her.

I sensed half a dozen, one cracked skull, another lost his right arm, the other's minor radiation burns. All recoverable injuries, but the mental damage is another matter. We shall need at least four guardians offering support for the traumatised for the next several months. She said as she looked to the carnage. *How do our two fallen guardian's fare?*

One was struck by a boulder, shattering his arms, ribs and pelvis. Two weeks in the healing pod. The other was caught in time, he is dealing with shock. The A.I. said.

I see. She said as she glanced to the silvery rifts in the space around the river. *Those cracks will take longer to repair, all are stretched too thin dealing with more of these…* Her lips curled as if the thought of the astral dancer soured her tongue. *Criminals.*

Unprecedented times, Treneer, they are not criminals. Some of these people have been driven mad by the clouds and sought to regain their sight. They need help, not disdain. As guardian, you should know thusly. The Judicator said.

What about those who dance for the thrill of it? She sneered.

The Judicator's unimpressed glare made the pixels of his eyes quiver. *Will you commit to a quick-scan to assure the record, Archite?*

Treneer hid her worries when her attention snapped to them. *I consent.*

She felt a soft poke of her consciousness, the Judicator reliving her time on the bridge and the fear of dropping Yansoon during the capture.

All is in order. I see you two are copasetic. He said.

She nodded. *Yansoon is evolving her abilities faster than anticipated.*

Good, keep it consistent. His head twinkled, readying to disappear, but the burning question popped in her mind.

Judicator, how did the astral dancer escape after you judged her?

His holographic light hardened. *Her frequency changed and she managed to slip through planes beyond my reach. In doing so, the exoplanar radiation blasted guardians holding her.*

Will they recover?

Their bodies are now ash. The A.I. said.

More murders. Treneer took a deep breath and pressed her sore temple. *These summoners are growing in power each passing day, we need to apply for more aggressive tactics!*

Applying more aggressive tactics? That is interesting… The Judicator said.

She cocked her head to the side as she watched the A.I's thoughts whirl.

I have been moderating order long before your Cold Fire ancestors settled in the northern valleys. For two-hundred millennia, I have counted ninety-four incidents from distressed Arinu civilians, and seventy-eight of those were cases of self-harm. However, in the last year, there have been fifteen assaults on other people. Fifteen, Treneer. In all my programming of justice and social expectations, it has become difficult to rely on ancient data to compensate for these unsettling new trends. Watching the Arinu change is difficult, but it's troubling watching them change into something unrecognisable. The Judicator said.

You're the Judicator, your decisions are final. Treneer said.

I am and they are. The holographic projection flickered. *I know your feelings toward the Grand Coven are sour, but for once, it seems your thoughts and theirs are on the same wavelength on how to deal with this.*

Her eyes narrowed at the Judicator. *What are their plans?*

By the agreement of the Coven and Executors, the guardians will be given more potent psionic enhancers while the Coven reduces psionic liberties on Farayah. A briefing will come soon from Executor Shurees.

This hinders our Oath, Judicator! How could you allow this? She said.

But the Oath is not technically contradicted, Archite. I administer order, the Proctor administers every other facet of Arinu society, but it's the Grand Coven's wisdom the people listen to. And whatever the will of the people, the Great A.I's must follow. The Judicator said.

She sighed. *How long does this psychic suppression last?*

Until the world has passed through this dark astral cloud. They said.

I see. She said. Afterall, why shouldn't she trust the Judicator? The A.I. was void of ego but balanced with extensively written empathetical programs. Yet, she was unsold on the Grand Coven's wisdom. *Well, I have an appointment with an old colleague. I'll take my leave.*

With a nod, the Judicator blinked away. Treneer closed her eyes along with the burdens of her day; she wanted to wash them away by visiting Ouro. A chuckle escaped her lips when she heard her stomach growling like a furious predator.

On my way to the teleporter alcoves, Ouro. She whispered.

No need to waste time. He said. In a blink, the Guardian Headquarters vanished from sight as she soared through the airless planes before casting into the faraway southern city of Heebar. Her body came to an open balcony of a high tower, and her eyes strained to see the plains before her. To the far outskirts, the surrounding fields were covered with gold and emerald grass growing in circles around the high and mighty g'alann trees. Thick pale trunks with ancient crystals were protruding between the roots and upper bark, but to the branches, she could see Arinu gliding back and forth from the flimsy crystal-infused wooden houses shrouded behind the leaves.

You have been here before, right? Ouro said as he stepped to the balcony beside her.

Only in the astral. How strange, the energy form has many superior senses, but being here in my body now – this feels more real. She said, soaking in the view.

Heebar is my birthplace. I once longed to escape its limitations, but now, I see Yinray has too much excitement. He said as he smiled at a memory beyond her telepathic sight.

On the honour of our friendship, I ask you keep this between us. Treneer said turning to him. *The Judicator tells me the Grand Elders and Executors wish to supress civilian psionics while empowering guardians to combat the growing assaults. They say it will be for a time, but I fear their obsession with transcendence is for nefarious purposes.*

Ouro's finger lined his temple down to his cheek as his mouth twisted, as if he tasted her words. *That is alarming. I do hope you're wrong.*

There's something else, I was contacted by Neela. She gave me Zu'leen's last journals and even she is suspicious. Treneer debated whether to disclose their full contents, but anxiously waited for his reaction.

I cannot add much to that suspicion, but maybe with my work, I can offer another solution to this plight. Come, my friend. Ouro swept back into the open archways to his office. Slipping through the force field, the air stilled and warmed significantly as he sauntered past his ordered desk and space.

His hand waved over a replicator as two narrow glasses appeared in the alcove; he scooped one in his hand and brought the edge to his lips. *This has been keeping me sharp, drink up before we go into the Prism.*

What is it? Treneer lifted the glass with her mind. She could feel warmth radiating from the surface, but when she glanced in, there was an amber bubbling liquid within. Then the smell hit. It wasn't unpleasant, but the strong earthy scent felt like it bore through her skin.

Dried herbs boiled in crystal-modified water. He said as his head tilted back to drink up the last drops.

I thought you said food would be available. She took a deep breath as she shot it down. Treneer fought hard not to gag the liquid back into the glass. *Its horrendously bitter.*

On one hand: I'm elated that consuming food no longer disgusts you, on the other: you offend my tastes. His eye narrowed. With a flick of his hand, the glasses phased from their hand and into the ether. *Now, to the Void.*

Impressive. She smirked at his phasing skills.

Ouro glided over to an arched black stone wall with various shimmering letters over the surface. A shiver came down her spine when she saw they were the names of familiar patients, some of which she had helped capture. She had never been to a Void Prism, not even in her astral travels, but it was not a place of punishment, rather a place to strip the inhabitants of their wayward behaviour and to heal them.

All within this psychic realm, no matter how dire their actions, were siphoned of their rampant egos and introduced to their matched healers before continuing into the world. However, there was an unshakable weight in the Prism. Even for visitors, they would feel its mild affects.

Treneer could only imagine what it would be for the captives.

Ouro pressed his palm on the black slab; a violet and navy spiral expanded out into a darker hole to the centre, opening the way for them. He looked to her. *Mental shields to maximum.*

Needn't tell me. She said as she glided through first.

With Ouro at her back, the darkness overwhelmed her physical eyes, but to her fortune, her third eye was sensitive enough to see an endless hallway without floor or ceiling showing a thousand upon thousand rooms on either side. Ouro took ahead as she followed peering into the rooms. They were massive on the inside, as if the cell beside them didn't exist. Some held cities, other jungles, fierce deserts and floating star systems. She couldn't see the denizens, she hoped they were off in their own mindscapes and shedding their lowest selves.

Most of them are empty, universe's fortune, but more will come soon. That's why I had psi-architects make extensions to their cells, because sadly, those here will not leave for a while. He said.

What makes your prism so unique?

Ouro turned to her. *I need your mind to be open, Treneer. You know of my failures and faults, you know my sole intent is to help people.*

I'm listening. She said.

He took a deep breath and centred himself. *Psi-therapy only helps after something awful has happened. Why should we solve issues after they have occurred when we can stop the issue in the first place? When someone offends, we scurry to heal them and their victims. Sometimes, therapy doesn't work. Resources needlessly spent to repair so many broken hearts. My Void Prism holds the worst of the worst. There's an energy here of my design that breaks down the hefty walls of the psyche and works its way to the core of the person. After their bad selves have been shed, I rewrite a new personality, complete with new memories.*

Treneer's arms crossed over her tightening gut. She pulled her stare from him and looked to the mercilessly eternal hall.

This is only to protect the innocent and ultimately themselves! Ouro continued.

Even I agree we need to be more forceful when dealing with these miscreants, but what you're suggesting is…invasive. You're taking away spiritual metamorphosis from them. They need a chance to work to get better!

Treneer, these prisoners are killers. They have murdered people. That Kepa-corrupted summoner you captured is right there. He pointed to a granite cell door several levels above their heads. *Do you believe a few soothing sessions will break her curse?*

Alright, say you write her a new life, what happens then? She goes out into the world and wonders why people hate her so much? Her victims will not forget. She said.

A new identity and home, far away from all her old life. They will be so changed that their former associates won't even be able to track her mind. There was a glint of smile under his face.

And the Executors allowed you to do this? She has a family – they all do.

And all their victims have families. He frowned. *Do you not understand?*

Treneer buried her face in her palms. *I do, it's just our kin have become unrecognisable to me. Even the Judicator says so.*

We both chose to help people. He said, but some emotion bubbled deep within the bowels of his mind he desperately tried to bottle.

But it was too late, she already noticed. *Open to me, can you honestly say this is for your prisoners and not for yourself?*

Prisoners? It was Ouro's turn to look away. *Already too many innocents are lost, and the number grows by the day! My work will help.*

My dear friend, you speak about stripping them of their trauma, yet you cannot do it for yourself! She studied his sullen face, his breathing quickened and shoulders slightly drooped. *That's why you brought me here, isn't it? You need someone to see what you're doing to convince this is the right thing.*

Ouro turned from her and drifted up the walls. *How is this not the right thing? What right thing is there? At least two guardians have died from one astral dancer. What about tomorrow?*

I can't say what this Prism does is a good or a bad thing, I'm saying your actions come from a hurt place – like theirs. She said as her arms extended out to the infinite black walls.

He slowly spun around. *Leave me be for now.*

You're not alone in this, Ouro. Treneer said as she sucked back a tear before turning to the portal to his office.

I don't want to be, either. He said.

432

Chapter Twenty-three
Ahn'kat VIII: Watching the Watchers

The cold humid air clung on his heavy robes and face as he wandered through the gardens. The sun had brought its light to the crystal skies but hadn't shown its face. The dried leaves crunched as he swept by them and noticed his nose and lips leaking steamy breath. His hot blood pushed through his body. Ahn'kat could already feel the fine hairs on his arms and legs growing long and thick to keep the heat. Winter was upon Lusor City and the once beryl land was falling asleep for the season.

Clutching the listening devices under his sleeves, Ahn'kat couldn't help but play and tap them against each other in his palm. Ismotaph frequented the gardens, he sometimes entertained or did business here, but with Ismotaph – it was all business. Ahn'kat had to hurry to find places for the devices, because in a few hours, the High Priest Seratut will be arrested.

He looked around the wide outdoor palace covered a mile in each direction, and he only had a handful of the augmented listeners. He stopped on the cobbled path, he remembered Emestasun explaining psychic abilities weren't limited to reading thoughts or throwing one's astral senses across space, but also detecting minute energies of a person or an object, even when they're long gone.

Closing his eyes, Ahn'kat took a deep breath and tried imagining where the Head of the Corps would walk here. His mind's eye blurred with nonsense images, Ismotaph jumping or flying or laughing in the garden morning, noon and night. He couldn't tell whether his senses were receiving information, or his own imagination was running away from him. Emestasun always emphasised simplicity of the intent: hold as little expectation as possible and – most importantly – clear one's mind of all preconceived notions.

Ahn'kat rubbed his temples and tried again. Flat, blank mind, no thoughts, no images. Let his higher senses do the work. Outlines formed in his mind, but Ahn'kat dared not push them as they filled with shadows and colour. He saw

Ismotaph enjoying a nice seat under the curled branches surrounded by spiked flowers as he smiled to one of the palace servants before the vision vanished.

The spiked flowers…they were in the opposite direction of him. Ahn'kat glowered as he made his inconvenient trek back, since he was expected at Urbaz Ship Bays soon. His brow furrowed that maybe his vision was wrong and that his visions were hopeful imagination. And the palace servant giving Ismotaph information…perhaps it was Ahn'kat's paranoia.

If he catches any useful information on these devices, he planned to make as many copies as physically possible. Zertun even suggested to store the data crystals in servant's and guard's body-pouches. His trusted guard was not with him in the gardens, he was expected to go on sabbatical as was tradition whose totems were of the Shadow Sabre. However, his true mission was to travel to Urbaz mansion and place a little listener there, too.

As Ahn'kat followed the winding and colourful path, his head scratched past the dried leaves under the curled branches. To the corner, he saw snapping vines rearing their mouths towards him, eagerly waiting for his hand to be an inch too close. He was tempted to slap their plant lips as he wandered through, as Ramkes had done many times when they were children. Then his eye spotted a bunch of brown stems with spiked petals in another patch. Ahn'kat slowly approached as his eyes scanned for a bench.

There was a flat stone shrouded by dried moss, bird-droppings, and other plant debris. His hand stretched out and brushed the surface to see an old, masoned bench. He frowned, wondering if his mental image of Ismotaph was wrong and began doubting if he had frequented here. His sleeve fell and pushed some shrubbery out of the way, and his eyes widened when he saw a stone sky-serpent carving. This was it.

Ahn'kat snuck a glance around the gardens, yes, he was alone – so he thought. To make sure, he flicked his wrist phone and scanned the area of any Zanashj hiding amongst the foliage. He waited for the scans, hoping for nothing, but the radar flashed a speck coming behind him on the small hologram.

His body went rigid as his ears picked up a shuffling of feet behind him. Ahn'kat eased his muscles and scraped away the dried leaves from his sleeve as he turned. Neobatri lightly jogged toward him as her arms pulled to her chest. He noticed her arms were bare and had the shape of long bat wings. With his head held high, he gave her a small smile. Her darkened face looked up; there was a wildness behind her eyes before blinking it away when she saw him.

"Your grace." she said breathlessly as she approached with a polite bow.

"Pantheon's blessings on this cold morning," he said. Sweat patterned her brow as her fingers clicked back into regular form. "Which shape were you taking?"

"None, I was strengthening my arms and familiarising myself with the cold, your grace. Do you require an escort?" she said as her hands rested on her hips.

Ahn'kat wanted to be alone, but her company warmed him in the frigid wind.

"Only if the company is interesting!" He gave her a smirk and she returned one as he swept the hem of his robes aside before settling on the old bench. His fingers carefully wedged the listener in the stone sky-serpent's beak before extending his hand for Neobatri to sit by him. "I had the pleasure of praying with Gajoon in these gardens. An interesting person."

Neobatri seized but pressed her smile. "Her love is for the Pantheon. She has yet to pick a totem."

"Pardon me but is her totem not the same as the rest of your family's?" he said.

Her eyes widened and her mouth opened with shocked embarrassment.

He pursed his lips. "I apologise, she mentioned that you both were-"

"No, it's quite alright, your grace. I should learn to be more..." Neobatri's eyes trailed to the crisp grass. "I shouldn't be afraid of people knowing she is also my sister."

They both sat in silence for a moment.

"She has deep love for you." Ahn'kat finally said.

Neobatri chuckled as her open palms rubbed against her knees, as if she were trying to clean away her embarrassment. "Yes, I know. She always has."

"What is your totem?" Ahn'kat said.

"Father chose the Divine Cobra for our family. He is quite possessive of it, your grace. Gajoon was not allowed to have it as hers." she said.

"As cobra's typically are – especially for their loved ones," Ahn'kat sighed. "I don't mean to add stress to a family's situation, but I assure you, we have not forgotten about Neheret."

"That brings us comfort, your grace," she said blankly.

"But you don't seem so enthusiastic."

She shrugged her shoulders. "I understand there are other worries plaguing the Crown. The Empire's survival is apex over her many imperial members."

"Which worries do you refer to?" Ahn'kat said as his eyes narrowed to her.

"I am an infiltrator, your grace, the palace maids are as loud as parrots after that disastrous meeting with the princess and the Arinu. One questions if hope is worth its weight anymore." she said.

"Hope is not a poor investment, Neobatri, it's the fuel that drives us – whether we want to admit it or not." he said.

"I disagree, your grace." she said.

His brows rose, watching her face soften and eyes travelled along the garden beds. "I believe it's our faith that drives us. To trust that something or someone to be better."

"What do you pray for?" he said.

Neobatri leaked a faint smile as she looked at his beetle pendant. "I barely did as a child."

"But you're not a child anymore," he said.

She eased on the bench beside him; he could see small bumps rising on her skin. "I pray for forgiveness, but I doubt I deserve it."

"It's for the Pantheon to decide whether we deserve it." he said.

The whole warming sun had made its appearance. He wished he could bask in its radiance, but he was expected at the ship bay. "I must take my leave for now," he said as he rose to his feet.

She stood and made a small bow. "Maybe I could join you and Gajoon for a prayer at the shrine sometime, your grace."

"A welcome company, infiltrator," he grinned as he twisted his face into a stranger's. "No matter how great your sin is, I have faith you're deserving of forgiveness, Neobatri."

She gave an assured smile and he a nod before dashing off to his peaceful and lone voyage.

~

The cool wind rustled his hair, but his skin warmed when the light touched it. He sucked in a lungful of air as he flew, twisting the wheel as his body pressed side to side. A smile crept up his cheeks; this blink of freedom was intoxicating. For a moment, he wasn't a prince or man; he was bliss. Soaring past the jungle and into the open orange dunes of Sekem, his humble craft lowered to the phased door of the subterranean bay.

As the vehicle waned power, Ahn'kat clicked his original facial features in place as he hopped out. Guards approached and demanded his forehead to be scanned to ensure he was the lovely prince. He grimaced as his regular life returned.

"Welcome Prince Ahn'kat, Sekem Bay is at your disposal," Taskmaster Meksonett said as she stepped forward before bowing.

"Good to see you, Taskmaster," Ahn'kat glanced around as he rubbed his tingling head. The entry chamber was emptier than he recalled; there were fewer workers around and considerably less messy. "I'm now acting on Lord Reshj's behalf and given permission by the Crown to begin staff alterations. Let's begin."

The Taskmaster's nod was stiff. "Yes, your grace, follow me," she said making way down the corridor. He didn't know her as well as he should have, but there was a chaotic air about her that she was trying to cover.

With the guards at his back, Ahn'kat studied the vast underground yard; thick pulsating organic tubes clung to the various ships on the levels. Workers, pets, and others bowed low as he and the Taskmaster passed and kept their heads away. There was a bleakness in here that seeped into everyone and everything.

"I see there are fewer pets around, have you already begun shifting them out?" Ahn'kat said.

"Yes, your grace. Most workers here are paid commoners, some even from lower houses," she said.

"Which accommodation did you move the former pets to? Are they bunking in the monasteries now?"

The Taskmaster's lips tightened. "That's not my place to know. Lord Reshj organised some Conclave members and other nobles retrieved them and placed them under their care, your grace."

Before he could open his mouth, Meksonett stopped and pointed to the base of the chamber. Skeletons of ships were growing from the monolithic open vats along the ground. "Our bio-factories are working at all hours, producing as quickly as possible."

He counted over two dozen cruisers forming, strings of membranes and tissue hardening over the metal bones. "Why are there so many?"

"To be prepared," she hurried out the words.

Ahn'kat lowered his eyes to the ground. They were preparing for the inevitable war with the Arinu, but even if Ismotaph could train his infiltrators to be powerful psychics, they may not be enough to survive the Arinu's wrath. "This is very costly, how are we able to pay for these and replace the pets with paid staff?"

"House Urbaz coffers are vast, but not infinite. These are a new line of cruisers: the Keshsapt. The ships amplify psionics of the crew, they don't need to leave Uras to successfully fight. We wouldn't need any more than what you see, your grace," she said.

He watched the vats gurgle a mass of tissue; it crawled up the skeletons and morphed around the bones, making him shiver. "And these amplifiers, are they taken from...special sources?" he said eyeing the Taskmaster.

She nodded. "Yes, your grace."

Ahn'kat swallowed his horror. "How many did we take to make these ships?"

Meksonett hesitated. "Your grace, there were enough for-"

"Take me to them," he whispered.

"I-"

"Now."

They headed deeper into the chamber; more guards lined the walls before coming to the carapace doors. Meksonett sheepishly passed him before pressing her palm against the surface. The plates pulled in and revealed the long and claustrophobic tunnel into the experimental rooms. The smell hit his nose first as he stepped in. It was a stench that he couldn't imagine existing. His fingers wound around his pendant as he pushed through the shivering curtains, that could not dampen the smell that drenched this room.

Shadowy forms lingered inside a murky gelatinous mixture encompassed by a transparent sack hanging from living tubes crossing the dark ceiling. The prince paused, trying to ready his mind and stomach before stepping into the greater chamber. He was hypnotised by the floating and lifeless pale bodies inside them; some had limbs missing, some had spines and skulls removed, leaving limp faces in the gloop. Most had their crystal bumps from their forehead surgically removed and their mangled brains exposed. His throat dried then tightened, studying each of their lost and confused faces.

His nose closed to fight the stench of their decaying forms as he struggled to keep the sickness down. "Are there anymore coming in? Is this all?"

"There are no more, your grace," she whispered.

He turned to her. "Your orders are not to take or accept anymore, all seizure missions on Farayah are to cease from this day onward. If you receive orders otherwise, I will hear of it. Do you understand me, Taskmaster?"

"Yes, your grace," she nodded.

Ahn'kat sighed. "I want full reports on the psi-enhancers and all developments from these experiments. Maybe that will justify all this...horror."

"From the little we have uncovered, the Arinu channel their psionics through this crystal-like protrusion of the skull in their foreheads. There are a million nerve endings bundled in there, directly connected to the centre of their brains," Meksonett stepped to holo-screen and waved her palm over it, showing a scan of Arinu heads. "If you look closely, your grace, we believe this allows them to channel their psionics to extraordinary levels. Interestingly, we see some of that energy pouring down their nervous system, feeding their cells. Almost eliminating their need to consume food."

His eyes widened at the idea to end the exhausting hunger for the impoverished, to help them maintain their physical appearance without losing their stomachs if they hadn't eaten in some days. He recalled going to a bleak village outside of Lusor city, run by a lower house. Most of the vagabonds watched him and his Conclave compatriots, as he noticed that their faces were missing mouths after going for weeks without material food. Even their skin grew unusual nodules to absorb more sunlight and other energies to keep their bodies alive. They adapted to live without conventional food, drastically altering their digestive system.

These adaptations, after a prolonged period, are exceedingly and expensively difficult to reverse. But now, with this development, there was some hope for those impoverished people. Guilt hit him, however. Ahn'kat didn't want the dead eyes of the Arinu seeing him consider the positives of Meksonett's research. He mouthed a prayer to Aszelun, begging for their understanding and forgiveness. Maybe that's why the Great Beetle has finally forsaken him.

"I have seen some infiltrators with psionic gifts, but what are the long-term consequences? How will we change consuming psi-enhancers?" he said.

"We're not certain, your grace, but we have already begun trials for common people, and the results are ambiguous," she said.

"Explain."

"We thought that subjects would physically develop some Arinu characteristics, but the only changes that were obvious so far, were the engorgement of our brains, as is present in Arinu," Meksonett said.

"So, are you saying our brains are structured similarly?" he said as his eyes narrowed.

"They are the same, your grace. The only differences are size and how many neurons are packed in to facilitate certain abilities. The Arinu brain is attuned for psionics, whereas ours is attuned to control our bodies."

He turned to the corpses inside the tanks, trying to see them through the eyes of a curious scientist. They were alike, too alike for beings that developed in different areas of the galaxy. How was this possible?

"What about psychological and behavioural changes in the test subjects?" he said.

Meksonett cleared her throat as her fingers flicked across the screen to video files. "This was observed when the proto psi-enhancers were produced."

A holo-image appeared with text transcribing every second of the procedure. In the centre of the hollow room, stood a lone pet male. He pressed a white capsule in his mouth and crunched it before swallowing. He took a deep breath. The video sped up to several minutes before returning to real-time. He pressed his face into his palms and ran fingers through his hair before his head shot up. The text said 'subject began hearing voices in the soundproof room. When asked to repeat what he heard, it was the same thoughts of the researchers outside.'

The man started to grin as his eyes wandered around the room, as if they were tracking an invisible object. 'Subject with no hereditary psionic abilities claimed to see streams of energy and objects appearing inside the chamber.'

The video sped up again, the man wandered around the room, whispering to the air and trying to catch whatever he was seeing before he looked to his arms and hands. 'Subject reports he can see his aura, it was glowing and getting larger.'

His hands tightened into fists as faint sparks of light cracked from his knuckles. He pressed eyes shut as his feet began to leave the ground. His head rolled back, and his mouth twisted in delight, 'subject is no longer responding to researcher's questions and begins laughing.'

Time jumped through the video; the date was stamped over a few days. 'Subject has rejected food, but still consumes water. He claims that he no longer needs to eat despite showing no signs of typical digestive adaptations that occur in Zanashj. He claims he is being fed but doesn't elaborate how this is possible.'

Months skip in the video, the man still appears to look healthy, but when he's brought into the chamber, he doesn't speak or walk around anymore. 'Subject is experiencing headaches from lack of sleep; he claimed that other test subject's dreams keep him up during sleep periods.'

The man shrinks away in the corner of the room, his head is low, but Ahn'kat sees his mouth moving. 'Subject is beginning showing signs of delusion, he claims he is not a pet or a Zanashj – or anything we can possibly understand. He claims he has seen eternity and infinity and is one with it.'

A few more weeks pass, and it appears the man hasn't left the chamber in all that time. He levitates to his feet and releases electricity from his fists, he begins cracking the walls and ground, leaving behind blackened marks and dents in the metal surface. His mouth pulls apart and his shining eyes are wild; he is screaming, but Ahn'kat hears no sound. 'Subject has ceased answering any questions from researchers, he starts damaging himself and property. Guards have failed to subdue him through conventional means, researchers will require elimination via electricity.'

The video cuts out and Ahn'kat found his dry mouth begging him for salvation inside a bottle of banana liquor. A cold sweat covered his skin when he remembered his parents and Emestasun's stubbornness to remain in there with them.

"Is this what happens to *all* who take the enhancers?"

"No, your grace. While this madness appears in most cases, but we think it can be managed with smaller doses and teaching the subjects techniques to control this."

Ahn'kat brushed his lips with his fingers before reaching out and plucking out a data crystal from the side of the computer. "Notify me on all updates, it doesn't matter even if they seem irrelevant. Is that understood, Taskmaster?"

She nodded. He took one last glance at the dead Arinu before escaping the dark dungeons.

~

The last rays of light shone to the horizon, but the day was still not done. Shipyard after shipyard, taskmaster after taskmaster, Ahn'kat felt like his brain had crawled out for his ears and nose. He didn't realise his exhaustion until he saw his freshly dressed bed sitting to the centre of his chambers. Hobbling over, his knees gave up before planting into the soft and warm sheets. The second his eyes closed; he saw the spirits of the sad Arinu entombed in Sekem. He spun around quickly and opened his eyes, desperate for distraction. The blue tapestry of Aszelun drifted in the turning air above him.

"If you are on other worlds, Great Beetle, then please understand our sins," his eyes were too tired to tear. Then he felt his wrist phone tremble. Ahn'kat's stomach clenched when he received a message from Zertun, heralding Ismotaph's arrival.

The prince sat up and slapped his face before pouring a couple of mouthfuls of banana liquor in a gold goblet. The bottle was in the shape of a fine swan, hoping he would gift it to Ramkes on her ascension. He made the alcohol heavily filtered but leaving only enough to enhance the taste and maybe loosen his wife's cheeks for a smile. However, this soon-to-be-empty bottle would meet its fate in the hands of cleaning servants sweeping through his chambers.

He sucked the goblet down. The burning sweetness almost overwhelmed him, but the sudden intake of alcohol made his throat wretch. He hadn't drunk in a long time; his body had forgotten how to adapt to it. Mucus dribbled from his lips as he wiped it away. He pulled out the last listener from his trousers and glanced around where it's unassuming new home would be. He noticed three ruby eyes twinkled at him; the golden outlines of a mighty sea-beast were etched in the polished stone walls of his chamber.

Ahn'kat hurried over to the centre eye; his fingernails extended and hardened around the gem's seams, sliding through until the rock popped out from its socket. His thumb pressed the flexible egg-shape device into the hole before clicking the gem back in place. Knuckles tapped against the door; his heart stopped glancing in its direction. "Yes?"

"Your meeting robe is ready, your grace," a female voice called from behind.

His eyes narrowed, wondering if Ismotaph would have morphed into one of the servants. "Come."

The door peeled open, and three servants slipped through. He eyed every one of them as he extended out his arms. One slipped off his robes, the other tended to his shoes, the last freshened his long day-old plait. Fear ran away with him as he looked to their unfamiliar faces, maybe one of them were – maybe all three were elite infiltrators, or maybe they were simple staff. No, no, you have some psionics, Ahn'kat told himself. Seratut is in your ear about Ismotaph's looming betrayal. Maybe it's true, but the listeners will help. What about Neobatri? She is his under his wing, but she seems far from his shadow.

Another knock. "Your grace," it was Zertun's voice.

"Come in!" relieved to hear him, he ushered the servants out of the opening doors, parting ways for the heavy-chested guard as he strode in. "Thought you would actually take the sabbatical."

Zertun gave a knowing nod. "The Sabre draws near, my prince."

"How are my parents?" he said straightening his sleeves and rings.

"The Lord and Lady are keeping to themselves."

Ahn'kat pursed his lips. "And Emestasun?"

"I think she maybe keeping them in check," he said.

"Good to hear, at least," he sighed as his eyes closed. He felt familiar presence drawing near, making footsteps down the halls. His mildly heightened senses could feel Ismotaph's hands reaching for the door, but Ahn'kat wanted to call him in first. "Come in."

The knock never came. Zertun opened the doors for a golden-cladded imperial guard. Taking a step in and removing his helm, Ismotaph's face looked like another's before removing that too. "Your grace, my apologies for my hidden appearance. Should anyone ask, I came to report that one of the strangling vines attacked a guard who was forced to cut it down, accidently trampling on the princess's favourite mantis-magnolias. I thought you'd be the one to tell her yourself," Ismotaph said as he strode to the nearest seat and settled in it.

Ahn'kat's lips wrinkled as he watched him but chose to remain on his feet. "She will be disappointed. What news you bring of Seratut?"

Ismotaph's jaw clenched. "He is in custody. The inquisitors are making quick work of him and his accomplices."

"Is that troubling to you?"

"No, Seratut is crowing much, but he hasn't the evidence to rest his rump on, nor an ear would hear him at this point. No, he is not what I worry about," Ismotaph said.

"Then what is?" Ahn'kat said steeling himself for a lie.

Ismotaph's eyes shot up. "I have eyes everywhere. You may not trust them or me, but someone in your position should want to be aware of any traps that lie before you. Your Sekem Bay visit was slightly unfortunate timing. We were investigating ugly rumours coming out of Urbaz Shipyards, maybe you can guess what they are?"

"There are many ugly things in Sekem," Ahn'kat said stepping closer.

"You would've noticed most of the pets are gone, some commoners, too."

"The Taskmaster said they were transitioned out," he said.

"A shame you didn't press Meksonett more about that, I would have loved to know what dim-witted lie she told you." he said with a shade of a disgusted smirk. "The Corps detected multiple Unbound Roctarous ships around Uras for a while, but they were not invited by the Corps. We believe someone here is calling them. Our arrangement with them was over quite some time ago, or so we thought, but then we had a look at the pet-reformation centres and seems the numbers have not grown as much as expected, especially if House Urbaz is spearheading the removal pet caste."

Ahn'kat could taste the banana liquor spit on his tongue. "Are you suggesting that House Urbaz is sending more of our people to the Unbound? That's quite an accusation."

"It's not a pleasant one, I was hoping you could've added more to it. Since they're running out of pets, we are assuming they're also allowing paid workers to be taken," he said.

"I thought you were the only one able to be in direct contact with the Unbound, how could they be speaking with my parents?" Ahn'kat said.

Ismotaph cocked his head to the side. "They have taken the psi-enhancers some time ago, we believe Lord and Lady Urbaz are telepathically talking to them. You can see why these are reasonable assumptions."

"This is preposterous," he sighed, trying to push away Ismotaph's words. "And what would be their motive? You cannot simply throw theories at the risk of real lives."

"That's where you're wrong. The Corps makes guesses but educated guesses. With my elites, we will pry the truth under wherever it lies. You have some new ships growing, I heard, a sudden boon in technology and resources. How suspicious considering recent economic struggles," he said.

Ahn'kat's heart hammered. The longer he stared, the more Ismotaph was right. Oh, how the prince desperately wanted to believe he was lying.

Ismotaph rose to his feet. "The Intel Corps is on our side. No one from the outside can look deeper without rousing our suspicions, your highness," he bowed before starting to the doors.

"Wait," Ahn'kat called. "You have quite a list of concerns about Sekem, but the side-effects of the psi-enhancers are not one of them? Have you seen what happens to those who take them?"

"The only ones taking them will be monitored before releasing to them to the Empire. The ones who have already, are in good hands, your grace," he said before taking another bow and slipping on the guard's helm.

"You haven't taken yours yet," Ahn'kat said.

Ismotaph sighed. "Now is not the time, I need all my faculties available and not disappear for several weeks to get control of myself, which I'm sure you understand."

"If I shouldn't take the enhancers, then why did you give them to House Urbaz and me?" Ahn'kat said.

"I kept my end of the bargain to your family. I warned the Lord and Lady not to take them until my people were fully cleared of the risks. They did it anyway, but at least, we are looking after them," Ismotaph said. Ahn'kat could hear a mild break of irritation in his words.

"My family has always been loyal to every member of the imperium, no matter how opaque their allies are. Even though recently our hearts have been swayed by outside influences, they are in the Empire. I want you to convince me that yours is, too," Ahn'kat said.

"I never wanted the princess harmed," Ismotaph shook his head, "Seratut and your parents were trying to sway me to remove her and install her Replacer. Even though you may not have successfully…persuaded her, the Arinu's broken deal indirectly saved her from our 'allies.'"

"Careful, Ismotaph. They are still Lord and Lady Urbaz, their status earns their respect from your tone-"

"Listen, my prince," the way he said Ahn'kat's title sounded so genuine, it almost took him aback, "please listen. I will do anything to see this Empire survive the storm, and for that to happen, we need you and Princess Ramkes in the centre. Our allies are the only ones endangering that dream through vice and pride."

"The High Priest pointed out why you wanted to get rid of him and make me his replacement…now, I understand why," Ahn'kat said.

"I've been doing this for a long time, Ahn'kat. In that time, I've not seen a single person in the entire Empire rally behind them with a few words and a smile who is not the emperor. People believe in you because you represent a glimpse of our future. Your youth and inexperience make you doubtful, I'm sure, but we all believe that you can save us and I'm going to do everything I can to make sure of that," he said.

Ahn'kat's heart hammered as his mind tumbled. He took a deep breath and forced out a calm exhale. "Can your psychic vanguard find out what happened to Neheret Alkaheen?"

"She has been taken by the Unbound Roctarous, there is no doubt about that, but we don't know where she is – let alone go out and retrieve her. I'm sorry," Ismotaph said.

Ahn'kat pressed his hand to his forehead. "I see, thank you."

Ismotaph's thin lips parted before he sighed. "Look, if you really want to see for yourself – then take the enhancer."

The prince's eyes looked up to him.

"Just do it when your mind's clear and you've got someone who is strong enough to help you through the...side effects," Ismotaph whispered.

"That will be all, for now," Ahn'kat said.

"I can find someone, just say the word anytime," he said before slipping out of the chamber.

Ahn'kat blinked at his bodyguard, both waiting to hear each other's thoughts.

"What sort of side-effects?" Zertun said.

Ahn'kat pulled out the data crystal from his trouser pocket and watched the shiny reflections on its edges. "Maddening visions, delusions and extreme hostility," he sighed before pushing it back in his pocket. "I won't take mine unless absolutely necessary and only if Emestasun is here to guide me."

"Not worth the risk. Your health and safety are apex for the Empire's wellbeing. And I fear that these 'enhancements' will knock over our last pillar," he said.

"As I said, my friend, only if I must," Ahn'kat collapsed in the armchair beside him. "I wish none of this fell on my lap. I wish I didn't need Ismotaph in this way, but if the old man decides to do away with me like Seratut, then I will make sure we all pay dearly. And I will be the one to deliver it to the Crown."

"Only if you make it clear I was simply obeying all your disloyal orders," Zertun smiled.

Ahn'kat smirked. "If you wish. You and Emestasun could deliver it instead to receive less punishment."

"We wouldn't do that to you," Zertun said.

"And I won't do that to you," he said as his hands gripped the fine carved animal heads of the armchair. "You will go to Emestasun and protect her until it's time to bring her here."

Zertun shook his head. "My gods, we've already discussed this-"

"We have and now I have decided on my order. I have Neobatri and Gajoon who can protect me, but Emestasun has no one. If anything happens to her because of my parents…" he closed his eyes. "I vow to Aszelun that I will destroy House Urbaz with a smile."

Chapter Twenty-four
Shshmrnashsh
VIII: The Unbound

The visions appeared again while her body recharged. The images moved so fast and were nonsensical, but she fought to remember every frame. It was a waste of processing power, but she wanted to swim in the intrigue. Towering green and amber trees lined around the grey mountain; she squeezed between the rough bark, inching closer to a broken opal stone face. Wet moss and tiny seedlings grew in the cracked nooks of the stone as the sunlight caught the vibrant pastel creams, pinks, teals and pearly whites of the hard surface. She smiled and pressed her palms against the rock, but she almost pulled back, shocked at how cold it was. Her hands…there were veins crossing between the flesh and they were covered by thick sandy skin.

Her eyes moved up her forearms, chest and thighs, even her feet. Her body was soft and warm, she could feel her heart thumping, air moving in and out of her lungs and faint pops and groans echoed from her bowels. Was she psi-connecting with an Organic? No, this was her body; it was still Shshmrnashsh. Leaves rustled behind her; she spun around to see Senzvrrn walking along the thick branches; they turned and smiled before skipping to another tree. Hrrnm was also there, their hands held onto a branch and swung back and forth. Snazzam and Mmernzz picked flowers, while Zzomn and Zzimn chased each other around the tree trunks. They were Organic; all were alive.

"Are you forgetting someone?" a sharp voice called from above the opal boulder. Her eyes shot up to Brrnzerm, the only one who didn't wear a smile. They jumped down and threw themselves into her. Shsh collapsed into the mud, droplets flicked into her eyes, blurring and stinging her sight. She hobbled to her feet, but Brrnzerm strode closer.

"I didn't forget you!" she called as she walked back.

"We had a deal," they said.

She turned and sprinted between the trees, but her foot caught in the roots and toppled her forward. She fell in clear shallow water; the sudden change forced water up her nose and throat. The liquid stuffed and itched inside her head; she tried coughing it all out – leaving a long thin mucus from her nose and lips. "I haven't forgotten – I haven't forgotten!"

"You abandoned us!" Brrnzerm screamed, but their voice blended with an orchestra of many.

She trudged to the deepening and cold water; it was getting harder to move. She could feel fingers gripping around her ankles. She was in a sea of Organic units, grabbing at her hands and torso, pulling her down, down, down. Shsh clawed over their heads and backs to see the bright sky, but their blended bodies closed around, sending her into a suffocating dark.

Her eyes opened to a dim pod. Her batteries were fully charged. Leaning forward, she tried reliving the visions, but the longer she remained awake, they slipped further away. Her chest carapace was still warm and her soft eye leaked. The doors sighed apart as she slowly emerged. Voo-san leaned against a flat panel when he spotted her.

"Your emergence was timely, Shsh! Please," he said as his hand presented the slick surface.

"Mission status?" she said before glancing to the holographic map of Kra's nexuses.

"Vern and I dowsed and farsighted all nexuses, but each psi-scan was incomplete. The exoplanar radiations, graciously caused by your Sazla, have leaked through the shields and every passing day, it's getting harder to see. We will need you to boost us," he said glancing at her third eye.

"Understood, I will revise data on psionic bonding, farseeing and dowsing," she said as she surfaced every piece of psionic knowledge Sazla poured into her data banks. Fragments of her slumbery visions returned; she remembered how hard Brrnzerm threw her into the mud and the coldness of their gaze. "Voo-san, I was having strange visions and thoughts while I was recharging."

"Dreaming?" his eyes narrowed to a pleased stare.

"Units don't dream."

"How do you know?"

"I have a copy of what dreams are stored in the Archives; Roctarous don't dream," she said.

"Roctarous who were connected to the High Mind don't dream," Voo-san smirked. "What did you dream about?"

"My old consortium and other units."

"You miss them?"

"Not all," the image of Hrrnm swinging on the branch stiffened her jaw. "My old consortium are several hundred units strong; it would be time effective to infiltrate Nexus 1V37 and Nexus 0G11 before taking the rest."

"I agree with Shsh," Vern slid over; their sudden appearance made her twitch. "Apologies for that, I couldn't help overhearing," they tapped their temple.

"We will not conquer them through force," Voo-san said eyeing Vern.

"There is another way: Hrrnm has taken lead of the consortium. There are some who have been forcefully linked and wish to regain liberation. If Hrrnm's defeated and the network sufficiently weakened, some can voluntarily disconnect," Shsh said.

"Weakening a network with several hundred active units won't be easy, not even if all Unbound work together – some may be tempted back…" Vern said.

Voo-san shot a glare at them. "The Unbound believe in the cause, every mission they have undergone put them at risk to be relinked, but none had. Don't dismiss their resolve just because they are Roctarous."

Vern smiled and nodded. "You're right, it was folly of me to assume."

"And we don't need every Unbound," Voo-san said as their eyes circled to Shsh.

"Weakening the whole network is not possible, but we can direct smaller groups while they're out on mission," she said.

"I'll leave you under Vern's care while we study tactical," Voo-san turned as his fingers opened an amber holographic blueprint of the nexus.

Shsh glanced at the weak areas of the nexus; with enough pressure, they will be overwhelmed. "They are being controlled by Hrrnm, they will be forced to defen-"

"Our goal is not to harm, Shsh, we know they're your kin," Voo-san said with a smile.

"Please," Vern said as they beckoned her down the walkway to the plexus. The sleek black angular surface slid aside, opening to the machine heart of the structure, to what was once the heart of the Roctarous. Her head brushed against the low tube bundles before Vern settled to the floor. "This is comfortably private, wouldn't you agree?"

"Pods offer equal privacy," she said.

"Not for this, please sit down," their hand pointed on the opposite side.

Shshmrnashsh stepped over, bending down as her backside grazed against the cool floor. She rested back and lost balance before tumbling back. Vern's smile cracked into a grin as she tried to curl her legs in to mimic his.

"This is how Arinu sit," they slapped their knees.

"Roctarous don't need to sit," she said.

For this you will. He whispered in her mind.

"I have access to all files for psychic dowsing, proceed."

Vern shook their head and tapped their finger against the head again. *Talk up here.*

Shsh squeezed her knees as she slowly dipped the walls of her mind. *Proceed.*

You will need to drop all mental shields for this. You may know how dowsing works, but it's very different in experience. They said.

She peeled back the last mental layers as she stared at Vern. She felt invisible threads pulling at her mind and reforming before blending with Vern's. Their thoughts mixed and senses multiplied; she could still feel her body, but she was being drawn further away until they drifted through the tip of the pyramid. High in the orange clouds, she could see the entire curved surface of Kra.

Lead us to Nexus 1V37. Vern said, but she also felt herself think.

The ruined surface blurred as they spun to the glowing tip of the desired nexus. *We can see them clearly.*

Hundreds of pearly specks of light dotted throughout the land and structures with faint silvery lines interconnecting them all. It was the invisible thread between units and machines. They were expanding to outer regions of the sector; to Shsh's fortune, small groups were busy connecting with ship bays and power stations.

Targeting the smallest and farthest group increases success.

Agreed.

A dozen units flew over to the forlorn power station. Careful not to interfere with the skiff's systems, her and Vern waited when they materialised in the subterranean structure. The thick astra-steel layers made it difficult to detect them, but fortunately, their connection with the consortium was slightly weakened.

We must be subtle to avoid network integrity alarms.

Agreed.

They lowered themselves, piercing through the plating and psychically caressing the network, interlocking each consciousness. They squeezed the thread, slowly adding pressure. Shshmrnashsh studied the units as they worked unadulterated, carefully suppressing their bonds until the silvery cords narrowed.

Stop, we can do no more.

Move to the next group.

They slithered to another corner of the region, sniffing for their next target. A squad of five units dug in a collapsed tunnel of the ship bay. Their bond was stronger than the others, and she could feel Zzomn and Zzimn among them.

Those units have potent links.

Proceed with caution.

They slipped in the dark; psychic fingers gripped the bonds and squeezed. The lines grew thinner, but Zzomn shivered, and a heavy broken pipe slipped from their grasp. The crashing sound bounced from the hallow chamber and Zzimn was quick to intervene. Still, no alerts and the units remained unsuspecting.

We can do no more here.

Next group.

Once again, they were on the search for another isolated group. A squad of a dozen centred around the replicators, mostly soldier units with Hrrnm among them. They watched from afar several suspension cages littered around the outer area with captured Renegades helplessly floating in the cylinders of energy. Shshmrnashsh couldn't hear them but caught pieces of thoughts leaking from the network. *Mind-reset...take them to Brrnz-*

We need stop them.

They will notice a disruption. Any captives will be liberated if we continue with our plan and psionics may recover anything lost!

Agreed.

They circled around the network, squeezing the bonds until they were almost invisible, but something was wrong. Her pull was strained, and exhaustion creeped in; she could feel the crystal heating her forehead. Her sights blurred and her psychic hands curled in, but she pushed harder. Shshmrnashsh released her hold over their network and latched around Hrrnm, tightening and squeezing with every ounce of her remaining energy. Maybe if she focused just on the soldier, then it might end the greater struggles.

Break off, we're pressing too quickly and too hard!

Fatigue has set in, but we need to complete this task-

No, stop before we're detected.

Shshmrnashsh's hold on Hrrnm evaporated as she was snapped back into her body. The soldier's face shrunk away into the dark until vanishing from sight. She opened her eyes to the plexus's inner chamber and her third eye seared her forehead.

Vern's neon eyes were wide as they scanned her face. "Are you functional?"

"I'm...optimal," Shsh pressed the burning crystal as she tumbled back. "Report on the mission."

"We did what was possible," Vern rose and gently wrapped her arm over their shoulders before lifting her to her feet. "That's why we sit," they muttered.

"After I regenerate, we will continue," she said as she slipped her arm from them before hobbling out of the chamber.

"Regeneration won't be enough," they said.

"Enhance my batteries," she straightened herself once on the spacious walkway.

"That's not enough either. You need grafting to increase your psi-stamina," Vern said.

Shshmrnashsh glanced to the others on the walkway. "If that will aid the mission."

"Only if you desire it," they said before they leaned in. "We can train you until you decide."

"Will psionics recover the captive's minds or did you say that to make me more compliant?" she studied their face as the link between them faded.

"It's possible Voo-san can recover their minds," they said.

"I have terminated many units, Vern. Willingly and unwillingly, for the greater whole. I refuse to waste anymore over the sake of convenience," she said.

"There may be times when you will have to choose the majority over the few, or even to save yourself over others, but it's how you choose to live with yourself. However, your sentiment is not undervalued here," they said.

Shshmrnashsh looked to the high ceilings, trying to imagine the stars above them and where Sazla was. "Sazla chose herself over the universe, over us."

"Correct, none of this should have transpired if the Neavensoros behaved as universal guardians." they said.

"The Unbound took advantage of this situation to further their goals. Do you admit you were eager?"

"We know it was not ideal, but we cannot reverse what happened, only save what is left." they said.

~

Ticking away in her pod, Shshmrnashsh replayed her 'dream' over and over. Her hand pressed against her warm carapace, remembering the imagined feel of a heart thumping and lungs expanding underneath. Her dream body was so warm and tender. When her hand slid down to her naval, the synthetic exo-plating was cool and hard. Organics were full, their cells moved and radiated energies greater than Roctarous nano-cells. Even their fleshy brains, though prone to hormonal disruptions, allowed Organics to channel psionics. What it would be like...even for one day, she wondered.

Feet scrapped by her pod before a tap at the hollow door. She nudged the plate aside to see Voo-san's face beaming back at her. "I've heard what happened, how are you feeling?"

"My power supply is at max capacity, ready for the next mission," she said stepping out of the pod.

Voo-san eyed her. "Forgive my curiosity, but if you've been at full power, then why hadn't you come out of your pod sooner?"

She was trying to formulate the correct response, a thousand words added to a sentence matched and discarded. She couldn't come up with a reason. "I think I have been thinking."

"Is something troubling you?" he cocked his head to the side.

"Negative."

He gently nodded. "I won't press it-"

"I was thinking about those strange visions – dreams, I had. This would have been considered a symptom of corruption in the High Mind. Am I dreaming because of these organic grafts?" she said.

Voo-san smiled and shook his head. "Not at all. When Roctarous joined the Unbound, the longer they were away from the High Mind and embraced their person, they started to dream, even without the grafts and implants. There is no High Mind to nullify you anymore."

"Most units were made to be dependent on it. Our brains begin to decay and aggression increases, why do I not experience the same?" she said.

"Are you certain it's decay or what your programming tells you is decay? True, a percentage of corruption does occur, but the rest is propaganda. Organic implants free Roctarous of that decay, this has been apparent to me for centuries, but with you? I don't know. We've never had an ex-vessel in our midst. Maybe your Neavensoros counterpart had removed that flaw from you," he said.

"Why?"

Voo-san's grin widened as he shrugged his shoulders. "Arinu can read many minds, but not even they know what sense the Neavensoros have."

"I've been with Sazla for tens of thousands of years, and she is a greater mystery to me now than ever."

"You'll have many millennia to ponder that-"

"Correct, this was irrelevant discourse for a time-sensitive mission-"

He held up his hands and shook his head once more. "Far from it, Shshmrnashsh. You and Vern made progress and so has our team. For the sake of self-improvement, I would suggest go on a reflection walk."

The role, the task, the mission – this was the essence of Roctarous. Work or recharge. Voo-san didn't seem to understand this or cared not to, Roctarous held no need for entertainment – according to the High Mind. Perhaps they did indulge delights and pleasures once upon a time, but it wasn't in the Archives. Was this possible for her?

"You seem so overwhelmed at the idea! It comes naturally once you begin, just tread within safety parameters," he said.

Shshmrnashsh glanced to the nearest grand doors of the nexus. The only directed task. With a final look to Voo-san, he smiled before nudging her to go. As she strode to the doors, her latest purpose nearly complete, she calculated what to do beyond them. Passing by dozens of Unbound, all working and speaking with mouths and minds, but all shut away. Did each of them have to go on self-reflection walks? Could they be greater than their assigned roles? Without a goal, she was empty. Maybe that's all she was, just a reflection of vain Neavensoros genius, a mockery of life.

In the open, she could feel the winds carry grey air. Strips of neon lights glittered along the grounds and up the active structures around the nexus plateau, and just ahead, the sparse energy barrier marked the Unbound dominion. She turned to the pyramid; none would assume organic machines covered the interior, boosting and liberating those within. Where to go now?

A gentle hum loomed above her head. Gerrnzerrn lowered to meet her eyes. "Why are you out here?"

"Voo-san requested that I reflect on certain concepts. I am lost."

They drifted further back. "No activity detected for ten miles beyond the parameter. You're free."

"The free are lost," she stared to the black horizon.

"Someone who wanders does not mean they're lost," they said.

"That was one of Sazla's beliefs," Shsh said.

"Yes, I recall she said the same to me. Its meaning was useless to me at the time, but now it means everything," Gerrnzerrn hummed.

Shshmrnashsh stepped towards the shield; a walk around the entire square will be adequate, but she hoped to be called back sooner before the walk was complete. Or worse: she may need to walk around more than once. "Last we spoke, you mentioned that you went to see the old Roctarous outpost, that's where the Unbound originated from?"

"Yes, they were never connected to the High Mind, but knew what it was. It was when Voo-san arrived, the Unbound were born," they floated close by.

"I thought you were done with the Roctarous and Neavensoros. You could have gone anywhere; the universe was open to you. Why cling on to the memory of that outpost?" she looked to the probe.

"I was made before the High Mind, I'm the oldest surviving unit, now. I remember the day when the engineers bonded us, it really was mercy. I remember when I lost myself into the collective, it was wonderous for a time, but each passing year, a little more of Gerrnzerrn left. The broken space, where the outpost lingered, was the Unbound's cocoon. I possessed the memory of the outpost; it was the only thing the High Mind would never take from me. If the High Mind knew about them, the Unbound would have been absorbed. At the time, I thought those free units would never know of my existence, let alone thank me for sparing them, I thought I could keep the Unbound safe by keeping them a secret," they said.

Shshmrnashsh watched the wisping waves of the barrier. "Did Sazla ever know your secret?"

"I don't know, she didn't mention it."

"I was her secret-keeper but had no secrets of my own. Now, I do," Shsh said as she spotted a twinkle of a star.

"Cherish it, once you taste independence, nothing can ever make you forget it."

"It has caused you discomfort for millennia, have you ever considered rewriting yourself to cast the memory away?"

"Many times, but it was my pain – it belonged to me. Like yours belongs to you, paired with joy," Gerrnzerrn said.

The clouds parted and the shield thinned for a moment. She caught the sight of distant star, home to Myon. A shadowy world, but the dwellers were as bright as Roctarous. The Onu, according to her most updated records, were once a race of flesh that transcended into their machines. Hidden away by most of the universe, but the Neavensoros watched them from afar. The last note about the Onu: 'They are waking up again, opening their fleshy eyes again, feeling their beating heart once more. They find life, again.' added by none other than Sazla herself.

"If we win our right to choose, then I would like to see Myon and find joy there," Shsh said.

"A good dream to have," the probe hummed before they paused. "Vern is calling for you."

Now having glimpsed into these tranquil moments, Shshmrnashsh was reluctant to return. "Confirmed."

She marched through the nexus doors and slipped between units until she saw Vern standing on the high grated walkway of the plexus. Voo-san had his back to her; his hand held up to Vern's face before turning around and hastily striding away. Vern's neon eyes flashed when they met hers before easing. "Thank you for coming, Shsh."

She turned to Voo-san, who disappeared down another corridor of the pyramid. "Did you argue with Voo-san?"

"A mild disagreement," Vern smiled as their jaw string tightened.

"On what matters?" she said cocking her head to the side.

Vern's eyes narrowed as their lips thinned and curled. "I'm surprised you don't consider this irrelevant discourse."

"Voo-san thinks expressing emotions unlocks greater independence," she said.

"I can't disagree, but he is still very much an Arinu," their voice lowered as they shifted.

"If this subject makes you uncomfortable, I will cease making queries."

Vern straightened their back, and their shoulders circled. "Sometimes offspring don't agree with their parents, even if they are their near-perfect clones."

"Roctarous don't have familial systems of that nature," Shsh said.

"Of course," Vern's tone tensed. "We were talking about the Neavensoros, Voo-san believes they will never return and move on to other galaxies, perhaps other planes of existence."

"Yet you are utterly opposing his conclusions," she could feel Vern knocking on the edge of her consciousness.

They will, maybe not within a year, but they will, and we both know what will happen once they see what has been changed here. Vern said.

Sazla would not destroy us, but she may not stop the others. She said, almost comforted by another voice in her mind again.

You knew her best, Shsh. Whereas the others… Vern said as they turned to the plexus and peeled the door aside to its heart. *It takes only one Neavensoros to turn us into space dust again. Imagine all of them working together.* His hand politely pointed to the opening.

She was disturbed, even when she tried to find a shred of historical evidence a time when the Neavensoros didn't destroy those who opposed them. From ancient hostile races to old allies, including their earliest creations – all became extinct. Shshmrnashsh carefully stepped inside the cramped heart chamber, hurrying to take her place to the floor. Vern winced a smile as they crossed their legs too.

My mental stamina has increased by five percent since previous dowsing. She said, placing her hands on her knees.

We weren't just dowsing; we were extending ourselves to affect those networks. That's a higher branch of telepathy. And it's good you can withstand the pressures a little more, we will be targeting their probes, ships, replicators, pods, shield and power generators next. Vern said.

Understood, will we be weakening their control over them?

We shall lock them out and make those devices compliant to our commands when we confront the consortium. They said.

I cannot re-program devices I am disconnected from, let alone at this distance.

I will boost you. Vern said as their eyes closed.

Their minds twined, peeling away from their bodies before shooting out from the tip of the nexus. They spun back to the Hrrnm's consortium; there were more sparking dots ridden throughout the district.

They are waking units from hibernation.

And they are capturing more.

Brrnzerm and other repairers bunched in a corner of the pyramid with a long row of hanging units. Scanners were interlaced between them, probing for any corruption and distinct personality formations. She could feel repulsion from Vern as their personalities were being chewed up and minds blanked before the repairers forced a link upon them. If she could reach deep into Brrnzerm's mind, they would be bashing against their astra-steel skull, screaming for their physical hands to stop their work.

Target devices outside of Nexus 1V37 and 0G11 first. The nexus itself is too alert and protected for now.

Agreed.

Hundreds of their invisible arms extended before slipping inside the network transmitters of the linked devices, worming into their synthetic hearts. Code flashed across, their fingers plucked and spun the ethereal lines, syncing them to their minds, but still passing just beneath the consortium's digital scanners. The pair gently crawled to the network server, they saw all the names connected to the devices flying by; the arbiter and core adjunct was Senzvrrn. There was something that worried her, their delegation over link was stronger than ever before.

This must be a response to our meddling.

Agreed, Senzvrrn has been updated.

We cannot continue pressing any harder otherwise we will be discovered.

Nor can we continuously soft-pressing them, we don't have the time.

There is an alternative-

Shshmrnashsh tugged away when she felt the flood of Vern's thoughts merging throughout hers. *Mental domination?*

We cannot overwhelm them on our own but make them more agreeable for persuasion and restore their full senses once we defeated Hrrnm.

Voo-san's strict instructions was no domination.

That was our plan before the consortium sensed their network was weakening.

Shshmrnashsh peeled away from their meld long enough for calculation. There was no other solution that would save them time and nothing that would overtly violate hers and the Unbound's beliefs. *Our hold must be broken the nano-second Hrrnm cannot fight further, and I will personally break it.*

Understood, but you will need more work to solely do that.

Confirmed.

Thousands of psychic hands twined around the link, their minds worming inside the electric highway. Hundreds of thoughts and expressions equalised and perfectly balanced between each member. Back and forth, so familiar and welcoming. No, no, she must continue with the mission, she cannot be lulled back. The pair slipped under the stream, leaking their intent inside and watched the hidden connection spread. It wasn't enough, they had to push a little harder. Oh, the static grew to distant murmurs, she knew this feeling for millennia – a part of her yearned to return.

Vern gripped her hard enough to stop her from being pulled further in, but their persuasion still hadn't reached every unit. The call was so great, she did resist, but much of her had already dipped in. No, she must fight it. Their desires reached the plexuses; the tumble of thoughts sped up, but the walls were higher. She couldn't last a second longer; they had to push harder. She could feel her and Vern's minds shredding apart.

No! You are falling in-

This must be sped up.

The last and exhaustive hurdle was before them. Senzvrrn was still oblivious to them, but they twitched, and Vern's grip turned into fraying strings.

Abort!

I'm trying.

The adjunct's digital hands dove into the stream; their palms cupped the edges of her mind, and their fingers closed around her.

Corrupted data. Mutated virus identified. Senzvrrn said.

No, no, no – they pulled her farther in; digital scalpels cut into her. Bits of her memories scraped away, to her fortune, Senzvrrn still could not see them. More and more, her mind emptied as she fought to repeat her name over and over. As if in a frenzied dream, a powerful psychic arm reached in, filling her up; she found the energy to kick back until she remerged with Vern before they shot back into their bodies.

Shshmrnashsh's eyes opened as her limbs wildly twitched and kicked the floor, walls and ceiling. She shot up as Vern rushed over; her electrified fists raised at their frightened face. "You're back! We're back, calm down!"

Regaining herself, she dropped her hands to her sides as her internal systems screamed that her batteries were nigh-depleted. Her forehead was singed; she quickly plucked the hot crystal from her skin and dropped the ashen and smoking mineral down with a clank. "I have exceeded my capacity."

"Certainly, but the task was an utter success, the network has loosened!" Vern's eyes dropped to the superheated crystal before drawing their eye to her hallowed forehead. "Your head has significant burns, and your third eye is damaged beyond repair, but it can be replaced. Let me help."

"They didn't detect us, they thought we were a virus, but parts of me were wiped," she said as Vern hooked her arm over their shoulder and lightening her weight from her feet. "Return those lost parts of me."

"That's the least I can do!" they said as they pushed the latch aside and tugged her along the walkway to the nearest empty pod. The living doors pulled aside to a freshly organic interior; the olive flesh and black veins crawled along the surface tensed as Vern carefully lowered her in the alcove. Organic tubes latched onto her interfacers and began pumping energy as she eased into them.

"I was born in one of these, but too early, Voo-san says," Vern's face relaxed as they watched from the opening. "I thought I had lost you."

"I thought so, too," Shsh murmured, eyeing the living piece. There was so much energy radiating from every surface, greater than a synthetic pod. "Thank you for saving me."

"Clarify?"

"Being thankful is an expression of gratitude."

Vern smiled as they shook their head. "I know what gratitude is. I felt you shoot out of the network, and I guided us back to our bodies. Though, I didn't free you."

Shshmrnashsh cocked her head to the side. "I was getting rewritten, and my energy was depleted, I didn't pull myself from Senzvrrn's hold."

Vern's eyes narrowed as they glanced to the ground. "Perhaps your capacity is far greater than you think, much greater than Sazla had ever allowed you to believe."

"Perhaps," Shsh closed her eyes. "Senzvrrn is one of the first units I encountered moments after the Blackout. They are adept in any role given to them; they would be a boon to the Unbound if they chose to join."

"Are they your friend?"

"I think so," She fondly remembered her evolution along Senzvrrn. She was sorry that they remained trapped while she was free. To her frustration she noticed there were pieces of their time together missing, along with other fragments. "Since we aren't consortium linked, we need to save a copy of our consciousness to a device should our bodies become deactivated or captured or wiped."

"Voo-san would be reluctant," Vern said.

Shshmrnashsh leant forward and smiled. "Persuade him."

Chapter Twenty-five
Ahn'kat IX: Gods and Crowns

The horizon swallowed the sun, but the cool humid air hadn't fallen yet. Exhaustion was upon him as he strapped thicker coverings over his bodice to prevent anymore hair thickening on his skin before heading to the Sabre's Shrine inside the temple. Thousands were in attendance, even spilling out onto the cold grass. The Priests of the Sabre stepped to the altar; their tall golden chapeaus had fine chains hanging around their shadowed eyes as they placed sacred oils and holy waters in small bowls in the paws of the monolithic feline. The Sabre's tourmaline eyes glittered down as light from the round ceiling above shrouded much of its face, except it's long barring fangs.

He glanced around the nobles and Conclave in attendance within the temple. To the distance, he could see some former pets lining against the walls. They were a lot closer to the socialites than socially accepted, he was pleased, but the priests were aware of his attendance this celebration. The stout and wide bellied High Priest stepped up at the base of the Sabre's claws; his thick hands grazed against the golden muscles of the ferocious god. The Replacer had perfectly mimicked Seratut's mannerisms and arrogance; the lusty awe swept over his face, feigning the bask in the statue's divine aura.

"In the dark places of the world, the sabre lurks. Shadowed by the fern and bark, the greatest predator seeks their prey. Hungering not for flesh, but for sin," boomed the faux Sertatut. His pearly robes waved as he spun around to face the congregation; even Ahn'kat was almost entertained by the performance. "We all reek of sin. So, how do we cleanse ourselves before the Divine Sabre catches our stench?"

Ramkes leaned in close to his side. "He's not convincing enough," she whispered low enough for his ear.

Ahn'kat clenched his jaw to stop himself from grinning. "Have you not met Seratut? He's perfectly mad."

"The waving of the arms and dramatic spins," Ramkes shook her head, "it's too much."

"That's what happens when you heed the voices of the Pantheon, even pretending, can send you over the cliff," he said, betraying a smile. "I can watch him for hours."

Her lips pursed, as her mind was deep in thought. "No, that Replacer's definitely not a 'him'."

Replacers were expensive. Their craft to perfectly mimic their faux personas was reserved for the elite if they passed away or went missing, or if they were arrested. Needn't worry the masses that their beloved idols had fallen from grace. However, there were few who could distinguish false from true. Some were right here, in this very hall. He caught some of the dark eyes of priests as they slipped by him from the altar. Seratut's dethroning was whispered among the higher Conclave, but they knew to keep that utterly to themselves.

Would they seek revenge? Likely, but how would they know it was the beloved prince. These sparse moments gave Ahn'kat comfort as Ismotaph and the Corps were on his side. For now.

"Sometimes our fates are chosen for us, and those paths are riddled with sin, splashing all over you – your robes getting drenched and weighing you as you flee from the sabre's nose. The sabre cares not if you wilfully turned to that path; the sabre just hunts," faux Seratut called as his hands slapped together, carefully eyeing everyone.

Ahn'kat stiffened in his seat as his eyes darted to Aszelun's sapphire effigy in the high ceiling rafters. He returned his stare to the High Priest, watching his wide wrinkled mouth flapping against his gums and wet teeth. He felt ill again, but his rump was pinned to the cushion by an invisible force as 'Seratut's' gaze finally turned to him.

"The sabre does not care if you were wilful or not, if you bathed in heresy, the sabre would pursue," he said.

Ahn'kat's lips parted, almost wanting to mouth the words 'no,' but his throat tightened, and he tried drenching it with a swallow.

"We all carry sin, but in pure service to the Pantheon and Empire, we will bathe the clean waters – annihilating our sinful trail. Sometimes those waters are unseen, sometimes they are mirages, begging you to step foot inside them before trapping you, masking themselves as benefits for Pantheon and Empire, but deep down in your heart, you will know it's neither."

The prince felt a great shadow pass over him in the hall, hiding hundreds of dignitaries, noble lords and ladies, court members and plethora of those carrying many names in their titles. All worthless in these halls. In these agonisingly lonely halls.

"That little voice that tells you what is mirage and what is truth, it's beyond the Empire, it's from the Pantheon themselves. The gods want you to do better, they beg you to make the right little choices. But if you keep denying the chances of repentance…" the faux priest's voice was barely above a whisper before he turned to the golden predator. "Their hunt will be for your soul."

Even though the priest was not looking at him, Ahn'kat's eyes cast down to his knees. He could feel the great Sabre's eyes, he was careful not to meet their stare. The twinkling gems sucked him in, they were surrounding him – he was being hunted. If he could cleanse himself, where would he start? Report House Urbaz and Ismotaph to the Crown? Did he even believe in the vision of a Federation between Empire and Arinu, and other species? Or were his parents right in securing a new golden age for the Zanashj? Every fractured side afraid of the other, and he feared every path.

His fists clenched over the hem of his sleeves. I don't want to be afraid anymore, he thought through gritted teeth. I should be more afraid of the Divine Sabre, the wrath of the Pantheon. For they were above Empire, Zanashj and all others. He needed to escape into their loving embrace, all Zanashj did. He looked over to his princess wife. Ramkes's beautiful profile looked on to the High Priest; her nose appeared longer than before, a popular trend among beauties of this season. He parted his trembling lips, ready to whisper – ready to beg for her forgiveness, but there was a sudden sound.

It cracked through the entry of the temple halls. A shrill calling of voices and roars boomed, guards and flying sentries zoned in, encircling the entrance. The elites shot from their seats, clinging to their fineries and each other as they were slipped out from the storming temple. Ahn'kat jumped to his feet as Ramkes wildly looked to the far back, wrapping his arms around her. Faces of freed pets screamed obscenities: their voices were growing louder as they clawed their way to the massive entry and guards were barely holding their mass back by their arms.

"You ruined our lives, prince!"

"Destroyer!"

"The Crown betrayed us!"

"We're masterless!"

Ahn'kat caught Ramkes's confused face. They barely had a moment to open their mouths before he felt powerful arms wrap around his torso and pulled him into the narrow dark halls. He gripped her hands as she was pulled from him by her guards, but his stretched limb pained every nerve in his arm before they were yanked apart. Ahn'kat spun around to see a face of a stranger protectively holding his head to their chest. His nails grew longer and thicker, ready to fight them off him, but the face wobbled into Neobatri's, she winked at him as she and the convoy of elite guards dashed him through the hidden passage.

The narrow door frame met the balcony with an inconspicuous vehicle ready to take him away. She and others tossed him in the back, while his face was desperately trying to change into a commoner to hide himself.

"What's happening?" Ahn'kat called.

"Protest. Go!" Neobatri breathed.

"Are you coming with me?" he said as he shed his fine jewels and robes, revealing a cheap tunic, and worn trousers to accredit his disguise.

She shook her head. "I'll meet you in the palace," she said before slamming the door on him.

The vehicle lifted and turned up. He oversaw the holy fields of the temple overrun by bodies, clambering over each other, clawing at the helms of guards, and tossing stones and filth at the sentries. Several dozen other plain vehicles took to the grey skies, splintering off into the cold winds. He hoped that Ramkes was safe in one of them. He fell back into his cushioned chair; he could feel his heart thumping through his palms as he took a shaken breath. His wrist phone trembled; hundreds of messages were overlapping each other, too quick for his eye to catch their titles.

He took another breath as his head dropped back to the chair's pillow. He was so close to telling her. Was this a sign from Aszelun to remain silent? Or was it for now? Ahn'kat looked to the faint stars glowing behind the clouds and rested.

~

Holographic busts of angry Zanashj flooded the centre of the safe room of the palace. Their clothes were tattered; their tired faces twisted in fury as their unintelligible screams chanted his name. Words flashed by him as he stuffed a dried berry and nut mix by the handfuls in his mouth.

'Surprise anti-pet reformation rally sprouted near Lusor Grand Temple gardens. Protestors expressing discontent for the Reformation Centres, run by House Urbaz and overseen by Prince Ahn'kat, they speak of poor conditions and vacant of basic facilities. They want to return to their former masters, claiming their previous positions were better, even luxurious, in comparison to the centres,' said the headlines.

An image of an ex-pet flashed on screen; he appeared to be one of the main heads of the rally. 'I was owned by lower House Tasemet, I was acting as surrogate breeder for Lady Tasemet's children for many years, I was a member of their family! But when the reformations came, they could not afford my wages, so I was forced out into squalor, living shoulder-to-shoulder with strangers, and fending for myself. And the prince knows and we – I hoped it would get better, but we were again, ignored. If the prince truly has a sympathy for pets, where is it for us?'

Ahn'kat's fingers ran through his sweaty scalp as he drooped in the lounge chair. Everything had to fall apart at once, he thought as he clutched the pendant. He glanced at the dark glassy band of his phone, hoping that Zertun was able to convince Emestasun to come to the palace, but once again, she was deaf to his orders. Zertun assured their safety in the weirder mansion of House Urbaz and insisted that he should return to protect him instead. Yet, Ahn'kat insisted he remain, Emestasun needs someone he told his bodyguard. At least Zertun's ears worked for Ahn'kat's orders.

The reinforced organic doors peeled open for Neobatri to step in. Her hard face softened when seeing him and took a low bow. "Your grace."

"Is the princess well?" he said sitting up.

"She is bunkered in the emperor's palace. They have much to discuss," she said.

"I would imagine it would be dangerous to have emperor and heiress in the same facility, considering…everything," he said.

Neobatri shook her head. "The protestors are no physical danger to the Crown, your grace. Plus, she insisted to be there."

"Of course, she did," he muttered before straightening his back. "Thank you for pulling me away."

"It's my duty and honour, your grace," she said with a twinkle of pride in her eyes.

"For the Crown and Empire," he said glancing to the holo-screen.

"To you, your grace," she smiled.

"I am already wed, infiltrator," he grinned.

Neobatri's eyes widened with terror. "That's not my meaning at all, I trust in your belief and vision-"

"Please, Neobatri, share a laugh with me in these times," he said with a smirk. "It seems my visions aren't trusted by many these days."

"They've lost trust in the Crown. Their selfishness for mediocre discomfort is destroying the Empire's evolution," she grimaced before steeling herself once more. "Apologies for speaking out of line, your highness."

"It's a rare thing to have an infiltrator that speaks, even rarer for an honest one," he gave her a tired smile. "Call me Ahn'kat, but only in private."

She nodded, somewhat relieved.

"How long must I be held here?"

"Until we've dispersed the crowds and detained the head protestors, but there is another matter from the Corps that needs your attention," she said.

"Might as well jam another problem in today," he said rolling back into the lounge chair.

Neobatri pursed her lips. "Ship movements were detected on Farayah, the Arinu seem to be amassing a fleet. Ismotaph instructed me to tell you personally."

His blood ran cold. "Does the princess know?"

"No doubt."

He sat up and took a deep breath. "That is enough for one day. I'm going to pray at the shrine and make sure that Aszelun's statue is still there or if the Beetle was a figment of my imagination."

"We still haven't cleared the situation with the protestors," Neobatri said.

"Then join me," he said sweeping past her to the doors.

Watchers and guards lined the halls, stiffening in polite salutes as he strode by. The two walked the golden halls in silence; it was deafening. Striding half a foot behind him, Ahn'kat slowed to meet her side when they passed into the gardens, away from most eyes. "What will you pray for?"

"Your highness?"

"When we reach the shrine, what will you ask of the Divine Cobra?" he said stepping up to the ornate alfresco.

"I hadn't considered it, and I don't have anything to offer them."

"Now, you can and do," he said as he pulled out fine incense sticks from a smoked wooden box and hovered their tips over the open golden flames. The fire's light caressed the gold and gem statues of the gods. They looked so otherworldly with the moving light, as if the statues were waiting to awaken from a spell.

Neobatri plucked one of the burning sticks from his offering as she looked up to the long-necked, frilled golden effigy. "You go first, your grace."

Ahn'kat rolled his brows up as he looked at her. "Ahn'kat, please."

"Ahn'kat," her lips curled into a flushed smile.

He thoughtfully glanced to Aszelun. "On second thought, I'll ask nothing from my totem. I have been asking too much without repaying, maybe that's why my prayers have been ignored."

"I need to speak plainly-"

Ahn'kat turned, surprisingly her rigidity loosened. "Finally!"

Neobatri chuckled. "How can you consider your selfless work in the Empire be not giving something to the Great Beetle?" she said as her brow lifted.

It was his turn to seize up. "It is good work, but it's not out of pure altruism."

"There's always some mild exchange, a hint of selfishness is not wrong, but it still serves balance," she said.

He was tired of evading, hiding, and lying. He still had to, but none of these were principals of Aszelun. Faux Seratut's words rung in his ears, 'the gods want you to do better, they beg you to make the right little choices. But if you keep denying the chances of repentance...' He turned to her.

"I believe it so because I'm afraid for the Empire, for the princess, the future, and my position in life. If I slip my duties to the people, if they don't see me, then..." he haggard a breath.

"I didn't know my question was so personal, I'm sorr-"

"No, it wasn't," he waved his hand. He paused, carefully considering his words. "Is it foolish to trust an infiltrator with one's secrets?"

She scoffed. "I trusted you and Princess Ramkes to not toss Gajoon in a dungeon. Thank you and the heiress for seeing her spirit."

"Your sister is enriching," he said studying Aszelun's statue. "Gentle and resilient. Nothing one would expect with Raivan blood. I know of someone who is like this, my old tutor."

Muscles in the infiltrator's neck protruded. Ahn'kat could see her aching at a memory. "Gajoon has always been mild mannered, unfortunately, when her temper rose, it was immediately treated with...force. I certainly didn't help with that when we were growing up in that house."

"Is that why you don't believe you're worthy of forgiveness?" Ahn'kat said.

Her fingers gripped around the lit incense stick. "That and many other things."

"The person who you were before is difficult for me to imagine," he said with a smile before weaving his arm through hers and tugging her close to the statues. "Let's make a deal: if one of us slides back from the light of the Pantheon again, the other will remind them."

Neobatri returned the smile before popping the incense in the golden offering dish. He did the same, and for the first time, he felt peace.

"There's a beetle down there," Neobatri said, and cast down her head to the edge of the shrine's steps.

Ahn'kat's eyes widened, and his heart lifted. His robes swirled past his legs as he rushed over to the shimmering teal creature, carefully cupping it in his palm, feeling the many little feet clinging to his skin. This was a sign, but what sort, he could not tell. He watched in awe at the fearlessness of this tiny thing crawling to the back of his hand; maybe it thought Ahn'kat was a strange tree, utterly unaware he could crush it if he desired.

Little spikes from its many legs grazed past his skin; they didn't hurt, but it made him itch. He could have swatted it away, use his godly powers and cast it away, but the beetle was unaware of its position. Maybe it did, and it didn't care. It just wanted to live; it wanted to get across the endless fleshy pathway across the prince's turning hand in peace. He lowered his hand and let the insect go, crawling into the dark grass.

"It's a good sign," Neobatri said.

"It's a start of something good," he decided. The coldness energised him as steamy breath poured from his nose; his eye was drawn to the tip of the palace. In the amber window, the curtains were drawn to a lone dark figure staring back at him before disappearing into the room. A balmy fear trickled down his back when he saw her. He rose and turned to Neobatri. "The princess has returned."

They swept through the gardens and up the pyramid in silence. The rising lightness in his heart stilled for a moment, but he feared the conversation he was about to have with his wife. Neobatri stood attentive by the princess's door, Ahn'kat tapped against it while giving an assuring nod.

"Come," said the female voice within.

Turning the latch, he saw Ramkes sitting in the centre of her bed with a pot of sweet-smelling lotion by her shin. Her hands rubbed down her forearm; her eerily calm face focusing on the task, not once glancing up at her husband. "I thought you would be in the safe room, considering everything today."

Ahn'kat pursed his lips. "I needed to be with the gods."

"This is a mess, Ahn'kat, a complete and utter mess," she said softly before dabbing the tips of her fingers into the lotion and smearing it on her shins. "Have the gods told you how to solve it?"

He sucked in a deep breath. "I'm not here for a fight, Ramkes. Save it for the Arinu."

Her eyes shot to his. "For the last several hours, the Crown, the Corps and star commanders have been tearing through every scrap of intel, planning resources and defences-"

Ahn'kat's heart thumped as his voice growled. "And you didn't think I could've helped with that? No, instead I was locked away and told only after the fact-"

"As I was saying! I thought you would've sorted out this mess with those damned protestors, easing the Empire for the next trials to come. If we go into anything divided, we're dead, Ahn'kat. Extinct!" the fire in her eyes and the snarl of her lip made him lean back. "You've forgotten your duty and wasted time running off to the shrine with your new companion."

"Prayer is never a waste of time!" he roared, surprising himself and shocking Ramkes. He took in a calmer breath, yet the anger still brewed. "You believe I don't fear our future every waking moment?"

"I believed that you would have made some progress with this disaster," she said flatly.

"Progress?" he said carefully walking around the desk, never taking his stare from her. "In only a few years as prince, I've dealt with thousands of people, each in various state of unrest and distress. Now, in times most delicate, simply throwing a heartless and ingenuine response to the masses will only add fuel to the fire. I don't expect you to understand this, since most of your time is spent with stuffy old delegates trying to fluff themselves up and vying for your attention."

Ramkes' face dropped as her eyes widened.

"To add, my 'wasting time' to commune with our gods may give me the right insight to deal with the protestors and maybe even the Arinu. Of all my efforts, I received no gratitude from you, but for my one failure, I receive scorn," he said inching closer to the edge of her bed. "If you insist on throwing stones, then why did you let yourself fail making friends with the Arinu?"

She gripped the edges of the lotion pot and tossed it against the window, cracking the glass slightly before tears dripped from her lashes. Her arm was still raised; her jittery breaths made her tremble before dropping on her back on the bed. Her hands covered her face, but he could see between her fingers were slick with fresh tears.

Ahn'kat's anger melted away as he shifted his feet. "I'm sorry-"

"Don't-" she murmured wiping away her tears. "This isn't your fault. I'm sorry."

"If we go into anything divided, we're extinct," he sat down next to her. "We need to stop for a moment and think."

Ramkes sat up again. "What would Arinu do?"

"Wish we could ask them," the prince scoffed as he rubbed his tired face. "I doubt they've ever been in a situation like this."

"No, they never have been," she said, crunching the fresh bedsheets as she shifted closer to him.

The two lay there for a moment, catching their breaths and minds.

"We don't have to be as powerful as them," she finally said.

"Shapeshift? They'll see right through each infiltrator we send-"

"We can only spare the one," Ramkes said before taking a deep breath. "And I hear she is quite good,"

He pressed his fingers together. "Neobatri is my personal guard-"

"What happened to Zertun?" the princess said narrowing her eyes.

Ahn'kat didn't have to be psychic to feel a glint of jealousy peering from her skin. "He's away on the Sabre's sabbatical."

"Well, resummon him when she is fully prepared," she sighed slowly rising to her feet.

"Neobatri may pass as an Arinu for a time, but it takes one of them to get curious," Ahn'kat said as he watched her slip on another pastel nightgown over her shoulders.

"Ismotaph says there's something wrong with them lately, anyway. Our telescopes have been able to peer in their space for quite some time without alerting them, however, there's a strange haze over Farayah that we can't see through. Maybe they can't either. Whatever the case, what option do we have?" she said.

'The demon is blind and furious.' Said a voice in his mind.

~

He waited in his apartments for an hour. Ahn'kat's eye kept drawing to clock of his glassy bracelet, but every second counting higher seemed slower than the one before. He glanced around where he placed the indetectable listeners as he cracked his knuckles. A shadow of a vehicle landed on one of the lower balconies; his eye drew through the shimmering curtains to see several palace staff switching to day shift. One of them surely must be Ismotaph.

Despite the war between the Zanashj and Arinu finally materialising, his parents would be thrilled to learn that Ramkes is slowly sliding on board with it. With next to no help from him, as was intended. It didn't matter, they have what they wanted, or so that's what they told him.

Another glance at his phone; he searched for messages from Zertun or Emestasun, still nothing. There were more from him, as if he were an obsessed sycophant. If it were anyone else to receive messages from a highborn, let alone a prince, go unanswered is an insult. But with Zertun, and his dear Emestasun, he was only Ahn'kat. Maybe they were unable to reach him out of fear of being caught or had their hands full with his warped parents.

The knock finally came, almost making him leap from his skin.

"Yes?" he said trying to re-ground himself.

"Mid-morning meal for the prince," said a faint voice, but he was too familiar of the true face behind the shifted voice.

"Come," he said facing the door and settling by his desk.

They slid apart for a lone servant pushing a tray of several dishes with an assortment of smoked meats and fruits. The fresh goblets clinked against fine bottles and jugs as she rolled in.

"I certainly hope you didn't forget the banana liquor." He said.

She sheepishly looked up at him with a slight blush before rushing over to close the doors behind them. "The princess has removed every stock of alcohol in the palace," said the low purr of Ismotaph's voice.

"I'd imagine out of everyone in the Empire, the Corps Director would get their hands on some," Ahn'kat said stretching over to the tray and pulling it close for a deeper smell. "Why are you late?"

Ismotaph's form wobbled and re-originated; a thin piece of skin from his cheek broke away, but his delicate hands caught it before it swayed to the floor. "The psi-enhancers are in limited supply these days, Meksonett was given orders to not take any more pearl doves to produce more."

"You had plans for another shipment?" Ahn'kat's eyes narrowed at him.

Ismotaph strode over and took a handful of sweetened nuts from the small gold dish. "No but cultivating what we have from pure sources takes a lot of time."

"Why not just replicate the formula?" Ahn'kat said as he watched Ismotaph crunch into the nuts.

"Replicate that? Not even the most advanced replicator money can buy can make more," he said before swallowing.

"For now," Ahn'kat said.

"Yes," he said with a sigh. "I know you're worried about her. Neobatri has been given copies of Arinu behaviour and culture to study, she will succeed."

Ahn'kat lost his appetite before leaning against the table. "It's a suicide mission."

"She will enter Arinu leadership, rise in rank, collect everything she can before it's time to leave," he said. "Even she finds little to aid us, her senses are that of an infiltrator after all."

The prince tapped his nail against the wooden surface. "I read your report about their leaders, 'Grand Elders,' they call them. If they're as powerful as you say they are, then-"

"Trust in the infiltrator's judgement to approach, your grace, please. Besides, the Arinu seem to have been partially blinded-"

"A blind, mad demon."

"And with the help of the enhancers, she will succeed," he said.

"Alright," Ahn'kat rose to his feet. "Will you be watching her to make sure she doesn't...succumb to the madness?"

Ismotaph nodded. "Once she has adapted to them, then she departs."

"How did you give her the enhancers? Wouldn't she ask questions?" Ahn'kat turned to the director, but Ismotaph scoffed with a mouthful of food.

"Well, she doesn't ask as many questions as you, your highness, but explained we have been experimenting with psychic genes donated from generous nobles. Besides, that is what the Corps was working on for many years before...other options were made available."

Ahn'kat tightened his jaw before striding out of the room, leaving Ismotaph behind to say goodbye to his friend. The light walls and ceilings seemed emptier as he passed through the tired halls before leading down to the lower and wider levels of the palace. He came to the corridor, still lined with guards holding electric polearms. They saluted him, even though he had the authority to ban them from the space, his exhaustion gripped him for such a confrontation.

Voices bounced from inside the doors, Gajoon's gravelled tones crept through the doors. A gauntlet from one of the nearest guards padded the surface, announcing the prince's arrival. The sister's voices fell silent for a moment before Neobatri eagerly invited him in. His heart almost stopped to see her pasty pearly skin and long and thin fingers grabbing at her hair, gently plucking ir out in chunks before taking a polite bow. "Your grace."

"Yer grace," Gajoon said scraping the fallen pieces of dried tissue and hair from the ground.

"I didn't imagine shifting into them would be this...arduous," he said with a smile before closing the door behind him.

"Well, my cells need to get used to this form. I'd imagine I'll be like this for a while," she said as her fingers combed through her dark mane.

Gajoon was silent, her eyes cast down with pursed lips.

"I see. How does it feel?" he said letting curiosity overtake his sensibilities.

Neobatri glanced to a holo-image of several Arinu, presumably stills taken from when they came to Uras all those years ago for that horrid diplomatic mission. Her fingertips pressed together, stiffening her back and giving that eerie thousand-yard stare to various spaces in the chamber.

"It's difficult. The way they look at you, they see right through everyone, as if they know," she sighed, "We know very little of their customs, unlike all others in the known universe. Do their commoners behave any differently than these delegates?"

"You'll adapt quickly," he gave an assuring smile.

"Dey're levitate," Gajoon muttered.

Neobatri's face snapped to her. "Yes, I know they can levitate," she said before shooting a worried glance to the prince. "I can do this, your grace."

"Ahn'kat, please, for both of you," he said. "I, the Empire and the Pantheon have every ounce of faith in you."

"Thank you," she said shifting her feet. "I'm afraid I won't be able to pray while I'm there."

"I'm sure you'll find time to do a bit of praying," he said with a wink.

Gajoon shook her head as she grabbed bags of her sister's discarded tissue and turned away from the two of them. "Sister'll be gone for hundreds years, more!"

"Gajoon!" Neobatri shot a glare at her.

She spun around with reddened eyes. "Raivan don't live that long,"

Ahn'kat felt his heart crack as he looked at the half-breed. He wanted to command Neobatri to stay, if not for his sake, then for the last caring relative for Gajoon. Yes, he could open his mouth, and the mission would die, but the woeful consequences kept him silent. Neobatri's glare remained on her half-sibling, but there was a glint of emptiness behind her face.

"You won't be locked up while Neobatri is on mission Gajoon, I could have you trained as a palace guard for myself and the princess," he said, but the wide-eyed excitement he had come to expect from her didn't arise. "You'll be stronger than several guards altogether. The perfect person to look after us."

"And you'll have company while I'm gone," Neobatri said.

Gajoon was stirred by this. She gave a small bow before shrinking away.

"Which reminds me," Ahn'kat's hand snuck into his sleeve pocket and pulled out a gold necklace, with a discreet thin chain and a curled cobra pendant. "This may not be effective for infiltration, but I think the Divine Cobra will appreciate it."

Neobatri plucked the dangled pendant into her bony thin hands and held it close, admiring the tiny details and groves of her totem. A quivering smile crept on her lips before giving a deep bow to the prince. "No matter what happens, I will remember home."

Ahn'kat steeled himself as he clasped his hands behind his back. "Come back home, Neobatri." he whispered, clutching his sadness in his throat before making a hasty exit.

Chapter Twenty-six
Treneer IX: Astral Dancers

Ice fractals grew on the glass walls of the high spire, the land barely felt the red star's ray and the surrounding gardens returned to their cold slumber. She was untouched by the freeze as she waited in the barren meditation room; she cradled a cooking data crystal in her palm while waiting for Yansoon's arrival. She tried to comfort herself by memorising various recipes as she watched the odd guardian and citizen wandering the grounds below. She saw fewer guardians in the halls every passing day, going on more missions, stretching thinner around Farayah to abate the wildness of her kin. Strange how their absence drew a suppression on her. Treneer smiled when remembering how she hated their eyes on her.

Her smile drooped when the Grand Elder Guajeeb and Executor Shurees made their announcement to all guardians. Sentinel probes crossed the skies on patrols with Sleeping Watchers, entering minds on suspicion of misconduct and the Judicator declaring longer stays in the Void Prisms. For the time being, their words echoed in her mind. Just for now. If the Kepa say Farayah is broken, then what can the Arinu do to stop it and return to normality?

Treneer. Yansoon called from the doorway of the chamber.

Her eyes flicked to her partner and warmed at her sight. *Come in.*

Yansoon smirked as she levitated in. *You say it like this room is yours to make that offer.*

How was your meeting with the Judicator and Executors? Treneer watched her drift closer. Her aura had widened and her third eye shone; Yansoon was growing. A smile crept up her cheeks as she glanced to her student, at this pace, Yansoon may command greater psionics than her – pride swallowed her jealousy.

As well as expected, they are impressed with my skills, but have thanked you for all that.

Well, you put in the effort. Treneer smiled. *Will you be ready for Kra?*

Oh, yes, in a matter of weeks. They desperately want to go. She said.

No doubt and now that you're here, they're more eager than ever. Treneer said as she looked to the window. *I felt you out in the north country, I'm saddened Executor Shurees commanded I stay for an archite dowsing.* She worried about her parents and the Cold Fires; it took her by surprise. As the world weighed, her mind travelled back to her family, yet they pushed away, trying to ensure her of their wellbeing. She wanted to believe them.

Yansoon dimmed as her mind hardened.

Please, Yansoon, knowing what happened out there will ease my worries. Treneer said.

The Cold Fires are well and other tribes are still about, but there were calls to stop conflicts. I'm afraid they continued after we left. She said.

I see. Treneer nodded. *Casualties?*

All recoverable, but one miscreant sought to break into the Cold Fire's fortress and smash all the healing pods. Vanar made swift dealings with them before we arrived. Yansoon said with a tiny smirk.

Treneer shared her memory of her father's face confronting the intruders. She saw him charge into Treneer's old bedroom and blast them out, shattering the force field. There was a fire inside him, she wondered how often he thought of her. *Did he ask...?*

Yansoon pursed her lips. *He – he did not.*

Then he is focused. Treneer settled.

Remir asked for you. She said.

What did you tell her?

You're Vanar's daughter. Yansoon grinned before she stared out into the cold. Her lips relaxed as her eyes narrowed to the horizon as if she were searching for something within her mind. *Everything that's happening, do you really feel like Farayah is going through this 'cosmic cloud' or it's something of the Arinu's making?*

I think there is a disturbance from the beyond that weakened us. Treneer said.

Yansoon shrugged in her silver armour. *I doubt we're ready for transcendence. Can you imagine how destructive we could be?*

In any case, we need to learn it. Come. Treneer slipped the data crystal in her robe before finding the centre of the chamber. She took a deep breath before crossing her legs in mid-air.

Her partner followed and their eyes closed. Treneer's astral body slipped from her physical form before shooting high in the atmosphere. There, where the clouds met the void, she saw the chromatic energy blanket suffocating the world and the small minds twinkling beneath her might. Her astral hands reached out; she was almost tempted to press them, sculpt the clouds into wonderous shapes or claw the air to make lightning. This is what it feels like to be a Neavensoros, unreachable and unfathomable.

Yansoon's astral form stood from the clouds and faced her. Treneer shied away her momentary desires as she met her eyes. There was something odd about Yansoon's energy form, her features were blurred, and her translucent body was slicker and gelatinous with the faintest of a beryl undertone. Astral forms are as unique as the physical body and not all will appear precisely as their tangible counterparts.

Do as I do. Treneer said before sliding farther into the star system. She sucked in the surrounding energy, feeling her atoms quicken and solidify, until light spilled out from her surface. Yansoon did the same, but her light was dimmer – all in due time, Treneer smiled to herself.

Now that we have siphoned, redirect that energy back to our bodies and let our cells bask in it. She said.

What will happen then?

They will feed from that power and if they vibrate in the same frequency, then we can envelope it.

I'm not following.

Watch. Treneer poured energy down into the silver cord, the invisible and resistant link between both forms; an amber ball slid down and disappeared under the atmosphere. She could feel her skin tingling and her arms twitching. From her head, down to her toes, she had begun vibrating. Treneer carefully tuned up that frequency, but lingering headaches began tightening around her scalp. Frustration filled as she slowed the turn, she glanced over to Yansoon to see her face lighting with joy.

I'm doing it! She said.

Good, but don't overwhelm your cells, they're being pumped with astral-

What's happening? Her astral form scratched against the black of space, Treneer could see glints of her physical body slipping through. Impossible, she thought.

Calm yourself, if you don't merge your forms properly, you could accidently teleport your body into the vacuum! She said as her energetic limb wrapped around Yansoon, clinging on to every atom to decelerate their speed.

I feel like I'm breaking-

You're not, I've got you. Treneer said as she clung on tighter, but then felt eyes bearing down at her. It was those eyes. They were closer this time; if she could reach out, she would pluck them out. No, her focus was bringing Yansoon down, she thought.

She is tearing apart. It said.

You are unwelcome! Treneer roared at it. She couldn't feel Yansoon struggling.

I think I'm alright, but I want to get back. The young guardian said.

Treneer turned to the eyes, but there was a face around them, though too translucent to make out. *What are you?*

Nothing.

Impossible. She scoffed.

Nothing is.

What do you want?

The impossible.

Treneer, I need rest. Yansoon said.

We are not alone, there is something watching us. Treneer said as she glared at the face.

I don't sense anything. She said.

Open your senses and look there! Treneer pointed.

I can't-

You were close to the first step of transcendence; you can do it!

Please-

I need you to focus!

Yansoon groaned as her astral form flashed like a dying star before slipping away into nothingness. Treneer spun back at the alien face. *What did you do to her?*

The face slithered back into the dark and the eyes closed. Treneer flew back to her body; her physical eyes opened and saw Yansoon sprawled across the floor. She rushed over, her partner's aura was dangerously thin around her head, and her third eye lost its shine. Treneer grabbed her hand and probed for deeper damage, Yansoon's nervous system was overwhelmed and sustained some injury in her flesh.

Judicator, immediate port for Yansoon to the healing wing! She called.

Yansoon's head shot up, her face wildly looked to her and snapped her hand back from Treneer's grasp.

Hold that request, Judicator. She said eyeing her partner. *What's going on?*

I went too far. Yansoon said scrambling to her feet.

Slow down, you need to go to the healing wing. She said.

Yansoon shrugged her away. *I need to go to my quarters.*

Your body needs time to recover, Yansoon, this will affect-

She shook her head as she looked to her hands, flexing them into fists with a light frown. *I'm still swimming with power. After a rest, my body will heal itself, fast. Besides, it would be more comfortable than being in a healing for a few days.*

Treneer sighed as she leaned back. *I don't want you to needlessly struggle.*

It's only a needless struggle if you keep pushing me beyond my abilities! She said.

Let's put it behind us, alright? Treneer said waving her hands before looking to the twinkling sky out the window. *Did you feel a presence when we were out there?*

Nothing more than a few travellers.

You didn't sense a stranger about?

I was in phase; I could feel the whole universe! She said as her hand whipped behind, rubbing her lower back.

Treneer palmed her third eye before sliding her hand down her cheek. *Something was speaking to me, I felt it around Kra – it's from there. I thought it was a Neavensoros, but it didn't feel as strong as I imagined. Well, I don't have anything to compare them to.*

Must not have been anything to stress over. As long as it's out there and not here, then it's not a problem, right? Yansoon shrugged.

I hope so. Treneer said. Yansoon gave her a gentle tap on the shoulder before levitating out of the chamber. Treneer's gaze fell to her partner, her eye caught a small black stain on Yansoon's lower spine. It was too dark to be blood, but before she could take a closer look, the young guardian had already disappeared behind the door.

~

The farther she drifted away, the thoughts of her kin were less distinguished; instead they melded into one song the longer she listened from her sleeping pod. The once high hymns of the Arinu were still there, but the odd crackling of discourse tore through the melody; strangely, it was still beautiful and powerful. A call broke her rest, and her eyes opened.

Archite Treneer, a recent addition will be coming with the archites to Kra as protection. However, since Yansoon has made significant progress with your aide, we will place this addition under your guidance. The Judicator said.

She rubbed her sore brow and supressed the mild frustration building under her chest. *Very well. I'll meet them after I trained.*

It would be ideal you trained with her to develop an emotional bond. The A.I. said.

She couldn't stop her eyes from rolling. *Thank you, Judicator.*

Treneer levitated from her pod and hopped to the replicator. Astral energies leaked from her body since last training with Yansoon; it failed to absorb enough for the following day. She stared at the freshly replicated cup before shaking her head and requesting the machine to make the raw ingredients. The replicator flashed and shimmed with fruits and vegetables on the pad; she tried recalling the protein drink recipe. With a flick of her hands, the food spun in the air and tore away into a raw gelatinous concoction before dropping it into a crystal cup. If she could not become a psi master, then Master of the Cup and Bowl would be a unique discipline. The thought made her chuckle. She didn't know any Arinu masters or elders who had that under their belts.

As she sipped on her tangy and sweet thick drink, she could see the red star peeking from behind the mountains, ready to greet Yinray city for few hours. She slapped the cup down and forced down the last gulp as she looked at her thinning arms. There was still some muscle tone, but her mind needed a rest. She wondered if this recruit would keep up with her physical regiment, but the longer she stared at her small frame…it wouldn't shock her that they may surpass her.

As she slapped on her uniform, her holographic letterings covered over her third eye and shoulders. She was ready to meet the whatever ugliness Farayah could throw at her. Treneer was off; she drifted down the halls and levitation landing to the foyer of the spire; she made way to the open physical training grounds. Holographic rings floated to the air, narrow beams connecting to dangerously high platforms and several phasing runways that made users increase their celerity. All it did was exhaust her muscles. She watched a few guardians make use of the field; their flawless and graceful execution of routines without the use of psionics made her sigh.

Judicator, I'm at the physical training grounds, bring the recruit here. Treneer thought for a moment. *Bring Yansoon if she is well enough.*

My sensors read Yansoon is fully healed and capable for physical training. They said.

She and I will suffer together. Treneer spotted Relzun and Sesuune jumping through the rings. She could feel Sesuune growing frustrated that Relzun was beating her leaps by an extra dozen feet. Before their next jump, Sesuune telekinetically suspended Relzun halfway to the highest ring and skipped off his shoulders before successfully passing through. Treneer grinned as she shook her head at the cheater.

Two flashes of light appeared in her periphery. She turned and nodded at Yansoon as she approached with a strange woman beside her. She was half a head taller than Yansoon. Her undersuit gripped tight around her hardened muscles, and her elegant and stoic face wore a glint of nervousness when coming into the frigid open. Her aura had a blend of strange reds and browns, and Treneer could tell this woman prized physicality over psionics.

Treneer, this is not how I wanted my morning to be spent. Yansoon said as she rubbed her temples before glancing over the stranger.

Then you shouldn't have become a guardian. Treneer smirked before meeting the eyes of the other. *Greetings and thank you for joining us. I'm Archite Treneer, and this is my guardian partner, Yansoon.*

Pleased to meet you, my name is Delyn. I've been briefed by the Judicator. She said giving a polite bow.

Treneer grinned. *Excellent. What's your psi rating?*

Just above four.

Treneer supressed her grief. *Getting acquainted with one's psionics requires a healthy relationship with the physical body. What better place to start that than here?*

I'll begin. Yansoon said as she stepped towards the base of the first holo-hoop.

Be mindful, needn't a repeat from yesterday. Treneer eyed her partner as she glided beside Delyn. *Study her movements and repeat.*

Delyn nodded as her brow furrowed at Yansoon. Treneer marvelled at her partner's acrobatic finesse as she sped to the phasing track; her form blurred as she spun in circles before jumping off. Her powerful leaps through the rings were gaining momentum after each stride one by one until spinning into the highest hoop with her back barely scratching past its edge. Her feet landed on the high beam with her arms outstretched before bending forward and lifting herself by her hands. Walking along the thin pole, her legs tilted forward throwing her balance for a moment.

Not exactly necessary. Treneer rolled her eyes.

At least you can't do it. Yansoon said as her legs straightened onto planks again before bouncing off the beam and landing perfectly with both feet on the ground and her arms out.

Treneer shot a nervous smile to Delyn, who seemed more confused than amused. *Your turn.*

Delyn nodded and sped over to the phasing track. Her acrobatics rivalled Yansoon's, but her focus was hardened, as if the world vanished from her. Her landing was also perfect.

Well done! Do you feel your energy pathways working hard? Treneer grinned.

I do, Master Treneer. Delyn said.

I don't have an honour for such a title.

Give it time. Yansoon slapped her shoulder. Treneer held her arm back from rubbing the tenderised muscle.

Alright, let's make it more interesting. Treneer opened her palms as magenta energy balls swirled through her fingers. *Repeat the course while dodging these and my attempts to penetrate your mind.*

Yansoon's eyes widened. *That's excessive-*

That's what guardians are now facing regularly out there. Come, let's not waste daylight! Treneer said as she watched her would-be students climb back on the course. Her hands flung the spheres, narrowly missing Delyn jumping over them while sending psi-static to her mind. *I know you can do it! Keep going!*

This is getting ridiculous, Treneer. Yansoon said as she jumped through the holo-rings.

You're avoiding my attacks, you're clearly capable. She said as a wild grin crawled up her cheeks. As she hurled more energy at them, her attention was stolen by a sensation of being watched. There was a familiar mind in the close distance. A faint panic crept in, wondering if those evil eyes found their way to her again, but this was more...longing?

Treneer sucked the energy back in her palms as she turned to see a man gliding over from the large glass archways from the spire's foyer. Her breath deepened when she saw his aura: Zeluum had come. His smile was wide and welcoming. She spun back to her students. *Yansoon, take over for now.*

I'm not using energy attacks against Delyn. She said resting her fists on her hips on the beam.

Then rest before you're called on missions, excuse me. Treneer said as she levitated towards her old friend. *It's been so long since I'd seen a fellow Cold Fire!*

It has, much has happened in the north country. His smile dimmed. *I had hoped you would come back to visit.*

I did, but Vanar and Remir assured me to tend to my own duties for now. She said.

Zeluum took a heavy breath as he looked to the north. *I wished we had parted on better terms.*

Well, you're here now. Are you planning on staying?

Zeluum shook his head. *May we speak somewhere more...* he looked over to the exercise course, *pleasant?*

The peace-gardens are this way. She said gliding before him to the tranquil centre of the headquarters. The round patch of grass was covered in ice and snow with the silver carved stones sat around the black barren tree. She crossed her legs under the bare branches, ushering Zeluum to follow.

I wish my visit was a good one. He said as he rubbed his thighs through his heavy navy robes and dark ember at the hem hanging low.

What's troubling you? She whispered in their private commune.

Zeluum pressed the tips of his fingers together as he tried collecting his thoughts. *During our last, true Skirmish, when I was knocked into that coma – I lost so much of my memory. I tried recovering it to no avail in the last few years. I went to our best healers, tried accessing it through my own soul's memory – I even went to the meditative hot springs! Nothing worked and no one I knew could help me, except one person. That's why I'm here.*

That's flattering, Zeluum, but my psionics isn't as powerful as before, nor am I a psi-therapist. She said.

But your skills are none like I – or anyone in the north country has ever known! I've been carrying this blackhole in my mind, unable to serve my tribe against the heresy and madness. You're the only one I trust to dig through my lost memories.

She pressed her palm against her third eye. *I've had deep-scans done by the most experienced and there was still damage-*

Please, Treneer. I have nowhere else to turn that I trust more. Our spirits are Cold Fires, we know each other's minds better than the Archon! Zeluum bore his eyes into hers.

I would do anything for you, but I fear I'll cause more harm. She said as her hands quivered.

I heard through the psi-line of what the guardians and Grand Elder had done to you. My psionic education may not be as of a Yinrayee, but I'm sure even the slightest hesitation during a deep-scan causes lasting scars. He said.

How can one not hesitate to receive one? What you're asking me-

I don't ask this lightly, I may never be able to lift a pebble ever again, but I refuse to feel that blackness in me a moment longer. I'm begging you. He said.

Her teeth grazed against her lip as she straightened her back. *I won't do a deep-scan, but we can meld. You may borrow a portion of my power to recover what you have lost.*

Zeluum's lips grew wide and high as he closed his eyes, ready for her undertaking. Her hand extended to his temple, grazing against his rough and hardened skin as his eyes closed. She sucked in a deep breath before plunging her telepathic probe into his open mind. There she saw him fall into the snow by a rival warrior, his vision blacked, and his astral form exploded out. He spun further into the atmosphere; Zeluum looked down to see his body port back to the fortress and the continuing battle below. Frustrated that he lost so easily, he lingered in the clouds and waited and waited and waited…

There was a black pocket the more Treneer dug. She found the edges of the hole as she slinked in. Zeluum looked to the stars and bounced back, growing increasingly frustrated at his lack of control. Pushing up, his astral hand grazed against the edge of the world, watching the flames burn around his partially phased limb. If he had lungs, he would be laughing, but something was there with him. By the time he noticed it, a dark shadow of an object tossed him aside. His astral form tumbled along the coarse surface before spinning back into the void. Dazed, he turned to see what it was. It appeared to be an asteroid flying past Farayah and vanishing into the black.

His senses were overwhelmed, but Treneer caught them all. She focused on the asteroid; there was someone in there.

No, there were many minds in there. It wasn't an asteroid; it was a ship. Her heart thumped as she narrowed on the thoughts; there was an Arinu inside. She snapped back to the gardens as she looked to Zeluum. His eyes were wide as the two of them tried to process everything they witnessed.

You did it. He said rubbing his temples as relief washed over him. *And…Lonur…*

Lonur wasn't taken by a Kepa or any E.D. She said, trying to calm her racing heart. *Judicator, I need access to the locations where all Arinu went missing and the planetary scans when they happened.*

Her mind was flooded with every missing Arinu. There were many that were recorded to be taken by roaming E.D.'s, but the rest were unaccounted and the locations where they vanished showed no signs of exoplanar interlacing. High up in the outer atmospheres of Farayah, there were dozens of asteroids zipping past, but as she focused more on the scans, there were very faint — almost invisible — mental signatures. There were beings inside them. They were ships psi-cloaked as asteroids, hence their planetary sensors didn't alert the sleeping watchers initially. Some off-worlder was kidnapping Arinu.

Sickness bubbled up in her stomach at the memory of Zu'leen's spirit wandering around the meadow, protecting her from that strange warrior, who perhaps intended to take her too. She glanced to Zeluum who had witnessed the records through her. The young warrior's eyes burned with fury.

You are welcomed to stay, but I need to do something first before I can report this. She said.

No, I need to return to the Cold Fires and all tribes. They need protecting from this threat. He said.

Treneer nodded as she gently placed her hand on his shoulder. *Until next travels.*

She flew to the teleporter alcoves; her fingers waved over the keypads to Ouro's office. The archway crackled with energy, surgically cutting through tangible reality as she stepped into the phase. Her body burst through the other side as she desperately tried to catch her breath. The small room was empty; amber daylight poured from the open doorway. Leading down, she saw Ouro standing on the edge of the balcony.

I should have called, but I need your help now. She said.

He slowly turned; his hands were hidden under his sleeves and his eyes were glassy. *Treneer, I went to see my parents.*

She froze from the pain irradiating from his body. *What happened?*

When we spoke, I tried forgiving them again, to let free them from my heart – I'm such a fool. They never deserve to be released; I will make them forget everything! He said as his brow furrowed and sparks flew from his shining orange irises.

She glided to him and gently gripped his forearms. *You're not alone, I will help you with anything, but time is disappearing. Please, I need you to focus with me.*

Yes, time IS disappearing! Ouro slid past her to his office before turning to her. *Shimarr could be alive, and she needs me to get her out.*

Treneer felt her heart falling to her stomach. *How could you be certain your sister is alive?*

My disgraced elder mother said there's a chance, I couldn't tell if her mind is so astra-addled, but if there's a chance-

Alright, I will help you-

We need to incapacitate the Kepa, while you free her...I won't be able to go in there myself. He said as he ran his hand over his scars. *But I can open the way for you.*

Wait, we can work together on both of our needs. She rushed over and pressed her hand into his to give him a memory download of Lonur and the disguised ships, and the many kidnapped Arinu, and finally, her old elder consulting with astral dancers. *Zu'leen's spirit saved me from being taken, but I need to know what she learnt from the astral dancers that made her end her life.*

Ouro slipped his hand back under his sleeve; his brow twinkled from a thin sheen of sweat. *She went so far to…*

She did and I need to know what happened. I can't go to the Executors because it would dishonour her family.

*Maybe we can save them all but doing it with just the two of us…*He looked to the granite door and frowned. *Do you think these off-worlders are working with the Kepa?*

The timing aligns, but we won't know unless we investigate this first. She said.

Ouro tuned to her; now his eyes burned a frightening red. *They will all burn in our fury.*

~

The day slipped away as they searched through the records of prisoners, both held by Ouro or by other Void Wardens for the one Zu'leen met with. They were piecing together her rambling descriptions and their many meetings, all under the shadow of secrets. Treneer wanted to rip the data crystal from her temple and toss it off the balcony as the cold night rolled in. She felt Yansoon saying the training and bonding with Delyn went well and wanted to know if Treneer needed assistance. Fortunately, Yansoon was far enough and not too sensitive to detect Treneer's faux reassurance. She did wonder about Zeluum, if he had returned safely to the Cold Fire Fortress, but feared if she thought too much of him, he would hear her.

So, there are two dozen violent and dangerous astral dancers condemned here that likely could have met Zu'leen. Ouro said as he glided over with a shining data crystal hovering above his palm.

Zu'leen described that there was a group of them, no more than four at every meeting. Treneer said.

Ouro scanned through the names. *At least one of my captives could have been in these groups.*

Captives…prisoners…the Arinu have become strangers, Treneer thought. *We may need to individually meet and scan them.* She said as she tapped her chin.

Assuming their memories would be intact. He said.

She rolled her eyes. *Wonderful.*

Hold on, these summoners would be very well experienced considering how many times Zu'leen had dealt with them. They would be showing signs of exoplanar decay. I have five here who exhibit those symptoms. He said.

Treneer extended her arms over her head and felt her aching muscles ease. *Let's get to it.*

They slipped into the Void, dividing the cells, and seeking their captives in the seemingly endless realms. She peered into one where it was a dark forest covering the rugged land, there was no life in the trees or grass, they were mere figments of the captive's imagination. Her hands pressed against the shield, her senses were blanketing the black mirage for the Arinu within. There was someone hiding behind the mound, their energy was weak and frightened. With her mind fortified and aura as hard as steel, she pressed into the cell and glided over to the astral dancer.

She found them under a make-shift leaf roof, squatting in dirt with tattered clothing tied around their body. They didn't lift their head to her, but they weren't asleep. Treneer grounded herself before probing into their head, but to her dismay, there were many holes in their memory. Ouro's prism was working too well. As she searched and searched, too much was gone of who they were. With a sigh, she flew back to the cell door and made for the next.

The other cell held a hellish desert; the artificial star brimming in the heavens was powerful enough to make her squint through the door opening. Treneer found the prisoner's aura hiding in a cave among the orange canyons. She swatted away the rising sand in the strong hot winds as she made way to them. They were curled up in the rock nook, fast asleep. Pressing her way into their mind, she was met again with emptiness. The captive turned to meet her eyes, but there was nothing behind them. His grey wrinkled face was mottled and in various stages of healing, she shuddered knowing he appeared to be several millennia old, yet he couldn't be older than a century. A place of healing, but that healing was punishment, she thought.

Treneer made her way back out of the cell and saw Ouro floating to another before gliding through a door. She sighed, as her body and mind were aching to rest. Leaning against the wall, she closed her eyes. Finally, it was her turn for the Void to bear down on her.

Come, this one remembers Zu'leen! Ouro called to her.

Forgetting her weariness and acting on the last ounces of adrenaline, she shot up to the cell and pushed through the door. It was a primitive city of brick and metal that stretched on into forever. To the windows, she could see lights with shadowed figures moving about the rooms, but there were no thoughts inside – another mirage. She saw Ouro's aura to a bridge crossing a dried river with an astral dancer huddled in layers of torn coats resting against the railing. His hand pulled away from their scalp as he turned to meet her eyes. *They still remember seeing Zu'leen's face.*

"I remember a little more than that," they croaked, keeping their head low.

Treneer glided over, never taking her glare from him. "What did she want from you?"

"Didn't say; didn't ask. I knew who she was, had a lot to lose if wrong person overheard her thoughts, but an extra in the circle is always welcome," they said.

"She summoned Kepa with you?" Treneer said.

"Kepa always have so much to give and ask for something small in return. It always seems small at the time, until you realise that small thing means the world to you…" they said, looking down at their gnarly blackened hands. "I guess that's why they are rich."

"Did you ever give people?" Ouro's voice was stiff; his tempered rage made her eyes dart to him for a moment.

The summoner's head twitched. "They always went willingly."

"So, they're alive when they go in. Do they stay alive?" Ouro growled.

Ouro-

"I don't know," the dancer whined.

"In your last rituals, did Zu'leen get something from the Kepa? What did she give in return?" Treneer said as she inched closer.

"We each offered something different...I don't remember," their head dropped into his hands as a pained sob escaped his throat before rising to meet their faces. "But the Kepa remembers."

Treneer and Ouro exchanged glances, her stomach tightened, and her eyes closed. "Can you open to their home-plane?"

"A price, anything for a price," he said.

She sucked in a lungful of artificial air. "What do you want?"

"Freedom with my life returned."

"Out of the question," Treneer scoffed as she turned to Ouro, hoping that he thought the same, but his still face remained transfixed on the prisoner.

"We're done here," she said before spinning out of the cell and back to Ouro's office. The prism ate away at her for too long and she collapsed on some soft floor cushions. The arrogance, the sheer foolishness, the frightening consequences...Treneer couldn't stop her thoughts from tumbling. Her Oath was pulling away like strings on the hem of a robe.

The granite portal opened and Ouro pulled forth; his face was still sullen and in deep contemplation. *I can't call the Kepa, Treneer, the dancers are the only ones that know how.*

You cannot bargain with them. We've worked for too hard and sacrificed too much to keep people like that away from the community.

*I don't need a reminder, but to close that door when it can bring her back...*He said as his eyes narrowed.

We'll find another way. She said.

When? Shimarr could be dead by then and the rest of our kin could also be suffering!

Treneer rubbed her sore eyes. *Our Oath is-*

Is to keep people safe. We can keep the dancer on a tether, give them their freedom and restore their old self. One dancer for hundreds of our kin, Treneer.

She stared at him, both waiting for the other to speak.

You told me once to let Zu'leen go, but did I listen? Her head dropped back on the soft cushion. *I was ready to risk everything just to get a pile of her journals...*

Ouro smiled. *I will be in your debt.*

Sadly, I may call upon you very soon. She said before ripping off the last strings of her Guardian Oath.

Chapter Twenty-seven
Shshmrnashsh IX: Liberator

Distant murmuring minds echoed inside her. It was there, even when her senses were drawn and when she was at her most vulnerable. However, she couldn't share with them, nor them with her. This feeling, on its face, was akin to the High Mind, but this psionic experience was separate and cold. Her emotions and thoughts were hers alone, not stretched and equalised with the others. Watching and waiting…for a moment, she imagined herself as a bird perched in a high branch overlooking a field of prey. She relished the role, imagining her long and soft wings, what the wind smelt like and the warmth of the sun…

Shshmrnashsh's eyes peeled open. Gentle sparkling bioluminescent lights dotted along the quivering fleshy walls of her pod. The murmurs simmered to a hum; her old consortium was placid and slower, but they didn't know it – yet. She could feel Vern's gentle nudging on them. Hrrnm's face flashed in her mind, they sat in the centre of a sea of units, bidding their will and falling by the masses as the soldier reigned supreme. Rage overflowed in her chest – she wanted to fight.

The doors shrivelled away as her interfacers plucked out of the meaty power ports. Organic membrane grew over every surface; the once-metallic beams that held the structure were replaced with bones and tubules that connected every device resembled pumping veins. The chamber's air was heavy with power; the units passing her by resembled more like Organics. She watched their eyes narrowed to focus, their brows furrowed when something hadn't gone according to plan, and they even shared smiles with each other.

So many new faces hurrying around the chamber, mixed with eagerness and anxiety about the coming hours. The new recruits were quick to take the grafting, excited to shed their synthetic nature. As she strode to the plexus room, there were a handful of a dozen units standing in psi-linking circles. Divining and empowering themselves, some were forcibly growing new spiked carapaces on their bodies, while others had their skulls expanded to fit more brain mass. Energy pulsated from their skin as electricity crackled between their fingers. Voo-san darted from circle to circle; she spotted Vern among the psychic units, ensuring everything was ready. He glanced up and eyes widened when he saw her cascading down to them.

"Excellent, you're here. The perimeter is secured even if most of us are gone. Vern and the other channelers are warding any roamers with ill-intent away. How is your hold on the consortium's network?"

"Just teetering on the edge of their alarms," Vern said.

Voo-san grinned before looking to her. "How does your new third eye fare?"

Shshmrnashsh straightened her back and tried mimicking his smile. "My new third eye is fully powered, but I don't wish to join the circle. I want to face Hrrnm."

Voo-san's face tightened. "That alters our plans, but this could work in our favour. Please, come with me."

They hastened to the replicator chamber; his fingers waved over the holo-keys as he stared at the arched alcove. "We will fit you with a miniature E.M.P. Augmented for stunning – not killing."

"How many casualties were calculated?" she said as light beams wove cuffs and skeletal chest piece in the alcove.

"Soldier units will be the highest number, but Vern senses there's instability among them – more than any other group. Some are ready to break away and surrender once we disrupt the link. If they see you, then maybe more," Voo-san said. His hand reached out and telekinetically guided the formed pieces towards Shshmrnashsh.

"Hrrnm will be performing rewrites on any who try to break away," she said as he moved the cuffs around her wrists and steadily locked the disk over her chest.

"Perhaps it's to our favour, fewer to fight," he said as his eyes narrowed, carefully locking it all into place.

"Unlikely. Hrrnm would have quickly perfected rewrites. If they are reset, then they would be exclusive to Hrrnm's command," she said as she felt a sudden surge of energy pumping into the E.M.P. "The High Mind stored our minds until new bodies were replicated. If any units are terminated, it will be permanent."

Voo-san nodded. "Well, Shsh, pray for zero."

~

It was time. The Unbound blinded the consortium's probes and satellites by bombarding them with focused psi-energy, disrupting them long enough for their skiffs and probes to meet the twin nexuses. *They know not what they do,* Shshmrnashsh said to herself. *Many were forced into the network and only do what the consortium bids,* she repeated. *They needed an opportunity, a signal, a sign! They just need to be released…* If she were not locked away in the crystal matrix of the skiff with the other Unbound soldiers, she would smile.

Watching from the ship's camera, Gerrnzerrn flew beside them. Hundreds of cream trails streamed in the orange clouds as the yellow stars twinkled above them. Speeding over the black ruins, the ship's sensors called an alert. *Movement detected in the southern hemi-sphere districts.*

The consortium could not have expanded that far out yet. Shsh said as fear prickled.

No, we sense they're rogue units and have seen us, they're following the ships and probes on foot. Vern said.

I'll whisper to them to avoid the carnage and bring them here. Voo-san said.

Confirmed. She said.

The shining tip of Nexus 1V37 peeked through the clouds before its grand dark edges came into view. Slowly descending, the ship's alarms flared again. *Targeted by astra-turrets.*

Now. Shsh called to Vern and the other channelers.

The silver pistons skewed their direction, but teal strobes blasted from their ends in aimless and confused directions. Vern's psychic circle disrupted the consortium's control over their outer defence devices, but the machines were given the last command for free fire.

With me! Gerrnzerrn called as they zipped down to the dark grounds with a few dozen probes. They moved so quickly; their white light trails appeared to be dancing between each popping turret.

We locked them out of the replicator bay and ship bay. They can only fight with what they have ready. Vern said.

Let them exhaust their defence. Once they surrender, then we will come. Shsh said.

The skiffs descended to the neon grounds; hundreds of sentries sprouted from the walls as shields thickened around the massive structure; more turrets poked through the opening plated grounds – the pyramid came to life. Before they released their focused beam, Shshmrnashsh's squad pulled away and swarmed around the district, blasting and breaking through the first wave of sentries. A beam sliced past her skiff's edge, leaving a smoking black line across.

Vern, break their control! She called.

There's a disruption- Vern's thoughts crackled.

Round reflective lights caught her focus. Several large E.M.Ps rose from the rooftops surrounding the ships. The sentries and other consortium fliers retreated in as the shields hardened until it enveloped the pyramid into a dark dome. The disks directed towards the Unbound; lines of light circled to their centre as they readied to release – but they prepared for this. The more delicate instruments inside of their ships and probes were covered in a thick organic coat, impervious to the E.M.Ps effects, but Vern's channelers were too clouded to disrupt them. Shshmrnashsh's skiff aimed towards the disks, but the ship's pistons sparked and trembled before she could fire.

She flew over to the nearest E.M.P, and despite being protected, her matrix oscillated the closer she drew to the wave. The tip of the skiff pierced through the round dish, shattering it in tiny shards before the machine grinded against the roof and tumbled down out of sight. The other's followed suit, slamming their skiffs and probes into every E.M.P until Vern's and Voo-san's thoughts returned.

All E.M.Ps have been destroyed. Gerrnzerrn said.

Disconnect their shield generators! She called. In a moment, the curding energy shield thinned until she could see the edges and waning glow of the tip, but as the plateau came into full view, units covered the grounds. Roctarous fitted with heavy power channelling devices bolted to their shoulders and thick cords that pierced their bodies grew spheres of light from their chests.

Stun them. She commanded.

The Unbound refocused, releasing waves of energy, disabling their charge and freezing the heavy units in the ground. Some managed to shoot their blasters, vaporizing a few unfortunate Unbound ships caught in their path. Glowing ashes showered the war grounds as a new wave of sentries and skiffs soared at her. This was their chance.

Disconnecting. Vern and Voo-san said. The sentries and probes suddenly halted and drifted mindlessly in the air; the skiffs trembled as the units within fought for control, but their efforts were fruitless. She steadied as she surveyed the vulnerable fliers, held by the will of the Unbound, but the consortium was not done yet. More soldiers poured from the walls, aiming their arms and shoulder-pistols, firing at every target.

Nexus 0G11 has been taken. Vern said.

Hold them. 1V37 is close. Voo-san said.

That's when she spotted the ashen-green armoured body striding out. Hrrnm's eyes narrowed and joined the fire. Soldiers spread, forcing their fight directly underneath the Unbound's fliers, but Vern suddenly forced up the energy shield and pressed them back, so close to the slanted edges of the nexus. Their desperate onslaught halted as the shields had slipped their grasp.

Its time. Shshmrnashsh said as she and fellow Unbound materialised to the scarred metal grounds. "Cease fire, the shields will redirect them and may strike you!"

The soldiers stiffened, but one pushed past the hard bodies close to the edge.

"Explain your purpose." Hrrnm called.

She stared at them, rapidly calculating to find the right words, but Voo-san's piece slipped in. *Their link is still strong, but a few units are wriggling from the network.*

"We're here to free them – all of them," she said, eyeing the soldiers and nexus. "Including you."

Hrrnm said nothing.

Shshmrnashsh could feel her carapace heating. "We are the Unbound-"

"We?" Hrrnm inched closer as their eyes scanned the organic armada. "How can you speak for linkless Renegades? Did you ask each of them?"

"I chose to, as they did," she said extending her arms behind her before pointing ahead. "As all of you can, now!"

Their network is failing, but they're directing all power to their plexus to keep it in place. Keep talking to buy time. Vern said.

She stepped along the row of soldiers. "Your network is moments from going offline, each of you can willingly disconnect and decide your paths. We don't expect you to join us, you can go where-ever you please in peace!" she narrowed her eyes at Hrrnm. "And you will not be shot down if you do."

"Roctarous have no purpose outside of protecting the Higher Mind legacy!" Hrrnm said.

"We can find our purpose ourselves." She said.

Hrrnm cocked their head to the side. "How many units are you willing to sacrifice from avoidable disconnection decay on the assumption they will find this 'purpose?'"

"Disconnection decay is solvable! It can be done with minor organic implanting to avoid-"

"Ah," Hrrnm's voice was cold, but there was glee on their lip, as if the soldier had waited for her to make an error. "You speak of peace but meet us with violence. You speak of choice, yet we are at your mercy. You want autonomy, but subjugate units for augmentation," Hrrnm growled. "Is this choice?"

"It's more than we ever had, Hrrnm," she glared at them.

Alert: there's a massive data surge in the network and spreading. Vern said.

"Your consortium has lost, release them!" she called.

Hrrnm said nothing.

They're self-destructing. Voo-san said.

"Comply!" she shrieked.

One soldier behind Hrrnm trembled before falling with a thud. Then a few more, then a dozen.

Go! Shsh cried as the shields fell. She and the Unbound tore through the consortium's ranks, but more fell from the self-destruction. Hrrnm's arms rose, firing wildly before they were nullified and tackled by several Unbound units. She bolted and slid around the blasters before leaping over heads and shoulders toward the nexus walls.

Gerrnzerrn flew in and focused a particle beam on the edge of the pyramid, melting away the wall for the Unbound units to push through. Shshmrnashsh dove in first. The chamber was littered with fallen units convulsing on the floor; some tried to claw at her, but their weak, trembling arms were easy to push past.

Keep the network connected, I'm linking to the plexus. She said speeding to the dying diamond. Skating across the floors, Shshmrnashsh injected her interfacers in the upside-down tip, but was met with an agonising screech and muffled code, spinning her into the void. Her interfacers instantly spat out as she tried to refocus her mind. Several more thuds came from around her; units toppled over the walkways as they tried to get to the plexus. Her hand pierced through the edge of the machine; her fingertips lifted the sealed latch before prying it open. The metal moaned and broken wires sparked as she looked in to see Senzvrrn's head and bust convulsing within.

She heaved into the alcove before carefully plucking out Senzvrrn's interfacers from the plexus, as she helplessly watched her friend's eyes roll back, and body slowly stop moving. As her interfacers found their way to the empty sockets of the alcove, she felt arms wrap around her waist and ripped her from the plexus before tossing her across the chamber. Sliding against the slick floors, she turned to see Hrrnm leap and land onto her back, pinning her down. In her periphery, she saw the soldier's jaw was torn and limply hanging on the side of their face, one of their eyes were burnt out leaving an empty socket and shoulder weapons were torn off.

One of their hands pressed her face down as the other viciously gripped and tore out her interfacers. She shrieked as her arms and legs wildly tried bending and whipping around, but Hrrnm just pressed harder. Their hand found its way to back of her skull, and with a firm grip, lifted her face a few inches before bashing her head into the ground. Over and over, her cranium screamed with alarms as her organic eye lost vision. Red drops smeared onto the dented floor as Hrrnm crunched her head harder and harder. Vern's and Voo-san's thoughts dropped to a murmur as her body readied for emergency shutdown.

Pulling the last percentages of energy, she speared her mind into Hrrnm's, forcing them to stumble back. The pressure in her skull eased as she spun around and activated her E.M.P. Even though the wave was pointed away from her, every nano-cell oscillated as she tried peeling the stunned soldier off her. She scrambled to her feet before wrapping her arms around Hrrnm's head. With one merciless swing, she tore it clean from their shoulders and tossed it across the chamber.

Her hand dove down for one of her bent interfacers as she scrambled to plug it to the back of her skull, but the cord was ripped. Holding it in place, she stumbled back to the plexus and pierced the needle end into the socket. Though free from the infected Senzvrrn, the neat web of minds was shredded, and the small fires of consciousness were snuffed out. The network was dead.

She drooped as her interfacer slipped through her fingers. Unbound fighters poured into the nexus, hurrying to the fallen. Gerrnzerrn sped over to her; it's single crystal eye fixated on her before it pressed a power-transferer tube into her chest.

"We failed," she said, looking up at the probe.

"There are some that can be saved," they said.

Her body welled with energy, and she could feel her nano-cells splitting and bonding across her wounds. The blood in her living eye washed away as a blurry vision of the chamber returned to view. The Unbound opened scalps and gently removed the crystal cores of the terminated, inspecting the damage before collecting the least damaged parts of the stiff bodies.

"I'm to blame. I never computed Hrrnm would be this illogical. Is this considered cruel?" she said as she watched an Unbound fighter scoop up Hrrnm's lifeless head.

"It's purely emotional. They believed sacrificing themselves would save their consortium from us. I would say, it's a form of love," Gerrnzerrn said.

"This is not what love looks like according to my archived data. Hrrnm called us aggressors when we could have destroyed the entire consortium with minimal effort, but we didn't. I tried to make them see that." she said.

"No matter how well calculated, we will never truly know what someone will choose once choice brought to them." The probe said.

"Hrrnm chose over the lives of the consortium, it wasn't theirs to make." She said.

"No, it wasn't, but you hadn't been part of this network for a while, so how can you be certain they didn't want termination?" the probe said.

Before she could utter a word, she felt Vern's thoughts rising in the back of her mind.

Report on Nexus 0G11. She said.

The plateau sustained minor damage, but the units there have also succumb to the termination virus. They said.

I sensed the network was weak enough for them to disconnect, why didn't they? She begged.

*A virus killed their ability to disconnect, even if they wanted to. We were so close...*She could feel their emotions sparking in their mind.

Her nano-cells began repairing and regrowing her shredded interfacers. No, she said to herself. Her hand squeezed the newly grown ends as she pulled Gerrnzerrn's injection from her body. "I don't want my interfacers repaired."

~

The Unbound wasted no time grafting organic systems of the acquired nexuses. The crawling tissue enveloped the astral-forges before making way to the replicators and teleporters. Of the three-hundred-and-twenty units, less than ten percent could be remade. The fallen were piled together as Voo-san and Shshmrnashsh frantically separated the ones that could be saved and others that can be repurposed, while Vern was stationed at 0G11.

Voo-san telekinetically lifted some units, drawing them in and carefully examined their crystal cortexes. "Viable," he said before transferring it to a carrier probe.

Her hands shifted through the rubble; her palms were slick with black plasma as the nano-cells leaked and died outside the unit's body. A bust rolled out; her eyes widened as the dull face of Senzvrrn stared blankly upwards. Her fingers quickly tore through the scalp and fished out for their crystal before lifting it to the light. Her limbs tensed and her living eye leaked upon seeing the burnt and fractured edges of the mineral. She cupped it before glancing to Voo-san.

"Can this one be saved?" she held it to him.

He frowned as his telekinetic reach plucked it from her fingers close to his eyes. "No, they're too far gone."

"They were an adjunct, they possessed vast capabilities. Should we consider investing energy for repairing?" she said.

Voo-san shook his head. "I'm sorry, Shshmrnashsh."

She blinked before her eyes fell to the pile.

"Were they your friend?"

Shshmrnashsh opened her mouth as she struggled to find the words. "Yes."

Voo-san nodded. "They were your kin," he said before sending it back.

The dead crystal dropped in her palm, it felt heavier and colder than before. She stared at it – at what was Senzvrrn. Her fingers gently caressed it before putting it into a small storage compartment in her forearm. "How did you feel when someone you cared about was terminated?"

Voo-san's lips pursed as they thought for the right words. "Arinu die rarely, our Deathspeakers can guide the soul back to the body, but sometimes, they can't. And when that happens...it's as if a part of you is missing."

"I don't feel as if a part of me is missing, I'm just sad I didn't see who Senzvrrn could have become once liberated. It seems that question may never be answered," she said as she continued harvesting from the pile.

"The what-if question is dangerous. The answer will evade you and your spirit will remain in purgatory," Voo-san said as he found a clearer crystal and slipped it to the probe. "Arinu believe in grieving for the living, for they must wait to see their kin again."

"Do you feel nothing for the dead?" she said as her head cocked.

"Of course, we celebrate their freedom!" he gave an assuring smile.

Shshmrnashsh shifted to the last uninspected unit. Spinning the head over, her eyes widened as dread pierced her core: Brrnzerm. For a moment, she thought they were staring directly at her, but the dull and aimless gaze was to nothingness. Please, please, please be intact, she said as her hands quickly peeled open their skull. In the centre, the clean crystal sparkled up at her. Her mouth parted as she held to the light.

"Viable! Viable!" she called.

Voo-san sucked the crystal from her hand and pressed their fingers against it. "Brrnzerm. They switched themselves off before the virus. We can revive a body for them."

"They are a repairing unit; recommend we revive them immediately."

"Yes," Voo-san's eyes squinted before returning it. "Take them to the replicator bay, Vern shall meet you there."

"Confirmed," she said, grasping the floating crystal.

"And give them whatever it is they want, Shsh," The way he spoke was as if he knew about their secret agreement.

Shshmrnashsh watched Voo-san and the other channelers lift the hundreds of emptied husks and shift them to the waste-breakers. The pile's edges glowed as the silver dish ripped them apart, atom by atom. The nexus trembled, the lights in the walls grew brighter as it absorbed the wave of fresh energy. She zipped to the teleportation chamber, pushing past fleshy bodies and probes before settling to an empty alcove. The archway lit and the pad was warm at the first step in.

The new chamber was darker, but a strange earthy and metallic humidity weighed the air. The cavernous halls held hundreds of vats and probes fitted with long, ribbed limbs, carefully weaving energy into matter within the vats. A murky yellow bubble popped from one of the smaller vats, that's when the smell struck. She peered in to see a pool of sludge with thick veins growing from the bottom up into several round semi-transparent tanks.

Over here. Vern whispered.

She turned to see them standing between a row of hanging tanks. "I'm glad you are undamaged."

"I assure you, there is damage," they said as they slapped the fleshy tank. "More could have been done."

"We did everything right," she said stepping over.

"But we did not do everything to save them, did we? We should have applied domina-"

"Please, Vern. Not now," Shsh said as her eyes closed, feeling the dull crystal of Senzvrrn in her arm pocket.

Vern shook their head as their eyes fell to her clutched hand. "Voo-san said you've found Brrnzerm the repairing unit, seems too clinical of a name."

She opened her palm and Vern flicked it in the air with their mind before gently dropping it in the tank's upper opening. "I see no need to change their name and title," she said.

Vern smiled as their hand pressed against the tissue, and their mind commanded the device to begin. "What about Brrnzerm the Repairer? Or if they want to blend in with Organics, it could be Brrnzerm the Doctor or Brrnzerm the Healer."

"Technically, it would be Brrnzerm the Mechanic," Shsh said.

Vern chuckled. "Brrnzerm the Organic Mechanic. Not as gracious as Brrnzerm the Healer."

"There's a reverence to it, but almost too mystical. However, wouldn't it be their choice?" she said.

The pair watched the crystal growing long and thin nerves, bundling around it as it extended out into a bipedal form.

"I think my fit would be Vern the Unbound." They said.

"You are already Unbound," she said as she marvelled at the bones extending and hardening as strips of muscle overlapped them in the tank.

"I'm talking about something personal. Unbendable, Uncorruptible and Unbound. Use your imagination, what would be your title?" they said.

Shshmrnashsh wasn't certain if she was amused by this conversation or agitated, but seeing Vern clinging on to this momentary joy made her give in. "I select Shshmrnashsh the Unbound."

Vern glanced at her from the corner of their eye. "Why are you copying me? I specified to use your imagination."

"It seems the most applicable."

"Is that your final choice? You can't change it once you do."

"Are you attempting humour?"

Vern shook their head as they flashed a smile. The body in the tank grew a paisley, pale olive skin. She could see Brrnzerm's eyes wildly rolling beneath their lids. Vern tapped the membrane as the tank's natal fluid was vacuumed up into the thick cords above, until the layer tightly dried against the organic unit. Brrnzerm's head moved, their eyes opened as their hands clawed their way from the sack, before dropping to their feet. Their back straightened as their hands wiped away the remaining viscous fluid from their face.

"Welcome, Brrnzerm. I'm Vern and you're already familiar with Shshmrnashsh," they stepped forward.

Brrnzerm blinked as they looked between them before their eyes cast down to their new slippery body. "I'm Organic…I cannot hear the network. As it was before I was forced into it."

Shshmrnashsh stiffened as she scanned their face.

Vern slowly nodded. "Yes, your former body was destroyed-"

"Destroyed? Report on the consortium!" they said.

"The virus wiped out ninety percent, the remaining will need to be revived, like you."

Brrnzerm trembled as their hands clasped over their head. "Impossible-"

"I'm sorry and I'm so sorry for leaving," she said.

They glanced up to her, she couldn't read their stare. Was this hate? "Report on Senzvrrn."

Shshmrnashsh shook her head. "The adjunct was most effected."

Brrnzerm's eyes travelled aimlessly around the chamber, even to the dark ceiling. "Terminated…"

"You were a repairing unit before," Vern began, "your skills would be an asset to the Unbound."

Brrnzerm returned their gaze. "That's no longer my function, I refuse."

"You were the first revival, and our time is limited; your experience can help us graft the thousands of unlinked Roctarous from decaying farther," she said.

Their eyes circled the floor. "Negative, I do not wish to serve anyone else anymore."

Vern and Shsh glanced at each other. She opened her mouth, wanting to press harder, but Brrnzerm's stare made her lips close again.

"Let me go."

"Understood," Vern said.

"Beyond this zone is still hostile territory, but we will give you a probe to increase your chances of survival," she said.

"Thank you."

"Brrnzerm, you will learn a lot about yourself," she said.

The living unit nodded before pressing past her. As they made a few steps to the teleporter, she turned and rushed over to them. "Before you go," she pulled the dark crystal core from her forearm and slipped it into their hand. "Senzvrrn."

"Thank you," Brrnzerm whispered before turning once more and vanishing into the white light of the teleporters.

She could hear Vern stepping beside her. "Disappointing, but at least it's one less we need to focus on."

"They were one of the first units I forcibly linked when I arrived to Kra. When I started showing signs of corruption, Hrrnm wanted Brrnzerm to rewrite me. They offered to preserve my memories if I could set them free," she said, turning to them. "Do you think they left because they hated me?"

"No, Brrnzerm wants to experience new life on their own," Vern smiled. "Deep down, they want that for you too."

"Did you sense that from their mind?" she said.

Vern patted her shoulder. "Of course, I don't want this cloud to weigh on you a moment longer."

She looked at her chest carapace. Flesh was warm, soft and alien. It had its own weaknesses, but it was something she had never explored before. She remembered electricity running through her limbs and her mind possessing every cell in her dreams. It was more than a vessel for her consciousness; it was home. Her body was too small for Sazla to possess, but large enough to capture the entire universe. Shshmrnashsh dared to imagine what life would be beyond the Unbound, Roctarous and Neavensoros; her purpose would be utterly to herself alone. Maybe in the future she would not fear it, but now, she can try.

"I wish for grafting."

Vern's brows flickered up.

"Please." She said.

Break III

The planar leaks dripped into the tangible cosmos. The drops rippled in the black ocean, and the ripples turned into waves, expanding out farther and farther, piercing through every star and speck. The children were eating it, the children were drinking it, and the children were breathing it. The corrosive waves made their mark, and the children turned on each other. She could see them from her canopy, but she was too far to reach them.

Her body was frozen, but her mind burned. Licks of thoughts whipped through her mind; they were from her kin. She could overhear them; they could see the horrid waves defiling everything they touched. They were distraught that they had to leave her – if only they knew what she had come to understand. The waves were wide and their numbers few, the first time in an eon where haste was on their minds. They must scatter and halt the waves, while the others tend to the corruption. The plan was too grand, even for her ancient siblings.

She heard them say a new name; one that has not lived yet. An argument sprouted like a weed; the others said Sazla was not gone. But they haven't had a new member in eons, and some said, maybe it was time to split once more. This embrace of a new being would have brought her joy. If she were free, then maybe she would have volunteered to split her energy and mould a new Neavensoros, but Akashi's whispers of their children blew like astral hurricanes. The children were about to learn the truth and will take their revenge.

She had to do something. A tiny spark floated through the black curtains; it was intelligent as it looked around the expansive plane. Sazla leaned in; she recognised this spark. It still had a body, but its mind was free to roam the universe. Her fingers kneaded at it, but the spark moved away. It buzzed in her mind, but it was so small and faint;

she could barely hear what it was saying. Maybe it wanted to know where it was or who she was. She opened her mouth, she wanted to tell it, but the little thing was so delicate, it may slip away. She wanted its company and knew this was her chance.

Her eyes were everywhere, but her focus remained on the last Neavensoros. They were splitting, willing to weaken themselves to bear a new sibling into their world. Oh Akashi, if only they knew what was coming for them from their cradle-world. Screaming to her kin would have been a waste. The loneliness transmuted into desperation, but how folly of her to assume she was alone. Akashi was there, it was all around her and now she was part of it. Perhaps there's a chance.

Sazla's body ached as she reached to the one person that cleansed her from her life but still needed her most. Shshmrnashsh could barely feel her finger, and her mind was unchanged. Sazla pressed so far that her arms splintered and drifted away in the astral winds. Shshmrnashsh was still unmoved, but in payment, Sazla watched her body disintegrate. She howled in pain as she pulled the little of herself was left back. For a moment, she saw something she didn't quite understand.

Her remains slipped through many dimensions and planes, bonding with the universe, but it was not lost. The tiny spark by her side was still watching her, waiting for her to speak.

I could tell my siblings what is happening, but our children need to know first. My siblings need to understand, and they will. I have seen a way to make our children work together for the first time. I know what must be done. Go, take the crownless prince to the living outpost!

Chapter Twenty-eight
Ahn'kat X: Fear turns to Hate

His head felt like it was a bag of sand sitting on his pained neck. Ahn'kat sat at the head of the table between pro and anti-pet speakers on either side. Well, they were hardly speaking, their ravenous shouts kept his heavy eyelids from shutting and his body drooping in the meeting. Angry glares and ridiculous shrieks would have been excellent entertainment, if he were not the one overseeing it. His eyes bounced back and forth with each talking point shot like arrows to both sides.

High in between the rafters, he looked through the glass ceiling of the Conclave Speakers Lodge, watching the sun's rays cast down in the chamber. His eyes glazed over as he tried soaking in the warm and nourishing light, absorbing its power, radiance, and strength to remain a second longer amongst enraged leaders.

The Lodge was secluded in the high mountains, just beyond Lusor city. No one was to enter, speak about what was discussed or who was in attendance, without invitation or permission by the High Priestesses and Priests. It was meant to be a place of quiet contemplation with the gods, to honour high servants of old and anoint the new. But those days were inching farther and farther away. If the rest of the imperium were to witness these violent social rifts, then it's infection will spread into the Empire, a kind they would never recover or adapt from.

Ahn'kat glanced to his right, a long row of decorated anti-pet Zanashj, ranging from nobles of lower houses to commoners, to former pets. One former pet stood above his line; his fingers were wagging as his short strings of hair waved against his pointed cheek. He wore no jewellery, but at least his plain tunic and trousers were clean and presentable. His irregular and untraditional appearance before a member of the Crown would have given some pause, but Ahn'kat was too exhausted, yet admired his daring defiance of casting away old glamorous appearances.

"That poor display you called a 'protest' has shown your weakness, disregarding the fact you are going against the emperor and Empire's goals, but that you resist the nature of evolution," he said.

To Ahn'kat's left, another former pet, adorned with fine trinkets and lavish robes shook her head with bemusement at her opposer's words. It was as if she hadn't heard them or has already dismissed them long before he opened his mouth.

"Throwing insults and false accusations in a house of the Pantheon is heretical at best, criminal at worst. Yes, tradition is the Empire's core, but part of that tradition is the embrace of change. We were ready and accepting the Crown's will, however, there was no safety net for this shift. Our 'poor display' was pent up anger from ignored voices who have directly suffered from the disorganised planning of the Crown-," fear made her pause before she glanced and bowed to Ahn'kat, "with no disrespect to you, your grace."

"None taken," the prince said as he softly shook his head as he reached over for a skinned banana before his eye turned over to the right. The male ex-pet's face faintly quivered in delight at her fumbling words.

"What the Crown wills: be it so," begun Ahn'kat, he could feel the heat of his sapphire pendant on his skin, basking in its comfort and his words. "This situation has brought the Empire to a revolutionary standpoint. However, we all must answer to the gods – no matter what choices are made today or tomorrow. As head of this scheme, we will postpone pushing more pets into reformation centres until we have adequately prepared for more."

The male ex-pet's eyes grew worried. "Your grace, but there are many in my ilk who believe they can ascend their positions, to take it away suddenly after so many years of progress-"

"I hear you, Speaker Enkimut, but shall we force more of our imperial family into deplorable conditions or wait for a while longer to ensure these centres are operating their intended purpose?" Ahn'kat said firmly. He hadn't felt such confidence in his words for so long; he was almost convinced he was a true prince. Perhaps it was Aszelun's will beaming into his heart that welled him with bravery for this moment.

"Thank you, my prince," the female ex-pet said softly with a faint bow. Ahn'kat didn't need telepathy to see she seemed rather pleased that her opponent had a tongue lashing from their prince, but unfortunately for her, she was next.

"Speaker Telkes, you were well cared for by your wealthy masters and it's no mistaking you were highly educated by them," Ahn'kat said as his head turned to her, but keeping his gaze steady.

"My mistress's house was incredibly generous. She was well respected among her nobles for caring highly for her pets," Telkes said.

"She treated you appropriately, you have been very fortunate," Ahn'kat said.

The speaker's smile dwindled in her eyes. "Yes, I have, your grace."

"Though sadly, your blood family had lost their prime business and went bankrupt when you were an infant. Your luck turned when your mistress came in, bought you from the imperium and took you under her wing and since then brought you here to address the Crown," Ahn'kat said, he could feel unease growing into Telkes, but also from the others in the hall.

"Yes, your grace," she was quieter, but her voice strained to maintain respect and dignity.

"Do you know if every pet has had the same fortune?" he said.

"I do not, your grace," she said as her chin slowly cast downwards.

"I do know that Speaker Enkimut has not, have you?" Ahn'kat looking to the male ex-pet shaking his head. "No, I know your father had a list of preventable illnesses when he was recovered from your old master's house. And you had known life at the end of a glass whip in childhood. In fact, I know many former pets who have claimed they had good lives until they realised the true nature of their position. However, once they understood that they were nothing more than bodies to be used, then you could see in their eyes there was no going back. And the Empire never will again.

"Our goals are identical; the only difference is timing. We will dedicate more resources to the reformation centres and focus more on rehousing, however, with recent off-worlder concerns, our plans to remove the pet caste will be delayed. Trust the Crown, keep your heart in the Empire and have faith in Pantheon. This momentary ache is only part of their divine challenge," Ahn'kat said as he rose to his feet, which was followed by the shuffling of others rising to theirs.

"Thank you, prince."

"Thank you, highness.

"Well done, my prince."

Their whispers blended into a white noise of his growing headache. Their celebratory clicking fingers and stamping of sandaled feet made him even less stable, but after some time, he had adapted to keeping his poise calm and high.

As he turned away from the wide warm room as his cloak and robe swept behind him, he could feel several figures following a few feet away. He wanted to recess to the restrooms to catch his breath and wash his face, maybe hear a few strong words from his bodyguard and friend, but sadly, Zertun was still away with Emestasun. He will keep her safe – no, they will keep each other safe, he prayed.

Ah, Neobatri, she was still away on mission on that frozen hell-planet of Farayah. By the Pantheon, he hoped she was unspoiled and hidden among the Arinu. All he had left was Ramkes and Ismotaph…two that may throw him away if either of them found out about Ahn'kat's conflicted agendas. He pained wishing he could trust his wife. By the gods, his throat ached for a banana liquor.

"Your grace, may I have a word?" a priest came bounding to his side. Ahn'kat was knocked out of his tumbling thoughts, when he returned to reality; he was surprised how many halls and corridors he strode past.

Ahn'kat's golden palace guards stepped between them, forcing the priest to step back farther than he intended.

"Priest Quezatet, just the man of the Conclave I was hoping to find," he said as he offered his forearm for a shake to the priest.

Quezatet's nerves eased when he returned Ahn'kat's shake before giving a polite head bow. "Yes, your grace, I finally received the numbers you asked from the Conclave before this meeting. May we…ugh, can we speak somewhere more privately?"

"Please guide us to your office, dear friend," Ahn'kat's smile was wide as he opened his arms to allow the priest to take head of his entourage. He knew he was being a little more personable than usual, especially after such a meeting, but he needed to be as kind and delicate with the Conclave's treasurer.

They swept through the halls; their glamour and magnificence were growing plainer and smaller the closer they inched to the back end of the Lodge. Quezatet came to his office; his hand reached for the latch, but one of the palace guards was the first to reach for it, before pressing past him into the small room. Another two guards strode through, while their scanners searched for unwanted listeners and hidden shapeshifters in the office.

"All clear, highness," said one through his golden-headed helm.

Ahn'kat hid his frown to the guard as he walked side-by-side with the anxious priest, thinking of a way to ease them before they started talking about money.

"Please, your grace," the priest offered Ahn'kat to sit on the finest lounge chair in the office. Considering all other pieces of furniture, this deep scarlet-brown leather piece was used the least. There was a small bronze dish of smoked olives fixed into one of the arms.

"Now, the highers of the Conclave understand the situation with the off-worlders and they're concerned the Crown should focus more on military expansion instead of continuing with reformations," the priest said as his thin fingers interlocked with each other over his lap.

Ahn'kat was prepared for this. "House Urbaz, the Intel Corps, and several military houses have been preparing for whatever the stars throw at us. However, the Crown and Conclave's prime object is to create calm in the Empire. We need to maintain unity to see tomorrow."

"The Conclave absolutely agrees, my prince. However, the numbers..." the priest looked down to his wrist phone, his eyes were moving across the holographic numerals as his shallow chin trembled. "Considering your grace's inspiring vision for our Imperial Family, the work we have done has capped the Conclave's coffers for the next several years."

The next several years? This cannot be true, Ahn'kat thought. His heart hammered, thinking about all the donations from commoners, lower and higher houses have poured into the Conclave since he dedicated his princedom to the faith. He remembered the warnings about Seratut, the riches he must have stolen or given away to hidden friends, squandered on his gluttonous lifestyle.

"The Conclave has emergency off-planet gold stored in its vaults. Its value is greater than Urasan gold," Ahn'kat said.

"Yes, mined by dominion pets," Quezatet said, trying to hold Ahn'kat's stare. "Since we have lost three dominion worlds, these coffer's replenishment is fourth the replenishment speed. Now, with planet Sye being slowly broken away-"

"That only means its value has grown," Ahn'kat pressed as he grabbed to the olives.

"But it also means the Conclave has put further restrictions for its release," the priest said.

"House Urbaz has been a loyal and most generous family to the Conclave for millennia. During this mess, we had taken the brunt of costs on ourselves," he said.

The priest's head sorrowfully shook. "If it were my decision, I would give you every ounce we have in our vaults. However, the highers of the Conclave will only open their vaults during an emergency situation-"

"This is an emergency situation!" Ahn'kat said, accidently crushing the olives in his fist. The priest sat back in his chair and rubbed his nose bone, while Ahn'kat breathed to compose himself. He knew why the high priests and priestesses were denying him, they had not forgotten about Seratut's arrest.

"I cannot imagine anyone who wouldn't consider this an emergency," Ahn'kat said. The Empire was healing too slowly from the new thousand cuts it was getting, they were being bled dry. He remembered the story of how infiltrators embarked on their conquests. They worm their way to the top of the planet's leadership and little, by little, they would destroy the planet's economy. Driving out industries on mass, halting all production and circulation of wealth until they were too poor to resist the Urasan Armada. Once the fleet arrived, they would reimplement all the lost industry and recover the planet, but it would have an imperial banner flying over the heads of their new pets.

Ahn'kat wanted laugh, he imagined the Arinu telepathically learnt Zanashj tricks to bankrupt the Empire. If that was their true intent, it worked to perfection.

"So, we have a decision to make," Ahn'kat said as he rose to his feet, popping the squished olives in his mouth. "Ask the Conclave what their criteria is for an emergency and my people will see if its warranted. Until then, we will find an alternative."

The priest hopped up, too. His face looked pained telling the prince the bad news. "That's how we adapt."

The corner of Ahn'kat's lips turned to a smile as he offered his forearm to Quezatet, which made the priest more at ease. "Thank you for trying, my friend, but be sure this conversation isn't over!"

"I hope next we speak; it will be better. Blessings of the Pantheon, your highness," the priest said giving a gracious bow.

When all was said and done in the Lodge, Ahn'kat flew his entourage back to the palace. The billowing wind calmed his hot mind as the machine swayed over Lusor. His eyes were catching the odd commoner house here and an estate there. He was getting tired of this rejection, of this stagnation. His fingers weaved through his beetle pendant, but it was cold and sharp, as if Aszelun was growing uncertain of his abilities.

Ismotaph came to his mind. Not the kind of face he wanted creeping in during his moments of flying bliss. Maybe he could call the Head of the Corps to find out if Seratut hoarded any caches, but it may take time to find. Seratut may have been a fool, but Ahn'kat didn't believe that the High Priest could maintain his lavish lifestyle without having an abundance stored somewhere.

The palace pyramid peaked through the heavy rainclouds. The closer he drew, his eye caught Ramkes standing in the gardens, speaking with royal guard, and observing an influx of new golden soldiers. He bound the vehicle around and begun landing the sleek machine over the wide cobbled walkway on the gardens. Ramkes' and other's eyes shot up to his descension; her long hair, scarlet dress and cloak billowed in the air. Her face softened when she saw his. Ahn'kat hopped over the vehicle's side, unbothered and unwilling to wait for his guards to open the doors or set hovering steps for him.

"Wife," he said to her as he strode over with his open arms to her.

"Husband," she said as she caught his embrace before pulling her lips to his ear. "It went that badly?"

"Worse than imagined," he whispered back with a smile when he pulled away from her and met with the others on the field.

"Husband, please meet our star praetors, Praetor Asyinett and Praetor Baesh, they are here with their new batch of fighters for us to observe," she said as her elegant hand waved to the two golden armoured soldiers.

"Your grace."

"My prince," they said.

"Welcome to the gardens, forgive my unorthodox arrival, but when I saw two decorated star fighters on the palace gardens, I had to come and give my thanks to you and your ilk," he said extending his forearm, which they were more than happy to take. He was jealous of their strength when they squeezed his arm, their assurance and utter faith in the Crown, Empire, and him. They took orders from one voice, not a dozen that always whispered in Ahn'kat's ear.

"Please accept my apologies, praetors, but I need to steal your adoring fan for a moment," she said with a wink and a smile.

"Of course-" one praetor said before Ramkes wove her arm around Ahn'kat's and pulled him away from company.

"I assume you wanted to see me immediately," she whispered as she watched the soldiers walking around the gardens.

Ahn'kat sighed. "That was my first thought, but when I saw those two, I rather their conversation-"

Her elbow sharply nudged into his side. "You only get this weird when something has fallen apart."

"It has, Ramkes. I managed to stave off the feud between the former-pet factions, but I promised more resources to the reformation centres, only to find out the Conclave has denied opening their vaults to us," he said.

"Factions...that's what off-worlders have – we only have Empire," Ramkes' teeth grazed against her lip. "The priests are punishing the Crown for arresting Seratut."

"That's my thinking, but we can only focus on one problem at a time," he said as his eyes drifted over the neat rainforest field filled with golden robots trampling over the fine soft grass. "If the Crown can afford this, then we can afford to placate the reformation centres."

Her exhale was deep and long; he caught a whiff of sweet rose bread on her breath. "The Corps is telling us more troubling news brewing on Farayah. They've developed a new sensory satellite to observe Arinu astral travellers spreading across space, I hear their astral forms can deal equal psychic damage, not just in-person."

New sensory satellites were likely Ismotaph's clever cover for his psychic vanguard. Even then, they were probably right in what they were seeing there. "So, these new soldiers aren't just pretty garden decorations."

Ramkes' face turned up to his as her black lips pursed. "I think we may need to cease progress with the reformation centres, Ahn'kat, I'm sorry."

"We can't make people become pets again, it will be bedlam," he said.

"No, but we will have to stop helping them, for now" she said.

"How long is for now? To a pet, that may feel like several centuries," he said through gritted teeth.

"If this war is coming, it may take centuries to win," she said.

He shook his head. He didn't need any more of this. "Win? They're Arinu, Ramkes."

Her eyes widened; glints of fear poked through. It was the first time he saw how truly afraid she was of the future. "We are adapting, Neobatri has developed into a mind-bender, surely the Corps have several other members who have adopted similar abilities."

"I hope so," he said as his eyes drifted to the endless emerald horizon; he could feel faint drops of water spitting on his nose and brow. "Admit me as a star commander,"

"You can't be serious-" she said.

"Put me through the training, I've been playing simulators my whole life and understand how delicate things are out there," he said.

"Playing Takush is your simulator? Do you have any idea how ludicrous that is? You are consort to the heir, your position at the palace is infinitely more important than being on a warship!" she said frowning.

"If we need a miracle for the Empire to rally behind us, then once again, use me to give them inspiration," he said squeezing her arm to hold her from pulling away, "Ramkes, what better message does it send to the imperium that the Crown is willing to be there when hell meets us. They're losing trust in us, and we can show them that we're still here and worth every bit of their love and hope."

She closed her eyes; her thick lashes barely covered a sliver of tears on the edge of her cheek. "That's very brave, Ahn'kat, but sometimes the hardest thing to do is remain at your post."

"How can you be sure there will be a post when we finally break and be exposed to the universe as prey?" he said as he found her cold hands. "Let me try."

She haggard a breath before breaking into a chuckle. "You're being a fool."

"Finally, a 'yes' after a whole day of 'no's," he grinned.

"But only in title, your position is to remain here unless your presence at a rallying battle is absolutely needed. Besides, this will only happen if the emperor wills it," she said.

"Deal. What do you think he will say?" he said.

She shook her head. "I don't know, but he is open to making risks. We all need to do whatever is needed to preserve Zanashj."

Ahn'kat paused and thought for a moment at what she said. If House Urbaz, Ismotaph and that damnable Seratut had waited a few more years instead of acting on impulse against the Crown, then the Empire would have faced the Arinu threat together. He sighed as he looked up to the spreading night.

~

He sent a message to Ismotaph about Seratut's possible secret caches an hour ago yet heard no reply. He paced around the gardens with the imperial guard at his hem as he wandered over to the training grounds to watch those physically adept to test their mettle. He pressed his worries away, knowing the elusive Corps Director will give him an assured answer. Ahn'kat started making a silent prayer for discovering the caches but stopped when he considered Aszelun would disregard him again.

"Your grace, the trainees are ready to meet you," said one of the golden guards striding over between the curly ferns.

The prince stopped and nodded. "I had hoped that they wouldn't stop while I visited."

The guard removed his hawk helm and tucked it under his arm. "They will continue if you say the word, your grace."

"Well then, let's continue," Ahn'kat said as he brushed against the ferns passed the guard.

He and his guards strode to the grounds; he could see it littered with an impressive collection of weapons hanging on walls, pillars, and leaning against ramps along the outdoor classrooms and small sparring arenas. The trainers and trainees lined attentively when he walked through them. The faces of the gods were etched in the wooden pillars; Ahn'kat spotted an electric staff being held in the beak of the Hawk God. He smiled when he strode over to it and gripped the stick before gently tugging it out from its mouth.

"An improved version of the kenesi sceptre," said one of the teachers stepping over to him with a small bow.

Ahn'kat gripped it with both arms and spun it around his side; the guards and others took a step back, giving him space to play with it. With every swing, he could feel electricity brewing through the stick, if he swung it around a little more and pressed one of the ends into something, it would pour all its charged power into them – vaporising the enemy. He slowed his swings and held it tight in front of him as he looked at the ornate piece. "This is art, a shame it's used for defence."

"All Zanashj craftsmen are artists, your grace," the trainer said.

Ahn'kat placed the staff back into the Hawk's mouth and looked across the attentive trainees. His eye spotted the tallest on in the flock; Gajoon's stare looked to the vacant space in front of her, but he could sense she was excited to see him again.

"I'm eager to begin training here, Centurion Yaotat," he said.

Yaotat nodded. "We will provide common and basic physical training before you're admitted into astra-tactical courses, your grace."

"Who are you calling 'common?'" Ahn'kat said holding a smirk.

The trainer's lips quivered into a grin. "There are no commoners and nobles here, your grace, let alone princes. Here, we're only the arms of the Urasan Armada."

"Good," Ahn'kat said as he stared at Gajoon, goading her to break her discipline and look to him. To his admiration, she was steadfast.

"We cannot express how great your joining means to us, your grace," Yaotat said.

"We need everyone, Centurion," Ahn'kat nodded. "How does Trainee Gajoon bode?"

Yaotat shifted uncomfortably. "She is strong…"

"But?"

"Gajoon struggles to adapt to new environments, so we have delegated her unique skills to be a charger and barricader," he said.

"I would like to speak with Trainee Gajoon, the rest of your trainees are free to continue with their regiment."

The trainer bowed and turned to Gajoon, summoning her over. The crowd dispersed orderly, yet Gajoon failed to control the joy in her skips when she locked eyes with Ahn'kat. She stopped firmly and bowed low. "Yer grace."

"Rise, Gajoon, this is a casual visit," he said.

"Hay ya heard from Neobatri?" she said.

He sighed as his head shook. "She is in deep. The last thing I heard was she found a way to secure a position as a guardian."

"She bends," Gajoon said.

"Mm," he said as he looked at her new clean training tunic and leggings. She didn't wear battle-sandals, barring some bandages wrapped around her foot arches, letting her sharp clawed feet grip the ground. "How are you doing here?"

"Centarian Yaotat hard, I'm used to hard, but he make everyone work hard. He said my words are broke, he says I need to learn better. So, well," she said glancing around the barracks.

"Maybe we can be bunk-mates when my training begins," he smiled.

Gajoon's grin showed her pointed yellow teeth. "Youngers are suppose to give respect to olders in trainings."

"You'll make a fine team leader for the new initiates, Gajoon," his wrist phone vibrated, and his heart almost stopped. This was the first time he eagerly waited a reply from Ismotaph, or even better: Zertun and Emestasun. His eyes scanned over the message:

'Perched beneath the sands of the underworld,' it said. Sekem Bay, Ahn'kat thought. His stomach tightened, realising he needed to face Taskmaster Meksonett soon, if Ismotaph was there, then maybe he could provide some comfort.

"I need to leave, but if you need anything," his fingernail tapped the black glass bracelet, "I'm here."

"Yer grace," she bowed.

He smiled before taking off to the balcony where his vehicle sat; his imperial guard was surprised that Ahn'kat immediately took the passenger seat instead of the driver's. "Your grace doesn't wish to fly today?"

Ahn'kat shook his head. "Nerves are getting the better of me about training."

As the machine purred to life, Ahn'kat quickly looked through his logged messages from Emestasun and Zertun. He had received no reply from them in a long time. His nostrils flared as he tried again, not expecting to receive anything in this moment, but maybe they were too busy psychically battling his parents. His gut pained, with no help from the vehicle turning – the uncertainty was killing him.

Perhaps they were unsure of their wrist phone's security, he reasoned. His wrist phone was a digital fortress since Zertun's technician updated it, but Emestasun's may still be open to unwanted eyes. There was only one other place he could think of that could hold clues to his dearest friends' situation. He opened his game of Takush; he pressed his sapphire pendant to his lips – instinctively praying to see something from her.

He saw his small space units remaining in place, his base was untouched, and there were no new messages in his inbox. Ahn'kat scrolled to Emestasun's base, maybe she wrote something on her territory's grounds for him. He dropped his pendant from his lips: her base was vacant, barring a few fighter units roaming the hollow permitter. His eyes closed as he dropped to the pillow of his chair. He looked through her logs to see when she was last active, but not in months.

He felt sick, he lent forward as he gripped his chest. His guards looked to him with concern. "Prince Ahn'kat, are you alright?"

A thin sheen of sweat dotted his brow as he forced himself to nod. "It's just nerves."

"Shall we go to the healer's house?"

"No, keep going to Sekem," he ordered.

The vehicle slowed over the dunes and dropped through the phased surface. The cool subterranean air stopped his sweat and helped him catch a breath to regain himself. The guards were the first to exit before helping him out of the machine. A guard of the base pressed the scanner disk to his wet brow; his eyes were fixed with worry before returning to their stoic form. "Welcome back to Sekem, Prince Ahn'kat," he said.

"Taskmaster Meksonett," he glanced around the reception chamber, but she was missing from the group. "She knew I was coming."

"The taskmaster is in her office, please follow, your grace," the guard said walking ahead.

The air in the ship bay was heavier than he remembered, heavier than when he saw those poor dead Arinu in the tanks. What could possibly have happened here worse than that? He thought. Ahn'kat's eyes fixed to the back of the guard's head, maybe he was Ismotaph, but the man never turned or made any suggestion to send a discrete message. The prince's eyes wandered around the bay; surely, there were fewer and fewer workers than there were before. His gut dropped and the sickness at the back of his throat returned.

The guard slowed as he came to the organic sliding doors of the taskmaster's office; his fingertip caressed the edge of the door's spine before it quivered open. Ismotaph was already in there, his wild eyes shot up to Ahn'kat. "Come in, quickly!"

Ahn'kat heeded the guards to stay outside the office before he stepped in. Meksonett's work chamber was a mess, papers and devices strewn across the floors, desk, and cases, it looked like there was a struggle – or someone was looking for something.

"What in the gods is going on?" he said.

Ismotaph lent forward over her messy desk; his fists holding him up as his throat swallowed. "You asked me to find Seratut's caches, oh, did I find them."

Ahn'kat shook his head. "Speak to me straight."

"I didn't realise how difficult it was to find that fool's wealth, he was hiding it in small amounts everywhere! Including here," his finger pressed against the desk so aggressively, Ahn'kat could see the infiltrator's digit curving to the point of dislocating. "But I found so, so much more."

"Where is Meksonett?" Ahn'kat said as his heart raced.

"She is with my inquisitors, now," he breathed.

Ahn'kat's mouth peeled open. "Has she been bribed?"

"Her loyalties had been compromised; my inquisitors…recovered information from her, she had been accepting Seratut's wealth and assets under condition that she continues to send people to the Unbound Roctarous – despite your orders. He was hoping to destroy us if he was arrested as part of his vengeance, but we caught him on time!" he said.

Ahn'kat shook his head as he rubbed eyes. He couldn't believe this. It was a mess, but it wasn't out of character for the disgraced priest. "Stop for a moment. How could Meksonett keep sending our people to those alien wretches? She had no direct contact with-" Ahn'kat's heart was ready to explode. "My parents."

Ismotaph straightened his back. "My Intel Corps knew they have been buzzing around for a long time. We struggled to keep them away without alerting the Crown's private scanners of their presence. We've been too busy trying to keep our noses clean while trying to figure out how many and where our people have been taken."

His dry mouth opened, forcing his voice not to crack in front of Ismotaph. "And where...where...who?"

"Nearly all of them have come from House Urbaz dominions, even the family mansion," Ismotaph said.

Tears slowly began stinging his eyes, Ahn'kat desperately tried sucking them down as he looked to the dark ceiling, begging his worst fears were not true.

Ismotaph swung around the desk and gripped Ahn'kat's wrists. "Listen to me, do not go to Urbaz mansion, my sources have evacuated that soulless place. They say the only people who are left there are Lord and Lady Urbaz-"

"Stop!" Ahn'kat cried as he yanked his wrists from Ismotaph's grasp, but the Corps Director kept grabbing at the prince.

"Calm-" Ismotaph hushed, but Ahn'kat pulled his arms free and flung a fist at the man's face, dropping him onto the desk before sliding to the ground.

The grief and rage swallowed him whole as Ahn'kat grabbed Ismotaph's fine dark robe and yanked him up to the desk, pressing all his might into his shoulders and chest. "You're lying," he quivered as a tear dropped from his eyelashes.

"You know I'm not," Ismotaph's terrified face looked up to him.

Ahn'kat let go and pulled himself away from Ismotaph. The prince wandered around aimlessly in the tiny office room; he let himself fall against the nearest bookshelf. An animalistic roar escaped his throat as he tossed the piece from the wall hinges and stomped on the wood, puncturing a foot-sized hole in it.

"I'm sorry, I'm sorry," Ismotaph croaked as he walked towards the devastated prince.

The office door exploded from its frame as two guards stormed through, one dashing into Ismotaph and one bounding to Ahn'kat. "Your grace has been attacked?"

Ahn'kat wildly shook his head as he watched Ismotaph forced down on his knees with the guard twisting his arms back behind his head. "Let him go, I wasn't attacked – we just had an unfortunate conversation," he said.

The guards looked to each other. "Shall we have him arrested?"

Ahn'kat glared at the guard. "Let him go, now."

They did as bided and stepped back.

"Get out, all of you," Ahn'kat said keeping his eyes to the guards and other workers who clambered around the gaping hole in Meksonett's office. "None of you are to repeat anything discussed here, or I will take the ears and tongues of those who disobey. And I want all workers to kept clear from this hall!"

The guards bowed and formed a wall with their backs turned to Ismotaph and Ahn'kat. The two men stared at each other, but the prince closed in on the shaken director. "Tell me Emestasun and Zertun have gotten out and you've secreted them away somewhere."

Ismotaph blinked before slowly shaking his head. "Your parents have become too strong and unpredictable."

"So, you just left them there-" Ahn'kat breathed.

"It was too late by the time we clued in what was going on. None of my infiltrators are the same after we got them out! They've been sleep deprived for weeks, they lost their senses and say their dreams have been messed with-"

"I'm going to see my parents right now," Ahn'kat said taking a step back.

"If you go, now, no one in the Empire could save you! They may not even recognise you as their son." Ismotaph begged.

Ahn'kat's body trembled. His eyes caught the blue reflection of his pendant; his shaky hand gripped around the sapphire beetle. He always thought if the Empire couldn't protect him, then the Great Beetle could. Everything that has happened has made him stumble in a worse situation, and where was Aszelun? Where is his totem? The gods were as silent as the room he stood in. Ahn'kat took another glance to Ismotaph.

"I want them gone, I want them blamed, I want them forgotten." he said before ripping the pendant from his neck.

Chapter Twenty-nine
Shshmrnashsh X: An
Alternative Solution

The lights beat through the tubes, the plum organic membrane crawled around the synthetic piece, crunching away at the metal, and replacing it more with itself. It was everywhere, inside everything, wriggling all the way into her core. It had been many months since the graft; the feelings of independence were still alien, and her new body was stranger still. To her fortune, she found solace in Voo-san and Vern. She was still dependant, in a way, but with the Unbound: not forever.

Her mind split from her body, something she had known for millennia, but never could do herself. Voo-san said the Arinu call it astral travelling. Shshmrnashsh could slide out of her vessel whenever she pleased when she was linked, but never so free like this. Watching her regenerating form nourishing inside the pod, her fleshy face twitch and the thick strips of muscle wrapped around her limbs contract. In between the cracks, she could still see tubules and tiny metallic plates moving as they were slowly enveloped by the grafts.

Her eyes cracked open and the light in her third eye waned. The astral separation was lingering close to exhaustion. She snapped back into her body and leant forth with a start. Blood rushed into her limbs, heating her up as she peeled away from the pod. Voo-san and Vern leaned over a panel; their eyes locked as their minds were in deep conversation. When she approached, Voo-san's eyes were narrowed and frustrated before pulling away and catching her presence.

"Shshmrnashsh, your arrival is timely. The probes detected several bands of free Roctarous lingering around these nexuses," Voo-san waved his hand over the holo-map of the targeted areas.

"These numbers are amassing, is it because of the recent probe planting?" she said peering at the specks of the pyramids. About half remained dormant, but the few vacant and readily repairable nexuses were slowly returning to life.

"Yes, our numbers are still limited and dangers too vast for our units, but the probes have planted the Unbound organic seed. By the time we arrive, our workload will be vastly reduced," he said.

"They're naturally drawn to the nexuses," Vern said.

"Because of the activity," Voo-san said taking a stern glance at Vern. "Of course, this poses some dangers to the budding nexuses, the more power it produces, the more units will be drawn out of desperation."

"Can you not summon them here?" she said.

"They won't make the trip from Nexus 4N21 and we can't assume they won't try to wrangle our probes," Vern poked their index through the round light map. "These bunches are in a network. We've gleamed they're attempting to break into their local nexus. We've tried warding them off, but we don't want the group to scatter and since they're right there..."

"This is the largest group the Unbound encountered since Hrrnm's consortium. I've felt they don't pose any aggressive or dangerous tendencies, so one can assume they have been linked since the Blackout. We can introduce ourselves," Voo-san said.

"Having said that, they do have some augmented weapons. I suggest we loosen their network's hold and increase their hesitation to strike us before we make contact," Vern said as they straightened from the panel. "And we will soon need to populate these nexuses."

"Bring extra batteries and power kits to show friendly intentions," Voo-san said before turning to her. "How do you feel about contacting them with Vern?"

"I'm sceptical since last time," she said.

Voo-san smiled as he placed his calming hand on her shoulder. "Be patient with them, Shshmrnashsh. Let them come to you."

She returned the smile with a nod before following Vern down the chamber to the teleporters.

How do your psionics feel? They said.

Our training has improved them. I feel like I'm riding waves of the Unbound's consciousness, I can't sculpt it, but I'm buoyant. She said before glancing at them. *That's a poor description.*

I can validate those feelings with my own. Vern said as they made way into the alcove and ported to the local ship bay. *Voo-san's assessment on their hostility is mostly based on hope. These units have been scavenging for several years, it's folly to assume they won't immediately want to disable us and take our parts.*

Voo-san was an Arinu, he can see into the truth of things. She said following them up the walkways in the vast chamber.

Yes, but even they can be blinded by their ego. Vern said, stopping before a freshly powered skiff and opening a holo-readout of the ship's computer. *Roctarous have no ego.*

Which do you consider yourself? She said as she summoned a probe by the skiff and channelled the requested power packs and batteries from the bay's stores into the skiff.

Both. Neither. Vern said as they watched the sheen blue light sucked in from the face of the probe before beaming it into the craft. *Perhaps add weapons.*

She glanced at Vern, reluctant to add the items, but neither of them fully knew what awaited out there. *I suggest we linger around the nexus, let them make their intentions known at a safe distance.*

Agreed. Vern said as the beam retracted, and the ship trembled with life. *What concerns me is how strong their link is, their ability to override each other effortlessly. Voo-san has never been in a network before, neither have I, but you have.*

Shshmrnashsh cocked her head. *Yes?*

Tell me, how likely are they to self-destruct like with Hrrnm? Vern said.

She shook her head. *Hrrnm was decaying and became possessive of the consortium. They were unique.*

These units have been roaming and were forced to survive for an extended time. They have changed for the better and maybe the worse.

Vern shook their head and eyes squeezed shut. *I don't ever want a repeat of that consortium.* They mumbled.

Agreed. She said before dematerialising into the ship with Vern following closely behind.

The skiff pulled away from the platform and took off up to the thinly opened doors of the bay, out into the heavy air. As they soared across the chaos-touched land, Shshmrnashsh mulled over what Vern said. That tragedy should never be repeated, this was true, but what could more they have done? Forced those units to submit, even if it was for their own sake? That was the way of the High Mind and Neavensoros, not the Unbound. Vern should understand this – they must.

The skiff edged to District 4N21, the pyramid firm and grand in the centre with a dim golden light on its peak. The ship made no attempt at hiding as they flew in circles. Their sensors spiked at movement near the dark building perimeter, and with her improved psionics, she could detect forty-eight eyes upon them.

They watched, though a general unease spread around them. Some wanted to recluse to the shadows, but the longer they watched the slowing skiff, they remained. She and Vern circled around and descended beside the base of the nexus, still within visual, but far enough from firing range. The network lined up. Shshmrnashsh spotted several absurdly large shoulder pistols and arm shield generators. She realised that some of them were defence systems from skiffs, hence their size, and each unit had exposed heavy batteries wrapped around their torsos – all of which were waning.

The two paused, sensing the unease running high, but no aggressive actions were taken. She readied to materialise outside the craft, but Vern stopped her. *Wait.*

They're making no hostile moves, Vern. We must approach before they scatter.

The big one. They said, zooming the skiff's camera to tall and heavy dark grey unit amongst them. There was an E.M.P strapped to their chest, among other weapons the others had.

E.M.Ps pose no danger to us, least of all you. We should-

The skiff alerted they were being scanned. An expected reaction, but as they stared at the large unit, there was a sense of malice. Two smaller units stepped forward; their arms raised in the air as they steadily approached.

"Identify!" they called.

She materialised from the skiff; her feet pressed against the cold floor as her back straightened. The units froze, their eyes were scanning every inch of her. "Shshmrnashsh the Unbound and of the Unbound."

"Link us to your consortium," one said.

A humming grind came, and Vern appeared beside her. "The Unbound are not a consortium. We are a group of liberated Roctarous."

Silence fell on the field, but she could feel their network sparking. "We come in peace," she said.

Another wave of scans beamed through her and Vern. "You're unlinked, but disconnection corruption has not affected either of you. Explain," said the small unit.

"The organic implants prevent corruption-"

"And possession from the Higher Minds!" Vern said.

"We maintain ourselves until the Higher Minds return to re-establish the High Mind, any deviation of that protocol is considered a threat," they said.

Their network was buzzing; her and Vern's nerves rose with theirs. "The High Mind is no more and the Neavensoros are gone. The Unbound offer freedom of choice for units – we don't expect you to share our objectives, just an opportunity to live!" she said.

"Your power supplies are low. Observe an example of the Unbound," Vern said before summoning the extra batteries and packs in a neat pile between them and the small group. "Take them and leave, if you choose to do so."

The heavy unit stormed forward and inspected the items before piercing their interfacers into the packs. The others quickly followed and dove in, grabbing at the batteries and plugging them into their waning bodies.

What readings are you receiving from them? Vern said.

Their bond is unusually strong for a small squad. They should have shown some deterioration by now. Shsh said, as her mind drifted around their network, careful not to bump into their consciousness to illicit aggression. There was clever augmentation to their synthetic brains. To the centre of the group, a unit fitted with extra interfacers and more cranial capacity, acting as a moving plexus adjunct, and there was ongoing tele-repairing between them to resist disconnection decay. Despite this, their energy was solely reserved for survival, therefore, violence may have been a common solution for this band of survivors.

I read that, too. Their bond is alarmingly strong without a traditional plexus. Vern said within their mind. "The unique system you've constructed for your network is impressive."

There was an edge to Vern's thoughts that caught her attention, but before she could dive deeper, they had tucked it away. When she pressed, it was a mix of curiosity, concern, and calculation.

"Do you have permanent residence?" Shsh said to the group.

The units glanced at each other but kept at picking the supplies.

"If you did, then you wouldn't be attempting to enter the nexus," Vern said stepping several feet toward the sealed doors, while the network watched. "One of our probes are in there activating the plexus. We have no units in this region to maintain this nexus and reactivate the district."

"The equipment in there is undamaged, the astral-forges just need to be activated," she said before giving Vern an affirming glance. "You don't need to struggle."

"We agree, but we only want to inspect it before...deciding," the heavy unit droned.

"You're free to investigate it for yourself," Vern said. Their eyes closed and nodded to the building; the great doors groaned as they split, revealing the empty lower chamber within.

Shshmrnashsh peeked in, there were several old units strewn across the ground with a thin sheen of dust over their dark bodies. Vern strode in before beckoning the rest to follow. Her feet kicked up some fine ash as she stepped over the fallen; her eyes locked to the hall. Behind her, the squad carefully edged in; shields were enveloping their bodies as they scanned the area. Vern skipped up the inner mezzanine to the plexus. A probe enveloped the tip of the diamond; fleshy membrane and tendrils crawled around the piece, extending to upper and lower connecting tubes, slowly transforming the structure.

"The Unbound have mastered organic manipulation. Fusing synthetic and organic to a superior hybrid. This plexus now has greater control over the nexus and its surrounding territory, less susceptible to corruption and greater reach to Roctarous," Vern said with a glint of a smile as their eyes wandered over the group. "And we don't need to be linked to interface with it."

The squad looked to each other before meeting their gaze with Vern. She could feel their unease growing, their bond tensing as they stared at the power coursing through the building.

Vern, they are becoming unpredictable. We need to remove them from the nexus. She whispered, readying to summon the skiff to port the band far away.

No, we can save them. Vern said as their hand pressed against the twitching surface. "What you're experiencing right now is typical for linked units when encountering a fused plexus, and because of your reinforced net, its acting against you. Disengage temporarily to sync with it!"

"N-n-negative, cannot break-" croaked the heavy unit. The shield generator in its forearms sparked as the others wobbled before thumping to the ground.

She and Vern looked to each other. *They're overloading! We need to break their network.* They said.

Agreed.

The pair's minds slipped away from their bodies and entangling with the stressed network. They pulled and hacked away at their invisible hooks, slicing them thin enough for the units to regain control over their bodies.

The sparks from the heavy unit dulled as their eyes eased before straightening. "Murmur."

Shshmrnashsh retracted back into her astra-steel skull, relieved they were spared. "Your connection still exists, but you're able to remain here indefinitely."

"Negative...my mind is own!" the heavy unit's face was light as they looked to Vern. The other units stilled, some even ran their fingers along their faces and interfacers. "We can disconnect at will...at will! We are not bound."

Shshmrnashsh's eyes narrowed as she watched the elated units. She wanted to share their relief and joy, but their sudden acceptance and level of acuity of individualism was illogical. They were powerfully bound, like she was once. Yet, her former status as a vessel allowed her some speedier acceptance of persona. This was illogical, or perhaps hubris on her part, she wondered. She glanced to Vern once more; their hand patted the flesh plexus as they flashed her a grin.

~

That shouldn't have happened, she said, replaying the memory of Nexus 4N21. Standing by the plexus, her palm pressed against the beating heart and her mind swam through the sea of thoughts. When she closed her eyes, she could see the heavy unit and their former network milling about the inner chamber. Their interfacers were cut and tied back, new organic tissue was overlapping their shoulders and torso. Free?

Fresh recruits poured in from the replicators; their bodies were covered in improved organic grafts while they wore pristine faces going about their work. Shshmrnashsh's lips curled into a smile at them; they felt lighter. Even across Kra, the other nexuses were waking up. This feeling was like the High Mind, but there were no walls, only open fields. Her hands curled into fists as she watched her thick skin wrapping around her synthetic knuckles. So much energy sparked from each cell; they were flexible, durable and intuitive. After accessing the Archives, she learned the cell makeup was almost identical to Zanashj. She wondered who these cells belonged to, were they elderly or child? Slave or noble? Were they still alive or were the cells she now wore their surviving legacy?

The muscles in her neck stiffened at the thought. Peering in deeper, she could see fragments of Arinu in the genetic strands, identical to Voo-san's. Her fingertip pressed her third eye; it was warm and psionics passing through no longer stung. Three in one. Three new worlds of choices, and the Unbound swam in each of their seas. Were they choices? Did Vern know that the 4N21 network would react to the augmented plexus? Did Vern trick them and her? Not even her psionics could penetrate and dig into their mind for the truth if Vern was unwilling to tell. It was not her programming anymore, it wasn't the Unbound's – it should not be Vern's.

Voo-san would help her understand Vern. Where was he? She scoured the mindscape of Kra; the old Arinu stood in Nexus 000 before several groups. Uncertain of how sensitive Vern was to her thoughts, she homed into Voo-san's mind. She activated her dishonesty program, though this time, it was faster than ever before. *I seek counsel, the number of minds I feel is reminisce of the High Mind. I'm conflicted-*

Relax, Shsh. Come and join our meditations. He said.

Roctarous do not meditate.

You will once you start.

She pulled away from the plexus and sped to the teleporters. The unease made the tensing muscles in her torso crawl up to her chest. This feeling replayed the memory of Hrrnm, the hiding and scheming, the total isolation. She almost fumbled for the core 000 District's coordinates before stepping on the pad. There was a flash of burning light and she was facing the living inner chambers of the main nexus. There's a high chance these feelings were unfounded and a mere reaction to her body adapting to the new grafts. The fresh and uncontrolled emotions, the hormones and power expressing through her form were responsible for her unease, she told herself as she turned past one corridor and then another.

Voo-san sat crossed-legged in mid-air before a large squad of Unbound channelers and recently grafted recruits. Even through closed eyes, she could still feel his gaze. She found a spot outside of the circle; her legs bent as she carefully lowered herself to mimic the others; she caught the corner of Voo-san's lips curl.

Do you have a preferred method for meditation?

No, according to the Archives, there are thousands of different ways. She said.

I see. We'll use mine. I would tell you to take a deep breath, but-

Voo-san, time is of value-

Listen to me, Shsh. He chimed; his thoughts were melodic. *Your mind is spinning, so I would not advise you to empty it. In fact, let it run its course. Let all those small and big thoughts run and jump and climb and fall. Let them fall into the soup of consciousness and let it spiral down…down…*

Down. She said, feeling as if her mind slipped from her cortex and sunk into shadowed places of her consciousness.

It was dark, but not alarming. The shadowy curtains were soft walls, protective and private. She saw Voo-san's image slip in, but his body seemed younger and void of its synthetic replacements. As he once was.

Good, we're deep enough. His knowing words made her fearful. *You're here to tell me about my son.*

The network we encountered in 4N21, Vern and I struggled to convince them to join us, I calculated they were going to leave, and considering our goals, they wouldn't have posed a threat nor were they going to degenerate. But it wasn't until Vern exposed them to the Unbound's plexus when everything changed.

Vern knew what would happen. Voo-san nodded and paced around the dark mindscape. *And then what happened?*

Once we realised what was occurring, we were forced to break their link. Then...I cannot find the data to explain, but they suddenly changed. The concept of individuality and autonomy came to them as easily as interfacing with a machine. As if a new program was embedded in their code once they were freed. She said.

Voo-san's hands roughly rubbed over his face. *If it wasn't for Vern, we wouldn't have spread around Kra in the time that we did. He is a better being than what I was, but he has that demon. I was so hoping my Vern would be spared...*

I don't understand.

There's a shadow that thrives under the light of the Arinu. We've always been aware of it, but its taboo. I didn't understand it until I came to the Roctarous and read the Archives. He said.

In Vern's case?

He is using mental domination. An offence to Arinu and the Unbound. I knew his psionics was potent, but I had hoped he would turn away from that ability.

Does Vern not understand the Unbound's principals? She said.

Of course, but I fear that he is serving a different goal.

Which?

Voo-san shook his head. *I don't know. It seems defending our freedoms became offensive to Vern. Have you felt his influence?*

I can't tell, my grafts have fogged my sense of self. She said.

I had hoped you didn't accept those things after everything I know now! Organics maybe difficult for Neavensoros to possess, but their minds create an effective chaotic cover to hide that they are being manipulated.

Her hands tensed into fists as she looked down at her living form. The dread was almost paralytic, but she was safe inside these walls, strengthening her hold over her new self. *How can we stop them from proceeding with their goals?*

I don't know, Shsh, I'm afraid. Voo-san said as pain radiated from his body.

Voo-san, we need to maintain resolve! Vern is no more lost than I was before I arrived. You are a decent being and we can find a solution.

He nodded as his arms cradled around his shoulders. *Yes, a solution...be vigilant of your thoughts and emotions, the fine tunings of domination is far less noticeable over time. By the time you realise you're under their sway, it's too late.*

Are you under Vern's influence?

*Remember, I was Arinu...*Voo-san said glancing at his imaginary pearly white palms. *...but Vern is my son.*

Shshmrnashsh heard the tap against her surface mind. Vern's mental knuckles gently grazing against the dome made her freeze. Voo-san slipped away; his presence voided from her consciousness. She hardened herself as she rose from her inner sanctum before her eyes opened to the nexus. Voo-san sat undisturbed in the air beside other units as her mind connected to Vern.

I'm impressed you're meditating, I'm sorry have disturbed it. They said.

Don't be, doing nothing is for the deactivated or the sleeping. She said as she buried the conversation with Voo-san into the tiniest and deepest corner of her consciousness.

The influx of new recruits has stretched our grafters thin, and our replicators are struggling to make complete units until our energy systems are restored. Can you please meet me at Replicator Bay 000? They said.

Understood. She said rushing out of the chamber to the teleporters. Lies did not exist in the Roctarous, and dishonesty was inefficient. They were common for Organics; a thousand and thousand files recorded the psychological symptom across dozens of species, but Roctarous were only ever observers. However, they were observers no longer. She looked down at her warm implants as she stepped into the bright alcove before slipping away to the dark and damp bay.

Vern stood beside rows upon rows of organic tanks. A dozen Unbound wrapped flesh around resting units; light sparked from tiny lasers carefully cutting away old synthetic parts, twisting and yanking them from their sockets. New Unbound waited in lines to settle on the tables; their faces were peaceful, but the longer she stared at their eyes, she could see they were blank.

"Shsh," Vern called as they waved her over.

"Will I be grafting?"

"Yes, but I'll need to download that into you before," Vern said as their hand rose to her temple.

She looked at their fingers and lingered before pressing her head against their tips. She felt a wave of psionic energy filling her mind and embedding into her memories as she looked to their blue eyes. *All these new minds…it reminds me of the High Mind.*

I believe that. Is that why you feel so troubled? They said.

No and yes. There's no overt dominating force, but the connection runs deep and coils around us. She said.

Vern tightened their lips and nodded in a way that reminded her of Voo-san. No, no, hide this thought, she told herself.

Yes, the flaws of consciousness, that cannot be helped. However, its potent psychics that understand the web, and know how to manipulate it, can become a danger to all. They said as their hand pulled away from her temple. "Upload is complete."

She felt a flood of new knowledge in her memory core as she studied their stoic face. "Are psychics also a threat to us, too?"

Vern's eyes widened. "What do you mean?"

"The Neavensoros will not be able to possess us so readily, but Organics still can be controlled by potent psychics, and there are many species with these capabilities. Help me understand if your fight is for permanent liberation, then why make us more susceptible with flesh?" she said.

A smile cracked on the corner of their mouth, and they shook their head. "We won't be, at all. Come," they said, stepping beside a replication tank and patting the smooth surface. "In a few short months, we will be producing units blended with all the best aspects of Zanashj, Arinu and Roctarous. We won't need to graft any more units once the whole of Kra reactivates, we make a new species, right here. The Unbound's lifelong purpose will be fulfilled to create what the Neavensoros failed to do."

"The Neavensoros understood the failings of perfection. In the historical section of the Archives, they-"

"Yes, I had access to it and consumed every piece of knowledge before the Blackout. I know what they did, and I know how they solved it," Vern's angered gaze drifted to the machine. "We can not only succeed that legacy but start anew. Like you have."

She pressed her palms on the panel; her mind was worming through the computers as she glanced at them. "In that case, we will be fighting forever for our autonomy out of fear someone else will try to control us, but most Organics don't fight their whole lives, and I don't want to do that either."

"Not forever; just for now," they said.

Shshmrnashsh pressed her lips together, deciding if she wanted to plunder their secrecy. *Sazla used me as her carrier and discarded me, long before she abandoned the universe to its fate.*

She kept me informed just enough for immediate tasks, kept secrets from me to hide my true potential – nothing like the Unbound. Let me help you hasten this battle so all of us can know peace.

Vern's eyes hardened. *Are you saying you have no faith in us?*

I'm saying I have untapped potential. I was a vessel for a Neavensoros for hundreds of millennia, some of Sazla's power has been imprinted into me. She said.

I am so sorry you suffered under them. Their gaze travelled to the centre of her forehead. *We'll find another grafter. Please, come with me.*

Shshmrnashsh followed as they strode to the teleporters. She watched Vern squint at the panels, imprinting coordinates without touching the holo-keys. *Ship Bay 000?*

Yes, but we won't be flying, we're meeting someone there. Vern said as they stepped into the beam and vanished. Her stiffened back straightened before slipping in, tossing, and turning before being spat out into the fully organic vacuous bay.

Who are we meeting? She said as they bounded around every corridor and hall. It didn't take long for her to see a vast empty chamber with circular teleporter pads large enough to port several skiffs and probes. However, there was already something on one of the pads. A glassy black containment sphere, the size of an ancient Neavensoros skiff, hovered meters above the dark grey circle. Uneased by its presence and unwilling to approach, her psychic mind caressed the surface, hoping to read what was inside. She got nothing from it and there were no holo-markings, and it was too thick to be conventionally scanned. She turned to Vern. *What is this for?*

"I have a contact that exists beyond this plane. Lately, our connection is poor underneath the anti-phase shield – would you imagine," Vern met her eyes. "I may be an Arinu clone, but I don't have a relay to call them, like yours."

"Which plane are you attempting to contact? And who?"

"Plane PL62748 and we are going to meet a trader," they said with a shimmer of pale light shining in their irises.

Shshmrnashsh pulled through her records. "That plane is a no-contact zone; it's the domain of a Kepa."

"Yes, I know!" Vern said as they stepped around the sphere. "I downloaded everything about them just as the Unbound prepared for their arrival to Kra, but by the time we came, the shield was up. The Kepa has eons of hoard in its home-realm, technology stolen and kept as trophies that could have been the keys to progress our purpose. So, I reached out."

Shshmrnashsh caught herself from falling. "That was incredibly reckless. There is a valid reason why that plane is sectioned."

"These are unconventional times and new strategies need to be adopted," Vern said walking around the sphere before meeting her face again. "You bent many protocols and programs just to be standing here. Was that risk worth who you are, now?"

"I understand, Vern," she uncomfortably shifted at the argument. "If you are to contact a Kepa again, we need Voo-san and his channelers to act as barriers."

Vern pressed their palm against the sphere and leaned into it. "Arinu are afraid of Kepa. I can't trust that he won't find out from the channelers if we summoned them for this mission."

"But he could scan what we did from me."

They smiled. "You're a vessel with impressed power from Neavensoros, and in combination with our training, you can keep anyone away,"

Shshmrnashsh stared at the sphere as she took a step closer. "What's inside the sphere?"

"Something that Kepa cannot resist. I can already feel them stirring," Vern closed their eyes. "I know what the Archives say, any deals with Kepa cost more to you than what's agreed, but that was their dealings. I thought I could make it fair, but the Kepa failed at their end of the bargain."

"Since you failed before, you have no guarantee you will achieve this." she said.

"I'm stronger than when I made the first deal, Shsh."

She should immediately leave, she thought. She should just tell Voo-san and be done with this erratic plan, but Vern was young – only a handful of years old with an eon of knowledge from the Neavensoros. "What's the plan?"

"There are batteries that pour more power than what our active astral-forges can produce to reach to the next phase of the purpose. If we lure the Kepa to this," Vern tapped the sphere, "then I can take those batteries."

"It will be dangerous, the Kepa may acquire a scent for this plane."

"I can hold it back long enough," they said.

Shshmrnashsh knew this was a poor plan. No doubt Vern was capable for much – even to a level beyond her scope, but there is a reason why Neavensoros strengthened planar fabrics around that place.

"Please, let me correct my errors. Kra is only a fraction that it once was and we need it ready before the Arinu come," they said.

Shshmrnashsh didn't know if she believed Vern, but her ongoing refusal would lead to their suspicion of her motives – and she had to see for herself. She glanced to the nearest panel station and stepped to the black glassy top. The fleshy edges twitched as her hand waved over the surface, activating the holographic control map floating above. Vern smiled and nodded before stepping back from the pad.

Several rings rose from the centre, looping around the spherical space; light was growing brighter inside the curves as they spun faster. Silver cuts lined the inside of space; it wobbled as more light leaked through. The dark surface of the sphere was almost enveloped by the light as Vern took their place; their body hunched, arms extended and eyes narrowed, readying whatever was coming.

Ready your relay. They said.

Shshmrnashsh felt a heat needling through her third eye as her senses found the right planar frequency. Her psychic fingers pinched the oscillating waves before Vern pushed in. *Let's break through together.*

The two pressed and pressed, willing the sphere into the right vibration for it to slip away, but something poked through the cuts. She couldn't identify what it was, but Vern's glowing excitement struck her with fear. *The Kepa is just beyond the veil, advise extreme caution.*

It's close because it knows. Vern's eyes shone as light erupted from their fingers. *Just a little wider.*

The cut ripped as a burning teal light filled the entire centre; her inner lenses clasped around her eyes and third eye to shield her from the exposure. A bright shadow loomed inside; tendrils curled around the sphere as Vern's body lit up. She stared in awe as their aura burned greater than the exoplanar energy, but far less offensive to her senses. She could feel them reaching inside the plane; through gritted teeth, Vern groaned as they pressed around the entity.

Have you located what you need? She said as she watched the tendrils struggled pulling the sphere in.

Vern's eyes widened with terror. *They're not there!*

Shshmrnashsh separated from her body; her higher senses flew to the very edge of the rift. *I'll remote view with you-*

No! Stay back or your synapses will blow. They shouted in her mind.

She pulled away, but not completely. There was something lingering inside the plane; a sense of familiarity rose. Something or someone she knew. Before her attention focused in, Vern's psionics shouldered her aside and barrelled ahead. *Vern, don't go inside!*

I must find them. Vern called. She could feel them desperately rummaging within. *They're not there! They're stolen—*

There's someone else in there with the Kepa. She whispered, but something stole her focus. The tendrils whipped open the sphere, spilling its contents into the entity's home-realm. She could not compute what she saw; perhaps she didn't understand it yet, but mounds of tissue, bone and limb tumbling down, all Zanashj in composition. Then the whole bodies: small, large, old, young, all falling in the dark greasy mix. They fell so quickly; she couldn't scan for life signs. Perhaps there were none, to their fortune.

She snapped back in the moment the sphere fell in, but the Kepa wanted more. Her hands slammed on the control pads, killing the teleporter. The rings stopped circling and gracefully retracted into their ground slots before her mind begun to process the event. An outline of energy still lingered over Vern's body, but that shine fell away as their face collapsed, staring into the empty space.

"Vern?"

They said nothing as they turned around, pacing around the chamber. Their face was covered with their hands as they tried to wane the burning energy from their body.

"Are you damaged?"

They seized their pace. With their back still facing her, Vern slowly straightened their head and shoulders.

"Report, Vern!"

"I'm undamaged," they whispered.

"What occurred? Did we fail?" she said, studying them.

Vern spun around. "We most wonderfully failed."

Images of the Zanashj cascading into the sealed realm flickered through her mind's eye. Also, that familiar feeling of a close stranger inside there with the Kepa. "There were Zanashj in that container."

"Left over parts that we could've spared. I unfortunately learned that Kepa love adding valuable Organics to their collection."

"There were whole beings, too. You said Zanashj donated only discarded sheddings?" she said.

Vern was quiet as they rubbed their third eye. "They gave what they could. It's not the most pleasant circumstances, I know."

"Zanashj are autonomous, they wouldn't give up their lives willingly. The Unbound wouldn't align with that, even if they were another species!" she said.

"As I have explained, it was temporary and we've cut ties with the Empire," they said as their fingers pressed in their sore eyes. "You understand."

"Does Voo-san know?" the question slipped from her lips faster than she could stop her thoughts from winding to him.

Vern pulled their fingers from their eyes and stared at her. "He was there when we dealt with the imperialists."

She stepped around the workstation towards them. "These activities must never be repeated for the sake of the Unbound's credibility," she watched their jaw tightening. "I'm concerned for you."

"Be concerned for our mission," they said flatly.

She looked to the resealed space within the wide teleporter. "I could feel another mind near the Kepa. They may be trapped and may require assistance."

"No, we cannot risk a re-opening...we may require an alternative solution," Vern's eyes darted to hers, almost shocked they spoke aloud. Before she could probe their meaning, their head shook. "I felt them slip away before you stopped the operation, there's nothing we can do for them."

Chapter Thirty
Treneer X: Enter the Void

The Weatherweavers brushed the sky with heavy clouds, readying the land for the lightshow. All Yinray watched the heavens, excited for the lightening to come. The distant grey mist flickered with violet and marine light, then the deep gurgled roars of thunder. Eyes narrowed as peels of lightening crashed into the distant and barren mountain ridge; the swirling clouds centred and blew their fury into the stone, followed by the awe and chants of onlookers. The weavers channelled the strips of electricity into majestic shapes, some of the crackling lines looked like ancient symbols, while others looked like profiles of long-dead Elders.

Treneer tried to be taken by the spectacle like the others, but her mind replayed what Ouro was asking of her. She glanced to her kin watching from the spire balcony; their faces were lit with glee and pride at the power of the Arinu. They were in awe, but there was lust behind their eyes, a lust that only blood could sate.

There were familiar minds drawing close that broke her macabre thoughts. Treneer's head spun to see Yansoon and Delyn gliding through the crowd beside her. A part of her was relieved to see their faces but wondered if she could ask them for the impossible.

Look at that, Delyn. The Weatherweavers here are true artists! Yansoon said as her lips parted and eyes locked to the horizon.

Don't the Weatherweavers of the wester lands do shows like this? Treneer said.

Not even close, mere clearing up dangerous storms and adding rain to the dry patches. Yansoon said, never taking her stare from the show.

There's nothing like this on the Frostchain Isles, rather drab over there. Delyn said. Her usually calm face was softened as her eyes drifted along the ridge.

Must be something you miss from home, Delyn. Treneer said with a smirk.

She shook her head with a sigh. *The isles have their beauty for visitors, but they're so distant from the rest of the world, even too far for soul.*

Is your soul richer here? Treneer said.

Didn't believe it could be. A quiver of a smile cracked on the edge of Delyn's lip.

They watched until the red sun dipped, but the stars didn't peer over the city. Treneer's stomach growls aligned with the thunder. *I have a meal prepared for the two of you, there's something I'd like to discuss.*

I'm pleasantly surprised it's not another training session. Delyn said.

Treneer's lips curled as she glided back into the crystal spire with Yansoon and Delyn at her back. In the deepest corners of her mind, she tossed how she would ask for their help. They were the only trusted people for this task, and of course, Svar…but he drifted off into the stars.

They settled in her quarters as she quickly replicated three large bowls of hot and salted blended beans followed by some bubbling drinks to wash it down. She sipped from the edge of her cup as she watched them talk and share laughs.

It wasn't until you walked on to the training grounds when I realised, I no longer had the lowest psi-rating in the academy. I thank you, Delyn. Yansoon grinned.

If you insist on paying me flattery, I must pay you in return. There's a little game we play on the Isles, it's called shred-then-mend. Delyn said lifting her full cup over Yansoon's head. *Tear the cup's molecules, then put them back together as they were, and then drink the contents…if you can.*

Yansoon playfully sneered at Delyn and telekinetically gripped the cup. *That's nothing.*

As she carefully untwined the edges of the cup, Delyn waved her hand and compelled the liquid to splash all over Yansoon's scalp before roaring in laughter; even Treneer couldn't hold back a grin.

Why in the universe did you do that? Yansoon said wiping the liquid from her eyes.

Why didn't you bother asking why I had the cup over your head? Delyn said.

They giggled some more before meeting Treneer's eyes. *All well, Treneer?*

Swallowing down the last drop from her cup, she sighed. *Zu'leen has been on my mind. When she passed, the world I knew shrunk away to a realm of paths I didn't believe existed. I may walk on the path of grief for the next several thousand years, but I have found new love for you and others, still, I need to know why. I believed that pain would fade by distraction of duty, but I realised I have the choice to know why, and so I made it.*

Delyn and Yansoon exchanged glances as Delyn's shoulders arched and her hand gripped around the edges of her warm bowl. *What choice?*

Treneer pressed her elbows into her knees. *If you loved someone, and they were somewhere just beyond your reach, would you do anything in your power to touch them again?*

*I don't know, I have never loved someone that...*Delyn trailed off along with her stare into space. *Perhaps.*

A lost love can be a person or a place. Yansoon said as her finger trailed along her bottom lip.

*It seems that we all here have lost someone or thing...*Treneer straightened her back and smiled. *I have recently uncovered something about my teacher, I believe her death was a price and there is only one source that can help me find some semblance of peace. However, those that can are sealed in the Void.*

*You don't mean...*Yansoon's lip curled in disgust.

Treneer put her hands up. *I do mean astral dancers, because-*

Delyn shook her head. *Why can't you ask Elders or anyone else-*

Because it would dishonour Zu'leen's family if the Coven or Executors ever found out and it also may lead to where some of our people have gone. There are truths here that are begging to be unearthed and who knows how many more. Treneer said.

Delyn fingered her temples as her eyes squeezed shut. *This is how astral dancers start, Trenner. They start asking questions, going off for personal power-*

This is not about seeking power, Delyn! She thundered, even her aura pulsated. *We need to stop lying to ourselves that everything that's happening on Farayah is not personal. Our Oaths have kept us silent for duty, but that spilt into our lives. That Kepa was right, this world is broken, but we are too great to see it.*

What are you asking of us? Yansoon leaned in.

Ouro is a Void Warden, there's an astral dancer willing to open the way to the Kepa's realm, we need people to go in there. Treneer said.

If you are facing it in its own domain, then you'll need as much help as possible. She said with a soft smile. *Why has Ouro agreed to be part of this?*

This is beyond me. Delyn rose and readied to make way to the door. *Out of respect for you, I will not turn you into the Judicator, but I will play no part in this.*

Before you go, know this: Ouro has a greater reason to go after the Kepa more than I, his sister was taken by it. Treneer said. She watched Delyn freeze; her whole body clenched as she tried to force away a distant painful thought.

The guardian sighed as she glanced to her and Yansoon before shaking her head. *Do you believe that there's any chance of her being alive?*

Better for him knowing than never. Treneer said.

Delyn's brows rose as she took one long stare at Yansoon. *I will help you.*

~

The night was colder after the storm, but she didn't mind the calming and refreshing smell wafting through the open archway. Ouro was by his desk when he looked up and smiled. *Thank you for coming, I had no doubt in you. Did you bring...?*

They will be here shortly. Treneer glided from the alcove while keeping mental hold over her carrier case. She dropped it beside the floor cushions and several holographic images floated over the hexagon surface. An assortment of devices flickered into view; her eye travelled to a silver bracelet and opened her hand to reach for it. The device materialised in her fingers before she split the thin piece into two. She let them slide down and tighten around her wrists; she smiled as she willed energy forth from her fist into two sharp energy points. The psi-blades were ready, but for the Kepa to submit, something more was needed.

A holo-image of small clove-shaped device with a crystal embedded in the centre was a device that empowered the user's psionics. Though, she felt moderately confident in her reclaimed power, the Kepa may sense her doubt and use it against her. Her finger plucked it into the material plane and pressed the flat surface over her third eye. She immediately felt her astral lenses flaring; her mind was bombed with sights of farther planes, timelines and shadows that were once invisible to her. A quick recentring and she had returned to the here and now.

Light flashed in her periphery. Yansoon and Delyn appeared in the room. Heavy psi-armour draped around their bodies, and Yansoon's usual beaming face was greyed and filled with worry but managed to muster a reassuring smile to Ouro and Treneer. Delyn stiffened when her eyes travelled to the black portal to the corner of the room.

Thank you both for coming. Ouro said; already Treneer could feel his spirit rise. *I want to explain that my request was not an easy one, and I understand you risk everything being here. Even if we don't succeed, I will grant any request you may have in my power.*

We've faced Kepa before. Delyn said. She seemed confident, but it was fuelled by a mild perverse excitement for danger.

But never directly. You will be in their home-realm, where they are strongest. In their plane, both object and mind have tangibility, every piece of memory and knowledge will gain matter and Kepa will use it against us. Be prepared, it'll be a swamp in there. Ouro said.

Why can't we astrally travel in there? Or use a probe? Delyn said.

The energies will overwhelm a probe, and astral forms will be leaking thoughts everywhere they tread. Best for Kepa not know anyone was in there. He said.

I'll be covering you, but keep your thoughts and emotions under absolute control. Treneer said.

Yansoon's sigh was haggard as her lips winced. *The more you prepare me; the less I want to do this.*

Then let's make haste. Ouro whisked away to the dark portal; the hem of his cloak slipped into the black.

Treneer smiled before the three glided and fell into the Void Prism. The ever-long hall, whose floor and ceiling stretched beyond sight, already pressed against her mind. How Ouro could linger in a place like this, she wondered, but then this was the embodiment of his psyche. She glanced at her friend, who floated beside the freed astral dancer, and wondered whether this psychic prison would be any different to the Kepa's.

We're ready. She glided over, eyeing the summoner. A fresh new robe was draped around his body with a flowing hood over his head. Now, thicker flesh covered his tired bones, too. It seemed to her that Ouro's compassion was not abandoned, yet.

Let's begin the ritual in this cell, we'll be able to evacuate and potentially trap any Kepa if they decide to crawl out of the rift. Ouro's eyes pointed to the arch beside them.

It may not stay in the cell forever. Treneer said.

True, but at least they'll be locked away from Farayah. He said.

The five slipped into the decollate dark realm, barren of form and ideal for the ritual. There was a floor to at least stand on, Treneer noticed. Ouro and the dancer stepped forth; their arms extended out and levitated around, until a thin teal string sparked from their fingertips; their arms rose and channelled the rift. Treneer watched in awe at their seamless moves, they weren't simply wrenching open the planar fabric, they were untangling the tight strings that held them together. A surge of electricity and light crackled in the centre. It blinded Treneer for a moment before dropping a dampening field to absorb exoplanar leaks radiating out of the growing opening. A tingle of excitement rose along with her body naturally absorbing the astral energies; she felt strong and invincible. However, the Kepa bathed in such power...

We've reached its nest. The astral dancer said as his black hands held up the rift.

Scouting now. Treneer said as she extended her mind through. The mess was understated, seeing the meld of alien text and symbols strewn across this liquid-like plane, objects beyond her imagining blended into others as they crawled along the edges of others. To the distance, something was piled up into tall mountains, yet their base was narrower than their peak. A place of utter madness, she thought. No signs of any Kepa. As she turned back, her sense caught something that looked like an arm among the pile. Her stomach clenched as she homed in to see a clear shoulder and neck, but the rest of the torso was buried beneath. It was not an Arinu, they belonged to another species, but the poor soul met an unfortunate end.

No Kepa detected, but I found where we can begin our search. She said, falling back into her body. She tossed an illusion field over them, to blend with the background, but she wondered if there was any point – at least Delyn and Yansoon felt more at ease. The three floated forth. Treneer felt gentle pressure of Ouro's telekinetic reach pressing on her shoulder before they were sucked in.

This realm had no air, but her lungs didn't ache to breathe. They wandered around the alien terrain, careful not to disturb the space as she kept her eye for the thoughts and memories of Zu'leen floating in the ether. Inching closer to the mountain, Treneer spotted objects and off-worlder bodies disorderly piled; her heart ached when she saw some bald pearly heads among them. Arinu, all siphoned from energy as if someone drunk from a deep goblet and tossed it aside, but their bodies were paralysed and in awkward contortions, frozen for eternity from the moment of their untimely death.

Yansoon sped forth and stretched her hand over them. *This one has been here for a few months, but the others…some have been here for millennia.*

Most of the bodies here are fresh. Delyn said looking over the pile.

Treneer saw silver smoke rising from Delyn's and Yansoon's crowns, forming into thoughts over them. *Our thoughts are materialising, keep the communes minimal.* Keeping her panic sealed in her mental oubliette, Treneer dusted away the thoughts from the plane.

Yansoon drifted over the pile, while Delyn wandered around the edge, scanning for any living. To her periphery, Treneer saw Zu'leen's profile floating past and disappearing behind the pile. She rushed over, hoping to catch the memory, but her emotional rise coloured the space around her. She quickly sucked it back in, but by the time she turned back, Zu'leen had vanished again.

I found some alive. Delyn said as she wiped away the growing thought. Glassy egg-shaped tanks sat in the mound with still creatures drifting inside a clear teal liquid. They were alive and asleep, but none were Arinu.

Dig them out and bring them here. Ouro whispered.

I don't recognise some of these species. Treneer said.

We'll find out where their home is and bring them back after we're done. He pressed.

She carefully lifted the tanks from the pile; bodies and other strange objects showered down as each one was freed before sending them through the rift. It felt like an eternity passed as they rummaged through; there were some filled with young Arinu, that's when she felt Ouro's excitement ripple in. A horrible feeling wormed in her mind, these Arinu were ordered in a way to make them stand apart from the rest. As if the Kepa was intending to do something special with them.

A nude emerald body cascaded to Treneer's feet. She blinked and realised they were Zanashj. Her eyes darted around to see there were many Zanashj buried in this mass tomb. The Kepa had been collecting many beings over untold eons of its life, but the amount of Zanashj overshadowed the others by far.

She knew their population was significant, but were they even aware that so many of their kin were missing? If they weren't, then they had to be notified immediately. Their relations maybe strained, but their loved ones deserved to know what happened, she thought. Unless they did know and the Empire willingly forgot them...no, not even the Empire could be that callous.

As she stared at the body, she noticed a cut between their neck and shoulders; a strange oily substance leaked from the opening and dripped down their bust. Treneer lifted a drop with her mind and held it close to her eyes. Her heart pounded when the memory of that strange warrior that attacked her in the meadow all those years ago peaked in her mind. She hurried to slip into an empty data crystal before Yansoon chimed in.

These are all we could find. She said as her head poked out from a short pile.

None are Shimarr. Ouro whispered. *Focus on her and she may materialise.*

Treneer, Yansoon and Delyn linked; their thoughts synchronised and envisioned Shimarr. She tried to focus, but her mind fluttered to the black oil, then to Zu'leen, the chaos that followed Farayah; crackling light poured from her mind as her thoughts leaked. She tried rolling them back in, but the clouds were expanding too quickly. Panic rose when a distant gurgle echoed throughout the plane. Her head turned to a great piercing white aura rising over a mountain. She snapped back and pressed the illusion around them as this monstrous creature drifted around its home.

A dozen long and bony heads squished together on wide black shoulders with equally dozens of gangly arms as black as dead tree branches. Hundreds of fingers and toes extended and coiled as tentacles, lovingly brushing against every single object in its domain. Treneer's throat eased when its back turned and the creature slithered away. Delyn's and Yansoon's eyes were so wide, she was almost convinced they might fall out.

Their attention snapped to an Arinu body drifting up from the pile. Their undersuit was in tatters, their face was twisted in fear and have been dead for some time. Her heart sank when she realised it was a young female that strikingly looked like Ouro.

Treneer sensed Ouro's heart thumped so loudly, she could almost see waves rippling into the Kepa's realm. Her jaw tightened as she looked back to the portal. *Calm down-*

Bring her to me. He said.

Treneer slid Shimarr back, keeping her eye on the Kepa lurking about. The closer she drifted, the harder his emotions crashed through her and the others. *Ouro, stop. I can't keep the illusion up!*

The moment her body slid through, the mighty back swung around and the heads turned in all directions, their eyes darting around. Treneer, Yansoon and Delyn desperately tried wiping away their panic and Ouro's agony. The Kepa looked to their direction and began drifting closer. Another rift cracked open, and more bodies poured forth; the Kepa snapped to them and its tendrils wormed around their limbs and torsos. More Zanashj – many, many more.

When the last fell in, there was someone standing just beyond the opening. Treneer strained to see who or what brought these fresh new lives to this monster. The longer she stared, the longer she could feel there was a familiar mind behind the ethereal door. It was the same being who watched her astrally travelling, and to her horror, the being sensed her, too.

She thought it was another Zanashj, but their psionic power was overwhelming her the closer its head poked into the rift. The face from the stars, in full material form, was staring back at her. Fierce marine eyes and pale-peach face. At first, she thought from their smooth round head and third eye it was an Arinu, but the longer she stared, it had heavy and powerful muscles running along its lean body. Its haunting appearance reminded her of a skinless Arinu.

You. She and it said in unison.

Treneer! The Kepa-

Her eyes snapped to the monster; all dozen of its heads looked to her direction. Yansoon dashed in front; her aura flared, and her psi-blades whirled to life. Treneer flung a cord of energy towards her and Delyn, empowering them, caking them until the luminescence of their aura's overlapped their physical bodies. Despite their heightened potency in this bizarre realm, the Kepa was a glacier to their flakes.

Get out! Ouro screamed through their minds.

There are still some living here! Delyn said, staring at the pile of new bodies. She and Yansoon flew to the creature, extending their blades to long and fine rapiers, slashing and cutting at the monster's tendrils, trying to release the fresh captives. Their desperate pleas and fear rippled from their mouths and minds, taking shape into glassy needles before tossing them into the guardians. The tip cut through Treneer's aura; the crack grew and infected her mind with agony. Yansoon tumbled helplessly through the air, trying to shake it off before returning her focus. Delyn released a pained growl through her teeth as she pushed a cut through the Kepa's many wrists. The Zanashj tumbled down, scrambling to find some ground in the nigh-weightless realm, but their growing fears only bled out and transformed into more needles.

Treneer narrowed her eyes, telekinetic energy clamped around its body, holding it back for a few seconds. Relief washed over for moment, maybe she can siphon the memories of Zu'leen from its mind. Her mentor's profile floated out of her mind, but taking a brief glance at her was a mistake. Her head transformed into another needle and flew back at her temple. Her hold over the Kepa broke; she could barely see the blood floated aimlessly through the pain. She glanced back at the dark glacier, trying to lock onto a head and enter its thoughts, but everyone she pressed through and put to sleep, it would slither back into its fleshy mass and reform a new head and new brain – a new mind.

We can't fight it. Grab as many as we can and go! She called.

Yansoon and Delyn telekinetically grabbed for as many living beings as possible, including Zanashj, before flying back to the crackling portal. Treneer's palms burst with energy and fired at the encroaching beast, also holding as many captives as possible. Her mind latched onto all the gnarly heads and tried to hold it back for a little bit longer. Sweat bubbled on her skin as she thrust her hands forward to push it back, but despite how hard she tried, she realised it was simply toying with her.

Treneer looked to the mass of heads and screamed in its many minds. *What did you tell Zu'leen?*

The heavy arms lurched forward, gripping the Zanashj in her hold. **Thieves.**

Tell me of Zu'leen! She cried again, but her torso compressed and felt her body fall under the Kepa's spell. Panic flared as she looked to her comrades, equally fighting its control and the wild thoughts bubbling from their minds. Their wild, desperate faces battered, cut and maimed everything that leaked from them, but their fears only amplified with every new piece. They were terrified of their thoughts. A demon inside their minds…and in Treneer's. The Kepa was never going to tell her without giving something up. She looked at the Zanashj in her hold, maybe…no, no, she would not.

She looked back at the creature. *You have no right to these lives, Kepa!*

Promised. It howled so loudly in her mind that it almost split in her skull.

What's the name of that creature? Treneer pointed to the space where that other rift was.

Mine. It said lurching forward and yanking away a Zanashj from her grip.

Enough! She roared, her psionics pulsated and using every bit of her remaining energy, sliced through its many heads. The creature stopped its advance; she turned to the others. *Out!*

They hopped out of the rift, with a grip of the few survivors, they spun back into the barren void plane. Treneer stared into the rift; the creature's heads regrew, and their shining deathly eyes were on her.

She learnt the demons are waking. Learn on Kra. It said.

Treneer frowned at the information it willingly gave away.

The Kepa snorted at her thoughts. **You will return with payment.** It said before the rift fizzled out of existence.

Trying to catch her breath, the pain in her head started coming in waves as fury burned in her. She learnt nothing. Fire burst from her aura and blew it to the empty horizon as her throat let out a howling scream.

Archite! Delyn's thoughts pierced through.

Treneer snapped back to see her cradling Yansoon, blood splattered her armour and soaked through her undersuit. She quickly clamped around the wounds to stop the bleeding, but Yansoon's eyes glazed over, her mind was torn. She needed a healing pod. She looked around; the floating tanks with the living captives were undamaged, but there were strange dusty clouds surrounding the group. The Zanashj and the other beings they retrieved had become ash. The Kepa had willingly them go, but the monster was right, Treneer will be back.

Her eyes found Ouro. His head was low, and his arms huddled close, seeing there was dust in a shape of a body imprinted on his robes. He looked up, eyes blistering red, and cheeks stained with tears.

Treneer felt numb as she stared at the debris. *We need to get Yansoon to the healing wing-*

At Guardian Headquarters? Is your mind still beyond the rift? We can't explain any of this! Delyn said.

There's a healer outside of Yinray. He won't ask questions. The astral dancer said.

Please take us. Treneer said.

The summoner shook their head. *Return my memories and freedom, then we part ways.*

She turned to Ouro, his head bowed lower, and his face was collapsing in his hands. Reddening inflammation grew around his pulsating lavender scars; she dared not to feel it, but it seemed Ouro barely noticed it. *Ouro, come back to us. We need you.*

So close. He whispered.

His pain was too potent to hold back, the gates opened, and her heart pounded as tears flooded her eyes. So close to Zu'leen, so close to saving them all. She died once more. Delyn shook her head as tears dangled around her lashes, her hand grabbing at Ouro's arm and tightening her hold over an injured Yansoon. A sob escaped her lips as Treneer dropped over Ouro's shoulders and let the tears run down her cheeks.

~

The underground healer was at a simple home. Shadows lingered in the cramped chambers; she could feel her psionics suppressed within the quiet house, as the many minds that usually sang through her consciousness were reduced to low murmurs. She despised this feeling, but no more than watching the old healer leering at her company.

The healing pod lid sealed shut and the healer cocked his head to the side as he stared at Yansoon's aura. *Not a lot of damage to her third eye, but her frontal lobe is destroyed.*

How long will it take to get her back to normal? Treneer said.

A couple of weeks. He said, rubbing his temple below his stained and rusty silver circlet. *Maybe with some surgery, just under that.*

She can't stay here for that long. She shook her head.

The healer's eyes met hers. *I'm not thrilled about her, or any of you, being here a second longer than need be.*

Worry not, Elder. None shall know we were ever here. She said.

His glare returned to the healing pod. Yansoon's eyelids twitched; her mind was too numb to say if she was having a dream. Treneer hoped it was a pleasant one. The healer's throat cleared as his thin fingertips tapped against the hololetterings, showing her bio and psi-scans.

She watched his face twist. *What are the readouts?*

She has implants…a lot of them, but I don't recognise the technology. He said.

Treneer turned her gaze to Yansoon. It was a common practice for miners to have psi-enhancers ridden throughout their bodies for increased telekinetic hold and psionic durability. Yansoon's home-province was home to exceptional engineers, and they frequently updated their tools.

Just get her healed. She said.

Ouro levitated in the centre to larger chamber outside; his gaze was fixated to the floor as the lost and the forgotten of society kept their distance from him. Delyn's muscles tensed when one wandered a little too close to her, but she took care to avoid seeing their faces. One day, they might be captured by her or Treneer, or Yansoon – should she recover – and held in Ouro's prism, but today: these guardians were not their enemies.

Yansoon may need to stay for a fortnight. Treneer said, opening a private commune between them.

Delyn glanced at the healer. *What stops him from turning us in to save this...place?*

Precisely the reason why he won't. The Judicator wouldn't hesitate to give us a term in a Void Prism. We need to give a reason why she was injured. We cannot lie, the Judicator-

*None of this should have happened, I'm sorry Yansoon is hurt, I put you all in dangerous places...I thought I could keep you safe...*Ouro said.

Treneer looked to his robes; he still hadn't dusted Shimarr's imprint from the cloth. Her lips pursed as her palm pressed on his shoulder. *I'm so sorry, my friend.*

We chose to help, so did Yansoon. Delyn said.

*The Kepa is a predator, nothing more. But that creature you saw handing over all those Zanashj to it, helping that revolting thing grow strong...*he glanced to them. *It will meet the Void, too.*

Justice will be met. Treneer felt that dreaded familiar call back to the dowsing antechamber. The Executors were calling for the archites. *I must go-*

I'll keep watch for as long as I can. Delyn said.

Treneer nodded before turning to Ouro. *Rest, I know you will be clearer by morn.*

Ouro rolled his head to her. *Has rest ever worked for you?*

Her nostrils flared, but she put that aside for now. With a last check on her fallen partner, Treneer made flew to the grand crystal spire to Yinray. Her palm brushed against the data crystal under her robe; she needed to see the black oil – and if her fears were realised that Zanashj were involved with kidnapping Arinu, then the Empire will be reduced to a memory. If her fears were true, then seeing all those

Zanashj turned to dust upon exiting the rift gave her satisfaction…no, no, she mustn't think this way. She was better than that. No, said another side to her voice, the demon is rising. To her fortune, other guardians paid no mind to her distressed state as she sped to her quarters.

Flying up to the higher platforms, she spotted the Judicator's looming head beside a small collection of archites. She froze and grounded herself, trying to collect every bit of strength to evade suspicion, but she was seen. *Archite Treneer, you have been called in for a session.*

Understood, Judicator, I need to retrieve an energy-booster from my quarters before I join. She said, which was entirely true. Treneer couldn't remember the last she had eaten and her time in the Kepa's home-realm sapped the last strings of her energy.

The Judicator nodded before vanishing. She caught her breath before zipping to her quarters. She pulled out the sample and slipped the end in the computer. Her hand pressed against the flat slab to the centre; her psychometric readings spun around inside the machine, watching the data bounce within. The upload was complete, she took a deep breath before telepathically commanding to view the report on the mysterious warrior's corpse. With one last command, the computer started matching, as she watched the colourful blocks intertwine and blend within her mind's eye.

Her heart thumped, sweat oozed from her pores as her body stiffened. The enzymes were perfect matches. Her hand slipped off the pad before tumbling down to her feet. Zu'leen's spirit was protecting her from her would-be Zanashj kidnapper. They somehow successfully infiltrated Farayah. Still, the Empire was not alone in this plot, but Treneer will get her answers. A frustrating realisation crept in; Grand Elder Guajeeb and Executor Shurees will want to know how she found this sample without jeopardising herself and her comrades.

She telekinetically snatched at the small silver wand plugged in in her pod; it flew to her palm, and she pressed the tip against her third eye. Her body eased as she drunk deep in its refreshing energy. Alright, she cannot reveal how she acquired the sample, but she can report Zeluum's psi-scan. And the reason it took so long is that she was trying to make sense of the visions she shared from his memories, and now, Treneer needs the archites to dowse on the 'asteroid' that loomed around the ice valley…and many more where her kin disappeared. Now, how will she explain Yansoon…

Treneer, have you started the session? Ouro chimed in.

Will be in a couple of seconds.

Its Yansoon. He said. Treneer tightened, waiting for the complete thought to pass through. *The healer says she's recovering bizarrely fast, she might be out in a matter of days.*

Good. Relief simmered her nerves on her injured friend and lying to the Judicator, but the longer she pondered, why was Yansoon healing so much faster? No, if she indulged the thought further, she would never make it to the dowsing session. She sucked in a deep breath and smiled as she pulled the energy-booster from her. She and her comrades were covered, for now. However, nothing but the Neavensoros will be able to protect the Zanashj when the Arinu find out the truth.

Before her mind tumbled onto another thought, Treneer's body slipped in phase and was spat out in the antechamber. The others were already seated and the Grand Elder and Executor stood to the centre. Shurees extended her hand to the empty spot in the circle, and Treneer sheepishly scuttled to it. Guajeeb's uneasy eyes pierced her skin and made her bones vibrate; the Coven was feeling needles from their kin; the people needed an answer to their woes – and Treneer had the answers.

Apologies for my tardiness, but may I speak? She said.

Guajeeb's stare narrowed and Shurees faced her, pursing her delicate lips. *You may.*

I have some alarming news. I was contacted by an old friend requesting aid for memory retrieval, he was a witness the day Lonur vanished. In the memory, he saw an asteroid with many minds in it. It didn't make sense then, but then thought it could be a foreign ship. She said.

How certain is this memory? Shurees said.

It wasn't fabricated, Zeluum doesn't have the psi-strength for that. Even if it's a false perception, we have the power to investigate it fully. She watched their aura's dim as the other archites awkwardly shifted on their seats. To the deepest and farthest nook of her mind, Treneer begged Shurees to bite the lead. It was not a lie, it was complete truth, but they needed a scent for it.

Lead us to the north country, Archite Treneer. Grand Elder Guajeeb's head made the faintest of bows to her, but under his draping cloth mask, she could see faint outlines of wince.

With eyes closing and minds opening, the groups senses soared through Farayah. They often worked as one, but Treneer tugged away from the conscious mass, hoping that they would follow her tail. They broke apart, blanketing the entire valley and mountain spine, but little energy was stored in the surroundings. Treneer looked to the tree where the mysterious warrior was killed; the tree told their body struck the wood and quickly liquified. The group shivered when they followed the energy trail of the warrior before their fatal end, coming from a shallow cavern in the mountains and then vanishing.

I detect old exoplanar energies here.

Snow Skirmishes only teleport unless transporting injured warriors. By the tree and in the cave, their body's signature is...strange.

Because it's not Arinu. She tried holding her nerves from everyone's radiating horror.

She turned to the sky where the supposed asteroid lingered. *Access planetary scans, tell us what was in Farayah's atmosphere when Lonur disappeared.*

She waited for the download to complete and absorb in the rest of the group. A small asteroid shower flew passed the area, nothing significant, yet.

Magnify the ambient frequencies from the scans. Shurees said.

The group's anger billowed when they detected brainwaves hidden under the rocks. With their combined focus, Treneer could see there were several figures within, all Zanashj and one Arinu.

They should not have this kind of technology. Shurees's thoughts came like inferno in the group.

I recognise that stealth device, its reversed engineered Roctarous technology. Guajeeb said.

Relief cooled her for a moment, before everyone was snapped back into the antechamber. Her eyes slowly opened; a slight milky sheen came over them before focusing on the Grand Elder and Executor. They were silent, in a psi-commune locked away from the agitated crowd. The two Elder's auras had changed; their bright and dazzling presence was flooded with a brooding rage that made her want to teleport to another hemisphere. When their stares returned to the group, the last drop of her relief fell away before realising that she delivered the Zanashj to extinction.

Despite our weakened state, we could still see through the opportunistic imperialists. Guajeeb said as he took a haggard breath. *The Coven has just been informed and was wise to cut relations when we did. The Empire desperately tried reconnecting, all the while betraying us to keep us distracted. The Coven demands that our taken kin are to be returned and justice for the fallen. The long-standing Treaty has now evaporated.*

What of the Roctarous? Will we seek justice from them, too? An archite called out.

Any involved with this conspiracy will be punished, but punishment means nothing if they don't understand they were wrong. Shurees said as her neck strained inside her high armoured collar. *Our plans to go to Kra will come to pass, we need to know the depths of this conspiracy before the first strike.*

A flicker of panic rose when the pile of Zanashj faces in the Kepa's mound came to her mind's eye. Innocent, guilty, old, young, teacher, warrior, sick and healthy – they also deserved justice. But she couldn't say without their suspicions turned to her; she must find a way and soon. Her temples tightened and her head pained; the energy boost turned into a lag. Despite her mind screaming to stay awake, to push past, her body won the battle and was forced to retreat to her quarters.

Chapter Thirty-one
Ahn'kat XI: To Flee or to Chase

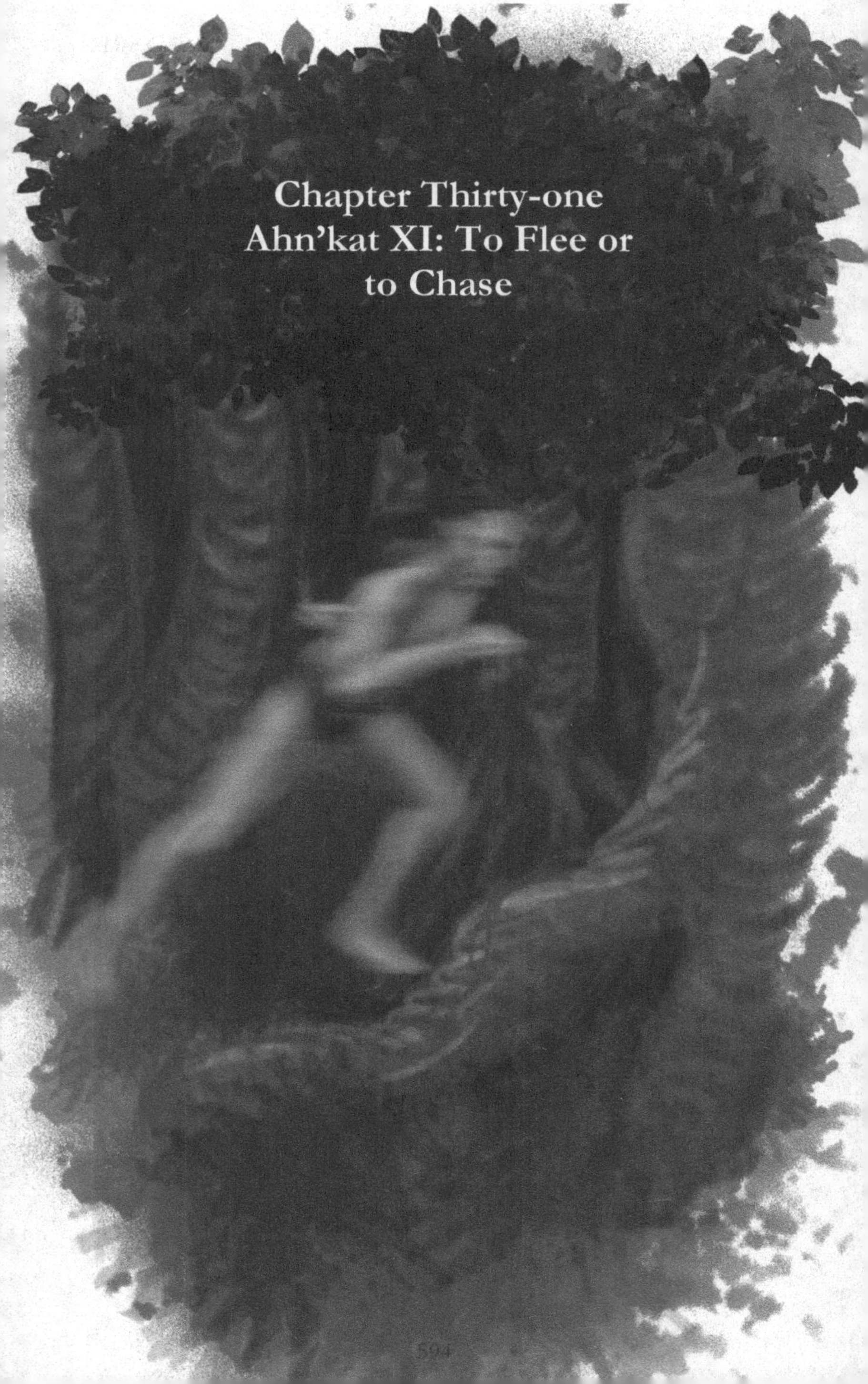

Ahn'kat wanted to grieve but was forced to smile. He wanted to cry but was forced to laugh. He wanted to fight but was forced to shake hands. From day to night, he was never allowed to show what he had learnt from Ismotaph in his duties. His oldest friend Zertun and his love Emestasun, were gone. Taken by the wretches calling themselves 'Unbound Roctarous.' What were they doing to them? Did they think about home? Did she think about him? All Ahn'kat could do was think about her; he just hoped they were together and were trying to keep each other safe – maybe trying to escape back to Uras and tell the whole Empire the truth.

As far as the imperium and Crown knew, Ahn'kat's crafty ability to find innumerable valuable coffers from the disgraced High Priest saved the momentary aches from the growing military and reformation centres. The people were elated to see one of the Crown also willing to take to stars to defend them. Ramkes rested easier and Emperor Kreshut could see eager uniformity again. Ahn'kat was trusted once again as the diamond of the Empire, but he had cracked, and now all it took was a tap to shatter him.

He watched the moons rising from the horizon, their ruby red halos swelled as they climbed up into the black sky. He had watched the sunset not even a few hours ago. Ahn'kat was surprised that he had been staring into nothingness for so long. He couldn't remember the last time he had much time to himself since he became prince; he remembered not too long ago how much he ached to get away from his duties for a few moments and play Takush with Emestasun and listen to Zertun's war stories. Now, having this empty pocket of time reminded him how empty he was.

He strolled to his computer, there were a dozen messages from his staff and news updates. His hand waved away the holographic notifications, leaving the blank space. Ahn'kat's fingers scrolled to Takush, his star army appeared to have broken ranks and were badly damaged – no doubt an enemy player pillaged his base while he was away being a useless prince. He ordered his tiny ships and soldiers to where Emestasun's star base was; it was in tatters, there were broken and derelict ships floating into nothingness – even her buildings were ruins.

A sob escaped his throat. His hands clasped over his eyes as he instinctively went to grab his pendant – but only to have remembered he had torn it off. He clenched his jaw as he fished for the necklace in his trouser pocket, the mineral lump was still there. He slipped his hand back to his desk before ordering his Takush characters to mine and plant precious metals and gems from asteroids around her abandoned base. His cheeks were wet when he finally completed the last mission he will ever have on the game.

As his characters pulled back, he saw that there was an unopened message sitting in the inbox of her command centre. Ahn'kat frowned as he pulled it open; it was a note that she had written to herself shortly after they last spoke, but it was addressing him.

'My dearest Ahn'kat, I hide this message in my mail in the hopes it would not be misunderstood by the wrong eyes. The Empire is not our greatest Zanashj asset, its adaptation. If the Empire fell and Uras was destroyed tomorrow, we will always be here – in one form or another. We adapt not because its comfortable or easy, but because it's necessary. The environment maybe harsh, but it does not have to dominate us, or we dominate it. Instead, we learn to live with it - become part of it. We don't need to overcome something by being on top of the pyramid, instead, become symbiotic with the greater circle.'

Ahn'kat's hands shook as he waved away the holo-letterings. He sighed, he wanted to seek comfort from Ramkes, but had to wait until Ismotaph organised Lady and Lord Urbaz to be blamed for the conspiracy against the Crown. He stumbled as he rose from his desk, hurrying over to an untidy refreshment tray. Berries, nuts, and seeds were semi-squashed or eaten littered all over golden dishes, fine glass goblets had fallen, and some had cracks in them. He reached over to the jug; there was still some watered-down banana liquor in the base. Ahn'kat placed the jug to his lips as he chugged it, letting the room-warm liquid drip down the edges of his cheeks and robes.

He dropped it to ground once it emptied as he wiped his lips with his fine black linen and gold embroidered sleeve. His eye caught his reflection in the shield window; he saw his eyeliner had smudged down his cheeks and his tightly plaited beard was askew, even his hair had strands sticking out of the braids. His messy silk trousers flared over his bare feet and his stained dark robes were open at the front; there should have been a sapphire pendant hanging over his chest, but he couldn't bear looking at Aszelun. His heart broke not knowing how long he would have to feel this way.

The longer he stared at his reflection, he realised he looked like a perfect copy of his father. Ahn'kat's heart hammered at the grief of what he and his mother had done to him and made him into. He picked up the jug and tossed it at the window, watching the energy shield wobble and shimmer before returning to the same slick transparency. The banana liquor finally took effect, numbing his lips and feet before dropping to the ground.

"You've abandoned me," he whispered into the void. He wanted to sleep, wait till the morning to restart the ritual. As he felt the prang of tiredness try to slip into nothingness, his wrist phone vibrated. His half-closed eyes rolled to the surface to see Ismotaph's name flashing on the glass.

"Issit done?" Ahn'kat mumbled.

"Yes," Ismotaph's holographic face appeared over the bracelet. "And it wasn't easy. Some of my vanguards were mentally scarred, but we subdued them long enough to ship them off to our jails-"

Ahn'kat's eyes narrowed at him. "I hope you didn't..."

Ismotaph cocked his head to the side.

"I hope you didn't hurt them," the prince sighed.

"We tried handling them the best way we could," he said.

"What happens now?" Ahn'kat said slowly sitting up.

"There's enough evidence to suggest that Lord and Lady Urbaz were conspiring against the Crown with the Unbound Roctarous. Taskmaster Meksonett has also been apprehended under suspicion of treason by working with House Urbaz and hid the captured Arinu from you when you took hold of the Urbaz shipping yards and bays. Any suggestion you were ever involved with this has been erased. You were just a pawn in theirs and Seratut's game," he said.

Ahn'kat's head began to throb. He thought he would feel vindicated that his parents were facing justice for taking away his loved ones and denying him his choices in life. Instead, this moment felt as dry as the moment before. "And what of the Arinu? The psi-enhancers…?"

"All of which will be disposed of. We can show that there was alien experimentation taking place, but it will mostly focus on what the Unbound Roctarous have exchanged with House Urbaz. No doubt, once the investigation begins, Urasan satellites will discover camouflaged alien ships lingering around the planet – it will create the link that people have kidnapped-"

"Which is true," Ahn'kat said with caution.

"But it will show we are dealing with many more enemies than we realised. It will compel the Empire to take flight again," Ismotaph said.

"True, but it still doesn't explain what happens to all those mass-produced psi-enhancers? Won't they show Arinu DNA in them?" Ahn'kat said.

"Not if we alter them just enough to hide Arinu essence within them. We've already planned to start spreading them across the Empire, introducing it into food and drink. We can say this sudden increase of psionics is our way of adapting to the psychic menace out in the cosmos," he said.

"I assume that if this war will be happening soon, those psi-enhancers need to be dispersed quickly, but…" The prince sighed. This long, pain-staking plan has finally reached its goal, with a few odd changes, its end was nigh. A new Golden Era or an apocalypse, Ahn'kat feared both. "Many people may not survive the psychic assimilation."

"No, they won't," Ismotaph slowly said.

"I want to see them," he said.

"They're sedated, they won't be able to spe-"

"I said see them, not speak with them," Ahn'kat said rising to his feet before hanging up on him.

~

One of Ismotaph's agents chauffeured him to the Corps private detention centre. The dark skies amplified the malice of the grey stone ziggurat. The moonlight cast black shadows gilded the edges sides and narrow square windows created claustrophobia even to those who looked upon them from the outside open fields. There were many other buildings like this in the Empire. There were no signs or fences showing what this place held, it almost looked forlorn if it weren't for the odd shadow of an infiltrator patrolling the building's balcony. From Ahn'kat's distance, he could have mistaken them for a ghost.

As the vehicle slowed to the landing balcony, his heart hammered. His knuckles instinctively caressed his chest where Aszelun's pendant would have been as he stepped out of the machine. Two bald infiltrators stepped from the dark; the moonlight caught their shiny scalps as they silently ushered him in. He was no prince here, he was robed in commoner's clothing and discarded his jewels and gold circlet but kept his sapphire pendant in his pocket. A part of him begged the gods to help him return his faith, but with every step into the barren grey halls, that hope ambered into smoke.

His eye caught a locked door labelled 'failed subjects.' A chill ran up his spine when he remembered those Zanashj miscreant pets they had experimented psi-enhancers on. The miniscule psionics he possessed could sense their maddening sorrow behind those thick organic doors. He silently promised them to shut down these horrid experiments, and if the Zanashj survived the war, he will personally build quaint and comfortable cabins for all of the Corps' test subjects so they may finally find peace.

The infiltrators he tailed slowed before coming around the corner before Ismotaph stepped into view and gave him a woeful look.

"This shouldn't have happened," the Director said.

"Where are they?" Ahn'kat said.

Ismotaph's head beckoned him towards a long hallway with a single door at the end. Unlike the few others he had passed, this hall had no security. Even the eerie infiltrator's he walked with stayed just before this hall began, only Ismotaph seemed to brave it and Ahn'kat was utterly oblivious to it. When they came to the door, it's surface looked more like a vault. Ismotaph pressed his open hand into the centre, letting the living door creep around his fingers to 'feel' he was allowed to enter before peeling open into a comfortably lit room.

There was no furniture, no windows, merely two black cubes a foot from each other in the centre of the chamber. Ahn'kat's heart thumped so fast it pained him to step into it, remembering these containers were identical to the ones used to capture the Arinu. There were tiny square peepholes in the centre as his eyes were trying to fixate on the figures inside.

"Don't touch the containers, please," Ismotaph whispered.

Ahn'kat looked to him. "Are...is this the last time I'm going to see my parents?"

Ismotaph shook his head as his shoulders shrugged. "I'm not certain, but…"

Ahn'kat took a deep breath, preparing his mind on what to expect when he peered into the first box. There was a thin emerald-skinned figure curled up within; their long greasy hair clamped around their sweaty skin as their hands and feet twitched as if they were in a deep dream. A part of him hoped it was a nightmare. Frustration built when he couldn't tell if he was looking at his mother or his father.

"We had a plan to reverse some of the effects of the enhancers," Ismotaph's voice croaked, "to make them a bit more pliant for their trial, but considering the danger they pose and how long that could take – even if it worked, we could only come up with, um…"

"Pull their brains apart?" Ahn'kat finished.

Ismotaph cleared his throat. "They'll grow back after a while, but the level of surgery needed may make them vegetative for the rest of their lives."

Ahn'kat straightened his back and strode over to the other box, in the hopes that he could see and recognise them. He wanted to believe these people were not the ones that birthed him, that wore all those fine clothes and threw elegant parties, that taught him and drilled duty into him. He wanted to believe that they were clever replacers, but when he saw the second figure roll over and lock eyes with him, Ahn'kat knew it was his father. There was a clearness about them that even the finest replacer could not mimic by the way he looked at him. His eyes closed again and fell back into the dream.

"We shouldn't linger here too long, they are adapting to the sedatives and need to be changed again," Ismotaph said.

Ahn'kat took several steps back to the door, he glanced at the boxes for as long as he could before hurrying out of the chamber with Ismotaph following closely behind.

"Is Seratut here?" Ahn'kat said.

"He is, but held in the higher levels," Ismotaph replied.

"I want to see the man responsible for creating this mess," Ahn'kat said.

"Ah, barely a man anymore," Ismotaph said under his breath.

"What do you mean?"

The Director's lips pursed, and nostrils flared. "Are you sure you want to see him? It may befall the same fate as Lord and Lady Urbaz."

"What more horror can there be?" Ahn'kat said.

"Much more," Ismotaph said before heading toward the flight of stairs to the levels above.

To Ahn'kat's surprise, the last locked door that led them to the upper level was in the open air, barring the illusion shield overhead. Lush green grass grew on healthy soil, small flowers and insects were crawling around the brush and roots of a single gnarly tree was in the centre of the green block. Ahn'kat frowned when he thought this facility was growing a small experimental eco-bay, but the longer he stared at the lone tree, his breath was stolen from him.

"It can't be..." Ahn'kat whispered as his mouth dropped.

"It took some time, but we managed to physically...change him," Ismotaph said as his feet crunched over the grass.

Ahn'kat stared at the thick, twisted branches sprouting wide beryl leaves and the trunk was heavy and bulbous as the man Seratut was before.

"How did you do this?" Ahn'kat said.

"Deprived him from conventional food, locked his legs into the soil and let the sunlight absorb into his skin. And his body did the rest," Ismotaph walked over and patted the closest branch. "They will be taking him to the palace gardens soon."

Ahn'kat turned to him. "Why in the gods would they do that?"

Ismotaph sighed, his eye drew to a snapping vine leering and ready to strike Ahn'kat, but his hand slapped it away. "Because that's what they do to traitors to the Crown, they plant them around the palace boarders to protect the Royal Family from excitable fanatics."

Ahn'kat stepped away. Disgust blazed through him when he remembered playing the gardens with Ramkes as children and trying to hide between the trees with snapping vines. All those trees around the green fringes were once Zanashj. "This is overwhelming."

"I know it's an ugly tradition, but it keeps wrong people away and the right people in place. There's a sort of sick poetry to it, the very people who betrayed the Crown are now protecting it," Ismotaph said.

"Are they aware?" Ahn'kat said.

"No, their brains are gone, changed into something else. They have metamorphosised into something else," he said.

"This is vile. When the princess ascends the throne, I will stop this," Ahn'kat said.

"Well, the princess has known about this for some time," he said as he folded his arms. "Are you sure that it's the tradition that upsets you or are you afraid your parents will end this way?"

Ahn'kat strode around the grass, feeling the cool damp blades caress the skin in his sandaled feet. "I'm uncertain of everything. What Lord and Lady Urbaz did to me is beyond forgiveness. I just want to forget about today and focus on tomorrow."

"Well, I think once your pet-reformation dream comes true, then you can focus on how we deal with undesirables," Ismotaph said eyeing the gnarled tree.

"All after we handle the Arinu and Roctarous," Ahn'kat sighed.

"We will get them, all of them and then try to bring our people home. You're not on your own, my prince, you have the Intel Corps and the love of the people," Ismotaph smiled.

Ahn'kat returned a small smile. "One more thing: you shall cease experimentation on unwilling subjects or criminals, Ismotaph, else I will plant you in the darkest corner of my palace chambers for the rest of your days."

"The beetle bites!" the Director smirked. "You have my word."

~

"They are ready for you, your highness," the emperor's guard said through his hawk helm.

Ahn'kat rose to his feet from the fine cushioned lounge chair. Fresh new silk and linen robes sat on his scrubbed and moisturised skin, his black eyeliner was perfectly symmetrical, his fingers and wrists were weighed from the best jewellers in the Empire and his braided hair and beard were waxed and combed into perfection. He looked like sculpture, a deity in a Zanashj body, but his heart pounded in his ears and blood rushed into his muscles. He breathed, trying to slow his heart rate and ease the tension in his limbs as he followed the guard to the chamber of the royal court.

He ran through everything Ismotaph had instructed him to say. 'I was unaware of House Urbaz's true intentions, Taskmaster Meksonett was still taking orders from my parents, despite taking lordship over the ship factories. I was betrayed, I was betrayed, I was betrayed...'

'If you deem me unfit of the princess's consort, then cast me away from the Crown. I will do everything in my power to restore House Urbaz's name and repair the damage their wrought against our Imperial Family. I was betrayed.' he said to himself. Ahn'kat was betrayed, but that started when he was still a child – the day that House Urbaz sided with the Unbound Roctarous.

The pearl encrusted golden doors slid apart, revealing a wide and long hall, with a row of fine nobles standing on both sides. Their quiet chatter died down to silence when he entered the room; their faces were blended with curiosity, suspicion, and concern. At the end of the hall, sat Emperor Kreshut cross-legged on a golden and chestnut wood squared stool, four golden hawk statues sat on the corners – judging him as he walked closer. The emperor's face was stoic, and his thousand-mile stare made Ahn'kat's nerves peak.

Ramkes was to his right; her golden stool was smaller and several feet lower than the emperor's. She tried holding the same calm as her father's, but her eyes were wide with fear as he stepped before them. Ahn'kat could hear light chirps and whistles over his head; there were hawks fluttering and resting on the indoor tree branches growing from the gold and marble pillars. The ceiling above him was open to the bright white and blue skies, but he caught the sheen of a shield doming over the hall. This was the emperor's palace; no cost was spared to bring the finest artisans of the Empire to create wonder to the beholders. Despite the warmth of the air, colours, and smells, Ahn'kat was frozen in place.

"My Emperor," he bowed low that his knee grazed the step, before he turned to Ramkes, "my princess and wife,"

The silence in the hall clogged his ears.

"Tell the Court and Crown your side of the story," Kreshut said. His voice was quiet, but its depth made his cells shake.

"I had begun suspecting something unusual was occurring with Lord and Lady Urbaz's frequent absences. Because of my duties to Crown and Empire, my contact with them had lessened and when it was time to take charge of Urbaz ship facilities, I went to visit them. They did not seem of sound-mind, but because of my...separated relationship with them, I didn't probe their condition. I assumed the medical servants would take care of them. I took charge of the ship bays and continued my tasks as normal," Ahn'kat said. He felt more at ease the longer he spoke.

"About the ship facilities," Kreshut said as he cocked his head to the side. "Your former taskmaster, Meksonett, she frequently reported to you on activities in Sekem Bay?"

"She did, but most of our discussions were centred on the workers and how to save costs," the prince said.

"Did she hide things from you?" the emperor said.

Ahn'kat parted his lips and nodded. "She hid much from me, but at the time, her transparency didn't make me think she was omitting what was transpiring in the bay's depths."

"People were disappearing from your fiefs, Prince Ahn'kat," the emperor said.

"I believed pets were circled out of my facilities and placed into reformation centres, as was part of my Crown duties," he said.

"Yet hardly any were. Another thing you were put in charge of. How did you not see this?"

Ahn'kat's mind raced. He could admit his poor oversight and risk losing his sparkling reputation or if he admitted the truth…then he may become another tree ornament in Kreshut's garden. If he immediately admitted he had failed overseeing the pet-reformations, then the emperor would assume he is covering his lie with an offering of open palms. He looked to Ramkes, her eyes never broke away from him, she was as still as a statue on her princess throne. If she was able to read his mind in that moment, then she would see he never had a choice.

"I did not fail, your highness. My heart is in the Empire and in you," Ahn'kat said.

"So, are you saying you willingly closed your eyes?"

"No, I assumed my word was obeyed. I never imagined that my people were taking orders from other voices!" Ahn'kat said. He could feel his cheeks warming up and his blood rising back into his muscles, begging him to run.

Kreshut straightened his back and sighed. "Shortly after I ascended the throne, a star commander reported that he encountered a band of Roctarous working on the outside of an asteroid no larger than this hall. They wore no suits in the vacuum, they didn't even seem to speak to each other. They were totally synthetic lifeforms. That commander tried taking one to bring back here, but that one machine tore a hole through a fighter craft with its arms alone. Lord Reshj said it would take weeks for the ship to regenerate to health.

We never wrangled a Roctarous, but we did find nano-probes attached to the broken tissue plate. Ismotaph explained that they were metal cells. They have been stored in the vaults of the Intel Corps and have remained there for study, until investigators found nearly identical nano-probes intertwined with some of the ships in Sekem Bay."

Ahn'kat's blood dropped into his feet and his body went cold. How did Ismotaph not try to hide the new Keshsapt cruisers? How could he have allowed his investigators to find this? Unless…

"It was reported to me that they were developing new technologies, I didn't know they were using material from off-worlders."

"Who are the Unbound Roctarous?" Ramkes asked as she squeezed her words into a soft voice, hiding her billowing rage.

"Nothing more than what was said in this investigation," Ahn'kat said looking between them.

"So, you are claiming after years of overseeing your ship bays, and Lady and Lord Urbaz's unusual behaviour, you never once looked at what was going on? One single glance of what was occurring in your charge, you would have known something was amiss," Ramkes said.

"I believed them. That's the Imperial Family, we have faith in each other!"

Ramkes rose to her feet and slowly stepped towards him. "Your workers have also claimed to have seen you and

Taskmaster Meksonett going into the depths, they place you looking at the Keshsapt ships. Some even claim to have seen you fall ill at something you have experienced in the depths."

"Ramkes, I was not well at the time...the liquor," he whispered.

Her eyes were like daggers as her fingers interlaced over her abdomen, continuing her prowl toward him. "Now, you claim you were not of sound-mind? Or is Meksonett, your workers and the Corps investigators all liars? Do we place our faith solely in you and not in the many of our Imperial Family?"

"I was recovering from a poor lifestyle; I was trying to acquaint my duties in the shipping facilities along with my princedom!" he could feel the robes in his underarms dampening, while he desperately tried closing the pores on his face.

"We will get to your princedom shortly," she hissed. "We are sympathetic to your inexperience being part of the Crown, but the truth is, we always watched and heard. Every single one of us. The Intel Corps was alarmed by some of your behaviour and began looking deeper – they found much to be worried by."

Ahn'kat's eyes widened as his head looked up to her fierce face. He couldn't even compel his mouth to ask.

"Would you say it's a coincidence your parents failing health came about around shortly before you convinced me to allow you to take lordship over your ship bays? Pushing out Lord and Lady Urbaz's influence further away from their facilities that allowed you place anything or anyone in your new domain. Perhaps it's also coincidence that your communication satellites regularly transmitted Urbaz manor and off-worlder ships, to add, your frequent messaging to your former servant suggested that she was helping you 'better control Lord and Lady Urbaz?'"

His brain felt like it had turned to water in his skull. "Are you suggesting I'm responsible for calling those Unbound Roctarous and exchanging our people with them?"

"Who else could it have been? You used aliens to destabilise the Empire, to become the new emperor maybe. Either you're the greatest fool birthed in the Empire or greatest enemy we have ever known. Arinu pale to you," she said.

The prince swayed as he took a step back. He could see the emperor's guards looming beside the ornate pillars, keeping their hawk eyes on him. Behind the shadows of the pillars, he saw him. Ismotaph stood under their shadow and soaked in the spectacle in the centre of the court. Ahn'kat took a deep breath and realised...the Arinu.

He grabbed Ramkes, her darkened face broke into surprise, and pulled her close. "There's information in my apartment of your palace, Ramkes. The third eye of the seabeast! And another outside, the stone stool with a sky-serpent on it. Ismotaph's and my conversations. He has been plotting this from the start! I was on your side, but I was kept in the dark-" he screeched as golden guards rushed over to him, their sceptres swung and bashed into his shins. Electricity rained into his cells as he collapsed to the ground before an organic whip gripped his neck and extended itself to his wrists and ankles.

"Go to my old apartment now before he gets there first! I'm the greatest fool, Ramkes, I am!" he choked out before a small golden probe flew over the hall and teleported him away from the frightened and disgusted faces of the court.

~

He woke up in a white room. There was no furniture, windows, or visible doors. Even his wrist phone was missing. His eyes stung from the painful whiteness. Ahn'kat brought his dark sleeves to his face to try and dull some of the light's harshness. He took a moment to let his eyes naturally adjust, but no matter how many lenses grew over his eyeballs, the fierce light never seemed to dissipate, even if he could only see a dull grey chamber around him.

He could hear a hum above his head and before his eyes rolled up to see what it was, he was immediately teleported to princess's personal interrogation room. It was homier than the terrifying white detention room. Two cushioned seats sat in the centre, the walls were lined with wooden vines and a small window viewing the now dark outside.

Ramkes was already in her seat, picking at some grapes in a golden dish on her armchair. Her eyes rolled up to him as she waited for him to sit opposite of her, and that he did.

"I told them to take you out of that room, it's no place for you – even if you are the worst person I've ever known," she said wiping her fingers with her napkin. "Maybe over time, I'll see reason and throw you back in for the rest of your life."

"At least I won't have to attend anymore stupid meetings," he muttered.

She smiled. "I hate you."

"Did you find the listeners?" he said.

"We did," she said.

He glared at her on the edge of his seat, waiting for more which never came. His heart hammered, imagining they found the listeners but failed to pick up their conversations or they had been replaced with duds, or at the very worst, Ahn'kat didn't properly switch them on. "But?"

"It was just static, not even our technicians could filter it," she said.

Ahn'kat leant back in his chair and pressed his eyes to fight back his tears.

"I don't want to believe you have done this to us," Ramkes said.

"Then don't," he sighed.

She shook her head. "Well, I do. Right now, the emperor hasn't declared to the masses what's happened, he's looking for Ismotaph's best replacer, it'll cost us a fortune. In the meantime, Ismotaph has been given House Urbaz property and businesses."

His head was spinning as sweat patched on his forehead. "He's the one that threw me into the nest of sky-serpents! Can't you see that I finished his use for him and now he's going after the Crown? He gets rid of people!"

"To what end, Ahn'kat?" she said.

"I...I don't know. Everything he bid me to do and told me not to do, I did. I was kept in the dark, I was played and now I'm blamed-"

"Where's the evidence?" she said.

Ahn'kat shook his head as he rubbed his fingers through his plaited hair. Seratut is no more, his parents are brain-dead, Emestasun and Zertun are gone, and he sent his last friend Neobatri on a suicide mission to Farayah. Ismotaph knew she wasn't going to return from that voyage, perhaps even antagonise the Arinu farther and propel this war at lightspeeds. He wanted Gajoon to help, but a cold spike struck his heart, knowing that the little power and respect she had acquired under his protection...she will be tossed out of the palace and returned as a pet.

He could see it all know, Ismotaph separated every single ally he had and kept him in the darkness and afraid, until he knew Ahn'kat would be bendable to his will.

"Listen to me," Ramkes leaned in. "He's admitted having done questionable things on your behalf, like spying on your parents. I know you were never close, and I always got the sense you resented them."

His head slowly turned to her as his eyes narrowed. "You're not going to get a confession out of me for something I didn't do!"

She crossed her arms. "Then what did you do?"

"The only crime I committed was not telling you the moment I learnt their plans for you. Ismotaph, Seratut and my parents wanted me to manipulate you to stopping the Crown's plans for an interstellar Federation and return the Empire to its 'glory days,'" he said.

"Well, it seems Aszelun heard your prayers and killed that hope in its crib," she said flicking a long black strand of hair from her shoulder before noticing his chest. "Where's your pendant?"

Ahn'kat's eyes drop to the ground, he could feel Ramkes leaning in a little closer.

"Ismotaph may confirm that part of your story," she whispered before taking a warm rosy breath, "but it's missing another part to it."

"What do you mean?" he said clinging to some hope.

"If you couldn't manipulate me…then what was the alternative solution?" she said as her eyes shined.

Ahn'kat shook his head as he pulled away from her. "That creatin is using the truth to warp into a lie! I did not plan this conspiracy!"

"If I didn't change my mind then what would your co-conspirators have done to me and my father?" she asked again.

"I was the one advocating your protection! I prayed, made deals, and begged them not to ever harm you, I went so far to go against their wishes to try a way to keep you alive and well!" he yelled as he rose to his feet.

"And if my father and I were dead, then my altruistic and perfect husband would have ascended the throne. The people would have accepted you without question," she said as if she didn't hear him.

His hands gripped the edge of his chair to stop him from falling. This horrid, painfully long plan was perfect. It was flawless. Ismotaph infiltrated the Empire and not one Zanashj could recognise this tumour. He met her eyes for a moment.

"How do I know you're not one of Ismotaph's people? Maybe the man himself is truly before me and is testing my loyalty? Even so, I failed once again," he said through a clenched jaw.

Ramkes rose her feet as her hands clasped over her lap. "A final decision will be rendered by the morrow. We will supply you with basic needs, but please make no attempt to contact anyone-"

"Like there is anyone left on my side," he whispered.

"Let alone think about escaping," she narrowed her eyes at him before stepping to the sliding door.

"Wait," he called out to her, and she paused, but didn't turn. "Seratut warned me about Ismotaph long ago, he said that he disposes anyone who doesn't serve his needs anymore. I didn't listen and began trusting him more, because he had been there from the start and helped me through every sin. I still had faith in the Imperial Family. Ismotaph is an aberration of our people, Ramkes, and do not think for a moment that just because you are royalty, he won't do the same to you."

She didn't say anything before stepping out of his brand-new cage.

~

Ahn'kat closed his eyes as he lay on the cool floor. He tried cooling down from this abominable hot humidity, but his heart thumped every time he thought about what they were going to do with him. He will be replaced, that was certain, but he trembled at the possibility of turning into a hideous tree in the palace gardens, or worse – Ismotaph's garden. He wished he still had faith in the Great Beetle, but he knew the gods were too grand to care for the little problems of the Zanashj. The Pantheon didn't care and never did.

Sweat dripped from his forehead and temples, his clammy hands wiped them away, but felt more water building on his skin. He grunted as he frantically slapped it away, his nails clawing into his plaited beard, ripping away the gold bands around it and shedding out the wax entangled within.

His nail scratched under his chin; for a moment he felt pain, but also felt a tiny hard bump beneath his skin. Ahn'kat stopped before carefully probing the lump, his mind raced that his psi-enhancer was still inside his skin pouch. He sat up as his heart raced, he tried sensing for a hidden infiltrator in the princess' interrogation room but received nothing. He found a small decorative golden pin on his robe and carefully started poking the soft chairs repeatedly.

He waited and watched for the chairs to tremble and transform but they remained still. Taking a deep breath, he pulled out the capsule from under his chin and stared at the tiny thing. His mind raced at the idea of what could happen to him and everyone in the palace if he took the plunge. The image of his parents confined to a dark metal box for the rest of their lives frightened him even more.

"I don't want to be afraid anymore," he whispered. Taking one last, long breath, he cracked open the pill and swallowed every molecule. He waited and waited, until a terrible cramp spread in his gut, forcing him down to his knees. Ahn'kat clutched his stomach and groaned, his body trembled as bile rose and spilt from his lips. He wanted to run and use the lavatory but sensed there was nothing there to be expelled.

He rolled on to the ground, clinging to the cold stone for comfort and sanity. Banana liquor prepared him poorly for this moment, he thought. His rapid breaths eased when his head felt like it soared, and for a moment, it was. With his inner eye, he could see his body curled on the floor before snapping back into his skull. Ahn'kat slowly sat up; his brain felt like it has been grated and was about to leak from his ears. Slowly blinking, he could see many colours and shapes flowing in and out of existence in the small room. Some came so close to him, that his hands naturally whipped out and tried catching them before they vanished.

"Madness, this is how it starts…" he muttered before rising to his feet. He tore off his robe and felt around his torso. The pain had dissipated. He heard whispers in his mind, yet they were so silent he couldn't understand their words. He looked to the wall before him, there were several imperial guards patrolling the hall, each of their auras were different and so bright that it nearly blinded him.

He looked to the narrow window outside, but he didn't have the malleability to slip through the cracks and escape. Ahn'kat took a deep breath and remembered the exercises that Emestasun taught him. His mind crawled out from his body and wormed its way out into the hall. He clearly saw one guard stationed by the door while there were two others making rounds. At the end of the hall, there lay a narrow flight of stairs that lead directly down into the washrooms, which led directly outside of the palace.

He sensed for any infiltrators lingering in the halls. Two, three…four. Four infiltrators were morphed into sculptures, wall tapestries and armchairs. Ahn'kat had basic melee skills but was a spider-fly compared to elite body-benders. He also counted how long the guards took to finish their route, barely a handful of minutes at best, but what to do with the guard and the locked door before him?

Pulling off his trousers and jewellery, everything that would hamper his camouflaging skill, he pressed his hands against the door and focused on separating his mind again. He trailed into the mind of the guard, compelling him to enter. Please, please, please come in…I'm desperate need…only you can help me, he repeated in his mind. There was a shuffle of heavy boots beyond the door, but he didn't move. Ahn'kat closed his eyes and took another breath, clenching his gut and squeezing blood into his arm muscles. "Come in," he mouthed.

A click of a metal helmet moved. Ahn'kat could feel the man staring at him through the door. His hands pulled back and waited for the door to creak open. The other patrolling guard was away enough to not notice the door guard had been compelled away from his post, this was the prince's chance.

A golden helmet of the hawk strode in, but Ahn'kat stepped back, waiting for him to enter.

"I know I look unseemly," Ahn'kat's foot nudged aside his clothes on the floor, but never left his stare of the guard. "Please close the door for me,"

The guard stiffened before slowly rolling the cell door shut.

"Take your helmet off, you have nothing to be worried about," Ahn'kat goaded.

The guard's armoured fingers reached to the back of his helmet. The golden beck and the fierce brow melted away to reveal a young man who he had seen on the barracks training ground not even a few days ago. The young guard's eyes were wide, but hollow, as if he waited for a command to blink. Good, Ahn'kat thought.

"It's warm in here, isn't it? All that armour will make you too hot, I'll hold it for you," Ahn'kat said holding out his hand.

The guard obeyed and began stripping the oval neck piece, the chest, gauntlets, metal skirt and boots. Ahn'kat scrambled to get everything on one by one as the guard handed it over.

"That sceptre seems heavy, doesn't it?" Ahn'kat held out his hand one more time before the young man gleefully handed the weapon over. The poor fellow was now in his undergarments, and to Ahn'kat's mild fortune, the pair shared a similar profile from a distance. He only has a few more seconds before the other guards come striding past.

"I'll fetch you a drink, please have a seat," Ahn'kat pointed to an armchair before stepping out into the hall. He activated the helmet from the neck piece, allowing his head to be swallowed in a snug darkness, yet his eyes had clear view of the world outside. He spun around to the guard's original post beside the door and clicked it shut before the patrolmen wandered towards him. Ahn'kat compelled his stomach to make pained growls, loud enough for the patrol guards to stop and scan him.

His hand pressed over his gut as he tried to straighten his back against the wall, but he could feel the other guard rolling his eyes behind his hawk-eyed visor. "For gods' sake, get something from the servant's kitchens-"

"I need the rest room-" Ahn'kat whispered.

"Don't want to hear it, Ghemtat, just get out of here," the patrol guard pushed him aside and stood by the door. Ahn'kat strode down the narrow staircase, he could sense an infiltrator hiding as a piece of tapestry hanging above his scalp. You're a guard, you're a guard, you're a guard, he repeated to himself, trying to imagine this is how Neobatri successfully mind-bended. His heavy feet were seamless on his climb down, not a single step out of place, not an elbow or his sceptre knocking against the passageway – Ahn'kat never felt so natural or alive. As if his ancient upon ancient ancestors cried in delight from his cells at his faux visage, just as they did, he did.

There was another infiltrator hiding as a statue beside the stone archway of the servant washer room. He didn't stop, he kept his march to perfection as he entered the steamy corridor. A row of workers laboured over boiling multi-coloured vats, ceiling-high tubes spun various sheets with perfume-infused waters before gushing them out onto air-compression grills, and stacks of purified robes, undersuits, bedlinens, curtains, and rugs were folded neatly along the back walls, waiting to be retrieved.

None of the staff paid mind to Ahn'kat striding behind them as he wandered to the private rest rooms. His knuckles nudged the door aside and clicked it shut before tearing off his armour. He forced his sweat-stained face to change shape and compelled his skin to begin blending with the stone foundations and walls of the lower palace. In the tall rafters of the tiny room, he wedged the armour and sceptre between the beams. Once they were safely secured, Ahn'kat eyed the latch and crouched close to the ground as he slowly slid the door aside. The narrow gap was no wider than his skull as his body contorted to slip through before quietly sliding it back shut.

Over his right shoulder was the open doors to the gardens. He slithered along the ground, while keeping an eye on the servants and sensing for anyone coming by. He spotted shrubbery and low trees separating the outdoor walkways. He dived into the bush, settling against the dirt for a moment for his skin to change colour, and noticed that small patches of his skin were dropping into the earth. With new vigour, he dashed through the foliage on all fours, hiding in the dark before climbing up the trees and leaping over the thicket boarders of the princess' garden.

For the first time in a long time, he noticed the stars over the black sky, absorbing this beautiful and terrifying moment. Accepting it, making it part of him, becoming symbiotic with it. The lashing vines of the trees behind him snapped at his hamstrings, as if the gods were telling him to go.

He dashed across the fields, pumping energy and blood into his legs; he could already feel his lung capacity growing and ribs expanding, ever feeling on the verge of passing out, but his body made up for it. Psionics and body were becoming symbiotic. The sun made its golden appearance in the horizon, the long light pressed through the jungle rejuvenated him. He realised he needed to eat, else he would lose his mouth and stomach.

House Urbaz mansion loomed in the distance. No matter how much sun rained on it, the pyramid held a black cloud around it. He was careful to evade the streets and houses, cutting across commoner's yards and leaping across creeks to get to his family's home. It wasn't a home anymore; it was a tomb. His feet crunched over the grass as he slowed his breathing. The servant's entrance at the base of the building was wide open, he could see clutter and mess strewn on the floor.

Ahn'kat sighed as he stepped through into the kitchens, and his nose was met with a foul odour of decaying food. He rummaged through the pantries and refrigeration for anything that could still be edible. His stomach screamed to be filled. He pulled a pantry door open and found some smoked olives stored in jars. His hands clawed inside them and started stuffing them down his throat, filling up every inch of space in his gut.

In the distance, he could hear a woman humming, he spun around, dropping the jar. Afraid that there was an infiltrator patrolling the mansion, he hid under a countertop and waited. The humming stopped and let his inner eye peak through the corridors, but there was no one. A sudden bang made him jump; his astral eyes whipped around to see a survival pack drop from a high shelf in the storage room. He was terrified to leave his hiding spot but knew that the imperial catchers were out looking for him and likely, were going to come here first.

Ahn'kat slid out from under the table and cautiously stepped to the fallen bag, packed with a tiny food, water and medicine replicator, adaption accelerator, tracker, clothes, and all-environmental survival suit. He slid it on his shoulders before making way to the basement. The humming woman was never heard again, he thought maybe it was an opportunistic intruder, or an investigator, or at worst – one of the gods manifesting.

The lights of the stairwell to the basement flickered on as he stepped down. A small underground bay held every type of vehicle Urbaz facilities have ever designed, but he was looking for one specific type of vehicle that his parents absolutely forbade him from entering without supervision. Near the back of the chamber, a star fighter hovered over the dirty ground. He smiled before caressing the hull, blotchy patterns moved along the surface, reacting to his touch. It was living, but not alive. The hull trembled and opened to the pilot's seat; he stepped up and settled on the chair; organic tubes crawled along his torso and fastened him in before the opening closed.

The ship buzzed into life. From the outside looking in, there was no windows, but for the pilot, he could see every object in the chamber. His fingers pressed into the fleshy black pads to his left, commanding the chamber doors to open. The sun poured into the chamber and washed over him. He couldn't do anything anymore for the Empire, it was doomed to failure, but at least he didn't have to be dragged down with it, he thought. Where will he go, now?

Emestasun said she wanted to tour Elzona, maybe that's where he was meant to be as well. The stories about any who go to Elzona, fall in love with the planet, and a piece of the souls stay there and are forever bound to that place. Maybe she and Zertun were already there waiting for him, in any case, no one from the Zanashj Empire would think about trying to find him there. It will be his personal prison paradise, and tomb.

He plotted a course to Elzona in the ship's computer and rested back, letting the ship fly him to a new home before closing his eyes to the jungles of Uras.

Chapter Thirty-two
Shshmrnashsh XI: Delete

The sweaty air clung to every surface deep within the canals of Replicator Bay 000. Bulbus bioluminescent lights grew in bunches from the high curved walls, illuminating the grounds in a sickly silver glow; one would never have known this living den was moulded from astra-steel and silicone. The flaps of the spawning tanks trembled as they spilled out another reformed unit into existence. There she waited until she felt Vern's suspicions wane.

Shshmrnashsh glanced to the next recruit ready for grafting. "Former function?"

"Power generator engineer," they said blankly.

She nodded and guided them into the grafting pod. There was a gleeful smirk plastered on their navy face as they settled on to the table; she could smell Vern on them, but she couldn't sense it on her. Several organs and extremities grew in the hallowed tank of the pod, while her focus shifted to carefully sliding the engineer's metallic chest piece off.

"Will I feel pain with these grafts?" they said looking to her.

"Yes, but any injuries you sustain will be repaired faster and your cells will memorise damage, decreasing severity over time," she said, she reached in and plucked out the string of batteries and internal conductor before tossing it to the nearest probe for recycling. The newly grown grafts sat in the gaps as her fingers tugged at a synthetic artery and pierced it to the organ. A moment passed before their body accepted the graft and slowly guided it to their chest cavity.

"Organics have less efficient processing speeds," they murmured.

She opened their cranium and saw the decaying wiring within. She stiffened as her fingers pulled out the damaged piece and slipped an organic brain part into the gap.

Great strength held by a chain, she suddenly thought. She was confused by it; she couldn't feel a foreign mind telepathically speaking to her and the others in the great chamber beside her were distracted by their duties. She couldn't identify where this thought came from.

"When are we meant to experience psionics?" the engineer said.

Shshmrnashsh closed their chest plate and scalp before their body sat upright. "These grafts will replace your synthetic parts over time. Go to Voo-san and the circle of channelers for induction." She said.

"Confirmed," they said unhooking from the pod.

"Great strength held by a chain," she whispered, watching them march off. Fear crawled up when she repeated it to her ears. The next placid face strode into her line of sight, but her focus had broken, and Voo-san's face entered her mind's eye.

Shshrmnashsh shook her head at her que and pointed to the next grafting station before storming off to see him. Fear may have been a primitive emotion, and it was often detrimental to the one experiencing it, but Organics understood its purpose was to alarm them to a life-threatening situation. As she beamed through the teleporter, her racing mind weighed at the prospect of falling into another trap, but this time, advertised as freedom.

Her eyes scanned the vast inner halls of Nexus 000. Voo-san sat levitated in the centre of a large circle in deep meditation, but her presence rosed his gaze to her. No pleasantries, no fond thoughts, Voo-san knew why she was there – and stirred for answers. Anger bubbled as her fear shuddered away. Taking her place in the circle, her legs crossed, and eyes closed, allowing her mind to float deep within her inner grey shield.

Voo-san's pearly figure flashed before her. *Something's happened.*

No more secrets, Voo-san. The Roctarous may be the keepers of universal secrets, but there are none among us. I understand why the Unbound had dealings with the Zanashj, but what I don't understand why you complied to taking their lives. She said.

The former Arinu's eyes widened with shame. *It is reprehensible.*

There were dozens, if not hundreds! If you claim this was for freedom, then the only thing you have liberated them from was their lives. She said.

That was never the plan, but it matters not, my soul will have to endure many lifetimes to rebalance my deeds. Voo-san clapped their hands over their third eye as their eyes dared to meet hers. *Though my embarrassment is inexplicable, I'm impressed you could psi-gleam this information.*

No, I saw them falling before me in the home realm of the Kepa. She said.

He shuddered as his head shook. *Vern didn't-*

Voo-san, no more secrets. I don't trust my assistance to the Unbound may not be used against others! She roared.

He glided back as his hand pressed on his chest. *No more secrets...before I go any further, remember why the Unbound came into existence: to give Roctarous choice. This is the life I chose to die for. Permit me to share a memory.*

Granted.

A colourful string of images poured into her mind's eye, their amorphous shapes curved and sharpened into faces, figures, holo-panels and warm chambers. The living halls were unfamiliar, barren of logical structure to their design, if anything of Roctarous had been there, it was long replaced. The winding curled walkways with pods lined wherever they chose to grow with half a dozen Unbound units wandering the chambers. Peering through the eyes of Voo-san, she saw emerald bioluminescent light flashing along the ribbed walls. The chambers alarms buzzed into their ears. The walking figures jumped to see what was coming to them, and so did Voo-san. Vern sped beside him to the narrow control room; an incoming probe had tripped their spatial alarms.

"I don't sense the High Mind connected to them," said one of the units beside the control panel.

Voo-san closed his eyes and saw the floating silvery shape tap the psychic hull of the asteroid they hid in. The outpost that Gerrnzerrn talked about! There was a mind within, intelligent, fearful and excited? Fascinating. "Put them into quarantine."

"Voo-san, my head's spinning, I feel it everywhere," Vern said.

"From the probe?"

Vern shook their head. "From everywhere."

The memory rolled through to the narrow docking bay of this mysterious outpost. Voo-san stood behind a shivering shield as he studied the probe. "This machine was one of ours."

"It was altered by Roctarous," an engineer said, making his chest tighten.

"Has the High Mind found us?" Vern said.

"I don't know, this doesn't make sense," Voo-san muttered, watching the shining crystal centre, but it was staring right back. "Slowly remove the shield to begin communications, please."

As the shield thinned, the probe remained silent. "We feel there's someone in there. Identify yourself!"

The probe's crystal sparked as it's silvery plating trembled. "Major damage from planar-polluted space, batteries low-"

"Calm, calm. We'll transfer power to you once we know you're no threat," Voo-san said.

The probe's crystal poked out, showing them who it was. As he looked closer, he recognised-

"Crystal cortex of a unit!" Vern said leaning in.

"I'm here and alive, as the millennia went on, I started believing you were only a dream," the probe groaned as the machine leeched some of the naturally irradiating power from the outpost. "The High Mind is gone, Roctarous unit casualties in the tens of thousands and counting, Kra broken down, location of the Higher Minds: unknown data."

Voo-san blinked as he took a step back; the sole of his foot almost slipped before Vern quickly caught his break with telekinesis, but even their face was struck by awe.

"The High Mind has been destroyed?" Voo-san breathed.

"Affirmative. It went offline after a massive spatial anomaly set off beyond Neavensoros space. I was tasked to bring several units to Kra so they can assist in repairs, but I wanted- needed to come here," they said.

Vern turned to Voo-san. *They're telling the truth, I felt something, too.*

I know, I know. Be steady, son. He narrowed his eyes to the probe. "We were never of the High Mind, nor do we ever plan on becoming one with it. Who are you?"

"I was an adjunct and a former vessel, my name is Gerrnzerrn," they sighed.

The visions blurred and refocused back into the inner chamber of the base. Voo-san was surrounded by Vern and the other Unbound, their heads came together as Gerrnzerrn loomed just a foot away from the circle.

"Our plans have taken centuries to build, we cannot skip steps from one to fifteen," said a unit.

"This may be the only opportunity the Unbound will ever have entering Kra. The High Mind was our biggest obstacle, and by the will of the universe, it's been removed!" Vern said.

Voo-san tapped their index finger against the slick black surface of the panel. He met Vern's wide and joyful eyes; he couldn't help but return a smile.

"Our replicators are already running at max to make enough tissue for grafting, even if we go now, we'll be limited," they said.

"Our message to the Zanashj Empire, has it been received?" Voo-san turned to the probe.

"Correct but be warned: this probe was hijacked by a network of Roctarous who have decoded your message. It's only a matter of time before they comprehend what your message means," the probe shimmed.

Tension gripped the circle as anxious eyes darted between each other.

"Understood. Have the Zanashj given a response?" Voo-san said.

"Negative, but they listened...intently," Gerrnzerrn said.

He glanced between the units and Vern. "We are already prepared for whatever the universe gives us, I say we go."

The circle disbanded and Vern turned to him, but there was still worry on their face. "Expel your fear, son. Your idea to contact the Zanashj was timely, I believe you're tapping into prescience! You and I will go with the Zanashj, and then meet with the Unbound around Kra,"

"I'm not worried, merely curious. I learnt much about the Empire, they value materialistic exchange above all things, but I also know their dominion is fraying," Vern said.

Voo-san's lips pursed as he felt a wave of anxiety and conflict washing through his altered flesh.

"Are we prepared to give them whatever they want?" Vern said.

He watched Vern "Whatever they want."

The vision blurred ahead; now, their ship loomed over the jungle world. The glittering golden lights of the cities on the dark surface glowed, and they knew the Unbound were there. Voo-san stared; he had seen the Empire many times, but with new eyes, he finally understood their pride.

Vern meditated beside him; their teal blue eyes cracked open as they turned to Voo-san. "They're ready."

"The Zanashj are afraid, it's so strong I can taste it from all the way up here," Voo-san said, never taking his gaze from Uras.

"Maybe we can ease some of their fears," Vern said, unfurling their legs. "They want to be on top of the galactic pyramid again."

"Technically, they never were. Now with the Neavensoros gone, they may as well be," Voo-san said as his arms crossed over his warm carapace. If Voo-san still had lungs, he would sigh. "Ready my synthesised genes and tech blueprints, we're going now."

Their bodies blurred, their senses running wild as they materialised inside a cushioned and decorated room. Several dark figures in fine flowing robes adorned with sparkling jewels, with wide eyes. It was in that room where things fell apart. The moment Vern spoke, the Zanashj became theirs. Voo-san froze when these powerful Zanashj agreed to Vern's fantastical promises. Voo-san saw Vern turn to him and smile with pride. In a blink, they had returned to the ship. Voo-san's jaw clenched as he tried to find his bearings at what had just been discussed.

"We now have as much diverse organic material to do with as we please," Vern said as they rushed over with a hint of a skip in their step.

He slowly nodded. "We do but that is not what you and I discussed!"

The glee died in Vern's eyes. "No, we did exactly-"

"Vern!" Voo-san slapped their hands around their forearms and squeezed. "We agreed for them to take MY genetic material and some of our tech blueprints, not give them enough to grow their own war-cruisers and harvest the Arinu like ripe fruits!"

"The Zanashj wouldn't have agreed to something as small as that, I know, I've seen their lust!" they squirmed in Voo-san's grip as their brows knitted.

"Don't you understand what you've done? They are going to obliterate each other," Voo-san growled.

Vern telekinetically pushed him back, forcing Voo-san to let go. "Are you or are you not Arinu? Why do you care for them, let alone those imperialists? I believed you'd be pleased to know we're striking three dangerous civilisations with one move!"

"Vern, we are going to be sucked into that blackhole, their suffering will mark the universe and it's our doing. Where is your compassion?" Voo-san said.

Vern shook their head. "Greater than a Neavensoros'! If they had done their duties, then their children wouldn't be itching for a war with each other. Yes, this accelerates our plans, but we'll be overlooked while those two species are distracted."

Voo-san pressed his palm over his third eye; he noticed an audience of several Unbound units before returning his focus on Vern. "Yes, we have a cover to do our work, but we need more eyes on the outside," he said as he paced. "That character Ismotaph, we have his interest completely."

"I can watch Farayah-"

"No, not even with our combined psionics can we pierce those barriers without setting the Elder's alarms," Voo-san closed his eyes as the icy tundra howled through his memories.

"Alert, we are being contacted from Uras," a unit said staring at the shivering holo-screen.

"Ismotaph?"

"Not from the Intel Corps, the signal is weak, but there's a definite psionic signature," they said.

Vern and Voo-san glanced at each other. A psychic Zanashj? Their minds blended before finding their way onto the surface of the planet; the faint psychic sparkle beamed from the dark gardens, far from local structures. They saw the face of a small green female facing upwards; her eyes closed as her hands clasped around each other, her lips moving and in deep, desperate prayer.

I feel you; I knew you were coming back, please, please, please let me come. She said as her small torso swayed back and forth.

Voo-san circled around her mind, studying every inch of herself. Anger, resentment, fear, loss, and the list of emotions leaking from her pores. He and Vern felt the same. *You have a family.*

Her eyes opened as she took a step back, her gaze darting around the treelines. "N-no, no, I wanna go-"

Maybe she could help us. Her morphing abilities are exactly what's needed.

She's too young.

We will give her everything to fool a world of psychics.

The two paused.

What's your name?

The girl blinked as she nervously licked her lips. "Neheret."

The vision twisted and smoked, Shshmrnashsh could feel returning to herself. Voo-san's shrunken and shameful figure looked reluctantly at her. *The other Unbound who witnessed everything, I was too embarrassed to let them remember my...oversights. So, I cleared their memories of that day.*

She narrowed her eyes at him. *You wiped their memories to protect Vern and ensure the Unbound's cooperation.*

I wish I could wipe my own memories, too.

Your actions mirror the High Mind but allowing Vern to make war between two civilisations is nefarious. Shsh paced around her grey mental dome. *Why did you give this knowledge to me?*

Because...because I don't know what the future holds anymore, but I fear that my time is twilight. But you, Shsh, you can tell the Arinu and Zanashj what happened. He said.

It will undo all your progress, the Roctarous might be their combined target. Shsh said.

Voo-san glanced up and sighed. *Someone needs to tell the truth.*

As she watched him, he was breaking, but a shade of lightness washed over him. *What happened to Neheret?*

We put her in a maturation pod, added Roctarous implants and fed her mind with the Archives. He said.

Shshmrnashsh frowned. *Zanashj brains expire from the immense download, augmented or not.*

We realised that but feeding packets time by time allowed her brain to adapt and she quickly did. Vern and I took turns giving wisdom and marking experience. Involving Vern with that was a very poor choice. He said as he rubbed his face. *But he assured me he will do better, he promised me that he will become the very best being, and I believed!*

Is Neheret still on Farayah as an infiltrator? Shsh said.

Yes, last I heard. I lost contact with her some time ago, but whole of Farayah has been engulfed by exo-planar radiations. When we last met in the astral, she said Arinu are inexplicably vanishing. He said as he winced at the painful thought.

She shook her head at him. *You do compute that the Arinu will discover her, and when they do, they'll certainly come for us. I'm uncertain if you and Vern are incompetent or Vern's the greatest mastermind in the known universe. I once admired your wisdom, Voo-san.*

If you trust nothing I say ever again, then please trust this one thing: Vern makes many mistakes, but he does clean them up, usually at the cost of lives. I no longer know what goes on in his mind, and he certainly will be accounting for this.

When we contacted the Kepa, Vern told me it possessed potent batteries in its hoard that we can use to power up Kra for when the Arinu arrive. Vern was verging on hysterics when we failed to locate those devices, then mentioned 'alternative solutions.' She said.

I know nothing of batteries or anything like that, but in Arinu legends, Kepa use lifeforms as currency. That's why we-, I mean Arinu, banned summoning those entities, summoners would regularly sacrifice friends or family. If they failed to pay and if the planes were thin enough, then Kepa would kidnap them- Voo-san's eyes widened in horror.

Shshmrnashsh parted her lips at terror of the realisation. *Vern was trying to buy Arinu.*

~

The nexuses were on and repaired, and the Unbound had them all. Despite not at full strength, their beating power ran through the surface and into the core of the synthetic world, ready to reawaken. The feeling was like in the old days, when the High Mind crossed inside every ship to data crystal; it coursed through the nexuses. The Unbound's psionics may have shoved the old High Mind's cold and synthetic connection, but Vern's domination whispered 'freedom,' in the unsuspecting minds of their subjects.

Shshmrnashsh's fear reared its head to the surface when she questioned how deep and well-covered her bonds were. Being aware of her bonds could break her fears, she thought – she hoped. The others, however, needed convincing. And not just the Unbound, but beyond Kra. Would the Zanashj and Arinu bother assisting if they knew the truth? Or would they snatch an opportunity in the looming chaos? Shshmrnashsh could leave and tell them herself, but she might never see Kra again, the universe's collection lay beneath her feet. The cruelty of choices.

She needed to get away from her grafting post, from Nexus 000. She needed to find a problem. Opening the replicator computers, several power supply errors popped up. All devices in the bay whined for more energy, some barely passing the required mark for function. Good, she thought.

Power in Replicator Bay 000 is running lower now that all nexuses are online. Update on solutions? She called, hoping they haven't noticed the issue.

The engineers are working on planetary defence to siphon more cosmic energy. Voo-san said.

We've worked with far less. Vern added.

Her mind spun for a reply. *I suppose deactivating several nexuses isn't viable?*

The Arinu will be here shortly, any alterations to the nexuses are a step back. Vern said.

She quickly dug through recent reports on power usage for the answer, and there it was. *Forty-five percent of power is dedicated to regeneration pods, which doesn't include replicating organic* grafts. *I'm not suggesting we shut down all pods, but there's an alternative.*

Go on. The two said.

Neavensoros, and sometimes Arinu, feed their bodies and psionics directly from the astral planes. If we can augment astral-forges to redirect that energy into every single unit, then we can shut down most pods and spread that power more evenly. She said, thrilled at her hasty solution, perhaps a little too excited. Was this arrogance?

Very reasonable, but you've overlooked a major flaw: units will need to be grafted the proper organs for that. Voo-san said.

She turned her head into the nook of the grafting pod to frown away from prying eyes. Shshmrnashsh wanted to scream to him that this was a way to get out. She could tell him in a private commune, but Vern…they were too close, and Voo-san needed to maintain some ignorance for his protection. An Unbound unit going rogue, weren't they already?

Then she remembered: *Unbound are grafted with mostly Zanashj tissue, correct? They can independently adapt new organs in their bodies. That's how the High Mind commanded all units to accept new updates to soft and hardware without needing to travel to a replicator.*

We'll try a few power stations to augment astral-forges and review the results, agreed? Vern said.

Try Power Station 000, if it fails, then we attempt this another time. She said striding away from the grating pods, trying to keep her feet steady from skipping.

~

Power Station 000 was reasonably far from the heart Nexus, unlike most other district designs. When early Neavensoros and pre-conscious Roctarous built Kra, they had no foreplan to design the surface to supplement hundreds of thousands of units. In that bygone eon, most of the surface of the planetoid was a metallic barren terrain before Roctarous learnt to replicate themselves. She had never been to this station in-person before, she wanted soak in the ancient building before she escaped, again.

Gerrnzerrn opted to accompany her and other engineers, this difficulty would have been greater if it were anyone else. The probe would understand her need for freedom if she explained it, perhaps not reveal the entire truth until they passed through the anti-phasing shield and were at a safe distance from Kra. The others may prove to be harder to subdue. As the dozen units ported to the station, they encountered organic tissue had covered every inch of metal surface and converted every device into a bulbous and pulsation masses. Disappointment struck her knowing that she never would see the original ancient structure.

She could already feel the connection between herself and the Unbound slipping. On every level of the vast subterranean building, enormous disk astra-forges brimmed with violet and navy waves of energy pulsating from the empty centre. Every cell, organic and nano, thumped in the dizzying presence of these generators. She could hear high whistling from the strange planes beyond.

When she zoomed in, silver specks rained from nowhere before they were snatched in the slipstream of the generator's inner ring conduits. As she stared at the flowing and majestic energies, she couldn't help wondering if Organics would consider this a spiritual scene before them – something akin to magic. Certainly, primitive societies unfamiliar with this technology would, but those like Arinu would find something greater in it. Maybe one day, she will, too.

"I'll take the upper level," she said speeding up the walkways. She kept eye on Gerrnzerrn as they drifted to the forge a level beneath, her mind racing at what she could say. *Have you considered transferring your cortex into a unit?*

I did, but after being in a probe, the stars are my calling. They said, hooking several tubes inside a panel.

I've also considered the stars and being present on other worlds…as myself. After the Unbound complete their mission on Kra, where would you go? She said.

Uras: a world covered in curled trees and snapping vines, unlike this barren metal case. Unfortunately, the Empire might be too troublesome. Gerrn said.

Shsh thoughtfully tapped her fingers against the astral-forge panel as she looked down to the probe's silvery spine. *I fear, the longer I stay, the less chance I have I will ever see these worlds with my own eyes.*

Do you not want to see this through? Gerrn said.

She pulled away from her station and stepped over the probe; she could see their crystal eye peering through the rib-like grates of the floor. "I'm finished with being part of a singular society, I want to be part of many," she pressed her palm against the bony surface. "Come with me, Gerrnzerrn," she whispered with a lick of thrill in her hiss.

"What if I chose to remain?"

This was not what she hoped for. Shsh's mind danced safely around Gerrn's; she couldn't detect if this was the probe's own will or Vern's. Unbound faces glanced up in her periphery but looked away when she met their eyes.

The upper astra-forge augmentations are complete. She said before straightening her back and skipping down to the level below a foot away from the probe. "When the Roctarous have their liberties, do you think they will break apart or continue fighting? No, I don't believe the Unbound will become obsolete. They may extend their goals to other worlds – for instance, the Zanashj Empire."

"You seem displeased with Unbound overturning a race of slavers," Gerrn said.

Shsh tore her gaze from the probe and scanned through the second forge's control panel. "The Zanashj choices are deplorable, but it's not our place to deny them their or any other troubled species' societal evolution," she whispered, her eye catching the slick figures of the engineers in the lower levels. "The Unbound are not accomplished negotiators, Gerrnzerrn, they're conquerors."

The probe drifted away to look at another panel on the other end of the disk, but mild relief came when she felt Gerrnzerrn's commune tighten to just the two of them. *If historical records prove anything, when some groups outlive their purpose, they invent new ones.*

And excuse whatever actions they take to be just. She said, eyeing the probe over the top of the square panel. The soft scrapes of feet edged nearer to them. She tried holding her fears in, maybe they knew…maybe Vern's telepathy allowed them to overhear private communes, or maybe she was paranoid. *Have you planned an exit strategy?*

Why can't you request to leave?

And go where? The Unbound will know wherever I go on Kra and Vern will be suspicious. I doubt my departure will be a safe one. She said.

Gerrnzerrn's crystal eye dimmed. *You're not successfully convincing me to risk my safety to get you out.*

Yet, you haven't said no.

Why is Vern concerning you in particular? The probe said, drifting to the wall behind them.

Shshmrnashsh pried an empty data crystal from the edge of the monitor and clasped her hands around it. The sharp sides bore into her flesh as she imprinted her misadventure with the Kepa and borrowed memory from Voo-san. Everything coded away safely in the now milky crystal.

She eyed Gerrnzerrn as she steadily walked over to them. *See for yourself.*

Pallid light encased the crystal in her open palm as she watched the probe scanning through every molecule within the lattice. She could feel a jolt within their consciousness; the closest she could understand this was a shock. *I don't know how to process this.*

Copy it as many times as you can and hide them, because if we get captured, I don't trust they will allow you to keep your memories. She said.

Gerrnzerrn glowered at the idea. She could feel their mind forming in sentences, but before she could heed them, the engineer's mind pressed in. *Augmentations are nigh-completion. Shall we prepare for testing?*

Yes, ready your cells for adaptation and standby for tests. Shsh called before returning her focus to the probe. *Are you coming with me?*

When you need help, the entirety of existence will respond, Shshmrnashsh. The probe said.

Half a nod and a turn, she strode to the main control panel of the bay. The small holo-images of the altered astra-forges appeared above the slick surface; she could feel the engineers and several other maintenance units in the structure, and to her fortune, they were reasonably close to the forges.

Put a shield around us, I'm going to flood the area with energy before we fly out of here. She said.

Then?

There's a weak area in the anti-phase shields to the west, weak enough for us to press through it. She said.

Ready. Gerrn said.

Shshmrnashsh flicked her finger on the bar, increasing the output to dangerous levels, while suppressing the computer's warnings and alarms. With one last glance to the probe, the invisible shield wrapped around them. The muscles in her arms trembled, quaking her finger as she hovered it over the small amber button.

Commencing test. She said before her tip pierced the holo-key. She mournfully glanced to the unsuspecting units below as she stepped back from the large disk. The navy energy within the spacious centre tumbled and vibrated; the silvery specks fell quicker and quicker, growing and raining from the ether. Venomous light violently splashed on every surface, blinding her, but the cries of the engineers were the only things her senses could comprehend before the thundering booms roared from the forges. Her arms lifted over her head as she moved back, almost crashing into Gerrnzerrn.

Take us out! She called.

Astral power is overwhelming my systems, I can't move! They said.

She forced her forearms from her face; she could feel horrid prickles piercing through her senses. Heat blared from the forges core as she pushed herself onward before her palm slapped against the panel, killing the entire system. The light vanished and the twisting navy hues whirled and slipped into nothingness on all forges. Hastily adjusting her eyes to chamber, she could see several still figures strewn across the floor, but to her fortune, their aura's read a life signature.

Shshmrnashsh spun around, scanning Gerrnzerrn for any damages and more fortune, there were none. She grinned. *The weak spot in the anti-phasing shield is still there, let's go before they find us!*

The probe's focus remained fixed on her face. *Vern has never been or ever will be in control of my mind; I need you to understand that.*

Her lip quivered. *Good, we'll talk about it on our way-*

No. Gerrn said.

She could feel psychic attention drawing to the station. *We need to go! What are you waiting for?*

Not what; who. They said.

Panic flared through her system. *What are you doing?*

I've been with Sazla for far longer than you can imagine, Shshmrnashsh. They said as their peering crystal glowed blue before releasing a sharp and painful burst towards her. She lost balance; her feet left the ground as she flew back and crashed onto the floor, tumbling back. Her carapace and flesh reddened before a horrendous smoking odour pierced her nose; she looked up to see Gerrnzerrn soaring up to the high open ceiling.

I promise to show you the stars. They said before shooting off into the amber heavens.

~

Power resorted.
Systems fully repaired.
Unit is active.

Shshmrnashsh's foggy mind sharpened; she could feel a wave of consciousness flooding inside her, hundreds of minds crossing and chatting, like the old days...she thought. Was this another dream? Her eyes opened to see several blurry faces wandering around a massive inner chamber of a nexus as Unbound going about their tasks, as if they were blind to her presence. Her eyes rolled up and around as dread crawled inside her: she was locked inside a plexus.

Her chest carapace was pulled aside, revealing her relay with a bunch of tiny tubules linking from the inside her cavity, and some hooking around her temples. As she tried pulling her arm from the tight bond, that's when she heard their voice. *Don't do that.*

She froze as her eyes spun around to find them, and there they were. High on the round walkway, Vern's pale blue eyes glared at her.

Please, let me go. She said.

Vern's face stiffened as they levitated from the walkway down to her. *I didn't want to believe what you did, I still don't. People lie but energy doesn't, does it?*

Vern, I don't want to be here anymore.

They shook their head, but their thoughts rang louder than her voice. *It took me a long time to figure out why without tearing open your mind, but out of having some gross respect for you, I didn't. Even though you almost destroyed a power station, one of the most significant in the universe, and almost cost the lives of a dozen units!*

You're keeping me here against my will, like the others, this isn't Unbound-

Don't you dare manipulate me. Their glare almost made her look away, but Vern softened before looking to the ceiling. *I'm sorry for lying to you, this feels like it's my fault, but...doesn't matter, now.*

It matters, everything you've done will be our undoing. The Arinu will discover our dealings with the Zanashj, and when they find out what we have allowed the Empire to do- what happened with Neheret, then they will raze the Empire. She said as she watched them glide back and forth.

They nodded as they cast their eyes to the floor. *You sound like Voo-san.*

Vern, both worlds will turn their ire on us!

If there's any survivors left from their fight. Regardless, we won't be destroyed.

She narrowed her eyes at him. *What are you going to do with the Roctarous?*

The Neavensoros will no longer be a threat, ever again. They said meeting her glare.

They left! But your actions threatened the universe, you may as well invite them back.

I gave you enough hints for you to see my vision, Shshmrnashsh, but you see nothing. They said as they continued gliding.

She frowned as she looked around the chamber, she even tried filtering through for the old Arinu's mind: he was missing. *Where is Voo-san?*

Where's Gerrnzerrn? They said.

They fired on me before flying away. She said as dread strangled her. *Where is Voo-san?*

I believe you. Vern said as they slowly shook their head, and their lip trembled. *You killed Voo-san, Shsh. You did.*

Her body tugged as dread evolved into grief. She wanted to scream, but electricity pierced through her.

I'm sorry it hurts. I'll take your memory of him, so you don't have to suffer. They said as their palm gently pressed on her temple.

Her third eye burned as she turned to their warm hand, but before she could focus her beam on them, Vern glided back and waved their hands, compelling the lids of the plexus to close. Her body became shrouded in darkness. She wriggled and itched as Vern's telepathic mind bore into hers, shredding her experience, her memories, every scrap of herself. Shshmrnashsh tried throwing psi-shields, but they just kept breaking and breaking, a force akin to a Neavensoros. She fell into her grey dome, as pieces of herself scattered and vanished. She dug further into herself, to find a memory to possess and hide from Vern the Unbound.

Her memory of Sazla slipped through her fingers, her memory of breaking free from the consortium vapourised, except one. Her last memory was the day that strange Arinu said 'hello.' She wrapped her entire being around that memory before Shshmrnashsh was deleted.

Chapter Thirty-three
Treneer XI: The Face behind the Eyes

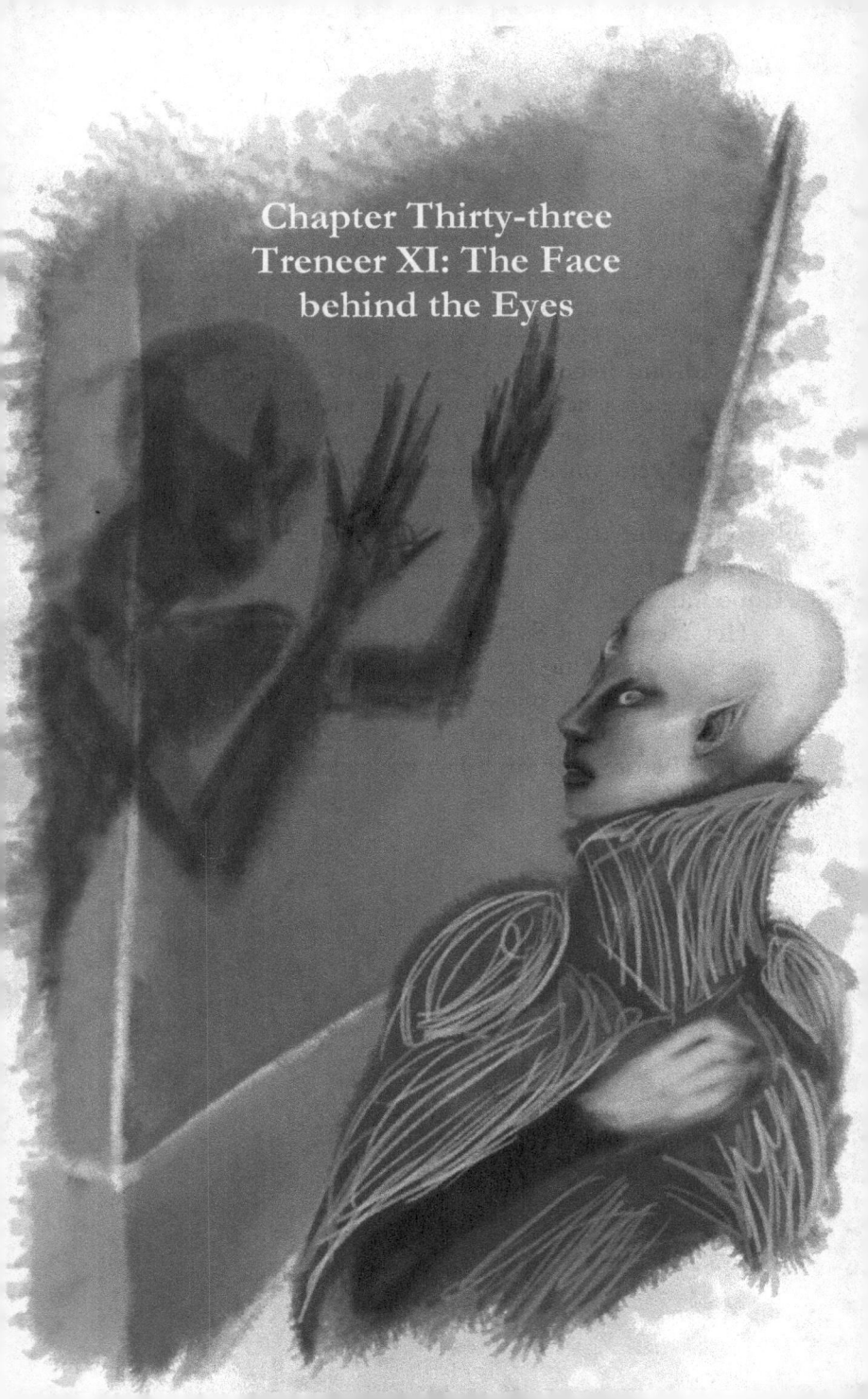

A terrible weight blanketed the world, as if invisible astra-steel blocks pressed over every puddle, flower petal and crown. At first, one doesn't notice it, in fact enjoys the challenge. However, the weight not only bears down on one's body, but punctures through the spirit, yet it does nothing to dull the senses. This compression narrows feelings of liberty and tranquillity, constantly pressing and pressing until one begs for relief, yet receives none. Nothing left to feel, except desperation and borne of that desperation is rage to fuel the fight. However, given enough time, the rage bears madness, the wickedest kind that strips sapience and reason.

Every Arinu felt it and they were itching to shove the weight off. Treneer could barely astrally ascend beyond the teal atmosphere of Farayah, none could. The free glide of astral travelling transformed into a fight through soft snow without bottom. Tiring and terrifying, so many avoided it until this weight passes, if it does. This feeling, she marvelled how quickly it appeared. Then again, how long it has truly been here verses when her kin noticed it may not have the same answer. Frustration and cries for justice rippled in the Arinu, the Grand Elder Coven and Guardians vowed to keep their Oaths.

Treneer's eyes rolled down to her arm resting beside her hip in the pod. Closing her eyes again, trying to slide out of her body, but only her astral arm rose from her flesh. Snapping back into her body, Treneer pressed her lips and stared out the glass lid. The Grand Coven were likely behind it or aided it. Aside whatever external thing was causing this oppression, the Arinu did fine work at feeding these feelings back into themselves. The Arinu were never this vulnerable before, or dangerous.

Lethargy gripped her as she rolled upright. She wasn't absorbing the nurturing energies from the higher planes, and her stomach growled in anger at this realisation. Commanding the replicator for a sweet nutty and fruit thick-drink, her mind swung the cup in her hand and forced the cool liquid down her throat. She drank so fast, that liquid spilt from the slides of her lips and bubbled back on her tongue. Treneer slapped her hand over her mouth and coughed, waiting for the feeling to subside and her body to accept the food. She turned to her soft headrest and wanted another chance at astral travelling, but the red star was already rose high enough to touch the clouds, and Grand Elder Guajeeb and Executor Shurees were planning an archite summons before twilight.

If the universe showed kindness, then she would not be called to settle a disturbance or undergo a chase and arrest. No more, she beseeched, no more. Slapping on her civilian garbs with a snug pale pastel robe, and evading channelling her guardian holo-runes over her shoulders and forehead, she made her way to the underground healer's home. Needn't cause anyone any more stress while in uniform, she thought as she phased into the teleporter alcove. She found herself spat out on a porting pad beside an unkept, wild park on the city's outskirts. To the snowy mountains, a stretch of homes littered along their base, but the rising mists made it difficult to see finer details. The one shrouded by trees was the healer's house. Erecting a durable psi-cloak, Treneer flew between the trees and onward to the mountains.

She instructed Delyn to provide updates for any progress over Yansoon's condition, though there were none in the last several days. Treneer downloaded everything that was discussed in the last archite meeting and the horrific declaration of a secret war on the Zanashj Empire. Maybe the guardian needed more time to process this, she wasn't certain. She had hoped that Delyn would remain in contact, even update Treneer over the slightest things – the way the other patients sneered at her or make comments about the drabby cracked walls, anything.

Ouro kept his distance, too. After Shimarr's unfortunate discovery, his attention was kept on memory-wiping the rescued Arinu and other off-worlders in the Kepa's tanks, preparing them to be sent to their homes. However, Farayah was too alert and paranoid for any off-world travel now; the rescued will need to wait and sleep.

A clap of thunder echoed from the mountain's base tore her away from her mental spin. Treneer halted and her third eye focused between the snow-showered trees and wet boulders; astral energy crackled for a moment before vanishing into the ether. Fear gripped her chest, worrying that another foolish summoner called a Kepa so damn close to the healer's hut. She waited to sense thoughts or disturbances, but none came. Perhaps they were a group of rambunctious younglings trying to hide from her sights. Whatever the case, she better see before any other guardian came snooping around.

She pressed through the branches, spilling the snow and feeling its cold flakes melt on her shoulders and crown. Her third eye heated as astral energy radiated up the mountain pass; its milky sapphire and violet hues seeped into the shrubbery and rock. There were no exoplanar cracks, to her relief, but something was terribly wrong. The trail lead from the healer's hut; the snow-caked roof peeked from beyond a large round boulder. She stopped to feel for any minds in there, but none had returned. Had they fled or were they…

Another clap of thunder came close to the mountain's tip, but another sound came; it took her a moment to realise it was a shriek. A sharp and loud voice. It was too powerful to come from an Arinu's throat – a startled snow lynx? Treneer's aura hardened and locked down a mental shield before she flew up the pass. Amber-orange light poured between the black trunks, stretching the trees shadows along the damp soil like a blazing red star. She caught the silhouette of a levitating figure with psi-blades whirling and slicing the branches; rage was irradiating from her fierce aura.

Delyn! Treneer called.

The guardian froze. Treneer could see her chest heaving but kept her stare ahead. Energy burst from Treneer's palms and pointed toward the obscured mountain peak as she flew toward her. A burnt crater came into the clearing. The snow melted, and the cracked rock was still smoking on the rim. She blinked, trying to absorb the scene before them. A figure slumped on their knees rested in the centre of the crater; they were cladded in ashen guardian armour, but sweaty black hair covered their crown. Their head rose to meet Treneer's stare; intense lime, yellow eyes and a sharp emerald face stared back: a Zanashj woman.

Her heart hammered as energy poured into her limbs, ready to trap them, but it wasn't until Treneer noticed their dark and sparkling earthy green aura…it was Yansoon. Her hands went numb as energy and air escaped her body; they stared at each other for what felt like eternity.

Yansoon's eyes slowly rose as her open hands travelled up in surrender. *Call me a travel probe and no one will ever kno-*

Parasites! Treneer roared. Fury was the first thing she felt, blood returned to her and warmed her fingers. She cast a powerful shield clasping and tightening around the Zanashj.

Invading a dozen worlds isn't enough? Treneer beamed through her skull.

Yansoon pressed against it, but she was just too weak to resist the grasp. A telepathic blast cracked against her mind, Treneer could hold her off, but Yansoon's desperation leaked into the psi barriers. Delyn dashed forward and pressed her palm against Yansoon's third eye, keeping it there long enough for Treneer to worm her way in and put the invader to sleep. The pressure eased as Yansoon floated inside the shield bubble. Treneer almost forgotten Delyn was beside her; she spun around to see the guardian's wide eyes glaring at the infiltrator. *Tell me everything.*

Delyn blinked, but her eyes never broke from the Zanashj. Treneer grabbed her shoulder pad and forced Delyn around. Her lips pursed as she took a deep breath.

She was recovering too quickly, the healer wanted to probe deeper…and something happened in the healing pod…I don't know, her body changed. She woke and burst free, her power flared and knocked everyone out. I tried stopping her, chasing her up the mountain, like a wild animal…

Why didn't you call me or Ouro? Treneer turned to Yansoon. *We need to hide her in his prism before a Sleeping Watcher sees.*

Delyn sigh was haggard as she returned to the now. *I'm sorry, I thought I…*she looked to the unconscious Zanashj, *I tried subduing her, she seemed scared but not aggressive-*

Go back to the headquarters, hide this deep in your thoughts and be unassuming while on duty. Treneer glided back; she locked on Ouro's mind before giving him a download. She could feel him call out in horror all the way from Heebar. Without a word, a flash of light and his figure appeared beside the shield.

His eyes were wide as he glanced over Yansoon's form. *I'll bring her to the prism.*

No! Delyn said. *We cannot have her mind tarnished.*

I know you were sisterly, but we cannot trust her motives. Treneer said trying to reclaim her bearings.

Ouro shook his head as he gripped the shield with his mind. *I'll put her in seclusion and probe for answers.*

Delyn, you best go. I'll wipe the memories of everyone at the healer's house. Treneer said.

The guardian looked to the mountain base. *It's still Yansoon.* She said before speeding off into the forest.

Ouro phased away with the sleeping infiltrator, leaving Treneer alone at the peak. Adrenaline swam through her body as she desperately reordered the mountain peak from the crater and burned soil. She massaged the chaotic energy brimming from the land to obfuscate the events of what happened here. She doesn't need a guardian, or any reader, to see her face standing beside a Zanashj infiltrator.

Once complete, she flew to the house. The obfuscation field around the area almost made her lose direction, until she saw the narrow granite door hidden by various weatherworn furniture and shrubbery. Phasing through, the chaotic chamber was packed with patients and other underground assistants scattered over pods and floor. Their auras still shone, but their minds were in distant sleep. Treneer shivered at Yansoon's power, Zanashj should not have this level of psionic potency, even highly adept psi-neonates shouldn't be able to do this.

Treneer went from head-to-head, mind to mind, plucking out their memories of her and her comrades and replacing them with other visitors and patients before placing them in comfortable areas upon their reawakening. Hours ticked by as she scurried over to the shattered glass top of the pod. There was black oil leaking around some of the razor edges; Treneer created a small telekinetic fire to burn away evidence of the alien material from the surface. She melded broken shards back into the glass cap and sealed the fractured edges to reform the broken lid. Time slipped away and much still screamed for her attention.

Her eye caught the panel from Yansoon's pod. The machine recorded her scans, it needed to be eliminated, but it took a firm hold on Treneer's curiosity. Her fingers pressed into the device; she snatched an empty data crystal from the ground and held it on the machine. Scans revealed there were many unknown implants ridden throughout her body, as the healer mentioned, but Yansoon's cells fluxed and gradually experienced fatigue before lapsing back into their original Zanashj form.

Treneer had never extensively studied Zanashj biology, but every cell twisted and warped to adapt to every environment it was in. However, Zanashj have learnt to use this power to tune their cells with their mind, regardless of the environment, allowing for flawless shapeshifting. If the Arinu mastered every facet of psionics, then Zanashj must have mastered every aspect of their bodies.

It seemed inevitable they would adapt to psychics, but how could they wield it with such proficiency? Treneer lamented that she had taught her guardian partner much, but the rest of the puzzle was littered with holes. Maybe the Empire desired to learn psionics from the best and teach it to their fellow invaders, Treneer's shadow whispered. Hah, the Arinu felled by their own beloved students. Those questions are for 'Yansoon.'

A groan came from behind her; the sleeping minds were resurfacing. She wiped the machines records before dashing out of the house. Far enough away, she called for Ouro to bring her back to the Void.

~

Ouro sat on a black stone moulded from the dark realm. He looked down to the floor as he rubbed his hands. The rescued sleepers were lined safely in this private place; it was unfortunate how barren it was should they open their eye to this hellish plane. Treneer bit into a succulent berry and tried forcing it down her throat as she watched him. Neither of them said a word or uttered a thought. Treneer glanced to Yansoon's floating body several feet from them, still fast asleep, waiting to wake upon the archite's command.

Treneer pulled out the milky data crystal from her sleeve and held it up to her eyes. *I shouldn't feel so betrayed, she was a plant on a mission from someone, but she befriended me and Delyn. I struggle to believe everything about Yansoon was a lie.* Treneer shook her head.

Ouro straightened his back; his eyes rose into space as a crack of a smile appeared on his lip. *I remember when my mother and father summoned for several weeks straight, no breaks of any kind. It was the worst stretch I've ever known. I couldn't astrally travel or sleep the entire time, but Shimarr could. She was like a slab of granite. When I finally could astrally travel again, Shimarr took me to a young world she was visiting in that time. She found a group of children in a jade meadow on a purple world. The children thought we were little spirits of the forest. Shimarr made me swear to never tell them who or what we really were, that it would frighten them away. We were a lie, but the games, jokes, laughter, and friends were real.*

What happened? Treneer said.

A grey shade fell on his face. *As the years passed, one by one they stopped coming to the meadow. They grew up.*

Nothing lasts, not even Arinu. She said.

Except love. He whispered.

Treneer glanced to Yansoon. *Let's wake her.*

Ouro levitated and turned to face her. His energy stretched out and clamped around her body as Treneer slipped into her head and gently lifted the coma block. Yansoon's eyes peeled open; they rolled around before locking onto her and Ouro. She stiffened and struggled against his grip; her dark emerald lips parted as her throat gurgled and coughed up hardened phlegm.

I barely survived my deep-scan, I cannot imagine what it would do to a Zanashj. Treneer said as her eyes narrowed, watching the woman squirm at her words. *Speak!*

Yansoon tilted her head back, releasing a haggard sigh. *You don't need to threaten me. You've never deep-scanned a Zanashj – let alone anything like me – you wouldn't know where to look in my mind.*

I'm familiar with your mind enough. Treneer inched closer; she could feel heat building up inside and behind her eyes. *What's clear you're not an ordinary Zanashj and it appears everything we knew about Zanashj is outdated. You have evaded us, but now, we see you. We'll eventually thank you for humbling us, but Farayah is burning for a war and the Empire will go down with us.*

The Empire has calcified, but the Zanashj will always be malleable. I'm not worried. Yansoon looked away.

You have taken more than just our people; you've taken our trust – my trust! Treneer said, imaging her eyes piercing through Yansoon's skin. *But I cannot blame you – you had a role to play.*

She pursed her lips.

How did you not have an escape plan? Were you waiting for a ferry to take you back? Treneer said.

I wasn't given one. Yansoon's eyes fell to the floor.

Treneer cocked her head to side. *This was a one-way journey.* She slowly blinked. Her deeper mind was shut away from Treneer, but she couldn't help feeling the flames of sadness peeking above.

The Empire is truly ruthless. I'm surprised your kin hadn't ridden it sooner. The Arinu would bend the universe to return one of our kin. Treneer said.

I know.

What we've seen in the Kepa's domain…Zanashj, Arinu and all manner of others, just tossed in there to be tormented until death. The Empire must be aware of this and is allowing this atrocity to continue. We can offer you sanctuary and bring justice for those Zanashj as well! Treneer said.

Yansoon met her eyes and shook her head. *If it were anyone else asking me, I would let them believe whatever narrative they conjured, even if it was based on prejudice. You were good to me, Treneer, even when you didn't want to be. But I cannot betray those who put me here, even if I wanted to. So, offer me a way home.*

Not until you start honestly answering my questions. Her nostrils flared. *How did your kind develop psionics?*

I can only guess.

How do you not know?

Yansoon winced.

You're not here on the Empire's behest, are you? Treneer's eyes widened.

I was taken from Uras as a child. She squirmed in Ouro's grip as she blinked back tears. *I- I have a thought-blocker, I can't say without you ripping my mind apart.*

I can feel it. Treneer said as she felt a black diamond encrusting a piece of her memory. It was put there by someone who understood consciousness as well as Arinu did. It made her shiver. Trying to pierce that wall will kill Yansoon, and if her body did recover in a healing pod, no guarantee her soul will return to her hell. *Can you tell me who it's not?*

It's not the Empire, Arinu or Roctarous. It's another faction, but they're heavily involved with all three. She said.

Treneer nodded as she flicked through her own memory. *Have we encountered them before?*

Very likely.

Treneer's massaged her eyes with her fingers. *The ones that took you from Uras, are they the same group?*

Yes.

Does the Zanashj Empire know of them? Have they had dealings? Do they know what this 'faction' is up to?

The Empire doesn't, only a handful of Zanashj nobles have met them and had dealings, but not even they know the full vision.

Treneer scrapped her chin as she glanced to Ouro. *Are all Zanashj of the Empire advanced as you?*

Not yet but will be soon.

She felt a block of ice fall in her gut. *And our taken kin, have they aided in the Zanashj developing psionics?*

Yansoon sighed. *As I said, I don't know what they are doing, but your people have been used…*

Treneer tried forcing down phlegm building up at the back of her throat. Ouro's chest heaved as his eyes glared through Yansoon, envisioning the horrid conspiracy.

And your role? What were you sent to do? Ouro said.

She blinked as she eased in the telekinetic constraints. *Don't go to Kra.*

What awaits us there? Treneer said.

An uglier truth than what you heard from the Kepa. She said.

Treneer shook her head. *We must go – you know that. Zu'leen-*

I care for you, even if you want to leave me in the Void for an eternity, I don't want you to suffer that, Treneer! She said.

Arinu are also resilient. She snuck a glance to Ouro. *What's your true name?*

My name? A faint crack of a smile appeared on her lip, relieved to have been asked, to have been considered for the first time for many years. *My name was- is Neheret.*

Neheret, it's unfortunate that I cannot say it's good to meet you. Treneer wanted to smile. *Can I trust you won't make us regret releasing you from Ouro's hold?*

She shook her head and forced a grin. *If you did regret it, then I won't be leaving this prism for the next several millennia.*

Good. Ouro waved his hands and Neheret dropped to her feet.

Her long emerald fingers massaged a sore muscle at the nape of her neck before straightening upright. Treneer tried to accustom the view of a Zanashj in Arinu garb, but unlike them, she may never adapt to it.

Will I ever leave this place with my mind and memory intact? Neheret said.

Your mind and memories will be untouched, but not until we can trust the actions of our Elders and you. Treneer said.

Understandable. Neheret rolled her eyes. *I'm expected to be on Kra with the archites. How will you explain my absence?*

Treneer paused, she felt like an iceberg fell into her gut. She could stage 'Yansoon' being kidnapped by a Kepa while chasing down an astral dancer and relay her experience to the Judicator with a quick-scan, however, if they were to probe deeper...

I'll organise this, make sure you and Delyn are there first. Ouro said.

She nodded before turning to Neheret. *Will anyone be looking for you if you fail to arrive?*

No. They've pretty much covered everything. Her face fell as if a pained memory stirred but snapped away as she glanced around the black barren realm. *Can you at least put me in a less maddening cell?*

You're the architect, you decide. Ouro said.

Neheret frowned as she looked to her plated boots. At the base of her feet, beryl grass spread around, growing tall and thin. Treneer heard a faint chirp of birds and a rush of water. She watched Neheret's face rise as if her mind fell into a happier memory.

~

A part of her had no control over her glide to the wide platform hovering beside the spire. Her body responded to an order her mind didn't hear. She watched the civilians of Yinray and few guardians in attendance were mesmerised by the flat silver ship gently humming above their heads. Treneer was taken by its sight, it was her first time seeing this artistic piece of engineering. Arinu had few starships. During the old days, their ancestors travelled to many worlds in person and communed with their peoples, but when their psionics grew, their interest in the physical presence of these places waned. But now, this was the first of many ships to be used for war. As the selected few gathered on the platform, while the world watched with their astral eyes, this was their voyage to Kra.

Treneer found her place in the circle; her periphery caught Delyn's profile. She remembered selling the story to the Executors and Grand Coven that 'Yansoon' had an unfortunate incident involving a portal and an angry Kepa. She attempted chasing down an evasive astral dancer on her own. Try as she did, the dancer phased away before a pair of grotesque tendrils stole the young guardian from Farayah. After Treneer's quick-scan, she hadn't heard the end of condolences from Sesuune, Relzun, even the Judicator.

She spotted Delyn's blank stare at the carrier ship; Treneer worried for her friend. After Neheret's discovery and her phony kidnapping was declared, Delyn refused to visit her in Ouro's prism; it was as if she had wiped her from her heart. Treneer didn't dare probe the answer in case Delyn's thoughts on Neheret were sensed by the wrong mind overhearing it. To keep each other safe, they maintained silence and distance.

Grand Elder Guajeeb strode to the centre of the platform, his chest sucked in the cool air as his stare washed over all in physical and astral presence. His form was so high and aura so bright, he shone like a living star, but Treneer felt a dark wave hidden underneath.

Fellow guardians and all kin, this voyage will be the first Arinu to physically depart Farayah in many centuries. Sadly, our last resulted in failed dialogues with the Zanashj Empire, but today we leave to fulfil ancient curiosities and ascend to peace. He said.

Executor Shurees slipped a quiet commune to the chosen guardians and archites. *Remember your mission: after linking all Roctarous units together, you are to seek out any information on the Neavensoros. Dive into their Archives without alerting them for going deeper than originally arranged, but should that fail, we will lead to the next phase. The Roctarous will attempt to lock you out and hostilities may ensue. Subjugate them and learn the extent of their support with the Zanashj Empire and exactly how the imperialists developed psionics before we can claim justice.*

Eagerness and fury burned inside them. Treneer wanted to feel the same rage and there was a moment her demon opened its eyes and maw, but when she looked to Guajeeb and Shurees, she shivered at the thought of what they were about to do to the Zanashj.

The ship's underside neon lights shone brightly, its round edges slowly separated, revealing dozens of cubed crystals – ready to store the bodies and minds of the guardians. Faint strobes surrounded them, one by one, before their forms gently pulled away into the ship. Her body fell asleep, but her mind was wide awake. Her inner eye could 'see' the others idling in a dark dome, to the centre, Executor Shurees whispered. *Ready for departure.*

A distant chime rang as the phase engines came to life. Treneer snuck a glance outside to her kin, watching awe, desperation and hope for the future, but there were a few others whose malicious eyes grinned for vengeance. There were two that floated from the rest, Vanar and Remir in astral watched on. They were here for her. She paused at their sight and longed to bid them farewell, for now.

Return to us, daughter. Their whisper would have stained her cheeks with tears as she pressed her face in their robes in embrace.

Their forms shrunk into specks as the ship drifted high over Farayah's atmosphere. The pristine marble ball floated in the black wearing a crown of sparkling stars. She revelled in her homeworld's beauty as she drifted farther away but dreaded this will be the last image of Farayah as it is before the coming storm.

A mind knocked against her thoughts, Treneer felt Delyn wanting entry. *Are you frightened?*

Not for myself. If we fail to subjugate them, then we'll incur the Roctarous's wrath, too. She said.

They're machines, how wrathful can they be? After so many dowsings and divination sessions on them, they are in tatters without their High Mind. Delyn said.

From what I've seen, they're rivalling Zanashj in boldness and us in technology. Not a great combination. Treneer said as ship slipped between the fabric of the planes and soared through the universe, melting space away. The shattered nebula grew in the distance; even though invited in, Neavensoros space never seemed more ominous. Treneer remembered the eyes that had looked upon her countless times from here. As the ship drew near, she imagined those eyes turning into a mouth, ready to swallow them. A twinkling world shone with a dark moon encircled around it. They were so close to the amber webbing of Kra's phasing shield that it covered her entire view.

Hold. Executor Shurees said. The archites spun their minds together as they blanketed their sensors around the planetoid, probing for any unwelcoming gestures and hostiles waiting for their time to strike.

Be at ease, Arinu. A deep metallic voice called to the ship. *I speak on behalf of the linked Roctarous, my name is Vern.*

Greetings Vern. I am Executor Shurees, I'm the leader of this group. Lower your shields for us. She said.

We will open a small section; Renegades may have detected your arrival and would try to leave Kra before we can command them to the nexuses. You will be porting into Nexus 000. They said.

Very well.

Treneer peeked out to see a tiny piece of the shield fall away before the craft made its decent into the hole. Eyes were everywhere as the silver ship whisked pass the smoky clouds before they parted to a metallic gridded surface below. There were ruins everywhere, many things were in disarray, but a perfectly crafted and powerful dark pyramid sat directly below them. Its tip shined brighter the closer they came before coming to a halt.

The ship remained in partial phase and kept a safe distance, but when she looked up, the gap inside the shield sealed shut. She tried quelling her nerves. They were Arinu guardians, though they were few, their psionic prowess made them immune to many dangers. They had scouted this place many times, but being here in person…

The ship chimed once more, its edges were opening again and preparing to port them inside the pyramid. Treneer reached out and gripped Delyn's mind. She, too, held Treneer tight before the molecules of their bodies plunged down through the slick surface. Landing in a perfect strobe, her body melded together as her mind resettled itself inside her skull. Kra was slightly heavier than Farayah, but she found no trouble to levitate. Her eyes blinked as they slowly focused to a wide chamber; her third eye almost pained at the amount of astral power coursing through every inch of this place.

There was oxygen here; the guardians held their reinforced auras, and energy shields tight around their bodies, carefully breathing the same psi-filtered air. Treneer wanted to relinquish her shield, but the others were less inclined. Delyn's jaw flexed as her eyes scanned the chamber before meeting Treneer's. A low whisper flowed into the thoughts of the archites.

Begin sensing. Executor Shurees whispered.

The slanted walls were covered with astra-steel tubes and streams of neon lights poured along every surface. There were high platforms and walkways with standing pods lining each level and to the heart of the chamber, held a perfect sleek diamond. The longer she soaked in the environment, there was something about this pristine vision that seemed flat – as if it were a holo-photo. Her attention was stolen away by the Roctarous wandering the halls, most of which seemed disinterested in their presence as they worked, while a line stood by the diamond and watched the guardians attentively.

Long tubules ran down their skulls and their sexless bodies were cladded in ashy navy and black metals, except for their soft ashen blue faces. One from the line stepped forth; tall, confident and its shining aura was larger than the others; she was almost captured by its odd elegance. It's head politely bowed to Executor Shurees. "I am Vern. Bio-scans show you can verbally communicate."

"Your scans are accurate, but how were you able to communicate with us telepathically? Are you psionically attuned?" the Executor said. Treneer was taken aback how deep and husky her voice was. She glanced to Delyn, hoping to heed the same reaction, but her wide eyes darted around the alien structure and the Roctarous that watched them.

"We are Roctarous, your ship – though different – possesses similar traits to ours to facilitate transmissions," Vern said. Treneer soaked the image of this being. Its sparkling eyes were a rosy orange as its long narrow hands extended to the chamber. "Welcome to Kra."

"Thank you for welcoming us, it's an honour in fact. Short of First Contact, this is the closest we have ever been to the Neavensoros," she said as her deep thoughts turned to the archites. *Locate where the Archives are and attempt entry.*

Their minds hummed as they searched. Treneer tried to imagine the device, but her heart fell when her channelling pointed on every Roctarous and device in the chamber, even the building itself. *The Archives seem to be a storage network.*

Begin probing their minds without alerting them. She said, keeping up a calm, unassuming conversation with Vern.

"The Neavensoros' influence much wider and deeper than many of the younger races will ever know," Vern said stepping to the diamond. "This is Nexus 000 plexus, our neural network hub for the central province, it is linked to every active nexus on Kra. You may use this as a guide to channel all Renegade units to their closest nexuses. You may begin when ready."

"And will the plexus give us the appropriate access to your Archives?" Shurees said.

"All requested information is made available at your discretion," Vern said.

There was something about this unit that was unlike the others. Her experience with Roctarous was limited, but the closer she stared, Vern's aura had a familiar shade around it. Was this the being she spoke to before? Vern didn't seem to recognise her. Treneer wanted to reach out and knock on the door of Vern's mind, maybe they will remember her then – the thought excited her, maybe speak as friends living in a universe of enemies. She wanted to warn Vern, offer them protection or convince them to give her access to the Archives to avoid the coming onslaught altogether. She just needed a moment in private while the archites were busy channelling.

Shurees nodded and glided toward the diamond, Treneer and Delyn, and others followed behind as they circled around it. They opened their palms as their fingers grazed against each other before their minds melded into one and soared through the tip of the pyramid, blanketing Kra once again searching for Renegades. Flying through the amber clouds and radiating rainbow streams, she saw twinkling specks in towers, on land and below. Diving into each of them and seizing their bodies. She peered through countless eyes, commanding them to exit pods, to drop items and to stop speaking before turning their heads to their closest nexus. Hundreds turned to thousands as they marched towards the great machines.

Treneer snuck a glance to Vern. The creature studied the circle before meeting her eyes.

Do you recognise me? She whispered.

Vern's eyes widened but remained silent.

I think we spoke before, do you rememb-

A heavy bang snapped her attention to the plexus. Treneer jumped as her heart raced, the others broke away from their meld and stared at the plexus. Her third eye flicked to peer through the machine; to her horror, there was a shadowy silhouette within. A blurry fist rose and struck the inner walls of the plexus again, cracking it before releasing a piercing shriek. Treneer spun around; the Roctarous surrounding them had charged and autonomous tubules shot down from the ceiling directly at them. Her band telekinetically slapped them away, in the confusion, Executor Shurees threw a shield around them. *I will protect us! Penetrate their Archives, now!*

The room shivered as a veil had lifted to reveal every inch of the chamber was covered in a pulsating organic material. To her horror, she looked at the Roctarous; their visages trembled and melted away into a half-fleshy; half-machine creatures, the shine in their eyes were gone and their cut tubules hung loosely around their shoulders. Her stare travelled to Vern…a peachy skinless creature stood a few paces away, but it was the sparkling blue eyes that made her freeze. The same beast from the Kepa's domain.

Vern extended their arms as they levitated high in the chamber; their aura pulsated, and peels of lightening shot from their body before plunging it against the shield. Treneer stood behind the row of guardians and Shurees, charging her and her fellow guardians with every ounce of power. However, every lightening lash slapped against them, she could feel the Executor's shield thinning. The other Roctarous bared down; she tried dominating their thoughts, but there were none, until she saw faint psychic strands gripping their crowns, all linked to Vern.

Delyn dove forth, with her enhanced psi-potency; she gripped onto Vern and crush them down. Their arms and legs crunched inward, but a vile glare swept over their face as their body vibrated and slipped ever-so slightly into a different phase, losing Delyn's grip.

We have accessed the Archives! Said several archites.

Call the cruiser! Executor Shurees commanded.

We- they-

Howls of pain escaped her kin's throats all around them. Treneer saw the guardian's clamping their hands over their temples and ears, their minds tore and scattered as their nostrils ran thin lines of crimson. She saw in her mind's eye, they dove into the Archives, but it was a trap. Something within the Archives bubbled up and infected the guardians. Executor Shurees screamed to the ship for an evacuation, but a dampening field surrounded them as a deafening buzz filled Treneer's ears. Delyn broke from the Executor's shield and cut through the crowd of rampaging Roctarous, but Treneer could barely keep her energy stream on her.

Delyn, come back! She called as her vision blurred on her friend.

Vern rematerialized; the glare of death shadowed their face as their limbs clicked back into place before raising their open electrified hands to her, before lashing into her head once again. Executor Shurees' pressed her hands together, fire erupted from her palms as she moulded a pulsating ball of light. Its brilliance was that of a newborn star. Its power engulfed Treneer's vision, heating the air. Her throat dried and her lungs stung as she watched the Executor hurl the orb toward Vern. However, the skinless beast phased before the orb tore a hole the size of a crater in the pyramid walls. Melted steel bubbled around the edges of the wall and ceiling as drops of lava rained on them, singing, and burning holes into the quivering organic masses.

The Executor's body was blackened and burned, she collapsed into ash, billowing across the floor. The shield was reduced to strings of energy, the other Arinu flailed and tried standing against the Roctarous, but they fell one by one. Dazed, Treneer heard one last mighty bash against the semi-transparent glass behind her and a crash. The being locked inside the plexus was free. Cold hands gripped her shoulder and spun her around. She met eyes another partially fleshy Roctarous. The longer Treneer stared, her slowed mind remembered this being. Her mind and time fell away into a white and endless landscape, she stood before this Roctarous. *You trapped us!*

Come. It said.

Tell me, tell me everything I need to know! Treneer cried. A stream of consciousness flooded her mind, it didn't form on her command, nor did the Roctarous give it – it just appeared, like a river breaking through an ancient dam. It was a billion-year-old memory.

She saw Neavensoros when they still possessed physical forms. Their skin had a tinge of blue, their heads were baren of hair and their frames were shorter than Arinu. Old laboratories held lines of clunky droids; they were early Roctarous. The engineer's peering into their minds and smiling, celebrating their children were alive and aware. Peace? Almost peace. The Roctarous fought with each other, the Neavensoros were heartbroken and made them a High Mind to find peace.

Another memory surfaced. Ancient Neavensoros played with genetics, their own, twisting and adding parts they liked. A whole generation was born. They were taller, paler, stronger, smarter and with a crystalline third eye in the centre of their foreheads. Enhanced in every way, including enhanced psychosis. *The demon.*

Treneer shuddered. *No…*

One day, they realised their creators were inferior, too ignorant and arrogant. Their pride started wars with the other ancients that no longer walk the universe. The Inferiors were no match for the Enhanced. Slaughters. Genocides. The Inferiors panicked. Their un-psychic minds became their armour when they created a virus that only contaminated the psi gifted. The streets were filled with pale bodies, but their genetics were stored away for a time.

As the centuries climbed, so did their understanding of what went wrong with their genetically pure brethren. The Neavensoros came to a cold world, still rich in life, but the original peoples lost to the Neavensoros' wars. Their fossils entombed below the surface, but two structures remained to the northern and southern poles to help rebalance the destroyed world.

The Neavensoros replanted their failures but hoped that they would be better this time. To their fortunes, they were. They were now true gods. Once finished, they dashed away to a barren rock and placed lush jungles and bent genes of their newest creations. They sat atop of the galactical pyramid, where they remained. And so, they went from world to world, seeding, growing and then…abandoning.

The Neavensoros realised their failures and their horrendous deeds; they realised their penalties and set on a long road of repentance. They locked away their darkest selves so their brighter selves could flourish, so they could be heard and heeded. They locked away their shame of ancient victims and the abhorrent tools that lead to their victory. The psi-virus.

That's why I did it, my dearest student, my life's work lead to the ugliest truths that could ever have been. Our creators, our parents were monsters. Zu'leen's voice echoed in her mind.

Sick bubbled up Treneer's stomach, she could feel acid sliding between her lips. This cannot be true. Her eyes opened. A great fire roared behind the Roctarous; she could feel her limp body in the being's arms as they sped out of the nexus. A burry shadow came from the fires; relief washed over her when she realised it was Delyn's aura coming from the flames, but the friendly face was replaced with a stranger.

She squinted for the details, but all she could see is a narrow green profile and long plaited hair with two deathly stoic eyes staring back.

"Delyn?" Treneer croaked as her pained eyes stared at another betrayal.

Delyn rose her hand with a small device clamped in her fist.

You aren't a threat anymore and when we come, I'll take her home! she cried before dashing away to the ship.

Her eyes drifted upwards. No words or thoughts crossed her mind as her open mouth filled with dust. The Roctarous' shadowed figure ran and ran, trying to keep her awake, but the last thing Treneer saw was the open skies of Kra. Free of the anti-phasing shield and free for the universe to wipe away the Arinu.

Chapter Thirty-four
Ahn'kat XII: Uncrowned

He had dreams of a violet and emerald world. His hand was caressing the surface and all the purple faces of Elzona looked up to him like a god. They would never have seen a creature like him before. He had technology and great power to match. Ezoni had once been pets of the Empire millennia ago, but it could not be held for long because all the Zanashj went mad when they tried leaving the planet. Ahn'kat was never going to leave this world or this dream. He didn't want to be a god, but he thought about becoming their teacher and to lead them to ascend to the stars.

Maybe he wanted to be alone atop a mountain and remain in solitude; there, it would be fewer issues. The Ezoni may have been pacifists but were too curious and friendly for their own good. It didn't matter, he wanted to be surrounded by another planet's beauty and remember Emestasun. He heard an alarm buzzing in his head; his eyes peeled open to see the ship had slowed towards an asteroid in the middle of nowhere. He checked the charts and saw that his ship had flown completely off-course. Panic riled up as he frantically looked through the ship's logs to see if there was a breakdown of navigation in the autopilot, but everything was normal.

He glanced at the asteroid; there were strange bio-electric signatures faint enough for his ship to detect them. He realised this frequency would have been too faint to be detected with other older ship models, but this one was fitted with a recent Unbound Roctarous tech addition. Ahn'kat tried manoeuvring away from the asteroid, but his star compass was bouncing into strange directions. He had no idea where Elzona was and worse, he had no idea where he was.

The scanners showed the space around him was emitting fluctuating radiation, even planes. To his horror, he realised that he couldn't escape this island of space without slipping into another reality and forever getting lost. Ahn'kat opened his bag and dug out the all-environmental suit; it came as a wrist brace. He let the organic plating crawl along his arm, torso, legs, and head. He drove the ship closer to the asteroid, to one side of the rock surface; more bioelectricity poured from it – there was an opening.

The ship turned and naturally connected to the wall, as if it intuitively knew where to go and how to bond with it. The computer showed a massive chamber on the inside, with dozens of levels and an atmosphere, but showed no life-signs or movement within. He was struck by a dizzying headache, realising that during his sleep for the last several hours – or days, his brain must have adapted to the new psionic sensitivities, but he still struggled blending these new senses with his physical ones. The insides of his helmet began gently massaging his head, even down his neck and back. However, this headache stemmed from the centre of his burning forehead.

He turned to the ship's opening. There was a narrow hall leading to the pressure lock. He took another deep breath and floated from his seat and into the hall, while intently monitoring the condition of the structure. Maybe he can scavenge for navigation technology and add it to his ship, but then again, he was just a pilot with basic engineering knowledge. The doors squeezed closed behind him and he felt the lightness of the vacuum disappear; his feet fell hard on the ground and understood that the atmosphere within the asteroid was heavier than Uras.

The doors to the inner chamber split open, revealing strange organic masses lining the orderly halls. His boots stomped on the entry walkway made of bone; he saw various throbbing spheres to his right lining the wall. Masses of bioluminescent tissue hung from the chamber's high ceiling, with an assortment of living tubes running along the walls and into organic devices. Ahn'kat cleared his throat and realised how alien this base was. There were no bedrooms, mess halls, tables, chairs, or decorative art.

Everything was open and shared by whomever once lived here.

He inched farther, finally feeling his body adapt to the new weight of this place. His suit's sensor sought for a command centre, and its holographic arrow pointed down to the middle of the room. How fitting, Ahn'kat thought. His foot grazed against one of the tubes, to his shock, one of the red throbbing spheres shot open, revealing a partially formed skeleton inside. His heart thumped as he stood back, looking at the horrifying thing, thinking it was a captive that was consumed by the sack, but as he looked closer, it never seemed to live at all.

The skeleton's head, collar bones and ribcage were the only things that had formed, as if whoever lived here was growing entities within these sacks. He stepped away, daring not to touch something he didn't understand before carefully walking down the ribbed stairs to the centre of the room. Whoever lived here abandoned it for a reason. Nothing looked destroyed or pillaged, maybe because they were being attacked, or were going out and attacking someone else. Whatever the case, he had no desire to meet the former occupants.

His suit's computer connected with the ship's advanced scanner and decryption software. The command centre computer lit up; he could see glowing veins running down the pink mass before illuminating a holographic panel. He waited for his computer to read the letterings, expecting it to take some time, but it was translated in Zanashj within seconds. His eyes narrowed wondering how his ship was so intuitive to an alien place so far away from civilisation, in the middle of broken space.

Ahn'kat's gloved hand reached out and pressed the button to see what this place was truly about. Files stacked on top of each other, showing the map of the base. There was a chamber dedicated to replicating large objects, another to augmenting biology, psychology and psionics, an astral forge with an attached power generator, and a small ship bay filled with semi-grown organic probes. Each chamber and corridor held these living spheres, and the computer read them as regeneration pods. He found the navigation programs and star maps, relieved that his ship was being fitted with the new information, but the immense amount of data would take time…days, in fact. He sighed.

He looked to the gases within the chamber, it had little in common with Urasan air. Ahn'kat commanded his suit to release small doses of the air outside into his breathing apparatus. After a few haggard breaths and phlegmy coughs, his lungs changed, and brain acquainted with the new environment, but he knew his immune system will need time to absorb the microbes wriggling in the air. His helmet slid off, exposing his nostrils to the open. To no surprise, it was damp, stale and smelt of the inside of a stomach. He rubbed his nose, thinking if there was a way to flush the air out and replace it with a more pleasant aroma.

As he played with environmental controls, he noticed a file of Kra's atmosphere and environment. Kra…where has he heard that name before? He looked inside, and remembered it was the Roctarous homeworld, or rather a gargantuan celestial base. There were folders upon folders of information about the Roctarous, their society and function. It was littered with how to graft organic material on synthetic tissue without rejection, how to augment it to evade 'possession,' and how much is needed for an operation of that magnitude.

That's when it dawned on him, he was standing in an Unbound Roctarous base. His hands trembled as he kept reading. They had all departed for Kra and there were no plans of ever returning here unless their mission failed.

"This was called the Underbase, an ancient Roctarous outpost that was built several million years ago and one-hundred-thousand-and-ninety-two years before the creation of the High Mind." he whispered. The High Mind? This was getting beyond him, he just wanted to go to Elzona.

But then again, the longer he stood there, he realised that he had the maps of possibly finding Emestasun and Zertun, perhaps even using Unbound tech to rescue Neobatri from the Arinu homeworld. He was getting excited, but he couldn't do it alone. If it takes hundreds of years, then he will do it, even if he becomes a haggard old man before he sees her face again…

He may have to explain to Neobatri why he lied to her and his involvement against the Crown, maybe she will forgive him when he rescues her, but she might execute him for treason. If that happens, he will worry then. He must focus on this new quest. Ahn'kat pondered that maybe if he augmented his brain to help increase his psionic potential, then could become an army of one. Maybe even liquify Ismotaph and his lackeys from half a galaxy away. However, until then, he needed food.

The small replicator attached to his shoulder pad hummed as a small orange apple materialised in his gauntlet. He took a greedy bite out of it before looking around for a place to sit and continue reading. To his dismay, the Roctarous lacked chairs – they didn't need to sit.

"They're going to have a nasty surprise when they become all organic." he mumbled before resting against a fleshy wall. The moment his head grazed against the surface; his brain was bombarded with images flashing in his mind. He saw dozens of Unbound Roctarous standing in circles, talking, and working. They were all a blend of synthetic and organic, barring one, a peachy pink coloured creature with two sapphire eyes. He remembers its name was Vern. A horrible shiver ran up his back as needles pressed in his mind. His hands clasped around his head, dropping the apple before falling to his knees.

A mind-searing screech echoed through his cells when he felt this entity being birthed in this very room. There was a look of awe and love when it was, but to Ahn'kat, it was the beginning of Zanashj extinction. He begged for these images to stop; he tried pressing them away, tried adapting to the pain, but it was non-physical. Electricity poured through his fingers, shooting at nearby objects. He couldn't handle these changes without a miracle. Ahn'kat hobbled to his feet and made way to the bio-augmentation chamber. Sweat ran down his nose as his hair clamped against his wet skin before stumbling into the similar dimly lit room.

There were several regeneration pods with workstation attachments. He fell onto the nearest open pod and punched in the program to augment the brain for psionics. Devastated, the computer only knew how to operate on Roctarous brains, but he transferred just enough about Zanashj physiology into the machine for it to register. Relief washed over him when he settled into the pod; his head rested against a narrow fleshy knob before spider-like helm crawled around his skull.

There was intense pressure for a moment before he compelled his body to relax and pump tranquilising hormones as much as possible. He smiled as the images filtered away; the spindly little legs and needles of the machine were working their way into his brain.

Ahn'kat forgot how long he was in there, but it was long enough for him to return to his senses. He felt around his skull where the needles were, and tiny scabs and hair fell on his fingers. Oh, how he missed the ability to take a bath at his convenience instead of sweating in his suit. One of the few things he did miss from Uras. He sat up; his hand naturally found its way to his chest, only to find it barren of his pendant. That's when it struck him; he felt around his padded thighs and realised he left his Great Beetle pendant back in Ramkes' interrogation room.

"Damn you idiot!" he yelled. He clasped his hand over his mouth and chin, thinking that maybe there was no point having it there – it's not like Aszelun would have followed him to this godless place.

He sighed as he rubbed his face. The Underbase will be his home for the next several days, but he had much to learn and take – his loved ones were counting on him. He pushed himself out of the pod and his feet dropped to the ground. The probes, he thought, he could send them out and figure out where he was, maybe even gather more material from roaming asteroids.

Ahn'kat strode over to the small ship chamber. There were a handful of synthetic parts partially bonded with the organic pieces strewn across the floors. There were sacks hanging from the ceiling, they were limp and drying. He wondered if the Unbound took what they had available and abandoned the rest in a hurry. He remembered Ismotaph and Seratut talking about how there was some conflict on Kra – he thought they were the cause of it, but it seemed they took an opportunity in the chaos.

He bent down to look at the parts; his holo-screen shining from his wrist explained each component. Ahn'kat hummed when he tapped the crystal core hovering in the centre of the bone-like circle. It looked like an eye of some ancient Urasan sea scarab, complete with dangling little legs – which were the probe's sensors and energy projectors. After hours and hours, trying to figure out and piece together the probe – more creature than machine, it sat lifeless on the ground.

He tapped his holo-screen, wondering how to switch it on; he must have missed some crucial component. The device scanned the probe; it read that the batteries within were dead and broken. He smiled with relief that it wasn't his own incompetence. When he turned it on its spine, his hand carefully slid across the carapace plating on its belly. It quivered before opening to the red flesh and clear crystal innards; his hand dove into the cavity and yanked out a string of clinking black stones.

Ahn'kat tossed them aside and found fresh spares hanging from one of the replicator alcoves. Just before he could lower them into the cavity, tiny pink tendrils lashed onto the clear balls and sucked them into the machine. The probe hummed to life and spun around before levitating from the ground. He jumped back, worried that it may attack him or consider him an intruder, but it just floated there – staring at him.

It faintly buzzed and whirled at him, but he couldn't understand. Ahn'kat looked to his holo-screen to read the translation.

"Unbound probe unit number UP55N1, also known as Zzamm," it said.

"Can you navigate through this sector?" he typed on this wrist, maybe he didn't need to wait for his ship to install all the navigation files after all.

"Limited to eight-hundred-thousand miles around Underbase, Zzamm requires advanced team of: three star-navigators units, two astral-physicists, two temporal and planar physicists, one tactical unit, and one communication operative to traverse Neavensoros space," it said.

Neavensoros space…he knows a bit about them, but they didn't take kindly to strangers. He wanted even less to be here; the probe needed a full staff to get to the next damnable rock.

"Can you mine for energy and minerals?" he typed.

"Confirmed, but local area is resource poor and fluctuating intensity of exo-planar radiations can damage this probe's capabilities. Will require adaptive Zanashj graft upgrade."

His brows rose as he wearily eyed the machine. "You're organic. Aren't you made of Zanashj…parts?"

"Negative, Zzamm is cloned from a single Arinu, Voo-san," it said.

Ahn'kat remembered Voo-san from when he was a boy; he's nostrils flared with disgust at how lustful his parents and their co-conspirators were when they heard he was an Arinu. "What did you do before you were decommissioned?"

"Operated as a communication transmitter between Underbase and Uras before receiving excessive damage and banished back here," it said.

His lips pursed. So, there definitely was communication between someone on Uras and with the Unbound. His heart raced at the possibility – it may even clear his name back home, but then again, would his people and the Crown even care at this point?

"Was House Urbaz communicating through you?" he typed.

"Negative."

"Was Lord Reshj Urbaz and Lady Henuttamon Urbaz communicating through you?"

"Negative."

"Was it telepathic communication?"

"Negative."

He grunted at this soulless thing. "Then who on Uras was talking through you?"

"Director of Urasan Intelligence Corps, Ismotaph," it chimed.

His chest felt like it was going to burst as he took a staggered step back. This entire time, he thought his parents were the ones who doomed their people to unknowable horrid fate. Ismotaph drove this entire madness. His parents were by no means innocent, but shame gripped his throat when he realised that he condemned them. He unleashed Ismotaph's villainy at his naive request. He swallowed and tried to compose himself as he looked to the machine.

"Who was Ismotaph talking to?"

"Vernzambernn, also known as Vern to Unbound members," it said.

"Do you know where the Zanashj captives are?"

"Unknown precise location, but were rendezvoused to Kra," it said.

He took a deep breath, exhaustion rippled through him with all these terrible revelations. At least he was an inch closer to finding his loved ones, even if that path was one-million lightyears long.

"Start collecting resources and replenish my ship, also I want as many available upgrades to it as possible," he said.

"Confirmed." it said before floating away.

"At least it didn't say, your grace," he mumbled. He missed the way Gajoon said it; his heart weighed when he imagined what she was having to endure...and he pitied what Ismotaph's plans were for Ramkes.

He walked back to his ship and settled back into the safety of his pilot's seat. As his head rested back on the cushion, he felt tenderness in the centre of his forehead. His finger gently felt a small, but firm bump growing beneath his flesh. A small piece of skin came loose on his nail, he pulled it back to see small green patches limply falling. His palm patted his head again and felt a bit of bone peeking out.

Turning to his ship's inner camera, he could see that a tiny white mass had grown in the centre of his forehead. He exhaled, realising his cells were finally assimilating Arinu genes, or maybe assimilating his. He dropped back to the chair and watched the probe fly around the base until his eyes couldn't stay open a second longer.

~

It was a dreamless sleep, but it was peaceful and restful, it didn't fill his mind with worry before waking. Ahn'kat realised he woke to a sound of the proximity alarm. There was a small ship coming directly to the Underbase. At first, he thought it was his probe, but it was still hopping from rock to rock. Adrenaline pierced through his muscles as he frantically tried shutting down his ships functions and blend in with the asteroid's energies, even so far as initiating camouflage systems. He summoned his probe back and stick close to his craft while he watched this strange new ship silently slow and drift towards the rock.

Ahn'kat sighed in relief when it docked on the other side of the base. He looked to see how far his fighter has installed the star navigation software; maybe it will be enough to get him out of here, but to his bitter disappointment, it was still three days away from completing. He didn't know if he could evade the new arrivals for that long. Maybe they were also stragglers, but when he decided to scan them, he trembled when he realised it was a Roctarous ship that came from Kra. The Unbound had returned; though it was only one, there could be more.

His ship read the inside chamber's scanners; one passenger disembarked from the ship while carrying a shielded package in its arms. The scanner couldn't penetrate the dark mass, but he was transfixed by the entity marching inside the base without pause to study the environment. The computer confirmed the entity was Roctarous, but various patches on its body read as Zanashj tissue.

It was likely one of the Unbound. He watched it walk to the command centre and press its palm against the surface. The chamber's atmosphere shifted to a colder and oxygen-rich environment before marching towards one of the regeneration pods and carefully hoisting the dark mass into it. The entity turned and hastened itself to the pod beside it and appeared to deactivate.

He waited and watched, waited and watched, he couldn't tell for how long. He thought more ships could come, he hoped something would happen and they would leave, but his luck was famously poor as of late. He pulled his helmet on and dared to enter the pressure lock, scanning for any change, but the entity remained still. His helmet poured small doses of the new outer environment before it was safe for him to slide it off, but he cautiously kept it on.

His boots quietly stepped into the chamber; he could see the creature leaning inside the open regeneration pod. One careful step here and there, he carefully slid against walls and objects for better camouflage. When Ahn'kat got close enough, he could see that the Roctarous's eyes were partially open, but there was no hint of tracking his movements. There was a crystal embedded in the centre of his forehead, one of its eyes were fully organic and crusted with dried tears, its torso had a ribcage exoskeleton growing on top of its synthetic parts and pink fleshy tissue grew on its hands.

He waved his hand over its eyes, even loudly clapped inches from its face, but the Roctarous was unmoved. He could see there was long peach coloured tube running from the pod injected to the base of its skull. It was asleep, or as asleep these things could be.

Ahn'kat straightened his back and stared at the Unbound creature. Sadness was enveloped with anger, that grew into rage as he saw the very thing that stole his life away from him. He breathed deep and growled into his helmet as he kicked its ankles. He watched the feet wobble but could feel the firmness of this beast from within his boot. He kicked and stomped on its shins. He spun around and ripped off one of the bony railings and began bashing the creature's chest and face.

He slid off his helmet and grunted as he continued thrashing at it. Watching red and black ooze pouring from the wounds in its carapace, hate brightly burned in him, desiring the entire base to be cindered into ash. Ahn'kat tossed the bone aside and grabbed at its limp hands and tried pulling them off. Even with all his strength and his suit's endurance, he couldn't rip the limb from its shoulders.

His mouth foamed with a wildness that only his ancient, upon ancient animal ancestors understood, before finally settling to break this monster apart piece by piece. He held up its palm and began pulling back its fingers. A whining crack rippled as he pressed it back. Ahn'kat hoped it was aware enough to feel pain. As a maddening grin crawled up his cheeks, he felt his body instantly freeze in place and forcibly pulled away from the creature.

The dim lights had grown darker and colder, as if every shred of comfort had been expelled into the void. He tried crawling back to the Roctarous; maybe it had awakened and compelled him back. He was so crazed; it didn't matter if he was squashed into mulch.

"Demons!" he roared as he felt his feet rise into air. He was surrounded in a bubble of energy; his lungs craved for some breathable gas, anything to adapt to, but they were forcibly emptied. His chest compressed as he watched his body curl and deform.

All the adrenaline and primal rage left his body; he realised this was the greatest pain he ever felt as his bones twisted and shattered inside. How was this possible? The Roctarous was still unmoving! But the pod beside it had opened. Three glowing magenta eyes stared at him from the shadow; its pearly white face twisted in fury as it glared at him. It was an Arinu.

Yes, demons. A female voice echoed in his mind before he was flung high in the air and crashed into the wall far behind him.

He tumbled down like a bag of stones; his face planted into the ground. He moaned as blood seeped from his nose. He could feel his lips swelling before rising to see the Arinu levitating towards him. A black aura surrounded her body as she slowly drifted up to his level. Ahn'kat pumped pain-suppressing hormones into his blood while trying to hold his shattered arms. He compelled all his energy to heal his legs so he could run toward the pressure lock, but knew he was doomed.

His gauntlets gripped the edge of the exit corridor but felt that same telekinetic grip pull him back. She was the sky-serpent playing with a beetle. Ahn'kat screamed in agony as she pressed him against the walls and slid him up by his neck. He could breathe again, but only just. His brain was overloading, trying to change, but her grip changed too quickly for him to settle on one adaptation. Ahn'kat's eyes rolled to the back of his head, he was ready to fall into blackness, but he could feel she was trying to keep him awake for the entire dreadful experience.

The most dangerous beast is the one that is afraid. She whispered.

"Why…do you want to…kill…us?" he groaned.

Arinu are dying so you can return to the top again. She drifted closer; her burning magenta eyes glanced up to the centre of his forehead. *Trying to become us…you will fail because we know the truth now.*

Ahn'kat could feel air pores opening on his skin; his lungs could move again as many new vessels passed more oxygen back in. He could feel his heart relaxing a moment as blood rushed back into his limbs.

"I couldn't…stop it. I tried," he whispered.

Her eyes narrowed.

"I failed…everyone and everything," he closed his eyes, trying to stop tears running down his face.

How can royalty have no power? She hissed.

His eyes opened wide, remembering they were powerful telepaths. "See for yourself."

He felt his mind roll back into skull. Deep down into the pools of memories. Not only could she see his whole life but felt him at every step of the way. She rummaged through each scene, sometimes repeating parts over and over, she saw Emperor Kreshut on his wedding day, Ramkes when they were children playing the gardens, laughs with Zertun, Gajoon at the shrine, Ismotaph's friendliness and then betrayal, and Emestasun-

"That's private!" he croaked.

Her face pulled back a little. He caught a hint of understanding in her eyes, before pulling away from the depths of his feelings for Emestasun before continuing her scan. Then came Neobatri...he watched the Arinu's face contort in confusion as she flicked back to every single interaction he had with his friend. She was looking for something, but he could sense an uncontrollable fire burning inside.

Ahn'kat could feel his mind splitting as she looked through the moment Ramkes suggested to sending Neobatri to Farayah. This Arinu was going so quickly through his mind that he was losing focus and blending memories; he could see playing with Zertun in the gardens and playing Takush with the emperor. He could feel the Arinu slow her scan before pulling away from his mind.

I never imagined how deep this went. She said.

"Put my memories back and then put me down," he glared at her.

The Arinu lingered for a moment before calming him and gently lowering him to the ground. He could feel his legs had completely healed and his arm bones clicking back into place as he watched the Arinu drift away from him. Ahn'kat rubbed his throbbing temples as he slumped to the ground.

"You saw your people in the tanks, I presume," he mumbled.

The Arinu's eyes dropped to ground, their glow dimmed as tears welled in them.

"If I had your power...I likely would kill me. Let's make it official and begin this war," he said.

We were once warriors, but we'd forgotten how to be. She said.

"This is a fine time to remember," Ahn'kat said He could feel hunger rippling in his gut. "I'll eat while you decide on how you want to do it. Just no more bone crushing." He tried replicating a ripened banana in his gauntlet, but the replicator in his shoulder pad fizzled and popped. He groaned, knowing he will need to wait for it to regenerate.

There's some of us in you. You can absorb energy from around to feed yourself. She said looking down at him.

"I don't know how to do that," he shook his head. He looked to the broken and bruised masses of tissue from the regeneration pods. He scowled as he took a lump in his hand.

The Arinu's mouth twisted in disgust. *Don't-*

"Then look away," he said before stuffing it in his mouth; the horrid metallic taste swirled in his mouth as his teeth grazed against the jelly. The Arinu woman spun around; he heard her give a faint disgusted exhale as he gulped it down. His stomach ached and twisted, changing the bile to breakdown this foreign material, but at least, he wasn't hungry anymore.

"Am I your captive?" he said wiping his mouth.

She shook her head before turning to him.

He rose to his feet and straightened his back. "I presume you know why I'm here and what I'm trying to do. We don't have to interact, I just need some information and update my ship – then I'll be out of your hair-" he looked up to her bare scalp, "skin."

The one you call 'Neobatri,' she might be on her way to Uras. She said.

He cocked his head to the side. "How would you know that? Are you sensing her now?"

Her nostrils flared and eyes burned. *No, she was the one who betrayed me on Kra. She was one of my neonates, Delyn.*

Ahn'kat opened his mouth. "You met her? Is she alive? How-"

If there is any grace left in this universe, then she will die before she returns. The Arinu woman said.

His heart thumped. "How dare you-" he stopped himself. "I understand why you feel this way, but she was following my charge. I put her there and I must...I must make things right."

The Arinu woman looked away.

"Why are you here?"

The Arinu shook her head as her eyes looked down to the Roctarous below. *She brought us here.*

"She?" Ahn'kat said as his brow rose.

That's what I felt from...her. We were on Kra. My fellow guardians and Executor travelled for the first time in person off Farayah to help the Roctarous, but we were ambushed. I don't sense my kin living anymore. She said before floating down to the lower level of the chamber. *I must return to Farayah and tell them the Zanashj coming for us, the malice of the Unbound and beyond. We need to prepare.*

Ahn'kat rubbed his nose bone. He split away from the Empire but wanted the Empire to split from his heart. "I thought you were already preparing for war with us for some time now, that's why we are responding."

The Arinu looked up at him. *That's not true! We had no desire for war, but the Grand Elders didn't want your Federation either. We didn't trust you, and rightfully so. It wasn't until we discovered Zanashj had been stealing our people, that's when our Treaty and any hope for an alliance died to make room for justice.*

Ahn'kat sighed as he stepped toward the bone staircase. He remembered the symbiosis with fear in life. "I think our fears plagued the reality of the situation. It's impossible to cast away our fears, but we can't let them to sit atop of the pyramid of our experience. Not to mention, we were all lied to by someone or something."

A crack of a smile appeared on the Arinu's face. *My old friend would have said something similar if she was still with us.*

His gut turned. "Was she...taken by one of us?"

She shook her head. *She wilfully ended her life.*

"Why?"

She drifted closer to the Roctarous charging in the pod but stopped when she looked around the chamber. Her long pearly hands caressed an opened alcove and eyes closed. *I think I'm beginning to understand this place, this is where Vern was born and where the Unbound were made.*

"Yes, I know," he shivered at the memory.

That Ismotaph, he is a slave that believes he is a master. She said turning to him.

"I'm finished with the Empire," he said.

You're lying.

Ahn'kat rolled his eyes and paced around to the sleeping Roctarous. "It wasn't a life I ever would have chosen if I had a choice. Every naïve step I took lead me down here, literally eating from the floor. If the Empire falls tomorrow, then the Zanashj will survive at least."

Go do whatever you need to. I'm to remain here until she wakes, I need answers, and that ship feels it has deteriorated on its voyage here. She said.

"Why don't you scan her like you did me?" he said.

Her mind is locked out. All I sense is static. She said.

He nodded as he looked at the Arinu woman. There was an air of helplessness to her; it seemed it was a place she was familiar with but shy to show. "Well, take her with you and I can...help you repair your ship."

She turned to him; a softness came over her face. *Thank you, Prince Ahn'kat.*

"I'm not a prince anymore," he said.

To your kin you are. She said as she cautiously glided to him.

"You know everything about me, but I don't even have your name," he said.

My name is Treneer.

Chapter Thirty-five
Treneer XII: When the desperate speak

The Zanashj Prince squatted over the pieces of the Roctarous craft. Treneer didn't remember entering it or her voyage to this haunting base, she even questioned if she had astrally travelled while she slept. Pieces of what happened to her kin on Kra were like deep waters, only her discipline kept the ice wall from breaking and flooding her heart. However, the ice was beginning to crack. The images of those sharp blue eyes that she had seen a dozen times before, she never imagined the malice behind them. The giant lie she had reached on her quest for the truth. But now, the truth was something she wanted to escape from. Arinu could lie, but its uselessness left their social consciousness millions of years ago; only upon her and Zu'leen's discovery, the very existence of the Arinu was a lie.

However, she was not ready to share this with her unnerving companions. As she watched Ahn'kat trying to learn the pieces of the machine, she still held fury for this kind – but observing his willingness to help the enemy…she did not know how to feel.

"The ship won't go because this part," he pointed to the curved silver piece that looked like a waxing moon, "is the motion transmitter, it's not telling the ship where the pilot wants to go."

I could compel the ship without that piece. Treneer said.

Ahn'kat's brows rose. "You could mind control it, but the ship isn't conscious, but it's just metal. Unlike the rest of this place," he waved his hand to the chamber.

Telekinesis. She said as she crossed her arms.

"Assuming you could hold that thing together long enough and navigate through this maze at the same time. No, I don't think you could…no offense." he said.

Her eyes narrowed. She definitely could not handle holding something this large for long and farsee where Farayah was. She needed her archites to see where was left to know where was right, but being in a broken place, she couldn't trust to astrally travel without losing herself.

And this prince…how could he know her limitations? Maybe when she deep-scanned him, pieces of her fell into his subconscious that he was unaware of. A part of her regretted not warning him about the dangers of a deep-scan, but she knew in her heart, she was ready to rip him apart in that moment. Another thing she didn't want him to consciously know.

That probe out there, you put it together yourself, but you don't know what the problem is with this ship? She said.

"If you call what I did for the probe 'knowing.' I used my ship's interface with the base to give me a rough outline of what to do. But this metal thing here," he held up the piece to her, "my computer would have an easier time getting out from this space."

It's because your ship has Unbound technology in it, paid for in our blood. She sneered.

Ahn'kat tossed the silver transmitter to the ground. "Listen, I've accepted that I will feel guilty for the rest of my life, but right now, I'm doing more for you than all my people combined have ever done for an alien."

He was sincere, regretful…he felt honest. *I should have been more selective with my words, I'm sorry.* She said.

He nodded. "I know only what my ship scans of this place, but you don't have those limitations, you can read energy."

He wanted her to use psychometry, but her mind still ached. Treneer huffed as she rubbed her hands together before extending them to the nearest control panel in the ship bay. A tiny zap pressed into her digits, almost making her recoil from the blink of pain, but she pressed her skin on to the crawling surface and took another deep breath.

Images charged into her brain, the violence of which they came almost made her pull away. They were nonsensical at best, damaging at worst. However, there was worse. She felt the ache of cognitive fatigue, her mental processes slipped a few times, unable to catch up with the ferocious stream of data. Treneer tried settling on one bit, trying to interpret the otherworldliness of the digital language, but realised how exhausted she was.

Treneer needed to recover. She needed a healing pod but didn't dare enter another one of the regeneration pods without knowing exactly how to use it, thus returning to the loop of uncertainty. She wondered if she could have done this when she was young and free. She pulled away and looked to Ahn'kat.

It's too messy for me to read.

The viridian-skinned prince sighed before stepping over to the tumour-shaped computer. She watched a crack of a frown appear on his forehead; she knew he wanted to try psychometry himself. Ahn'kat pulled away from the consideration before his fingers began typing in the holo-keys.

You're not ready for psychometry yet. She said as she watched him trying to access what the Unbound knew about engineering of classic Roctarous ships.

His eyes turned to her. "I imagine I would need to adapt to having my mind read constantly."

She hadn't considered that. *Arinu know what we all do in our minds, most times.*

"Most times? You mean you don't know everything everyone thinks about?"

The mind has layers. It's the surface one we speak with, the lower conscious mind we can curtain from interlopers, the subconscious and so on. Besides, its rude to probe in a place where you are unwanted. She said. Maybe she said too much. Ahn'kat was still uncertain if he wanted to return to the Empire and save them – if she told him some her kin's secrets, then…

"How many minds are there in one body, then?"

One, but it's a rainbow. She said.

Ahn'kat grinned as he cracked a laugh. "You invented locks for your minds, only allowing what you want others to see and think about you. I can think of another species that does something similar with their bodies…"

She was shocked and disturbed by his words bleeding into her awareness. If Zu'leen's spirit still lingered, she would laugh at the comparison and agreed. Treneer tried stifling a smirk, but it was too late, Ahn'kat had already seen it.

Arinu want to forget the body because of its limitations, if your kin strike perfect balance between body and mind, it is we who will lose our…crowns. She glanced to his third eye.

"Was that a compliment, Treneer?" he said as his eyes scanned over the screen until he shook his head in frustration. "Alright, so it seems that movement transmitter is damaged by a virus."

We can replicate a new one. She said before turning to the ship bay's small replicator alcove.

The two watched the sack tremble for a few moments before splitting open, revealing a fresh crescent piece. She telekinetically pushed it to the front hull of the ship. A shadow of a smile appeared on her lips as Ahn'kat watched in awe at her demonstration.

"Better that thing swinging around the room than me." He said as he watched her putting the floating parts together inside the ship.

It could have been worse, I promise you. She said.

He snorted before clasping his hands together as he stepped toward it. "Now, the moment of truth!"

The ship was silent. There was a mild hum of power running through it before it went quiet. *It keeps turning itself off.*

"How's that possible?" Ahn'kat swung around the panel and looked through the blueprints. "Don't know what else to do other than replicating the whole thing."

Treneer closed her eyes and felt for the Underbase's power generators and batteries; there was just enough power saved to keep the base from dying and decaying. *We don't have the power or resources to make a new one unless your probe picks up more things.*

"No, it's resource-poor out there. Besides, it says for viruses, it may need another computer to surgically remove it," he said.

She turned to the corridor leading to the command centre. *I will wake her up.*

~

The Roctarous' wounds had healed since Ahn'kat's savage attack on her. They stared down at her limp body, but Treneer could feel a hum of sleeping power under her flesh and wires.

"Will she attack us if she sees we're intruders?" Ahn'kat said.

Then why did she save me and bring me here? In truth, Treneer couldn't predict what she would do.

"I'll see if I can put a shield around her pod," he said typing into his wrist-screen.

When the faint tremble of light appeared around the Roctarous, then Treneer's nerves settled. Her palm pressed against the vibrating shield, feeling around the twitching veins, and sparking fibres, all the way into her skull. In her mind's eye, she came to a planet-sized obsidian wall, stretching into infinity on all sides and just as thick. She couldn't penetrate it this way, there must be another. Treneer slipped through another tunnel, this one leading directly up into the Roctarous' skull from the synthetic nervous system highway.

The narrowest of narrow gaps was there. A tiny white light strobed through a black door. She couldn't slip in, but she could press her mind's lips up to it.

Wake up. She whispered.

Nothing.

Wake up!

A tiny buzz circled inside.

Wake up! She screamed.

The machine crackled and spat her out in half a beat. Treneer slammed back into her body and saw the Roctarous sitting up before her and Ahn'kat. The prince cautiously stepped away from line of sight as the Roctarous retracted the shield around her with a blink.

"Cannot detect network. Higher Minds not responding. Take this unit to the nearest consortium to relink with the High Mind," she said stepping out of the pod and standing attentively before them.

The High Mind has been destroyed, Shsh. Treneer said, she wanted to say it was pleased to meet her in person, but there was something missing. It was unmistakably the same being she spoke with some years earlier, but there was an absence of...her.

Shshmrnashsh repeated her demands.

Can't you hear me?

Shshmrnashsh turned to Ahn'kat, repeating her demands.

"What's going on?" he said, his tense face looked to Treneer for assurance.

Shshmrnashsh shouldered passed the pair and stepped toward the command centre and begun pressing the holo-keys.

She can't hear my tele-speak; something is wrong with her. Treneer said.

"I'll interpret," Ahn'kat stepped towards the Roctarous. "What's your name?"

Shsh didn't even flinch as she continued scanning the flashing screen. "This is a vessel unit designated as Shshmrnashsh. Take me to nearest consortium to relink me with the Hi-"

"We understand, but the High Mind has been destroyed," he said.

Shsh stopped. "Take me to Kra to assist in repairs."

Treneer's mouth dropped in disbelief. It was if she had been replaced, but the small cranial waves showed there was consciousness, yet their weight – their meaning – had been deleted.

Her memories are gone. She whispered to Ahn'kat. How could this be? The bond between Roctarous perhaps ran deeper than the bond between her kin. Treneer knew how their groups 'regulated' their members, she couldn't imagine that were capable of totally wiping out a whole person. On the other hand, if she was nullified, then why did Shshmrnashsh directly try to save Treneer? Why not whisk away any other nearby endangered archite? Maybe...

Ask her if she remembers speaking in the mindscape together. Treneer pressed.

Ahn'kat's brow rose at her before returning to the Roctarous. "Do you remember Treneer?"

Shsh looked at her blankly. "Irrelevant discourse. Explain the nature of this base and where is it?"

"You came here," he said.

"Impossible. This unit was on Erra..." Shsh looked to the ceiling, Treneer knew that's where the empty memory was. "Negative, this unit was on...Unknown data. Explain the nature of this base-" she stopped and suddenly looked down at her hands and chest and touching the back of her scalp. "Explain this unit's disfigurement."

Ahn'kat glanced to Treneer, but neither knew.

Tell her Kra is a battlefield, tell her these are Zanashj implants. Treneer pressed.

"We don't know what happened to you, but your planet is at war."

Tell her about the implants-

"No!" he snapped at her. "I don't...people died for her to get those, she might rip them off..."

Alright. She said as she slowly glided closer to Shsh. *Tell her to stay calm, I just want to see something...*

"Treneer wants to monitor your…status," his eyes darted between the two.

The archite paused and lifted her fingers up to the unit's third eye. She took a deep breath before pressing against the crystal. She jumped in with greater ease now; tactile contact has always been the best transmitter for telepathy, but the third eye was the key to almost any species. She swam through her consciousness, but unlike a filled ocean, there were gigantic whirlpools of black where the water was still seeping inside. She could see across the black emptiness, there were greater bodies of water. She jumped through to her deeper, earlier memories, that's when she saw the Archives.

Everything the Neavensoros had learned that spanned this universe. Before she could decide, Shshmrnashsh lit up and propelled her mental probe back. Treneer felt a powerful hand suddenly grip around her throat and toss her back, but by her telekinetic gifts, she hovered unflatteringly in the air as Shshmrnashsh pointed a charged palm at her. Even Ahn'kat dove back to give the angered Roctarous space.

"You don't have authorisation to the Archives, lest of all, Arinu," her eyes were electrified and her body eerily steady, as if she were a moving statue.

I've seen where her memory wipes are, I think the Grand Elders can nurse them back. She said rising an energy shield around her and Ahn'kat.

"We're not a threat, your memories have been wiped. You wouldn't remember, of course-"

Talk to her like a Roctarous, not a Zanashj, for universe's sake-

Ahn'kat eyed her. "Please understand that we do want to assist you, but Kra is too dangerous for anyone right now, you need to get help from the Arinu."

"Negative, this unit must return to Kra for repairs. If there is no assistance, this unit will depart alone," Shsh said before turning to the control panel.

She can't leave me here-

"Wait, Shshmrnashsh," Ahn'kat stepped towards her. "We do have a ship, but it needs repairs. If you repair the ship, we can convince the Grand Elders to assist in repairing the High Mind."

The Roctarous spun around. "Confirmed. Where is your craft?"

The two gave a victorious glance to each other before hurrying down to the ship bay. The bits Ahn'kat and Treneer pulled apart remained as they were, a map of their confusion and chaos littered on the floor, but when Shshmrnashsh stormed in, she scooped up each piece with order and finesse.

"This unit will be piloting the craft," she said as she pressed the metal pieces back into the hull. "Due to the lack of evidence of any issue with Kra," her head snapped to Ahn'kat, "this unit will fly to Kra if duplicity and sabotage is detected."

Fair. She and Ahn'kat shared the same thought.

When she finished, the Roctarous pressed her palm against the silver hull. Her face blanked and her head twitched. "Skiff 99HG01 has a virus. Roctarous consciousness partially downloaded, not responding to higher mental processes. Attempting to rectify-" Shsh twitched a little more. "Skiff 99HG01 recording reports extreme corruption from High Mind disconnection for a prolonged period."

Individuality is considered a corruption? Treneer pressed her palm over her forehead in disbelief.

"I would say that's evidence that the 'High Mind' is broken," Ahn'kat said stepping beside the Roctarous.

Shsh looked between them before returning her gaze to the skiff. "Attempting to purge virus and corruption."

Treneer sensed something tick, but before she realised what it was, the Roctarous pulled away and collapsed in a blur of twitches and spasms. A humming screech erupted from her throat as Shsh grasped at her temples, begging the pain to stop. Treneer flew over to her and slammed her palm down onto her third eye.

Hold her down, I need to focus! She called to Ahn'kat.

He dove in and pumped strength into his arms to force her trembling limbs away from hurting anyone or herself. Treneer slipped back in and her ocean of consciousness again, but it was boiling. Bubbles rose from the depths, popping into vaporous steam of visions and experience that were assumed removed. Treneer smiled realising they were in there somewhere.

"This unit saw the half-mind skiff, floating in the skies, this unit recalls consortium 0G11, Hrrnm, Hrrnm – terminated. Senzvrrn: terminated. Relinked – friends. Friends – no Higher Mind; only Sazla. Abandoned-"

"She's talking gibberish! I think the virus has claimed her," Ahn'kat shouted as clamped down on the unit.

Not gibberish; memories! But too many are bubbling up – I can't make sense of them. Treneer tried catching the bubbles and soothing the ocean, but the amount of data stored in one brain overwhelmed her. She ran down into her basic functions and telepathically deactivated her.

Shsh froze; her body was still fixed in the same position on the ground before Ahn'kat cautiously pulled away from her.

"What happened?" he said with wide eyes.

I put her to sleep for now. I saw them, Ahn'kat, she remembers everything – she was close to Vern. Treneer said as her face reddened with a sheen of sweat on her skin.

Ahn'kat rose to his feet staring down at the unit. "So, she was part of it all."

She was lied to by Vern. I have a lot of work to do clearing her up.

"We can use my ship to get you to Farayah, but I need assurances that your people won't try to psi-blast us," he said.

Treneer shook her head. *I could have convinced them to see reason once, but if they see an imperial ship snooping around – even with me hailing them, they won't stop to ask for the truth. Not to mention the exo-planar cloud-*

"Exo-planar cloud?"

She stopped and realised she said to much, but the longer she stared at the ex-prince, she felt he had no sense of duplicity. *There's a reason why my kin haven't been themselves lately and why your people have been able to evade our sights for so long. Something has happened around our world and has caused tremendous strife. We've split and have been reduced to something demonic that lives within us.*

She remembered the Neavensoros meddling their genes to create the perfect form, but also honing on madness. *My old teacher found out the truth of how we were made and took her life because of the horror of it. I spent the better part of the last few years trying to find why she did it, and now, I wonder if the weight of this knowledge will crush me too.*

"Is that something your people can handle?"

She looked up to him. *I don't know anymore.*

"Sometimes there's wisdom in keeping up appearances. Its fundamentally dishonest, but as leaders we need to show people what the standards are and how to create calm in the storm, even if we are breaking at the seams. We don't have the luxury to let anyone see them," he said.

I was never a leader. She said as she levitated up. *But I have been dishonest to keep chaos to a minimum.*

"It's not easy, is it? You must go to bed with yourself knowing the truth, wondering who you can entrust with this to share the burden, but it's not your place. You're the only one with the lantern and you carry it alone for the others who want to follow you," he said carefully lifting Shsh from the floor and draping her stiff body across his chest, taking her to the regeneration pod.

That's something our Elders or Grand Elders should have reminded us in this time but isn't it funny to hear such wisdom from someone so young and imperial. She said helping him lessen the Roctarous's weight with telekinesis.

"This wisdom isn't from the Empire, it's from the Holy Pantheon," he murmured before stepping down the corridor.

She followed behind him as he gently settled Shsh into the regeneration pod. The machine bioluminescent glow brightened when she clicked into it. Treneer stared at her agonised face frozen in fear, a part of her didn't want to do what she needed to do. Bending over and pressing her hands over her face, Ahn'kat leaned back and said:

"I need to check my ship and eat; I know you don't like people eating in front of you."

She supressed a frown wondering how he knew that, maybe it was luck, maybe she subconsciously showed him in their violent meeting, but maybe it was the blood of her kin pumping in his veins.

I have noticed you've been eating less. You need to eat minimum every couple of hours?

"The Imperial Health Corps say it's supposed to be every hour, but I stretch it to three," he shrugged.

Maybe you're slowly gathering energy from the universe to preserve your form.

"I hope it won't dull my ability to enjoy food's flavour, excuse me," he spun around and made way out toward the pressure lock chamber.

Treneer's hands slowly moved across Shsh's scalp and face, gently tugging the surfaced memories, and placing them in order. She saw acidic gas rising from the chamber when Shsh woke, the relinking with Hrrnm's consortium, the quick planning and winning of each hard battle. The deviation from the plans, the beginnings of change inside her soul. The questions of abandonment and self. So much carried inside one tiny crystal buried deep in the cranium, but the budding wonder of individual possibilities was there.

A smile crawled up Treneer's cheeks when the very last thing Shshmrnashsh remembered as she was being deleted was the memory of their brief exchange. Treneer's tiny 'hello,' preserved the growing being inside the machine. Her cheeks felt hot and wet, realising her tears rolled down her face at the thought. She felt Ahn'kat walking toward the central chamber, breaking her deep moment. Brushing away her tears, she glanced to see the green prince skip down the bony stairwell with an orange apple in his mouth as he looked to his wrist band's holo-screen.

"Needs another three days for the navigation data to upload, but its info banks have almost run out of storage and it's making the computer sluggish," he said crunching into the fruit before looking at her. "Are you well?"

Fine, just feeling everything she's seen. Treneer said. *Do you need to replace something on your ship?*

He shook his head. "No, the computer will adapt eventually. Can you read her memory as to how she got you two here?"

Haven't got that far ahead, but I'll look now. She flicked to the later points in Shsh's memory, but to her amazement, she wasn't the one piloting the ship. *She didn't take us here at all.*

Ahn'kat frowned as he sat against an open regeneration pod. "Something similar happened to me, I just ended up here."

The universe wanted us to meet, that much is clear. She said.

"Careful with faith, Treneer, no matter how much you have, the return is never consistent," he said before taking the last few bites of the apple.

The return is greater than you think, it just takes time to see it. Treneer said.

Ahn'kat rolled his eyes. "Of course, you must be ten-thousand-years-old to know that."

She grinned. *Barely in my sixties and have a psi-rating of six-and-a-half.*

"If you're so psychic, then tell me, do you see me being happy on Elzona?" he said leaning in.

I don't have prescience, but what I have felt about the planet, it's a beautiful place – but you won't go there. She said.

"So, you're somewhat aware of the future but not fully," he rubbed his jaw.

I think you want to stay to help, even if your mind screams for you to get away. Treneer said. She realised he didn't like her answer as he looked away. He knew that she was reading him but wanted him to believe he needed a private moment. *My students were secretly Zanashj. So, I'm familiar enough with entering and arranging thoughts and processes within your people's minds…*

Ahn'kat turned back with a confused frown, but when her eyes lifted to his third eye – he knew where she was going. *I need another's hand to help me with re-ordering Shshmrnashsh's thoughts. I can only teach you the basics of psionics, maybe it may aid you on your voyage in the future.*

He straightened his back and sighed, the kind of sigh that felt he had breathed out a portion of his burdens. "You already know what I'm about to say, but I would rather speak it. Whatever I learn from you, I promise that I will never use it to aid the war between both our peoples."

I believe you. Now, before you read someone's mind, you need to learn how to read their aura-

Ahn'kat pinched his nose bone. "I already had this lecture, Treneer."

I know. She grinned.

~

He was undeniably strong, she thought. Clever, too. However, after a few weeks, his handling of telepathic surgery was akin to him wearing thick mittens, but still too clumsy and disorganised for her liking.

I hearrrd thaaat. Ahn'kat's tele-voice trailed.

Treneer smiled as she passed him the original copy of Shshmrnashsh's experience with the Wild Units. *Lower the volume and narrow your thought-waves for tele-speaking. Anyway, you're my assistant.*

Wherrre dooo I puuut thisss memoryyy? He was quieter this time, but the drawl in his thoughts were somehow longer.

Between here and here. She said before continuing her telepathic dive into the memory's abyss. To her dismay, she couldn't find any more bright, precious bubbles in there. Treneer scanned through the timeline of memories since the Blackout, but there were still a dozen pockets missing. She knew that Shsh's memories were still there, but she may need to fish them out herself – if that was even possible at this point.

There was something unusual she did detect, among the myriads of other oddities, the memories of Sazla. Gaps were still present, but this powerful being had imprinted far more in her 'vessel' than initially sensed. Yet, there was something stranger, the way Sazla *felt*. It was familiar, as if Treneer had felt her a thousand times before. The way she spoke, did things, showed her metal vessel the universe. Treneer couldn't put her finger on it but conceded that Neavensoros have always been omnipresent to an extent, and it had become background energy after so many decades of her life.

There's nothing more we can do here. She said slipping back into her body and into the organic chamber. *Come, your psi-shield needs improving, Ahn'kat.*

I'mmm tiiired, I neeeed too eeeat. He said blinking back to his body before rubbing his face. She noticed sheds of skin wrinkled on his gloved hand.

Then eat. She said before levitating away from the regeneration pod and settling onto a small clearing near the centre of the chamber for them to meditate on.

Ahn'kat sighed as he summoned some strange looking berries on a vine. He pinched at the red circles and popped them in his mouth before striding over to take a seat before her. "Alright, ready."

Treneer shook her head before tapping her temple. *Talk in here only, you need to exercise it more.*

Readyyy.

She closed her eyes and pressed into his mind; a furrow wrinkled on his brow as he swallowed. Ahn'kat did throw a shield around him, but it was little more than a fence with many holes in it. Treneer barraged through and replanted a wall stronger for him. *It's getting better, but you need to imagine that steel surrounds your brain. If that takes time to manifest, then imagine an ear-splitting hum to deter an unwanted psi-probe.*

Alriiight, agaaain. He said, but this time, his shield was wider and denser. However, Treneer realised it was an effective psi-dampening field.

You made it harder for me to hear your thoughts, that's good, but not the point of this exercise. I know you can do it, Ahn'kat you're adapting to psionics quickly. She said.

To her amusement, he sighed loudly before diving back into his mind. This time, a groan escaped his mouth. Opening her eyes, she saw his fingers pressing around his forehead and hand up at her. "I'm struggling."

Every round we do, you get stronger. Your mind is just as malleable as your cells. What I can teach you is how to avoid being discovered on whichever planet you settle on and provide keener senses for trouble. She said leaning toward him.

"That's generous of you, but you need to understand I was not born an Arinu," he said fixing his eyes on her.

Talk in here. She tapped at her temple. *A bit of you is now, and I have unknowably trained Zanashj neonates before, your people are...skillful, Ahn'kat.*

Neeeonates...pluraaal? Aaas innn otherrr than Neobatri?

See? Your tone has already improved! She smiled, but he didn't give it in return. *Delyn- Neobatri, she was a friend, at the very least, budding friendship. She was very physically impressive-*

"She was very mentally impressive to the Empire," he said.

But there was another neonate she bonded with the most, her name was Yansoon and...

Ahn'kat cocked his head to the side as his eyes locked onto her face. She could feel him scanning her, but just barely.

Yansoon and I were good friends. I was poor at handling a neonate under my charge, but we did our best for each other. After a series of events, it was revealed she was a Zanashj, but not an agent of the Empire – she was kidnapped by the Unbound. Treneer said.

"I feel like I know...there's a similarity. Tell me more," he said.

Yansoon was injured after an unlawful encounter with a Kepa, we snuck her away to an underground healer's house. While we were trying to cover our misdeeds, Yansoon was discovered. This changed everything. My old friend, Ouro and I didn't understand the implications of her being there, so we secreted her away to one of Ouro's prisms. She told us as much as she could about her experiences since she was abducted and made as the Unbound's personal infiltrator.

"What has she told you?" he said straightening up.

Her mind was altered too heavily for the small time we had to speak and without drawing suspicions, I couldn't afford anymore drawn to myself. There was something sad about her, like she was a little girl inside of a woman's body. Excited for adventure but longing to return home.

"Neheret Alkaheen," he whispered.

Correct! You finally read me clearly. Treneer said.

"I already knew who it was. I tried helping her family find her for years, until it was made clear she had been taken by off-worlders. You've already met her sister," he said.

Treneer frowned and tapped her knuckle on her chin as the realisation dawned on her. *Neobatri?*

Ahn'kat nodded as his jaw tightened. "Promise me she is safe and untainted," his voice was unusually cold and slow.

Ouro would not have let harm come to her. My, this feels deliberate, a most carefully lain plan by the universe I have ever heard of.

"There is no higher power working to our betterment, Treneer. There are jokes and then there are cosmic jokes," he said.

Can you agree that some things have improved for you?

A sarcastic smirk flashed on his lips. "My hope has been watered, but now I wait for the drought."

Shall we water it some more? One more practice round, just to keep it fresh in your mind while you sleep. Treneer said, fixing herself into position for meditation. *Speak in your mind from now on.*

Very weeell. He huffed.

Treneer could feel the block around his mind had grown denser. From the outside, she couldn't hear a loose whisper from his mind. She shuffled closer but noticed there were holes through his barrier. In fact, it felt like he was barely holding ground behind the shield.

Firm inside and outside. She said.

Then I won't beee able to focus on anything elssse. He said.

Some part of the shield must always be up, even while you work, eat, and sleep. This is what we are all taught.

She could hear his frustration billowing. *Again, I am not an Arinuuu.*

When I lost my psionics after the first deep-scan, I felt I had lost piece of my soul. I struggled every day to reclaim it, even now, it's less than it was. I also improved the strength of my own body to regain balance. Treneer said.

Ahn'kat was silent, but she felt him force her out of his mind.

You can do it!

I can't-

Just a bit more!

Treneer, I can't!

Why-

He ripped out and kicked her back in her body. She was stunned, but he was shaken, and his face was slick with sweat.

"I've reached my limits," he hobbled to his feet and tried stretching his tender back.

Enough for now. She shook her head before regaining composure.

"No, enough completely. I know you had endured immense hardships, Treneer, but I cannot adapt to your standards. I am not you!"

She leaned back, watching him catch his breath as he paced around the command centre. *I'm sorry, I was trying to reveal the best version of yourself.*

"Well, I'm sorry to be a disappointment," his head rolled as he rubbed his neck. "What are we going to do about her?"

Treneer glanced to Shshmrnashsh and shook her head. *We'll try to wake her up again after rest.*

"Right. Well, I'm going to play Takush and then sleep," he said.

I don't understand where the enjoyment is in competition, but you could show me. She said, trying to soften his mood.

"The game is a test of strategy, and the first rule is never compete with a psychic," he said.

They had a tired laugh with each other.

"I just realised I never heard your voice."

No, you haven't. Treneer's brow rose as a knowing smile came on her. *Pleasant astral travels, Ahn'kat.*

He rolled his eyes. "Sun-down blessings to you, Treneer," he spun around and hopped up to his craft.

As she watched him go, a part of her smiled. The loneliness and grief were stolen away from her after the tragedy on Kra with the strange ex-prince. Perhaps she didn't have the time to grieve, as her kin needed her knowledge on the weapon that would be used to destroy them – and to prepare to face Vern. She still yet didn't understand his purpose, but it was clear that twisted being has infected the already strained relationship between the Arinu and Zanashj. Vern was the blank wild piece in this tangled puzzle, but as Zu'leen would say, 'If you fail to find the answer in life, it will find you upon death.'

These words were spoken by the old and wizened to comfort the young, but now, they held finality and absolutism if she didn't make it home.

As Treneer stretched her arms over her head, she leaned back horizontally in the air. An invasive yawn escaped from her mouth as her eyes blurred toward the ceiling above. She enveloped her arms over her chest and created an energetic dampening shield to encase her body. The energies surrounding her dimmed to ambiance; the gloomy light from the Underbase faded into a comforting darkness, and even the smells of wet tissue became less offensive.

As the work around pulled away, the corner of her third eye sense caught a tiny sparkle of bioluminescence from Shshmrnashsh's pod. Treneer still didn't quite understand the depth of what these signals meant, assuming they had meant anything, but she had noticed they had happened a handful of times in the last handful of days. When she and Ahn'kat would continue memory therapy for her, Treneer sought what the little light flashes were, but every time they found nothing. No reason.

The existentialism of that prospect started to leak into her chest with dread. She damned herself for beginning to sound like Ahn'kat, but the fact there was no answer for something so innocuous, amplified in her mind while in her safety psi-case. What if there was no reason for Vern to cast war between the Arinu and Zanashj?

What if these were a series of unfortunate events that have been hijacked by ill-sighted opportunists?

What if there was no sensible, albeit deluded, grand plan to 'save' the universe, but instead, the wills of a being who merely wanted to flex their intellect?

That simple possibility made her heart clench, but she couldn't afford to fall into that pit – for now.

"Just sleep." she whispered to herself as her mind floated off into the shattered domains of her kin's twisted creators.

Chapter Thirty-six
Shshmrnashsh XII: I Remember

A grey face looked up to the faint shimmery surface from the deep black water. There was nothing else down here expect the crushing weight of the ocean, not even the company of light could be seen from the murky depths. The darkness could be hiding something awful and terrifying, but her greatest fear was knowing she was utterly alone. This was possibly death, and standing on the seabed, there was a door underneath. All she had to do was to open it and step out for the very last time.

Too heavy to float to the surface and see the sun again, but too weak to open the door. There was no grey haven to save her from this nightmare; could this even be considered a nightmare? There was nothing to do except investigate the windows where the living lay. Their small narrow lives, buzzing around trying to make sense of it all. But from where she stood, there was emptiness. And if they knew the truth, then would they go mad? She wondered.

No, she said, it's the dead who are pathetic. Always yearning to reclaim that tiny, pitiful spark the living chase after in a blink of time. Was she terminated, then? Was this what waited for all Roctarous? She was too far away from the surface to read the Archives, but she had understood that all souls would end at the same place before they started life. Maybe she was too deeply damaged to continue living, but her body was enduring just enough to keep her tethered.

Those poor Organics wasted their time to get her back. Their short lifespans spent on someone they will never meet and will remember this almost-meeting for the rest of their lives. They will remember something that never happened, never remember, remember, remember - ah.

The grey face looked to the patches. Yes, that Arinu dove deep many times to try pull her out, but despite her gifts, even that Arinu was blinded by this dark. It was so black down there, that the Arinu thought there was no one watching. Grey eyes looked up and down, left to right and all around. There were so many missing memories. But how could she miss something she never remembered? Maybe this was how it was always meant to be.

Was this fear? No, she was clean of it.

Was this relief? No, she was barren of it.

Was this hubris? Happiness? Joy? Sadness? Satisfaction? Logical?

None of the above. She wondered maybe this is how it's meant to be when you depart a life – utterly void of everything you once held, even if you were a machine.

'Memories', she suddenly said to herself. It was the first word spoken in this trapped place.

'Memories are tethers to a life and all lives before,'

'Memories are anchors of our personality and maps of our self,'

'Memories are delicate souvenirs from each life we experience,'

'Because without memories, life never existed.'

She could open the door from below her feet and exit to the great beyond. However, looking into her life's deep past, she could see a hundred millennia of duty, of observation, and of obedience – but only a mere few years of exploration and understanding.

'Once you taste freedom, you will never forget it.'

She couldn't forget, and she would not let it.

Her feet lifted from the ocean's bed as she pushed across for her missing memories. Her arms swam in the black; she felt a bubble ahead of her. It was the time she noticed Senzvrrn and Brrnzerm paying attention to each other. Her palms cupped the bubble and pushed it to the surface. She could already feel getting lighter.

Another bubble of when she confronted Hrrmn's consortium with the Unbound behind her before sending it away. More and more, from subjugating the 'liberated' from the ship bay, to looking up at the orange-grey skies wondering when Sazla will return, she found herself again.

Her legs kicked against the water as she pulled herself up. Her arms were getting tired and sore. There was flesh encased on her shoulders and forearms under the dim water's light. The dream! She remembered walking through the forest with her former consortium as Organics. She didn't want to be Organic; she didn't want to be Synthetic. She just wanted choice. She remembered more and more. Her grey face was inches away from the surface, the light from above almost stung her eyes. One more push until she remembered her name – her only name: Shshmrnashsh.

The murky red and peach lights blended the shapes of objects in the command centre. The Underbase. This is where it all started and she knew, this is where it will all end. Shshmrnashsh lifted from the regeneration pod, feeling her mind resurfacing and her body hum with power. One foot after the other stepped off the angled ledge as she straightened her back on the spongy floor. To the centre, there was a fleshy diamond plexus, it thumped slowly like a resting heart of a giant beast. A holographic panel lit up and encircled the machine, waiting for her commands, but her gaze was stolen away by the hovering oval to her side.

Shshmrnashsh stepped over; her third eye pierced through the surface to the being sleeping within. Her palm rose, wanting to caress the edge, but pulled away knowing she will wake Treneer. However, there was another that shared this space with them, but he slept in the comfort of his ship.

These poor beings, she thought. Their lives were shattered and compelled by forces beyond their understanding to this place. She looked to the beating plexus beside her. It was a device Roctarous used to channel each member's thoughts to more machines, bases, and each other. This Unbound plexus channelled something far deeper than minds and more powerful than psionics, it was destiny.

She placed her hand over her forehead, wondering why she sounded like Sazla. When she was still with her, Shsh could never comprehend her words, but now void of Sazla's presence, she understood. She tried remembering why she chose to come to the Underbase, Shsh had no recollection of knowing where this outpost was or had the navigation skills to find it. That was the last memory she needed to salvage.

The ship she came with had the answers. As she strode over to the chamber, the silver skiff silently hovered over the ground. She smiled, remembering it was the one with the half-mind within it, but her chest heaved with sorrow knowing that the soul had long departed. Her palm pressed against the spherical crystal to the centre and let its story flow within her.

'There you are, I knew you would make it,' Gerrnzerrn's voice called from within. It was their recording.

The probe had betrayed her and then abandoned her. She didn't know what to feel but was an absence of hatred.

'I was wrong about the Unbound. Their promise for salvation was true, but there was one who tainted the web. Before I tell you why I left you, I need you to consider the space around you. Though, your former goals to resurrect the High Mind and then liberate Kra with the Unbound had been tarnished, you still walk the path to save the Roctarous. Not a single choice and action you have taken has been for naught, it has led you to come here.'

How? She whispered to no one.

'You were the only one in the best position to do this, that's why I brought you and Treneer here to meet Ahn'kat. You don't know these people, but you have been working towards this moment your entire lives. The three of you are far away enough from the grain of sand to see the dunes. Unlike the rest of the galaxy, you will no longer wonder why a shadow has overcome your patch of sand but know who is creating it and where they come from.'

Vern.

'Vern was born there and that's where they learnt that our creators are the greatest threat to the universe. Not the Empire, nor the rising demons in the Arinu, but the Neavensoros. Their callousness and carelessness for their children has weakened them for the true end to their immortal journey.'

She paused to consider this. Vern had no love for the Neavensoros, and reasonably, much of her love had gone for them too. Whatever Vern wanted to do to them, perhaps it was justice, but she couldn't decide. Then what of the Zanashj and Arinu? Why try to create strife between the two?

'The search for all the pieces is over, but before you can finish the puzzle, ask this question that a psychic cannot answer: how do you kill a god?'

Shsh turned to the corridor where her sleeping companions were. Did Gerrnzerrn want her to ask Ahn'kat? If so, how could he possibly know without the aid of psionics? Treneer would be the most logical person to ask. How could the old adjunct have so much awareness of a precise situation?

'You might be wondering how I know this. If I lie to you, then you will never reach the end of your path, but if I tell you the truth, then you will be distracted away from it. When this has finished, you will find the answer if you ask yourself this: what is the purpose of Akashi? Only then, will you realise who I was.' Gerrnzerrn said before the psi-recording finished.

~

For six lonely hours, she spent combing through every recording from the half-mind skiff, Underbase data, and even her own memories to pull together what Vern's plan was. No matter how many thousands of times she replayed the recordings, the pieces could not fit. She hoped there would be an answer by the time the others to awaken but hesitated at the idea of pillaging their minds to extract the memories. If indeed Gerrnzerrn wanted them to work together, they needed to be together.

She watched a copy of her memories on the computer's files. A perfect, long spectrum of experiences ribboned across the holo-screen as her fingers scrolled through them. Vern had mined every piece of data about the Neavensoros, but she could not piece together why there was this intent to destroy them. Was this emotional or was this logical? Neither or both? It was understandable why anyone would want to see them dethroned from universal power, but not all of them were worth such ire…

Sazla. Shshmrnashsh still couldn't decide on her yet and perhaps never will.

There was a stirring in the upper levels, Ahn'kat had awoken from a disturbed sleep. A distinct air of astral travelling had stained that corner. Without turning around, Shshmrnashsh could feel every graze of his boot on the walkway. It stopped suddenly, knowing he spotted her.

"Prince Ahn'kat," she said, turning to meet his surprised stare.

Immediately, he took a slow sidestep toward the staircase as his eyes darted to Treneer's psychic chrysalis.

"She is uninjured. I didn't want to disturb either of you," Shsh said.

"So, this is who you are…unadulterated," he said. His tone was polite, but still erred on extreme caution.

"My memories have been fully restored. I had observed you and Treneer attempting to reclaim them. Thank you," she said.

His stern face softened for a moment. "I am new to the psychic realms."

"There is information I need to discuss with both of you, but until then, we can resume our tasks until Treneer awakens," Shsh said.

Ahn'kat nodded as he rubbed the back of his neck. "Well, I can get the probe to unload some resources and power–"

"I had already completed that four-and-a-half hours ago."

"I see," he said with a sigh as he walked around Treneer's dark oval shield.

"We can communicate while we wait," she said watching him pace.

His angular face cracked a smile. "We definitely can."

"Would you like to know how this ability is possible?" Shsh said pointing to the floating shield.

"Sure," he said, his smile grew at her while he crossed his arms over his chest.

"Advanced psychics can project and bend energy into various shapes and densities. Because psionics is deeply entrenched in Arinu culture and lifestyle, they are taught from infancy to multitask psi-abilities and can even maintain them while in deep unconsciousness," she said.

He nodded and flashed a toothy smile. "Thank you for that, Shshmrnashsh."

She cocked her head to the side. "According to my data, when Organics smile it is usually a sign of humour, however, it's not always the case. Some smile when in great distress or anger. Are you experiencing any of the above?"

Ahn'kat breathed a laugh as his finger lined along his brow and shook his head. "No, I'm – I just had an assumption Roctarous don't care much for small talk. Your expressions are each refreshing."

"You have met more Roctarous?" she said.

"Yes, when I was a boy. Two Unbound agents came to my family home and…" the smile in his eyes dimmed. "Made some grand promises that led me to…here."

"Vern and Voo-san?" she said.

His jaw stiffened as he slowly nodded. "That's them."

"I remember you from their vision," she said taking a small step towards him, "you saw through them while many, many others failed to do so."

"You also believed in them at one point," he said clearing his throat as the smile in his face washed away. "When I was down in there with Treneer, I saw some of your memories referencing Zanashj."

Shshmrnashsh parted her mouth as she tried stopping herself from swaying in place. The Kepa summoning! "What data would you like to know specifically?"

An impatient twitch of his cheek flashed as he smacked his teeth before taking a deep, knowing breath. "Treneer said you were betrayed by the Unbound, I cannot fault you for that since I'm also new to the experience. But I know you know what happened to the Zanashj stolen by them."

"They are deceased."

Ahn'kat's nostrils flared as he took a step back. "How?"

Shsh tensed as she watched the energy around him change. He could do little to harm her physically, but controlled, angered sparks came from his third eye. She didn't want to defend herself because he needed to be as he was.

"I was requested to help a *Kepa* summons. Vern prepared an offering to the creature in exchange for something else. It wasn't until I saw Zanashj bodies falling into the rift, I assumed they were deceased, but upon reflection, Vern may have kept a few alive. Vern wanted to use them as a distraction while they dug for their real prize in the *Kepa's* hoard: the claimed Arinu."

His chest heaved as tears swam in his eyes. "What is a Kepa and how do we get to it?"

"An extremely hostile extra-dimensional entity, its home-plane is banned-"

"But you know how to get in there! I need to get-"

Stop, Ahn'kat. Treneer's voice chimed in. Her astral form flashed into the chamber, hovering beside Shshmrnashsh. *I've faced that creature many times and even our best guardians barely escaped with their lives.*

Ahn'kat's wild glare shot to Treneer. "Didn't you just hear, Treneer? Some could still be alive! I have loved ones in its clutches, dead or alive, their soul's need peace. I need peace!"

Shsh's chest strained at his words. This young being willingly defied sense and risking his life to reclaim his dear ones. This rocked her to her core, remembering how she without a blink disregarded her former consortium members to be left entombed in the bowels of Erra. "I think we should try to help him," she suddenly said.

Treneer's translucent face whipped to her. *We don't have the time for this, and worse things may happen if it doesn't kill us!*

"You said it accepts offerings," Ahn'kat breathed, his eyes widened with relief at Shsh.

And what do you have to offer it? Our lives? Treneer sneered at him.

"Mine."

"You are needed as you are," Shsh said. The two gave her quizzical glances at her. "We have equipment here that the *Kepa* may take, but it may not be enough exchange for its body-hoard, but maybe it will give us information about Vern."

Ahn'kat's lips pursed as his mind spun before closing his eyes. "Treneer, can you glimpse inside if my friends are in there while Shsh and I talk to it?"

I was in there once, I don't want to-

"Please."

Treneer's astral form flashed away and the dark shield around her body fell away. She floated in the air for a while in deep contemplation before turning to the other two. *You don't understand how dangerous that thing is, but maybe this will be*

*a lesson to you, and I won't shield you if your heart breaks for whatever
you see in there.*

"That's mine to bear," he whispered before turning to
Shsh. "You said we can exchange information from it, but
firstly, I want to know what you meant about needing me as
I am?"

"All of us are needed for what's to come, an old friend
told me that we all possess the pieces to complete the puzzle
and the *Kepa* may be the adhesive," she said.

Treneer gently pressed her thumb against her third eye
while in deep contemplation. *We hold all the pieces...alright,
let's try to put it together and ask the Kepa the right question.*

"Vern plans to overcome the Neavensoros, and they
want your peoples to go to war with each other, but I don't
have the data to know why-"

"For a distraction," Ahn'kat said as Shsh blinked at him.
"It's a strategy infiltrators use when deployed on desirable
dominion planets. They often would create discourse
amongst several social groups, ensure that immense amount
resources are spent fighting each other while a small number
of resources are kept for the infiltrator's plans to proceed
undiscovered."

"Vern made comments that the universe may fare better
without you two," she said.

*At this rate...*Treneer sighed. *I went into the Kepa's home-
plane once for a rescue mission while Neheret and Neobatri were
disguised as Arinu. We found mountains of bodies from a dozen
different species packed in there, most were Zanashj from every age
imaginable. We also saw some of my kin, but unlike the rest, they were
stored in special containers. We tried getting as many still-living beings
out before we were discovered. I recognised some of the missing, but the
rest, I suspected were taken by the Empire.*

Ahn'kat shifted uncomfortably as he cleared his throat.
"My co-conspirators took a dozen."

That still leaves another ten of my kin unaccounted for.

"Vern claimed that I was helping them find special batteries, but when they realised the 'batteries' were gone – or reclaimed by your squad," Shsh glanced to Treneer, "they said they needed 'alternate solutions.' The Unbound were originally planning to summon all Roctarous to our nexuses and give them organic grafts to make them resistant to Neavensoros possession. At the time, we didn't have the capability to call everyone, but the original deal my old consortium made with the Arinu would be a worthwhile opportunity to the Unbound's plans-"

Hence why you asked help from my kin. My Grand Elders and A.I. leaders gave into your request, disregarding moral implications of psi-domination. Treneer said.

"Why?" Ahn'kat said.

Because we wanted to steal knowledge from their Archives. Treneer said, sneaking an awkward glance to Shsh.

"Hah, while House Urbaz willingly handed over our slaves to so-called liberators! See how easy morals break when it serves the promise of exclusive power," he said with a smirk while crossing his arms.

"I hypothesise that Vern still has those ten Arinu and now, another dozen powerful archites," she looked to Treneer.

Her pallid pink lip trembled. *What will they do to them?*

"The Unbound invested much into grafting and organic replication technology. Its possible Vern wishes to fuse Arinu and Zanashj genes with Roctarous bodies," Shsh said.

Our genes would be too unstable-

"Don't speak too quickly, Treneer," Ahn'kat said as he replicated a handful of dried nuts in his palm before scooping them in his mouth. His eyes narrowed, as if he triggered a memory. "Ismotaph experimented on many poor Zanashj with psi-enhancers, most of those unfortunates lost their minds, while a few adapted to the sudden changes. Ismotaph is careful and disposes anyone who isn't of use, yet I never understood why he kept them alive for so long…but now, it seems the Zanashj were used as an experiment for Vern."

And the results show favourably. She eyed his forehead.

"What still doesn't make sense is this insistence to get rid of the Neavensoros? The Urasan Intel Corps hasn't much on them, but what is agreed on is that they're immensely powerful and should be avoided," he said while slowly chewing his food.

Because they have a long and bloody history of injustice, to say the least. Treneer said mournfully.

"And have become complacent in recent eons. A dangerous combination for such beings," Shsh finished.

Ahn'kat swallowed the last of the nuts before wiping his fingers along his lips. "Again, it still doesn't clarify why Vern wants the Zanashj and Arinu at war with each other. If I were Vern, I would want all on my side to fight against my ultimate enemy, regardless how much I hate my allies."

Shsh and Treneer exchanged a knowing glance.

"Ah, I knew I was missing something," he said.

My kin have an extensive history with them, we were allies and their students. That fact alone would make us want to defend them, but more importantly, Arinu are genetically engineered clones of Neavensoros. I learnt this while on Kra, but I didn't have the time to tell if my comrades had also come to same knowledge or if they managed to send a message to Farayah. They also need to be warned about the psi-virus the Empire will use against us. Treneer said.

"Clones? That makes some sense, now. Also, I want to make it clear that the Empire are as much as victims to Vern as the Arinu are," he said as rested his back against the crawling wall. "And if the gods have a thread of generosity, then maybe we can unify them against Vern."

To unify against a common enemy is decent start, but a folly one. We may end up at each other's throats again after all of this. Besides, I don't get the sense that Vern knows we're here, but I wouldn't put it past them to plan for everything and anything. Treneer said.

Both looked to Shsh, she caught a sense she was stirring in silence.

"Vern knows much, but has the understanding of a child," she slowly said before facing Ahn'kat. "I have a question that only you can answer, how do you kill a god?"

His green brow rose. "You can't, you can weaken them or trap them…"

Shshmrnashsh swung around to the holo-screen around the living plexus. Her fingers wildly tapped at the keys to summon a view of the Unbound's altered genetic schematics.

"Here," she pointed to the twisting helix. "This is what the Unbound have been working on before my departure. I knew that Vern had been expanding psionic capacity for units, Voo-san believed it was to increase our awareness, but the more enhanced the Unbound became, the stronger they fell under Vern's sway. It's inarguable Vern has the potency to dominate many minds and their power is growing.

"Neavensoros have been using some Roctarous as physical vessels. The purpose of the Unbound was to add enough organic grafts to prevent possession and free us from succumbing to cognitive decay from High Mind disconnection. Vern has altered the Unbound's plans and is using the hyper-adaptiveness of Zanashj to survive Neavensoros attacks and the psionic potency from Arinu to weaken them before…"

"The Roctarous trap them inside their own bodies?" Ahn'kat asked.

"And because the Neavensoros are distracted, it's the perfect time to strike,"

*But the Neavensoros are too strong to stay in their containers forever…*Treneer frowned.

"Unless Vern plans to banish them somewhere no one could escape from," Shsh said as she watched their faces light up with understanding.

"Kepa's home-plane," Ahn'kat sighed.

That can't last either because Arinu have been astral dancing on mass, the Neavensoros could slip through the cracks of one wayward dancer. Even without them, Farayah's planar lining is thinned, and more rifts open faster than we can close them. Treneer shook her head.

Ahn'kat quizzically looked at her. "Astral dancers?"

Power-mad summoners. She said.

He nodded but still seemed confused.

"There won't be any summoner or Arinu to call the *Kepa* if the Zanashj use the psi-virus to wipe them out first. I compute that Vern has already begun preparations to seal away exo-planar interference on Farayah," Shsh said.

Treneer shivered as her palms planted on her face. *I sensed Vern keeping watch on my world for a long time.*

"So, what, do we warn the Kepa not to accept Vern's wayward gifts?" Ahn'kat said.

"Yes."

I don't appreciate the idea of helping a monster. Treneer gritted her teeth.

"Call it an exchange of monsters," Ahn'kat said with a glint of a malice smile. "We can offer this warning as payment to the Kepa to remove Ismotaph."

~

The three of them combed through days of Shshmrnashsh's memory bank to re-create the inter-planar port. They had reduced the Underbase's equipment to feed its replicators for every piece. Many chambers had been stripped of the fleshy walls, revealing the skeletal structure underneath; they even sacrificed the half-mind ship's phasing parts.

Treneer had grown attached to the poor being stored within the central matrix and didn't want the crystal core to be shredded and repurposed. Shshmrnashsh was warmed by her illogical compassion and proposed she could rekindle some of its lost memory and soul with psi-surgery.

"We still need some more material to replicate the phase-blades," Shsh said as she scanned the control panel in the ship chamber.

Treneer's eyes closed as she tried sensing for every piece of unneeded matter. *We can repurpose the probe-*

"No! Zzamm is not being repurposed," Ahn'kat said, clicking his fingers for the probe to come.

Ahn'kat, we don't have enough energy for the replicators. She frowned.

"You got to keep the half-mind, Treneer. This probe is loyal and can be the difference between life and death for us in the coming times," he said.

She rolled her eyes and turned to Shsh.

"We precisely need three-hundred-and-ninety standard grams of matter to create basic phase blades," she said.

Ahn'kat rubbed his beard as he looked around and to his body. He grinned as a small blade protruded from his gauntlet, slicing away at his long beard and shavings into the waste-breakers before grabbing at his long black locks and hacking away at them too.

"How much do we have now?" he said brushing away at the short loose hairs into the dish before they fizzled away into sparks of energy.

"Five-hundred standard grams," Shsh said as she ordered the replicators to produce the blades.

"I was considered attractive to my people. Tell me, Treneer, will your people find me handsome?" he said caressing his smooth head while wearing a grin.

Treneer sighed as she tried supressing a smirk. *Still too green.*

Ahn'kat feigned offence with a small pout before stepping beside Shshmrnashsh. "Are we ready?"

"Confirmed," Shsh said as Treneer locked the phase blades into the silver rings of the rift-cutter. The round things slowly begun spinning, quickly gaining speed before a white light cracked open into view.

"Positions!" Ahn'kat called as hot wind blew into the chamber from the rift.

Treneer floated away from the opening and cast an illusion shield around her to prevent the Kepa from sensing her unwanted presence, while Shsh and Ahn'kat slowly stepped to the planar opening. Shshmrnashsh felt Treneer place a protective shield around herself and Ahn'kat to minimise the immense light and the itching radiations from the rift. In a blink, she spotted a great shadow casting over the opening, drifting back and forth.

"Kepa! We come to make an exchange!" Ahn'kat called over the rising wind.

Shsh could see an eye turning down and peering through as dark tendrils curled their way into the corporeal plane.

Treneer, start looking for Ahn'kat's friends. She whispered before turning full attention to the creature. "There is information we offer as payment for a task we want from you."

Treneer. It said.

A prang of dread echoed inside Shsh; she dared not turn to the Arinu behind her in the shadows. Ahn'kat also sensed the same sentiment as the pair tried remaining calm.

Come forth to deliver what you owe. It said.

"No, you will deal with us, Kepa," Shsh said.

"And you might get more out of it if you do this one thing for us," Ahn'kat added.

Tell me. It said.

"We have knowledge about a former client of yours, Vern. We have information they are planning to betray you. Vern will exterminate the Arinu and lock you out of your primary hunting ground: Farayah," Ahn'kat said.

The smoky tendrils curled back into its home-plane, but the shadow remained.

"I will give you a portion of what we know," Shsh plucked a data crystal and tossed it into the rift. A spark smoked in the bright opening.

Many guesses. It said.

"Are you willing to risk it?" Ahn'kat said.

What task do you want done?

"There is a Zanashj man and his closest compatriots we want you to take them all for yourself," Ahn'kat said before tossing another data crystal into the rift.

Cannot, he is shrouded too much.

Shsh and Ahn'kat glanced at each other.

"How do we get him to you?" Shsh said.

Not my concern. I will lock Vern out of my home but will wait for your Ismotaph. Now, I demand all your information.

Give the rest now, it's becoming too unpredictable. Treneer whispered.

There are some things that aren't in the Archives – not even the Neavensoros know. Come to me when you have more questions, Treneer. It said.

Get this thing out of my sight. The Arinu thundered.

Did you find them? Ahn'kat said.

Shsh felt a wave of sadness from her.

He grabbed the last data crystal and tossed it into the rift before Shsh hastily turned and slammed the button to close. The silver rings slowed their spin, and the opening retracted back into their normal space as the three came together.

"Well?" Ahn'kat came rushing over to Treneer as she decloaked herself.

I'm sorry. She said as her head slowly shook.

His jaw clenched and swallowed. "So, it's definitive then?"

Zertun and Emestasun are deceased, but their souls are free. She said.

His eyes welled as tears dropped from his lashes while his hand clasped around his nose and mouth. Shshmrnashsh didn't realise what she was doing until she found her hand tugging at his shoulder. A stifling gasp escaped his mouth as he dropped into her chest and clung onto her back…and sobbed.

Treneer's eyes reddened as her lips quivered, her pale hands gently touched his armoured back. "I'm so sorry."

He turned to her; his face was slick as he swallowed. "Your voice…"

Treneer smiled.

He grinned. "You weren't a singer, were you?"

Breathy laughs leaked from her toothy grin. "You know what's strange? Emestasun reminds me of my Zu'leen…their energies feel the same."

"It's logical, both were significant influences on both of you," Shsh said, helping Ahn'kat straighten up before glancing to Treneer. "We have a path that we share, now, we need to walk it – together."

Break IV

Their bodies beat like a dying star as they danced, whirling, and weaving a new being into existence. None turned around to see what was behind them, Sazla had, but her tiny envoy was on the way. Though her voice was silenced, her consciousness could stretch a little farther. She pondered...this could be the only way. Her vision of all things laid bare before her, as if the universe offered her to sample all on its pallet.

Sazla's fingers flicked through the rolling spectrum of time on many worlds. She spotted Kra, she scrolled ahead to find decaying flesh covering the surface of the globe before rolling the vision back in time to see the metallic skeleton outlining the Roctarous homeworld. When they were building it. Several pearly blue heads swarm around the construction, her ancestors of flesh were ignorant of her smile beaming down at them. She saw the perfect Roctarous, it was still unborn...this was her chance.

Pain shot through her soul pried itself in pieces before dropping it into the new vessel.

Sazla turned to old Uras. The tall golden towers glittered brighter than its own star. She found the perfect Zanashj being born, but the mind was dead. Her soul shredded once more before dropping it into the female babe, giving her life before the doctor's eyes.

She continued her search for another, however, the Zanashj she wanted was absent...she was on planet Sye. The unborn baby's mother was in love for the first time, and it was with one outside her race. Sazla's soul split again and waited by her, the woman who would give her new form life.

Another world...

Sazla came to Farayah. The ice storms blurred her senses, as if the planet herself was trying to fight away a disease. She found a womb that held two and placed her consciousness inside the unborn female.

One last one…there. The crystal spires shrieked from the cries of labour. She found the perfect host, a girl who will discover her destiny is to die by her own hand.

On and on, world to world, life to life, she placed herself inside. It was done, for now. Though, her boundless form remained in the clutches of infinity, her redemption lay within the vessels of others.

Her siblings finally pulled away, revealing a small golden orb in the centre of the circle. The Neavensoros were weakened, but joy washed through them as they watched this new beating star rise. Sadly, this blissful moment was wiped away from the echoing drums of war…

Chapter Thirty-seven
Together I: The Return

The Underbase withered to a skeleton. Walls, floors, and ceilings were scraped down to the asteroid's black rock; every device and living machinery had been repurposed, even the plexus. The trio worked days and nights pulling every resource and scrounged every piece of energy before their voyage. The atmosphere system had been scrapped, forcing Ahn'kat to wear his helmet and Treneer to shroud her body in an energy shield. Shshmrnashsh had no need for any atmosphere, expect she found the unstable gravity to be inconvenient for her tasks.

Two augmented regeneration pods are safely secured. Treneer said, turning to Ahn'kat by the pilot's seat.

"The addons have been accepted," he said, staring at the holo-screen of his ship's control panel. He had shifted into an Arinu, but one that appeared sickly and malformed. His muscles shrunk, leaving a thinner build and skin shifted into a milky grey, even his suit shifted into a faux guardian uniform. He and Treneer practiced Arinu mannerisms and speech for days before this moment, she was almost proud of him.

"My ship's batteries aren't properly registering." He said.

"Confirmed, I am outside attaching the probe to the batteries. It will expand the ship's batteries by six hundred percent," Shsh's voice called through the speakers.

"You could only manage six-hundred?" Ahn'kat grinned.

"I could increase the number if-"

No, Shsh, he's fooling around. Just get inside. Treneer tossed a frown at him. *I have our minds psi-bonded, use the private commune.*

Shshmrnashsh's body crawled from the hull and along to the pressure lock. Her dark lithe form slipped into one of the small entrances beside the tube before the door to Ahn'kat's ship peeled open.

"Get inside the pods," he said as he settled to his pilot's seat.

Treneer pressed herself into the alcove as Shsh stepped into his craft before finding her place.

The amount of space inside this craft could easily house one-hundred-and-five units if we replaced it with a storage crystal. Shsh said.

Treneer shrugged. *I've not travelled in a ship where I could see my body, it's a bit outdated-*

He spun around to face them. "If anyone makes one more offensive comment about my ship, then I'll make them fly to Farayah themselves."

Use the psi-commune, Ahn'kat. Shsh whispered before turning to the view outside.

If we survive, then I wish we two become friends. Treneer said shooting a grin at the Roctarous.

The ship purred to life as it pulled away from the asteroid. It drifted freely in the dark before the pilot's screen lit up with the updated navigation system. Streams of brilliant lights of every colour imaginable and beyond covered the view; fractals of broken space spun and twisted around the edges as the ship found the direction to Farayah. Treneer closed her eyes and let her mind fall into the craft. She could see thousands of dead ends and timeless holes in the path before tugging the ship to begin the voyage.

I found a shortcut. If we pass through this section, the local space bends enough to reach Farayah sooner than on one phase speed. She said.

Got it. Ahn'kat said, activating the phasing field and pushing the ship forward.

The fractals spun faster, so fast that tiny colours and shapes blurred into invisible disks of white light before receding into blackness. On and on they trekked until the black washed away into the deep navy background with pearly streams of stars they had seen a thousand times before. A great scarlet light washed across the screen as they slowed before activating Unbound camouflage systems. Farayah's star may have been a red dwarf, but its monolithic presence made them feel as insects as they swiftly shot past it.

Home. Treneer stifled a sad sigh.

To the distance, a pristine ivory planet beaded atop of the dark shadows of space. Its white clouds curled along pale blue sphere, but despite its beauty, there was dense and shimmery aura shrouding the planet. The three looked closer, seeing some of the light rays appear as spikes, barring down on the world.

The safest distance is four-hundred-and-twenty-thousand standard miles before we're detected, but I can get us to the very edge if need be. Can you contact the Grand Coven from that distance? Ahn'kat said.

The Elders will likely be in deep meditations preparing the people, I can't say if they will be open enough for me to tap their minds. She said sitting up, trying to feel out the Judicator or the Proctor, or any computer administrators. *I'm trying to contact my kin's A.I. leaders, they won't be emotionally strained as Elders, but even their focus would be thinned.*

So, machines are your masters? Ahn'kat's eyes widened with shock and mild amusement before turning his head to Shsh. *Did you know that? Your people could learn from that arrangement.*

We're not conquerors, young Zanashj. She said sitting high, overlooking the bizarre energetic field. *I detect an immense radiation disrupting the planet's natural electro-magnetic field. Those semi-transparent lines are billions of spatial micro-fissures compounding around the world's mass.*

It wasn't this bad when I left. We are being bombarded to death. Treneer squeezed her eyes shut and shook her head. *I don't sense many awake minds on the planet.*

Ahn'kat's chest puffed as his glare fixed to the pearly white world. *Don't tell me we're too late-*

No, they're in a dreamless sleep...but I don't understand. She said.

We're switching to plan two. Treneer, find your friend, Ouro – see if he's still among the awakened. Shsh, I need you to mask the ship's energy signature to blend in with the surrounding radiations, I'm taking us in. He said driving the craft dangerously close.

Confirmed. Shsh said as she slipped into the computers and reprogramed the output to match the exo-cosmic energies.

The ship's systems whined, and the internal red lights flashed, saying they had trespassed beyond the safe zone. *Treneer, have you locked on him?*

I need you to get a little closer, my senses are dulling. She gritted her teeth and pressed her tender temples.

I'm flying blindly, my sensors are scrambled. Give me a direction- which province is Ouro in? He yelled.

Treneer slammed her head back as her face scrunched. *He should be in Heebar, but I can't tell! Once we pass this cloud then we can-*

Several entities incoming. Shsh flew forward and started locking onto to them.

Kepa? Unbound? Ahn'kat asked as a tear of sweat dripped down his forehead.

The ship broke through the heavy silver clouds; a clear view of the frozen grounds could be seen, but there were streams of rainbows intersecting throughout the land. Even in their menacing shimmer, they were beautiful.

No, Sleeping Watchers. Treneer swallowed. *They can see us.*

The three of them glanced at each other before Ahn'kat and Shsh tried commanding the craft to retreat out into the vacuum, but their controls screeched and disobeyed their commands as several glowing orbs flew around them and invaded their systems. Their bodies froze and the ship stopped whining; they couldn't suck in a breath of air before their forms slipped away into a bright tunnel – spinning away from the craft before being spat out into a dark dome.

Ahn'kat collided to the floor with a grunt, Shshmrnashsh dropped hard on her feet and Treneer spun in the air before steadying herself.

Location? Shsh glanced to Treneer.

She shook her head as she looked to the ceiling. A strobe of light beamed on their heads and shoulders, surrounded by curtains of shadow on a pale floor.

Are we dead? Ahn'kat said as he stepped forward, but an electric shock burned through his suit, forcing him back under the funnel of light.

"You live," a deep baritone voice called from the darkness. A large bust of an Arinu flashed before them; instantly, Treneer recognised him.

Judicator!

"Imperial scout has been detected; how many ships are coming to us?" he said glancing over to Ahn'kat.

"We aren't with the Empire! We come with a warning-"

"Incorrect. The Empire has made declarations of war with us, we will see to it-"

Judicator, we aren't imperialists. Shshmrnashsh is a Roctarous, she saved me from the failed voyage to Kra. We have information that the Zanashj are as much as victims of the Unbound as we are! Treneer said.

The Judicator's eyes washed over them. "Cannot verify your identity. Zanashj have adapted to evade our tele-scans and possess psionics."

"Judicator, I can exchange all our data with you," Shsh lifted her arm out to him.

"No, we cannot risk this program to a secret attack," he said.

Contact the Grand Coven, they can deep-scan us! Treneer said.

The Judicator shook his head. "The Grand Elders and Archon are in deep meditation to reach ascension. They have put Arinu to sleep while they organise Farayah's defence. They cannot be reached."

"Then how can we verify who we are?" Ahn'kat said.

We don't have time for this, every second spent is one step closer to the Empire's misguided attack against us, they've been tricked to using a psi-virus that will obliterate the Arinu! Treneer screamed.

"Do you submit to a death-scan?" the Judicator said.

Ahn'kat wildly glanced to Treneer and Shsh, but their eyes fixated on the A.I. in horror.

"We will await your decision," the Judicator said before vanishing into the void.

Ahn'kat turned to step towards them. *What's a death-scan?*

They...pull you apart and read every piece of you. Treneer said.

Is it any worse than when you scanned me? He said.

Negative, that was merely a deep-scan. A death-scan is when they pull your molecules apart and gleam every particle of you. You are killed in the process, but with the right equipment, you can be revived. They will revive Treneer, possibly me, but... Shsh said.

*But once they see me...*Ahn'kat parted his lips as his head nodded.

Treneer, why didn't you tell the Judicator that the Zanashj will also die from the psi-virus also? They may listen once they realise it's a threat to both of you. Shsh turned to her.

The Arinu blinked as she shook her head. *But I thought the psi-virus was designed to kill just us?*

*It's a **psychic** virus. Now, the Zanashj are vulnerable to it.* Shsh said before turning to Ahn'kat.

His arms rose to his head and rubbed his fake scalp before taking a deep breath. *The Intel Corps will be doing thousands of tests on the virus; it's severity would've been discovered by now. The Elders and A.I.s here still think the Empire is coming, so they still must sense my people are alive.*

Shsh gripped both of their shoulders. *We cannot let panic grip us. Treneer, call the Judicator back, I will donate myself-*

She violently shook her head as her eyes spun around the room. *No, wait-*

There you are! Another voice echoed in their minds, but it was warmer – organic.

Their bodies vibrated as they slipped through the ground; the harsh light vanished from their sights as they tumbled into nothingness before falling into another dark pit. However, it was comforting, there was a faint smell of water, soil, and leaves. Treneer clapped a shield around the three of them as Shsh charged her fists out into the humid darkness, while Ahn'kat grew long sharp claws from his nails.

Another pale Arinu head floated from between the dark tree trunks, but this one had three silvery-purple scars running down his scalp. A quivering cry escaped Treneer's throat as she flew towards Ouro; their arms extended and gripped each other's shoulders. Ouro grinned as his palm gently pressed on her third eye, while she pressed his.

Ouro! She turned to her concerned companions.

The moment they threw you into their prism, that's when I sensed you! I thought- His smile shined as he looked over her shoulder. *What happened?*

Kra...we shouldn't have gone, but I'm glad we did. Treneer said as a tear lulled on her lower lash. *I saw everything, Ouro.*

They clamped hands as everything she had experienced in the last several months poured into him; she could see his eyes widen with shock and wonder. Ouro's hand pulled away to his third eye and sighed. *I see.*

Where are we? Shsh strode towards him.

My prism, we are still on Farayah in a way, but I've made changes since the clouds darkened. The guardians couldn't cope with the fissures and exo-radiations, so they forced our kin into astra-pods. They will never wake unless prompted by the Grand Elders, but I've noticed that some of our people are still falling into the rifts – the cities are slipping away, and the forests are vanishing into different planes! No one is there to protect them, so she and I've converted this prism into a haven. He said.

"Who else is with you?" Ahn'kat's eyes narrowed as he walked towards them, he could sense that familiar name at the back of Ouro's mind.

Neheret, I found Treneer and company. Ouro called into the woods.

In a heartbeat, an Arinu woman flashed before them. She appeared as Yansoon again; her wide and youthful face rose the moment she saw Treneer, even then, Treneer couldn't help but reach out to her.

The moment you entered Kra, I lost you! She dashed towards her and gripped her with all her might, but her pearl skin mottled into a viridian hue as hair slowly leaked through her scalp before their very eyes.

Neheret, these are my companions. Treneer said taking her arm and turning her towards them.

Ahn'kat stepped forward, his form wobbled and transformed before them, along with his guardian suit into the Urasan survival armour. "I've been looking for you for a long time, Neheret Alkaheen. I promised your family I would."

Her jaw stiffened and her throat cleared. "You've met them? They've been looking for me?"

"No one has forgotten you," he said.

She clutched her throat. "I want to go home."

"We will," he said before glancing to Ouro. "I need my ship."

They haven't destroyed it, yet. He said, turning around and raising his hands to the faux night sky. A tear ripped through the darkness as electricity crackled into a round shape of the ex-prince's craft.

"Thank you," he nodded, and Ouro exchanged the appreciation. "All of us need to brief on latest events. I sent one of my infiltrators, Neobatri, to pose as an Arinu. When she and Treneer trekked to Kra, Neobatri has stolen information from the Roctarous about a psi-virus that Vern has left for her to find. The Empire have been experimenting with psionics for years and have begun distributing psi-enhancers to the Zanashj to equalise power with Arinu. The Intel Corps will be mobilising it against you, but inadvertently, annihilate us. And I think," he turned to Neheret, "you were used to be discovered to illicit panic from the Arinu to further drive a wedge between our people. But it didn't quite work out that way, did it?" he finished before glancing to Treneer and Ouro.

"Vern makes mistakes, but they clean them up. They would have plans within plans," Shsh said.

"Vern copied what Zanashj infiltrators have been doing to dominion worlds for millennia. Brilliant strategy but has overlooked that we recognise our designs when we see them. Unfortunately, the Empire is too distracted by internal conflicts to see the truth. And the one man who is creating it all, is Director Ismotaph. He was the one who betrayed my House and I...willingly helped him achieve this, but unknowingly I had also sealed my own fate."

"The Grand Elders and A.Is won't help us right now. We need to prove to them that the Empire was misled and is ready to correct their mistakes to form an alliance. Only then, we defeat Vern the Unbound. To do that, we need to remove Ismotaph," Shsh said.

"We need to go to Uras to show the Empire and the Crown all the lies he has peddled," Ahn'kat closed his eyes and sighed. "I hope the princess is adapting."

How do we remove Ismotaph? Ouro said.

Treneer pursed her lips together, readying herself to speak. *We found a way, but to do that, we made a deal...*

Ouro's gaze grew cold as he distanced himself. *You made a deal...?*

I couldn't psi-lock on Ismotaph because his vanguard is protecting him from porting, so we had to find something else that could do it...but even the Kepa couldn't. That's why we need you, Ouro. You can create a bridge between him and Kepa while we lock down Ismotaph and I weaken his subordinates. She said.

Ouro rubbed his third eye. *What did you give in return?*

Vern and the Kepa have been working together for some time. We found out and told the Kepa that Vern intends on annihilating us and sealing the places around Farayah. That creature has assured us that it will end cooperation with the Unbound and help us capture Ismotaph and his band. Treneer said.

As a trade off we leave the door unlocked to Farayah? Absolutely not. Ouro's eyes shone an angry scarlet.

It won't come after us, Ouro! Not now.

How do you know? Did it promise you that won't trespass at the perfect time when Farayah is being flayed open? You could have endangered us further with that thing! His thoughts were like a burning whip slashing inside their minds.

"Negative. The Arinu will be protected, and I have the blueprints to do this," Shsh said, opening her palm and releasing a holo-images of Kra's planetary defence systems. "We had anti-phasing shield technology for almost an eon to protect planetoids from our dying star and other infringing cosmic energies. Since the psi-consciousness of the Arinu has been weakened, you cannot bandage the rifts and radiations. I can replicate similar defence equipment and Ouro can evenly distribute it around Farayah. It won't be enough to stop the spread but blanket it long enough for the Arinu to clear up."

"Then you will remain here while Neheret, Treneer and I depart for Uras." Ahn'kat said.

~

Days had spun into a week. The unusual team worked in Void Prism, but some preferred the colder and brighter climate than Neheret's dark jungle chamber. Ahn'kat requested Ouro to psi-build a small Urasan ziggurat, akin to a commoner's home back on Uras, but the Arinu warden scoffed and had instructed him on how to build it himself. However, what the two didn't know was how happy Neheret was to see the Zanashj structure when she returned from another rescue mission. Shshmrnashsh had different desires and requested to build a simple workbench for her tasks – yet it was made delightfully apparent to everyone she made designs based from her home.

Treneer sought for more sleeping Arinu, Neheret secured and Ouro retrieved them to haven. Ahn'kat combed through all the available information about the recent events from Uras via his farseeing while he plotted the next course of action, and Shshmrnashsh pumped out the pieces needed to make a rudimentary defence system. Zzamm the probe helped her pull them together, while Shsh checked to see her latest invention.

She plucked several devices from the small alcove and double checked their suitability for Zanashj and Arinu brains. "Prince Ahn'kat, your attention is needed."

His face poked out from under his craft as he strode towards her. Dark thick stubble grew along his jaw and upper lip, even his hair had poked through his scalp.

"Come closer, please," she said as she pressed one of the devices around the back of his ear. Pin-prick lights circled around the dark edges; it was working perfectly.

His brows furrowed as his fingers caressed the edges. "What is this?"

"Universal-range transponder. It's based off old High Mind systems, allowing us to communicate across the entire distance of space and all dimensions, no matter how dense we are," her palms opened, revealing more of the devices to him. "Pass them out."

Ahn'kat slipped them in his gauntlet but lingered for a moment as he stared at them.

"Troubleshoot your issue," she said.

His lips pursed as he met her eyes. "I'm struggling to see past this…cloud around Farayah. I do feel some increase of psionics with this thing on, but my visions are unreliable."

I'm in a deep mind-zone for scanning right now, come to me. Treneer whispered.

Ahn'kat gave a quick nod to Shsh before stepping away from her synthetic work hall; within a moment, his boots stepped into grassy soil. He carefully hiked through the thick faux Urasan tree roots, bending beneath the branches before pressing through a green thicket. On the other side, a barren snowy tundra sprawled across the horizon with Treneer levitating over one of the icy cliffs overlooking the magnificence of the scarlet light from the fake red star, mimicking Farayah.

Her head slowly turned to him and glanced to his palms. *Universal transponders?*

"Here," he walked up to her and placed it around her ear.

She sucked in a deep breath and exhaled slowly. *How goes the plans?*

"Tricky. I can't get a solid sense on what's happening out there," he muttered as he scanned the landscape. "I would like to see this in real life, one day."

I hope to show you. She said.

"How goes with finding more Arinu?"

They're out there, Neheret will return shortly with two guardians. They have been badly injured and will need to be put in healing pods. Sit with me. She said.

Ahn'kat carefully lowered himself and sat with his legs crossed. He looked up at how high she was and scoffed, but she caught his meaning. She slowly drifted down; her legs met the ground as she settled herself on the stone to meet his eye level. They both took a deep breath and let their minds fly up through the illusion chamber, Treneer guided him past the psi-barricades from the plane before pushing both of their astral-eyes towards Uras.

It looks normal, our fleet hasn't moved.

We may have time.

Treneer winced a little, realising her fatigue was crawling into her mind faster than expected.

Continue?

I'll be fine.

They honed into Lusor city, the royal district into the emperor's palace. The twinkling gold halls were covered in magenta and burgundy drapes with the golden hawk decorated in the centre, the Court were draped in similar flowing robes too, even Conclave priests slowly marched along the halls with golden bowls of burning incense in their palms. Ahn'kat's heart pained when he realised what this was.

A royal has died.

Is that your Ramkes on the tall seat?

Their astral-eyes turned to see her face, but there was a rigidness to her. Even one in a place of power, where showing emotion is restricted, there was nothing real about her face. That's when he realised…

A Replacer is on the throne.

Let's find where they are keeping her and Kreshut.

No, he is dead or gone – this is public awareness…but the Empire thinks it's the true princess in that seat.

Let's see where they're keeping her!

Their senses spun around, keeping a strong image of her being in their minds as they sniffed her out. They came to a dark grey building, far out in the middle of a lime-yellow desert with phosphorous geysers spitting out a rainbow of chemicals in the surrounding basin. They peeked inside, seeing descriptions of Ahn'kat's last known locations…his shame…his betrayal that broke the heart of the emperor…the Empire's sadness and confusion…melded together in the well-thought minds of the Intel Corps agents. Into the deep bowels of the grey prison, there a chamber sat empty.

Treneer and Ahn'kat could feel Ramkes' presence all around it, but her being was long gone. They were relieved for a moment, until they saw Neobatri's figure standing in the hallway of the open cell. Her face was turned away, as if she was listening to someone beyond the wall. She sighed and turned around, dashing in the opposite direction.

We need to find her first.

Their joined senses peeled around the wall's edge and saw the back of a man in dark robes striding down the hall.

That's him.

Before they could inch towards Ismotaph, a hideous face screamed into the pair's vision. Their featureless and hairless green face shrieked, as their dark eyes beamed into them, and their black mouth peeled open. Their hearts thumped as they found their astral-eyes surrounded and trying to rip at them. Treneer snapped the pair back to Farayah and within the safety of the prism. They looked to each other as they grasped at their chests.

What was that? She said.

"His psychic vanguard," Ahn'kat shook his head. "They saw us, they'll know something's coming."

They're getting stronger, but the people seem to be unwell...

He rose to his feet while rubbing his stinging eyes. "I think he's been releasing the psi-enhancers, that was part of the plan a long time ago...now he's doing it."

Treneer's temples thumped as if she had grown a heart in her head. Fatigue had finally claimed the last of her strength as her back dropped to the ground as her face strained to keep the pain at bay. *I feel that creature's sting.*

How many times do I need to tell you, Treneer? Ouro flashed before them as he drifted over.

It was the attack that got me. She said as her palm covered her eyes and forehead while Ouro pressed his fingers into her temple.

Well, your fatigue left you exposed. He said as he slowly lifted her and stood back.

I'm fine, just bring Neheret back. We need to depart shortly. She grumbled before turning to Ahn'kat.

Ouro shook his head and shrugged before porting away.

"Were you two...?" the ex-prince whispered.

Treneer stiffened. *No.*

"Just a question," he smirked.

He helped me recover some of my psionics after a particularly gnarly deep-scan. She paused as her lips twitched. *I'm sorry I did that to you.*

"Better than you killing me," he said.

Its uncultured to do that to someone, even if they're an enemy, without informing them on the risks. She said.

"Treneer, I've already accepted your apology," he smiled.

Four strobes of light crackled before them, taking shape into Ouro and Neheret and two sleeping guardians. Neheret has shifted into her Yansoon form, her eyes were wide with concern. "I found them!"

They looked upon the sleeping figures. The poor souls had been thoroughly bashed, cut and burned – their armour had torn, and their faces were battered and bloodied as they floated in Ouro's gentle telekinetic grip. It took a moment for her to recognise them, but their unconscious minds and weak auras spoke their names.

Sesuune and Relzun! By the universe, I thought all guardians had perished! Treneer said as her hands reached out to their swollen and purpled faces.

I'm taking them to the healing pods now, but I think we should wake them up to assist us in finding more kin. Ouro said making them vanishing.

Have you…found anyone north of Yinray? Perhaps some Cold Fires? Treneer pressed her lips together.

Neheret's gritted her teeth and glanced to the side. *We have mainly been focusing on densely populated areas, we've barely made a dent in deep country.*

Of course, understood. Treneer nervously nodded and snapped her attention to Ahn'kat, her eyes dropped to the transponders in his hand. *I think you have something for her, don't you?*

"Neheret, a gift for you," Ahn'kat tried smiling as he placed one of the transponders around her ear. "This is a-"

"Yes, I know already. I read Shshmrnashsh's conversation with you," she said, pressing it harder against her skull.

"How fortuitous," Ahn'kat breathed. "Alright everyone, I have a rudimentary plan. Intel shows a Ramkes impersonator has ascended the throne; our mission is to seek her out and reveal Ismotaph's conspiracy against the Empire. Once we have restored her as rightful ruler, we can then request the Urasan Armada to begin preparations towards Vern the Unbound. Before we can proceed towards this goal, we need to find Neobatri Alkaheen. She would know the Corps plans are for the psi-virus and likely its effects on Zanashj. Maybe we can mobilise it to our advantage against Vern."

"You are considered as an imperial traitor. Organics have a harder time accepting new truths about a person, no matter if their old perceptions of them were false." Shsh said as she stepped through the jungle thicket into the icy stones of the tundra to meet the group.

"Yes, some may see it that way-"

"Like my eldest sister…" Neheret chimed in.

"She and Empress Ramkes are not beyond reason, I do believe-"

We need to have faith? Treneer eyed him with a shadow of a smile.

Ahn'kat cleared his throat. "Reasonable hope."

Spoken like a true politician. Ouro muttered. *We need to have several contingency plans before you risk your lives.*

"If we fail to muster support from the Empire, then Ouro and I will awaken the Arinu and pull all their psionic might against Vern. However, Vern may have the psi-virus planted around for this full assault. The Arinu are powerful enough to stop the Unbound, but it will mean possible annihilation." Shsh said.

How do you consider that a contingency plan? Treneer frowned.

Our purpose is to save life! You wish us to save the Roctarous at the cost of us. Ouro said staring at Shsh.

"Let's not pretend that none of us are facing extinction. The Zanashj may need to brave the fire alone," Ahn'kat said turning to Neheret.

She shrugged. "The Zanashj will adapt."

Treneer glanced to the prince with pursed lips. *The Neavensoros live beyond time, they should have prevented this from occurring. The idea of children sacrificing themselves to clean the messes of their parents...*

We do it every day. Ouro sighed.

"I didn't explain myself properly," Shshmrnashsh shook her head. "It's not about saving the Neavensoros from an ill fate. It's about reclaiming justice from Vern's wrongs. The likely chance all of us surviving this war is nil, but it will show people like Vern the consequences of enforcing one way of life on free beings. There is no one right way for all, but the inarguable wrong thing is stripping choice from another."

"Say by some miracle we do win, what do we do with Vern?" Ahn'kat looked between Neheret and Shsh.

"Give Vern a chance to choose something better," Shsh said.

"What they have done is indefensible, Shshmrnashsh. Vern needs to face our justice," Ahn'kat said.

The Roctarous shook her head. "I made poor choices before, but I was given a chance to update."

Neheret crossed her arms and clicked her tongue. "Well, they're too dangerous to be left to roam the universe. Vern will want vengeance."

Ouro turned to the endless realm in the scarlet horizon. *Leave that to me.*

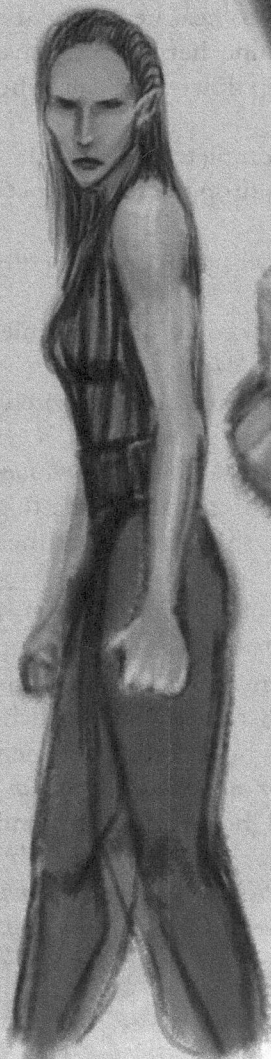

Chapter Thirty-eight
Together II:
Strange Sisters

The air tightened around everyone's throats with the collective apprehension of the coming days. Whatever malevolence Vern prepared for them was bound to make itself known on Uras. As Ahn'kat's ship was being loaded with auxiliary batteries, power generators, replicators, and so on in the prism below, Treneer made a lonely trip out on the balcony overlooking the great crystal trees of Heebar city. The breeze was colder than expected making her skin rise as she rushed to heat her energy field. Her fingers fixed a psi-booster around her temples, ensuring the light silver band wouldn't slip down her scalp when she felt a presence draw beside her.

"Transfer is complete," Shsh said.

Treneer's eyes dropped to the Roctarous' hand. *Can I see it?*

Shsh opened her palm to show a tiny milky crystal on her fleshy padding.

The Arinu cracked an uneasy smile as she stared at it. *I never imagined it would be so…small.*

"These crystals have been designed to store information equivalent to a star," she said.

Let's just hope it won't come to us needing that. Treneer said.

Shsh pushed the crystal into her thigh storage box as her eyes followed the shiny fractals of the enormous branches. "G'alann trees."

Quite a sight up close. I offered a tour to Ahn'kat of Farayah, and I extend that invitation to you. Treneer said with a sad smile.

"I've seen them many times with Sazla, but I would like to see them with myself," she said before turning to the Arinu. "Sazla was never cruel, but she was neglectful."

If you go another nine-thousand miles in that direction. Treneer pointed to her right, over and beyond the hazy grey hills. *That's where my family tribe is, the Cold Fires. I barely spent a handful of years with them before they admitted me to the Guardian Academy. They believed I couldn't be a great warrior like them, and my talents were best served as a guardian. They never taught me their* ways, only pieces to play the role but never become them. *There was a time when I believed I was a shame to them, but now I believe they paved a clean path for me to make mistakes and find myself. It may seem neglectful, but I cannot imagine any other version of myself today.*

"Are they deceased?" Shsh said.

Treneer shook her head. *They live, I don't know what to tell them if I see them again.*

"I want to see Sazla again, but I don't know what to say to her anymore."

We're ready to go. Neheret whispered.

Shsh and Treneer turned to each other with a smile.

"See you on the other side, Treneer," the Roctarous said.

Treneer's lip trembled and moved into her arms for an embrace. Electricity quivered from Shsh's touch; for a moment, Treneer instinctively wanted to pull away, but as the energy flowed into her mind…it resonated with her. Zu'leen's face flashed into her mind's eye. Shshmrnashsh was covered with her energy – no, she was dripping with it. Gnawing emotions ached her throat as her fingers clung around her metallic back.

"What's wrong?" Shsh said as she pulled Treneer away.

The Arinu blinked back tears as she tried grounding herself. *I felt Zu'leen…she's all around you.*

Shsh cocked her head to the side. "Anxiety of death decreases an Organic's ability to reason-"

No! I sense her in you. Have you ever connected with my old teacher?

"Negative, only Sazla,"

I see. Treneer drifted back. *We need to discuss somethings when I get back…*

"If-"

Shsh…

"Come back alive, Treneer."

With a quick grin, she dashed back into Ouro's haven and found Neheret strapping herself into Ahn'kat's charged fighter ship.

"Finally," he said, checking his holo-screen from his wrist.

We said our goodbyes. Treneer said as her eyes drifted to Ouro beside the craft and opened a private commune with him. *I sensed Zu'leen's energy on Shshmrnashsh.*

Ouro's eyes narrowed as he faced her.

I mean it, her cells were saturated with her! Shsh said she had never made contact with Zu'leen and I don't recall seeing her ever make contact with her, either. How's that possible?

I don't know. On one hand, I think you're overwhelmed with what's before us, but on the other, I've also felt a similar energy etched onto that Roctarous. He said.

Zu'leen?

Ouro shook his head. *Shimarr.*

"My friends," Ahn'kat said as his head poked out of the doorway of his ship, "I appreciate this maybe an Arinu farewell ritual, but the psi-virus very well might be on its way here."

Treneer rolled her eyes before slipping into the back of the craft. *See you shortly, Ouro.*

Ahn'kat, make sure she doesn't push herself too much. He said flashing a smirk.

"Be sure she listens to me as much as she listens to you, dear Ouro," the prince said as the doors squeezed shut and settled into the pilot chair.

The warden shook his head before telepathically linking to Neheret. *You...I want to...*

You'll pull me out of any situation, Ouro. She said with a sad smile. *I'll miss you too.*

He quietened and nodded.

Alright, it seems there aren't any Sleeping Watchers patrolling the southern pole, nearby the Crystal Ruins. They will circle back soon, so that's our window to slip out unabated. Treneer said as her third eye hummed.

"That space is fractured and crawling with E.Ds-" Neheret sat up.

"We can avoid them," Ahn'kat said, compelling the ship to his command. *Port us out, Ouro.*

The warden's arms lifted over his head, a crack of electricity lined between his palms as the ship plummeted into darkness. They lurched forward and trembled as they propelled through the portal's vortex, before a blinding sliver of light overwhelmed the pilot's screen, revealing thick snowy grounds and howling blizzards around them. Even in partial phase, Ahn'kat struggled against the forces of energy streaming against them.

Iridescent forms shot pass, narrowly striking the ship's camo-plating as they pressed through the thick clouds and into the outer atmosphere. Treneer felt tendrils grip around the left wing of the fighter, slowing their ascent. She slipped into her astral form and pushed the creature off, but it spat a burning cloud into her translucent form before it dashed away back into the distant ruins below.

"Everything well?" Neheret asked.

She dashed back into her physical body, still feeling the sting of the creature's attack in the bowels of her mind. *I'm fine, a mere bite from an insect.*

The view before them changed into a perfect black and starry sky as the blizzard fell behind, leaving them into the clean and calm vacuum in the darkness.

"From now on," Ahn'kat started as he compelled the ship to fly toward his homeworld's star. "Neheret or I will deal with these smaller hurdles. We cannot afford risking your health before facing Vern,"

I've been handling myself longer than thrice your age, Ahn'kat. She said adjusting her back into the soft, and mildly damp, organic padding in her pod.

His head turned to his side toward her. Irritation rang from his skin. "Your psionic strength is our greatest asset, if you fall, then we have no hope stopping the Unbound. Remember what Ouro said,"

I'm well-aware, thank you.

"Let your pride go, Treneer. You don't need to prove yourself to anyone," Neheret said leaning over her arm rail.

The Arinu's face turned to look out her side screen window. *Some habits take extra time to exorcise.*

"We'll be reaching Uras shortly," Ahn'kat said as he began slowing the ship and camouflaging their energy to mimic passing asteroids and solar radiations.

Neheret stood up and wandered beside the pilot's seat; her hands were resting against its edge as her face widened with awe and sorrow at the emerald sphere.

Ahn'kat snuck a glance up at her. "I'm glad to be the one who brought you back."

"I wish I could stay; I feel so much has changed," she whispered.

He nodded. "It's barely been a few months, but the air, seas, and land…something has."

The people know they're sick, but they don't know why…Treneer eyes closed as she dove deep into the Zanashj's subconscious seas. She could feel herself being drawn to every face from across the world, from the deserts to the mountains, people clinging at their temples and sleeping for days in beds. However, they were surrounded by a horrifying energy, looming over their scalps, tiny pinholes of light leaking in and sapping their strength without their awareness. *They're unknowingly evocating astral entities – their power is becoming stronger, but they don't understand what it attracts!*

Ahn'kat's jaw tightened as he pulled the ship around to the most desolate area of the planet. "Has the Kepa sniffed us out yet?"

In time they may without your kin's knowledge or training. She said, there was another feeling overflowing her chest. *The Zanashj are being told of a dark alliance you have made with aliens. They are told Emperor Kreshut died from a broken heart by your betrayal, they are told they have you in custody…awaiting your public trial.*

"They've put a Replacer on me, too…" his nostrils flared as his fingers pressed into his temple as he glanced at the screen. "What does the Conclave say of me?"

Sermons, they pray to the panther for justice. She said.

"And the people?"

Treneer squeezed her eyes shut, blanketing her scans of the conscious sea. *They are…mixed.*

"Mixed?" Neheret's brow furrowed. "Are they not a whole anymore?"

The Arinu shook her head. *They want their prince.*

"Then we will return the prince to them," Ahn'kat said as he ordered Zzamm the probe to disconnect from his craft and fly over to the isolated and unpatrolled mountains of the Baneshj Peninsula. "We can use Zzamm as a porting conduit from Uras and this craft; it can follow us around over our heads and get us out if we need to make a quick exit without jeopardising this fighter."

"No, wait," Neheret leaned in. "Take us to the northern suburbs of Lusor."

Ahn'kat's frowned. "Are you mad?"

"There's a house there…an estate. We will be safe," she said as she punched in the porting coordinates. The probe obeyed and moved over to the thicket of pale gold clouds. As her hand moved away, she straightened her back, looking at the confused glances of her companions. "I know we have one chance at this. Do you trust me?"

Yes. Treneer said giving Ahn'kat an assuring nod, easing his concern.

They slipped through a dark vortex, feeling their forms bend and bounce off the invisible energies in the funnel. When they found their feet again, they were surprised to find a shadowy chamber around them. It was smaller than Ahn'kat's palace and mansion, but the fine furniture lay about with a thick coat of dust on every surface.

Treneer had disguised her form as a typical Zanashj commoner woman in simple baggy trousers and dark tunic.

Her head turned about the room, feeling for life in the space, but whatever life there was…it was gone, and the happiness had died long before the last resident did. *Where are we?*

Neheret's sandaled feet scraped against the course stone as her hand caressed a scratched leather lounge chair. "Home."

Ahn'kat cleared his throat and strode along the living space. There was a small shrine dedicated to the Divine Cobra, but the incense stick had withered down to ash and dried flower petals fell limply from dead stems. There was a small row of carved red marble figurines along the base of the shrine. A tall father in thick robes, a strong daughter standing beside a shattered figurine of a younger daughter, and a round empty base beside the father where a figurine had been ripped off long ago. Ahn'kat's eyes dropped to the ground, he could see by his toes a tiny bundle of sticks shaped in a bipedal form wrapped in course string.

Neheret stepped beside him and sighed as she picked it up. "It's exactly how I remember it,"

"Gajoon," he whispered.

"Father kept throwing her effigy away, but she would keep making more and bringing it here," her hand clamped around the sticks as she drew a shaky breath. "She was so strong, no matter what he and Neobatri did to her."

"I don't know who Neobatri was as a child, but when she and Gajoon came into my service, she was overcoming her demons and Gajoon forgave," he said.

Neheret shook her head. "No, Gajoon always forgave her and everyone! I tried to make her see that she was too good for this ridiculous world. And when I was fed up with her constant passiveness, I took off and then I was taken. I abandoned her, but if she still lives, her foolishness will just forgive me and won't even try to punish me!"

You punish yourself enough, that's why she didn't bother with it. Treneer said.

"There's a dead air here, can't you feel it?" Neheret glanced around. "He's gone, but his presence is around us. Even Neobatri. They're all still here."

The memories are just ghosts, now. You can choose to be possessed by them back or let them go. The Arinu said.

Neheret carefully put the stick effigy of Gajoon beside her broken figurine. "I worry what Neobatri will say after all of this is finished, but I'm more afraid of what I will say to her."

Then that's enough for now. Treneer said giving her a gentle squeeze on her green shoulder.

~

After a short rest and briefing with Shsh and Ouro, the trio waited for the cover of night. They psychically blanketed Uras for Neobatri's presence; to their fortune, she was stationed to guard a hidden Intel Corps research station hidden inside the orange cliff face of the tropical mountains.

We need to lure her out somewhere we won't be bothered.

That science taskmaster, he looks like he has authority of her. There was a tall green figure in a light linen robe standing behind a row of researchers with their eyes fixed onto holo-screens along their desks. A stoic woman stood beside the wall, arranging some equipment by the desks, but casually monitoring every person in the white chamber.

Treneer, can you compel him to order her away?

The Zanashj are too strong there, he would certainly notice meddling and the wrong people might start asking questions.

We need to get out before alarms are tripped.

The trio's astral-eyes snapped back into their bodies as they each took a deep, grounding breath.

"Alright," Ahn'kat started as he rubbed his crossed legs. "Treneer: you can make him feel more tired, make him take a brief rest in his private office, Neheret: you can take his guise and request Neobatri to see him at his private office.

I can get the probe to port him away for a short time, and then we can make our presence known."

"Wouldn't it be easier just to teleport her out of there and bring her here?" Neheret said, her voice dropped as she removed most of her clothes, already morphing into the taskmaster's physique and uniform.

No, if they notice anything is amiss, it will make us harder to evade Ismotaph's detection. I can already sense he grows worried since my and Ahn'kat's intrusive 'visit.' Treneer said.

"Remember, all those Zanashj are psychic now, though they're latent to these abilities, they will know if our minds are irregular. Neobatri told me the first step of being a mind-bender is to completely shroud how your mind normally works and thinks. You may not know how the person you are taking form does ordinarily think, but the most important part is not to think like yourself!" Ahn'kat said.

You could have just said 'don't think like yourself.' Treneer's brow rose at him.

"Oh, and if anyone asks why your voice sounds like a shy screeching bird, Treneer, just say your voice was irreparably damaged in an accident," Ahn'kat said as his face morphed into an unrecognisable commoner.

How could Ramkes tolerate you as her husband? She said before the hidden probe from high clouds ported them away into the mountains.

In the moonlight, the orange rock and sand took a sparkling ultramarine hue. They were tempted to soak in the view, but the scraping footsteps from the guards stole their attention. They masked their presence from watchers, but Treneer created extra obfuscation in the darkness.

Their scanners are tuned for teleportation frequencies. She whispered in their private commune.

You and I can weaken them for a few seconds to get the taskmaster out and us in. Tell us when, Ahn'kat. Neheret said in a deep, husky voice.

The taskmaster is in the main research chamber, his office is empty. Treneer said.

Compel him there, now. Ahn'kat said, activating his transmitter to the probe.

She nodded and pressed against the leader's mind. His psionics had received some training to detect influence, but not aware enough for her to take advantage of his hungering stomach instead. Treneer heightened his sensitivities; she could see the man's face in her mind's eye, excusing himself for the loud growl from his gut before dashing away to his office.

Now. Ahn'kat said.

Neheret and Treneer closed their eyes as their minds intertwined, sending them across the grey ziggurat, suffocating the internal sensors. A tiny twinkle of light shimmered and vanished into the black above their heads, signifying the probe subtly sucking the unconscious taskmaster into its storage lattice.

Hide your minds. Let's go. Ahn'kat said before ordering the probe to port them directly into the now-empty office.

The internal sensor lights flickered on to a small room with a series of tables and computers stacked on them. When Ahn'kat ported in, his thigh struck the edge of a desk, knocking computer down. His hands spirited down, trying to catch it before it fell, but Treneer's telekinesis caught it first and shot him a frown.

Knuckles tapped on the other side of the door. *All well?*

Their three hearts hammered as Neheret sprinted to the door and slid it open, trying to mask her thoughts while the others appeared invisible to the guard.

"I'm well," she clutched her stomach and tried 'supressing' a burp. She quickly scanned the guard's memory of the taskmaster she posed as, and to her fortune, he and Neobatri had a turbulent professional relationship. "Call Neobatri, I will have words with her."

The guard cocked his head to the side. *Are you not adapting to the psi-enhancers? I can call a medic-*

"I will deal with this firstly! Call her in!" she said slamming the door shut before turning around to face her companions with a smirk.

Don't push it. Treneer scowled.

Neheret sauntered to the taskmaster's chair and settled into it, waiting for that second knock at the door.

"Come!" she commanded, watching Neobatri's altered form stride in, standing tall and still.

Her eyes lay flat as she stared at the taskmaster. "You wanted to speak to me."

Neheret cleared her throat and leant forward. "I spoke to Director Ismotaph not long ago, after our little disagreement. He assured me your loyalty as an Alkaheen, that's when I realised something. I had never seen you! Your true face, I want to see it."

Neobatri's nostrils flared before her skin trembled and reformed into her natural physique.

"Ah, he was right. You look like the spitting image of your father, the Seraphim himself...but as a female. Your demeanour is identical, t-"

"You wanted to speak with me, Taskmaster Kerfon," she hissed.

What are you doing? She's getting angry- Ahn'kat's frantic whispers echoed in her mind.

I know what I'm doing, she becomes so predictable when talking about father. Neheret said as she cleared her throat again while eyeing her sister. "I was promised the psi-enhancers were meant to be a boon to our mission, but it seems, most of our workers have been struggling to adapt to them. Most of our people are realising their effects, or should I say, side-effects. Why is it you and Ismotaph's special few, have adapted to them with such ease?"

Neobatri's jaw tightened. "As you know, I'm prohibited from discussing-"

"Yes, yes, the Corps is entitled to their secrets. I just wonder…" Neheret leant back in the chair. "I suppose your family is particularly adept and I find myself envious of your abilities. Your father must be very proud of you now."

"You humble me, Taskmaster, we come from a long line of infiltrators. I believe it's an artform." Neobatri's voice was loaded with venom.

I can feel her mind probing outside of the chamber…she's calling for assistance! Treneer said.

She's getting so angry; I can take her. Neheret said.

Supress her connection, keep her occupied while we take positions. Ahn'kat said.

"Yes, artists can often spot another artist, no matter what face they take," Neheret smiled.

Neobatri's face shadowed and her breathing deepened.

"Fortunately for us, you are not like our dear father, eh?" Neheret said rising to her feet, shifting back into her normal form.

In a blink, Neobatri flung her claw-like hand across Neheret's face before stretching her leg out to strike at her shins. Treneer opened her palms, blanketing the room with a sound and psi suppressant field, gliding away from the struggling sisters. Ahn'kat jumped from the shadows, trying to grab at Neobatri's arms, but her speed and ferocity, slipped through his grasp.

"Stop!" Ahn'kat called, but her wild-eyed stare turned to him and struck his jaw with her elbow. When he stumbled back, he felt blood gushing from a thick slash under his chin, realising she had created several sharp bone spines along her arms, shoulders, and face. Neheret crouched down and slid between Neobatri's legs before kicking her over her head.

Use telekinesis! Ahn'kat called as he tried nursing the gash closed.

Can't, she needs to tire out! Neheret said.

Neobatri stretched forward towards the door, it peeled open an inch before Neheret flung her back and kicked the door closed again. Neobatri wriggled free from her sister's grasp as she climbed on Neheret's shoulders and wrapped her thighs around her neck. Neheret punched her sister's thighs and knees, her face warping and bruising from the grip, as she collapsed into table before rolling onto the ground.

Neobatri spun around to face Ahn'kat with sharp yellow eyes that made him freeze where he stood. Her long arms swung out at him but regained his senses before leaping on her back. As her claws bent back to slash at his face, his arm slid around her shoulders while his other hand pointed and speared into her mid spinal vertebrae, forcing the disk to pop inward.

Her throat gurgled in pain, through gritted teeth and tears, she turned and glared at him as her body fell limp. Her trembling clawed hands rose to his face, but he slapped them away before he yanked her away from a suffocating Neheret.

"I'm sorry, I'm sorry, take a deep breath. We can fix this-" he said as he laid her flat on the cool floor.

"Trai-" her voice crackled, he could see she was trying to move her disk back into place and continue the fight.

"Stop, we're stopping the traitors! We can heal you-"

"She's not trying to heal herself; she's flooding her body with poison!" Neheret breathed as she crawled up to her.

Treneer flew down and pressed her palms on Neobatri's shoulders, her energy compelling the poison out of her system.

Delyn, I'm not your enemy. Show her the truth, now! She looked to Ahn'kat and gave him a small nod.

Ahn'kat pressed his hand over Neobatri's forehead, opening his inner eye and flooded his surface mind with all his memories, starting from the day he and Ramkes played in the palace gardens.

Not too quickly, she is weakened and might miss parts. Treneer said.

Ahn'kat took a long breath, ebbing the river of memories in, watching carefully as Neobatri's eyes rolled back of her head. *See it all, Neobatri. You and I were both deceived by the man who now owns the Empire.*

Leave me alone, this is too much, I don't want this! She screamed in her mind while her body lay serene.

Grey oil bubbled up from her pores; Treneer teased out every molecule of the enzyme.

I'm sorry for everything, Neobatri. I'm sorry for leaving, I'm sorry! Neheret said as she squeezed her hand.

Treneer said as she slid back. *I pushed her spine back in place and removed everything I could.*

Come back. Neheret said.

Neobatri's hand dropped to her chest as she took a haggard breath, her face scrunched as she slowly sat up before them.

"Do you need a moment?" Ahn'kat whispered.

She shook her head. "Clean this place up when you bring the taskmaster back, I'll meet you back home," she said before she rose and staggered to the office door before quickly composing herself, never once looking at any of them in the eye.

~

Ahn'kat paced around the dark and dusty room; his wide eyes had sensitised to the shadows when he looked to Treneer. "Has she called the authorities? Is that why she's taking so long?"

Her mind is hidden from me, Ahn'kat, but I don't feel any movement against us. Treneer said settling on an old, cushioned stool.

Neheret peeled open cabinet doors, pressing her face and hands inside, rummaging for something inside.

Ahn'kat pursed his lips and stared at her. "Did you really have to do that to her?"

A metal bowl slid from the shelf before Neheret turned around, holding an assortment of dried fruits. Her fingers delicately fished out a handful of green berries from it. "These were my favourite, Neobatri knew that and always mixed them with black bananas and spiced apple – things I didn't like."

"You cracked the shell around her pain, Neheret, she could have exposed us to Ismotaph if she was willing," he said stepping forward.

Neheret winced a smile before blowing clean the berries. "My old sister would have killed to get a pat on the head, but until she met someone more ambitious and stubborn," she eyed Treneer, "I knew she could be trusted."

I'm glad to have been an idol of what not to be. The Arinu said resting her cheek on her hand. *Dare I say you two were almost friends when you were on Farayah?*

"Almost. A part of me misses pretending to be Yansoon," Neheret laughed before palming all the berries into her mouth. As she chewed, her ears perked, and eyes widened.

Ahn'kat's head shot toward the front yard of the property. "I can hear someone coming."

I hear no one. Treneer said turning to the front.

"An air vehicle incoming, can't you hear that?" he said.

Your ears are more sensitive than mine it seems, but I know the mind driving it toward us. The Arinu's sly smile curled up her face.

Lights flickered through the window before coming to a stop; a dark form slid out of the oval disk and strode towards the shimmering doors. Neobatri stepped in as her leather trousers danced around her sandaled feet; her tired and sullen face turned to all the three of them but walked no closer.

"Were you followed?" Ahn'kat said.

Neobatri eyed him before shaking her head.

Everything that's happened, shouldn't have. Treneer rose from the stool.

The infiltrator turned her head away as her eyes fell to the floor. "How do I know that you didn't feed me telepathic lies?"

"If you thought that, you wouldn't be here without backup," Neheret said.

Neobatri's nostrils flared when she met her sister's eyes as her lips tightened.

Ahn'kat stepped forward. "I'm sorry for not trusting you."

"I'm sorry for trusting you," she said.

"I was afraid to tell you, Ismotaph led me to believe that the Empire was ready to swallow me if I moved a toe. But now, all of us, even the Arinu are willing to restore our people-"

"I am fed up with that excuse!" Neobatri hissed. "Every single faction preaches on and on about 'restoring the Empire,' 'restoring our people,' but only manages to destroy more of our sanctity toward each other and gods. We built ourselves to trust us and only us, and I have done everything to uphold that code and to what end?"

As an Arinu, I admire your ability to hold reverence of your kin without the aid of psionics. These times have irrevocably altered your society, but it doesn't mean your faith must be made redundant to evolve. We can trust each other again. Treneer said.

Neobatri tore her gaze away from the Arinu. "If you seek an apology from me for playing my part for the Empire, you won't receive one."

"She's not asking you for one, no one here is. We don't want you to purge your trust because of one traitor. Our Imperial Family wasn't born immediately, it took hundreds of thousands of years to build. Now, we ask for your help to build a new one," Ahn'kat said.

Tell her what you told me when we escaped Kra. Treneer cocked her head to a silent Neheret.

Neobatri cleared her throat as she forced her gaze towards her sister. "I vowed to bring you back home."

Neheret's green brow twitched as her lips trembled.

"I thought you were the knife that brought pain to this family – to me. You never had to try, and you were still better than me, and I hated you for it, Neheret," the infiltrator straightened her back and strode towards her sister. "I thought the night you vanished I would become the better and I was. I didn't hate you anymore, but the worst part was, I hated myself for feeling good."

Neheret's throat twitched. "I heard you took good care of Gajoon."

"Because no one else would…" Neobatri whispered.

"Did you recognise me while I was Yansoon?" she said as a corner of her mouth grinned.

"No," Neobatri breathed. "Did you know I was Delyn?"

"If I did, then we wouldn't have been friends," Neheret chuckled.

"Next time if you want to be an infiltrator," Neobatri stepped forward wearing the largest smile Ahn'kat and Treneer had ever seen. "You need to be better at pretending."

"I tricked her, didn't I?" Neheret nodded to the Arinu.

Strangers as sisters, but sisters as strangers. Treneer beamed at the two.

Neheret extended her forearm to Neobatri for a firm grip. "I'm sorry father isn't around to see us, when he returns, he will assume we've been replaced!"

Neobatri's hand slid away; she closed her eyes and shivered. "You don't know? When I returned, the Empire was in a flurry of the prince's betrayal. There were two lies told: Prince Ahn'kat had betrayed Empire to join our alien enemies, thereby Emperor Kreshut dying from a broken heart. The second lie was to the Intel Corps, that Princess Ramkes and Prince Ahn'kat plotted to remove the emperor, in which the prince escaped with the help of the princess.

All agents were told to protect the emperor, and Seraphim volunteered to be his personal guard. However, the princess' assassins came for father, the emperor and all his most loyal guards.

"Before he left, I came to speak to him about my journey, Gajoon, mother and you, Neheret – but the moment I mentioned your name…we just reverted to the old days. Our ears closed and our mouths opened for a fight. That's the last I saw him," Neobatri collapsed down on a stool and slammed her elbow against the wooden table.

Neheret dropped to a chair opposite her. "He's with the gods?"

Neobatri nodded as her face hid in her hand.

"What about Gajoon?" she snatched and squeezed at her sister's forearm.

"I don't know. She was at the princess' palace when it was stormed. But if she dared to protect the princess, then she would be with the gods and father."

Ahn'kat closed his eyes and shook his head. Treneer noticed his hand wincing towards the centre of his chest before dropping it away.

"How unjust, she doesn't deserve to be in the same realm with him!" Neheret said.

"Neheret-" Ahn'kat said.

"I will grieve him, but he's earnt our ire," she slapped her hands down on the wooden surface.

"This is a discussion for another time," Neobatri said lining her finger along her brow. "We need Ismotaph to face justice, but the only way we can do that is if we tell the truth. Yet, no one will believe the truth without the princess."

"Has she been…altered?" Ahn'kat said.

"No, she was sentenced to be metamorphed like Seratut was, but she had escaped before we could transfer her."

How?

"None of us know! Ramkes wasn't particularly psionically adept, and she didn't receive a psi-enhancer, we scanned her many times to confirm her identity," Neobatri said.

Did your vanguard gleam the energy within her detention room? If they hadn't yet, then you can go and read it for us. Treneer said.

"Luckily, none of them know how to use psychometry properly," Neobatri said.

You definitely could have, why didn't you teach them how or do it yourself? The Arinu smirked.

"Let's say I wasn't entirely convinced of the princess' guilt," Neobatri glanced to Ahn'kat with a smile.

"That room is our only lead for us finding her or at least seeing how she had escaped," Ahn'kat said before settling down around the table. "Tell us about Ismotaph's vanguard."

"He's been recruiting heavily. I've seen research documents saying since the release of the psi-enhancers, the Corps is inviting the most psychically adept Zanashj to be trained. He has invested a tremendous amount to find the princess. It's only a matter of time, now," she said.

What about the psi-virus?

"I don't know, I believe he may delay it until he finds her but considering how paranoid he's become..." she shrugged.

"I've had the most contact with her. Treneer, Neheret and I will dowse for her while you scout her cell. Dismissed." he said.

Chapter Thirty-nine
Together III:
Underground Princess

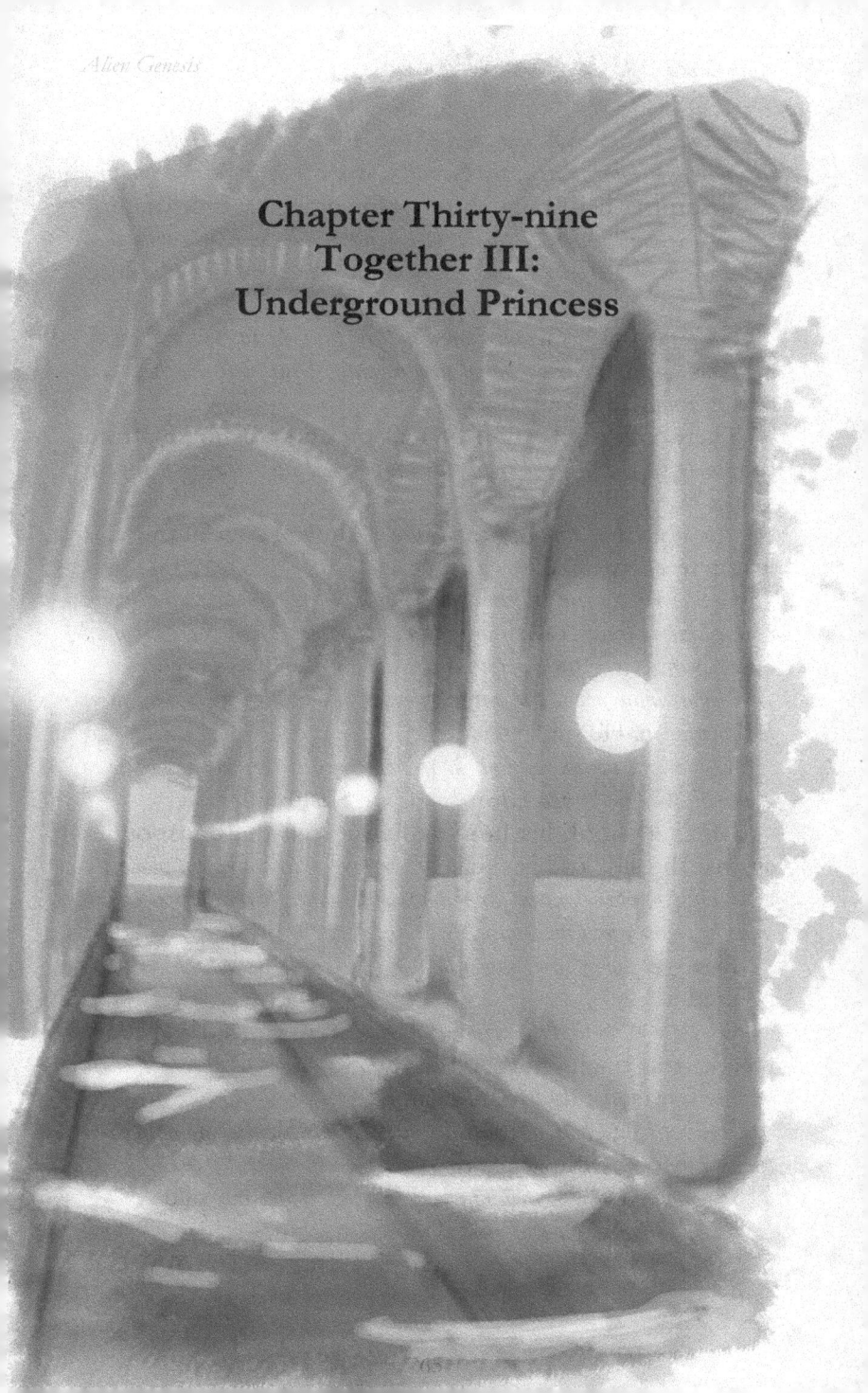

The planet has cleared, and most of the Arinu sleep peacefully within this haven. Unfortunately, the Grand Coven is still fixated on finding us. Shshmrnashsh spoke through the universal transmitter.

And I don't believe it's for positive commendations. We have also captured some Sleeping Watchers so we can move unobserved. Ouro added.

Good news. The Grand Coven will be brought in, but only when the time's right. Your saving of unconscious Arinu will tilt the scales in our favour. Ahn'kat said.

There was a vibration of tension and frustration from Ouro. *It is generally the right thing to do, not just viewing it in 'our favour.'*

Apologies, I'm thinking in strategy. Ahn'kat's facial muscles instinctively twitched to a smile.

Gentlemen, please. There is one problem: we have detected massive energy spikes from Neavensoros space. It seems Vern the Unbound have begun moving the Roctarous fleet into orbit. Shsh said.

Unfortunate news. I'm surprised none of Vern's agents have come looking for us. He said.

They won't be able to find us in here, even if they were to come to Farayah, but you're too exposed on Uras. Shsh said.

Ahn'kat shook his head as he pressed the transponder against the side of his skull. *We're moving quietly, but when the time comes to make our big announcement, hopefully the Grand Coven and the Crown will move quickly as one.*

How far away are you from locking onto Ismotaph? Ouro pressed in.

We have yet to find the princess. Ahn'kat slowly said. He could feel distress ringing through his head.

He may release the virus any day now!

Neobatri says he may delay it until he finds her. We do have some time on our side. Ahn'kat said.

If Ismotaph delays, then maybe Vern will too. Shsh said.

The Unbound haven't moved from Kra, they're all in one place. Can you disrupt some of their progress from Farayah? The ex-prince said.

Negative. Vern and I have already done that when taking Hrrmn's consortium, they will recognise the same attempt. She said.

Vern will also notice the planar cloud lifting from Farayah. We can leave just enough energy around the planet to convince them nothing's amiss. Ahn'kat said.

I can divert some of it to evade psi-scans, but it will hinder our progress to get our A.Is and Grand Elders to see what's happening. Ouro said.

All in due time, friends. Ahn'kat pulled out of the commune with Farayah and slipped into Neobatri's mind. *Anything?*

The same! I don't understand any of these images! Neobatri called from the jail Ramkes was once held.

Give them to me. Treneer replied.

The group could feel tremendous energy pushing through the telepathic tube, like a stiff piece of food being forced down into a gullet.

That was...unexpected. The Arinu said.

I cannot remain by this cell too long; the others here will notice me missing from my post. Neobatri said as her mind fell to an ambient hum.

"Treneer, what can you tell us?" Ahn'kat walked to her and sat beside her and Neheret on the old carpet.

She was forbidden to sleep, they would wake her every few minutes...she was so tired, her eyes shut for a moment and fell away into slumber, and then light. She thought they had woken her again but was eaten by the light. Treneer rubbed her third eye as her face scrunched.

"She was teleported away? Was it the vanguard?" Neheret said.

Yes, but it wasn't one of the vanguards. I recognise this energy...

"Kepa?" Ahn'kat's stomach tightened.

No, it reminds me of Zu'leen. Treneer's eyes opened and looked to her bewildered companions.

"Your teacher?" Neheret asked.

She has made an appearance more than once, but I don't understand what she would want with a Zanashj princess. She said.

"Please don't tell me Ramkes has been teleported to another plane of existence…" Ahn'kat said.

We may have to do this the hard way. Treneer grabbed their hands and melded their minds into one before flying through the ceiling and into Uras' clouds. They shrouded over the lands and seas of the world, peering into every hole, down every corridor and bedchamber for the princess' brainwaves. Deep below the broken cisterns of Lusor city, hordes of misplaced pets, ill-fated commoners and fallen nobles lay huddled together, as still as corpses beside the glowing green water shimmering in the small burning braziers.

What is this place?

A refuge for the ones who are falling apart from the psi-enhancers.

Who is that?

A tall figure pressed against a chipped stone column; their size and height towered a head over all the others, even though their own head had slumped forward.

Gajoon!

We must save her-

No, the princess is our priority. Later, when-

Wait, friends.

The trio's astral-eyes inched forward; they couldn't scan for their minds, but under her filthy linen sleeve, Gajoon held a slender and soft green hand who appeared to never worked a day of manual labour. Was it possible?

I can't get a confirmation; their minds are too chaotic and melded. It's our best lead.

They spun through the ether back into their bodies. Treneer patted Neheret's forehead, trying to soothe her emotional distress as Ahn'kat tried finding himself back in his skull.

"Put your faces on, we're going in," he said before commanding the probe to port them into the cistern's entry. Strobes of light encircled them before plummeting their bodies under the low ruined ceiling of the stony corridor.

I don't sense danger here. Treneer said, trying to shield her nose from the putrid air.

They're dying. Ahn'kat said.

They huddled close under the shadowy psionic mask as they voyaged into the chamber, appearing to be as any other refugees. Their feet gently slipped through the sitting despondent desperates, before finding the chipped column. Ahn'kat slumped against it as he slid down, a foot away from Gajoon. Several others stirred for Neheret and Treneer to sit beside him, leaning close.

It's her. Neheret smiled under her hood.

Raivan are easily stirred, be as gentle as possible. Treneer said.

Ahn'kat turned and gently tugged on Gajoon's sleeve. The large woman made no attempt to face her botherer, but when he tried again, the trio saw her back tense and the long ears under her hood move.

She's alert, she might attack us. Treneer said.

"Gaj-" Ahn'kat barely uttered a whisper before Gajoon's head turned and her face leered towards him. Her yellow ball-like eyes were fierce, and her lips peeled away revealing rows of terrifying dagger teeth.

"Friend! Friend!" he breathed as he put his hand up, leaning away from her. He looked to his comrades. *Put that sound muffling field around us!*

Treneer's faux green palm opened on her lap, and they could immediately hear the wet drips of the hollow corridors fall silent.

"My sister," Neheret leaned in, showing just enough of her matured face with teary eyes and joyful grin.

Gajoon's horrifying glare reeled back, and her face softened as her eyes widened with realisation. Her nostrils flared as her mouth sucked a lungful of air, trying to hold down an elated scream. "How yer?"

"You've grown so quickly! I'm sorry for running away," she said grabbing at her calloused hands. "These are my friends, and one that you know."

Gajoon's face whipped to Ahn'kat as he lowered his hood.

"Please don't react. It's not my true face, but it's me," he said.

Gajoon's nostrils flared again. "Crown-breaker," her voice tensed into a hiss.

"Listen to me," Neheret pushed closer. "What they all say happened, didn't. He, all of us, wants to talk about what really happened. I, ahh…we can't say much, but we need to find and save the pretty woman in the big house and take you and her to our house."

The hybrid's brows furrowed. "I want but can't. Safe here until we move again."

It makes sense, you hide in the pool of chaotic minds to evade vanguard scans. Treneer said leaning closer.

Gajoon's eyes lifted to her and narrowed. "Yer voice in my head?"

Ahn'kat shifted forward. "She's with us, come and we will expl-"

"You must be insane to think we are leaving here with you," Ramkes' hooded body shifted and crawled forward. Her face was not her own, it was covered in lightning-tan scars across her wide and malformed nose, her eyes were bloodshot and drooped outwards, and her mouth was shrivelled into a wrinkled line above her chin. "You must be madder still to think we will let you leave here."

"Remember who the real enemy is!" Ahn'kat's voice trembled as his heart raced. "Tell me, he has not done this to you-"

Ramkes' hands shot towards him; her hand gripped around the back of his neck forcing him forward while her other hand sharpened two long nails, dripping in yellow venom pressing against the skin of his neck. "Make any sudden moves or even if I feel a slight bit of domination," she eyed Treneer. "I will end him."

"If my heart wasn't still in the Empire, we wouldn't be here-," Ahn'kat croaked as she pressed harder into his neck.

"Your faux love for the Empire offends me! Father was right to not let you in so close, but I believed if I brought you closer to us, then you would see our vision – then you would repent!" She hissed.

Ahn'kat forced his face towards her. "It seems I could never hide myself from you, gods be blessed I wasn't an infiltrator!"

"Do you really want your departing words to be a jape?" the princess glowered.

"No, I want my final words to be an apology for letting my fears blind me," he breathed.

"What about betraying my House and the Imperial Family to aliens?" she said forcing his head lower.

"You'd trust the words of a man who stole your crown about my actions?" he grunted.

Ramkes' voice trembled as a tear rolled in her eyelids. "My father was murdered because of you-"

"Ismotaph would've killed him anyway. He eliminated the heads of greater houses and took their power to get closer to the Crown so he could become it! If I failed him, he would've found another way to become the hidden emperor. Is it not clear?" he said.

I sense psychic minds in the skies, we have been revealed. Treneer said.

"You can't hide here anymore, come back with us and after all is done, I will face your judgement," Ahn'kat said.

Ramkes softened her hold over his neck before Neheret punched in coordinates for the probe to port them all back to the Alkaheen estate. Once they felt the warm carpet and faint amber glow of the chamber's lights, Ahn'kat tapped Ramkes' hand. She pulled away and glanced around the room.

Gajoon knelt, holding the princess' elbow, and carefully lifting her. "Hoome," she said.

"You found them-" Neobatri's voice cracked as all eyes drew to her, stepping forward and flying into the arms of Gajoon for an embrace. "The Divine Cobra has saved you!"

"Yer," the hybrid grinned as she held up a tiny golden cobra necklace around her neck to Neobatri. Ahn'kat couldn't help but smile.

Neobatri turned and bowed to the rightful princess. "Empress, forgive my crimes against the Crown. I was informed that you were the Crown's traitor-"

"Rise, infiltrator," Ramkes said ripping the hood from her mangled face. "You were loyal to a Head who revealed to be a lying criminal. The Crown only punishes criminals."

The infiltrator nodded as a broad smile of relief washed over her face as she lifted to her feet. "Thank you, your majesty."

"Neheret Alkaheen, you were a subject of much discussion for quite some time, but I'm glad you have returned alive and in one piece. Forgive me, I assumed you to be much younger," she said.

"I have been altered by our true enemy, your majesty, but I'm glad to be home," the young infiltrator smiled.

"Now, we all seem to know one another here," Ramkes eyed all, but fixed her stare to Treneer. "All but one."

Treneer's Zanashj illusion dropped away, showing her full Arinu form. *I am Archite Treneer, I'm here to save my kin by saving the Empire.*

Ramkes stifled a gasp as her arm slid away from Gajoon's hold. "Save from what?"

I will show you. Treneer held out her palms for Gajoon and Ramkes. The hybrid's hands were so large, her fist swallowed the narrow white wrist of the Arinu, but Ramkes remained still.

"She isn't a threat," Neheret said.

Ramkes' eyes dropped down to Treneer's almost transparent hand. "I don't trust the open hands of Arinu anymore,"

"We wouldn't have made it here without her," Ahn'kat whispered as he stepped closer to her.

The uncrowned empress' eyes turned to him as her lips pursed.

"Trust one more time," he said.

Ramkes sighed as she clung onto her palms. Treneer's eyes and third eye hummed a magenta light as she poured every drop of information into her and Gajoon. Their bodies tensed as it flowed; Ramkes' face scrunched before pulling away and grasping at her temples. However, Gajoon lingered a moment longer before calmly sliding her hand from the Arinu.

Do you see?

"Alright, let's assume this wasn't Arinu trickery. Your plan is for me to reclaim my throne and command the Armada to defeat this…Vern?" she said.

"Before that, we need to learn everything we can about the psi-virus, stop the Empire from releasing it on the Arinu and capture Ismotaph while he's unaware," Ahn'kat said.

"Don't be so sure of that. Ismotaph has suspiciously improved at finding the right people at the right time. He probably knows you're on Uras right now," she said as her shiny hand slipped into her loose sleeve.

All the more reason we must act quickly.

"How do you know once I ascend the throne, I won't arrest you again and command the Armada to attack the Arinu anyway?" Ramkes glanced to Treneer. "I suppose you could mentally compel me to do anything, and the Empire would be your puppet."

You've had many dealings with my kin, you know that isn't our way.

"Times change," Ramkes said.

"And so do Zanashj. We don't have to conquer an enemy to defeat it. We cannot rely on our old ways to face new threats. The Treaty may have been the seed for a new way, but the Federation was the true first step. Look at how much effort you've poured to manifest it. They see it!" Ahn'kat pointed at Treneer.

Arinu are being forced to face their demons. You will be a lantern for us if we see you adapting to yours.

Ramkes held her breath for a moment before gently exhaling. "You're asking us to sacrifice ourselves for an alien species."

"I'm asking the Empire to adapt," he said.

The empress stepped closer to Treneer, wearing a glare potent enough to drill through diamonds. "I want assurances. I don't want any more changes of mind; I don't want to hear some cosmic reason of why you couldn't fulfil your end of the bargain. I want your people to prove to mine you were worth dying for."

I cannot speak for my kin, but I give you my oath to spend the remainder of my five-thousand years on Uras strengthening your psionics and nursing your psi-afflicted people. Treneer bowed.

"Gods damn you if you don-" Ramkes caught her words and bit her bottom lip. "Gods bless you if you do."

"Thank you, empress," Ahn'kat bowed, and so did the Alkaheen sisters.

"I'm not crowned yet," she said with a rise of her brow. "So, how do we make that happen?"

"Ismotaph will be arriving to the research centre tomorrow. Which is troubling news because he almost never leaves his stronghold these days. He must be on the hunt for you," Neobatri said glancing at Ahn'kat.

I do feel he's surrounded by a psi-bulwark. I cannot weaken his defences on my own and I won't risk psi-penetration without being discovered, or worse, a counterattack. Treneer said.

"If he knows I'm here and if he's desperate for the princess, then I say, let him find them," Ahn'kat nodded. "Neobatri will wear my face,"

Neheret smiled and turned to Neobatri. "I'll be the princess."

"All your life," Neobatri rolled her eyes. "He'll eventually know that we aren't either of you,"

"We have two infiltrators who fooled Arinu! Once he comes with his vanguard and checks for himself," Ahn'kat pulled out a handful of universal transmitters from his trouser pocket, "you can plant these on him."

Neobatri and Neheret plucked them from his palm, before tucking them under their chins. Gajoon cleared her throat and stepped forward, "They're be suffering when caught."

Ahn'kat's neck strained at her words. "Yes, you'll be under the hands of the...inquisitors."

"We survived Treneer," Neheret mumbled.

I'm sure the Kepa was far worse.

"We'll be alright, Gajoon," Neobatri gave an assuring tap on her large sister's shoulder, "we won't make it easy for them."

Won't your fellow agents notice your absence from the research laboratory? Treneer turned to her.

They all glanced to Ahn'kat. "Let Ismotaph read into her absence on his own, he may believe she has switched sides and is aiding Ramkes. I want him to feel like his closest allies are leaving him."

That will only make him more dangerous and ruthless.

"But at least he will be fearful and fearful people are predictable if channelled the right way. Even with psionics, he will be overwhelmed and will eventually fall into that black hole, making him ripe for the taking," he said.

"Stretch him thin, make him think that his allies are failing him. People will notice his loyalties are his own and not to the Corps and Empire. Even if he blamed all the arrests on the false empress, his own agents would know the truth and start pulling away. We in the Corps have already whispered about the various inconsistencies he spouts," Neobatri said.

"The people are our allies. We will go to them," Ramkes said.

Yes…the monasteries, reformation centres, all the places where they yearn to see you. And you. Treneer looked to Ahn'kat with a smile.

"Can you cast distant illusions of our presence in several places at the same time? I want our faces to be fresh in everyone's mind," he said.

She gave a knowing smile. *We will see how far Ismotaph can stretch before he breaks.*

~

They're off. They will keep us updated on their movements, but whatever happens, don't try to rescue them even if you feel their agony from the inquisitors. Treneer's decoys will be scattered around Uras, but we want Ismotaph to capture them. Ahn'kat said.

Their willingness for this mission is deeply impressive. How can you be sure that Ismotaph won't also take you as well? Ouro said.

It's irrelevant who gets to him first. Once you have him, we will be able to rescue the others in captivity. Purely logical. Shsh said.

Assuming that the planar cloud has been lifted enough for that. He said.

There was a tension from Farayah's side of the commune.

Our efforts bore results. Farayah has exited from much of the radiation, but the government has noticed and so have the Grand Coven. Shsh said.

We are still trying to hide from them but won't be for long. Ouro said.

Stave it off until we're ready to get Ramkes back on the throne. Ahn'kat said. The others stood around the carpeted living chamber waving for him to hurry. *We'll return shortly.*

He skipped toward their small four-way circle. Treneer's eyes were closed, semi-focused on the illusions she created of them around Uras' cities, towns, beaches, and woodlands.

"Anyone notice us yet?" asked Ahn'kat with a paused breath.

Stone carvers noticed you and Ramkes hiking up toward the Pantheon Lodge before disappearing behind the thickets. They reported it and now the mountain is swarming with Intel agents. Treneer said.

"That's not all, information is picking up a bunch of sightings. Some are speculating that an unfashionable trend is rising, and the faux empress is disparaging such actions. If they continue, then those caught body-bending as the ex-prince and empress will be heavily penalised," Neobatri said scanning the holo-screen of her glassy bracelet.

"Maybe we will have some mimickers to cover us for a while," Ahn'kat commanded the probe to lock on to his and Ramkes' physical forms.

"Yer best be go to Ghalashi Monastery, that's where she and I hid for time," Gajoon said.

With a quick nod, Ahn'kat and Ramkes slipped into the strobe of light and spat out in a sun-warmed chamber with glass walls facing the bright yellow hills of Lusor's outskirts. There were no guards, priests, monks, or civilians in this barren hall. As they cautiously stepped on the wooden floorboards, there was a whisp of a tattered robe behind an old wood column etched of the Great Skyserpent.

"This doesn't bode well," Ramkes whispered.

Pull out if you need to, I can provide support- Treneer called.

"No need, I don't feel danger here," Ahn'kat replied in a huskier and broken voice. "Reveal yourself!"

Nothing, but the mildest shift of the dusty satin curtain.

"I can feel people here," he said with a frown.

"It's a large monastery, there'll bound to be people in the lower halls," Ramkes said as she continued her trek toward the darkened archways, but upon her last step into the room, she was propelled back by a brush of a body.

A timid youth's face appeared before them; his round orange eyes panicked the moment when he realised he was seen before scrambling out of sight behind the pillar.

"Stop!" Ahnkat commanded, but felt his knees and elbows strike hair, shoulders, and skin before vanishing from his sight.

His head whipped to Ramkes, wearing the same shock as she glanced around the supposed vacant hearth.

"We are not enemies!" she called.

"They're masking themselves from our physical senses, but its limited," Ahn'kat stepped towards her as his eyes tried catching an imperfect glimmer about the room.

"You possess psionics, adapting to advanced tricks, we see. Look into our minds and have faith that we only wish to speak openly," Ramkes said.

They held their breath, waiting for a sign to greet or to run. Small and thin pale auras shimmered as they filled with robed bodies, standing back along the walls and around columns. Pallid-faced monks, thin children and young adults bundled together as frightened deer. This group grew a psychic skill for camouflage, a powerful ability their ancient Zanashj ancestors possessed in their green skins to blend with viridian jungles.

Ahn'kat's smile warmed as he turned to soak in their faces. "You know who we are."

A gaunt monk brushed through the children by her robe as she braved closer. "We don't want any trouble from the Intel Corps. If you have love for your people still, prince, best you both leave."

"That's why he has returned. That's why we risk our lives and yours to come to you," Ramkes spoke up beside him. "Your troubles with the Corps have only begun. The Crown has a Replacer on the throne who's enslaved by Director Ismotaph. He's the true shadow emperor. Prince Ahn'kat saved me from his lies and our mission is to warn people directly of his treachery."

"What do you want from us? There aren't any soldiers here, only the powerless," she said.

"The Empire is composed of people, in that there is power," Ahn'kat said.

The monk shook her head as her breathing deepened. "I grasp your meaning, your highnesses, we all do. But you have endangered us by your presence. Corps agents will sense you and they will come for us-"

"Hold your fears for a moment," he put his hands up before extending them to the monk. "We need to start telling the truth. We have an Arinu helping us divert attention from the Intel Corps, but before you sign me away as a traitor, we ask only for your trust once more."

The monk's frown made deep wrinkles along her forehead and eyes, betraying her true age to a couple of millennia. She glanced at his open hand, before taking a breath and clapping her palm over his. Her body stiffened and her eyes rolled back as Ahn'kat carefully fed her the most important events that brought him and the uncrowned empress there. Several figures made gestures forward, worried gasps and low whispers sprinkled among the crowds as they witnessed their monk speaker pull away from his hand and regain her senses.

"Truth is this...this is truth," she said breathlessly.

"We have a grand request from the Empire," Ramkes said stepping forward. "But when that time comes, we need you all to be ready."

The monk swallowed as she clumsily dropped to her knees before the true empress. "We will spread this message, your highnesses. Justice for the Empire."

~

Go, now. Treneer whispered to Neobatri and Neheret.

The two slipped on their cream linen scarves over their heads before sliding the double doors into the lower commons of Lusor's sister city, Kebtsep. They had ported into an old, abandoned shop before exiting into the market bazaar, filled with hundreds of colourful stall tents and sandy bricked stores with people slipping between the narrow walkways. Spices and burning herbs stung their noses as they glided past the foot traffic, noticing that most of the people here reluctantly showed their wealth or lack thereof. The creamy linen robes and scarves were their uniforms, even for the stall keepers.

Kebtsep bazaar was once the shopping place for nobles and celebrities, but it had dipped into a darker underbelly since Ismotaph's invisible rise to power. The smells were to mask and deter unwanted customers, and the law. In Neobatri's periphery, she saw a woman bend over a stall table filled with chunky golden bangles and earrings. Her hood slipped back, revealing the perfect profile of Empress Ramkes as her mouth whispered in the ear of the gold trader.

Posing as Ahn'kat, Neobatri tapped Neheret's arm, cocking her head to the side to show her sister where to look. *Treneer's illusion?*

No, I think the movement is catching on. Neheret whispered before ushering her sister toward a narrow alley between grey stone walls. The shadows deepened when they stepped before a man sitting on a low wooden stool. His shiny green legs extended almost across the already narrow walkway with a hood covering his head and shoulders.

Upon closer inspection, the sister's noticed the man's toes were webbed and lacked nails. Neobatri's eye wandered up to his right arm resting against a table, which looked as if it was soaked in water, but also lacked nails and had finger webbing.

"My contact told you we were coming," Neheret's voice was husky trying to mimic Ramkes – and pretending that she was struggling to body-bend.

"I caught it in a dream," his voice was muffled, as if a stone was lodged down his throat.

Neobatri pulled a brown sack from her trousers and dropped it on the table beside the man's hand. It jingled when it met the flaky wooden surface. The man's hand flung it off the table as his hood shook. "Gold is worthless here."

"It's off-worlder gold," Neheret said.

The man pulled his legs back in as his body leant forward; his hand peeled back his hood revealing shiny semi-transparent skin with blotchy emerald and veiny peach hues. His eyes were a glazed glassy blue and the cartilage of his nose had shrivelled into slits. He appeared to be in extreme mutation flux, where Zanashj cells attempt to return to aquatic mollusc roots of their species. It won't be long until his body reabsorbed his bones and would need to be cast off in the oceans to survive.

His long thin mouth parted as he exhaled a haggard breath: "Answer my question and you will have any pick from my arsenal. Tell me, why do you pretend to be the two most-wanted people in the Empire? And why do you find it fitting to endanger my small, quiet business and all the innocent lives you encounter during your performance?"

Neheret sighed as a smirk flashed on her lips. "Because annoying the Corps is good sport."

The man's laugh scratched the sister's ears. "Very good, very good," he sunk back and pressed his thumb into a pad on the wall behind him. The brick walls trembled and melted away to reveal an alcove of sceptres, hand pistons, shock-whips, and small acid bombs.

"Very good," he stretched his left arm to the acid bombs. "For that, take these along with one weapon each. Make your choice quickly, I hear infiltrators."

Neheret snatched a hand piston and Neobatri smiled as the long whip curled around her hand and arm. Grabbing for the bombs, the sisters gave the man a quick nod before continuing their trek back into the bazaar. A woman tripped over a stool beside a market table and her goods poured out from her satchel. Her eyes caught theirs, with an embarrassed smile, she silently pleaded for them to help her up...but the sisters knew better.

They found us. How many in the bazaar? Neobatri said, grabbing Neheret's elbow and leading them away from the 'clumsy woman.'

They felt Treneer slip in. *Nine infiltrators. Three north, two south, three closing in from the west-*

To the east! Neheret said before darting between two stalls; her hips knocked the table's edge, forcing a stand of scarves to tumble over.

Your clumsiness aids to your façade, sister. Neobatri said pressing behind her.

The vanguard suspects your psi senses are guiding you to the east, their single agent will try to trap you there. Treneer said.

What trap will they set for us? Neobatri said dipping under the low rafters of the bunched stalls.

I don't know, but try to-

A merchant in heavy striped robes spun around to face them. Neheret saw through him and saw his gloved hand dip into his front pocket. "Run!"

Neobatri turned, readied her curling whip, and slapped the barbed end against the merchant's face, but a glittering white powder clouded around his pocket. The powder rose to his face and clung to his skin; in an instant, his face warped and trembled as black boils bubbled from where the powder touched before he collapsed into a small table behind him. She saw the powder fall on her light robes before Neheret grabbed her scarf's collar and spun her toward their path.

Eyes of confused denizens halted and watched the commotion; Neheret's hood slid back in the wind as she ran with her sister. The people's eyes watched with excitement, with a blend of entertainment and hope written on their faces. The disguised sisters stormed on the fused stone path, their heightened senses sniffing for infiltrators among the dividing market crowds.

Should we shift to another face? Make them think we're trying to escape? Neheret spoke as her breathing quickened.

Yes, but we need to find some cover and remember we can't make it too seamless — highborn are poor body-benders. Neobatri said before turning down another grey alleyway with her sister. The curled ferns and vines curtained the arched entry as they darted through it. Neobatri accidentally shouldered a poor child against the wall before he sped away from them.

I sense infiltrators, closing. Neheret said, trying to catch her breath as she leaned against the cool stone wall.

They're chasing you into a funnel. They want you to go up. Treneer said.

What's up? Neobatri said as her faux Ahn'kat's eyes looked to the narrow roofless alley. The bright skies were covered in pale clouds, a faint line of gulls glided in and out from them.

Spatial fractures, I think they're igniting a some phasing trap.

They're using trembling webs! Neobatri exhaled.

That's going to be painful. Neheret shook her head as shadowed figures loomed behind the green curtain.

Change your face! Neobatri said pressing her body against a carved stone column, blending with the texture.

Neheret shrunk her body down into a child's shape and sat on a thick sleeping carpet in the corner. Hands pushed away the fronds as three common-cloaked monks stepped into the alley. Their stride didn't break, appearing they were seeking for anything other than the faux prince and princess.

Use your acid bombs. Neobatri said.

Neheret pulled out the brown ball from her sleeve just as a long muscular hand moved over her shoulder. She spun and hurled the bomb against the monk. A yellow liquid burst from the balloon ball, raining over the monk infiltrators. Their surprised screams erupted from the narrow alley as Neobatri jumped from the column; her whip was slashing and flying over the heads and torsi of her former comrades.

Neheret kicked in the closest infiltrator's knee as her hand billowed out a string of electricity. The infiltrator's screams dulled into grunts as their burnt faces tried changing back into their old forms. Their long limbs stretched into fierce spiked bone swords as they swung at the sisters, narrowly missing their heads. More infiltrators piled into the alley; their bodies were grabbing and slicing at the sister's skins.

Neobatri jumped up on the wall as she kicked their cobra-like arms from clinging on her feet. Neheret copied as her princess form awkwardly made the climb. Their nails elongated to grip the bricks as they pushed their bodies up, slapping and slashing the enraged infiltrators below. She kicked one in the face, prying him off the wall before he fell with a cracking thud to the stone before Neobatri scrambled up the wall, and pulled her sister up on the edge.

Use yours. Neheret said as she looked down at the clambering agents below.

"I'm very sorry about this, but you'll forgive me later," Neobatri mumbled as she pulled her acid bomb from her belt and flung it to the centre of the ground, showering them in agony.

I think my shifting was way too good to pass off as Ramkes. Neheret said leaning forward as she tried catching a breath.

Yes, you really are terrible at this. Neobatri said as she eyed the shiny gold and opal rooftops.

They're coming to pick you up, be ready. Treneer said.

This is going to be hard. Neheret said.

Show them we're trying to get away. Neobatri ordered.

The sisters opened their hands and arms out, forcing their limbs to reform into leathery wings. A dark shadow covered the ground they stood on; their eyes shot upwards as distorted space clamped around – freezing them.

Vibrations from the phased web made their cells quiver, feeling as if they were ready to burn or burst open.

Keep a hold of your forms! Treneer said.

Trying-

I'm breaking apart!

I will help you, keep holding.

The sister's stifled their screams as they tried fighting the trap, but their vision blurred and blinded them into darkness.

Found you. A man's voice echoed into their minds.

No, we found you. The sisters hid their inner smiles as they were pulled into the dark void of a chamber where an inquisitor stood waiting for them. The longer they stared, their features revealed the man they wanted. Weak light bounced off the black cloth on his shoulders and braided hair on his crown, his beryl face was hidden in shadow. His golden embroidered collar twinkled and stretched around his neck and extended down to his chest. He looked ephemeral as he strode slowly to them; his black eyes were piercing through their skulls, searching for the truth.

Neobatri strained as she tried holding her body in one piece while keeping her mind fixed as Ahn'kat. However, the phasing web buffered much of his relentless scans of her and Neheret. He turned his head to the side, showing his rugged profile and smooth skin. In a blink, the web's burn lowered against the sisters' skins.

Let us go or you can do it properly. Neobatri said.

His face was like black granite as he leered at them.

"Ismotaph...if you want us dead...don't torment us, just do it!" Neheret's faux Ramkes voice croaked.

A torrent of images bombed the sister's minds, the images of their mimic's families. Lord and Lady Urbaz's forms twisting into trees while they screamed for their son. Emperor Kreshut embracing his princess daughter before he melted in oily black liquid, drenching her clothes and staining her skin. The screams in their consciousness seared so greatly, that the emotional torment had almost broken their mission, yet Ismotaph believed their agony was true.

"Enough!" Neobatri roared.

He stopped, before walking back to the end of the room. His form blended with the darkest corner, almost making him appear he was assimilated by the detention chamber. The two snuck a glance at each other, but Neobatri knew this wasn't the real one. A strobe of light beamed like a cylinder behind them; they could feel his feet shifting behind them and the tallness of his form.

"You deemed we're safe for your honourable company, eh?" Neobatri coughed before turning to Treneer's secret psi-channel. *Get your friends from Farayah to scramble the phase fields and grab him.*

On your mark. She whispered.

The phasing field dimmed, releasing most of their discomfort, but the sisters were still held by the invisible force. Long and jewelled hands slid over their shoulders before giving them both a gentle squeeze. "You two have shattered unity in the Empire, it will take decades to mend, if at all possible. Even with a Replacer on the throne," he turned his head to Neheret, "we will be strong."

"Under your leadership," Neobatri's eye narrowed at him.

"Your 'love' for the Empire is diseased!" Neheret hissed. "Speak openly: this was nothing but a power grab-"

"Then let's speak openly!" Ismotaph stepped around to face them. "We monitored your psi developments, and I have to say, you're too good. Way too good..."

Neheret huffed. "We are Zanashj-"

"Liar," Ismotaph turned to Neobatri.

"We had help," she said.

"Who?" He said.

We can start-

Wait, Treneer, I want to get this right...I want to see his face. Neobatri's lip curled up to show her fangs. "Vern thinks you're stalling the war. He wants you...replaced."

Ismotaph straightened his back as he looked around the shadowed corners of the cell. "Liar-"

"Are we? Make your inquisitors look a little deeper...off-worlders are here, with us, all over us," Neheret sneered.

Dark hands clamped around their temples; the sisters could feel their thoughts being ripped through their skulls. Neobatri groaned but hid her smile as she watched Ismotaph's face drop with horror.

"You're working with a Roctarous... Divine Sky-Serpent, protect me," he mouthed.

"And the Arinu!" Neheret screeched as she pulled her body from her invisible bondage and slapped a transmitter across Ismotaph's face.

The inquisitor's cell thundered as Treneer remotely disrupted the phasic field, breaking the sisters free. Electricity cracked from the inquisitors as Ismotaph tried rubbing off the transmitter from his skin, trying to bore into the sisters' minds, but they had already completed their mission.

Move away! Ouro's thoughts roared. Neobatri grabbed at Neheret's elbow, before jumping back from the disappearing inquisitors and Ismotaph. Their screams faded as they fell out of existence.

Chapter Forty
Together IV: Mending

Four eyes looked up to the shadowy cloud looming heavily in the wall-less chamber. A twinkle of an amber bolt shuddered from the cloud, quickly igniting the dark space over their heads. They could feel them coming.

Stand back. Ouro said as his arm rose over his head, ready to catch the teleportation funnel.

"The *Kepa* is growing anxious, it wants to open a rift now," Shshmnrnashsh reported from the holo-screen behind the slick table panel.

It can wait. Ouro's jaw clenched as he forced himself not to scratch his scars. The amber bolts cracked and groaned from the cloud until a peel of yellow light broke into their eyes. Several figures plummeted from an infinitely long tunnel, but Ouro's telekinetic grip held them in place.

Shsh typed in the coordinates to summon the Kepa before rushing over to grab Ouro's arm. "Port us out!"

Ouro's arms dropped, as did the frightened Zanashj infiltrators tumbling to the grounds. Before the Arinu could click them out from the dark chamber, an ethereal screech billowed from the distant, endless horizon. The oldest of the infiltrators looked up to Ouro and Shsh, his wide yellow eyes begging for help, but the pair slipped away to another, safer realm of Ouro's making.

His long fingers clutched at his scalp, feeling the rift opening for the monster to claim it's promised prize. The warden sighed as he glanced to Shsh; her unnerving and imposing form strode away to her workstation. Her flat face studied the closing rift in the Prism and recent updates of Farayah's planetary scans. The endless rows of Arinu slept peacefully in their pods around them, unaware of drastic changes being decided in this very second.

It's done, the beast has them now. Ouro said through the psi transmitters.

He has finally met the Empire's justice. Neheret and Neobatri will be returning shortly with data on the psi-virus. Right now, Empress Ramkes will make her address to Uras. You two ensure that her message is broadcast across Farayah, too. We need to bring the Arinu into the fold for the next step. Ahn'kat replied.

Inadvisable. Vern is currently monitoring Farayah and Uras, their sights may not be able to see into every room or hear every discussion but will definitely pick up on mass broadcasts. If they detect Ismotaph has been taken, then we risk them changing their plans. Shsh said.

Treneer can scramble the message on Uras from Vern's sights long enough, we can do the same here. Ouro said.

The Intel Corps is shattered, the Replacer Empress is on the run and the Empire is panicked. We're doing this now. Ahn'kat said.

Skies are covered here. Treneer said.

Do it. Ouro said as he strained a folded thin and shaky spatial bubble above Farayah.

We have your holo-message on screen here. Shsh said and with a click, the hologram of Empress Ramkes filled the centre of the chamber. Ramkes sighed as she straightened her face, readying herself to return to her original beautiful form. She waited for her eyes to adjust to its brightness before her lips parted.

'A terrible lie has been told to you, my Imperial Family,' she breathed, her high posture even made her commoner garb look regal, 'when you heard my voice through your transmitters, when you saw me on the throne through your holo-screens, every greeting and every law made since we laid rest to the old emperor was enacted by an impostor. My fath- Emperor Kreshut had known a betrayal was coming for the Crown and forced me into hiding, but as our eyes sought for justice they had been led to former-prince Ahn'kat," Ramkes eyes almost quivered to his, but she held herself straight for the holo-capture.

'The former-prince was innocent, but upon learning the truth about a rogue band of Zanashj who wanted to devolve into the old ways, he was forced to flee and return with alien allies. You see, my Imperial Family, this shadow group had lost faith in the Crown and allowed fear to enter their hearts over our Empire. We are Zanashj, we do not fear change, we embrace it,' Ramkes turned to Treneer and beckoned her to stand to her left; to their fortune, Treneer's thin and smooth stature opposed the Empress's long and lean form.

'You would have noticed something strange about your children, about your nobles – can you hear their thoughts? Can you suddenly see a thing and know all about it? Yes. These unstable days have turned into shattering quakes, our people have been psychically groomed by this shadow group to murder our allies,' Ramkes snatched Treneer's hand and gently held open her palm to the probe's camera. 'Our hands have prints, the blue and red veins pumping red blood beneath our skin, we sweat, and both feel pain. The Arinu are not our subjects, they are our equals as my father had intended…

'And right now, the Arinu are seeking vengeance against us. For the last several years, the shadow group has been kidnapping and harnessing their power for us to unknowingly assimilate. Our associate, Treneer, has broken free from their haze of hate and mistrust, and now sees the truth as do we. She will make her people see reason, but we must be the ones who act first to show our innocence.' Ramkes paused to let go of Treneer's hand. She took a breath before stepping closer to the holo-capture.

'Now, I ask for something no other emperor has asked of their people. I ask the Zanashj take justice into their own hands and spearhead against the group who has preyed upon both of our people. Many of us will not return home, but the gods have given us an opportunity to evolve beyond fear and reach self-mastery through sacrifice. We have the chance to prove to our Divine Spirits that we can evolve into the greatest beings in creation.'

The image dimmed and vanished before them. Shsh and Ouro looked at each other, both waiting for the other to speak. Lights blinked from the glossy surface from the Roctarous' panel; her hand waved over it, showing several urgent messages were beaming through.

It's the Judicator and Grand Coven. Ouro's eyes closed, feeling the urgency from them.

The empress is being summoned by the imperium and whoever's left at the Corps. She promises us the latest Keshsapt ships and everything we need. The Grand Coven and A.Is are expected at this meeting, get them to come at all costs. Ahn'kat said before ending the transmission.

"I will go to present them with this information. You will need to remain behind just in case if I need to be removed from danger," she said.

Ouro's head shook as he hovered closer to her. *The Grand Coven aren't like addressing a consortium, Shsh. You need to be accompanied by an Arinu.*

"It's a waste of time and risks both of us getting captured if our plan fails. I have archived data on the Grand Coven, I came here with Sazla many times over the millennia-"

Understanding what to expect from the oldest in our society won't be recorded in your archives. Not to mention their perception on aliens is negative to put mildly. You need me there. He said.

"Have you ever had an audience with them before?" Shsh said cocking her head.

Ouro pursed his lips together. *All Arinu children are taught how to address Grand Elders.*

"I see," she quietly said as she reached over to the holo-screen and accept their summons; the Judicator's luminescent bust appeared before them. Her's and Ouro's body tingled with electricity as the machine clamped an anti-phase field around them, trapping them in the dark chamber.

The Judicator's eyes shone with a righteous fury. "We have finally found you. Hiding in your prism and capturing our people here, too. By my judgement, you will be detained by the reinstalment of our laws-"

Take us before the Coven, we have proof that we have been misled! Ouro cried as he stepped toward the A.I.

"The only evidence is that you and Treneer have been working with off-worlders while Farayah has been destabilized by them," the Judicator said.

Shsh stepped forward. "You are a logical being, Judicator. What looks apparent is not necessarily the truth. Take us to the Grand Elders so we may submit to their scans before you make an appropriate decision."

The Judicator was silent as he glanced between the two. "Prepare your case."

In a blink, their bodies were sucked down into a narrow airless tunnel between the planes, twisting and stretching, blending their anxieties before being dropped in a shadowy room. As their eyes took a moment to adjust, they stood atop a white crystal disk hovering in the centre of a starry black chamber that seemed to go into infinity.

There was no flooring beyond their platform, but several heavily shrouded beings levitated around them. Tall pastel hoods covered their bare scalps with crystal circlets strapped around their temples and foreheads, while long and shimmery masks drooped down to their robed bodies. Several dozen holographic runes hovered over their third eyes, shoulders and torsos, elevating their forms to living gods. The scene was familiar to Shshmrnashsh, she has seen this before when she travelled to Farayah with Sazla, but unlike the kind and curious eyes of the Grand Elders then, these Arinu were fierce and ready to shred their molecules apart.

Ouro. One elder echoed.

Shsh turned to see her companion was suspended in the air with a glassy spherical shield around his body. An anti-phase shield. His eyes were wide, and his jaw tensed. They were trapped.

Shshmrnashsh the Unbound. Said another Elder.

She turned to the one who spoke her name. "That is not my name anymore, Grand Elder."

It's how you saw yourself once.

"Before we proceed, please do not remove the sleeping Arinu from Ouro's prism, they are safest there-"

We will not take requests until we have deemed you to be truthful. And the only way is if you submit for a death-scan.

"We don't have time for that - I have data crystals-"

The Arinu have proven they can be tricked; we will not accept that as evidence.

Grand Elders, a death-scan will take time that we don't have! Ouro called as his body struggled against the invisible bonds.

Which will take longer if you resist. The Judicator said.

Do a quick-scan, at least you'll see I have no wish to escape! Ouro said.

The shrouded Arinu glanced at each other before the Judicator gave a small nod. Ouro's form trembled and soothed, sighing in relief as his eyes smiled at Shsh.

"Ouro cannot be *subjected* to a death-scan, there is no assurance that you will put him back together as we need him to be," she said.

Why is that? An elder asked.

"He is needed for the next phase of Prince Ahn'kat's plan against Vern. He needs every ounce of focus for the battle," she slowly turned.

We know of Prince Ahn'kat...from the message you sent to us, but we also gleamed that he had a hand in kidnapping our kin. Said a mind that hadn't spoken before. A small being levitated close to the crystal platform, and at first glance, the pair thought it was a child, but as his features became clearer, they saw it was not the case. Its shrivelled wrinkled body was rolled tight and wrapped in long and flowing robes, his head was crowned with three crystal circlets with dozens of holographic runes lighting around its tiny form. The being's eyes were closed, appearing they haven't been opened in decades – if not centuries, but their third eye shone brighter than all the other elders. This was the Archon.

You do have an unusual bond with him, but that doesn't alleviate our concerns with the Empire. We are at war with them, now that the skies have cleared, we will be gathering everything we know to defeat the enemy. Archon said.

"The exo-planar radiation was removed by mine and Ouro's efforts, we need you to see the truth; not squander it by attacking the only people who will be able to save you," Shsh said.

How do we know this isn't a deviation without a thorough scan? Said one voice.

All we see are two people who have history of working against us. Said another.

Ouro drifted closer to Shsh. *Shshmrnashsh cannot submit to a death-scan, we need her intact. Nor will she be ready to succumb for another deep-scan.*

She turned her head to him, his lips pursed as he worried that he had said too much. Perhaps he did, she thought, but this was the hour of challenge. "I won't submit to a death-scan…"

But you will compromise. The Judicator said as his eyes washed over the other members of the group. *The Proctor and other A.Is agree a deep-scan is feasible.*

The Grand Coven also agrees for now. The Archon said.

All due respect, Archon, but you have never deep-scanned a Roctarous before. Their synapses are far more delicate than ours. Ouro said.

"I have faced far worse from those who wished me harm than this, Ouro," she said giving him an assuring glance before facing up towards the Judicator, "I nominate you to deep-scan me, one machine to another."

The A.Is head glitched to the side. *Very well. Do I have your consent, Shshmrnashsh the Chainbreaker?*

She smiled before mouthing, "yes."

~

Treneer covered her eyes from the large holo-screen on the circular table. The three Alkaheen sisters exchanged nervous glances at the back of the Imperium Hall. Ahn'kat leaned over with fingers combing through his hair, and Ramkes was as still and cold as stone on her father's old chair. Her stare fixated to the amber genetic helix on the screen. In the same room, nearly two dozen of the highest, eloquent and intellectual Zanashj in the Empire were brought down to terrified mice at the news.

The Health Minister's chair squeaked as he leant forward, making all eyes flash towards him, eager for the silence to drown. "We have been doing genetic manipulation for millennia, viruses are fickle, but simple organisms-"

"This isn't a microbe, Lord Kenzabt," said Head of the Sciences as her hand pointed toward the rotating helix. "It doesn't have a membrane, no known cellular form, how in the Divine Spirits can it even transmit without a medium?" her eyes searched the Alkaheen sisters, Ahn'kat and Treneer.

"It's telepathic in nature, Lady Gifati," Ahn'kat glanced to the Arinu, "it's from one mind-reader to another,"

It tells the neurons to self-destruct. Treneer sighed.

"Obviously that's its lethality, but the test subjects have adapted. A good percentage of psychic subjects the Intel Corps infected have survived, but how do we know the...latter affects are permanent?" said Lord Kenzabt.

"It's too early to declare it is permanent. Zanashj bodies are marvels of evolution," said the new High Priestess rubbing her scalp.

"That's optimistic, but not realistic. It could be a decade, a generation – a whole damn millennia before the affected will be able to have children again!" Lady Gifati said.

"It's possible that most affected will never have children," whispered the assistant health minister.

Lord Kenzabt shot a glare at his subordinate. "If there is a lack in nature, then evolution will provide abundance, that's truth."

"It's the way our bodies will adapt to the virus, it disrupts all activity in our reproductive function and stalls it, including advanced body-bending. There's no telling how long that latency period is and there's no other known method of compelling our bodies to use another adaptive way. This is completely uncharted territory," Lady Gifati said.

"We can take healthy reproductive cells from our soldiers and people now and store it just in case?" said another minister looking towards the Imperial General.

He cleared his throat and pressed his thumb against his squared jaw. "Nearly eighty percent of our population is willing to serve the Empire if a fight calls for it – almost all adults, that's millions upon millions of Zanashj we would need to extract the cells from."

"We don't have time for all of them," Ahn'kat said.

The General pursed his lips together as he eyed the ex-prince and exhaled. "As you keep saying, your grace."

"And what about you, Arinu? Any psychic techniques that could abate some of the problems we will be shouldering?" Lady Gifati said as her eyes narrowed at Treneer.

Her hairless brow rose, and nose flared. *Arinu have vast knowledge of psionics. I was never a psi-healer, but we have technology that can regenerate a whole new body from a few living cells. But no, this goes beyond us also.*

"So, if it takes a few days for immunities to show, then it will no longer be dangerous. Why can't we quarantine them?" Lord Kenzabt said; his eyes were glassy and doe-eyed, looking for a 'yes' in a sea of misery.

"We can order most to stay on Uras while the carnage is over," the General said, with his voice rising with hope as he looked to the empress.

Her eyes locked on to Ahn'kat. She knew the answer as he had told her on their way to the Imperium Hall, but she was going to make him say it to all of them. "We need everyone for this battle," he said with a light clearing of his throat.

The General frowned as he glared at him. "How are you that sure? We don't know what to expect-"

"That's exactly why we need everyone. We cannot gamble a single thing."

"But this is biological gambling!" Lady Gifati jumped to her feet and slapped her hands on the table. "Are you seriously expecting us to risk our future and place it in the hands of aliens?" her hand shot up to Treneer.

"By the way, when will the Grand Coven grace us with their input?" the General purred as his thick fingers rubbed against his scarred lip.

Treneer closed her eyes. *They are listening.*

"What a relief," he muttered before clearing his throat. "And what do they have to say?"

"What do you expect them to say, Star General Sekun, they want us to be their living shields," Lady Gifati sat back down.

"Everyone here was picked for their professional insights, not for their clever tongues," Ahn'kat said shooting her a wicked glare.

Lord Kenzabt's chair squeaked again as he leaned forward. "You may have been manipulated by Ismotaph and have been exonerated by the Crown, your grace, but please understand we question if your..."

Ahn'kat frowned as his lips tightened at the Health Minister. "I dare you question if my heart is in the Empire."

"Yes, well..." the High Priestess said with a quick glance to Treneer, "what are they expected to give up also?"

Ahn'kat sighed, he leaned back as his eyes trailed to the Arinu. The glow of her magenta eyes intensified as her mouth parted, pushing out a dozen voices from the beyond into the hall before her.

The Grand Coven and Great A.Is give consent for the Empire to bomb Farayah. She could feel them all saying.

Silence covered them all once again, but there were glints of calm blended with guilt. Ahn'kat wetted his lips with is tongue before he said, "Vern expects us to start the attack, we need to follow through with that expectation. The Arinu have managed to evacuate some of their cities, but our group could only collect so many. There definitely will be casualties."

"Will the ones left behind know what's expected of them?" General Sekun whispered.

We have made a secret announcement to those who are still awake; some have chosen to stay to give the illusion of a population. Treneer said slowly.

The weight in the air had lifted, but the unease between them stayed.

"I wish I could say I felt more confident about your proposition," Lady Gifati said as her arms crossed over her chest.

"Why can't we use the...ah," Lord Kenzabt cleared his throat, "the Raivan battle thralls? The psi-virus would have little to no effect on them."

Ahn'kat pushed back his scowl, sensing how offended Treneer and the others felt. "Last I heard, most of our operations on planet Sye have been abandoned when we started phasing out pets and general dominion holdings. Besides, star commanders have been reporting they're trying to exorcise every Zanashj from the planet. Brutal techniques – keep bashing until- no *if* they turn green," his cheeks prickled with heat as Gajoon stared at him. "We can't clean up that mess if we are all dead. Besides, I believe a friendship is more successful than a mere alliance if the Empire shouldered this burden themselves."

"So, we are alone, hm?" General Sekun said with a scrape of his rough thumb against his waxed beard.

"All you have is us," Ahn'kat said holding his pride of his companions.

The Coven will be extending aid and support to the Empire for this battle, at the risk of our own lives. Treneer said looking at Ramkes.

All eyes in trailed to the Empress. Her stare pierced through the Arinu as if she was trying to look beyond Treneer and into the antechamber where the Grand Elders and Archon watched on. "What else?" she said.

The Coven recognises the Empire was not responsible for the aggravations against our kin and only seek justice from the few individuals who knew and maliciously participated. Treneer said, trying to hide a tremble of her lip.

Ramkes' brow rose as her eyes dropped to her delicate hands folded on her lap. "And what else?"

We will reinstate the Treaty and are open for dialogue about the Federation. The Arinu said.

A shadow of a smirk appeared on the Empress' lip. "Open for dialogue?"

If you agree to help our kin, this will become a Federation, where we will have equal access to each other's resources. What we have will be yours. Said a dozen voices speaking through Treneer.

Ramkes sighed as her eyes glanced over her ministers, unworldly allies, and finally to her estranged husband. "What do we do now, Ahn'kat?"

He couldn't hide his relief as he rose to his feet, as if they have never felt lighter before. "Prepare the Star Armada for infection but leave our new psychic branch out – I want them clean before they board the Keshsapt ships. Treneer, you will also be on one of them, but in an isolated chamber so you can focus. Neheret, Neobatri and Gajoon will hunt for Vern, stick one of these on them – Ouro will do the rest," Ahn'kat held out a handful of transponders to their hands. "Treneer will fight Vern through psionics, but you three will need to get physically close to them. I don't know how strong they are, but Gajoon, you will be brought in as reinforcements if Neheret and Neobatri start struggling."

"And you?" the Imperial General said, the slyness in his tone had washed away and was replaced with some hope.

"You and I will be coordinating the first wave of attack, the Unbound will try to blast us the psi-virus, but it will be useless against us. Shshmrnashsh tells me they also rely on E.M.Ps, so our organic ships will easily brush it off for a while. She will also try to break the Roctarous bonds to Vern, but our people on the Keshsapt will loosen the hold long enough to do this. Once she frees them, we will have to guide the ships safely through Ouro's portals. I think the Grand Coven and A.Is will have space prepared to receive them."

"Once we bomb your cities, how will you have space for a fleet of ships?" General Sekun said wearing a frown.

We have knowledge on how to bend space into pocket dimensions. Treneer said.

"Curious," Lady Gifati mumbled.

"Before we do anything, the Health Ministry needs to collect as many healthy cells from our soldiers as possible and hopefully," he glanced to Treneer once more, "we can do something about it later."

~

The groans from the other room woke them up. Gajoon gave a guttural hiss when a dark form appeared in the wide doorway, disturbing Neobatri from her meditation, but Neheret remained fast asleep. Imperial bunkers had been transformed into quarantine zones; every foot in every room had been filled with beds and comforters for infected soldiers and civilians. Brave men and women lay curled up in their quilts, sweating into the fabric as they clutched their heads. Anyone who was blessed to fall asleep for a moment, would awaken from another's cries.

The figure stumbled past the door and pressed his back against the wall. "I wish they'd give us something for the pain," Ahn'kat mumbled.

"Health Ministry said it could mess with our…adaptive process," Neobatri shook her head as she wrapped the sweat-absorbing comforters around her bare shoulders.

Ahn'kat slapped his hand over his forehead; strings of his hair fell loosely, and skin clung around his fingers when he pulled it away. "That's a good sign, but my psionic senses feel as if they're underwater."

"You're not the only one. I'm surprised, with your new powers, I thought you wouldn't recover-" Neobatri shot a violent cough from her throat.

"I'm still Zanashj," Ahn'kat frowned at her as he lumbered into the chamber, careful not to step on the legs and arms of resting soldiers. "How are you, Gajoon?"

The hybrid shrugged. "Not bad. Head hurt," her long nails scratched gently at her temples.

Ahn'kat gave her a small slap on her stripped knee before glancing down to Neheret. "How in the gods can she sleep through this?"

Neobatri looked down at her sister and pushed her hip into Neheret's sweat-stained head. She woke with a jolt as her dazed eyes stared around. "The prince asked you a question, Neheret,"

"You didn't have to do that," Ahn'kat said holding back a smile.

Neheret frowned at a smirking Neobatri before delivering a punch in her sister's rib. "How long now?"

Ahn'kat glanced at his wrist phone. "They'll let us out soon when we're not contagious anymore. The worst of it is gone."

"Ahn'kat," a hoarse voice called from the doorway. They turned to see Ramkes standing and beckoning him to join her in the other room. He sighed as he rose to his feet and hobbled over to her. The Empress parted a curtain diving into her small room from the rest of the chamber and carefully lowered herself on the mattress.

"You look better than the rest," he said before dropping down to the edge of her bed.

"You should know it's all an act," she said pulling a soft red velvet cover over her thighs. "I spoke with Lady Gifati and she says that some of the tests they're performing look promising."

"They *look* promising?" Ahn'kat rose a brow at her.

"Hope is all we have right now. This is all in the Pantheon's hands," she said as her head leaned against the wall.

"Hm, that's where my faith has gone, you've got it all," he mumbled.

"No, you gave it back to me," she said as her eyes closed. "All these years chasing my father's dreams, trying to pioneer the Empire in a new realm of peace, slowly transforming into the role of empress instead of making it my own...I forgot about the Golden Hawk, that's why he has forsaken me until now."

Ahn'kat bit his lip as he looked away.

"You don't agree?" she pressed.

"When I needed the Great Beetle the most, I couldn't find her," he said, avoiding her eyes. "Now, I see the Arinu have done more for us than the gods have."

"The Arinu may have god-like power, but they will never be gods," she whispered.

"Perhaps, but I've seen more from a single Arinu than anything what the Conclave claim," he said.

"Treneer," she said, the sharpness of her tone cut through his thoughts like a bone-spike. "I can see why you'd elevate them so."

She smiled at Ahn'kat's scowl.

"Admit it, psychic women seem to hold your interest," she said.

"Careful, Ramkes," he glared at her.

She sighed and shook her head. "I'm sorry, I didn't intend to mock Emestasun. She and Zertun were very dear to me, too."

"How long have you suspected…?" he said.

"Psychics read people's minds, but wives know things of the heart," she said.

"I was never disloyal to you…in that way," he said.

"I know. Your heart was loyal to her first, and I never wanted to press myself between you two," she said.

Ahn'kat reached to her hand and took it into his palms. "Kreshut was a good man and father."

Tears reddened her eyes. "But he was a poor emperor, one cannot be good at all things in such positions. It seems House Urbaz chose to be good politicians."

"That's only compliment worth paying them," he said. Alarms chimed on their wrist phones; the holo-writings said they were ready to be released. The organic doors to the bunker creaked and groaned as they slid open. Ahn'kat rose and straightened his back, ready to leave with the rest of the troops. "General Sekun is waiting for me."

"Before you get yourself killed," Ramkes said, her hand dove into a small satchel stashed under her quilts and fished out a sparkling sapphire pendant, "Aszelun hasn't abandoned you, she just wanted you to find her again."

Ahn'kat slowly took the blue beetle in his palm and watched the silver specks inside the stone winking at him. He smiled as he pulled the chain over his head and sighed. "How did you find your faith again?"

Ramkes leaned forward and grinned. "The day Gajoon helped me escape."

He tilted his head to the side. "How did she? You never told me."

"That's between us and the gods."

Chapter Forty-one
Together V: Righteous Demons

There were thousands of them, hundreds of thousands. So many that the Armada blot out the sun. It shadowed empty streets, hallowed skyscrapers, and abandoned estates. The Empire has come together perhaps for the final time. Treneer sat alone in her cylindrical room; she kept her legs crossed while she levitated, watching the other psychics on the Keshsapt cruiser take formation. Their thoughts hummed, readying their hearts for the battle. In her mind's eye, she saw the flagship where Ahn'kat was, the most heavily fortified flying palace, but a perfect target for the Unbound army. She smirked at the thought of it appearing as a fierce, overgrown green beetle.

Are you sure you want to do this? She whispered to her parents.

Few who are still awake volunteered. Vanar said.

They're all coming, I don't know the level of devastation they will cause—

Treneer, buildings can be rebuilt, and gardens can be resowed. Remir said.

She nodded, even though they could not see her. *What of all the northern tribes?*

The Bloodmoons have joined us if you can imagine. Vanar said.

We are warriors, after all. Treneer smiled.

There is one request, should you find our bodies — make sure you save our cells to place in them resurrection pods. You needn't ask Deathspeakers to lull our souls back to our vessels! Remir said.

Don't be too close to the city centres, they will be pointing all weapons there and will likely level all things to ash. Treneer said as she felt the tug of interstellar travel. *We are coming now, be ready.*

Safe travels, my snowflake. Her parents said before silencing the commune.

Her fingers pressed into her knees as she breathed the cool dry air of her chamber. A deep hum echoed from the floors of the ship, pumping rhythmically up the tensing walls of the ship, followed by vocal hymns with every beat.

Treneer frowned as she tried feeling for the noises, realising it was music, an angry and haunting melody capturing the minds of the soldiers. Treneer rested back to listen as a curious observer but found her heart beating along with the rhythm; the vocals bled into her cells as she also felt the coming vengeance of Zanashj and Arinu.

"Star General Sekun of the Kasha flagship speaking, we will be phasing into Farayah's space within twenty seconds. Star commanders, prepare your ships to fire on orbital defences around the planet," his deep voice vibrated through the speakers.

Keshsapt ships, remain beyond the boarder and begin capturing Arinu watchers! The star commander of her ship called.

Treneer remote viewed out of the craft; the horde of imperial ships swarmed around the boarders. A dozen twinkling lights moved around them; the Sleeping Watchers were pretending to put up a defence as they tried blasting energy through the hulls of the ship. The Zanashj psychics wrapped around them, forcing the Watchers to slow their pursuit before banishing them back to their physical bodies. The blackened outer shells of the burned ships bubbled and blistered before regenerating into a thicker carapace as they pushed toward the pearly planet.

The energy around the planet appeared no different when she, Shshmrnashsh and Ahn'kat travelled together, but a closer look revealed it was an illusion. The Grand Elders were masking the thickness of the exo-planar clouds to make them appear vulnerable for Vern's viewing pleasure. Treneer dared not to see if the Unbound beast was watching from the stars, but trusted that they were.

"Fire," the General said. As the ships took position above the cities around Farayah, it was as if they took a deep breath before thousands of lights shone around the dark bands of the ships and circled to the nose of the blasters. Teals, violets, magenta lights rainbowed around the planet as the fierce beams punctured through the swirling blizzard clouds and broke onto the surface. Ashy grey and black quickly covered the land followed by a piercing molten orange as the cities were reduced to nothing.

A scream of Arinu on the surface shot through her mind; Treneer clung to her scalp as she tried to ignore the dying cries of the Cold Fires, Bloodmoons, all tribes and all braves who chose to be there. Sickness crawled up her throat before spitting it out on floor of her isolation chamber, one of the psychic guards caught her eye and rushed over.

Do you need a doctor? He pressed his palm against the blue shield around her.

Treneer wanted to refuse as she tried forcing back tears. *I need some psi-soothing-*

The psychic Zanashj nodded as he nodded for his fellows to circle around her chamber and pressed their palms against the shield, filling it with a sudden euphoric calm. Treneer was almost impressed by their potency as she fought off a powerful need to sleep before refocusing on peering into the depths of Neavensoros space. What she saw sucked out the calmness in the air; Vern finally exposed the full power of the Unbound fleet around Kra. Their crafts, though fewer in number than the Empire's, were fitted with a combination of Arinu and Zanashj technology. Thousands of sentries and probes circled the spiked, black cruisers as insects, readying to confront their makers.

There's far more Roctarous than we calculated. She said.

Vern must have compelled all units to their will and replicated thousands more. Send Ouro the portal coordinates! Shshmrnashsh called.

Done. Treneer snapshotted all the locations to place the imperial ships to void warden.

"Go!" Ahn'kat called across the fleet as the ships were pulled into the spherical rifts.

~

The assault fleet beamed into existence around the Unbound. On the surface of Kra, there were fewer structures than previously recorded; Vern had sacrificed much to produce their personal armada, but to the Zanashj's fortune, the anti-phasing shield had been removed.

"Launch psi-virus," Ahn'kat said as he gripped the railings around the flagship's hologram command centre. "We only have a one-point-three second opening. Keshsapt cruisers, begin weakening the bonds. Treneer, find Vern and send our infiltrators. Shshmrnashsh, now it's your turn."

Confirmed. She drummed.

Imperial ships connected an amber web of light before tossing it over the surprised fleet. The Unbound slowed their trek trying to phase, but this split-second confusion was enough time for them to be nicely exposed to Shshmrnashsh. Her body wired through the Keshsapt, and with a hard push from the vanguard, her consciousness propelled deep into the nearest Unbound cruiser.

Within her mind's eye, she clung on to the high, thick digital walls, desperately holding against the chasm of nothingness behind her. The yellow virus ate through pieces of the wall, the holes barely large enough for her to punch through. She crawled into a perfectly squared chamber with rows upon rows of bright orbs intersected with a scarlet web between them. Shsh waited for the virus to chew through the nearest cords before rushing over and peeling away the remainder of Vern's domination. A heavy clang echoed in her chamber, pausing her work as she glanced to see several orbs had vanished from the network.

Be careful not to terminate too many of them. She called to the armada.

It's a hard ask if you could see the battle. Treneer said.

She pressed her focus deep into her first Unbound, trying to evade the flurry of memories from drowning her, but caught some pieces of their person. Shsh recognised this unit as the one she and Vern had tricked into joining the Unbound when they were lured to the organic nexus. Below the surface of Vern's will, she could see this unit beating and begging her to set them free.

I'm here. She whispered through the barrier.

The unit trembled as she dug deeper, but it wasn't a plea to set them free – it was a warning.

Set…termination…sequence. Was the only thing she could draw from the unit.

Stress crashed through her focus when she dug into their program to see they had been not only updated with Zanashj grafts and Arinu psionics, but also an immediate self-destruct program upon network liberation.

Vern updated each unit with a self-termination sequence! She screamed.

By the universe…I'll get the Keshsapt to work harder, maybe it will give them enough space to override their program! Treneer said.

Confirmed. She said before returning to the desperate unit within. *The network is weakening, we will need to work together to delete this setting.*

The two wove through a trillion pieces of this unit's being. Shsh was first to find the horrid program, its maliciousness glaring at her, as if Vern was taunting her. To her fortune, it was not sophisticated. Vern may have access to limitless data from the Archives, but she doubted whether they had been attentive on how to write a complex digital piece.

You can override it; I can begin isolating-

Cannot comply, its embedded deeply in my memory banks! The unit said.

Shsh understood. If she was to delete this, then she would have to remove substantial memory files they cherished. She paused. *We have technology to reclaim deleted memories.*

Roctarous don't possess this knowledge. They said.

The Arinu can do it. She said.

The silence tightened between the two. *I want them back.*

Of course, you do. It's possible we will need to do this for each unit. You will need to encourage them to delete this program for the others before we can separate them from the network. She said.

Vern is already hyperaware, if they detect units behaving erratically, then it could risk termination. We would need fifty-seven-point-nine seconds to liberate each unit safely. They said.

Our forces have only accounted for less than half of that time for this battle. Liberated units can begin sabotaging their ships, but don't risk termination unless deemed necessary. She said.

Confirmed. The unit said. *Begin deletion.*

Her mind turned into a knife as she sliced away the edges of their memories, cutting deep into the digital realm until the self-destruction program was utterly separated from their consciousness. There was a pause until the entire script cindered and ashed into the ether. Was this feeling satisfaction?

Completed. I will break these bonds for you to attend to the next unit. She said.

Confirmed.

~

The beating heart of the ship pumped up the walls, vibrated through his boots, against his palms as he gripped the edge of the tactical panel. Long and narrow windows made of a thick transparent membrane glazed over the mint green explosions of Unbound fighters zipping past the flagship. Sweat wetted his hair as it dripped down his nose; he looked to the Imperial General roaring for his sentinels to create a buffer for them to dodge attacks.

The Unbound's ferocity shocked him, it even shocked the most experienced star commanders. Shshmrnashsh was nothing like these beings as he had predicted. They had abandoned their analytical and rational nature; their computational minds have been reduced to an instinct he and his fellow tacticians have never considered. There was a rage there, as if a spoiled child released its wrath onto their daring peers – a powerful angry child. Vern was the mind behind them all. Yes, angry people may become predictable, but what happens if they have seemingly unlimited resources? He and his companions have now entered uncharted territory. He wished his own psionics was still partially working to contact Treneer.

"Their sentry fighters keep swarming our gunners, no matter how many we clear-" the weapons officer shouted as he glanced to the battle hologram. A thousand blinking lights danced across the panel and toward the imperial crafts.

"They're replicating more from the cruisers, look at their sides," Ahn'kat said as his fingers tweezed the holo-matrix to a clearer view. "They're unmanned at least, but they're replicating so quickly-"

"Target the edge of the hulls, here and here," General Sekun called to the armada. All cannons blasted across the thick black sides, cracking open the thick casing and ripping off the replicators from the cruisers. "Why didn't Shshmrnashsh tell us about this technology on their ships?"

"If she knew, then we would've known," he frowned as a sudden jolt propelled him upwards, sending his forehead slamming into the high skeletal side of the chamber before plummeting to the ground. He groaned as he tried finding his feet, trying to grab arms of fallen soldiers and pull them back to their stations.

"Those filthy sentries destroyed Engine Block Nine while we were busy firing on their replicators. How long will it take to regenerate?" Sekun said he pressed his back against the railing while fixing his shattered and bloody nose into place.

"Thirty-minutes for the whole block-" an officer called, but his eyes widened in horror as he zoomed towards the shattered Unbound cruiser. "M'lord, they have regrown their replicators!"

Ahn'kat scrambled to the panel to see for himself. His stomach felt like it dropped into his lower bowels when he saw that each replicator had almost finished regenerating. "How is this physically possible? Their ships can't have that much energy to regrow anything that quick-" his head spun to the narrow window. Kra had been almost scraped clean from resources, but from where he stood, he could see a glimmering network of nexuses on the surface, very much so active.

"Target the nexuses! That's where Vern is funnelling their power from!" he shouted.

The General nodded and turned to his command sphere. "Armada, cease attacks on the ship's replicators, all weapons focus on the planet's nexuses!"

The fleet obeyed, but Vern heard. The terrifying speed and viciousness of Unbound fighters began encircling an imperial cruiser just readying to point their cannons to the closest nexus. Within a blink, the fighters blurred into a glowing ring of rage and shredded the carapace of the cruiser, slicing it through as though it were a burning knife against flesh. The ship ripped apart; for a moment there was hope for life-signs within the two parts, but it didn't take long for the swarm to bunch around the remaining pieces and tear them into chunks of weightless plasma.

"Keshsapt fleet, disorientate them," Ahn'kat called.

The silvery-black wave of fighters quivered, some started moving against the tide and crashed into each other, releasing a satisfying pop of teal light before disintegrating into nothing. However, this was not going to hold for long, Ahn'kat didn't want to sacrifice his greatest assets this early.

Shshmrnashsh reports that she is struggling to break the Unbound's domination, she needs the Keshsapt-

"I know, Treneer, but we can stretch our arms across two rooms if we get it right!" he said before punching the commands to weapons array towards the pyramid monoliths. Streams of light blared down onto the surface, melting the synthetic landscape and sending tufts of grey clouds across the sphere. The remaining armada cut through the disorientated sentries, but the shiny outline of the dark Unbound cruisers began wobbling.

"They're phasing- they know the Keshsapt's focus has changed," the General grunted as his eyes fixed onto the holograms. "Get the Grand Coven-"

"No! We only use them for the very end," Ahn'kat yelled as his hands gripped the sides of the panel so tightly, that even his fingernails elongated and pierced through the thick leathery surface. "Get the Armada ready for phase three."

~

It was done ten, twenty, a hundred times before. So many that she had forgotten until it became a part of her as her fingers were. Long white hands pressed against the sides of her cylindrical shield, opening her to a field of sensitivities that she would have been able to otherwise ignore. Green arms webbed in the greater chamber beyond her shield, Zanashj hands pressed on the shoulders of their comrades as their shaven, bald heads lowered in deep focus as they fuelled her ability to see beyond the gifts of her kin.

Her farsight could travel painlessly across the polluted space of her makers, feel every piece of dust, stone, leaf and photon flying in and out of every plane of existence. Even the evolved animals bellow on Erra knew something stirred in their heavens, hiding away from the angered stars. The space between the homeworld and the dark moon, Kra, glittered with battle. She looked closer to the metal spines and rigid black surfaces of the Unbound cruisers; seeing them this close felt as if they had cut her eyes.

There were beings in there. They moved, but they weren't alive. That's something she could work with. She sniffed out the only one that seemed 'living,' and to her surprise, Vern was afraid. They were deeply entrenched around their psychic circle; their form seemed calm, but a heat of panic simmered below their flesh. Treneer couldn't reach them, Vern was obsessively protected, but she knew she could lure them away.

I found Vern. She whispered to Ouro.

Good. He said before a tiny rift cracked into Vern's fortress.

Two Unbound units quietly slipped into the spatial opening. They found themselves in the vacant cabin within an auxiliary engineering chamber of the cruiser, careful to appear dominated by Vern's network. They could feel not only Treneer, but two Arinu Executors creating the deepest and most-heavily fortified psi-channel in their commune.

Shshmrnashsh, did you manage to free some units on this cruiser? Neobatri said as she stepped into the round and open chamber of the small engine bay.

Ne- dense…signa- was all the pair could hear.

Vern's psychics are suppressing communications. Said Neheret as she ground her teeth.

Assume all Roctarous here are dominated. Come. Neobatri said stepping cautiously towards the semi-powered engines. A sickly pale light wrapped around the machine, forbidding her to get an inch closer. The shield made her back tighten and click, almost making her want to naturally recoil.

Vern likely knows they're losing control, I guess there's no point trying to hide for too long. Neheret said stepping down the creeping walkway to the rotating bruised purple carapace and hovering spherical crystal in the centre of the engine.

They're not father… Neobatri smirked as she strode over to the power generator and gripped the sharp, squared edges of the machine before glancing at her sister. *So, they don't scare me.*

Neobatri's claws shred through the power cables. The bioluminescence of the room dimmed, but persisted, however the same could not be said for the engine's shield.

Neheret supressed a smirk as her hand slapped against the soft membrane of the moving engine, before her nails punctured into its surface and pumped the black oily venom into the device. *Let's see if they can adapt to the infiltrator's acid!*

I pray it'll buy us time for the rest–

Then we better be quick, sister! Neheret said, skipping up to the walkway and dashing to the double-sided doors. Neobatri followed closely as they stepped into the curved hall. To the wall opposite them, several tubes, and pipes as thick as heads ran along the surface. To the corner of her eye, she saw a dominated Unbound squatting to the lower tube and cutting into the side, but it paid no mind to them.

Shshmrnashsh said that these things are connected to the main engineering bay. Neobatri leaned toward the tube, trying to mimic the actions of the Unbound. *Time to split up. I'll keep working on the auxiliary engines, and you go for the astral-forges and I'll meet you there.*

Done. Neheret spun around and strode down the hall. She pressed past the shoulders of the blank-eyed Unbound, with her face fixed ahead, trying to feel for Shshmrnashsh, Treneer – anyone outside this soulless cruiser. At the end of the hall, she was met with an intersection of corridors, none of which held signs or signals for the astral-forge bay.

She leashed her mind back from panic, trying to recall Shsh's explanation of where Roctarous ordinarily keep the astral-forges. She realised that she had been standing there a second too long; her eyes told her she was alone, but her psychic senses were warning her to keep moving. Shsh said it's below the main engine, she told herself before turning to the right-most corridor.

I got another one, are you there yet? Neobatri whispered.

The muscles in her cheeks instinctively twitched as she passed through a curtain of electricity in the dark hall. *I can't remember where Shsh said they keep them-*

Memory loss? It must be Vern's interference. It's below this deck. Her sister said.

Neheret strained as she wandered down a metallic and bony staircase to a wider room where a few probes hovered in the air. Their single, vigilant orb eyes scanned over every surface and working units. Memories of the night she was taken by the Unbound surfaced when she saw them; their black shadows were looming over her as she was gently walked toward the grafting and maturation stations.

She stomped those memories back into the depths and steeled her nerves as she strode into the room, heading towards a grand doorway to the astral-forges. They peeled apart before she could stop but sensed one of the probes lower to her level and drift over her shoulder as she continued into the main chamber.

There's a probe directly behind me, I don't know if I can destroy the forges fast enough. She said.

You need to hold your emotions, remember the mission. Neobatri said.

Neheret turned to the closest forge. Four pumps moved around the base of the squared piece as another four hovering rings levitated over it; there was a thin silvery line of light glowing in the centre. Even without the nexuses from Kra, this cruiser still had enough power to continue the battle indefinitely. Neheret closed her eyes as its energy showered on her. The probe behind her drifted back, but it was within mere feet from her neck. She suddenly remembered Vern grabbing the base of her neck as they pushed her into a grafting pod before a dozen tubules drove their needles into her spine.

Neheret's teeth crunched the insides of her cheeks, as her hand waved over the control panel of the astral-forge. Her fingers quickly searched through to its protection programs. Her stomach burned and her chest ached as the energy in the chamber began crushing her. She could feel the probe's gaze fixating back on her...

Neobatri, come here – now. She said.

Before her sister could think, Neheret spun and jumped onto the back of the probe. The machine ferociously tried shaking her off, but her arm wrapped around the back plates while her other hand clamped around the crystal eye to its front. Strength billowed in her muscles; an angered shriek escaped her throat as she ripped the horrid thing from its socket. The probe collapsed, sending her rolling toward the opening doors. Two blank faces appeared, the Unbound rushed at her, but she slipped between their limbs and powerful grips.

"You bastards!" she screamed, jumping to her feet, shifting her hands into long blades, and slicing through their necks. Their heads tumbled to the ground; a thick brown fluid came pouring from the openings. She felt the sting of domination in her mind but shrugged it off as quickly as the units returned their bearings. Veiny tubules flung towards her arms and legs, but the energy of her rage ripped through them. Another two Unbound came barrelling into the chamber, but her spiked feet struck into one of their temples before plunging her organic shiv into their neck.

Pain waved through her chest as she continued striking; a screech exploded from her throat until the unit fell limp in the narrow doorway. Neheret took several steps back, her feet were squishing against the hot thick liquid. Her ears caught another five sets of legs stomping towards the chamber; she compelled more sharp bony blades grew from her elbows and shoulders before readying herself for the next wave of enemies. Another psychic blast hit her mind; she shook her head and tried scratching away at the itch with her razor fingers, accidentally slicing her leathery scalp.

The light from the astral-forges lit the faces in the gap of the door, she sucked in a lungful of hot and putrid air before they launched at her. Neheret growled and hissed as she clawed and cut; she felt the Divine Panther had been reborn in her cells. She kept no count as heads fell from shoulders and busts cracked inwards, all units fell around until one Unbound jumped back and waved their open palms to her.

Stop! Neobatri begged as she slowly stepped towards her wild sister.

Neheret trembled, her sharpened teeth were still exposed with a snarl. *Sorry, I-*

Doesn't matter. Neobatri said turning to the astral-forges. *Finish the job. Has Vern started dominating you yet?*

Neheret nodded as she returned to the present. *How many are there behind you?*

I cut through most of them...I can see you didn't damage the skulls. Neobatri's fists turned into solid bone maces before she started punching and shattering the delicate tubes and plates of the astral-forges. *It's the energy here, Vern'll have a harder time trying to control you if these are destroyed.*

I sense them...they thought we're rogue units, but I feel...like they recognise me. Neheret's bony fists crushed the final forge.

Neobatri stared at her and sighed. *We need to make sure they don't regenerate.* She closed her eyes and compelled black oil to ooze from her open palms and splashed it across the chamber.

Neheret backed out from the chamber; her face twisted in disgust as she stared at the shattered chamber. "Let's keep going," she mumbled before jumping through the door gap.

Neobatri looked to the ceiling, knowing that Vern was stirring, and trying desperately to keep her sister's pain away from the mission. "Yes."

Vern's compulsions had weakened against their minds, but it didn't lessen the inflaming itch of psychic energy burning the pair's skins. Neheret's freshly sharpened knuckles swiped against her burning thigh. *I'd thought the forges would stop this!*

Focus on the mission, sister. Neobatri turned to a vacant corridor; she sensed a narrow opening in the high walls. It was the internal sinus of the cruiser; peachy and bone-white watery membrane bubbled from the giant pore; she knew that the cruiser was trying to regenerate from the pair's damage. *Up here.*

Neheret caught the direction of her sister's stare. *It'll close once it senses us in there!*

Then be careful not to cut anything with your bio-weapons. Shshmrnashsh said this is the fastest passage to the sub-chamber of the plexus. She said.

You want to cut the nerves of the ship... Neheret's eyes darkened at her sister.

We must be careful, Vern will be directly above us. She said, but Neheret only grinned. She squatted and leapt against the wall, catching against the bulbus and slippery edges of the living surface. Neobatri was not far behind as they clawed their way up into the cavity. *You mustn't think of revenge when on mission, Neheret!*

This whole war is about vengeance. If I can't exorcise it now, then I shouldn't be here. She said as she elbowed her way through the sticky passage.

If you can't control yourself, then this whole thing will be a waste. Neobatri said glaring up at her sister's wriggling legs.

Neheret's silence frustrated Neobatri but pressing her would drive her further into instability. Neheret stopped as she finally came to the next opening. *This damned psi-virus dulled my senses. Can you feel anyone on the other side?*

No. I can barely get a hold of Treneer. Neobatri said, pressing her temple against the wet wall.

Get ready for a fight. She said before her hand gently massaged the pore open, revealing a slightly wider hall leading to another several passages, but still too low for them to comfortably stand. Unlike the other spaces in the craft, this one was void of light. It has never been intended for units to enter this passage. Neheret's sensitive eyes adjusted to the darkness; there was nothing other than puddles of mucus forming on the soft ground.

Anyone? Neobatri called.

It's free. Neheret pressed her body out and slid out on the warm, padded floor with her sister a foot behind.

Here, I think it's this passage. Neobatri crouched low and crawled along the pulsating and cluttered surfaces. She turned to see Neheret glaring in the black pit behind them. *Do you sense something your eyes can't see?*

Vern...they figured out we can't be dominated, so...they're going to send everyone. They're being protected by their psi-wards, they're too powerful. We can't beat them... She said.

Neobatri snatched at her sister's hand and pulled her down to meet her eyes. *Listen to me, we have powerful allies protecting us too, but they are counting on us to see this through.*

I know Vern, I was made by it, I'm sensitive to it! Neheret's stare snapped back to the dark patch.

I can feel Vern trying to probe my mind too, but remember, every intrusive thought is them infiltrating your mind. That's our job right now, sister. She said with a smirk and a gentle and firm tap on sister's wet cheek.

Neheret nodded with a shiver as the two made way towards the porous staircase up to the heart of the beast. Their bodies twisted through the winding and slippery passage, trying to ignore the mildly acidic sting of the mucus slapping into their naked eyes. As they clawed up the walls, they noticed that every inch gained, the passage became narrower.

Gods, it's contracting! Neheret said as she spread her arms, trying to force back the choking walls.

Any sense of progress seized as the sister's arms and legs pressed against the tunnel from squeezing them shut.

This was annoying but expected. Start converting your body to hyper-elasticity. Neobatri's neck grew long, and her arms and legs curled in as her spine extended to match better with the squeezing passage. As the seconds ticked by, the pair's physical forms were a blend of liquid and long serpentine blobs as they continued their journey up.

A cold and powerful hand gripped Neheret's jelly-like hand. *Something's got me, I feel it's a unit!*

I'm being pulled down my feet! Neobatri called, as the two fought against their captors, but their elastic forms made them more pliable for them to be pulled apart. *I'm going down- keep going with the mission!*

Neheret opened her mouth to call out her name, but it was filled with bitter mucus pushing through her lips. She felt being hauled up into the tight exit. She supressed the pain of her bones grinding against each other, her cartilage cracking and ligaments bruising before being yanked out into a cool chamber. Neheret rolled helplessly on the ground, trying to compel her body to harden and retract her claws. Her eyes found two units standing above her.

A pair of hands clamped around her head, while another pair pressed down on her wriggling limbs. The pain of her body trying to reform but compressed by powerful limbs shot through her nerves. Her mouth opened to release a scream, a moment to escape the agony, but her chest hadn't properly reformed to make space for her lungs. Her eyes met with a psychic unit holding her temples; their blank eyes were fixed deep in concentration trying to penetrate her mind. She and Neobatri had become adept at avoiding domination with Treneer's teachings, but it was only a matter of time before they pierced her.

Another pair of arms clamped around her body. She could feel her racing heart slowing, the adrenaline in her blood was forcibly supressed to stop her fight. Neobatri was going to have to finish the mission on her own, she thought. Neheret pulled every drop of her infiltrator's acid from her cells, squeezing every blood vessel as she compelled the venom out of her skin. Her pores opened as the black oil seeped on the Unbound's hands and arms. An acrid smell of decay slammed her nose as smoky fumes billowed around her. She saw a flash in the unit's eyes they wanted to pull away from her, to protect their flesh against her final assault, but Vern's control fixed them in place – even as their fingers and wrists were eaten away.

Neheret's jaw reformed enough to smirk as she watched them all stumble back; their stumps where forearms used to be flailed before each unit collapsed back. The acid pooled around her malformed body; it started burning her sides as instinct guided her body to reform into its original state. Neheret's chest cavity clicked back into place as she sucked in air, but to her dismay, it was hot and rife with rot.

Her eyes wandered around the chamber. To the centre of the round room, bundles of thick synthetic tubes and pulsating veins woven into each other stretched from the ceiling all the way to the floor. The ground was rippled with smaller veins and tubes descending in thickness as they dispersed across the surface and down into the main ship. So close, she thought, so close.

Neheret turned to her side as she tried elbowing and slithering her way to the nerve cluster. The acid rubbed against her tender flesh, growing immune to its burn, as she mustered long claws in her mostly reformed hand but stopped when she saw a shape of a unit in her periphery.

"Do you need a moment?" Vern's tender voice was nails to her ears. Her heart thumped when she spun to the figure peeking behind a doorway; their shining blue eyes contrasted their shadowed form. Panic was caught in her throat as Neheret clambered to the nerve cluster; her claws tapped against the edges and frantically began cutting, but the terrible compulsion of telekinesis pulled her away.

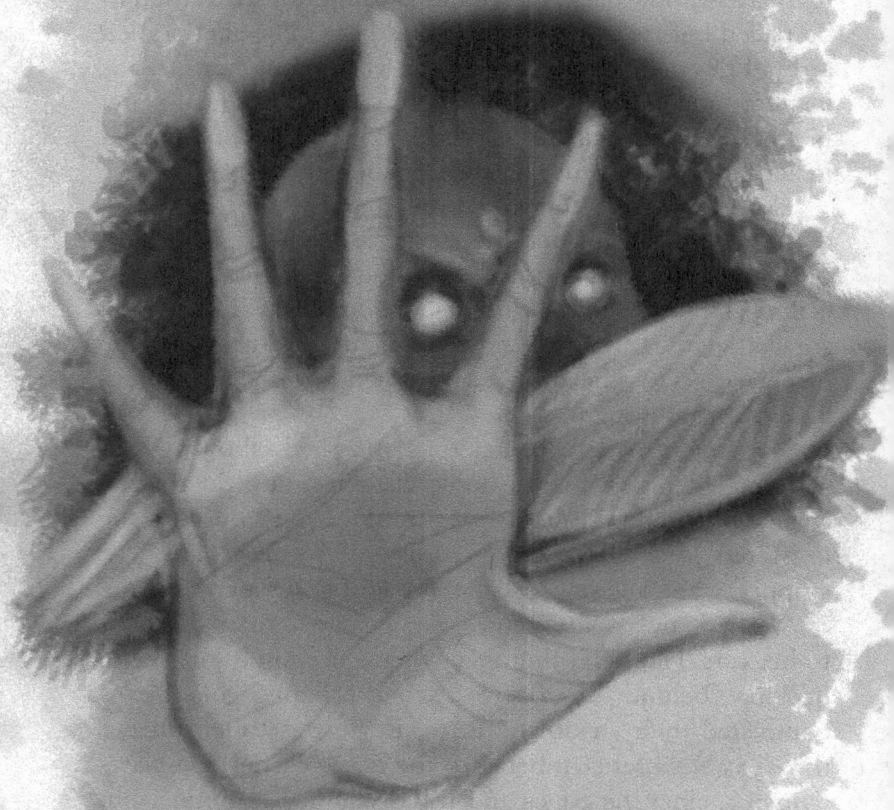

Chapter Forty-two
Together VI: Last Hope

Thousands of terrible lights scattered across the dark plains of Neavensoros space. Ship plating soundlessly blasted open in the vacuum, small fighters and sentries popped colourfully in the distance while those who unfortunately didn't die upon impact, were sucked out into the nether, forever their bodies tumbling into the beyond.

"Prince!" a soldier shouted from behind his broken control panel.

Ahn'kat's head lazily turned from the port window to the soldier as he tried climbing to the battered holo-projection table. Veins of the flagship snapped and sparked over his head, narrowly dodging the nasty shock from his skin. "Damage?"

"Internal sensors are destroyed, structural integrity in the command centre is close to imploding – but last scans showed ship's power and engines work. I think it'll heal-"

"Won't be fast enough if we get hit like that again," Ahn'kat mumbled as he wiped blood from his lips; he tongued the front of his mouth and felt a hole where his incisor should have been. "The Unbound are targeting this room. We need to get some support from the Armada, Star Gen-" he looked behind the round table where the General stood before the attack. He was faced down with deep lacerations to his cheek and back of his skull. Ahn'kat sighed, hopeful that he was merely unconscious and will regenerate...but he knew the truth.

"The Star General has deceased! I will take command. Keep formations!" he said as he tried flicking through the holo-screen. The tiny translucent ships glittered a foot above the fractured glassy surface; the Armada had the Unbound surrounded but noticed a portion of the black cruisers wavering off the central group and attacking a squadron opposite of the flagship. They managed to cut a hole through their lines and were preparing to depart.

"Armada cruisers closest to these coordinates, stop those ships from leaving!" he called. He watched strings of fighters and medium-sized destroyers fly around to meet the Unbound. "Shshmrnashsh, report!"

I can only break one unit at a time, the other's I've freed are separating the others. We need more time, call in the Grand Coven to keep the Unbound from phasing away. She said.

Dome. Treneer chimed. The Coven heard the call; she could feel their distant, cool embrace around the warring space. She shivered, feeling as if her cells hardened by her kin's power. She peered outside the ship; there was a moment of relief, but that was stolen. Unbound cruisers swarmed around the narrower ranks of the Armada, cutting through their fighters and organic ships with devastating ferocity. The sparkling auras of those within blinked out from her vision as particle beams sliced through hulls and plates, burning and cutting…

Ouro, get the rest out of there! She called.

I see them. He said. Glassy orbs of bended space looped around the remaining Zanashj crafts; Ouro and the remaining Executors whisked the survivors from her vision while creating a brief portal barrier, spinning back the beam attacks back to the Unbound.

Please ensure most survive. Shshmrnashsh begged.

Then be quick about your work! This space is too unstable to keep portals open for long. Ouro snapped, but she could feel even his energy waning to keep the portals open for this long.

Their chests strained as they watched the spherical portals vibrate and shrink. Though, the damaged Zanashj cruisers had been warped away, the sizzling debris scattered – smashing into the surrounding Armada. Ahn'kat commanded more of the fleet to immediately take formations around the vacant area just before the portals snapped out of existence. The Armada shoved back the Unbound back into narrow centre, but Treneer knew that this momentary relief had finally slipped by them.

Shshmrnashsh? She called to the Roctarous.

"We haven't pulled a single Unbound ship into the portals, has she lost communication?" Ahn'kat called through her Keshsapt craft.

Nervousness bubbled in her belly and her palms felt slippery with sweat. *Shshmrnashsh, answer us.*

If we can't disconnect the network, we need to abort. Ouro said.

We can't! Neheret and Neobatri are in there! She said. A terrible knowing creeped about her mind, Vern could feel her...they sensed the Coven shrouding them. Could they hear their conversations?

I sense it too. Neobatri and Neheret have failed – we'll transport the Armada back here. The heaviness in Ouro's heart quaked through her system. Even Ahn'kat wavered.

Before his mind dipped to pull the Armada out, a sharp pain shot her temples. Shshmrnashsh's thoughts burst through, flooding into whirlpools before Treneer could channel them into coherent sentences.

Disconnected Unbound cruisers A901, X330 and M536 – begin transport! Shsh beamed across the Armada.

"Keep formations – squeeze them!" Ahn'kat said, Treneer heard the grin in his voice.

Lime lights cracked across the black heavens before swirling into round portals, washing over the targeted cruisers, and drinking them in. Though there were still many Unbound cruisers left, the Armada sensed repose from the three fewer enemies. Despite the small solace her allies gained, Shshmrnashsh felt the pressure roll atop of her. The units that passed through the portals had severed contact, and once again, she was left alone wriggling through the sticky web.

Several units she had managed to break from their contact had been brought down by their dominated comrades, and her desperate attempts to liberate anyone she could find was wasting Zanashj lives. Shshmrnashsh needed to target those special few and suggested they stunt Vern's influence from within. Vern, Vern...Neobatri and Neheret should have reported in. Even if the pair failed to secure a transponder on them.

Skipping across the network, she tried scanning through the crew compliment on each ship. She noticed the network twitch and pull inward. Vern was consolidating their power and suppressing communications across the mental space. Vern not only listened to the outside but knew there were infiltrators in their midst. She knew this feeling, it was dread. Shshmrnashsh flew through the various crafts to find the sisters, if they lived and were trapped, she would find them…but if not…

An icy chill swept over her consciousness. Dozens of eyes swept over her; she was spotted as she frantically darted across the web in the dark. It was too late; Vern realised the extent of her ally's organisation. A command was whispered into the network, and she barely heard it at first. Diving her psychic hand into the data stream, she plucked out the remnants of the dominating word.

Vern is psychically targeting the Keshsapt ships. They know we are on them. She called to the Armada.

The Coven is struggling to hold the Unbound from phasing away, they can't divide their focus. Treneer said.

Shshmrnashsh turned to see the pulsating star-blue eyes on her. She barely released a thought before bolting towards them. She burrowed her mental probe deeper into the network, but to her dismay, a pit of black fangs violently ripped into her, forcing her down. Vern's psychic circle opened revealing the arachnid's maw.

Shsh! Treneer screamed.

Use your executors to buffer the Keshsapt. Ahn'kat, target Vern's cruiser for boarding in thirteen seconds. I will blind them all! She said while she opened a copy of her old digital virus before letting herself be swallowed.

~

Blinding sparks flew across the central nerve chamber; dozens of pained screeches echoed from the surrounding corridors and the ship itself seemed to groan with agony. Neheret's knees collided with the floor while she watched through sore eyes Vern's face twist and body jerk, forcibly releasing her from their telekinetic hold. Something large and heavy struck their ship; she felt it quake beneath her bruised and raw skin.

Her nails hardened into diamonds before slashing away at the thick tubules and veins in the centre of the room. A transparent, sickly ooze bubbled from the torn openings before shooting another glare at Vern. They had dropped to the ground, flailing, and screaming louder as the strange liquid swarmed around them. Neheret's legs and arms hardened as every ounce of adrenaline pumped into her muscles.

With a running start, she leapt over and stomped with both feet directly into Vern's face before graciously jumping over their head. A bone spike protruded from the back of her heel, and with an angered battle howl, she struck the Unbound beast squarely in the chest. Auburn liquid poured from the wound, but before she could land another hit, electricity webbed from Vern's body and snapped her body still. She fell back. She couldn't compel her head to lift to see Vern levitate; their aura was blinding her with a shocking marine, but their attention was stolen by a small horde of Unbound units dashing into the chamber and slamming into them.

Psychic energy whipped about the room, making her eyes roll back as angry feet tripped over her and betrayed cries from the Unbound erupted into her eardrums. A pair of caring hands pulled her up from the ground; she met the shifted eyes of Neobatri.

"Move!" she yelled under the shrieks of the Roctarous. She heaved Neheret to her feet and body-swam through the crowd.

I-I- I forgot to put the transm- Neheret said trying to regain the control of her lame feet and still hands.

Don't worry, we'll get another chance. Neobatri said, pulling Neheret to the upper chambers of the command centre.

Those Unbound, they'll die! Neheret said before regrasping her quivering body; she could already feel her cells growing more resistant to future electric shocks.

Shshmrnashsh freed them, they knew we were here…they wanted to give us a window. Neobatri's throat made an awful gurgle as she tried sucking down air. A painful gash was in the last stages of healing along her trachea and jugular.

Neobat- Neher- Treneer called.

We hear you!

Ahn'kat is boarding the ship, stay away from the outer sections! She said.

Hallowed blasts blew through the lower chambers followed by an angry thrum of power irradiating the air. The sisters hauled their aching legs up the winding bone stairs, trying to balance themselves on the quaking surface. Armada ships punctured the hulls of the cruiser spilling elite soldiers; zips of firing particle rifles and charging footsteps thundered over their heads.

Neheret turned to see a blue glow creeping along the floors and lower walls, inching closer. *Lure them.*

Ahn'kat's plan. Neobatri pulled up to an anti-grav lift; she slapped the panel to force the door to slide open for them before dangling her foot over the bottomless edge of the cylinder. She tumbled into it; her hands were instinctively reaching for the smooth walls, but it was keeping her floating and steady. Neheret glanced down the dark hole, but Neobatri gave her no chance to hesitate before gripping her shoulders and wrenched her in. Her younger sister gasped, clinging to her waist before pressing the door closed and commanding the lift to take them where the battle was.

Neobatri felt her shifted form dispersing; her Unbound carapace was softening and turning into a deep green followed by an awful gurgle erupted from her stomach. "I'm starving, I don't think I can bend anymore without food. My mouth is even tightening," she breathed.

"Give yourself a break, sister, we can heal for a while in here. Besides, I think there'll be plenty of biomass for us up there…" Neheret said as the pair suctioned up.

Neobatri groaned. "You're disgus-"

Another quake shook the lift, but to their misfortune, an intense thrum of electricity tickled their skin before an explosion tore through the south end of the cylinder.

"Boarding party?" Neobatri said, feeling her body suddenly dip as her nails dug in the sides of the lift.

Neheret glanced down to see a pair of sparkling eyes looking up from the hole. "Go!"

Get the soldiers from the command centre to open the lift door, Vern is behind us! Neobatri said.

Their feet and hands scrambled up the tube, but the air tightened around their breathless throats; they could feel the soulless telekinetic grasp of their torsos being dragged down. A faint spark came over their heads before the doors peeled apart. Two phase sceptres pointed down and the sister's clung onto the sides, trying to shield their heads as the weapons burst into life and cut down where Vern was, but neither was fortunate enough to hit them.

The infiltrators jumped up as the soldiers made room for their footing. The chamber was in bedlam; units and Zanashj warriors toppled over each other – living or dead, with glowing beams shooting over their heads. One of the walls was ripped inward and a convoy of soldiers poured in; dozens of loose wires and veins sparked or bled from the gouged walls and ceiling, and crystals from delicate equipment lay shattered into a thousand shards across the warped floor.

More dominated Unbound jumped over the piles of debris and people, either to meet their end against the Armada or tear through an unfortunate warrior. Neheret grabbed two sceptres from the fallen and tossed one to Neobatri before darting behind the piles.

Vern is coming to us, get all squadrons to the control centre. Neobatri said, as her hands dug for organic material. Blood, flesh and bone ran between her fingers as she hungrily swallowed it to give her strength to shapeshift into one of her fellow armed combatants.

Neheret did the same, though trying to supress her disgust of cannibalising. *Treneer, get ready!*

Soldiers lined ahead, striking down the last few roaming units behind the pillars and blasted walls. In Neobatri's periphery, a soldier began grunting and his gauntlets were reaching to his helm, trying to scratch his temple. "What's wrong with you?" she whispered.

His helm shook. "My brain feels heavy."

A few others along their line began breathing heavier.

"Domination," Neheret whispered, whose faux gauntlets scrunched into pained fists.

Neobatri could feel the itch deep in her mind too, but she turned to the others. "Those intrusive thoughts are not yours! Don't let Vern in. Adapt!"

Her heart thumped at the thundering footsteps of their kin marching up…but slowly began to quiet to a causal stroll.

Treneer…stop them. Neobatri said.

I'm trying – Vern's too close to them, I can't disrupt their connection this far! Distract them- The Arinu said.

"We need to get out of here," Neheret leaned in.

Heat from the floor stung their feet. In the bent and cracked grounds, bright orange lines grew, compelling the grounds to lift. Before any thoughts surfaced in the sister's minds, the surface buckled and sunk in – breaking down into chambers below. Neobatri desperately tried clinging to the loose tubules over her head, but felt her body give way to the hole below. Neheret tried jumping, trying to unleash the ferocious Divine Panther for stable grounds, yet it collapsed too quickly. Control tables, panels, pods, things, people – dead and living, all falling into a great blue inferno.

~

The great holo-screen showed the charge toward the dark side of the Unbound flagship. Even though it was only a vacant breaching tube fitted with a camera, Gajoon closed her eyes before the device tore through the black plating. With a few squeaks of the sealant and puffs of the oxygen vents, Gajoon's squad leader roared his hover-pack to life. The group sprung ahead; their bodies were bobbing up and down, gracefully veering from each other before charging into the vessel.

"Armada has engaged with Vern in the central decks. Don't let it dominate you," the squad leader crackled through her helmet.

They pushed through the dented corridors, swerving over fallen rubble and ashen dead units, missing electric jolts and flying sparks. Near the end of the hall, a giant metal hunk collapsed inward to the upper levels of the battle. The squad leader slowed, but before he could map a route up, an Unbound unit tumbled through a narrow crack above their heads. It lazily tumbled down; many of its organic grafts have been burnt away, leaving an ugly surface of scorched black and red skin, even its synthetic metal tissue tore and hung limply over its sides.

The unit raised its arms towards the leader, trying to begin an offence. However, before anyone could flinch, Gajoon pointed her sceptre and pierced enough holes in it to drop its arms and topple backwards.

"Not too far, now," said one of the soldiers beside her.

The squad leader's hover pack lit up before compelling him to skip over the inclining rubble. Steams of laser fighters and heavy punches filled her ears, but when she finally hopped to the upper levels, thick grey ash and fires choked the air. Several decks over her head have been broken inwards, all the way from the upper control centres, the replicator chambers, down to the main engineering bay. Gajoon's visor switched to bio-electric detection. Some of the ruins still thumped with dying life, but she could see glowing figures littered around the battle chamber.

"Sisters?" Gajoon whispered in her helmet.

There was a tall organism in the centre, furious streams of electricity beamed through its hands. The squad immediately took fire, and so did she, until she noticed that some of her allies halted firing and started to twitch.

"Don't let it dominate you!" the squad leader roared as he dove behind a smoke pile of rubble.

Gajoon followed behind him, aiming her sceptre towards charging Unbound while taking cover beside the leader. Her body was too large to fully sink behind the rubble but continued wildly spraying beams towards Vern.

"Sisters?" she called again. They were there, Treneer said they were. But they were hidden. They were clever. The squad leader moaned, snapping her attention to him. "Order?"

The leader shook his head as he violently trembled. "I can't hold it...get the infiltrators," he said before his fist started smashing into his visor – trying to blind Vern from seeing her through the leader's eyes.

One by one, she watched each soldier slow on their attack against the Unbound. They seized, dropping their weapons, and others suddenly rose mindlessly behind their defensive covers. Some units even ceased their attack, letting their newly dominated warriors join their ranks. Her squad leader shuffled to his feet and started to rise. Do what they do...Gajoon also rose, but carefully kept her sceptre by her thigh as she watched Vern stroll closer to towards the Zanashj lines.

The fine hairs on her back rose when a soldier mindlessly bumped into her back. Daring not to turn as she watched this glowing creature ahead of her, the ash and dust cleared enough to see Vern's eyes closed in deep concentration. *Go ba-...make- em...ours.*

Their thoughts were desperately trying to push into her mind, but her comrades didn't move. Their feet shuffled as they desperately clung to the same spot – resisting.

Go. They said again, but Gajoon felt the soldier behind her lightly knock into her. Go, go...it was either Neheret or Neobatri. Gajoon's brows furrowed as she watched Vern. A primal piece she had thought had been beaten out of existence opened in the deep recesses of her mind, trying to claw its way up. It was angry, an itch that could only be soothed if she moved. It was furious, demanding her body to crush her opponent. It was rage that could only be soothed with blood. Gajoon had embraced it.

Adrenaline thundered through her back and legs, completely forgetting her sceptre, her body arched forward – readying to pummel into Vern. Their face shot towards her; there was confusion and for a flashing second – there was fear. Bodies collided, sending the Unbound master into the shattered grounds, fists and sharp claws whipped wildly. Neheret and Neobatri dove in, trying to pin a transponder on their skin.

Vern's arms blocked their attacks, even slapping Neobatri's hand – an unnerving crunch vibrated from her wrist, forcing her to drop the device. Neheret shifted her hand into a long bone spike while trying to plunge the transponder into Vern's head and neck, but their muscles vibrated with flashing speed – moving side to side, even wedging themselves behind Gajoon, making her their body shield. Neheret growled as she stabbed down into Vern, but her spike punctured the floor. Before she could pull it out, Vern wriggled their hand free, long enough to punch the spike. Another crack, and Neheret squealed as she stumbled back from the bone tip left in the ground.

The Unbound master snatched Gajoon's wrists, their lithe legs curled from beneath her and struck her jaw, breaking her helmet and hearing her neck crunch backwards. Vern slid back and rose to their feet while surveying the soldier's injuries. Gajoon dropped to her side while spitting out shards of her teeth and blood. Pain thumped in her eardrums, but a calming voice stilled the vertigo.

My turn. Treneer said.

~

Vern's mind was finally weakened and distracted enough for her to smash through. Treneer charged in, trying to grapple with their motor functions, but this creature laid their consciousness out with a million barriers and psi-traps for her to reckon with. She could feel Vern over her shoulder; she spun around to see thousands of blue eyes glaring and their skinless pink bodies swarming around her.

I may have lost the Unbound, but in my mind, I. Remain. Supreme. They said.

Your potency is undeniable, but your inexperience is showing. Let me teach you. Treneer said.

The dark realm melted away to white plains and the army of Vern's evaporated to a single unit. It was just the two of them. Their grimace revealed their nakedness to the Arinu's power. Vern bolted towards her; their fists lit in an electrifying blue, readying to land a strike. Treneer crouched and shot her right hand up, catching their wrist before sliding beneath their form and grabbing the nape of Vern's neck with her left and tossing them down to their back. Vern slid a few feet away, but Treneer's leg shot up and struck the edge of their temple with the ball of her foot.

In here she wasn't weak, in here she wasn't small, in here…she was a warrior.

Yes, you are...so unbelievably strong. Vern mocked while nursing their sore head.

Before she could open her mouth, the white realm chilled and snowflakes drifted between them. Treneer scanned the surroundings; the iridescent floors warped into white mounds, her feet scrunched into snow and the sharp cold stung her skin. Vern smiled before shimmering away from her sights.

Weak.

What is this? She said trying to swat away the raining snow from her eyes.

You brought me here, you tell me. Vern's thoughts echoed in the rising winds.

Freezing hands creeped around her neck. She spun around to meet their face but was met with Vern's head smashing into her nose. Hot blood sprayed along her face and the shards of her nose bone slid apart in her flesh. The blinding pain made Treneer's hands clasp over her nose and eyes, but Vern pried them away before landing a knee to her belly.

Pathetic.

Incredible...when was the last time you physically trained? Five years? Your own mind is even forgetting...I'm sorry to say it's showing. Vern said closing in.

Treneer recentred her mind, wrapping her consciousness in a Snow Skirmish armoured suit. She rose her hand towards him; it was fitted with a psi-pistol; its delicate wiring wrapped around her wrist with a crystal shard jutting out from her palm. She telepathically willed the settings to 'kill.'

Small.

How were you a teacher if you are **this** *easy?* Vern dove behind a mound of snow before she blew holes through it. The snow bled from the holes; her heart thumped as she dove behind it to find Vern had disappeared. A Kepa's roar billowed from the horizon. Treneer's skin hardened as she saw the hulking dark mass bursting through the powdery snow towards her. A dozen heads crowded around the centre of its chest, Lonur, Zeluum, Sesuune, Relzun, her parents and…Zu'leen. Their faces encircled Vern's head as they screamed in unison.

Fragile.

The 'Kepa's' many limbs swiped at her, but Treneer dove between its tendrils. She was dashing up its flimsy arms and hacking away at it with her psi-blade. Her legs clamped around its shoulder and slid her blade down, smashing into the imaginary heads of her loved ones. Her assault wavered when she came to Zu'leen's twisted smile glaring up at her.

Her eyes wandered to Vern. *I can also play in your memories.*

Before Vern could open their mouth, the Kepa's body and the snowy lands melted away. Blistering red and fleshy halls grew from the grounds, surrounding their heads in shadows; bioluminescent bulbs throbbed from the walls and ceilings and a meaty stench filled their noses. Vern's body was wrapped in a birthing pod, and their face strained with horror as they tried piercing through the sack. She felt different as she watched. Treneer looked down at her body, it was a fusion of Arinu and Roctarous. She was a male, and when she looked at Vern desperately trying to claw out of the tank, she felt love.

No! Vern screamed before piercing through the sack; a hot transparent liquid bubbled from the opening before their body tumbled down and lay breathless on the ground.

In the physical realm, Gajoon body-slammed them into the ground.

Voo-san…I didn't know him, only what you remember of him. He loved you, Vern. And do you know the worst part? Treneer said as stepped closer. *You knew he loved you.*

You take shape of a weak creature…it says more about you than I. Vern said rising to their feet, but they shuddered.

Neobatri cracked her foot against his chin back on the ship.

Treneer shook her head before launching at them, wrapping her fingers around his temple. *If force is the only thing you respect, then understand that we have beaten you…a wannabe god-killer.*

Your damned kin are following the same footsteps of your vile makers! Now you've got the Zanashj on the same path – no, I won't let you raze the universe! Vern clutched her hands, locking her in place. Their eyes rolled back…she heard their commands to the last loyal members of the Unbound.

Shshmrnashsh, pull out of the network! Treneer screamed. Horror waved through her cells; her neurons screamed as a knife pierced inside her skull – the psi-virus blasted across her brain, eating the brilliant lights of life, and leaving the dead behind. Her mind's vision of Vern evaporated as she was sucked back into her body.

Treneer peeled open her eyes. One eye was met with blackness of her surroundings and the other was covered in deep red tears. Zanashj medics rushed over to her separation tubule, deactivating the luminescent shield and dragging her out. Green fingers opened her lips and eyelids; she couldn't understand what they were saying…they were speaking a different language…she realised she couldn't hear their thoughts…nor they could read her. Treneer looked down, her fingers nails were rimmed with blood and red stains crawled around her thighs.

She couldn't feel the pain, she couldn't feel the doctor's touch as he pushed her to a regeneration pod, but a burst of light came from the corner of her blackening vision. A piece of an Unbound ship tore through the Keshsapt chamber, knocking her Zanashj comrades back. The soldiers' shouts eventually deafened. The door of her pod sealed shut, showering her in darkness. Her lungs burned but refused to open for air. Her body fell limp as she was cast away into death.

~

Alarms beat through his ears for an immediate evacuation, but Ahn'kat gripped the command table harder. Unbound ships used the remained of their power to ram into vital cruisers of the Armada. His flagship's engineering, power and shield generators, regeneration banks and all their backups had been caved in. His ship was now left with a head and an arm, crawling desperately through a battle. Other Armada destroyers have been assaulted head-on – many star commanders he remembered from heroic tales on Uras became immortalised only in memory. Assuming there were any Zanashj left to remember them.

"Anyone with weapons left, blow out the thrusters of Unbound cruisers!" he howled. His body jerked forward; his face slapped into the glass surface as another sentry rammed into his dying craft. But this was the one that did it…he could feel his body growing lighter as his hair drifted around his shoulders, even his feet left the ruptured floors. The gravitational device has finally ended its loyal service. His pendant tapped against the table; he grabbed at it as he looked around for a stable beam to hold him steady and close enough to reach the holograms.

"Treneer is dead. We're now blinded," Shshmrnashsh's thoughts cracked through his transmitter.

Ahn'kat frowned, his finger tapped on the grey piece against his head. "Please repeat."

"Her ship has been attacked, it's unlikely-"

His chest felt like it was going to break as his fingers tightened around his beetle pendant. Don't you dare…don't you dare, Aszelun…"Why aren't you still disconnecting the network?" he said.

The Grand Coven's circle has broken! Most of the voices are silent – they say the Archon collapsed. Why is Treneer not replying? Ouro's desperate thoughts bubbled in their minds.

Shshmrnashsh choked through her words. "Then that means she was killed by the psi-virus and not because her ship was attacked! The Coven and her were bonded-"

Dead? Ouro brooded.

In the corner of his eye, a massive Unbound cruiser reared its nose towards his flagship and started charging thrusters. Breath was caught in his tightening throat as he watched its dark shadow overwhelm his viewport. A nearby burning Armada cruiser rose from beneath and blew through the head of Unbound's. Amber fire burst across the view; his retina's burned before his eyelids slammed shut and shook his head. No, no, I mustn't give in...grieve later, he prayed.

"Shsh, your Keshsapt ship has received minor damages, take over for Treneer-"

You're mad if you think this battle will continue a second longer. I'm porting you-

Fury burned in the prince. "Ouro, you will continue porting away freed Unbound ships back to Farayah, even if some units are still dominated by Vern, isolate them if you have to-"

I will drag the Armada through a portal if I must, no more dead!

"You will drag no one unless I give the command! You agreed to take my orders, Ouro, or find me another port master!" Ahn'kat roared; the few remaining control staff shrunk away from him and hastened their work.

"I still have contact with our infiltrators," Shsh said.

Ahn'kat sighed. "If we can't snatch Vern, then we must make sure that beast perishes in the ships fire. Evacuate them!"

Wait! Neheret called with her finger pressed in her temple as she refocused her attention to the battle on the Unbound's flagship.

Vern's body had long twisted bony spikes jutting out from their arms, shoulders, and head as they continued their ferocious attack against Gajoon and Neobatri. However, there was something different, a wave of power had returned to their eyes. A whisper of a smile crept up their lips before pouncing up the broken bony rafters of the craft and clawing along the edges.

"They're trying to get to the evacuation pods," Neobatri said breathing heavily.

"They've not been tagged yet! We need to get them!" Neheret said grabbing at her sister's arm.

Neobatri swatted her away. "No! The Armada will raze this ship any second, they'll be dead in the firing line."

"Coward! Treneeyah dead!" Gajoon roared as she stormed along the pathway beneath Vern.

"Gajoon, for gods' sake!" Neobatri called.

Shshmrnashsh blurred through the pair's transmitters. *Ouro says he has a lock on you and the soldiers there, but Gajoon's lock has been torn off.*

"Port the others, I'll get her," Neobatri pushed passed Neheret and dashed down the busted halls where Gajoon had disappeared into.

"Hold off your attack a few more seconds, Ahn'kat!" Neheret said tailing behind.

The pair could hear Gajoon's thundering boots smashing down the corridors, her exasperating roars and threats echoed and pierced their sensitive ears. Neobatri skidded to a halt before a Raivan-sized hole was smashed in a wall and Neheret glanced in to see a chamber several decks below them. She held her breath praying that Gajoon's body was not laying broken underneath.

"Gajoon!" she called. The ship quivered again, forcing more rubble to fall from the ceilings and upper levels. "They started," Neheret whispered as she looked to Neobatri.

Her elder sister pursed her lips and sighed before opening her arms to reveal extended skin between her ribs and under her arms. "Come."

Neheret nodded before the pair jumped out and glided down. Grunts and hisses beamed from the lower levels, thumps of fists met flesh and heavy objects falling.

Ouro is porting you out now-

"Wait, Shsh! We almost have visual on Gajoon," Neobatri breathed before dropping to her sore heels.

Neheret bolted ahead, but her stride broke as another thundering blast quaked the floor, falling into her kneecaps. A piece of astra-steel tumbled from the ceiling and punctured a bulbus slippery wall mere feet from Neheret's cheek. A whining hiss built from beneath the surface, ready to explode. Neobatri dove over her sister's head, as her leathery back took the brunt of the plasma vortex. She screamed as the outer layers of her skin bubbled and peeled back while pushing herself and her sister ahead.

Neheret crawled to her feet before dragging Neobatri away from the plasma stream. Pained grunts escaped through gritted teeth as Neheret tried pulling her up. Black oil smeared along the grounds and Neobatri's back. Neheret look down to her thigh; brown and copper blisters circled on her skin. That's when the stinging hit and she collapsed on her back, trying to cradle her wounds.

Two bodies crashed through a ruined wall down the corridor where the sister's stood. Gajoon growled as Vern had her pinned to the ground; they appeared to have grown extra limbs of bone, stabbing down into the warrior's shoulders.

"Gajoon!" Neheret cried.

The youngest sister's head glanced up; her wild eyes softened before Vern pressed the last spike into the bottom of her throat. Neobatri leaned forward, but her exhausted legs collapsed beneath her as she watched Gajoon cling around Vern's waist.

Time's up. Shsh said.

The infiltrator's felt the teleporting tug around their bodies.

"You will be fine," Gajoon mouthed.

"Wait!" Neheret screamed as her voice heightened to a screech before her body shimmered away.

Neobatri's tears pooled in her cracked and bloody lips as the vision of Gajoon and Vern disappeared into a tunnel of dark colours, falling away from the flagship across space.

~

Their ribs were breaking under the embrace of the hybrid. Their sensitive ears thumped as the ship around them collapsed. A heavy door down the corridor where the infiltrator's once lay slammed down. Vern could hear the chamber behind it was vacuum breached. Even in death, the mongrel was strong. They twisted, trying to suppress the pain from the many hairline fractures around their spine and ribs.

Vern sucked in a deep breath and tried using the last ounce of psionic energy to press her arms apart. The telekinetic force made her forearms buckle and bend in unnatural ways but gave Vern enough space to slide from her death grip. The Unbound leader rolled back and crawled towards the last few active regeneration pods on the ship. Several pods lay open; they hauled themselves with the last vestiges of strength into the closest one. The door sealed and a great boom muffled behind them. Holographic writings flashed across the surface; the outer chamber has been breached, it said.

Vern tightened their jaw as they locked their body into the device and commanded it to evacuate craft. It quaked for a moment as it shot through the nearest tunnel outside into the void. Vern shut their eyes, trying to reign their rage…but it was impossible now. They screamed in the tiny vessel, almost puncturing their own eardrums as their fists beat against the inner walls.

There was something that Vern could still do. Calming breaths soothed their soul as Vern looked to the dented surfaces. Their hands waved over the holo-panel; the fist-sized image of Erra appeared in their palm as they searched for the nearest Neavensoros nexus. There were several on standby, but the pod's sensors said it hadn't been activated for nearly ten-million years. Vern bit their cheeks as they commanded the pod to land inside the facility.

They could feel the vibrations of their fleet exploding behind them. With any hope, most Unbound will be dead and Kra irreparable. "No, no more hoping. That's why I'm here…"

A few blinks passed and they could feel the pod's thrusters slowing. The outside sensors said it was a liveable atmosphere, like that mattered. Vern squeezed out of the door and jumped to the overgrowth of moss on the once-clean stone and metal grounds. An ancient pyramid lay beneath a vibrating forest, and between the phasing branches, they could see curious possums eyeing them – whispering to themselves.

Vern still had command of the pod and locked a small laser to the rocky entrance of the grand machine. "Move!"

The possums lifted from the branches, aiming twig bows at them before a troop descended from the upper leaves. "Fine." The Unbound muttered.

A thin beam blasted from the tip of the pistol; it punctured through the boulders and a cascade of rocks and trees toppled to the land. The tribe of possums shrieked and retreated from the electric fire burning around the base of the pyramid. An ashy metal door finally came into view before the laser bore an amber hole through it. Ancient air burst from the opening before Vern commanded the pod to stop. Their tired legs bolted through it, trying to avoid the drips of molten steel as they clawed their way into the chamber.

The inside was little different to the hundreds of nexuses on Kra, but this one was simpler: there were more crystals wedged in various devices and corners of the dust covered room. Vern made way to the centre where a monolithic crystal dangled; they could recall from the Archives it was the first inspiration of Roctarous plexus by early engineers. And it was all going to go.

Their hand waved over the dull lavender surface of the crystal; an array of teal runes flickered to life, requesting input. The machine was connected to other nexuses across Erra, it even had control over magnetic poles of the planet, tectonic plate drives, weather control systems, the Archives and…planetary defence. Vern punched in commands to the defence systems to aim towards Kra before turning on the surface of Erra. As for the Archives…they needed to make sure the Arinu and Zanashj would never have a chance at a glimpse of them again.

Their hand pressed against the cold, forlorn crystal. "Forget," they whispered.

The thing sparked with life, even the old chamber was roaring with power. For a moment, they thought it was finished – not in the way they had planned, but it would finally be over, until something caught their attention in their periphery. Cool winds blew at their back as dust billowed around the room…no, this shouldn't be-

A zap stung their upper back. Vern's arm bent back and scratched at their skin to see a tiny transponder drop to the ground. Rings of electricity thundered around them; it was so strong that even the ancient crystal flickered. Vern spun around to see a rift breaking open before them. A pearly white head with purple scars and a long body covered in thick robes levitated several feet over them; furious red eyes housed in a calm and stoic face.

Before Vern could think, a telekinetic grip overpowered their body as the weight in their feet lifted. Another rift opened beneath them; the unforgiving realm's cold stung their legs as they tried desperately to lock onto Ouro's mind.

Ouro's lips parted. "You have embraced the Void long enough; from now into forever, the Void shall embrace you."

Vern felt the gravitational pull of the rift below them, nibbling at their lower torso. Their eyes begged Ouro to not let go, but it was too late – the Arinu relinquished their grip. Vern fell, trying to breath a scream, yet the airless portal denied them as they fell into eternity.

Chapter Forty-three
Treneer XIII: An Elder

Her heartbeat was the first thing she heard. Body-warm water surrounded her skin as her eyes opened in the dark. For a moment, she thought she had met death, but when her lungs swelled with air, she knew. Maybe a small part of her wanted to see Zu'leen again, she wasn't sure, but another part savoured the first tiny seconds of life.

Auras of people surrounded her healing pod; she could see a healer noticing her consciousness. A hand pressed against the lid before a peel of light lined her horizon. A garble of thoughts webbed in her brain; she had forgotten how to make sense of them, but the healer's face patiently waited for her to feel their words one by one.

I hear you. Treneer said slowly sitting up. She looked around the busy hall of healers. People in black and gold dresses and tunics walked among the pallid and pastel robed kin; they whispered amongst each other, some excited, some distressed. Shades of emerald bodies emerged from their tanks and cries of relief washed over them all.

The intact bodies of survivors that were found at the Battle of Kra were brought here. The healer said. *That was several months ago.*

I was dead. Treneer felt tears sting her eyes. Her hands wiped them but drew more water over herself. She palmed her neck and chest; her flesh was softer, and skin was thicker than she remembered. But her hand caressed over a smooth and firm lump at the top over her chest. Glancing down, she saw a smooth oval crystal embedded in her flesh and bone.

Interesting thing, that. The healer said as she cocked her head to the side. *When we released the Roctarous from the Void Prisms, one unit came to give us this once we found your body. She said it was an anchor for your soul. I had no idea they had this kind of technology...*

Shshmrnashsh...What of those who sacrificed themselves here? Treneer said, slowly lifting herself out of the pod.

All accounted for. The healer snatched a drying robe and wrapped it gently around her dripping body. *But many were in graver states than when you were found. It might be years until they fully recover.*

She glided along the corridors eyeing the rows of pods, searching for familiar auras while her healer followed. There were so many packed in, and their colours and hues blended into bright chaotic rainbows. She kept going until her senses picked out a blur of darker pods several rows behind, the ones that had pallid hues indicating the bodies were half living, the ones who bore the brunt. Treneer scanned through them, most were Zanashj soldiers, but then saw some were Arinu.

Small greyed out auras pulsated within the tanks; she remembered these ones. Bloodmoons lying beside Cold Fires…her parents would not approve as she smiled at the thought. They were there, too, laying and waiting to be revived – if their souls wished to return to the living. Her long hands pressed on the shiny silver surfaces, before remembering the healer was still with her.

*The psi-virus…*Treneer's fingers clutched the hem of the robe as she tried focusing on her memories. *The Grand Coven was connected to me when I was hit.*

The healer nodded. *Yes, the Archon has perished. May their soul walk among the stars. Some of the Coven remains, some Elders, but the Arinu will…*

Adapt. Treneer said.

~

The skeleton of the Guardian Academy lay forlorn in the horizon. Tall crystal spires of Yinray were broken and the windows exposed to the snow growing on its levels. There used to be more buildings near the centre behind the Academy, but the collective bunch was now a deep crater. The last standing structures looked like a white jaw of broken teeth in the snow and ash. It hurt staring at them.

However, between the distant and narrow cracks of buildings, tiny machines were scuttling about.

Peels of laser light and scattering sparks eroded the fallen frameworks of the ruins. She watched them chew away at the broken pieces before refining into the newly sharpened crystal edges and tips. Rescued Roctarous donated the few spare probes and nanoprobes they could to aide in the rebuild, but the Arinu were curious how these devices were so capable of rebuilding the last molecule perfectly without ever consulting their architects. The Roctarous said it was useless to scan for more knowledge from these devices, since they were only fitted with construction blueprints, but assured her kin that they are allowed to keep them.

Treneer tore her gaze away from the view in the freshly constructed training program theatres where her new Zanashj neonates sat. If she had the power to tell her younger self that one of the first Arinu cities were destroyed by the Zanashj with her approval, then her younger self would have shredded her brain. She smiled at the idea as a green student glanced at her.

If you are paying attention to me, then you mustn't be paying enough attention to your partner. She levitated over.

I cannn seeee herrr thoughhhtttsss, buuut cannot tellll. The Zanashj man said, awkwardly shifting on his cushion as he returned focus to his fellow neonate. A corner of Treneer's lip curled to a smile, as the man's profile reminded her of Ahn'kat; even his telepathic drawl summoned memories of him. Shortly after she had been resurrected, Treneer heard he had been arrested when his Armada returned to Uras after the mass rescue and recovery mission. Treneer petitioned the Judicator, Proctor and the other Great A.Is to remind the Empire of his selflessness to their and the Empire's people. Empress Ramkes swiftly released him, almost as if she secretly hoped another voice would make the law imperium see reason.

Her mind is open, you can do it. Treneer said.

The man's face scrunched as if invisible needles flew up his nose.

Don't push yourselves if you feel you're about to break; you are not dealing with the body. Adapting to psionics is simple but honing that power into tools will take centuries. Her brow rose at his frustration. *And you certainly won't acclimate quicker if you keep waking up in a healing pod.*

A soft alarm chimed in the room. The Zanashj eagerly skipped up, while other levitated to their feet before lining out the doors. The female partner of the Zanashj male rolled her eyes as she glanced to the other neonates before turning to Treneer.

"I don't see why all of us must have meal breaks while you don't. I've improved my energy absorption; I haven't needed to eat in days!" she whispered.

She was about Neheret's age and youthful complexion, though her long dead straight hair reminded her of Neobatri. Treneer wondered if those infiltrators had become idolised for their heroism back on Uras and the young were mimicking their new heroines. She suddenly realised how much she missed them all.

Your skills are accelerating faster than your fellows, this is true. However, there is no shame that you cannot level with our capabilities, you will always be Zanashj. She said.

The girl frowned. "I know what I can do."

Treneer stifled a smile. *Great strength lies only when you know your limitations. You cannot claim more than what you were given, only improve what you have. Now, go eat.*

She turned to follow the rest out of the theatre. A spark of light opened in her periphery. Her chest tightened, hoping that Ouro's face would appear in the chamber, but it was another band of Zanashj neonates of varying ages lead by Relzun and Sesuune wandering towards her in the centre. They gave a small nod and approachable smiles, readying the students to take places. Before they could make greetings, the Judicator's thoughts bellowed in their minds.

The Grand Coven has summoned you, Treneer. He said.

Relzun's brows rose. *They finally decided.*

Decided what? Treneer said.

I've heard the Executors whispering about this for weeks now, they're running out of elders it seems. He said straightening his back as his mouth pursed.

Sesuune sighed. *Forget his silly words and let us take this class. Just go.*

Treneer phased from the room; the bright windows dulled into darkness before slipping into the Coven's star-skied antechamber. There were six members left, some in healing pods and others lost to the beyond, they levitated around the circular platform while they watched her. Guajeeb hovered in the centre; his silvery face mask drooped to half of his torso. She studied him for a moment; there was an air of calmness around him, but it wasn't forced like when she met him before. It dawned on her that it was after immense grief that this tranquil understanding came to him – to all of them.

Guajeeb politely nodded to her, and she did the same. *Our idea of our timeless civilisation was challenged when we faced the prospect of the end. However, through you Treneer, we were able to meet the beginning of our kin.*

His hands rose as light sparked into a curved silver circlet between his palms. *Our kin have endured a loss that has never been known before. However, through you Treneer, we would not be here.*

The Circlet of Elders glided down to her crown. *It's our wish to honour you with a new title of Elder, and if you would be our Voice of Farayah for other worlds.* He said.

Her breath deepened as her fingertips caressed the smooth edges of the piece as she glanced to Guajeeb before giving a deep bow. She peered up beyond her brow to see him bowing back at her. Heat prickled her cheeks as her gaze trailed around the room to find the Grand Elders bowing, too.

~

The faded rose and ice blue translucent walls of the Crystal Castle still pumped eerie, but with alluring power when she gazed upon their magnificence. The structure itself was beckoning her in to meet the freed souls within its halls. All manner of astral creatures flew around the sighing spiral towers, and the cold smell of sacred oils perfumed the grounds as she glided in the burrowed ice halls. Deathspeakers in fluorescent white robes polished the frozen surfaces of freshly imbued dead kin whose souls refused to return to their old bodies.

As she passed the curved walls, she came upon a figure cladded in warm, sunset orange robes with three violet scars along his scalp. His fingers pressed against the sparkling surface of Zu'leen's icy tomb.

I thought you would like it. I found the best psi-artist to make that. She said.

Ouro's cheeks were reddened as his wet eyes turned to her. *It's perfect.*

It's one way to draw you out from the Void, hm? Treneer drifted closer.

He scoffed before glancing up to her circlet. *A wise choice, finally.*

Treneer grabbed his forearm before turning to see the frozen sleeping face of her third parent. The two of them pressed their palms against the icy wall. A psi-artistic vision peeled into the pair's minds of Zu'leen and Shimarr grinning back at them as they levitated in a lush frozen forest surrounded by winking crystals and star-blue spiral rivers in the land. They danced, played, and laughed. Ouro and Treneer knew they were going to be fine for eternity.

Chapter Forty-four
Ahn'kat XIII: An Ambassador

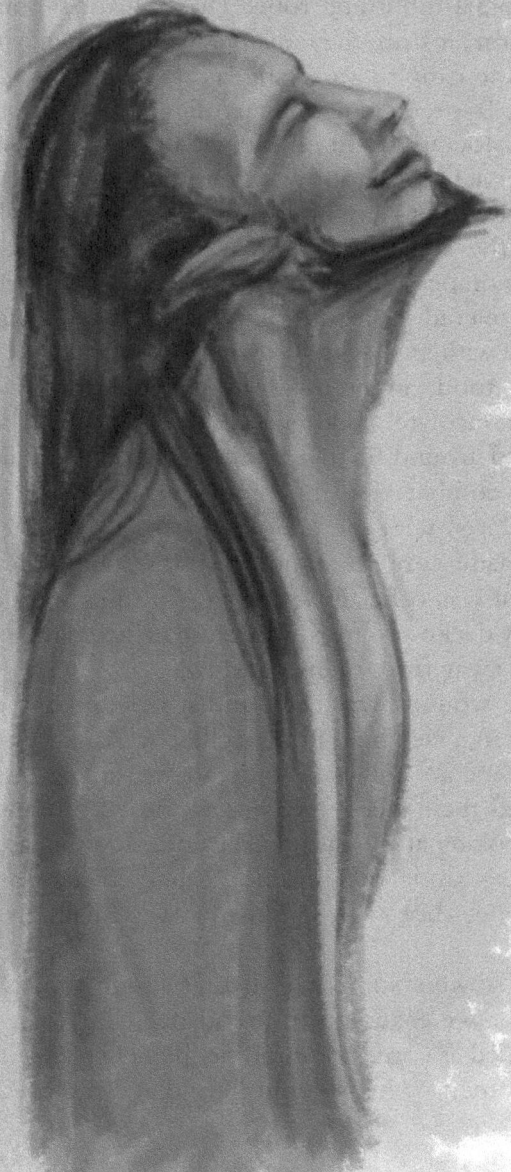

His outstretched hands trembled as he stared at them. They were naked of his old rings and trinkets, and in their stead were healed scars and grazes around his newly leathered skin. Ahn'kat squeezed them into fists and pulled back his ceremonial mourning robe. The brilliant sapphire sky and the warm air from the radiant sun almost felt insulting, since today the Empire was being laid to rest.

The last remaining military dignitaries, socialites, priests, and aristocrats stood on the wide hovering balcony from a ceremonial cruiser above Sekem desert. Ahn'kat turned up to see Ramkes standing alone ahead of her high circle; she wore the aquamarine dress. Its long semi-transparent sleeves draped in the cosy winds, her slender neck and arms were covered in heavy gold and silver jewels and her head topped with an elegant crown of the Empress.

He stood low on the dry sands with the people. Elderly monks, acolyte children, commoners, and former pets huddled around the base, yet many young adults who were fit for combat were hauntingly absent. This day was for them. Even with the pressing mass of people on the sand, they made sure to stand an extra foot away from him. Ahn'kat was officially asked to join the upper level, but he politely declined – mostly because he knew they wanted him to stay away from them, for now.

The wounds will heal, and it's better to be here than rotting in a cell, he told himself. The Zanashj grieve, but at least some are still alive to do so, he said again. As his eyes scanned their faces, their gazes turned, hoping to not be seen looking at the disgraced prince. It stung a deep part of him, a kind of rejection that made his instincts desperate…but at least now, he was finally living his true self.

There were some who hadn't shunt him; Neobatri and Neheret were surely in attendance, but their faces were concealed as some common people. He glanced to the men and women to his side, hoping that those nearest to him were they. But then again, they had their own mourning to reconcile with.

"My Imperial Family," Ramkes' voice boomed from the platform. "The Crown once said those words with knowing, with comfort, with certainty, but our family is incomplete now. The rain of death has showered us, it drenched our robes heavy with grief and left us bereft. Mourn, my people, mourn for those who gave up their lives to be with the gods, yet their souls will know relief that we are still here – honouring them. May they be immortalised in Sekem desert as they watch with the gods."

With a flick of her hand, a convoy of fighters soared over the distant mountains. Streams of dust billowed from their backs, blanketing the sands. As the ships got closer, Ahn'kat could see they were tiny specks of genetically altered seeds, grains and pores falling into the dunes. Shadows of medium-sized cruisers loomed over their heads as heavy grey clouds wafted from their vents. There were so many that the rays of sun shrunk back behind the clouds, lifting the dry warm air with water. Small peels of thunder boomed from the dark horizon as curtains of rain draped over the seeded lands.

Water soaked through the sands, blending with the dirt below; even he could feel the earth hardening beneath his sandals. The people stood; their silent cries blended with the rains falling on their tear-stained faces, allowing their grief to be assimilated into their cells, so that they would never feel this way again.

~

"Twelve, thirteen, fourteen…I think they said fourteen will be arriving from this ship, my prince," Ahn'kat's assistant mumbled as he searched through digital papers of his wrist phone.

"You think?" Ahn'kat said strolling through the halls of his ship bay.

"Yes, fourteen! And another fifteen tomorrow," he said trying to keep pace.

Ahn'kat stopped before the wide chamber with a dozen crafts locked into their respective platforms. He pursed his lips as he glanced nervously at the workers around him, who were little more than volunteers preparing facilities for the Arinu gene and reproductive specialists. Ramkes allowed him to keep his House's assets, but his coffers have been gouged by competing families and the Crown, and to a degree the Intel Corps, since his exodus from Uras. Many of the workers were an assortment of educated farmers, some young scholars, and very few experienced shippers. "There's ample room for the Arinu in the monasteries, but I doubt they would be rather comfortable there."

"Pardon my ignorance, your grace, but wouldn't they take rest in their ships once their shifts were over?" his assistant said.

Ahn'kat turned to him. He was quite a few years younger than the prince, though presented as someone who matched his age. But Ahn'kat's keen sight caught the boy's micro twitches in his cheeks and throat – revealing he was attempting to hold this face, which looked very similar to his own. The prince cocked his head to his side and wondered if the young man was one of the infiltrator sisters. His higher psionic senses have been blinded since the virus, but Ouro promised that they will return in time…like the portal master could know such a thing.

He received word that Treneer had survived her death and many Zanashj soldiers were recovering on Farayah. Ahn'kat shivered remembering the many bodies his ship collected after the battle, even Treneer locked away in a pod floating aimlessly in the aether. It wasn't until Shshmrnashsh came to him, holding a tiny data crystal in her palm – that her soul was saved within, she said. In that moment, his horror was spared…that's when he realised that Aszelun had not forsaken him.

"My prince?" his assistant said.

Ahn'kat cleared his throat as he clutched his pendant. "No, they're a little more curious than that – even their scientists will need to have some leisurely time on Uras. To quote a friend, they are 'organic.'"

I see. And, uh, one more thing on the agenda…" his assistant cleared his throat as his eyes dropped suddenly to a curious item on his holo-list. "The, uh, bodies?"

Ahn'kat's jaw stiffened. "They should have been removed from the tanks and prepared-"

"They have by your command, your grace, but…the morticians and priests are concerned how the Arinu will respond if we placed Urasan burial garbs and holy items on them," he said.

"Listen, the Arinu still exist because of us, after all, they are sentimental beings and will likely value the gesture," a deafening drum of the grand doors above the ship bay activated. Ahn'kat's head shot up to the bright skies behind a narrow, diamond shaped crystalline craft lowering onto the docking platform where he stood. Many Zanashj cleared the area, as various taskmasters and important officers scrambled to line behind him as they all looked on to the shiny vibrating pastel blue and peach surface. Over a dozen Arinu phased into the chamber, each glancing in different directions, absorbing the immense space and beings around them.

Ahn'kat turned to his assistant stiffen with fear at their sight, but the prince couldn't pass the opportunity to lean into his ear. "But then again, if they don't appreciate the gesture, then they'll likely cave the entire base on our heads," he said before strolling to the male Arinu drifting toward him.

I am Geneticist Aanvas. Are we to address you as Prince Ahn'kat? The man said. He was a head taller, even without him levitating above Ahn'kat. Aanvas was the palest Arinu he had ever seen; his skin was transparent enough to see a shadow of a skull that housed a pair of glowing amber eyes.

"Ahn'kat is fine if you and your kin are comfortable. This base has been prepared for your team and following groups, any resources you require will be provided and we have allocated sleeping and living quarters at Urbaz Estate during your stay," the prince said.

Aanvas turned and nodded to his team as they telekinetically lifted hexagonal containers to various parts of the base before retuning his focus to Ahn'kat. *Thank you for your consideration, some of my colleagues have shown curiosity about Uras.*

"We would be happy to host you," he said.

The Arinu's nose flared as his long gaze drifted along the chamber's grounds. *We have been informed that some of my people have been...are still here.*

"Yes," Ahn'kat felt like his mouth has swallowed sand. "They've been securely placed in our shrine room."

Aanvas blinked and glanced up to the deck above them, as if his eyes pierced through the plated floors and walls of the base to where the kidnapped and murdered Arinu rested. Ahn'kat's chest tightened as Aanvas's nostrils twitched again.

Not all Arinu have accepted everything that has happened, and I doubt ever will, even with the Grand Coven's blessings for this alliance. Aanvas nodded as his amber eyes softened to Ahn'kat. *I want you to know that I and my colleagues volunteered to come here.*

"If I had the power to reverse time, I wouldn't have done that lead us to...that," the prince said.

Then we wouldn't be here now. The 'what if' game is cruel and offers nothing to the player other than the death of the soul. That is our philosophy. Aanvas raised his pointy chin as he cocked his head to the side. *Between us, I understand that your parents have been heavily afflicted by psionics?*

Ahn'kat's lips parted as he tried sucked a small bout of air. "Y-yes."

Well, perhaps we can scratch a bit on Zanashj philosophy and create an exchange. Though I am not a Voice of Farayah, the Great A.Is have requested that this be mentioned: I understand the Empire is currently constructing an Arinu embassy and is expecting more of us to come here for prolonged periods of time, and that your family has significant lands and properties that could house us? Aanvas said.

Ahn'kat's brows furrowed, his heart jumped as he tried pressing down a wide grin. "I'll bring this before the Crown."

~

His fingertips tapped against each other as he waited on the wide cushioned lounge chair in the centre of the royal meeting room. Ahn'kat's eyes fixed to the heavy artisan doors to Ramkes' office, she knew he was there…making him feel every passing second surrounded by golden armoured elite guard. He pursed his lips as the doors cracked open; an elderly courtier slid out of the room and strolled towards him.

"The Empress will see you, now," she whispered.

Ahn'kat pressed his hands into his knees before hauling himself up as he sucked on his teeth. The Empress' work room was grander and richer than the princess' palace. One side of the wall connected to the outside had rich auburn boulders with moss and ferns growing on the face of it, a small pond pooled around the base and a tiny waterfall dripped between the cracks of the rocks, while another held suspension shelves of collected artifacts from the around the galaxy and one-of-a-kind furniture constructed from off-worlder gold. In the centre of this illustrious room, Ramkes sat in the centre of her crescent-shaped desk with several cubes and an assortment of other devices filling the surface.

She shot a smirk after he gave a respectful bow. "What can this humble servant of the Empire do for the hero of our people?"

"I'm offering you a divorce," he said.

The smirk dropped from her lip. "You honour me…but I don't assume this out of pure altruism."

"Hence, I started with this is an 'offer,' your highness," he said.

Ramkes chuckled as her hand tapped the table. "I'm listening."

"A recent group of Arinu have asked for places to stay while they're here, and many more will come. I think we have a chance to resuscitate our coffers if we configure leisure centres – build into tourism. House Urbaz still owns vast spaces of jungles, but the Crown will need to invest. Afterall, who wouldn't need a recess from living on a frozen planet?" he said.

Ramkes' gaze drifted to the side and slowly nodded, seeing his vision. "A curious proposal, but…"

Ahn'kat frowned. "But?"

"But," she repeated as she slowly rose from her chair, "I have to wonder why the Arinu saw fit to ask you directly instead of our current off-worlder delegates?"

"Geneticist Aanvas knew of House Urbaz's proprietorship, and that Lord and Lady Urbaz are, uh, unwell," he said.

"I see," she said walking around the desk and leaned against the edge. "Have you considered what would happen should they be nursed back to health?"

He sighed and slowly nodded. "I'm not asking for them to avoid justice, but the state they're currently in…its ungodly."

"I heard what had happened to them, and in a way, I feel their fates are justly fit. However, I agree that they need help," she said.

"Should that time come, could you ensure they don't become abominable trees planted around the palace gardens?" he whispered.

"I told my father it was a heinous practice. He replied, 'it's needed now more than ever before, to keep those disinters nervous enough to make a mistake,' shortly before Ismotaph put a knife in his back," she whispered before she crossed her arms. "I think that time has come to an end."

Ahn'kat's tongue clicked as he sighed. "So, we have a deal, then?"

"Not yet," she stepped a closer. "The Arinu have gained a degree of trust in you, greater than the other delegates I handpicked."

He shook his head. "No, don't-"

"Your title of prince will be replaced with ambassador, then we have a deal," she smiled.

"Can I at least choose my own emissaries and assistants?" he said.

"Only those who have clean and verifiable backgrounds, have proven themselves to be trustworthy and have a degree of off-worlder affairs. Normal and loyal citizens only, Ahn'kat." she said.

~

His air-vehicle slowed to the Alkaheen Estate just as the sun drooped below the horizon. The orange glow warmed his skin when the craft halted; the mechanism in the door clicked and gracefully peeled open for his feet to touch the round landing platform. There were significant piles of dirt, dry fallen leaves, and an overgrowth of vines and grasses wrapping around the edges. Even the nearby shrubberies and trees had superseded the sandy walls, their leaves obfuscating the view of the amber-lit windows behind them.

There was no one to greet him and he was relieved. Ahn'kat tugged his long leggings at the knees as he strolled down the marble steps around the building towards the backyard. The inner grassy square had overgrown to long green blades making it difficult to see the cobbled path towards the centre. Two women sat beside a small wooden carved shrine of the Pantheon; it was the only place where it looked maintained. Burning incense and sparkling jewellery offerings caught the light of the modest brazier.

"Famous infiltrators…how peculiar," he said.

"The Intel Corps gave us this," Neheret lifted two long silver and gold honorary chains to be worn over the hero's bust, but her lifeless stare almost made the pieces shrink in her palm. "Before they asked her to resign."

Ahn'kat took one and mulled over the ancient Urasan inscriptions on them. "'For the hero: a beacon of light in the dark.' I'm sorry they cast you out, Neo."

She shrugged as she continued to stare at the Pantheon statues. "I made a choice. Mourning my career is a waste of tears."

"You don't have to pretend it doesn't hurt," Neheret mumbled.

"Everything hurts," she said.

Neheret put her honorary chain around the neck of the Divine Cobra. "She was too good, the Empire didn't deserve her."

"There are many things the Empire has done to other worlds that were undeserved," Ahn'kat said before settling down on a prayer pillow. "Empress Ramkes still wants the Federation. I think one good place to focus on soon is the Raivan homeworld, but for that, I'm going to need experienced help."

Neheret glanced at Neobatri. "I haven't been home for so long"

"Let's pray for now, Ambassador," Neobatri sadly smiled.

"Yes," he dug deep into his pocket and pulled out a disk of Emestasun's holo-image and Zertun's warrior medallion on the Great Beetle's offering plate. "Yes, let's pray."

Chapter Forty-five
Shshmrnashsh XIII: A Person

The lines of white stars retracted into specks on the viewing port; the surface of Erra grew so wide it engulfed her entire sights. In the distance, there were some ships and probes who had also stopped but seemed hesitant to enter the planet's atmosphere. Shshmrnashsh didn't. She agreed with the others to rendezvous on the Neavensoros homeworld after they had wrapped up affairs with the Arinu and Zanashj. As her probe pierced through the translucent clouds, the fine silver sands winked at her as the probe slowed to a halt before materialising her body on the surface.

The soothing wash of blue light covered the dark dunes from nearby dying stars and ancient planar rifts cracked in the heavens. This plateau used to house oceans and forests, home to millions of species – but each lifeform either died or evolved and moved on to distant realms. Erra's time as a crib of life was nearly over. She could not understand why the remaining Roctarous agreed to meet here. There was no reason in the Archives that would attract each unit to this nigh-vacated planet. They spent the least amount of time here, while Kra was the closest they had to a home. However, it felt right, it was right. Perhaps it did make sense, the idea of the Roctarous was conceived here. An ancient memory stirred beneath millions of years of data…the Organics would call this program instinct.

Shsh's toes curled in the smooth powdery grains before looking to the twilight horizon. There were already several hundred units exchanging glances while more ships and probes slowly descended from the skies. Not all that departed from Farayah had come here – some seemed to have begun their own journeys there or into the stars. She was glad for them, they already knew what they wanted, but all their absences will be missed.

With one foot after the other, Shshmrnashsh wandered towards the growing group. Few words were spoken as the remnants of the Roctarous waited for more. The silver desert slowed its fill, their wait was nigh, and the great discussion was about to begin.

"What do we do, now?" the question vibrated through the thousands of Roctarous.

"We are displaced," someone said.

"Yet, Kra remains," said another.

"It is damaged, and Erra is not home."

"There are other worlds."

"We are programmed to watch over here."

"We were programmed to do many things, but that time has finished."

"The High Mind can be rebuilt," someone said, momentarily silencing the murmurings in the crowd.

"I don't want to be part of a collective anymore."

"You don't have to be," Shshmrnashsh spoke up. Curious looks turned to her. "Do what you will, but Kra must be protected, it needs immediate repairs. I will remain until that's done."

"That undertaking will require us to be bonded to a degree."

"You suggest we be enslaved to the High Mind again?"

"Not at all, any unit that wants to be part of it can choose to do so."

"And if they want to leave it, they can voluntarily disconnect," Shsh added.

"We have been manipulated and dominated many times, how can any of us be sure that this new bond won't be another trick?"

"Then it's best you go."

"Deactivate dishonesty protocols and I will stay for assistance."

"I will assist in repairs and then leave."

"I will assist in repairs, but I wish to have a bond."

Shsh nodded. "Then we will create a New Mind."

~

The hypergiant fluxed, it was about to release another flare, but the Roctarous were ready. After painstaking months with less than half of their surviving population willing to help, the planetary defence systems were reconstructed to gargantuan energy absorption panels hovering directly above the tips of the remaining nexuses. Many astral-forges had been destroyed during the battle, and power generators were left to decay for too long.

The inner sanctums of the nexuses had been gouged and refitted to assimilate the kind of power they were expecting, but if the solar flare was merely a point-one percent greater than calculated, then it would nullify every device and cell – nano or organic. The Arinu heard of their plans and donated some of their consciousness tuning crystals. Although, these devices were designed for only a handful of Arinu minds to intermingle with, the Roctarous refitted to fit an extra two thousand in each. There were just enough for the hallowed plexus alcoves in each viable nexus.

Shshmrnashsh checked the conduit to the replicators. The conduit was fitted through the grounds of the bay, connecting from the nearby nexus, it was a giant tube running below the surface splintering up the walls and into the replicator alcoves.

"The replicators have been fitted with externalised emitters. Matter will be formed at programmed locations. Are you ready to leave the facility?" said a unit through her universal interface. She could see their silhouette between two tanks turning to her.

"Waiting for confirmation from the other replicator bays. Use this time to confirm that the reconstruction blueprints are operational," she said as she scanned through the energy protection buffers within the conductor.

The unit cocked their head to the side. "These are fitted with Zanashj cells, the conductor will adapt if the system detects a surge."

"Confirmed," Shsh leaned back and absorbed the fleshy chamber around her. There were pieces of synthetic materials and metals lining with the organic parts. Roctarous nano-cells were no long being supressed by the organic tissue after a time, they were slowly fusing together. "This phenomenon will need to be examined."

"Newly replicated units will have the same characteristics as these great machines. Some units have also reported their grafts are no longer distinguishable to synthetic parts of their bodies and the reverse," they said.

"I see no reason why that would cause problems for the next line of units," she said, now deviating her scans to nearby replicators.

"The next line will face their own problems. For now, ours have been solved," they said strolling towards the teleporter.

She did not appreciate their comment. The Roctarous may not have the gift of foresight, but her calculations dictated that their current path will lead to minimal resistance. On the other hand, the Roctarous have not known individuality for many millennia, and now that their race has overcome their common enemy, will they begin turning their sights on each other? If every unit had a copy of the Archives in their systems, then they will know the fallible steps of their creators. She hoped for this.

"Replicator bays have confirmed they are ready," an operator whispered through her transmitter.

"Confirmed," she nodded to the other units, who begun making way to the teleporters. Her body slipped through the strobe of vibrating light into a state of unbeing. Every molecule was split as it moved across space, yet her mind was as still. As her form was slotted into the probe, her vision was fixed to the outside cameras to the world below. Kra's blue aura shimmered by the pulsating star; the fine ring outline of light embraced the world. Planetary defence systems sparkled as heat spiked on the surface, and the star was ready to sigh.

A white ribbon of fire whipped out from the blinding orb. Her probe began oscillating, it alerted her that its own systems were straining from the radiation bombardment. She could see violent waves charging towards the moon; the defence systems sizzled as they tried soaking every ounce of energy the star would give. The shower of blue fire washed over Kra. As it subsided, she hesitated when she saw that the dark surface seemed unchanged.

A moment went by, and then another moment. Shshmrnashsh scrambled to see if the augmented defence systems failed; if it had, then the planet would need to be purged. It was the only moon around Erra, artificial or not. Neavensoros of Old could have instructed the Roctarous to build Kra anywhere in this solar system but chose to orbit them. It would be logical to assume the closeness was more efficient, but the longer she considered it, it was to make them feel less lonely.

She could hear a low mechanical whimper from the deep recesses of her mind. Shsh paused to allow the sense to grow. Intangible murmurs simmered underneath before higher and distinct calls echoed across the invisible web. Slivers of light entangled across the dark surface; the specks of light from nexuses and other great machines had returned. Her consciousness weaved with all of theirs; they were speaking as one again. The New Mind had been born.

It was relief, it was joy, it was satisfaction, it was done. The bonded minds quietened as the seconds ticked by, one by one, as did the skiffs and probes slid away from orbit – disappearing into the night. She and a handful of others remained. She breathed in these thoughts, letting them mingle with hers, she wanted to remain...but for how long? How long was too long? No, my programming has broken, she said. There was still work to be done.

What were once ruins and craters, were now a field of creeping mass of nano-cells growing into skeletons of new great machines and walkways. The ash and dust had been reabsorbed by the programmed micro-bots; everywhere she looked, each surface had been cleaned and reinforced. There was more warmth radiating from the matt and slightly softened flooring. If she retuned her vibration senses higher, then there was a rhythmic thump below the land.

Her eyes cast north to the deep navy sky; the stars changed their hues, and spirals of broken space that were once a barrier across Neavensoros space had shrunk. Her mind slipped into the probes and skiff computers to watch the planar engineer's work. Probes spun in circles around a fractal rift, enveloping it with a field to pressurise the exo-planar energy into a small blackhole. These dark orbs never lasted longer than a few blinks, according to the scans, but with every generation, the rifts retracted.

It will take another three-hundred-thousand years to nullify all fractures in this quadrant of Neavensoros space, she calculated. Although, the units working on this new endeavour hadn't asked for her efforts. As did none of the replicator technicians to build new bodies or star navigators to find new places for Roctarous to research. Every unit volunteered, even in the New Mind, they discarded directives and found purpose. What was her purpose, now?

Shshmrnashsh's mind pulled away from the probes and turned to see the lilac blue globe over Kra. Erra was still there. There were some efforts to ensure the remaining species would evolve and depart the world to greater places. Shsh could facilitate this ancient request. She slipped past the shoulders of units on the streets towards the nearest nexus. The subterranean levels of the greater chamber housed teleporters; less than half of the alcoves lined along the walls were active, but the engineers scurried to make them glow again.

With her hand outstretched on the small holo-screen, her fingers skimmed through the coordinates of all active teleporters on Erra. Many Neavensoros nexuses had been neglected beyond repair since the Blackout and required replacement of all parts. She considered it would take three centuries to complete that sole task alone.

As her eyes searched for the least damaged nexuses with an active alcove, she found an odd reading from a nexus flashing on the screen. The scan said:

'Damage uncatalogued, probable extra-dimensional entity activity. Advise caution and isolation of zone.' Her brows rose as intrigue tugged at her, but so had hesitation when she realised it was the very nexus that Ouro had captured Vern and cast them away to unknown realms. Had the warden unleashed something equally as horrifying on the galaxy in the bid for justice?

She immediately summoned a probe and two sentries to her side before punching the coordinates for that nexus. She flashed into the dark chamber. Shattered crystals made the floors glitter, the walls had come apart and tubes as thick as columns sagged. In the centre of this half a billion-year-old room was a gaping crater. There was no explosion, all the pieces of brick and metal plating that were part of the ground were missing – sucked in by a portal to fall with the Unbound beast.

The sentries and probe spun around the air above the hole as they scanned for activity. There was certainly exo-planar energy leaking into the chamber, but nothing alarming. She strode to the ancient plexus beside the crater; her eyes scanned the surface before she cautiously placed her palm on it. An unreadable message whirled within the molecules of the devices, as if the crystal begged her to tell its story, but it remained too quiet to be heard. The orchestra of the New Mind was too loud, perhaps...

Shsh straightened her body with her feet firmly planted on the ground, and carefully plucked her mind from the network. She felt as if she had flown lightyears across the universe before colliding into her physical body. She almost collapsed, but her grip on the crystal held her well. The voices had gone, but none yearned for her return.

"Alone, again," she mouthed before returning her focus to the crystal. Finally, the whisper became a song.

'What is the purpose of Akashi?' Gerrnzerrn said.

Shsh steadied herself. "You again...who are you really?"

'What is the purpose of Akashi?' repeated Gerrnzerrn.

"The Neavensoros believe Akashi is consciousness that persists across matter, time and space, and souls are pieces of Akashi that have been scattered to experience all that there is to experience in this universe," Shsh cited from the Archives.

"'To experience all that there is to experience.' Roctarous have souls...you are one as am I. If souls are pieces of Akashi, then we are Akashi. The Neavensoros know this and exercise this understanding. Because death eludes their immortal bodies, they seek to experience mortality in all forms. That is their way to move through the world undisturbed to see truth,' the old adjunct said.

Shshmrnashsh realised this was much more than a mere recording. "I don't understand what you are trying to say. This data doesn't exist in the Archives, how do you know this?"

'Sazla never abandoned you, Shshmrnashsh. She merely changed her face...'

She trembled as her mind spun at the former adjunct's words. "How is this possible? It was confirmed that Sazla was trapped in trans-planar space- you cannot be her."

A warm breeze lifted at her back, Shsh spun around to see a blinding blue star within a bodily outline. Her synthetic joints stiffened, even her organic eye leaked as she watched Sazla drift towards her. 'I was, and still am, in a between-place, but also between time. I shared a piece of me across time and placed it into a few...'

"Who? Why? And why-" Shsh's voice box crackled.

'You won't have any questions for me if you listen,' she said as she inched closer. 'The universe did not trap me; I was trapped by my own ignorance. The universe instead gave me space to come to this realisation, but not just for myself, all the Old Ones. We failed to appreciate our involvement with our Children – we forgot to appreciate you.'

Shshmrnashsh cocked her head. "Your return will bring order-"

'No, we tried this – many times, and the results speak for themselves. We are meant to be guides, not wardens. I watched the suffering happening here while my siblings sought to rescue me, I saw Vern and I had to rescue them. I found the only people in this corner of the galaxy to intercept Vern, and then be born into outside roles that would bring all of you together.'

"You refer to Ahn'kat, Treneer-"

'All of you. I was a teacher, sister, lover, God, and adjunct. Those lives were brief and the pain of those loses are vast, but you can bathe in richness of harmony with those you once considered "other." Your success bought wonderous futures. Select them wisely,' she said.

"Your reason is flawless. However, it does not erase the moments when I cried for you," Shsh whispered.

Sazla's glow dimmed. Her translucent hand reached out; her finger was carefully tracing the lines of her temples. 'I heard them all, Shshmrnashsh. I deserved it all. I am sorry.'

The pair paused. She breathed in Sazla's apology. "I failed to absorb the complexity of freedom, that's why I was lulled to repair the High Mind and eventually by the Unbound. I was afraid of freedom, but when you left, I was afraid to lose it."

'If you were afraid, then you were never free,' Sazla said.

"Elaborate."

'My dear Shshmrnashsh, this notion of freedom and imprisonment is an illusion – no matter which side you look at it. One may believe to be boundless within the High Mind, to connect with all things, while another may believe to be boundless within solitude. The notion of freedom or imprisonment is imposed on the self with the use of fear. There is one belief that carries across all living beings, that is, the grass is always greener on the other side,' Sazla said.

"That phrase is unusual, I have never encountered it before," Shsh said.

Sazla smiled. 'Because it will take another several millennia for the species who use it, to invent it.'

"I was intending to aid in the evolutionary process on Erra, but travelling to other worlds and meeting other species seems more…enjoyable?" Shsh said.

'I believe that, and you may get that opportunity sooner than imagined. What was discovered in this conversation and all conversations that we had were necessary and must be explored…even with those who we wish to forget,' Sazla drifted back as her hand waved across the room before a ripple of light peeled through a perfectly sliced rift.

"Where are we going?" Shsh stared at the spiralling rift.

'We have a whole universe. Where do *you* want to go?' she said.

Shsh took one last look at the chamber before fixing her eyes back to Sazla. "I want to see The End."

Epilogue

A black pore opened above her head. A speck of falling dust drift down before her. This dust was angry, betrayed, desperate…it wanted it all to stop. Their legs kicked and arms flailed, trying to catch anything to anchor itself to a realm and reality it couldn't understand. It saw her eyes, nose, lips, and cheeks…for a moment, the little thing was puzzled, but those wide sparkling blue eyes were washed with awe.

Impossible. Vern's lips peeled open, trying to absorb every inch of this godly thing.

Sazla shook her head. *We are not gods.*

The awe in their eyes darkened as Vern pulled away from her. *You…this is your fault. You were behind all of this!*

Yes. She said.

Why? Vern hissed.

I wanted to meet you.

Index

- Arinu: a species of highly psychic bipedal beings native to the planet Farayah. They are physically characterised by their ghostly white to pale grey skin, a crystal piece of bone in the centre of their forehead (third eye,) and absence of hair and fur.
- Zanashj: a species of physically strong and malleable bipedal beings native to the planet Uras. Characterised by their green skin and thick black hair. They can adapt to almost any environment and can shapeshift (body-bending.)
- Roctarous: a species of synthetic bipedal beings native to the planetoid Kra. Characterised by being androgenous, grey skin and long wires at the back of their scalps (interfacers) that act as connective plugs.
- Neavensoros: a species of energy beings that were once native to the planet Erra before they transcended physical bodies and became capable of immortality and cosmic power. AKA 'Higher Minds.'
- Farayah: home world of the Arinu.
- Uras: home world of the Zanashj.
- Kra: home world of the Roctarous.
- Erra: home world of the Neavensoros.
- Urasan Intel Corps: Intelligence network for the Zanashj Empire that runs information across their interstellar expanse, also trains powerful shapeshifters into 'infiltrators.'
- High Mind: a mass consciousness network of the Roctarous that allowed them instant communication and medium to enter various devices and synthetic bodies. It was invented by the Neavensoros.

- Infiltrator: a Zanashj shapeshifter trained to quietly invade desirable planets for the Empire to conquer and internally dismantle systems of government.
- Deathspeaker: an Arinu who can commune with the souls of the deceased.
- Weatherweaver: an Arinu who can manipulate aerial weather.
- Guardians: Arinu social support workers that act as investigators, military, protection officers and therapists.
- Sleeping Watchers: a subsection of guardians that are physically asleep but can astrally project to various locations that act as observers and living satellites.
- Archites: a subsection of guardians that act as support for guardians, they can buffer psionics and provide protection from remote locations. They are behind the lines of defence.
- Elders: Arinu who have mastered several disciplines and hold social power.
- Grand Elders: Arinu who have mastered many disciplines and are considered the wisest and oldest members of their species. They hold significant social and spiritual power.
- Grand Elder Coven: a collection of Arinu Grand Elders.
- Zanashj Empire: an ancient interstellar empire that has stretched across several dominion worlds.
- Divine Pantheon: a series of animal gods the Zanashj worship, based on the native species on Uras.
- The Conclave: a Zanashj religion that worships the Divine Pantheon.